FLORA LEWIS

ALSO BY FLORA LEWIS

CASE HISTORY OF HOPE (1958)
RED PAWN (1963)
ONE OF OUR H-BOMBS IS MISSING (1965)

EUROPE

A TAPESTRY OF NATIONS

SIMON AND SCHUSTER
NEW YORK/LONDON/TORONTO/SYDNEY/TOKYO

PUBLISHED BY SIMON AND SCHUSTER
A DIVISION OF SIMON & SCHUSTER, INC.
SIMON & SCHUSTER BUILDING
ROCKEFELLER CENTER
1230 AVENUE OF THE AMERICAS
NEW YORK, NEW YORK 10020
SIMON AND SCHUSTER AND COLOPHON ARE REGISTERED TRADEMARKS OF
SIMON & SCHUSTER, INC.
DESIGNED BY EVE METZ
MANUFACTURED IN THE UNITED STATES OF AMERICA

1   3   5   7   9   10   8   6   4   2

LIBRARY OF CONGRESS CATALOGING-IN-PUBLICATION DATA
LEWIS, FLORA.
EUROPE.

INCLUDES INDEX.
1. EUROPE—DESCRIPTION AND TRAVEL—1971–
2. EUROPE—CIVILIZATION—1945–   .   I. TITLE.
D923.L47   1987   940.55   87-12878
ISBN: 0-671-44018-7

CONTENTS 7

PART II • EASTERN EUROPE

THE SOVIET UNION—A Continental Weight	353
EAST GERMANY—State Behind a Wall	365
POLAND—The Malady Is Geography	390
CZECHOSLOVAKIA—A Sullen Quiet	418
HUNGARY—The Most Amusing Barracks	444
ROMANIA—The Lights Went Out	466
BULGARIA—The Soviets' Most Loyal Ally	484
YUGOSLAVIA—The Undone Puzzle	504
CONCLUDING COMMENTS	525
EUROPEAN INSTITUTIONS	529
BRIEF FACTS	535
BIBLIOGRAPHY	549
INDEX	559

INTRODUCTION

WRITING ABOUT modern Europe is so vast and ambitious a project that the first problem is deciding what to leave out. Thousands of books have been written in recent years about almost every country, almost every aspect, of the continent that gave rise to Western civilization. The origin of this work was repeated requests from people to recommend "a book about Europe." There are so many, but I could not think of one to suggest as a general survey, an introduction to Europe's diversity but which also took account of the growing homogeneity and convergence of outlook. I was emboldened to try to produce one. In many ways the societies have changed profoundly, influencing one another and responding to common pressures. In other ways they remain deeply anchored in their special pasts and stubborn customs.

The salient fact about Europe remains the nation-state. There is a sense of shared Europeanness which has waxed and waned in the last two generations, but it is still secondary to the sense of unique nationality which began to arise after the Renaissance and the decline of feudalism. Therefore, I decided to organize the book on a country-by-country basis. At the same time, there are themes which ignore borders and catch everyone up in the same kinds of problems. That too is an essential facet of modern Europe. In order to deal with the particular and the general, I have tried to organize warp and woof, weaving the themes one by one into the country chapters. The selection was necessarily arbitrary—identifying the topics which modern Europeans perceive as most important in their world and assigning each topic to the country which most vividly represents the way Western Europeans see themselves and their role in the world. Withdrawal from what is now called the third world was traumatic for each "mother country," to use the once common phrase. This is emphasized in the chapter on Britain. The revival of industry after the devastation of war is taken up in the chapter on West Germany. The scourge of terrorism in a continent that seems to have abandoned war between nations as a tolerable ambition is discussed in the chapter on Italy. The resurgence of regionalism within the nation-state is examined in particular detail in connection with Spain. The special role of intellectuals in defining the issues and prejudices of modern Europe finds its place in the chapter on France, and so on. Each topic affects many countries. Selection and matching reflect an effort to synthesize.

The nearest to an official political definition of Europe that exists is the list of signatories to the Helsinki accords in 1975 at the Conference on Security and Cooperation in Europe. There are important anomalies. All of the members of the East's Warsaw Pact and the West's North Atlantic Treaty Organization signed, including the United States and Canada, which are obviously not part of Europe. In addition, the signatories included neutral countries—Sweden and Austria, among others. Albania, totally isolated at the time of the negotiations but a little less so in subsequent years, deliberately stayed away. Some but not all of Europe's ministates took part—the Vatican, San Marino, Lichtenstein. Andorra did not. Cyprus and Malta, not geographically in Europe but the only independent islands in the Mediterranean, were included, an indulgence which many of the others later regretted when the Maltese government took it upon itself to intrude the Palestinian and Arab cause into the discussions and to block consensus at several crucial points. Switzerland, so adamantly neutral that it has refused to join the United Nations and many other international organizations, was an active participant. The Soviet Union refrained from demanding, as it had done when the United Nations was founded, separate membership for its Byelorussian and Ukrainian republics.

All together, thirty-five states signed the Helsinki agreement. The document served as a substitute for a World War II peace treaty with Germany, which remains politically impossible to negotiate because of German partition. The "Final Act," not a treaty but a declaratory document with no provision for enforcement, commits the signatory states to a series of principles and obligations. They are divided, in the diplomats' jargon, into three "baskets," one dealing with military security, one with economic affairs and one with human rights, flow of information and cultural matters. From the Soviet point of view, the key provision was renunciation of any attempt to change existing borders by force. This was not quite the endorsement of the post–World War II partition of Europe that critics impute to Helsinki, since it leaves open the possibility of changes by negotiation, improbable as that now may seem. From the Western point of view, the most important gain was the formal recognition of human rights as an international, not an exclusively internal, concern. This was not the great step forward which determined optimists hoped to see, but it did undermine the legal argument that the way a government treats its people is its own sovereign affair and that no one outside has a right to interfere.

For my purposes, most of the signatory nations are included. The exceptions are the two North American countries, the midgets, the Mediterranean islands and Turkey, which for all its ties with Europe is more truly a Middle Eastern society than a European one and cannot be approached in a purely European context. The book is meant to be an overall account of the current European scene, with some logical sequence as it proceeds across the geographical and political map, and a quick reference to specific questions. The Contents is a guide to the order I have chosen; the Index is a guide to the interweaving themes.

This kind of composition inevitably produces some overlap. Moreover, it doesn't pretend to be complete. The approach is both impressionistic and analytical. To avoid weighting the text with statistics, I have included a list of basic facts about each country at the end of the book. There is a degree of bias in the length and detail accorded each country. It reflects in part a sense of the importance each plays in current affairs, in part the fact that some societies are more transparent, livelier and easier to discern than others. The countries of Eastern Europe are no longer the opaque enigmas they seemed in the years following World War II. But neither are their workings and assumptions so visible and decipherable as those of the noisy, bustling societies of the West. Sometimes the West is hard to set down because it is so open, so shifting that clarity is lost in the complexities and the frothing surface. In the East, there are secrets and deliberate deceptions on the surface that confound the observer, but the undercurrents are strongly marked.

It is impossible to discuss Europe without reference to the Soviet

Union, the Eurasian land mass that weighs on both continents. But it is also impossible to give even a hasty idea of the brooding, self-conscious giant in this format. So the Soviet chapter is focused not on the country itself but on its impact on the rest of Europe. Russia has been there, as friend or foe, since the defeat of the Tatars. One way or another, the rest of Europe has always lived with it and knows it always will. That is a crucial difference between contemporary Europe and America. The Russians are inextricably present in the European tableau, yet always as outsiders. They cannot be called a bridge between Europe and Asia; their lands and their power are too vast. Neither are they a separate continent. They are a presence that tells of another world far beyond the horizon, like a pervasive wind that brings the scent of distant climates without a glimpse of the topography.

Nor can history be ignored, though there is no presumption of presenting even the most superficial account of so rich and well preserved a past. Again arbitrarily, snatches of history are mentioned as they shadow the contemporary scene, past events that color current concerns and fears. History helps get inside the minds of people as they face the problems of the day, as a knowledge of their customary food helps get inside their skins. Some periods recede to a dim, subconscious background, while others, possibly older, take on immediacy in shaping present attitudes. Indulgence must be asked for the idiosyncratic, incomplete way that history is introduced in some accounts and skipped in others. This is not an attempt to judge what mattered from the historian's long and careful view, but to give an inkling of the elements of the past which influence people's awareness of the world they now confront. It changes from country to country; people don't remember the same periods.

My view of Europe is inevitably that of an outsider. I have spent most of my life there, living at various times in England, France, Germany, Switzerland, Holland, Czechoslovakia and Poland. But it didn't make me an Englishwoman or a Frenchwoman or a composite that might be called a European. I have an American cast of mind. It helps me to notice the difference in the way each society sees itself and others. There is always some truth in the stereotypes. Caricature is a form of portraiture. Yet the stereotypes are contradictory. The English see themselves as, above all, civil and honorable, and view the French as sly and greedy but also joyous and adept at the good life. The French see themselves as cultured and tolerant and the English as crudely mercantile but also sedately, imperturbably elegant. Stereotypes are by definition superficial. Each society is a potpourri of flavors, with different ones dominant at different moments. The effort is to present them as they see themselves and as they look to neighbors. Their people ask themselves different questions as they grope to define their own identity. Polls and surveys are now commonplace in most countries, and they do produce a silhouette of nationality that often conflicts sharply with the traditional image of each society. They must be read not only by the answers, but by the questions. The questions show what the societies want to know about themselves even more perhaps than what they really are. On the basis of polls and official statistics, an identikit picture has been drawn where that is possible, offering an artificial assemblage of traits but which nevertheless does reflect the people who ask and answer the questions.

Most of all, I have tried to show that there is such a place as Europe, such a thing as European, even though the moment you approach to look more closely it breaks up into kaleidoscopic fragments. My wish is to bring both the unity and the complexity within grasp. It is the same old Europe, and it changes every day. Certain undercurrents make the trends of change visible. The shape of the future can be discerned in the present and the parts of the past which remain alive. This book will serve its purpose if it conveys a sense that Europe is moving and shifting in interesting ways, reliving and also remaking civilization. It can be no more than an introduction. I hope it will whet the appetite for knowledge and spread the admiration and affection that I feel.

PART I

WESTERN

EUROPE

EUROPE
A Civilization

THERE MUST BE a tacit understanding before people can be sure they mean the same thing when they speak of Europe. It is commonplace among the politically aware in Western Europe to use the name "Europe" when they are talking about no more than the European Economic Community, the exclusive group of associated countries which numbered first six, then nine, ten, and now twelve. The second smallest continent, comprising 7 percent of the earth's total surface, Europe is really a large, irregularly jutting peninsula of the great Eurasian land mass. But it is not myopic to call the Common Market "Europe," although it leaves out many important states in the West and all those east of the Elbe except Greece. It is a reflection of great aspirations, of the founders' hope that one day it would designate a mighty union worthy of a continental name, as the United States is often called simply America. That is not going to happen in this century, perhaps not in the next. But the ideal, the sense of a special family, persists, echoing in the ambitious name which refuses the primacy of any single nation.

Charles de Gaulle, who did a lot both to establish that organization of Europe and to stunt its growth, spoke of another dream of Europe "from the Atlantic to the Urals." That is even further from realization and carries an unrealistic implication that the Soviet Union will collapse, fracturing at the range of mountains which cut off the European lands of Russia from the steppes of Soviet Asia. There is no evidence he was really thinking in these terms.

21

Rather, de Gaulle was trying to remind the world that the contemporary partition of Europe by pure power politics is unnatural. It belies geography, history and deeply rooted custom. It has endured since World War II because of a tenuous balance of power that prevents either East or West from dominating the other. Nobody can foresee how the rift might be healed. As unsatisfactory and painful as the division is, any credible way of removing it must instill great dread because it would almost certainly bring cataclysmic violence. Europe is the only continent where there has been no war between nations since 1945. In the nuclear age, Europe is the continent where any war is likely to bring about the end of human society on earth. Even in the unlikely event of war in Europe without the use of nuclear weapons, the existing non-nuclear arsenals are so huge, so destructive, that the fate of the world would be at stake. So it is still true that the destiny of the whole world hinges on events in Europe, even though the lords of Europe no longer rule the world. The Europeans must continue submitting to partition for their own survival and the safety of mankind. Yet it goes against the grain. Each succeeding generation feels more uneasy with it, more resentful at what weighs as an unreasonable, illogical constraint of natural tides. King Canute, in the guise of the superpowers, has raised his hand and dammed the movement of the waters. It cannot last indefinitely, yet it dare not be breached. There is at present no way out of this dilemma.

Solace is sought in another ideal of Europe, the old united Europe of Christendom, which long existed in men's minds and in their prayers if scarcely ever in their daily lives. It is a definition no longer of religion but of a blend of cultures that developed on the basis of a religious identity. Europa of the Greek myth, a maiden so beautiful that the enraptured god Zeus changed himself into a bull and carried her off, is said to have been a Phoenician princess, possibly from Tyre, south of Beirut on the eastern shore of the Mediterranean. The Roman Empire, which stretched from England to Constantinople, brought a certain unity. But after the fall of Rome the organization collapsed and the continent fell into largely tribal darkness. It was the spread of Christianity and the medieval Holy Roman Empire (under mostly Germanic kings) which gave the peoples of this land a first sense of European identity. They fought about everything, especially about the rites and dogmas of religion, though this was often the excuse and justification for wars of conquest and dominion by monarchs on secular or sacred thrones.

Concourse with the culture of the Arabs brought the beginning of enlightenment to people who had fallen into barbaric times, reviving lost knowledge of their own Greco-Roman heritage as well as bringing word of new sciences and techniques, in mathematics, astronomy, chemistry and medicine. But learning was the preserve of a privileged few. Confrontation of the "people of God"—as Christians called themselves—against "the infidel," the faithless, as they called Moslems, created a bond of community among the quarrelsome Europeans. They gradually expelled the Moors from Spain and southern Portugal, which the North Africans had begun to conquer in the seventh century. The decisive turn of the Turkish tide into Europe after the fall of Constantinople in 1453 came with the Ottomans' defeat at sea at the Battle of Lepanto in 1571 and on land near Vienna in 1683. However, it was not until the end of the fifteenth century, in the same year of 1492 when Columbus discovered America, that Islamic rule finally ended in Iberia. Only in the nineteenth century, with the liberation of Greece in 1829 and Bulgaria, Romania and Serbia in 1878, was Turkey forced out of the Balkans, except for a small area on the western side of the Bosporus, the border with Asia.

For the most part, Europe was poor, ignorant and brutally oppressed in the centuries that followed the fall of Rome. The glories of classical antiquity were forgotten. The skills disappeared. Life was short and rapacious. The Crusades, supposedly organized for the purpose of saving the Holy Land from the Turks, were largely a pretext to send roving bands of starving marauders off to distant lands so that some semblance of order and fruitful economy might be maintained at home. But they too served to broaden knowledge and reawaken a thirst for commerce. The fourteenth century was the watershed. Historian Barbara Tuchman quite rightly saw in it "a distant mirror," as she called her book, of the way modern Europe evolved. The great disasters of the period changed men's attitudes and broke open stultified societies. Some historians specifically point to the ravaging epidemics of bubonic plague and typhus, which literally decimated populations, as the mainspring of European wealth and power to dominate the world. The ratio of people to land was drastically changed.

When the terror passed, presumably because survivors had gained some immunity, there were many fewer mouths to feed with the same arable land. It was possible to accumulate surpluses to support manufacture and enliven trade. That brought a period of relative plenty. People began to rediscover their ancestors' skills and to seek learning.

With the Renaissance came a new refinement of spirit, a delight in beauty, artistic creativity and invention. It began in Italy, and the contrast was so striking, so alluring, so promising of pleasure that all who could brought the magical craftsmen to their courts or attracted them to their cities. That was the real emergence of European civilization, built on the rediscovered skills of the Greeks and the Romans and impregnated with a new, adventurous humanism. The Russians, still under the thrall of the Asian Tatars though loyal to the Christian Church of Byzantium, were left behind.

The age of exploration brought the Europeans, newly emboldened by their growing knowledge, to the age of expansion. They developed nation-states, wealthy enough to finance voyages of conquest to the other continents. The booty and the trade brought new riches, new ideas. Europe reached its zenith. By the nineteenth century, it was truly master of the world. It had absorbed what it chose of other civilizations and proclaimed its own unchallenged superiority. Colonization followed conquest. Spaniards and Portuguese went off to seek their fortunes in what became Latin America, parts of Africa, even distant Asia. The British, French and Dutch moved to the New World and the far Pacific. Emigration from other parts of Europe came later, in successive waves stirred by famine, unsuccessful revolt and repression, the lure of land and adventure.

The Industrial Revolution which the new spirit made possible confirmed Europe's supremacy. It was sparked by the rise of new ideas, the drive for invention. The result raised living standards on a scale never known before even as it turned large numbers of the peasantry into miserable proletarians. A new middle class developed, spreading the privileges of burghers and guildsmen on a far wider scale. The watchword was progress. It seemed inevitable. Europe carried the torch by which the rest of mankind would see its way to unending ascension from the primeval struggle for existence. New political ideas and associations arose to force a better distribution of the marvelously expanded ability to produce wealth. Revolutionary France proclaimed the rights of man. Authoritarian, Protestant Prussia founded a system of social security, creating the idea that the state bore a responsibility for the well-being of citizens alongside the traditional obligation of the Church to dispense charity.

The political division of Europe today is predominantly east-west (except for Greece and the extension of the Western military alliance to Turkey). But the older, underlying division is north-south. It is a gradation, without a sharply defined border like the military line dividing east and west. But it seems to have deep geographic, ethnic, and cultural polarities. North-south has become a way of describing global cleavages, between the bulk of economically developed countries and those still struggling to move beyond earlier stages of production and distribution. But there is also a north-south declension within Europe, approximating levels of industrial advance. The breaking line is more or less the direction of access to the seas, on one side countries that face the Mediterranean and on the other those that look to northern seas through the great north-flowing rivers or from their own shores. The only state facing both ways, and thus considering itself part of both communities, is France. (Russia, with its access to the Mediterranean through the Black Sea and the Dardanelles, has a certain geographical claim, but then it is an exception to practically every European denominator.) France considers itself a Latin country and takes an active interest in the Mediterranean, but in fact it has long been dominated by northerners.

Almost every European country has its own internal north-south division, with the north figuratively as well as literally on top in terms of wealth, culture and influence, until it gets too rugged and too cold. Scandinavia and Britain alone are dominated by their southern regions. There is no self-evident explanation for this repetitive pattern, but it is striking, even in small countries such as Switzerland. The north-south contrast plays an important role in the domestic affairs of almost every nation. The American humorist James Thurber once suggested another kind of division, between mountain people and valley people. In his stirring little cartoon book *The Last Flower* he used it to explain the recurrence of war. Life is hard in the mountains, Thurber said, so the people who live there become strong and tough. They look down with envy on the valley people, who grow soft and complacent in the embrace of a more generous nature. Eventually they attack, to secure the benefits of valley life for themselves, driving the losers up to the mountains to seek survival. Changing places, the people change habits and character, and the cycle resumes. Thurber's theory doesn't hold up well on closer examination, but it does convey a feeling for the ebb and flow of tribes and ethnic groups, which has been the throbbing rhythm of European civilization. There isn't any area which hasn't been overrun at one time or another, often from several directions. The tides left their traces.

The great powers of the world in the eighteenth and nineteenth centuries were England, France, Austria, Prussia and Russia, the powers of Europe. There were other advanced cultures, some much older, but they lost confidence before the might, the self-assurance and the demonstrated capacity of the Europeans to advance their nations' interests. The awe and admiration they evoked were intense and lasting. A generation after the independence of India, a culture so endowed with the graces which enhance life that early European visitors were overwhelmed, the place of honor in Calcutta was still the old British club. The change was in the skin and costume of its members, nothing else. *The Times* of London, freshly ironed, was on the tables. Ceiling fans, from Manchester or Glasgow, cooled the white-clad dignitaries as they sipped their gin and tonic or, good Hindus, lemonade. It didn't matter. Being there pronounced them members of the company of English gentlemen. Western civilization was bred in Europe, and the hegemony of Europe established it as the model for the world's ambitions. The supremacy of Europe enshrined its cathedrals, its monuments and arts, its prejudices, tastes, and politics as the very definition of excellence. It is a mistake to consider the reign of Europe only in terms of military dominance and colonial greed. It brought an excitement and a romantic vision of human perfectibility which still inspires, and perhaps deludes, the world.

The extraordinary success of the European powers brought their decline through national rivalry. Now some wise men talk of a near millennium of European conflict as "our long civil war." But the Europeans taught nationalism to the rest of the world even as they exhausted themselves in its quarrels. At the Congress of Vienna, which ended the turbulent Napoleonic period in 1815, the fussy protocol of rank and prestige was the first order of business. None of the five rulers preparing to make the peace for all of Europe could tolerate the idea that one of the other delegates would precede him into the room set aside for the negotiations. After weeks of haggling, the Austrian emperor arranged for five doorways to be made. The five great powers entered simultaneously. It is not a large room. It is in the Ballhausplatz Palace, now the Austrian Foreign Ministry, and is still used on occasion, a reminder that the alternatives for nations are still only diplomacy or war.

The Congress of Vienna, which reestablished a balance of power after the vast upheaval of the Napoleonic Wars, did succeed in keeping the Europeans from general war for a century. But there was no abatement of national antagonisms. They were simply redirected to the race for empire in the rest of the world, and the tensions finally exploded in World War I. That war is seen now as a tragic folly, a series of stumbles and miscalculations which could have been avoided with statesmanship and a little more supple thought, a little less jingoistic bombast. But it was a collapse of systems as nations sought to dominate trade and capture colonies, as ethnic groups sought independence and escape from imperial rule.

When he brought the United States into the war in 1916, President Woodrow Wilson called it "the war to end wars." He articulated the ideals of national self-determination which were to stir the whole globe and liquidate European dominion half a century later. But the attempt to achieve a new order foundered in a single generation. The new borders were contested, and most of the new states had noisily discontented minorities. Irredentism, the demand to redraw maps to meet their aspirations, became a major continental political issue. The League of Nations, a visionary attempt to create a new international concert, was toothless, polemical and ineffective. America's refusal to join capped its incompetence. The harsh provisions of the peace treaties prolonged and deepened the economic ruin of Germany. The intransigence of France provoked a yearning for retribution. The political systems built on the wreckage of the nineteenth century's imperial balance were weak, not only in Germany and Austria, but in Italy, in the Balkans, in Poland. Dictatorships were imposed in many countries, in reaction to a sense of chaos and impotence. As the French poet Paul Valéry said, there are two dangers which never stop threatening the world: order and disorder. Whole populations were driven to desperation when the world economic structure was allowed to break down in the Great Depression. These developments spawned World War II just twenty-one years after the Great War.

Nobody has yet managed to explain the fanaticism Adolf Hitler was able to induce in the Germans, who had considered themselves Europe's finest example of dignified culture, nor the methodical, cold-blooded barbarity of the Nazis. It was modern efficiency run amok in cruelty and hatred. Perhaps the concept of a "master race" was nourished from the same sap that produced Europe's greatness and sense of superiority. Italy and Japan, also discontented powers seeking expansion and resources, joined Germany in the Axis pact. They did not share the Nazis' peculiar ideology, but they too were hungry for lands to dominate, pleased to share in the search for spoils. They were defeated by a grand alliance of most of Western Europe, the British Commonwealth, the United States and the Soviet Union in a crusade that changed the world. The end of World War II in 1945 was the new historic watershed. Modern Europe flows from that event.

As soon as the Allies turned the tide and could anticipate victory, though well before they had achieved it, they began to think about how to avoid the mistakes which brought the second catastrophic war so soon after the first. The leaders were men who had lived through World War I, the illusion of the 1920s that war had been outlawed, the self-deceiving notions of the 1930s that a new war could be avoided by appeasement of Germany's aggrieved demands. Their first concern beyond victory was to make sure the same tragic pattern was not repeated.

For a short time, the victors focused on preventing any possibility of German resurgence. The most common attitude was punitive, to limit German sovereignty and economic capacity so severely that it could never again mount a war machine. But the lesson of the years between the wars forced awareness that an indigent, totally dependent Germany in the heart of Europe would become a permanent drain on the rest of the continent and impede, if not actually preclude, the revival of its wartime victims. It would become a source of infection that eventually would turn into another threat. At the same time, the fractious wartime alliance was quickly breaking down in the Cold War confrontation between the West and the Soviet Union. Churchill had repeatedly warned Roosevelt during the planning for victory that Moscow's expansionist appetites must be forestalled.

But the need to enlist the Soviets in the Pacific war against Japan left Roosevelt little choice but to seek an agreement with Stalin at Yalta, in February 1945. The nuclear bomb had not yet been tested, and there could be no assurance that it would end the war in the Pacific, expected to require an invasion numbering a million men. Besides, a cooperative future depended on being able to project the wartime alliance as the basis for an orderly postwar world. Roosevelt did not want to foreclose that possibility by early confrontation even before the German surrender, which came on May 8, 1945. So there were compromises, soon breached as Moscow made clear its determination to exercise full dominion in the lands occupied by the Red Army. As that came to be seen as a threat to the areas farther west, many Western leaders saw Germany's manpower as a necessary bulwark for the latent conflict with the Soviets.

Even before the Cold War, however, one man at least was working out a different approach to the problem of Germany. He was Jean Monnet of France, a businessman-statesman who had helped organize supply lines in two world wars and who understood the importance of economic resources to political as well as military undertakings. And he had an idea of bringing Europe to peace through economic integration. Germany's remilitarization between the wars, he was convinced, was made possible by its superior access to coal and steel. Instead of imposing limits on German production, he believed that guaranteeing equal access to France and the Low Countries would build a secure future balance. Monnet saw cooperation and integration as the way to safeguard France, not the constraint of force. He was a visionary, dreaming of supranationalism as the remedy for the plague of nationalism which had all but destroyed Europe. He believed in institutions as the only way to instill the lessons of history over generations. And he was practical, pursuing the goal step by step as he worked on the master plan for French recovery. He was frustrated at many points.

With the vital help of the U.S. Marshall Plan, Western European recovery came much faster than anyone had expected. The aid was deliberately provided in a way that buttressed European cooperation and stability in the West. But it helped to sharpen the division from the East. The partition of Germany, and thus of Europe, was imposed first by force and then sealed by the steps taken to promote recovery. Ironically, it was the Cold War and the threat of new hostilities which eventually made possible the peace structure based on Franco-German reconciliation which Monnet had envisioned. The Federal Republic of Germany was embraced in the West, and it warmly welcomed the offers of cooperation with France when Paris grew ready. France gradually moved from seeing German rearmament as a threat to seeing it as an essential protective shield against the military menace farther east. The German Democratic Republic meanwhile took shape as a member of the Soviet bloc. As they rebuilt, each of the two Germanys became the most important European member of the antagonistic alliances.

The war, which had reduced the European powers, also brought the rise of two extra-European superpowers to dispute the fate of the continent. There was a strong current of resistance to the encroaching shadows of the giants on both sides. In the West, this bolstered development of institutions such as the Common Market, which helped revive a sense of European self-reliance and specific identity. The United States, which really had not sought to dominate, encouraged

these efforts, maintaining military support through the North Atlantic
Treaty Organization. Still, many argued for a European "Third Force,"
a neutral or at least noncooperative opposition to what Americans
called leadership and these critics called hegemony. They were mostly
on the left, but there were also those on the right who saw a surrender
of independence in participating in an American sphere of influence.
But the majority were pleased with the direction taken and its rewards
of security, freedom and prosperity. In the East, Soviet might quickly
crushed opponents of the new Communist regimes, and subsequently
also those Communist nationalists who balked at submitting to Moscow.

At the same time as it saw the rise of the superpowers, the postwar
period brought the demise of the European empires. Decolonization
was almost completed in one generation. The world was simultaneously
polarized between the two giants and fragmented into myriad bits, more
than 160 countries, some with scarcely more population than inhabits
a few square miles of apartment buildings in a modern metropolis. The
Europeans emerged as middle powers, vibrant, influential in many
ways, but no longer able to dominate the world.

The development of two global powers, first America and then the
Soviet Union, decolonization with its subsequent perception of north-
south strains, and the drive for modernization to adjust to these two
profound changes are the three major facts defining modern Europe as
a whole. None of its countries really escaped the devastating impact of
World War II, not even Britain, which was never occupied but spent its
substance fighting back. The first concern after the war was reconstruction, which came to mean not just rebuilding but starting afresh. Britain, with its Labour government, set out on a brand new course.
Technological and commercial leadership had passed to the United
States. The Europeans struggled to catch up, though many resented
the drive for change. At first some saw modern techniques as an insidious American domination, an attack on their old identity and cultural
bastions. Gradually, they absorbed new methods and regained self-
confidence.

The Common Market served not only to invigorate and expand the
economic organization of Europe, but also created new social and political networks binding the Western societies, even those which did not
join. The initial six, which signed the Treaty of Rome in 1957, were
France, Germany, Italy, Belgium, Holland and Luxembourg. Britain

had taken part in the negotiations almost until the conclusion, but then walked out. It was still fearful of a continental union and hoped to break it up with competition from a much looser organization based on mutual trade concessions. But the Common Market flourished, and Britain regretted its decision. Finally, in 1973, it entered along with Ireland and Denmark. Norway had planned to join at the same time, but its voters rejected the idea in a referendum after the completion of negotiations. The tenth member admitted was Greece, in 1981. In 1986 Spain and Portugal brought the membership to a dozen, probably the limit for at least a generation because alliances, policies of neutrality or other basic considerations make further accessions unlikely.

Even beyond the borders of the European Community, a certain homogenization took place, tangible in pizza parlors from Stockholm to Lisbon, blue jeans and Adidas shoes, French cheese, the moment's fashionable haircut or hair-straggle everywhere. Modern communications and transport, the vast expansion of trade, made Europe seem much smaller and borders far less an obstacle. A generation of growing prosperity brought rebellious youths and waves of immigrant labor, the seed of future problems, to almost every country. Barriers dropped, restoring freedom from official restrictions and ease of movement, fine new trains, superhighways, mass air transport. The look of the cities changed. Telephones that work, good plumbing, skyscrapers, dreary housing developments, traffic jams came to be taken for granted, no longer characteristic of one country or another but simply of the times. People got in the habit of expecting modern comfort and efficiency everywhere, and it tended to look the same. Language and currency, politics and laws still differed from nation to nation, but there was an interweave of the texture of life which swept throughout Western Europe.

European societies were becoming stabilized. Old patterns of politics had left their traces. There were still extremes, but they had become marginal. In the 1930s, the system of democracy itself was the central issue. Half a century later, the idea of revolution, whether Communist or Fascist, had receded to dwell in a few feverish, impotent minds. Prosperity played an important part in wiping out centuries-long conflict. But attitudes had also been changed by the experience of two devastating wars and the disastrously failed promises of militant ideologies. Western Europeans had, in their variegated ways, become moderates. They had learned to suspect panaceas and to appreciate mild, steady efforts to find practical solutions to practical problems. Above all, the nuclear age and the superpower rivalry made war unthinkable. Though different people had different notions about the best way to preserve it, fighting, quarrelsome Europe had come to cherish peace.

All the boundary disputes, all the irredentist friction that had fed military rivalries for centuries, were swept away. Only at the very edges of the continent, in Northern Ireland and the conflict between Greece and Turkey, are there people who look across the border and perceive the face of an enemy. The same is not true of Eastern Europe. There, almost every border is still disputed. Apart from the frontiers imposed by Soviet incorporation of parts of Poland, Czechoslovakia and Romania and all of the three prewar Baltic states—Lithuania, Estonia and Latvia—almost every Eastern border remains a grievance. Poles and Czechs do not agree on their border. Hungarians yearn to recover Transylvania from Romania. Bulgaria has claims on Yugoslavia. The stability of frontiers in the East is sustained only by the Soviet army. Despite their Communist systems, the Eastern countries have not achieved the mutual consent and forbearance for the post–World War II map which was reached in the West.

There has been a resurgence of nationalism in all the Eastern bloc countries, especially in Poland but even in truncated East Germany, which has launched a rehabilitation of the history of Prussia and Saxony. The countries of the East did not reach their present situation through consensus, free debate, the open consideration of alternatives that permitted the Western nations to reach their mutual accommodation. Their systems, and the World War II border changes, were imposed on them from outside. No one can say how they would behave toward one another if each were free to decide its own fate. But it remains evident that their forced alliance has not put them through the process of rethinking their historical relation with neighbors that has afforded reconciliation in the West. Should the East-West divide ever be healed, there would still be a question of consent to the borders within the East.

At this period of its history, however, peace for Europe is entirely a matter of East-West confrontation. With increasing discomfort in the era of Soviet-American nuclear parity, Western Europe relies on the United States as guarantor of its security. It is at once a blessing and a burden as the Atlantic alliance strains and seeks to mend itself. Not surprisingly, Europeans complain that their protector neglects their interests when Americans are preoccupied elsewhere in the world, as during the Vietnam War, or too provocative toward the Soviet mammoth, as in the first Reagan term. They are no longer economic and political wards and feel a right to self-assertion. Americans, not surprisingly, complain that Europe takes advantage of them, saying the Europeans are not doing their share in paying for their own defense or joining in political offensives. Cyclically, these tensions provoke talk of organizing a more independent Western European defense, loosening the unprecedented bond with the United States that has lasted for two generations. It is a futile cycle that comes to naught because, when the irritations boil over and the steam clears, it becomes obvious that this epoch offers no serious alternative. Until the world takes another drastic spin, any relation other than close alliance would be far worse for both Europe and America.

But there is more than common danger and common advantage tying Europe to America. While it is possible to stress the differences in their development, these are minor compared to the heritage they share, all that is implied by the idea of Western civilization: the arts and sciences, the rule of law, political freedom and the rights of the individual, the notion of humanism. The great achievements of Europe had their seamy side. Europeans imposed much cruelty on the peoples they snared by conquest into their own world vision. They offered a model of nationhood which encouraged war even as it helped to organize societies. They exploited others mercilessly to enrich and oblige honor to themselves. But they also developed the idea and the techniques of progress, of the duty to improve man's condition, of the need to respect him, even if at times they spectacularly rejected noble ideals. Europe is no longer master of the world, but it is now an indispensable mistress, seductive, fecund, sparkling and consoling. It is not fickle, but its lively spirit continues to metamorphose and fascinate.

BRITAIN
After Empire

I T TOOK AN AMERICAN, then Secretary of State Dean Acheson, to put the diagnosis clearly. "Britain has lost an empire and has not found a role," he said in 1962. The British were shocked and angered. They were recovering from the exhausting effects of two world wars in a generation, but proud of victory and unmindful that their reassuring old slogan had become an empty echo. Schoolchildren were still being told, "The sun never sets on the British Empire." "Rule Britannia, Britannia rules the waves . . ." stirred hearts and was believed. At first, the feeling was that the Americans were simply being peevish, brash upstarts as usual. Harold Macmillan, even before he became Prime Minister, had said of wartime relations with the United States that "we played Athens to their Rome." Many thought that, despite a few economic and technical problems left by the great struggle, Britain really was the senior partner in the "special relationship" with America.

Later, American writer William Pfaff devised a theory that the "special relationship" was the insidious cause of Britain's decline, because it provided a false sense of importance and discouraged efforts to restore national vigor and productivity, which the continentals were straining to achieve. Perhaps feeling themselves the wise head on brawny American shoulders did contribute to the slack that overcame Britain in the years after the war. But I think other causes were more important. Apart from a few neutrals, Britain was the only European country that had not been occupied. The British were the only ones who thought they had won the war. Everybody else had tasted defeat at some point. The sense of triumph provoked a psychological disarmament.

So the British were the first to insist on sharing out the political rewards of victory. The ordinary people who had borne the heaviest burdens demanded, as is usual after wars, that they be recompensed with profound changes in a dramatically unfair social system. Even before fighting came to an end in the Pacific, they turned out their beloved, tenacious war leader Winston Churchill and installed a socialist government with a mandate for a welfare state. Equity was the first concern, before renewal. Rationing of food and clothes continued for several years. There were no more bombs or military campaigns. But the grayness remained, unrelieved by the urgent sense of heroic struggle when life had been at stake, yet scarcely infused with the vision of a fine and just new world worthy of yet more sacrifice, which the socialist Labour Party promised.

A few years later, in 1951, with "cradle to the grave" social security laws in place and a number of institutions nationalized, Churchill and his Tories were recalled to power. They did not, could not, dismantle the major reforms and the unprecedentedly heavy taxes. But they lifted a lot of restrictions and constraints. Spirits bloomed. The time for free-wheeling had come again. If enterprise was unleashed, it was a special kind, for the quick return, the easy way, the gleeful "nick" that got one ahead at the expense of the next man. Britain had its "me generation" without rebellious teenagers and unkempt hair long before other countries. Twin brothers John and Roy Boulting captured the cynical exuberance in a brilliantly perceptive film called *I'm All Right, Jack*. The phrase was the maxim of the time. It meant, I'll look after myself and too bad for anyone in my way. It wasn't class war by any means. It was a gentle, nonviolent, usually witty, sometimes hilarious, British form of anarchy. The result, of course, was continued erosion of the economic base just when the rest of Europe was seriously back at work turning reconstruction into sturdy new growth.

At the same time, the illusion of successful emergence from the war worked as blinders for the British leaders looking at the rest of the world. They clung to traditional formulas of a balance-of-power policy toward the continent, seeing bits of what had to be different according to their lights, but without grasping the large pattern of a changing world or preparing their countrymen for a new role. Prime Minister Clement Attlee, who succeeded Churchill while the war in the Pacific was going on, had a general understanding that the colonial system could no longer be sustained as it had been. His government received credit mainly for the welfare state, which would have come anyway and perhaps more rationally. But its greatest contribution to history was to launch decolonization with independence for India. Churchill, who had said, "I did not become His Majesty's First Minister to liquidate the Empire," would almost surely not have done it, and Britain could have been dragged into utter collapse and disorder by the drain of vast colonial wars. As it was, the British departure was precipitous. Up to 100,000 people died in communal fighting, and many millions became refugees in the new states of India and Pakistan. History exacts a high price for undoing wrongs. Still, Britain was saved from catastrophe.

There was a similar experience with Palestine, which was mandated to Britain after World War I. It left an even more troublesome legacy for the rest of the world. After the murder of six million Jews with scarcely a whimper of resistance, and the cold indifference of Western leaders to these people's plight, militant Zionists resolved to take responsibility into their own hands for the survival of those who remained.

Ernest Bevin, the Labour government's Foreign Minister, became increasingly angry and frustrated with the conflict in Palestine. He was a man of vision in many ways, but he had a streak of narrow, working-class anti-Semitism. Finally, in the spring of 1948, he decided the solution was to give up the mandate, pull British administration and forces out of Palestine abruptly and let the Jews and the Arabs fight it out among themselves. The State of Israel was proclaimed on May 14, 1948. All ties with Britain were cut.

In Britain, the process of decolonization was gaining momentum, though not without domestic controversy. Labour Party anticolonialism was rooted not only in impatience with the costly, bloody effort to put down insurrections when the country had had more than enough of fighting. There was also a strong element of ideology, in sympathy with what later came to be called liberation movements. Also, Labour's leaders had long been "Little Englanders," focused on domestic needs and suspicious of involvement with foreign powers. Ready as they were to abandon far-flung possessions, they shared with Conservatives the conviction, traditional from the first Elizabeth's reign, that Britain's security required a continental balance of power. The European federalist ideas of France's Jean Monnet, who had worked closely with

Britain during the war, looked distasteful and even dangerous to London, which opposed continental union. Britain not only refused to join the building of an organized, institutionalized Europe; it fought rearguard actions to dilute and weaken the trend. Only later did British governments come to see "joining Europe" as an alternative to empire, another role in which Britain could not rule but would have had a dominating influence. By then it was too late, or, for France's Charles de Gaulle, too early.

De Gaulle blackballed the British from the new continental club in 1963. Whether he really believed the British were "America's Trojan Horse," as he said, or whether he was primarily swayed by the long history of Franco-English rivalry can only be guessed. Certainly, de Gaulle never doubted that France must continue to have a leading role in the world and, given its weakness, he feared it would be dwarfed by making common cause with Britain. His public argument was based on the "special relationship" of Britain with America, a link based more on perception than on solid fact.

George Bernard Shaw had called Britain and the United States "two countries divided by a common language." But there had always been important ties of culture, law, sentiment. Despite much bickering, the wartime alliance cemented them.

The great decisions on the conduct of the war and the planning for a new world structure were made by Roosevelt and Churchill, though often after sharp disagreement. But the implications were not so far-reaching for the future of Anglo-American relations as de Gaulle professed to believe, a fact sadly demonstrated when President Harry Truman cut off all Lend-Lease aid for depleted Britain immediately after the war. Nor was Britain given extra privileges a few years later when America realized that, in its own interests, it must help finance European reconstruction through the Marshall Plan. Still, the United States tended to maintain closer consultations with London than with other Allied capitals. London's views weighed a little more. And the wartime atomic cooperation, sustained on a more limited basis when postwar spy scandals broke, gave Britain piggyback nuclear power status, which de Gaulle particularly resented. Britain remains the only nuclear-armed country which did not develop its own weapons.

Obsolete psychological and diplomatic assumptions were matched by industrial obsolescence. The Industrial Revolution began in England, draining the people from Scottish valleys and Midlands fields into the grimy mills. It was England's ordeal and the degradation of its workers, far more than Prussia's belated attempt to catch up, which inspired the German social observer Karl Marx to his theories on inevitable developments of capitalism and communism. Coal, iron and textiles, railroads and steamships were the base for the extraordinary expansion of productivity which permitted the second major transformation of human society, first converted from wandering tribes to agricultural communities, then from agriculture to industrial cities.

There was no prodding incentive after the war to renew factories and equipment. After having been so far ahead that the whole world followed, Britain rested and found itself lagging behind. At first, there was a sense of relative advantage. Britain had not suffered as much physical damage as most of the continental belligerents. Engrossed with the thought of well-deserved respite, the British didn't notice for a long time that the desperately impoverished Germans were building new, advanced mills and factories to replace those destroyed by war or dismantled in defeat, a renewal which eventually became a competitive boon. Capital reserves had been drained, limiting investment, at the same time that demands for social justice had been sharpened by sacrifice. This was true everywhere, but continentals and especially the vanquished felt the prior urgency was to rebuild a productive base.

Moreover, in Britain there was little change in structure to match the profound changes in circumstance. The labor unions, formed in fierce struggle with the old industries, reflected the early patterns based on crafts. There is a federation, the Trades Union Congress, but its 105 member unions have intense jurisdictional disputes. Over half the working force is unionized, a high figure compared to France or Germany. Four out of ten working women, who now total a third of the labor force, are union members, compared to only a bit more than two out of ten a generation ago. Particularly important to the power of labor has been unionization of the public sector, itself greatly enlarged by nationalization. In state-run enterprises and services, 85 percent of the employees are in unions, compared to 42 percent in the private sector. Nearly half of the white-collar workers belong to unions, a drastic change from earlier industrial dominance of their membership.

Union spirit and solidarity remain high, reflecting the fury of long-remembered battles. It usually is not hard for a relatively small group of workers with a grievance to bring a dozen or more related unions to the picket line. But bargaining is a game of leap-frog, in which each leader needs to show he can do as well or better by his men than his fellow union leaders. A manager may have to settle fifteen or twenty separate contracts to keep a plant going. Man-days per thousand employees lost by strikes in Britain in recent years were third highest in the Common Market. The tide was turned on union strength by the policies of Prime Minister Margaret Thatcher in the 1980s, however, with laws banning secondary boycotts and lifelong election of leaders and the government's success in breaking several big strikes. The unions also lost their power to deliver their members' votes to the Labour Party in a solid bloc.

The TUC is really the base of the Labour Party, founded as a socialist party by intellectuals but rooted in the union. Yet the argument that a Labour government can rely on better industrial relations and thus produce better than the Tories keeps breaking down in the instinctive adversary role the unions take, even when their party is in power. Len Murray, who became head of the TUC in 1973, was a remarkable change in the traditional style and personality of union leadership, an Oxford-educated man who spoke foreign languages, dressed well and knew which fork to use. He was not touched by the distinctions of accent, clothes, vocabulary that still emblazon class in Britain. But when I asked him in 1967 what the unions really wanted in their rough conflict with Harold Wilson's Labour government, he said, "To bargain as an equal." If the government is the union's bargaining partner, rather than management, then who is to speak for all the other parts of society—the consumers, the professionals, the pensioners, and above all, the general national interest? Murray shrugged at the question. "Let them organize and bargain for themselves," he said. I reminded him that the Marxist dictum said not only "to each according to his need," but also "from each according to his ability." Murray snapped, "I never said I was a Marxist. I'm a union leader." Later, Britain's first woman Prime Minister, Margaret Thatcher, was to make this attitude and union power the prime targets of her economic counterreformation, "privatizing" many of the nationalized industries.

Partly history and traditional attitudes, partly postwar nationalization, which gave government the responsibility of management for large sections of industry, made British unions another serious factor in the loss of economic momentum. Whether nationalized industries are run well or poorly, and there are some of each in several countries, there seems to be a threshold where public ownership becomes an almost unbrakable motor for inflation. It lies at the point where the number of workers in the public sector, with job security and other benefits, set the yardstick for the national wage level in direct negotiations with government. Their combined economic and political leverage applied to a single bargaining partner distorts the production system. Crossing that threshold stopped Italy's "economic miracle," though Italy has had conservative governments since 1945. Socialist-run countries, with a strong egalitarian bias and generous welfare systems but a relatively small public sector, as Sweden and Holland were for long periods, have not encountered the same problem. Wage levels continue to be dominated by accords between unions and private management, with the government outside the process in the role of social and political arbiter.

To make matters worse, the vigor of British democracy imposed excessive economic zigzags. Steel was nationalized, denationalized, renationalized. The reversals and uncertainty about the structure of the economy were more of a restraint on investment and enterprise than continuity of either public or private ownership would have been. Robust British politics, with the secure confidence that alternation in power is possible and peaceful, is an important element in the civility the country has developed. A coup or a dictatorship is unthinkable. Democracy works in the most profound sense that everyone can take for granted their side will have its chance if it can persuade the majority. So there is no impulse to upheaval or constraint on freedom. But like so many virtues, it imposes a cost when the issues are fundamental and the pendulum swings too often. There is broad consensus on the most important values in Britain, but not on certain economic and social policies. Yet real growth requires longer foresight and stability than the electoral calendar can provide. Regular switches in ideology when a government falls from grace weaken the base of production.

It is a national paradox that such a humane society, so dedicated to liberty and decency, so protective of animals, so imbued with individual pride, should remain so rigidly conscious of class. After *I'm All Right, Jack* came the era of the Angry Young Men, epitomized in John Osborne's play *Look Back in Anger*. The young men from the industrial cities of the Midlands and the north were infuriated to find that the tremendous reforms, the egalitarian generosity of the welfare state, still had done nothing to break the invisible barriers to opportunity and social reward. The country had settled down cozily in its old habits,

assigning each to his "place." "Knowing your place" remained the by-
word to getting by without friction. But youth's moral rebellion at the
maintenance of strictly, if subtly, defined layers in the social pyramid
was short-lived. Acceptance, indeed assertion, of the right to class consciousness is too deep, almost as though class were an inalienable aspect
of identity.

The attitude is not one-sided. Shaw thought it was. He pinpointed
accent and vocabulary as the great barricade erected by the establishment to keep the lower classes down. In *Pygmalion*, he argued that it
could be overcome if only the English would "teach their children how
to speak." In his will, he left a lot of money for development of a
phonetic alphabet that would make it easier for all to speak English
"properly." To highlight the absurdity of English nonphonetic spelling,
Shaw offered "ghoti" as the logical way to spell *fish*—*gh* as in *rough*, *o*
as in *women*, *ti* as in *station*.

Long afterward, the novelist C. P. Snow recalled the launching of
the British Broadcasting Corporation in the early 1920s. For the first
time, national radio would tune everyone in to the same diction. The
question was which should have preference. "We thought we could
undermine class by offering a standardized pattern that wasn't linked
to any level or region," he said ruefully in the 1970s. "BBC English"
was no accident. It was a careful, conscious attempt to destroy the most
immediately recognizable label by which the English sort themselves
out and thus to create equality of opportunity. Snow conceded the
failure. "BBC English" itself became a label of pretension, of a lack of
authenticity, and an object of ridicule. Every layer clung to its own
speech pattern. One of the most insistent demands of the Angry Young
Men was to be respected for speaking in the manner they had learned
at their mother's knee. They succeeded. The BBC abandoned the attempt to create a model English and, in what Americans came to call
"affirmative action," put a variety of representative voices on the air.
When money, education, fashion and political power made it possible
to get rid of class as an institution, the British refused almost unani-
mously. They may argue about which "place" is more honorable, but
they intend to show they know their own. A poll published in *The Times*
in 1980 showed that when it comes to aspirations, 79 percent of the
people wanted their children "to do better in life" than themselves, but
only 7 percent said they would like to know "a better class of people."

A little scene at the time of the chaotic Conservative Party Conference which chose Sir Alec Douglas-Home as leader and thus, eventually, Prime Minister in 1963 illustrated the automatic reflex. The conference was in Blackpool, a rather garish seaside resort which has some grand old hotels but caters primarily to the boardinghouse set. Strings of colored lights in arty patterns adorn the streets to give a holiday atmosphere. There is a huge convention center, called the Winter Garden, with rooms for several large gatherings at the same time. As the tall, pink Tories filed in, the women powdered and pearled, the men tweedy or pin-striped, another flow of chunky, dark people went through the same doors. The men were in cardigans and cloth caps, the women in dowdy prints. They walked alongside each other, but they never mixed, and they knew immediately they were headed for different auditoriums. No one made the mistake of going to the wrong place, all followed their kind. There wasn't a hint of resentment on the workers' faces nor a word said about C. P. Snow's description of the "two nations" of England. It was obvious that both were more comfortable with segregation. That fact underlies the "us" and "them" of politics, with the middle class arbitrating to provide the healthy rhythm of change and consolidation.

There are many things to override the schism nonetheless. The advent of "swinging London" is one example. That was the time of the miniskirt and the Beatles in the 1960s. There was enough prosperity for young people to have money of their own to spend, for the first time. The new market imposed new styles and a new disregard for quality. Victorian standards were enthusiastically shooed away. It seemed liberating to buy cheap and often, to be daring, to rip away the shame with which the prudish Queen had staunchly veiled the enduring foibles of the British. The period provided the revenge of the uppers and the lowers against the stolid middleness she had enshrined and brought a long-awaited release of gaiety and self-indulgence after the grim years of war and the worried years of Whither Britain.

Of course, it couldn't last. "Stagflation," the puzzling combination of industrial stagnation (considered normal to recession) with galloping inflation (supposed to revive the economy by stimulating demand) first appeared in Britain. It brought what are now seen as predictable results. The proud pound sterling was buffeted into repeated devaluations. It became impossible to maintain sterling's role as a worldwide reserve currency and measure of value, a function ceded in the 1960s to the U.S. dollar alone. Britain would have had to export more and more to buy the essential imports of food and raw materials, but it could not. The standard of living not only stopped rising well before continental Europe felt the pinch of slackened growth; it actually began to decline. People talked of the "British disease," of Britain as the new "sick man of Europe." North Sea oil production, spurred by soaring OPEC prices, offered a respite but it was understood as a windfall. The middle class reasserted itself. A new leader, remarkably a woman, but tough-minded, her voice ringing with conviction in praise of the mythic "old values," was given power in 1979.

Margaret Thatcher was almost a caricature of Victorian virtues— patriotism, discipline, a degree of masochism in the belief that a bad taste means the medicine is good. Her sculptured hairdo, the jeweled brooch above the bosom, the impeccable propriety of appearance and manner offered nostalgic reassurance that Britain was back on the familiar track where rewards were won by good behavior. She promised to "squeeze out the fat" with a policy of austerity that further threatened Britain's flabby industrial muscle. Unemployment soared well beyond a record three million before idle productive capacity began to be used again. Many from the dying industries would probably never find another job. Prospects for the young were bleaker than they had ever been since the terrible 1930s.

Still, Mrs. Thatcher's Conservatives were reelected in 1983. A surge of old-fashioned flag waving, generated by the expensive but successful expedition to retake the bleak South Atlantic Falkland Islands after an Argentine invasion in 1982, made her a temporary heroine. Britain rode high again, for a nostalgic, almost Disneyland moment of recovered righteousness and self-confidence. But it was a passing thrill. Mrs. Thatcher's overwhelming majority of seats in Parliament was not a measure of solid popularity. The Labour Party had lurched leftward, ever more Little England and archaically ideological in response to Mrs. Thatcher's ideological conservatism. It repelled much of the moderate left.

A new party, groping for the abandoned center, was founded by breakaways from Labour. They called themselves Social Democrats and made an alliance with the hitherto ineffectual Liberals. Together, they polled almost as much as Labour, but they won few seats because their support was dispersed around the country. In any case, it would have been miraculous in a country that clings so much to habit if the Liberal–Social Democrat alliance had achieved its goal of becoming a balance wheel in a single election. Founders of a new party in Britain have to expect to wait a generation or so before achieving a solid, mass base. The combined opposition results showed that there was no question of dismantling the welfare state even under Thatcherism, only of paring benefits to revive work incentives and cut government spending.

An important part of Mrs. Thatcher's support came from the very success of the welfare state, from workers who had built up a new stake in the economy, which they wanted to protect. Shrewdly, she had enabled them to buy homes cheaply. With a stronger sense of security, achieved over years of Labour reforms, they too had come to resent the bossiness and constraints of their unions. A photograph taken during the campaign illustrated other factors that tipped the scale in that election. It showed three smiling women with a banner that read "Maggie Is Our Man." For all her talk about old values, Mrs. Thatcher was a new phenomenon for 10 Downing Street, home of British Prime Ministers, and not just because she was a woman. Resolutely middle class, her accent, her clothes, her cheer embodied what many determined should be the real look of Britain. She was the second Tory Prime Minister to come from a state-supported rather than an elite school. She spoke with pride about having lived above her father's grocery store. But the luckless Edward Heath, who had made it to the top before her, was seen as a wishy-washy man, uncertain, pouty, without grit. People who didn't like "Maggie" or her ideas believed what she said.

Arch-Tory writer Peregrine Worsthorne, whose aristocratic refinement matched his name, said thoughtfully after rejoicing at Mrs. Thatcher's victory, "She considers the idle rich as reprehensible as the idle poor." A teenager, ostentatiously punk with brush-cut green-dyed hair, huge safety pins dangling from his leather jacket, defiantly trying to be cynical, said nonetheless in Trafalgar Square on election night, "Better an Iron Lady than those men of cardboard."

Born Margaret Hilda Roberts to the son of a shoemaker and the daughter of a railway porter, the future Mrs. Denis Thatcher learned to admire hard work, individual responsibility and adherence to principle. Her mastery of political skills she acquired on her own. But she gave her father, a Methodist lay preacher, credit for her steadfastness. "Pa made me a conviction politician," she said later. She divided the people around her into loyalists, whom she praised as "one of us," and "wets," a schoolgirl expression for weak-kneed, irresolute boys. "I usually make up my mind about people in ten seconds, and I seldom change it," she said. As the chance arose to push them aside, she ruled out of date the continental vision of the "English gentleman," so long envied, imitated and ridiculed. She chose self-made men—Leon Brittan, son of a Lithuanian Jewish immigrant, Norman Tebbitt, an ex-airline pilot and union organizer, Nigel Lawson, an arrogant, witty, biting former journalist. It was the beginning of a revolution for the old Tories, and perhaps for Britain itself, substituting a meritocracy for the hallowed notion of "place." The ideal she set forth for the country was self-improvement through individual effort, in effect the transformation of the middle class from a state to be derided into a national aspiration.

The 1982 war to recapture the Falkland Islands from Argentina had a lot to do with both her popularity and her sense of "what Britain stands for." It was Mrs. Thatcher's war, fought on the sheer principle of keeping the Union Jack flying, at high cost and no direct benefit. But Britain won. The faraway battle had coalesced and mobilized spirits as nothing since the blitz in World War II. The victory loosed a surge of national pride and a new sense that "Britain can do it," after the waning years. The smoldering embers of patriotism, even jingoism, burst into flamboyant, near unanimous community. But the economy was still sluggish, and social grievances mounted again.

In the 1970s, before Mrs. Thatcher became Prime Minister and when the economic doldrums had become overwhelming, a Labour member of Parliament suggested that, far from falling behind, Britain was once again out in front of the world. He was William Rodgers, one of the bright, urbane, intelligent young men in the new leadership when Labour's Harold Wilson ousted the Tories' Harold Macmillan, whose image as "Super-Mac" had been too shiny not to tarnish. Rodgers was on the wrong side then. He was ousted by his own constituency party committee for being too reasonable, too moderate. But he said he didn't mind because it meant he could spend more time sailing his dinghy, cultivating his garden, devoting himself to the private pleasures that determine the "quality of life." His point was that just as Britain had led the Industrial Revolution, what was called its decline could in fact mean that it was leading the postindustrial revolution to a more serene, humane way of life. He didn't grow long hair, wear beads and sandals, or make his own yogurt. But he did epitomize the way the British had turned inward, lowering their sights, retreating into the old, traditional solace of "every Englishman's home is his castle." The mood didn't last as the irritations with decline piled up, nor did Rodgers' retirement. In 1981, he broke from Labour to help form the Social Democratic Party, becoming one of its principal strategists in the effort to establish a choice between Mrs. Thatcher's hard right push and Labour's sharp swing to the left.

Britain was almost alone among the industrial or industrializing countries in not having suffered an acute spasm in the enigmatic year 1968. It had had earlier spurts of youthful irreverence and rebelliousness, but they had been absorbed, more or less accommodated. Titled dowagers with blue-tinted hair had been as enthusiastic participants of Beatlemania as pimply schoolgirls. The British aristocracy and the working class had always shared a disdain for the industrial rat race, the assembly-line mentality. It wasn't hard to adjust to the idea of making do with less if it meant less work and more leisure. *The Times* poll in 1980 showed 51 percent of the people saying they would refuse to work longer hours for more money, against 45 percent who would have been willing. And only a bare majority, 52 percent, said they would prefer to continue their five-day week with more money, against 44 percent who wanted work time cut to four days at their current pay. Ambition, getting ahead, might be economically satisfying, but in Britain it is socially suspect and earns a certain smug contempt. It is possible that the British were in the vanguard in seeing endless material growth, permanent appetite for consumption no matter how pointless, as an illusion, or anyway not worth the candle.

The aphoristic "stiff upper lip" is not really stoicism but disdain for what is seen as minor disturbances of the good life, ruled by good manners. "Mustn't grumble" is the ideal British response to trouble, the real display of superiority over other peoples who allow life to harass them. It has been said that this attitude makes the British the world's best airline passengers and has given them one of the world's worst airlines. Such behavior is incomprehensible to continentals. Jean Elleinstein, a French Communist historian who became disillusioned with his party and began traveling to see the world with freshly opened eyes, returned to Paris appalled at what he had experienced in London. "The British really have lost their spine," he reported. "They are down and nothing can stir them. They stand patiently on the sidewalk, waiting in line for a taxi like sheep. I ran ahead and grabbed the first one, and nobody said a thing to me. They just stared." The Frenchman assumed they were staring in awe at his audacity, in timorous resignation. It never occurred to him that the kind of British stare he received is infinitely more insulting, more damning by British standards than the crudest, most outrageous flow of French obscenity.

Civility, "what is done," remains the central factor of British life. Like the unwritten constitution, the unwritten rules of behavior pervade all attitudes and undermine all attempts to transform the society. Ralf Dahrendorf, a German sociologist who went to live in London and analyzed British society with an outsider's eyes, came to the conclusion that its quintessentially middle-class Prime Ministers Edward Heath and Margaret Thatcher were really trying to change the country into a kind of Germany with their appeals for a different approach to work, a greater respect for the demands of efficiency. They were doomed to failure, he maintained, because of the stubborn British insistence on "the way we've always done it," the way people cling to their own idea of themselves. It misleads some foreigners into the notion of British untouchability. It is also expressed in reverse, in the accepted right to flout norms and try to shock in dress or speech, a kind of acknowledgment that the rules are still omnipresent. Such a web of subtle, intricate and almost instinctive rules make planting bombs or organizing riots unnecessary. The punk style took particular hold in Britain, with middle-class boys and girls who would have been radicals or perhaps even terrorists in Germany or Italy dyeing pink or green streaks in their hair, dressing in the rebellious uniform of the moment, wandering in the streets and crowding the discos in harmless but apparently satisfying defiance of the rest of society, which refused to conform to nonconformity. A special place of indulgence, even affection, is reserved for the eccentric, because he or she is the exception that proves the rule.

A great many things can be taken for granted in such a climate. The streets of London and the other major cities are allowed to deteriorate with rows of tacky, peeling houses. Self-respect is preserved by tending the roses and geraniums in the little garden plot behind each home. Eighty-five percent of Britons' houses have a garden attached, far more private gardens than in any other European country. There are 100,000 miles of public footpaths for the pleasure of walkers.

The most important effect of the British sense of the "quality of life" is the meaning of work. Statistics show the British work longer and have fewer holidays than continentals, but they refuse to work very hard. The tea break was hallowed long before American offices began to permit coffee breaks. Dahrendorf observes, "Any foreigner who watches the British at work cannot help being amazed at their leisurely pace. In this, the division of labor helps; few people would dream of helping out if something has broken down. Instead, one waits for 'the experts' to turn up. Indeed, it would be interesting to know how much time working people in Britain spend waiting for something. Work is about life, not life about work. Britain's version of liberty is living at work rather than just living for work, and this may well be a more plausible liberty than that of the Continental who works his guts out on some other job when he has left his job, and who never stops working."

Egalitarianism is of a special kind, the equal right to defend a traditional privilege or custom. That applies not only to the adoration of royalty, the determined maintenance of titles used just as enthusiastically by a socialist elevated to the peerage as by an heir to the distinction. A British Leylands automobile plant was shut down by a strike for months in 1983 because management ordered an end to the workers' right of six minutes' "washing-up time." Half a century earlier the union had gained the concession of ending the workday six minutes early. There had been all sorts of changes since then, of course, in overtime pay, work rules, the organization of the factory. The labor force had turned over many times. But even a threat to close the plant, which had been losing money, could not budge the refusal to surrender in the name of productivity a right that had once been "won."

To stand on an issue of established principle is widely understood. That was what rallied the British to the perilous adventure of recapturing the Falkland Islands from Argentina to preserve the right of 1,200 residents to live under the British flag. It was at the root of the painful, nerve-wracking dilemma debated throughout the country over issuing guns to certain policemen obliged to risk their lives in trying to arrest armed criminals.

Street crime increased significantly in the 1970s and early 1980s, as in virtually all countries. Chief constables banded together, however, to resist arguments from a few in the public and insist that their officers should not be armed except "as a last resort where conventional methods had been tried and failed, or must from the nature of the circumstances obtaining, be unlikely to succeed if tried," in the words of Kenneth Oxford, chief constable of Merseyside and president of the Association of Chief Police Officers. The chairman of the Police Federation, representing rank-and-file policemen, said, "I want to make it clear that our policy on the use of firearms remains the same as it has always been."

The perennial argument about schools, a national obsession, also has to do with questions of principle and the right to choice as essential to the quality of life. On the continent, the traditional argument about schools has to do with religion and whether the state should support education sponsored by the Church. A whole series of governments in France's postwar Fourth Republic fell over the dispute between the traditionally anticlerical left and the church-respecting (but seldom churchgoing) right. There are not many vocal anticlericals in Britain. That role is replaced by chapel and the Low Church (as opposed to the officially established High Anglican rite). The British issue is elitism, whether the expensive "public" schools, totally supported by privately paid fees and donations, should be allowed to continue alongside tax-supported education. The Duke of Wellington's alleged remark that the Battle of Waterloo was won "on the playing fields of Eton" is often cited to defend the notion of excellence sustained only by maintaining an elite.

The burden of school fees has much impoverished the upper and middle classes, along with heavy taxation. Still, they persist in straining their finances to make sure their children will have access to their idea of a quality life. In fact, these schools have had a great deal to do not only with the continuance of a fragmented class structure but also with cementing the nation. The children come from various areas but they are molded into a single, lifelong community. To judge from the endless number of plays and books about life at boarding school turned out year after year for greatly appreciative audiences, it must be a searing experience, never forgotten by those who participate and always regarded with fascination and a twinge of envy by those who do not. It homogenizes the people who run the nation even as it divides them from the rest. It is the channel for passing from generation to generation that unwritten set of rules by which the country lives.

To the extent there is a special British attitude to sex, that too is a product of the school system. One need only mention Shakespeare and Sheridan to demolish the myth that the British don't like bawdry, that something about the climate or geography or race turns them against sensual frivolity and passion. True, the Victorian ethos forced interest in sex behind heavy curtains, or behind stairs. But even then, anything was permitted except being found out. However, the widespread practice of sending the children who will grow up to set the standards away to a kind of cloister at puberty does leave its mark. Not only are adolescent boys firmly separated from adolescent girls, with social meetings made fearsome by careful control and contrivance, but they are also kept away from their parents. Just when they are likely to take notice of what they see and hear among adults and absorb it as natural, they are excluded.

Conversational taboos guarantee acute embarrassment in investigating the subject, which of course they do nonetheless. One result is a particular, schoolboyish humor about sex that can last for life, and makes the British seem odd to continentals. Even now, the BBC can broadcast as uproarious comedy a skit about a young cleric seeking advice from his seniors on marriage. It goes on and on with contortions of innuendo on how to relieve him of innocence. The denouement, which rollicked listeners, was that the cleric was going to perform a marriage and had questions about the ceremony, not the consummation. Only the British would find it funny. The assumption that upper-class boarding schools foster an inordinate amount of homosexuality among the British is widely held, but dubious. It may be that their sense of the proprieties makes them more aware of it and more sensitive to the knowledge. Italians, Frenchmen, Germans may be homosexual, or may feel revulsion or indifference to it, but they don't pretend to be surprised that homosexuality exists.

Britain's birthrate is going down, as in most of Europe. The number of illegitimate births, divorces and couples cohabiting without marriage is going up. But most people who are married say they are quite content with the arrangement, and most marriages are made between people who were born within twenty miles of each other. This is despite the fact that there has been a very substantial population movement reversing the earlier trend toward the cities. Greater London lost 10 percent of its population in the last fifteen years, Merseyside 9 percent, and more rural East Anglia and the southwest gained. It is a reflection of the concern for a greater easiness of everyday life even at the loss of urban advantages. There are other signs that this postindustrial change of motivation is general.

Pollution, once such an English specialty that London's "pea soup" fogs were legendary, has been effectively combatted. There are strict rules about what can be burned in city fireplaces, and while homes are often still cold, many more have some form of central heating. There is still fog in the winter, of course, but no longer the dense, yellow blanket that once stifled cities and stopped all traffic. The poisoned rivers are being brought back to life. Even the highways, indiscriminate killers in the rest of Europe, have been tamed. With twice as many cars on the road as a generation ago, the highway death toll has actually been reduced.

There is another side, however, to renewed dedication to the quality of life. It has led to letting things run down. If repairmen don't want to work at odd hours or at times reserved for leisure, the indispensable machinery of modern life cannot be well maintained. Efficiency often has a low priority, and Britons will put up with poor service and shoddy goods that people of similar economic and social standing elsewhere would not tolerate. The older sense of quality, insistence on the best, has been undermined. That is really what Mrs. Thatcher means in her harangues calling for greater effort at keeping up standards and values.

The identikit portrait of the modern Briton, drawn from polls and statistics, yields a thirty-seven-year-old woman, married, probably at work. This is a numerical paradox, because the excess by almost 3 percent of women over men in the population is primarily found in the older age groups, owing to longer female life expectancy. Despite the 1975 Act Against Sex Discrimination, women earn only 65 percent as much as men, and they have actually been losing ground in the last decade in upward job mobility. In the enclosed little world of "Oxbridge," the number of women students admitted to the once all-male colleges of Oxford and Cambridge has dropped dramatically a decade after the sex barrier was officially removed. The American feminist Betty Friedan had a hard time in a Cambridge debate trying to argue that women's liberation brought advantages to men as well.

Only two out of five families now conform to the traditional pattern of working father, housewife and dependent children. Gardening is the favorite hobby, and walking is the favorite sport. The overwhelming majority is Protestant, and large numbers regularly go to church. *The Times* discovered, to its surprise, that more people go to church on Sunday than to football (soccer) matches on Saturday and that "the clergy maintain a high place in public esteem even if the image is one of slightly dotty eccentricity." But churchgoing doesn't imply austerity of habit. The consumption of alcohol has risen sharply, mostly beer, though Britons still drink only half as much as the French and suffer only 7 percent as many cases of cirrhosis of the liver. Gambling has always been a widespread national indulgence. Of all adults, 39 percent are regular bettors, and 60 percent of the men and 40 percent of the women bet at least occasionally. The type of gambling tends to be a class affair. The uppers bet on horses and go to casinos. The lowers favor dog racing and bingo games. Weekly football pools have the same compulsive attraction as national lotteries in Latin countries. Watching TV, the best in the world, consumes twenty hours of the average Briton's week. Social life tends to consist of going out to a pub or a club for a drink rather than giving and attending parties, except for the upper classes.

Travel, once reserved for aristocrats and colonial administrators, has become a mass phenomenon, though the British retain their disdain for and suspicion of the natives of "abroad." One in every four Britons takes an annual vacation outside the country. That experience plus the free entry of Common Market foodstuffs and the immigration of workers have changed eating habits. It is still as hard to get a good meal in Britain as it is to be well served in France, but the variety of foods and cuisines available has increased enormously. That hasn't dulled the national sweet tooth, induced no doubt by the traditional dullness of British food. The country is one of the world's largest per capita consumers of candy and chocolate.

More than half (52 percent) of the families own their house, and practically everybody has a bathroom now, definitely not the case in the 1950s, when a majority did not. But fewer have cars than elsewhere, 256 per 1,000 people, compared to 346 in Germany and 536 in the United States. On the other hand, most people own tools and do their own odd jobs around the house, often because it is so hard to find a willing professional craftsman, and so expensive.

The average Briton is, of course, both a reality and a mirage. The United Kingdom of Great Britain (England, Scotland and Wales) and Northern Ireland is in many senses four distinct nations well aware of their differences. The whole U.K. is slightly smaller than Oregon, with a population about equal to that of France or Germany. But it is heavily concentrated and there are striking differences of landscape, which have almost as much to do with cultural contrasts as does history. In southwest Cornwall, where Land's End pokes out into the warm Gulf Stream, there are palm trees. Wine grapes are grown, though more as a hobby than in serious competition with France and Italy. The "home counties," clustered around London, look so much like Normandy that they are a reminder of the ancient connection, with gently rolling fields, narrow hedged lanes, square stone church towers. The regions are similar, that is, where the countryside has not been submerged by the highways, huge squat factories and dormitory towns that spread across the "Golden Triangle" of the southeast during a spurt of construction in the late 1950s and 1960s. This is the area of gracious living for those who can afford it, and of memorable cathedral towns which were the market centers when England thrived on agriculture and wool.

The Midlands was the early center of industry, based on the coal mines and the once great port of Liverpool. It is the home of squat, dark people, such a contrast with the rosy-cheeked rural squire-archy. Whether they had different origins among the waves of conquerors and migrants who washed across the British Isles since pre-Roman times, or whether their shape and mien were changed by many generations of back-breaking toil and bad diet, can only be guessed. Nobody goes to the Midlands for soothing immersion in the beauties of nature, but it was a crucial source for the great burst of energy which made Britain a global power.

Wales lies along the west coast, its bright green valleys despoiled in places by coal slag. The Welsh come from the same people as the Gauls of Brittany, and they share an ancient poetic mysticism. The local languages are similar. During the intense regional surge of cultural separatism in the 1970s, Celtic conferences were held, bringing together Welsh, Irish, Scots and Bretons, who tried to talk to each other in dialect and nourish ethnic revival. It didn't last long. The nation-state remains the basic European unit. But the Welsh are deeply attached to their land and their memories. They emigrate less than others. They tend to keep apart.

The lovely Lake Country lies below what is still called "the Borders" with craggy, damp Scotland and its forbidding offshore islands. Life in Scotland is harder. It makes for dour, weathered people who warm themselves during long northern nights with good stories and their magic brew. Their innate sense of practicality, and perhaps lack of access to London's closed circle of political, financial and cultural dominance, have turned many Scots to engineering, medicine, the applied sciences. Their ancestors were adventurers who roamed the world, driven by politics after the Stuart wars, by need when industry sprouted to the south, and later by the opportunity to practice their skills. A failed history that promised glory, but lost, weighs on them. The clannishness bred by the rigors of life in mountain bands persists in social ties that defy the English class and occupation strata. The castles of the

Frasers and Athlones and others are still the sites of the great summer gatherings where the laird and his clan celebrate their old fealties, a belonging that transcends status; it is a vast family reunion.

Oddly, the assertions of regionalism in these self-consciously distinct lands fluctuate in inverse proportion to the government's control. The British system is at once highly centralized and meticulously observant of certain local rights. With the exception of Scotland, which maintains its own laws on a few subjects, such as criminal justice and inheritance, the writ of the Houses of Parliament runs absolute throughout the land. The splendid halls at Westminster, topped by an ornate tower holding the clock known as Big Ben, have given their name around the world to the political structure called the "Westminster model." The architecture itself helped shape the system. The long narrow chamber of the Commons is lined with benches. The government members sit on the front bench to the right of the Speaker, supporters on the benches behind. The opposition, its "shadow cabinet" in front, sits on the Speaker's left. They change when the voters transfer power. As a result, "right" and "left" never accumulated the heavy emotional baggage they have in semicircular continental legislatures. Over the centuries, the House of Lords has gradually been stripped of its predominance. Now it is primarily a debating society; it can delay legislation for a year, but the Commons can pass the same bill again and put it into effect. Ministers must be members of one House or the other, but it is no longer considered acceptable for the Prime Minister to come from the Lords. Lord Home had to renounce his peerage to head the government as Sir Alec Douglas-Home.

The "Westminster model" implies a system that assures full opposition rights, a government that can be turned out by vote of a majority, and a Prime Minister's right to call elections at will. There is no separation of powers, as in the United States. The judiciary has rigorous independence, but cannot void an act of Parliament. Many former British colonies in the third world sought to copy the system. Few succeeded. Citizens' rights are assured by an accretion of parliamentary and judicial custom as firmly anchored as in any constitution, but there is no sacrosanct text.

The other traditional limit on Parliament's power is local government, which is strongly entrenched. It runs its own police force and school system, under a national framework, and provides community services. The British, unlike the continentals, are strong on voluntary associations. They take a lively interest in the performance of local officials and supplement their function in many, often generous, ways. "Authority" is never the awesome word it is for most of Europe. Bureaucracy, inevitable in the welfare state, chafes. That is one major reason for the popular swing against statism.

There is nothing in between the highest and lowest levels of government, despite occasional efforts to build a buffer. All though the 1970s, regional nationalism waxed. The Welsh demanded new privileges for their lilting, unpronounceable language and the BBC had to give them local television time. Scotland made "devolution" of powers from London to regional government a key political issue. The urge for separatism was fueled by discovery of North Sea oil, which some Scots thought belonged to them and could be the base for viable economic independence. Finally, when Parliament agreed to a referendum on the issue of autonomy, the Scots turned it down and agitation subsided. Local nationalism was seen as a stirring emotion, but not a practical project. The ebb and flow of regionalism in Britain more or less matched similar movements on the continent.

Northern Ireland, of course, is a special case. It had its own legislature and Prime Minister, until they were suspended because of communal violence, though London always retained primary powers. Now that is more of an obligation and a headache than a determination to rule, despite the claim to the contrary of Irish nationalists. There was a time when immigration lines at British air- and seaports were divided and labeled for "British" and "Irish and others." Today there are three lines, one for British, the second for people with passports from European Community countries, and the third simply "others." Republic of Ireland passports come under the Community heading, and the aura of opprobrium has gone. The tragic civil war in Northern Ireland has led to spates of terrorism in London. But disgust with the murderous tactics of IRA fanatics has not led to any serious revival of the old anti-Irish feeling in England. As much as it demands of the British, Ulster (the six northern counties of Ireland) is seen basically as an Irish problem, the unpleasant residue of ancestral ambitions and injustices which the rest of the United Kingdom would be glad to shuck off if it could find a satisfactory way.

Xenophobia, in fact downright racism, has been transferred to immigrants from farther away, with darker skins. It has old roots, in geography as well as habit. Insularity is a way of rejecting aliens. When

Britain considered itself at the apogee of global involvement, between
the two world wars, a famous headline in *The Times* announced one
day, "Heavy Fog Over Channel, Continent Cut Off." But there are
divisions, and subdivisions, and sub-subdivisions of opinion on the
exact location of the navel of the universe, outside of which everyone
else is alien. "Natives" aren't people born in Britain, but the people
Britain once ruled. An elderly Englishwoman, transported to Germany,
remarked with surprise "how many natives there are in the American
army," meaning blacks.

The British are more cosmopolitan about Europeans now. People
from the third world are a different matter. They have brought the
vestige of empire back to the metropolis. But the old colonial color bar
works quite differently where black and brown people are not "natives"
under British rule but newcomers. Britain is not alone in this respect.
All the countries of Europe welcomed immigrants in the period of
expanding prosperity, and began to consider them trouble when recession set in. They are the problem of the future. The existence of the
Commonwealth brought large numbers of Pakistanis, Indians and West
Indians to Britain, along with a flow of Greeks, Italians, Spaniards and
Portuguese from impoverished southern villages to the richer north.
One in twenty people in Britain now is foreign-born or the offspring of
the immigrant generation.

It is a shock for an insular nation accustomed to dealing with "others"
only on its own terms, in the others' far-flung lands, and on the basis of
assumed superiority. The look of London has changed dramatically,
with whole neighborhoods gone black or brown and the gamut of
human skin tones bustling along the main streets. Regent Street, Oxford Street, the Strand have lost their staid dignity and taken on the air
of a bazaar. The immigrants do the dirty jobs and live in rather dirty
places, clustering together for protection against their unfamiliar and
sometimes hostile surroundings. There is a tension between the customs of British democracy and British courtesy established for the
homeland and the habits of condescension and command established
for imperial rule.

The British did not set out to conquer the world or paint the map in
their colors. They were seafarers and traders. Colonists were either
refugees, as the Pilgrims in Massachusetts, or adventurers seeking new
homes and better fortune. London's interest was in the business they

brought, and the rise of the merchant class in England was the impulse for mercantilism. After the ouster of the Stuarts in 1688, Parliament gained a new preponderance and with it the traders expanded their power. Gradually through the eighteenth century, they established more and more outposts.

It was an irony that while Britain lost the thirteen colonies which became the United States because of American revulsion against mercantilist excesses, it began to accumulate its global empire as a result of the Napoleonic Wars which followed. There was no concerted policy of aggrandizement. At each stage there were political quarrels about whether it was worth the cost. What in modern terms could be called the liberals and conservatives found themselves changing sides from period to period. The American Revolution led some to conclude that the old colonial policy was too severe and that mercantile interests could be better preserved by local self-government and looser ties to the Crown. But the dominant view was that the colonies had been given too much freedom and that stricter government control was needed.

Colonial policy wavered from place to place and time to time, but always serving the essential aim of trying to keep order at the least expense and greatest reward. The decision to abolish the East India Company and subject the subcontinent to imperial domain after the Mutiny of 1857 was the watershed. What came after was spurred by strategic concerns to keep the sealanes open to India, rivalry with the other European powers who developed colonial ambitions, and a messianic belief in Britain's "civilizing mission" which justified territorial conquest in the name of ending slavery and uplifting the natives. Rudyard Kipling and his compatriots were truly convinced of their generosity in taking up "the white man's burden." To lessen the strain, the British sought to rule through local chiefs and nabobs.

In India particularly, where they were dazzled by the luxury, the sensuous delights of bright colors and exotic spices, the refinement of art and divertissement, they accommodated very well to local society in what were often considered mutually advantageous relations with native rulers. It wasn't until the colonial administrators and officers started bringing out their women that race became an issue. The memsahibs, it must be suspected, realized they could not easily compete with the seductive local lovelies and their amiable ways. A painting made before the Englishwomen arrived now hangs in a home in the London borough of Kensington. It shows Englishmen and Indians sporting uproariously at one of the many festivities. The painting was true enough to life that when it reached England the family of one of the revelers recognized him. He was immediately reproved and disinherited because he was obviously gambling, which he had promised to quit.

Although the Pope had divided the world beyond Europe between Spain and Portugal in the sixteenth century, it wasn't until the nineteenth century that the great scramble for empire began. Spain and Portugal were already exhausted and forced to contract. But the rest of Europe plunged headlong, following the maxim that God helps him who helps himself. If the continental empires are taken into account, Russia, Austria and Prussia, then Switzerland was about the only country that did not seek foreign dominion. Sweden had already been pushed back from its incursions into the lands of the Slavs. All the others pushed outward. Germany and Italy were late to consolidate as nation-states, but they entered the race enthusiastically soon after they achieved a domestic power base. Holland and Belgium took part successfully. The biggest contest was between Britain and France in Asia and Africa. It nearly led to general war at the time of the Fashoda incident in Upper Egypt in 1898, the high point of the long clash, which surprisingly is still kept alive between French- and English-speaking African states. U.S. intervention held off the dismemberment of China. Washington was not up to full-scale competition and chose instead to prevent exclusion of American traders by using its leverage among European rivals to impose its "Open Door" policy.

There is something disingenuous about nostalgic admiration for the Congress of Vienna in "keeping the peace" in the century between Napoleon and World War I. In fact, the nations of Europe were so busy amassing lands and subjects in the rest of the world that they were diverted from trying to seize each other's lands. Eurocentrism was no delusion in the nineteenth century. Europe came to own much of the world and ran it all. The powers were the powers of Europe.

Britain, however, succeeded far more than any other country in settling new lands and installing replicas of English society, which left no role for decimated and dispossessed natives. With the exception of the rebel United States, the emigration produced the white dominions, Canada, Australia, New Zealand, and the special case of South Africa. World War I had its origins in this explosion of European expansionism, but apart from the transfer of German-held lands to the victors, its impact on the colonies was not quickly felt. The first major step was the emergence of the British Commonwealth. The white dominions had supported the mother country during the war, but in the process they had developed their own national consciousness. The Imperial War Cabinet in 1917 proclaimed that future constitutional relations should be based on a "full recognition" of the Dominions as autonomous nations of an Imperial Commonwealth. It took until 1931, when Parliament passed the Act of Westminster, for it to become fact. Along with the colonies, the Commonwealth nations all remained pink on world maps and there seemed no real change in Britain's place in the sun. But certainly seeds were planted that were to grow into the drive for independence that burgeoned after World War II.

The decision belonged to Clement Attlee's Labour government. The Earl of Mountbatten, uncle of Prince Philip and the last Viceroy of India, played an important part in transferring power in such a way that India chose to join the Commonwealth instead of breaking away completely. Thus began the modern multiracial association that remains a major institutional bridge between Europe and the lands it conquered, transformed in many ways and finally left to self-government.

British politics, British insight and British moral character permitted the withdrawal with relatively little cost to Britain. France fought two big wars, in Indochina and Algeria. Holland considered fighting for Indonesia, but the United States pushed and wheedled it out. Portugal was the last to cede, and it took a revolution at home. In the wake of the struggle against colonialism, the intellectual fashion was to denounce the period of European expansion as wholly evil. It changed the world profoundly, not always for the worse, and still underlies the bonds and patterns of culture, trade, political experience and expectations which wrap the globe. Decolonization, along with the emergence of the Soviet Union and the United States as superpowers, was the great historic aftermath of World War II.

Europe was left in a peculiar position. Some Europeans suddenly noticed that, as a Frenchman said, it was "a mere peninsula on the great Eurasian land mass." Still, it maintained its links to the lands overseas, its memories and its sense of being natural leaders in the story of civilization. Commonwealth ties were a major argument in Britain for refusing to join continental Europe's effort to unite in the postwar period. When Britain did join the Common Market, in 1973, it was halfhearted. The loss of empire had not been emotionally digested and there was a feeling of comedown in being just another member of a middle-power club. The embers of pride and responsibility for far-flung possessions flamed for a moment during the 1982 Falklands war, but even then, a few in England saw it as a farcical replay of the old melodrama.

Meanwhile, the traces of the colonial past were penetrating British society, bringing the multiracial flavors of the Commonwealth into everyday English life. After a number of nasty arguments, immigration was controlled and the flood diminished. But, in the words of M. Collett, a conservative councilor in Birmingham quoted in *The Times* of July 26, 1976, it was too late. Collett said he had campaigned for twenty years to stop the stream of immigrants, mostly dark-skinned, and no one listened. He found himself, as he had warned, with an East African refugee family as neighbors. "They are charming," he said. "It is too late now. We have to accept it." Not everyone did. The ugly American pattern of ghettos and race riots in the big cities took hold, exacerbated by the decline of grubby industrial centers and docks. Lacking America's experience of absorbing waves of newcomers or its later, hard-learned lesson that extending civil rights requires active effort, British politics did not move to assimilate new groups. There is integration in lowly posts, in hospital wards and among customs officers at the airports, but not in Parliament or other seats of power. All that is yet to come, and how hard and violent it will be is for the future to tell.

As the rise of the superpowers and the end of empire changed the role of Europe after World War II, the aftermath of decolonization and the new migrations posed a new problem of identity for its countries. It is not a problem for Americans. A citizen is a citizen, no matter where he or his forebears came from. Discrimination exists, by race, creed, ethnic origin, but the question of who is an American does not arise. For Britain, France, Germany, Holland, Sweden, the question has only begun to be acknowledged. Is the Brixton-born child of a Jamaican an Englishman? Is the Glasgow-born child of a Pakistani a Scot? Are the Algerian children around Place Pigalle Frenchmen, the Turks in Munich Bavarians, let alone Germans? European nationalism is largely ethnic. It is not so much a passport but a language, a shared culture, a tradition, a custom of behavior, that defines identity. In the past, absorption of newcomers was virtually complete in a generation or two. But the ex-colonial immigrants are so different that it isn't just a matter of taking them into the society. Their presence will change the very notion of how the society defines itself.

Empire did not last so long for Britain as the distorting effect of nostalgia makes it seem. It did change the nation's sense of itself, and the loss of its vast domain was disorienting. The postwar phenomenon of immigration will work profound new changes over time. They might not have been so difficult to accommodate had the early promise of a united Europe, a new polyglot superstate, been fulfilled. But it wasn't, and isn't likely to be in the lifetime of any European alive today. Britain has joined Europe, but "European" has not become a nationality.

IRELAND
The Republic and Ulster: Neutral but Not at Peace

For too long to bear, Ireland's only riches seemed to be its lyricism, its boisterously romantic spirit and its acerbic wit. From the great famine of the mid-nineteenth century to beyond the middle of the twentieth, its major export was its young people. While the population in most of the world was expanding, the Republic of Ireland's declined by well over half, to below 3 million, only starting to rise again in 1971 to the current 3.6 million. The United States alone is estimated to have 40 million citizens of some Irish ancestry, though of course that represents several generations of immigrants. Its other most notable export was literature, poignant, satiric, hilarious, angry, abrasive. If ever a people survived as a nation above all by the charm of their culture, it was the Irish.

Successive invaders, including the Danes, who founded Dublin and other major cities, were absorbed. The Anglo-Normans, who conquered the island a century after the Norman invasion of England, became thoroughly assimilated. They settled mainly in eastern and southern Ireland. By the time of the Battle of the Boyne in the seventeenth century, the Irish fought so fiercely against new expeditions from England that they were subjected to special punitive measures and expelled from their lands. For eight hundred years, culminating with the independent Irish Free State in 1922, which became the Republic of Eire in 1949, the people stubbornly preserved their sense of separate identity. It was based on legend, tales, song, a love of the wet green sod and the blue mountains and lakes, religion and an ancient language.

Yet, in less than half a century as a modern state, Ireland has reversed the dream of its nationalist revolutionaries. The issue of the six northern counties of Ulster, still dominated by Protestants under British rule, remains a fierce and deadly cause among those who live there, though by no means the prime concern of people in the twenty-six counties of the Republic. But the effort to revive Gaelic as the language of currency, to enshrine the old rural ways and to celebrate unchanging Irishness in a self-sufficient, isolated society has been practically abandoned. Nostalgia is greater among the emigrants and their descendants. The citizens of Ireland prefer the access to the wide world which English gives them. They are well aware that Britain itself has subsided to the ranks of the middle powers. But the sun never sets on users of the English language, even if it no longer illuminates a global empire, and the Irish do love using language to move people.

In place of the initial attempt to shield the old way of life with high protectionist barriers and modest industry, Ireland has adopted one of the most generous systems of incentives to foreign investment. Willy-nilly, the country has been urbanized. A third of the people now live in metropolitan Dublin, the capital. Sentiment lingers in the law, nonetheless. It is made very difficult for foreigners enchanted with the scenery to buy land for vacation homes in the often abandoned countryside. The Irish will not tolerate an equivalent of what Spaniards came to call their Costa Concreta of touristic overdevelopment. But writers of any nationality who choose to reside in Ireland can receive tax indulgences, not unlike the enticements Monaco extends to attract the idle rich.

Some analysts ascribe the abrupt change of course from the proclaimed goals of the rebellion to the new search for development and involvement with the world to the experience of World War II, which the Irish euphemistically named "the Emergency." They chose neutrality, risky for a time when the continent was overrun by Germany and Britain was fighting alone. Either Britain or Germany could have opted for a preemptive invasion to deny Ireland's strategic position to its enemy. A minority, especially extremists in the underground Irish Republican Army, was pro-German and sought to provide espionage. Most people were glad to be out of the war but hoped Britain would win. Neutrality demonstrated national cohesion. The Irish were prepared to fight in defense of their new state, but for no other. The identity problem was resolved.

The isolation of neutrality brought other problems. Bread, tea, sugar and fuel were rationed. There were good jobs available, for those willing to go to work in Britain's tight war economy. But the lame Irish economy stagnated further, for lack of vital imports and markets for exports. The country was cut off, more than the nationalists had intended and by circumstances beyond their control. They found that they minded, for cultural and psychological as well as economic reasons. After all, as the later reaction showed, the Irish wished to join the world as Irishmen, not to barricade themselves in their bogs.

Emigration had been largely blocked by the war. Instead of journeying to distant lands and losing ties, young people went to England and were able to visit home a few times a year, or to the Irish cities, returning to the village every weekend or so. They brought back a new view of rural life, no longer the glorious rustic idyll of man in nature which the poets sang and which the old-timers thought the very essence of Irish character, to be defended against all comers. To the newly urbanized, it seemed dull, stagnant, stifling and mean. The advent of communications—not TV, which came much later, but the cinema, radio and mass-circulation magazines—spread the word of amenities and excitement to be found. In 1946 only one out of twenty farm dwellings had indoor toilets, only four out of twenty anything but the most primitive sanitation.

The milestone came in 1959, when the old rebel leader Eamon De Valera moved into the president's mansion in Phoenix Park (formerly the British viceroy's home) and Sean Lemass became Prime Minister. It was a change, not only of generations but of outlook and attitudes. There was a new air of optimism, a spurt of energy, a determination to modernize and leave the ancient grievances behind. A fluke of history brought an unforeseen tragedy, but it only became apparent later. Britain was planning to join the Common Market. Ireland would go along. That was expected not only to freshen the society and broaden its vistas, but to blur the border with Northern Ireland in such a way that the contrasts would gradually disappear. The idea of Europe had a substantial political and social content at that time. A dilution of nationalism was enthusiastically anticipated.

One morning in the early 1960s revealed the startling movement of minds for this visitor. I went to see President De Valera in his stately white house surrounded by the carefully laid out English gardens. His tall, imposing figure was stooped by then. He wore thick glasses. Nearly blind, he held out a small map of Ireland with the north in bright orange and the rest in gleaming emerald green—a map specially made for him. He could still distinguish colors. He spoke of the partition sadly, the remaining shadow on the dream of independence, which had come true. But the fire had gone out. There was regret, not bitterness.

The elderly taxi driver who had waited to drive me back to the Dáil for an appointment with Prime Minister Lemass began to talk on the way downtown. He was a child at the time of the 1916 Easter Rebellion, which he remembered vividly. He had been an ardent member of the Irish Republican Army for most of his life. But now, he said, his sons were grown. One of them was a doctor and the other an engineer. They had no use for violent plots. They were busy getting on in the world, quite successfully. He said they had told him, "Da, what do you want with those worn-out notions? That's old history. It's child's stuff to keep playing at it." They convinced him. He quit, and got rid of his guns. He predicted that the IRA would soon die out. "The young want none of it," he said.

Trim and lively, Lemass was full of plans for the future. He talked of attracting industry, educating technicians, building roads and housing. He planned to meet with Northern Ireland's Prime Minister Terence O'Neill to discuss the advantages to both sides of joining the Common Market. Even the leaders of the two churches, the North's Protestants and the South's Catholics, were establishing friendly contact. The past was slipping away and prospects looked bright.

Then, early in 1963, France's President Charles de Gaulle vetoed Britain's entry in the Common Market. Ireland, with its currency tied to sterling and its economy tied to Britain, could not think of trying to go in on its own. A decade later, both were admitted. But in the meantime, the Northern Irish climate changed. Impatient Catholics demanded the civil rights which had always been denied. Extremists came to the fore. The IRA was revived. Frustration burst into terrorism and renewed hatred. Hopes for peaceful erosion of the old hostility and reconciliation of the young were drenched in blood. The "Irish question" had not ebbed away.

The Irish are not quite the unique race they consider themselves, but a mixture like most Europeans. No one knows who the first inhabitants were, Stone Age people who left few traces. Archeology shows an active society by the Bronze Age, people who built massive and sometimes richly ornamented stone tombs and worked metal with artistry. Copper and gold were abundant, but there was no tin. The wide use of bronze leads to the presumption of regular trade with Cornwall, which had tin mines. The ancient people of Britain and Ireland seem to have been of the same stock, dark and short, later called Picts. The Greeks called their two islands the home of the Pretani, a name rendered by the Romans, and some scholars say first by Julius Caesar himself, as Brittani. The first arrival of the Celts was probably not before 400 B.C. They were a Germanic people, fair-haired and tall, who introduced the use of iron. There is also evidence of population moves between Iberia and Ireland. The Romans did not enter Ireland. But the Irish learned about Roman military tactics and fortifications in Britain, and when Rome's power receded in the fourth century A.D. they set out to raid and colonize in the empire's wake.

The Druids developed out of a class of seers and sorcerers among the pre-Celtic people and became not priests, as is sometimes said, but a caste of philosophers and wise men. The Celts seem to have entered Britain from Ireland, not migrating first to the island nearer the continent. *Scotti* is an old Celtic word meaning "raiders," apparently the initial mission of the people who settled in Scotland. The Irish established colonies all along Britain's west coast, from Argyle to Devon. Their dynasties lasted for centuries in Wales. But while the Celtic language submerged the earlier Pictish in Ireland and the ancient Picts were taken in vassalage, they were not then absorbed.

Christianity began seeping into Ireland very early, through lingering Roman influence in Britain, but mass conversion came when St. Patrick arrived as a missionary bishop in 432. He was a Briton, probably from Gwent in Monmouthshire, and had been captured when he was sixteen years old along with thousands of others in an Irish raid during the reign of Niall. He was held as a slave in northeastern Ulster but escaped after six years, probably in 407. When he returned, his mission succeeded rapidly and he chose Armagh, near the ancient Ulster capital, for his see. In 438 he was received with honors at Tara, seat of the high king Loiguire, son of Niall.

The Norse first arrived in Ireland at the beginning of the ninth century. They raided, traded and founded cities, subduing both the Celts and the remaining Picts, who united in opposition to the invaders, leading to ethnic assimilation. Full conquest was averted, however, by the victory of the Irish king Brian Boru at the Battle of Clontarf, near Dublin, on Good Friday, 1014.

The ensuing period was one of tribal wars and rival claims. Attempts by various Irish kings to impose a central royal suzerainty as William the Conqueror did in England after 1066 brought continuous fighting. As a result, there was little capacity left to resist when England's Henry II came in 1171 to claim what was said to be a grant of Ireland by Pope Adrian IV, in return for restoring order in the Irish church and state. Ireland accepted its status as a papal fief under the British crown. Throughout the Middle Ages, the Church flourished. The monasteries produced illuminated manuscripts and artifacts of great beauty. Learned Irish monks traveled widely on the continent, and the Latin classics were copied and preserved for posterity.

There were continuing disputes over the grants of Irish estates to adventuring Anglo-Norman lords. The distant English monarchy did not require its colonial envoys to extend the rights of emerging English law to Irish subjects, who clung to their Gaelic clans and land tenure. Once again, it took a blow from outside to bring the Irish people together in their distress. That came in the sixteenth century when Henry VIII broke with Rome, proclaimed the Church of England and was excommunicated, along with his subjects. The Irish had no desire for a reformation. Only in a small, protected area were abbeys converted to English speech, education and loyalty. Outside, Gaelic culture was sustained and the English king's legitimacy challenged on the ground that his rights had derived from his allegiance to Rome.

Religion was only part of the issue. The Crown was intent on reducing the feudal lords, which both the Gaelic and the old Anglo-Norman aristocracy resisted. In the seventeenth century, Oliver Cromwell's Puritan revolution cemented the mutual enmity. The Irish race was held in odium by the Cromwellians, and the sentiment was returned. Protestant English and Scottish colonists had already been sent to Ireland under the Tudor kings, and they took the best lands. Unlike earlier settlers, they did not fuse with the local population because of their different religion. The "plantation" (implanting of English colonists on expropriated Irish land), which began after 1603, brought not only new Anglo-Saxon landlords but for the first time farmers who worked the land themselves and drove away peasants as well as feudal proprietors. There was an uprising in 1641. Mercenaries and troops used to crush it were promised compensation with Irish land. Many Irish of all classes were driven away to poorer areas, and their fertile holdings were put under Protestant ownership. Those who were allowed to stay were made tenants, who could be evicted at will.

Under Cromwell, who led an invasion of Ireland in 1649–50, the Irish lost most of their remaining rights. They placed their hopes in the restoration of a Catholic monarchy under the childless King Charles II, who succeeded Cromwell. But when Charles's brother and successor, James II, had a son and reversion to a Catholic dynasty seemed inevitable, English noblemen summoned the Protestant William of Orange to the throne, which he ascended as William III. James fled to Catholic France. He collected money, arms and officers from King Louis XIV and landed in Ireland to raise an army. Protestant Europe sent Dutchmen, Danes, Germans and Huguenots to join the English forces, which William himself went to lead in Ireland. The "War of the Two Kings" was decided on a single day, July 1, 1690, when they faced each other across the narrow River Boyne.

Defeat at the Battle of the Boyne was the end of the Irish cause. The victors exacted harsh retribution, to crush the majority so it could not rise again. Settlers were sent, mostly from Scotland, to "plant" new overlordships. Landowners who did not "conform" (become Protestant) were impoverished. Catholics were barred from trades and professions, education, public office, juries, the vote and the right to arms and to a horse worth more than the equivalent of ten dollars.

The religious hostility prevented intermarriage, which had reduced ethnic differences in previous ages and promoted assimilation. Thus began the long despair and decline. Consolation was taken in remembrance, keeping the long story alive as though all these events were compressed into yesterday. Perhaps no other European nation save Poland lives so intimately with its history. The Poles share many traits with the Irish, a habit of reverie, reckless romanticism, a volatile spirit capable of intense sorrow and equally intense gaiety, a stabbing, ironic humor. For them, too, the past seems ever-present. An English traveler noted how near the Irish memory remains to the surface of everyday life. A tablet was erected in 1969 to commemorate Henry II's arrival at Baginbun in 1171. Within a week, it was smashed.

The harshness of English rule nourished both the resentment of the victims and the fear of the "implanted" settlers lest they lose their dominance. They accepted for safety's sake a union within the United Kingdom, enacted in 1800 with abolition of the Irish parliament and completed with establishment of a common currency in 1821. It brought no relief to the peasantry, left illiterate and miserable. But the population grew rapidly in the first half of the nineteenth century, estimated at more than 8 million in 1841. Then came a new disaster. Potatoes, brought from America in the seventeenth century, had become the poor man's staple diet. The potato blight arrived, also from America, in 1845. Within five years, about a million Irish died from hunger and disease, and the flood of emigration began.

Forced on London's attention by tragedy and agitation, the "Irish question" became a major issue of British politics. Land reform was a constant source of dispute. "It rained outrages," one historian wrote of the period. In 1880, tenants on a large estate on the shores of Lough Mask not only refused to pay their exorbitant rents to the agent, one Captain Boycott, but shunned him in every way. His name became a method of resistance. England was incensed at the campaign of civil disobedience, assassination and bombings, some of it organized from America, which amounted to a wave of what would now be called terrorism. But it was also impressed by the passion of the Irish and the eloquence of some of their leaders, notably Charles Stewart Parnell, an Anglo-Irish Protestant who was the main spokesman for the nationalists in the Westminster Parliament.

Prime Minister William Gladstone is said to have been on the verge of granting the demand for fairer land laws, when two tragic incidents caused such shock that conciliation was prevented. Just after their arrival in 1882, the new Chief Secretary of Ireland, Lord Frederick Cavendish, and his deputy Thomas Burke were murdered with long sharp knives on their way to dine with the Viceroy in Phoenix Park, at the approach to the mansion. Cavendish was a nephew of Mrs. Gladstone, and the Prime Minister had come to consider him almost as a son. Parnell was also deeply shaken. He denounced the act. But the ensuing fury of the English, and counterfury of the Irish against a Dublin city councilor named James Carey who turned state's witness and gave hanging evidence against the perpetrators, foreclosed the chance of political settlement. Seven years later, Parnell, who had introduced a home rule bill in Parliament, was named co-respondent in a divorce suit brought by his friend and co-nationalist Captain W. H. O'Shea against Kitty O'Shea. It was a great scandal, the subject of a theatrical drama later. It enabled Parnell's enemies to destroy him. He was hounded to his grave and Ireland lost its most eminent spokesman.

The Phoenix Park murders were the work of a secret society, the

Fenians, whose members called themselves "the Invincibles." The gang was broken, and Irish frustration mounted, giving rise in turn to the secret Irish Republican Army. The House of Commons finally passed the Irish Home Rule bill in 1912. There was disagreement with the House of Lords, and it did not become law until September 1914. But by then, World War I had started. Implementation was postponed. On Easter Monday, 1916, rebels rose up in Dublin. The fighting was ended within a week and the leaders were summarily executed. They became martyrs for the national cause. In the first election after the war, the nationalist party Sinn Fein ("We Ourselves") won a decisive majority of Irish seats. A campaign of killing policemen was launched at the same time and escalated rapidly into another Anglo-Irish war, called "the Troubles" by the Irish. It could have been a model for modern guerrilla warfare.

Finally, in 1921, a treaty was negotiated with Britain giving the twenty-six counties of the present Republic dominion status as the Irish Free State. The six northern counties remained in the United Kingdom, to the unabated fury of the nationalists. The firebrand leader of the Fianna Fáil ("Soldiers of Destiny") party, Eamon De Valera, became Prime Minister in 1932, moving on to the presidency in 1959. He retired in 1973 at the age of ninety-one, after more than half a century of rousing nationalist leadership.

When he died in 1975, the Ireland he left was not the one he had envisioned. Instead of sweeping across the island from the Gaeltacht, the isolated western villages where the old tongue remained in use, Gaelic receded. The new Irish cause was material improvement. As the poorest member of the Common Market until Greece joined a decade later, Ireland began receiving large EEC subsidies, amounting to $250 per capita by the early 1980s. Cheap labor, English-speaking and increasingly educated, added to the appeal of government efforts to attract foreign industrial enterprises. The proportion of people in agriculture dropped to 22 percent, though 37 percent of exports were still off the farms and 17 percent of gross domestic product came from the farms. Trim modern houses went up in place of the insalubrious old cottages. The new generation married earlier, and the population was rising again. With half its people under twenty-five, Ireland is now the youngest country in Europe. The country supports as many sheep as people, and twice as many head of cattle, on the lush, moist meadowlands.

The Irish came to appreciate the economic value of their rolling, wooded hills and quiet valleys, their old country manors and graceful horses. Tourism is encouraged and rewarded with traditional hospitality and lilting, friendly gab. The geography that was heartache can be seen now as a blessed rentable refuge to people from the hectic world outside, where young Irish men and women go to study and travel. Dublin has retained its charm, with broad squares lined with Georgian houses and the bridges across the River Liffey. It is a quiet, easygoing city, graceful and supremely conscious of its cultural tradition. Theater is the most celebrated art, though the most popular is probably the sing-alongs of old ballads in pubs where everyone joins in. The more sophisticated take tea and scones in the well-appointed lobby of the Shelbourne Hotel, but they often talk racing and horses like most everybody else.

Some intellectuals, arguing compulsively in the crowded pubs, bemoan the subsidence of passion and rhetoric from the hard old days and deliberately set their novels and poems in an earlier time when the gorge rose. They boast that "we're all lawbreakers at heart," with a taste for anarchy sparked by long oppression. But they say it with a smile. It is an attempt to recapture the fantasy, which has been called "the escape of the powerless," and for which George Bernard Shaw had berated his countrymen. "Oh, the dreaming! the dreaming! the torturing, heart-scalding, never satisfying dreaming, dreaming, dreaming . . ." he said. The country remains deeply conservative, "full of solid petit bourgeois, small farmers and minor officials," the intellectuals sniff.

But after the boom of the 1970s, which churned up the beginnings of a new disdain for materialism as well as great expectations, came a bust. At the beginning of the 1980s, the title "the sick man of Europe," which had passed to England, then Italy, then Belgium, was handed on to Ireland. Although it had the Common Market's second-smallest population (after Luxembourg), it had the highest birthrate, the highest inflation, the highest foreign debt per capita (more than Poland's and equal to Brazil's), the highest youth unemployment, one of the highest overall unemployment rates and one of the highest tax rates. Farm income dropped by half in real terms in two years. High growth and high government spending had to give way to austerity. From rejoicing at the rejuvenation of a trampled old society, the Irish began to be afraid of their newly surly youth. In the slums, 30 percent of the young

people were unemployed with no real prospects. Emigration was difficult as jobs dried up everywhere. Older Irish had always burst out of
boredom and guilt with drinking and brawling. That was indulged. Now
young Dubliners in districts grown tacky with neglect were taking to
drugs and street crime. That was shocking. "What else is there to do?"
they told posses of inquiring reporters.

Some new foreign factories, which had turned somnolent villages
into hubs of prosperity, closed down because of inflation. It brought
again a sense of being at the disposal of merciless outsiders. But others,
especially in forward-looking industries, kept on. The underlying momentum was still there, the ups and downs aggravated no doubt by a
tendency to the manic-depressive overstatement which the Irish had
long considered their warm distinction from the cool, tight-lipped British.

The change has not persisted long enough to remodel ingrained habits. But there have been telegraphed notices. The campaign to
strengthen the legal ban on abortion in the constitution, so that it might
not easily be repealed, was one. The voters supported the amendment
overwhelmingly in 1983, by 66 percent to 33 percent, but the idea that
a new bulwark was needed surely stemmed from a sense that traditional
certainties were being undermined. The Irish church, like the Polish,
had long been the deeply rooted assurance of nationhood. Owen Dud-
ley Edwards, a contemporary historian at the University of Edinburgh,
suggested that the British might have converted the canny Irish to
Protestantism, as they converted it to Christianity long before, if they
had made a "serious, constructive effort" instead of putting rapacity,
security and continental diplomacy first. So the Church provided what
the British-run government refused—accepted community, support in
time of need, staff for hospitals and schools. When the Irish government began to pass welfare legislation, Cornelius Lucy, Bishop of Cork,
saw it as a challenge not only to economic and social conservatism but
implicitly to the role of the Church. "Now, under one pretext or another," he proclaimed, "the various departments of the state are becoming father and mother to us all." Of 3,500 primary schools, 3,300 are
Church-owned or -controlled. The proportion tapers off further up the
educational ladder, though it remains high. Trinity, founded by Elizabeth I to produce an English-speaking, Protestant educated class, now
has a majority of Catholic students and high esteem as a quality university, but its integration is an exception.

The Church adapted itself to a rural society. It remained the true center of local life, so much so that there was scarcely a secular breeze in Ireland when most of Europe was driven by anticlerical winds. There is probably no Catholic country where more people attend Mass every week—still 90 percent of the Irish do, despite urbanization—though the average is 70 percent among university students. Independent Ireland never formally established the Catholic Church as the state religion. There was no need, outsiders commented, it was so deeply imbedded. But the preamble to the 1937 constitution mentions devotion to Jesus Christ, and an article on the role of women says: "The State recognizes that by her life within the home, woman gives to the State a support without which the common good cannot be achieved." It provides that women should not be obliged by "economic necessity" to work outside the home.

When the problem of national independence was gone, the central issue for the Church moved to focus on sex, specifically to oppose contraception, abortion and divorce. That stand stirred no great opposition when the country was depopulated. But attitudes changed as the population grew, mainly because emigration had dropped so substantially. Because of the nineteenth-century famine, 2.15 million people out of a total of 8 million left in the years 1845–60. Another 3.8 million emigrated in the following decades. In the decade 1971–81, there was an emigration of 103,000 people out of a population of 3.5 million. Their isolation was ending; the Irish learned what was going on in the rest of the world, including the rise of the feminist movement.

Membership in the European Economic Community brought outside support for the educated Irishwomen who felt the same urges that stirred feminist movements elsewhere. The European Parliament and the European Court of Justice, empowered to hear individuals' complaints against their own governments for breach of human rights, took stands which highlighted the contrast between Irish law and what had become the norm elsewhere, even in Catholic countries. Slowly, slowly, the climate was also changing on the deeper level of long-held assumptions as well as in the economy and demography. James Joyce, who left home in the early twentieth century hoping through art and exile to open Ireland's eyes to its stolid, inward-looking sectarianism, wrote that he sought "to forge the uncreated conscience of my race." The official censorship, and the far more pervasive censorship of closed minds, served to shield Irish thought from his explosive impact on English and world literature. But time was weakening the barriers.

The explosion of youth beyond the society's absorptive capacity in recent years sharpened questions raised by modern trends. A few liberal Catholic clergymen saw a need for shifting preoccupation to the problems of the country's still numerous poor (25 percent), to more concern for tolerance and less for dabbling in politics. But the threat of waning influence which the Church foresaw was being met primarily by an energetic counteroffensive on behalf of tradition. The fighting in Ulster provided a certain prolongation of the role of national champion. A French commentator, Huguette Debaisieux, writing in the weekly *L'Express* from her country's more relaxed point of view on both sexual morality and the role of the Church, found the Irish overwhelmed with priest-induced guilt. "The worst sin," she said, wasn't "the act but finding pleasure in it." Thus, the Irish church with its obsession about sex could deplore specific deeds of violence but refuse to condemn the supposedly chaste IRA overall. (The Dublin government does condemn terrorism.) It is hard to overstate the part played by what most of Europe considers quite personal issues in the continuing Irish conflict.

Declan Deane, an outspoken priest in Northern Ireland, wrote in the liberal Catholic monthly *Doctrine and Life*, "If you want an ecumenical spirit, you do not look to priests, ministers or preachers for it, you look instead to the ward sister, the pigeon fanciers, and the drunks." Efforts to lead to moderation on humanitarian grounds have repeatedly foundered on the reefs of dogmatism. Mairead Corrigan and Betty Williams, the Belfast housewives who won the 1976 Nobel Peace Prize for their attempt to inspire reconciliation and a halt to the killing, were soon brushed aside and forgotten. Wars of religion, archaic to other parts of Europe which had gone through them on a devastating scale in past centuries but had left them behind, continued in Ireland.

In 1984, a group called the New Ireland Forum, which represented the three leading parties in the Republic and the mainly Catholic Social Democratic and Labour Party (SDLP) in Ulster, issued a report suggesting several possible approaches for negotiation with Britain on Northern Ireland. More important than its proposals was the underlying recognition of some new facts. One was that the British were no longer clinging avariciously to a colony, that they had gotten rid of most of their colonies a generation earlier and resented the cost in soldiers' lives and treasure which their commitment to Ulster's hard-minded Unionists imposed. There were even complaints in Dublin that the Irish question no longer stirred British politics. A second was that after nine years of civil war, Northern Ireland was no longer the relatively rich part of the island trying to drain the substance of the South. Turbulence and the decline of its old industries had made it little better off than the Republic, while Dublin had increased social benefits to a point where there was no longer such a wide gap with the British-subsidized Northerners. An abrupt decline in fortunes and entitlements had been a major fear of Ulstermen if the British withdrew. But most important was the understanding, expressed openly by Prime Minister Garret FitzGerald, that the Republic would have to move away from sectarianism, toward pluralism and tolerance in law as well as mentality, if it were ever to induce the Northern Protestants to reunite the Irish lands.

FitzGerald, the leader of Fine Gael ("People of Ireland"), was a big, burly man with a long, jowly, rather melancholy face and tousled hair, a well-educated intellectual. Britain's *Economist* described his party as "staunchly conservative" compared to the "implacably conservative" major opposition party, Fianna Fáil, led by the emotionally nationalist, populist, hearty Charles J. Haughey, who became Prime Minister after 1987 elections. The two had become alternates in heading the government, a reflection of the tentative advance and retreat toward transformation. The choice of the relatively small Labour Party, which named Dick Spring as its leader in 1982 when he was thirty-two years old, made the earlier decision favoring Fine Gael. Spring gave the support necessary for a coalition majority to FitzGerald as coming closer to his ideas for a more socially oriented, modern Irish politics. He was himself a sign of shifting standards, not the usual union official leading Labour but a lawyer who had married an American Protestant woman. Fitz-Gerald, a man of considerable culture and fluent in French, became one of Europe's most impressive statesmen, moderate, imaginative, lucid and steady. If he had not been obliged to preoccupy himself with Irish troubles, he might well have won a leadership role in the whole European Community.

In 1985 FitzGerald persuaded Britain's Prime Minister Margaret Thatcher to sign an agreement giving Dublin an ill-defined right of consultation in Ulster affairs for the first time. Britain made no concession of sovereignty, but the hope was that Dublin's intervention to assure the rights of Catholics in the North would turn them away from support for IRA violence. If calm could be restored, the two leaders reasoned, then reconciliation might follow. The British were no longer adamant about Northern Ireland; their position was that they would stay as long as the majority there demanded it. The clear implication was that if ever the majority of the feuding people of Ulster voted for it, the British would leave and Ireland would once again be united. That has always been the goal of the Northern Catholics and the government at Dublin, a goal firmly enshrined in the Republic's constitution. Mr. FitzGerald lost the subsequent election and withdrew from his party's leadership, but the Anglo-Irish agreement was maintained despite harsh opposition.

But Ireland cannot easily throw off its heritage of violence. Neutrality kept it out of the foreign wars of living memory, but it still has not stopped fighting at home. However, neutrality no longer means a desire for isolation. It was the only European neutral to join the Common Market, with relish and reward. It still looks to the United States with family feeling; there are so many Irishmen there. But it is no longer on the margin of Europe. It is a full member and coming up in the world as it strives to improve its economic base.

ULSTER

ULSTER, the northernmost province of Ireland, was traditionally composed of nine counties. Five were predominantly Catholic and three of them were allowed to join the Irish Free State when it was formed in 1921 and the island was partitioned. The two others were kept in the North for geographical coherence. The most adamant Nationalists still refuse to use the official name of Northern Ireland, or even Ulster, referring instead to "the six counties," which they are determined to incorporate in the Republic of Ireland. But Ulster is a fully constitutional part of the United Kingdom of Great Britain and Northern Ireland. Therefore, it isn't neutral. Its territory forms part of NATO along with the rest of the British Isles. Its status is roiled in bloody controversy.

The Protestant majority, called Unionists or Loyalists or sometimes Ulstermen, insist that their province has rights and duties no different from any other part of the United Kingdom and that they are totally loyal to the Crown, though that doesn't keep them from harshly opposing the British government at times. Their color is orange, after William of Orange, who became William III of England and consolidated the establishment of Protestantism. The Catholic minority, called Republicans or Nationalists, insist that the territory is an integral part of Ireland, that partition was a forcible abomination, and that by right the six counties should be merged with the twenty-six in the South to form a completed thirty-two-county Republic. Their color is green, for the

77

Emerald Isle. Until 1985, they were not allowed to fly their flag of preference, the Republic's orange-white-green tricolor, although the Protestants flew their Unionist banner marked with a red hand.

To outsiders, the dispute put in these terms is an anachronism. The border in Ireland is the last under dispute in Western Europe, which has ended its thousands of years of local territorial wars. The Nationalists are the last Western European irredentists. Everywhere else, ethnic minorities have been accommodated and postwar frontiers accepted. Technically, Northern Ireland should be discussed in the chapter on Britain. But in fact, the troubles among the Irish no longer really concern the British. Most of them wish only that the issue of who should run Northern Ireland would go away, that British troops, which have tried to impose communal peace since 1970 at considerable cost in lives, could be withdrawn, and that Westminster, the government in London, could divest itself of direct responsibility for rule. There are still many people in the North convinced that everything wrong there is the fault of the British and everything could be resolved if they would only pull out. But the problem is really an Irish one, between two old and hostile communities, separated into ghettos but too intertwined by history and economics to go their separate ways in peace.

The most partisan among both the Catholics and the Protestants insist that the conflict "is not a war of religion." The more they talk about it, though, the more they make clear that they define themselves and their communities, their friends and their enemies, by their religion. "I don't hate Protestants," said an ardent Catholic woman of twenty-one in the town of Lurgan, near Belfast. "I just hate what they stand for. They made us their white niggers. They've been masters in our country for too long." "I don't hate Catholics," said a forty-five-year-old Protestant gunman in Belfast, "but I have a right to my own way of life. They have too many children, their churches are smelly with incense, they kneel to popery."

Both sides appeal to history as though it were yesterday's Supreme Court decision. A ten-year-old Catholic boy, caught stoning British troops, was asked by one of the soldiers why he was doing that. "You've been oppressing us for eight hundred years," the child said defiantly. Peter Robinson, the strident deputy leader of Ian Paisley's hard-line Protestant group called the Democratic Unionist Party, said, "England is obligated to remain here and treat us like all other parts of Britain. It is a solemn commitment under the Act of Union of 1800"—the law that formally incorporated the whole of Ireland under the British crown. On a wall in the Protestant part of Belfast, a graffito read, "To hell with the future and long live the past, May God in his mercy look down on Belfast."

Both sides argue the righteousness of their cause. Thugs on both sides murder and bomb to force their way and intimidate their co-religionists into opposing conciliation. Moderates are made to feel weak and almost futile. Recognizing that there could be no hope for a solution through direct negotiations between the two sides in Northern Ireland, the governments at Dublin and London concluded an agreement over their heads at Hillsborough, Northern Ireland, in 1985 which imposed a modest compromise. Britain would retain full sovereignty so long as the majority in the North wished, but accepted an "Irish dimension" for Northern Ireland, granting the Republic an institutional right to consult on local affairs and to take up the grievances of the Catholics.

The nub of the problem is that the Protestants are a minority in the island as a whole and will not submit to the Catholic majority in a united Ireland. The Catholics are a minority (35 percent) of the 1.5 million people in the North and have been kept powerless, the object of fierce discrimination. In the circumstances, the principle of self-determination works for the Unionists and infuriates the Republicans. The moves toward reconciliation in the early 1960s collapsed because the underlying fears and grievances were still too raw. What Northern Irish now call "the Troubles" bubbled up with the civil rights movement in 1968–69, when London was "swinging" and youth was stirred to rebellion in countries around the world. Catholic demands were not so different from those of blacks in the American South. But unlike the U.S. government, which sent troops to enforce school desegregation in Little Rock, Arkansas, London sent troops in 1970 with the single mission of putting down violence. The Stormont, the Northern Ireland parliament, heavily dominated by Protestants, remained the local political authority. Though at first Catholics welcomed the British as protectors, they soon came to consider the soldiers as enforcers of the Protestant order and therefore as enemies.

Violence soared. From thirteen deaths listed by police as "due to terrorist activity" in 1969, the figure increased to 467 in 1972. At that point, London suspended the Stormont and instituted direct rule as an interim measure while it tried to mediate a political agreement for a new provincial government. A pact for "power sharing" was signed at

Sunningdale, England, in December 1973. But there was a violent reaction from Protestant militants, who declared a general strike. In the meantime, the Labour Party's Harold Wilson replaced the Conservative's Edward Heath as Prime Minister of Britain. London bent before the Unionist storm. The agreement collapsed in 1974 and direct rule continued.

The British proceeded to impose important reforms. Proportional representation was established in municipal elections, getting around the gerrymanders which the Protestant elite had used to shut the Catholics out of office, and providing one-man one-vote. Civil service jobs were opened to Catholics, but as they had been rejected for so long they were not able to rise quickly through the system of seniority. A housing authority was established to provide new construction in the slummy Catholic areas neglected by Protestant officials. Housing was a major Catholic grievance, though by the time new buildings went up attitudes had hardened so much that ghetto lines remained tightly drawn.

By 1985, the British were spending $3 billion a year on subsidies for Northern Ireland. Terrorism deaths had declined to about fifty a year, a total of some 2,500 since 1969. Parts of Belfast, a grimy dock and shipyard city, looked like Beirut with gutted buildings and stretches of rubble. But most of the devastation was from neglect or demolition to make way for new construction. There was bombing damage, but not so extensive as appeared. Unemployment, which was 6 percent at the end of the booming 1960s, had risen to over 20 percent and up to 50 percent in some areas. Ulster had always been far more industrialized than the South, and its aging industries suffered heavily in the recession.

The long "Troubles," really an endemic civil war, took a toll not only of the economy but of human resources. People were frightened, and tired of being frightened. Yet life went on behind the strict security precautions. Guards checked each car entering the main shopping district, taking names and license numbers and checking again when they were driven out. Armed cars patrolled the cities and soldiers in battle dress stood warily on the streets. The countryside was green and gentle, like other parts of Ireland, but the people were bitter.

There is a wall in Belfast, partly cement, partly brick, partly tin, separating the Catholic Falls Road neighborhood from the Protestant Shankill Road area where they meet back to back. People refer to it as the "Berlin Wall," though of course it isn't at all the same. Anyone can go around it, but it reduces the chance of sneak attacks. Still, it symbolizes the ugly barrier which attitudes have erected, between lives which have so much in common.

John Hume, a Catholic, is leader of the moderate Social Democratic and Labour Party, a husky man with rumpled brown hair and large, sad eyes. He tells of his youth in a family of eleven children, sharing a two-bedroom house with his aunt and uncle and their family. Through scholarships, he received an education and was elected as one of Northern Ireland's seventeen members of Parliament. Recalling that his father was unemployed for twenty years, he tries to rally support for compromise by stressing economic and social progress. "But the young don't remember when the problem was eating," he says. "They respond to the emotional arguments."

Andy Tyrie, a Protestant, heads the paramilitary Ulster Defence Association, the vigilante force which confronts the Irish Republican Army. Shorter than Hume, he is square-shouldered, with confident dark eyes and a black moustache. He too grew up in a two-bedroom house with eleven children. "We'd have liked better housing, jobs, one-man one-vote too," he says. "The only difference between the way we lived and the Catholics was that we weren't allowed to complain about anything, we had to support the state because it was supposed to be ours."

Relatively, the North has always been better off than the South. But it is still a land of rampant poverty surrounding the self-important gentry. Belfast has none of Dublin's Georgian grace and little of its cultural effervescence. There is a Protestant Church of Ireland, modeled on the Church of England. But most of the settlers came from Scotland and cling to austere Scottish Presbyterian ways. Looking back, a senior British cabinet minister was prepared to say, but only off the record: "We were extraordinarily brutal, insensitive, we made terrible mistakes in Ireland." Now Britain is trying to resolve the consequences and work with its Common Market partner, the Republic of Ireland, to bring a settlement acceptable to both sides in Ulster. But the past won't fade away. Livid with each new generation, it rises to stir the embers of old wars, old atrocities, old hatreds, and to inflame emotions in a cold country.

For all the lilt of its language and the warmth of its passions, Ireland has been an unhappy land, left behind too long as transformations brought other parts of Western Europe out of their painful past. There are people who know this and are pushing for openings, pushing for change. Ex-Prime Minister Garret FitzGerald is one of them, but he knows the drag of the people who cling to old habits, old emotions, old privileges, old fears. The ultraconservatism of the Catholic Church, more rigid even than the Church in Spain, which managed to evolve more with the times, has fed the fears of the Northern Protestants that they would be saddled with restraints if the six counties were subordinated to Dublin. The ultrarighteousness of the Protestants and their insistence on mean discrimination has fed the grievances of the Catholics.

The IRA, an illegal and secret society, has frightened authorities in both North and South with its fuzzy slogans about a "workers' republic" and its ties to armed radical and terrorist groups in other parts of the world. There is evidence that in its search for clandestine aid, it has turned to Soviet and Soviet-backed sources. Asked directly about his aid to Irish terrorists, Colonel Muammar Qaddafi of Libya did not deny it but justified it, saying he was prepared to back all manner of "freedom fighters."

Sinn Fein, the legal, political branch of the movement, makes little effort to conceal its close involvement with the underground. In its shabby, impoverished headquarters off Falls Road in Belfast, there are somber, menacing murals of fighters with the legend, "Guerrilla Days in Ireland." Greetings from a dissident Palestinian group in Damascus are taped to a mantelpiece, along with posters extolling Nicaragua's Sandinistas, El Salvador's guerrillas and others. The headquarters of the Ulster Defence Association, about a mile away, are a little less grubby but only by a degree, with the same ugly air of deadly desperation. There the posters are of anti-Communist guerrilla groups, including Nicaraguan *contras*, and Angola's Jonas Savimbi. It all has so little to do with helping people to live in Ireland.

And yet there is hope, hope for economic improvement with Common Market help which would lay the basis for more confident, relaxed societies. There are surges of gaiety and delight, of tenderness and wisdom. Even when they are miserable, the Irish know how to celebrate themselves.

FRANCE
The Reign of Intellectuals

THE GALLIC COCK SAYS *cocorico*, not *cock-a-doodle-doo*, and it crows for France. It is proud and independent; self-assured and self-mocking; vaingloriously top of the heap and prudent; gorgeous and self-conscious. Other countries choose an eagle, a lion, a unicorn, an elephant, a serpent as their national symbol. The French enshrined a barnyard fowl, but the scrappiest, noisiest, most brilliant. They are perfectly aware of the contrapuntal undertones, and they relish both the bravura and the satire. Nuance is everything. Everyone else considers the French the most nationalistic people in Europe.

Chauvinism takes its name from Nicholas Chauvin, a Napoleonic soldier who was very brave but so demonstratively, militantly patriotic that his comrades found his posturing ridiculous. The other word for it is *cocorico*. But the late President Charles de Gaulle, who seemed to admire only Jeanne d'Arc as a historic model, always worried that his compatriots would lose their sense of nationality and fall apart into bickering tribes. He considered their national community dangerously fragile, in constant need of arousal to sustain cohesion. "How can you govern a country that makes 365 kinds of cheese?" he asked disdainfully. He had "a certain idea of France" which he pronounced his sole and unwavering guide.

De Gaulle understood and appreciated the idea of a Europe that would encompass and surmount a thousand years of internecine wars to restore the medieval vision of a great power of Christendom. But he

83

adamantly opposed the moves toward integration that could coalesce the powers of Europe. It must be a *"Europe des patries,"* a Europe of fatherlands, he insisted, because he feared that France would somehow lose itself in the dilution of a larger union. André Malraux, the distinguished writer and art historian who was his Minister of Culture, admitted after de Gaulle's death that for all his exalted vision of a noble France, the leader didn't think much of his countrymen, didn't really trust them to live up to the privilege and responsibility of being French. And yet, Malraux also said, "Every Frenchman was, is, or will be a Gaullist." He was right. The tall, rather awkward, intransigent general, who in World War II fled to England when France fell to urge his country to fight on, embodied the nation's honor. De Gaulle was loved for that.

When he returned five years later in triumph, he knew that the resistance had been weak, that many had collaborated with the German conqueror, that most had simply plodded on under the occupation trying to survive. But he proclaimed that the glorious spirit of France had never flickered except in a few traitorous hearts, a tacit absolution. De Gaulle was loved for that, too.

It wasn't until the 1970s that the complicity of silence about France under the occupation began to be probed. An acerbic film called *Frenchmen, If You Only Knew* showed a clip of more than a million Parisians jammed into the great square in front of the City Hall in 1944. They had come to cheer Marshal Pétain, the hero and symbol of victory in World War I, the man who had signed the surrender to Adolf Hitler and established a subject state to rule over part of France from Vichy in cooperation with the Nazis. Then the film showed a clip of just as big a crowd cheering just as enthusiastically in the same square. The man on the balcony that time was General de Gaulle, who had just liberated Paris from the Germans. "The population of Paris did not change in the three months between the two events," the film's narrator said tartly. "So it has to be supposed that the people in the two scenes are the same."

De Gaulle stalked away from power in January 1946, less than a year after the war ended, and did not return until 1958, when France was being torn apart by another war to maintain its rule in Algeria. His coup was wildly welcomed by those who thought he would never give in. But he negotiated Algeria's independence, and went on to legitimize his rule by the constitution of France's Fifth Republic, centralizing power in his own hands as President. He was prickly, aloof, impervious to criticism, galling to the Allies, headstrong and unyielding to anyone's opinion. Eventually, de Gaulle was loved for all that, too.

He never really explained his special "idea of France," nor for that matter what he meant by his cryptic "I understand you" to the Frenchmen of Algiers in 1958 or his disturbing "Long live free Quebec" in Montreal in 1967. The ambiguity of abstraction is a pillar of national strength, the bastion of Frenchness. The French think of themselves as the most lucid of all peoples, their language the true tongue of clarity. René Descartes, the father of deductive logic, is revered as the essence of the orderly mind. "Cartesian" is the French way of describing good reasoning. The intellectual tradition emphasizes abstraction. The ultimate Cartesian deduction is "I think, therefore I am." But like most French conclusions, it is a paradox. It is not really a final idea, it also implies a new beginning—I am, therefore I must think. The French higher education system gives great importance to the capacity to develop abstractions and present them with elegance. In this way, French senior officials and establishment figures develop a special polish, which others cannot help but admire.

Yet while the facts exact their due, they must not be allowed to get in the way of a pithy generalization or a clever ambiguity, *la petite phrase*, a few sharp words which imply much more than they say. Frenchmen are perfectionists in many practical and agreeable arts, but the acme of respect goes to the intellectual. Nowhere else do intellectuals rule so supreme. No other society bows before them so unquestioningly. They set themselves apart, so that commerce, farming, government, family life, all the vital everyday activities, go on around them without undue disturbance. But the intellectuals flavor and shape society's sense of itself in a way that politicians, tycoons, labor leaders, leftover aristocrats and run-of-the-mill celebrities can rarely manage to do.

Ideas are always important, and the people who best generate and articulate them have a special role in history. All the countries of Europe have had their giants of the mind and the word. When Europeans extol the civilization of their continent, it is art, literature and philosophy they have in mind more than social organization, politics, engineering or even science. The traditions of the academy are sacrosanct. The rulers, warriors, traders molded the nations of Europe. But the intellectuals provided the currents of universality. They are at the origin of the very notion the world has of "Western civilization" and its values.

Considerable debate has arisen about the importance Europe still holds for the earth's other inhabitants. It is small, densely populated, with relatively few resources. On global maps, it doesn't represent much, and other areas are growing faster economically and technologically. But the Europeans, along with their descendants who settled and built nations in the Americas and the western Pacific, produced a culture so rich, so creative, so bold in its vision of man's capacity, so challenging to his ingenuity, that it remains dominant. Europeans established the foundations for hope of a humane future, and discovered the principles for building a device that could end all hope. Culture, the source of Europe's ascendancy, remains its greatest treasure.

Intellectuals are recognized in each country as a national resource, and they weigh on the feeling of what it means to be a Spaniard, a Swede, a Greek. They help to provide identity, and to cement or move society. Yet France, the country that pays the most attention to the earthy details of existence, eating, dressing, flirting as well as possible, is also the prime example of the sovereignty of intellectuals. "Put Imagination in Power" was a slogan of the rebellious students at the Sorbonne in the upheaval of 1968. Nobody was quite sure what it meant; nobody is ever quite sure what the assertions of grandeur mean. But the whole country caught its breath. The impish idea resounded.

Because of their penchant for abstractions, the French tend not to make much of what really happens in their country. "Plus ça change, plus c'est la même chose" is a French adage that never wears out its usefulness, but it can also mislead. The country has changed dramatically since World War II, which brought stunning defeat as well as final victory. There is a railway car in the clearing at Compiègne, where the 1918 armistice was signed. It has been turned into a museum to commemorate that event, but there is nothing to show that Pétain also surrendered there in 1940 and Hitler danced a jig on the spot. The French remember everything, but they don't make a point of noticing. The old *pissotières*, with their aroma of urine and the unmistakable evidence of trousered legs, had been as much a part of Paris as the Eiffel Tower. They have gone. For a few years, there was no place on the streets for men to relieve themselves discreetly. But the need remained. Modernity arrived. The new installations are called *sanisettes*. They are completely enclosed. It takes a coin to open the door. When it closes, the toilet is automatically flushed, cleaned and disinfected. In a bow to both technical progress and changing attitudes, the amenities are now unisex, equally available to women, whose needs were previously ignored. Of course this is a trivial example of change and continuity, but it is also an example of the way change continues to pay heed to the inevitable minutiae of life.

More evocative of French circumstance, perhaps, is the change in the wording of signs in French subway trains reserving a certain number of seats. They used to command priority for *les grands mutilés de guerre*, people seriously injured in war. The new métro cars, quiet, clean, well appointed, still have signs reserving seats, but now they are for "pregnant women and the handicapped." War victims are no longer a numerous social category.

Details matter enormously to the French, and they go to great efforts to make sure they are just right, whether it is a swirl of cream on a pastry, the color of cloth on an old chair, the seam of a dress. Parisians are not often hospitable, not because they don't like inviting people to their homes, but because it takes so much trouble and expense to assure a perfect menu, with just the right wine, that few can manage very often. They would rather not have guests than entertain in a mediocre style.

There are still great street markets, but now it is possible to choose your oranges from Spain, Italy, Israel, California, Algeria or elsewhere. Modest families can buy fresh green beans or pineapples from Africa in midwinter. The somewhat more affluent can have "wild strawberries" (now grown in greenhouses) or kiwis and mangoes, previously unknown, at Christmastime. Not long ago, only the rich could eat fresh produce out of season. The traditional glory of French cuisine, with all its sauces and herbs, developed because it was so difficult to obtain good-quality foodstuffs. At first, the innovation of nouvelle cuisine, which was the rage of the 1970s, was, above all, the emphasis on top-grade ingredients and abandonment of heavy disguises. It was soon elaborated into the baroque, as practically everyone could afford mere quality. *Le biftek*, once a luxury, became an ordinary dish. So the chic chefs forgot steak and, at absurdly exalted prices, began to offer the tripe, brains, sweetbreads which had long been the diet of the poor who couldn't pay for red meat and settled for carefully cooked offal. A reverse snobbism. The fashion waned, as excess usually does among the down-to-earth French, but not the passion for well-prepared food.

Yet supermarkets, which were once considered an intolerable intrusion of Americanism, flourish even in small towns. Few people who work still go home for lunch. *Bistro,* the Russian word for "quick," was the fast-food emporium of the nineteenth century, established to serve impatient soldiers who swarmed into France after the fall of Napoleon. Now bistros are good if not grand restaurants where it's possible to have a meal in less than two hours instead of three or four, and the French put up with snack bars, pizzerias, and frozen, microwave-heated quiche at the corner café.

For some mysterious reason, modern was colored orange. In a frenzy of modernizing, bars, offices, hotel decor, fast trains and storefronts were redone in bright orange to show they were up to date. New buildings, glass and concrete, are usually garish or dismally ungainly. To the French man in the street, "modern" means efficient, clean but ugly, and it's easy to understand, given the dreadful excuses for modern architecture displayed all over a country which reveres elegance and taste.

In immediate human terms, the most important change in French life has been the advent of the mass-market automobile. Possession of a car is a declaration of independence, an achievement of power and liberty which at last gives tangible meaning to the idea of equality, even as it saps fraternity on the streets and roads of France. The inexpensive car came along just in time to ease the exodus from the countryside. From 25 percent of the French labor force engaged in farming in 1945 (nearly half the population lived in rural areas), the number working in agriculture dropped to 6 percent in 1983. The European Community's Common Agricultural Policy, reinforced by de Gaulle as the price of France's return to active participation after seven months of sulkily leaving an "empty chair," and continued intervention by successive governments to help small farmers, stemmed the flood to the towns. Only 6 percent of its gross national product comes from agriculture, but France remains intensely conscious of its farmers, and they weigh heavily on its politics. The southerners among them are traditionally leftist, the northerners traditionally conservative, with the result that no matter who governs, the farm bloc is assured an attentive ear at the top.

Still, large sections of the country have been depopulated, particularly in Brittany and in central France. Villages, which by traditional definition have at least a few shops, have been downgraded to hamlets, mere clusters of houses with no commerce, not even a café. Local schools have been emptied. Often only a few old people clinging to the soil are left behind in a once thriving village. But they seldom stay isolated so thoroughly or as long as might have been expected by the demographic trend. The automobile and the French attachment to the land brought another kind of renewal, the "secondary residence." Restoration of abandoned farmhouses became a major avocation, while developers rushed to build concentrations of vacation bungalows. These new country homes are sprouting everywhere, not just in resort towns or near big cities. The population map of France ebbs and flows with every vacation season, almost every weekend. Highway disasters are a staple of TV news and the press. A high proportion of French families have a second home, either for sole use or to share with grandparents and relatives. The ties of city-dwellers with rural France, and a strong sense of roots, are thus intimately maintained.

Awareness of the long past is nourished, partly by deliberate policy of the centralized education and cultural administration systems, partly by this insistence on regular returns to home turf. School texts are the same everywhere, and were throughout the days of the French Empire. It is a sour joke among Algerians, Senegalese, Vietnamese and other former colonial peoples that the zeal to spread an all-embracing French culture required them to recite, as all French schoolchildren do, a history book that begins, "Our ancestors the Gauls . . ." The decline of French as a world language, especially as a lingua franca of the world elite, is a source of pain and recrimination. A substantial budget is dedicated to countering this trend. So is the care and restoration of monuments, including even unimposing private houses if they form part of a street scene or neighborhood considered to have historic value. They are ever-present reminders that the past lives on, and they are objects of the kind of intense concern that environmentalists in other countries show for nature preserves and endangered plant and animal species. Passing the Cluny Museum with its medieval treasures, a very modern-minded Parisian banker murmured in awe one evening, "A thousand years, we have a thousand years of culture to support us. That's what France represents. That's why we are so sturdy and so rich in spirit."

It is a form of ancestor worship which imposes a certain sacrifice. Malraux presided over the period of renovation when, after the years of depression, the years of war, the years of struggle to revive, France began at last to build. He paid great attention to scrubbing the grimy old façades of Paris until they glowed rosily again, to regilding the gates of the palace at Fontainebleau, to establishing Houses of Culture in the provincial cities and restoring once lovely neighborhoods that had deteriorated into slums. But he did not consider plain housing or a landscape lacking memorable echoes of the past as part of the cultural scene. As urban real estate soared in value and metropolitan populations swelled, the poor and the not-so-affluent were forced out to suburbs where developers planted row on row of tacky high-rise or barracks-style apartments. The population shift conserved the grace of city centers. There is no urban blight, American style. Instead, there is suburban drear and despair. It erupted in the 1970s when the angry refrain "Metro-boulot-dodo" forced authorities to notice at last that large parts of the population had reached a point of utter disgust with lives that consisted of jamming into subways (métro), days at work *(boulot)* in vast, impersonal office buildings and a return to bleak anthills and a sleep *(dodo)* of empty exhaustion.

Still, change is as alluring a promise as continuity. It has brought comforts. Telephones became easily available and they work very well. Proper plumbing, still something of a privilege more than a decade after the war, was accepted as a rightful necessity. And change brought prosperity and a renewed self-esteem to nourish confidence in a secure future. De Gaulle, with his contempt for the prewar Third Republic which crumbled before the Nazis and for the postwar Fourth Republic and its petty political bickering, shrewdly combined the emotional enhancement of a mystical past and the allure of a bright future to get his countrymen working and hoping again. He didn't start France on the road to becoming the fourth nuclear power. That was decided by his predecessors. But he gave the weapons program its substance and its special meaning of independence, self-confidence, world standing, of France as a nation to be reckoned with in the age of the superpowers. It mattered little that the meaning was largely mythic in strategic and geopolitical terms. The nuclear weapon made security more an issue of perception, one's own and that of others, than of hardware bought never to be used.

Oddly, de Gaulle bet badly in his choice of high technology to vault a floundering French economy to national strength and vigor, but he was not an economic animal. He was more sensitive to the psychological impact of proud modern skills. He also knew that unbounded rhetoric could not change the fact of France's limited means, so he picked three specific, glamorous areas on which to concentrate French efforts: supersonic transport (the Concorde), computers and a special system of color TV (Secam). All three were brilliant technical successes, proving French competence, and all three were economic duds. The failure was due to inadequate concern for cost and marketing calculations, the unglamorous part of technological Cinderella stories. But the lesson was learned, and the message absorbed that in order to remain "la même chose," France must plunge to the forefront of change.

The immense diversity of France, which so stirred de Gaulle's fears for its sustenance of united nationhood, also made change easier than might have been supposed. No other country of its size has such a variety of landscape, flora, and custom. Modernization required similar efforts from everybody; it worked as an equalizer.

Brittany, in the northwest, is rocky and poor, bright and fresh in summer, bedrizzled and befogged most of the rest of the year. It was the home of Asterix, the doughty hero of cartoonist René Goscinny, who used the history of the Gauls fighting off mighty Roman legions as an anachronistic satire of modern French foibles. Breton, kept alive by peasants and stubborn local patriots, is a Celtic language, with links to Irish, Scottish and Welsh. The mysterious dolmens, huge stones that may have served in druidic rites or astronomical calculations, attest to a lively prehistoric civilization in the region. Brittany is windswept, with its face to the ocean, and there is salt in the air. The men are sailors and fishermen, a rough life that gave both the courage and incentive for Bretons to provide the wave of French emigrants to the New World in the centuries of colonization. Later, Bretonnes provided the maids and concierges of Paris. But they moved up, or rather down, from their mean garret chambers. Their places have been taken by immigrants from more distant lands, Spanish and Portuguese, Algerian and Moroccan, Vietnamese, even Sri Lankan and Filipino.

Normandy, just to the east, is quite different, largely protected from the fury of the Atlantic storms but well watered by their rainfall. It sparkles in the deep green of prosperous temperate climes. If it weren't for the Channel, it would be hard to tell where Normandy stops and southern England begins, so alike are the fields, the narrow lanes with high hedgerows, the roses, the exposed-beam cottages and the ancient square church towers. The Norman conquest created deep ties with

England, of the family sort that mean quarrels. In 1966 the Harcourts celebrated a 900th anniversary reunion in the Château du Champ de Bataille, from which their noble ancestor set out with William the Conqueror to found the flourishing English branch of the family. Now, thanks to Common Market subsidies, Normandy contributes substantially to the mountains of butter and cheese and other overstocks which plague the European Community and drive the English to exasperation with their continental club. Normandy is comfortable, fashionable, a part of the country that, along with the gentle Loire Valley, gave rise to the notion of *la belle, la douce France*. The idyllic description is true, but incomplete.

The industrial northeast, flat and grubby, primed the wealth of France in the nineteenth and early twentieth centuries and was defaced by it. Like other centers of the Industrial Revolution in Europe, it has been left to decline and stagnate, angry but impotent at the dethronement of steel and coal. From the Middle Ages to the recent past, the area was a hub of trade and manufacture. Its flourishing cotton and wool industries and its position on the flat northern invasion routes made it a battlefield for centuries; it was the scene of some of the longest and bloodiest battles in both world wars. The city of Lille was subjected to seventeen sieges and was demolished several times. At times it was Flemish, at times French, Spanish or Austrian. Louis XIV claimed it as part of his heritage through his mother, Anne of Austria, and since then it has been French. Though the people are hearty and industrious, the region has lagged socially and culturally. Rimbaud wrote scathingly about dull petit-bourgeois life in poems inspired by his youth in the bleak town of Charleville. More assiduously Catholic than other parts of France, the north is poorer and has the highest infant mortality and the highest birthrate. One in every three persons is under twenty, compared to the national average of about one in four. The climate is cloudy and cool, the scenery uninteresting. No one goes to visit unless they have business there or are traveling to neighboring Belgium. People feel left behind, and they are. The effort to modernize, to leap forward with the newest industrial technology, is only beginning, and it is a bitter wrench.

Eastern France, Alsace and Lorraine, is solidly continental, turned away from the sea and its weather, facing the German plain with its broad avenue deep into Europe and, farther south, the mountains. It presses on the Rhine, to be connected one day to the Rhone by a canal that will transform the economic geography of the continent as much as the development of highways did. There are fields and forests, Alpine peaks and narrow valleys that lie dormant and white in winter and burgeon with dark green northern vitality in summer. It seems somehow less French than other areas, more absorbed into Europeanness. That isn't only because it was so fought over, so often detached and reattached. There is a different, heavier scenery, a solidity that is less fanciful and dreamy than other regions. Alsatian is a German dialect. Despite generations of hostility with the Rhinelanders on the German side, the people of Alsace feel Rhenish. They eat sauerkraut and live in towns of cobbled, medieval sturdiness little different from those across the river. But their white wine is a bit drier, more to the French taste.

The Savoy, where the French Alps rise, is almost indistinguishable from neighboring parts of Switzerland. But there are clues in the border area to the peoples' different habits. The verges of the road are more scraggly on the French side, the orchards less precisely planted, the houses not quite so freshly painted and maintained. But the mountains and the lustrous, deep lakes give the same sense of natural majesty imposing a certain orderly humility and patience on mere man, and the area is neater than the rest of France.

Burgundy, the center-east, remains enthralled by its ancient power and splendor, which flourished earlier and more luxuriantly than in other parts of France. Unlike people in other provinces, Burgundians cannot be called nostalgic or restless at their integration in the nation-state because they never really conceded superiority to Paris. There are limestone caves in the Périgord, to the west, where prehistoric clans lived at least 25,000 years ago and left cultural traces. But in northern Burgundy, there are remains of a highly developed civilization some 2,500 years ago.

Excavations of the Greek colony of Vix, near Châtillon-sur-Seine, revealed not only a magnificently decorated, perfectly formed vase the height of a man, but medical instruments, jewelry, even golden hair curlers, as fine as any ancient Greece produced. The countryside rolls softly, exposing fertile fields to warm but never ardent sun, which sweetens the grapes. Dijon, the old capital, uses its filigreed palaces and medieval monasteries as part of city life, as though the dukes and learned doctors still sauntered through the streets.

The Rhone flows through thriving Burgundy into sun-baked Provence, also once an independent realm, and spills into the sea at Marseille, already a great port in classical antiquity. Provence is Mediterranean, ocher-earthed and silvered with thin southern pine and cypresses. Northerners, who developed the Riviera in order to repose in perfumed breezes and yachting blazers (and now on its topless beaches), take home bouquets of mimosa or bowls of olivewood. Early in World War II, emboldened by the successes of its German ally, Italy laid raucous claim to the "recovery" of Nice and Marseille. Now that border is friendly and open. The last abrasive border dispute was settled in 1945 when the Val d'Aosta was awarded to Italy. Provençal is a romance language, nearer to Latin than is French. It enjoyed a literary surge in the late nineteenth century, due mainly to the efforts of the famed poet Fréderic Mistral. His name is also that of the fierce wind which blows down the Rhone Valley from the Alpine glaciers at certain seasons. Now Provençal survives mainly in the names of farms and villas sheltered in the valleys and of tourist establishments in villages cresting the sharp hills.

The French consider themselves primarily a Latin, Mediterranean nation, but that is part of the cherished myth. The Frankish tribes from Germany and the Viking Normans who settled above the Loire established dominion. The Languedoc region in the south (from *langue d'oc*, literally the language of "there" as opposed to *langue d'oïl*, the language of "here" in the north) was murderously overrun. Yet the people, called Occitanians, retain folk memories of independence and ties with Spanish Navarre, still visible in the ironwork balconies of towns such as Montpellier. Languedoc drops down to the southwestern coast, touching the Basque country at the foot of the Pyrenees. Marshy in places, rainier than Provence, the land is often sandy and grudging to the cultivator. But there is still a Spanish-style pride among the Occitanians and flickers of resistance to the north, dating from the bloody thirteenth-century crusades sent against the Albigensian heresy centered in Languedoc. High-spirited students, home in the lovely walled town of Carcassonne on vacation from Paris, amused themselves scrawling "Français Go Home" on police stations in the years when the favorite graffito of their comrades in the capital was "Amis [Americans] Go Home."

Aquitaine, the Atlantic side of the south, shares the Bay of Biscay with Spain but it has looked to England since Queen Eleanor married Henri Plantagenet, who became Henry II, King of England, in 1154. Her son Richard the Lionhearted lost most of the French territory which she brought to the English crown, but the British ruled Aquitaine for three hundred years, developing the export of claret, the red wine of Bordeaux. They left behind rugby as the local game, whereas the rest of France plays football (soccer) or *boule*, and a habit in upper-crust families of naming dogs Rover or Sport. As François Mauriac showed in his biting novels, nowhere in France does the ranking bourgeoisie maintain such a stiff hierarchy of snobbery as in Bordeaux, site of the great English-founded wine merchant dynasties. Aquitaine is a cool, fairly dry region, generously wooded where the land has not been cleared to the horizon for endless rows of vines. Like Burgundy, and unlike several other provinces, it does not resent Paris. Disdain suffices. Girondins, from the banks of Aquitaine's broad Gironde, argued bitterly during the Revolution with the more radical Jacobins for a French republic built on largely autonomous regions. They lost, but never really ceded.

The true center of France is the Massif Central, rugged, isolated, often forbidding. The Auvergne, in its midst, has a reputation for thrifty, not to say miserly, querulous people. Clermont-Ferrand, home of Michelin tires, and Limoges, home of fine china and elegant carriages named for the province of Limousin (origin of the word *limousine*), are manufacturing cities, dull, flat, offering little distraction.

But the center is not the heart. That is the lands of the Loire valley and the grain fields that encompass Orléans and spread up to Paris. It is traced with rivers and streams, its forests filled with game. Its smoothly heaving horizon beckons, and its climate soothes without smothering. The Renaissance princes, rich and secure, built vast, extravagant châteaux in the valley, for they no longer had need of fortified castles. The delight in refinement, festivity, lightness of demeanor and spirit that the French call *savoir vivre* was nourished by the region's bounty.

Ile de France, Paris and its environs, is a mental island, separate and above everything else. Its beauty comes especially from the sky, seldom empty, seldom still, diffusing a soft, reflective light. It can be no more of an accident that the Ile de France gave rise to the Impressionist painters, fascinated with the subtleties of light and tint, than that the art of Egypt is stark as the glare of the sun above the Nile. The rivers meander between grassy banks, even the broad, commerce-laden Seine. There are industrial suburbs, dormitory suburbs, and country-club suburbs, but Ile de France still has charming villages and small towns with a life of their own, as though they were far from the capital.

Paris is a spectacle, with an intense sense of its uniqueness. It is not a big city as modern metropolises go, some two million people, administratively and politically cut off from its surroundings. It seems even smaller because it is a city of neighborhoods whose residents do not usually mix. They have their own way of dressing, eating, talking. In the home of *bon chic, bon genre* (usually abbreviated to BCBG), which is the well-to-do Sixteenth arrondissement, there are tea shops, sedate department stores and an air of propriety quite unlike the rest of the city. Other quarters have their busy cafés, their saucy street life, their luxurious elegance, their street bazaars, each with its own flavor.

In the older parts, it is a city of walls, with only the squares, the avenues, the parks to give a sense of space. But the huge, heavy doors which breach the walls open on unsuspected marvels of gardens, ornamented courtyards, hidden villages of little houses. It is hardly possible to see all of Paris, so much of interest is tucked away. The city's special grace is in its grand vistas, sweeping scenes of harmonious proportion, but there are details everywhere, in dull-seeming back streets as well as on the magnificent monuments and bridges, which suddenly catch even the jaded eye. There is always something new to be noticed on the most familiar façades. Paris is proud of its beauties, and it cares for them well, with seasonal flowers in the parks and some of the large intersections. For a hundred years, from the time of the Commune uprising in 1870, the city had no mayor because the government did not trust Parisians with local responsibility which could challenge the state. But now there is an elected mayor, and he sees to it that the city is clean, well marked and well lit, flaunting its sense of being by far the best place for a civilized soul to enjoy life.

Paris isn't France, but it completely dominates the country. It is still difficult to cross France by train or plane without going through Paris. Everything starts and finishes there. The supremacy of the capital has something to do with geography, the convenience of the waterway, but more with deliberate strategy.

France was not the first part of Europe to converge feudal domains into a new idea of nation, but it started early and went about it thoroughly. Arms mattered, of course, as they did in the birth of nearly all states. The main tools, however, were finance and culture. Cardinal Richelieu, chief minister of King Louis XIII, dreamed of great reforms, colonies and trade, and sought to impose the authority of the King on the grand nobles through taxation. He also recognized the unifying power of a common language, and in 1635 he founded the French Academy to produce a dictionary. To this day, it is still engaged in revising definitions and ruling on the propriety of language, the first delineation of the borders of Frenchness and the connecting thread of French culture.

Under the ambitious Louis XIV, Jean-Baptiste Colbert, the Minister of Finance, established a centralized treasury and created the economic doctrine of Colbertisme, nationalist, mercantilist, state-directed. Whether the government of France is conservative or leftist, it still takes for granted the right of the state to a position of dominant power over the economy. With Cardinal Mazarin, the chief minister, Colbert added beaux arts to the concerns of the Academy. Together they enabled the King to complete the task of subduing the recalcitrant nobles.

France, then, in the seventeenth century was the most populous and the wealthiest of European lands. Louis XIV used the bulging royal purse for armies to expand his kingdom, and for a gorgeous court to reduce his vassals by the seductions of pleasure. All the arts were summoned to attract provincial aristocrats into magnificent dependence on the King. They flitted like butterflies competing for the brightness around the royal light. Those who balked at the gaiety, frivolity and sumptuous luxuries of subjection at court in favor of being their own master were banished to their fiefdoms, where life was tedious and banal in comparison. But few could resist partaking of the Sun King's glory. Force and intrigue helped complete the glittering triumph.

Louis XV knew where such absolutism was leading and suspected the ultimate consequences. His prediction, "Après moi le déluge," was fulfilled with the overthrow of his successor Louis XVI in 1789 and a rampaging revolution.

A school of historians holds that the tremendous virulence of the French Revolution was a reaction not only to the arbitrariness and opulence of the monarchy, but to an underlying allegiance to the provinces against the center. The King's exactions were added to demands on the peasants by the local lords and the Church. They were an unbearable total burden, adding nothing to the laborer's defense in daily life. The ferocity provoked can still be seen in provincial cathedrals and chapels. While the rabble of Paris gathered around the guillotine in the Place de la Révolution to cheer the severing of noble heads, the provincials beheaded statues of saints and earlier kings. Men climbed hundreds of feet up precarious spires to wreak symbolic vengeance on their masters in the capital. At Chartres, and in many country places, headless stone figures still adorn medieval splendors.

As often happens when nations are stirred to blind fury, success went to the most radical of the revolutionaries, the Jacobins. They were determined to seize power, not to disperse it. They tried to overthrow everything, including the calendar, and redrew the map of France to wipe out provincial borders. But they kept the centralized system. The excesses of their terror brought exhaustion and a new demand for order, resulting in the dictatorship of Napoleon. It is another French myth that the revolution was a full republican success, one that wiped out the privileges of rank. Only fifteen years after the fall of the Bastille on July 14, still a national holiday, Napoleon crowned himself emperor in lavish rites, and gave princely titles to his family. The belief in Napoleon as the liberator, the nemesis of crowned rulers, was nourished by the reaction of Europe's other sovereigns, who were aghast at the challenge to what they claimed to hold by divine right. But far from practicing the republican promise of equality, the Emperor installed himself as the source of power and centralized it more than ever before.

Nonetheless, the aspirations of the revolution marked a watershed for France. Its idealism is still central to the way Frenchmen think of themselves. Deep chords are struck when their leaders speak of France as "the homeland of the rights of man" and of the generous tradition of political asylum. Liberty is considered a birthright, an immutable part of what it means to be French. The American Revolution influenced the thinkers of France and helped shape their vision of the rights and duties of a citizen. But the social upheaval in France was far more profound, leaving a permanent challenge to privilege based on birth and property. Some Frenchmen scoff today at the idea that America had a real revolution. It was only a war of independence, of national liberation, they say, which did little to change relations within American society and did not even abolish slavery.

In France, the mighty were toppled and power changed hands. The revolutionary fervor did not lead other Europeans to rise and overthrow their rulers at the time, but it signaled the beginning of the end of monarchical tyranny as an acceptable form of government. The banner of republicanism was raised as the ideal. Through the nineteenth century and well into the twentieth, the intellectual leaders of Europe drew support and courage from the example of France. Paris remains the mecca of expatriates from unhappy and ill-governed lands. Utopian socialism has French roots. *Commune* is a French word, derived from what is common, what is shared, and it is applied to the autonomous, collective institutions of village life. This is the origin of the word *com-*

munism, first tested in flames and dire misery in the Paris uprising after the 1870 defeat of the Second Empire (proclaimed by Napoleon's nephew, who took the title Napoleon III) in the Franco-Prussian War. The experience of the Paris Commune was brief and extraordinarily bloody. It was put down in 1871, but it left scars that still throb when Frenchmen feel emotional tugs to choose one side of the barricades.

Napoleon I's totally centralized administrative system endured through all the battles. The provinces and their historic names, Burgundy, Aquitaine, Brittany, and so on, were abolished by the revolution. They were chopped up into departments to which Napoleon appointed prefects with great powers, answering only to Paris. Now there are ninety-six, usually named for rivers or mountains in the area. But the old allegiances and the old names never died. When regional councils began to be established in 1964, it was no coincidence that the new jurisdictional level between the capital and the departments closely followed the outline of the ancient provinces. Decentralization became an important plank in the reform platform of the Socialist-Communist coalition which won power in 1981 after a generation of rule by de Gaulle and his heirs. The regions were strengthened, the prefects curbed. But once again the changes only echoed the old adage of continuity. The important powers remained with Paris. Modern France is still the most centralized of European countries, for all its diversity.

French politics are also intensely polarized. The revolution and the reaction it provoked were so extreme that nearly two centuries later the swing of the emotional pendulum had scarcely slowed to moderate oscillation. Only the Bolshevik Revolution and the Spanish Civil War, in the twentieth century, tore their countries apart in so great a rage. Perhaps the mullahs' revolution in Iran will eventually be seen as an equally deep historical wound.

The much-used phrase "a man of the left" is not just a party label, it is a declaration of faith and heritage. Jean Daniel, editor of the pro-Socialist magazine *Le Nouvel Observateur,* was once asked what he meant by it. He groped for a definition of something that seemed to him so all-encompassing and yet so obvious that it wouldn't need explanation. Finally he said, "It means a person of heart." Touching his left breast, he repeated the old aphorism, "You know, the heart is on the left." Danielle Mitterrand, wife of the Fifth Republic's first Socialist president, François Mitterrand, said something similar when she was talking about her attachment to the party. "It means caring about peo-

ple, trying to help." This exclusive claim to the humane virtues by the
left inevitably inflames the political discourse, with the conservatives
laying counterclaim to the entrepreneurial, civic and patriotic virtues.
French politics are seldom violent nowadays, though they often sound
so. The vocabulary leaves little room for the moderation most people
basically espouse, and which many politicians delight in deriding. Lio-
nel Jospin, who succeeded Mitterrand as head of the Socialist Party
after the 1981 elections, defined the political center. "It's like the Ber-
muda Triangle," he said. "Whoever approaches it disappears."

In France as everywhere else, politics are mostly about personal rivalries and power relations. But to admit anything less than noble aspirations is considered demeaning. There is a disdainful phrase for it,
la politique politicienne, the politics of politicians, meaning the cheap
little tricks of the game as opposed to the high aims of public policy.
There is no other way to distinguish "policy" from "politics" in French:
both are *la politique*. As a result, French politicians ascribe great importance to programs, which are elaborated with a great deal more care
and endowed with a far longer life span than American party platforms.
Party names matter little, and often change. But the abstractions they
are meant to project are crucial.

After the war, "the right" became a pejorative, a word of opprobrium
used by the left but never by the left's major opponents. From the time
de Gaulle founded the Fifth Republic until Mitterrand's election, they
called themselves "Gaullists" or "the majority." Afterward, they made
do with "the opposition," and then, back in power, "liberal." In European usage, "liberal" alludes to the nineteenth-century argument for
individual rights, free enterprise and private initiative.

Since the Fifth Republic's introduction of a powerful presidency, the
names that matter in French politics are the individuals vying for the
post. So long as the President's supporters have a majority in the National Assembly, his writ is probably stronger than that of any other
elected leader in the world because the legislature tends to behave as a
rubber stamp. The President can appoint and dismiss the Premier at
will, and call new legislative elections at any time. But when the Socialists lost their majority to a conservative coalition in March 1986,
France faced a new, delicate experience of divided powers which it
called *cohabitation*, a suggestive phrase which accurately reflects neither love nor marriage between the head of state and the government,
just obligatory sharing of responsibilities. This was imposed by the fact

that the President's term lasts seven years, while the legislature must be renewed after five years. When the right won in 1986 and Jacques Chirac became Premier, it set out to undo many of the reforms introduced during five years of Socialist domination, including nationalizations, proportional representation and laws which confirmed government monopoly of TV but challenged concentration of power in the press.

The underlying purpose of all political maneuvers, however, was to jockey for position in the next presidential election, in hopes it would restore the previous single-handed leadership. There was talk of a need for constitutional reform and a more clearly defined separation of powers in the event the experiment broke down or drifted into paralysis. The Fifth Republic had taken root, and no one suggested going back to the Fourth's system of fragile parliamentary coalitions. But the French are not so wedded to their constitution as Americans and see nothing wrong with major changes when they seem necessary. "How can you live with the same old constitution for two centuries?" one politician asked an American. "Don't you think it's good to freshen up now and then?"

The shifting kaleidoscope of political alliances imposed adjustments in France. There never was a two-party system, though there have practically always been two well-defined sides, left and right, republicans and monarchists, statists and liberals. When they coalesce on each side of the gap, Frenchmen complain that the country is "split in two," driven to confrontation. When, as more often, they fragment in competitive rivalries on each side, the complaints are of lack of coordination and coherence. Despite all this, the Gaullist legacy of stability has come to be cherished. The French vaunt their individualism, but, or perhaps therefore, they like strong, decisive government and leaders with a clearly established, self-assured personality. The antipolitics, antigovernment politician who campaigns against *le pouvoir*, the way the French often refer to government, is not for them. The leader is expected to have a certain elegance of speech and demeanor and even some aloofness of manner, an aura of superiority to represent the country, not to embody the man in the street.

Even the Communist leader, Georges Marchais, would not appear in working clothes or a hard hat. He is a burly figure, with an improbable ski-jump nose and mischievous dark eyes, whose ranting, taunting, ridiculing performances amuse his compatriots but attract fewer and fewer of them. The decline of the Communists has been the most important political development of the Fifth Republic. From a steady quarter of the vote in the postwar period, they have sagged to a marginal 10 percent or less. There was a period when they seemed on the way to power, and a Socialist premier warned that they "are not to the left but to the east," referring to their dedication to Moscow's aims. They still have strength in the largest labor union, in some municipalities and other fiefdoms, and in their closed, protective society within the society, which runs summer camps, forms of welfare and a kind of parallel police. But they are no longer a serious contender for leadership.

The Socialists, revived by François Mitterrand over a decade and a half from a moribund fringe to become the strongest single party, took over the Communist role as potential alternative to the right and center-right. They achieved it by forming an alliance with the Communists which made the drive for power numerically credible. Then, when the Communists broke away in frustration, they began a bumpy evolution toward moderation, more like the Social Democrats of northern Europe. It was Mitterrand's shrewd helmsmanship which steered them. But he is more a literary than a political type, with a cool, impersonal aura that is almost secretive. He was able, without a visible wrench, to transform himself from supreme magistrate to a sort of reigning arbiter when the voters obliged him to accept an opposition Premier, and he gained popularity and admiration in the process. Several figures in his party are vying for the succession. If they don't force a split, one of them will eventually rise to it, for French politics has entered the post-Gaullist phase where fairly regular swings of power can be anticipated.

The contenders on the other side came from a variety of parties and groups organized more around their personalities than any clear-cut platforms or traditions. Jacques Chirac, who radiates ambition, is a long-limbed, energetic man with powerful hands and a practiced smile. He is the quintessential political tactician, who rose through Gaullist ranks and sought to use Gaullism's base to launch a tough-minded conservatism in the style of Ronald Reagan and Margaret Thatcher. He conveys a sense of force and momentum which exhilarates his supporters but seems ominous, to the point of revulsion, to others. He became an open rival to former President Valéry Giscard d'Estaing, whom he helped elect in 1974 and who first made him Premier. Giscard initially modeled himself on John F. Kennedy, but once in the presidential palace he withdrew into the aristocratic pose he really preferred and gradually chilled the public. Tall, slim, sporty, he is a handsome figure, but somehow he seemed a worn leftover from the past when he tried to make a comeback. Raymond Barre, the second Premier who served Giscard as President, seemed more in tune with the prudent, unemotional, conscientious France of the 1980s. Rotund, with all the mannerisms of the economics professor he had been, betraying no sign of humor or fantasy, Barre incarnated reliability without illusion.

The crux of French politics is the perennial contention between the right and the left. But a far-right group arose as the Communists lost appeal, to complement them on the opposite margin. There has always been an endemic far right in France, waxing and waning as issues shift, often expressing the frustrations of the petit bourgeois with social change. In modern times, the catalyzing issues have been taxes, the struggle of small shopkeepers against retail chains, and then, more impassioned, immigrants, especially North Africans. The latest version of the far right is a party called the National Front, led by a pink-faced, roly-poly, skillful demagogue named Jean-Marie Le Pen. The party has been openly denounced as racist by most of the other politicians, but the immigrant issue cannot be ignored and it casts a shadow on France's image of itself.

The real political counterpower is held by intellectuals. They form a vocal class, creating a tension between the great man who claims to embody the nation and the stubborn individuality of the French. This tug of visions between France as one and France as myriad is deeply embedded in the society. The pendulum swings but never comes to rest. It is a source of French vitality and creativity, a cherished paradox.

Intellectuals are more easily recognized than defined, though they are hospitably willing to include more or less anyone who seeks admission to their company. The emphasis is on philosophy and the arts. Scientists can choose whether they wish to belong. Unlike the Russian notion of "intelligentsia," the title doesn't designate just anyone with a higher education; a French intellectual must show appropriate gestures and sympathies.

The French educational system, culminating in the *grandes écoles*— exclusive top-level graduate schools with stiffly competitive entrance exams—tends to create and renew the class. The intellectual elite is no longer on display in a few cafés on the Boulevard St. Germain in Paris, as it was in the early postwar period. The garrulous flocks at the Café Flore or the Deux Magots in those days had more to do with poverty than with public display of clannishness. There was no heat and few had space and resources enough to gather their friends at home. Cafés were the cheap, natural place to assemble. Now, with decent housing, there is much more dispersal, though leading intellectuals still have an acute sense of a special role.

The war and the occupation branded the intellectuals far more severely than it did most other Frenchmen. By definition, they argue principles and theories, judge and take sides. As Simone de Beauvoir made clear in *The Mandarins*, they were unforgiving, even vengeful, toward their countrymen who were indifferent to the resistance, let alone toward collaborators. They emerged at the liberation with a sense of historic responsibility to remake the country in the image of their dreams. As she also showed, they immediately fell to squabbling, pontificating, denigrating, and their visions tarnished at their touch. But they reigned with supreme self-confidence. Those who had been active in the resistance—and many played an important role—felt themselves responsible for the honor of France and its regeneration into a purer, idealized society. They had published underground journals which kept up hope and morale and served in maintaining communications with the resistance and the rest of society. After the German invasion of the Soviet Union, the Communists also developed an energetic resistance movement, though at times in rivalry with the Gaullists. The Communist wartime record was courageous and patriotic. They were skilled at clandestine organization, and it won them many sympathizers. That was an important factor in the strong postwar Communist influence on the French intellectual elite.

The king of them all was Jean-Paul Sartre, with Simone de Beauvoir as his consort. He was a small, puckish man, with thick glasses and a biting wit, great erudition and an even greater sense of his profundity in sorting out the world. It is hard to understand now how Sartre and his court managed to impose near absolute tyranny on the intellectual order of his time, but tyranny it was. Soon after he died, in 1980, a group of young writers and editors gathered to talk about the succession and the heritage, and found to their surprise that it was dust. Sartre was no longer read or quoted much. His vast strictures and perceptions didn't seem to apply.

Yet in his day, few dared challenge him. Albert Camus, who opposed a tragic, resigned view of man's capacity for wisdom to Sartre's activism, died young. His was a great and haunting talent, deeply humane and essentially pessimistic. He could not be ignored because there was too much recognizable truth in his descriptions of ordinary people driven to terrible acts through what they considered the best of intentions, exemplified by the war in Algeria. Camus was made unwelcome in Algeria, his homeland, by Frenchmen who believed themselves patriots, and while he captured the imagination of critics of the war, he had no simple solutions to offer them. The tragic sense of life does not enthrall. In contrast, Sartre stirred up passions, issued calls to action.

Raymond Aron, a pithy journalist and professor of sociology with a dry, polemic style, outlived Sartre by a few years. But it wasn't until his late years that his stubborn insistence on moderation, common sense and a certain tolerance in social analysis won support from intellectuals of fashion. "Intellectual and spiritual pluralism," Aron wrote, "does not pretend to offer a truth comparable to the truths of mathematics or physics. But nor does it offer merely opinion. Pluralism justifies itself by the falseness of the beliefs that oppose it." An American might simply say, "The know-it-alls don't."

That was typically French, Aron's way of fighting what he called the "messianic" dictates of totalitarianism with as much vigor as those who proclaim a single "truth" to be revealed, by divinity, by history or by dogma. Sartre did not fall into that simple trap, but he held that truth could be made to reveal itself through action. He preached "engagement" (commitment), plunging into issues, and his doctrine of "existentialism" held that commitment would bring forth truth enough. "Sartre magnificently orchestrated the adventures of youth," wrote the critic Jean-Marie Domenach when Sartre was gone and the metaphysical passions had subsided to reveal how "naïve, silly, like an angry child" Sartre had been, in Domenach's words. There was not really a hippie counterculture in France. It was the rebels who ruled.

Although he never joined the Communist Party—he insisted on being his own self, unlabeled, even refusing the Nobel Prize so as to be unique—Sartre probably had more influence in nourishing a cult of the Soviet Union and hostility to America than did the Communist leaders. His concern was to give no comfort to anti-Communists; as another critic, Alain Finkielkraut, reflected once the idol fell, Sartre equated ethics and morality with the left, so that to be against the left was moral turpitude. In Sartre's way of thinking, the will to remake man in optimism and idealism excused all mistakes, while a pessimistic acceptance of human imperfection was in itself an evil. Like de Gaulle in politics, Sartre overwhelmed his intellectual opposition by a combination of disdain and grandiose promise which seemed irresistible. Modesty, humility, reality looked dull fare in comparison.

The dominance of this approach crushed not only other ideas but careers and hopes. Writers had trouble being published, actors had trouble getting jobs, professors had trouble getting audiences if they did not go along. The immensely popular singer Yves Montand, whose wife, the actress Simone Signoret, was even more involved in left-wing causes, changed abruptly to an anti-Communist view in 1983. He admitted that he, like many others, had been a "reverse bigot" and had concealed what he knew so as not to help the bourgeoisie or earn the contempt of his friends.

Just when the passions of the early postwar years were beginning to cool in the face of European realities, the Algerian war revived the sense of outrage. France had fought to keep Indochina and had finally withdrawn in exhaustion. (The ambiguous settlement set in motion America's war in Vietnam.) But Algeria was considered different, not a colony but an integral part of France, administered under the same system as the mainland. The war against the Arab Algerians' demand for independence tore French society, especially as reports seeped out of the use of torture and brutality in the attempt to suppress the rebellion. The divisions it provoked brought France to the verge of civil war, and that was what brought de Gaulle back to power. Decolonization was a bitter and costly experience, so soon after the ordeal of World War II, and France did not weather it well.

Sartre was a leader of French opposition to the "dirty war." It refurbished his claim to purity, renewed the assertion of revolution as the true expression of culture, and led him to endorse terrorism as the justifiable rebuff to stifling authority. And he was followed as a prophet, a "master of thought," as French intellectuals in earlier times had enshrined Voltaire, Hugo and Zola to head their ardent cult. The student explosion of 1968 extended his mandate. By then, he had to jostle to keep up with the new slogans, but he would not be left behind.

Alexander Solzhenitsyn's book *The Gulag Archipelago* had the impact of a bombshell on France. The rest of the world had long been aware of Stalin's terror, of labor camps, of massacres, of thought control. But it was only then, in the late 1970s, long after East Berlin,

Budapest, Prague, Gdansk, that the collective blindfold of Paris' Left Bank intellectuals was allowed to drop. Some of the firebrands of 1968, a decade older, reflected on the ashen remains of their romantic illusions and wrote with pensive new sobriety. They enjoyed a brief celebrity as the "new philosophers," but their influence faded too. French intellectuals like intensity, big words and vehement adjectives. A new group emerged on the right, calling themselves GRECE. It was an acronym, deliberately chosen to read as the name of Greece in French, symbol of an intellectualism that rejected "soft" Christian values and extolled tough pagan valor. That was a reaction to the development of a Catholic left, sometimes more radical than the Communists. But it was quickly co-opted by the standard political right, and its leader, Louis Pauwels, became the editor of a weekly magazine inserted in the bourgeoisie's daily bible, Le Figaro.

It came as a distressing surprise to the Socialist government after a couple of years in power to discover that their intellectual chorus had faded away. They had so long considered themselves the natural habitat of the artists and philosophers that they took it for granted they were entitled to the enthusiastic, thunderous support they had received as the opposition. It never occurred to the Socialist politicians that the intellectuals tended to be critics, people whose mental comfort resided in opposition to constituted authority and who could not be dragooned to the side of power just because power had changed hands. Nor were the intellectuals much interested in the responsibilities of government, the compromises that office imposes. Mitterrand himself was caught in the squeeze between the practical politics of governance and the purity of rhetoric which is the luxury of the opposition. He and his government had reached the position where they could be judged on what they did, not just on what they promised, and the incumbents saw the intellectuals' inevitable use of their right to criticize as a sign of disloyalty.

Pierre Mauroy, Mitterrand's first Premier, made a long, embarrassingly plaintive appeal in Le Monde, asking why the leftist intellectuals had gone "mute." The Communist director of the House of Culture in Nantes, ousted after the opposition won back city hall, said in astonishment, "We always thought culture belonged to us, that the right really conceded it." Jack Lang, Mitterrand's effervescent and unrepentant Minister of Culture, was stung to find himself under attack by certified big-gun intellectuals when he came home from a UNESCO conference in Mexico. He had been a smash hit there with a tirade against "American cultural imperialism." It wasn't particularly new; it had been a refrain among defenders of French culture since the complaints of "coca-colonization" in the early 1950s. The difference was that the Left Bank claque had disappeared. Some even switched sides and denounced Lang for a philistine failure to appreciate American creative work. In any case, by the time the left established itself in government, with a documented intellectual as President in François Mitterrand, the intellectual tide had turned. There was a swing to the right in politics and a surge of interest in technology ahead of philosophy and the arts.

Of course, French intellectuals do not march in lockstep. There are always conflicting trends, but there is usually a dominant tide, especially at times of crisis. It may be that the spread of higher education, the development of a technological class with its own more concrete and less polemical concerns, was eroding the preserve of the intellectual caste. Or it may be that a time of confusion, of transition, brought a dispersal of views that would coalesce again later when issues seemed clearer and more morally compelling. The Socialist government, after a short and heady period of political will overriding the facts of the society's life, came to seem more like the end of an era than a harbinger of the new days it had proclaimed.

The difficulty was that the disappointed intellectuals had yet to mark out a new direction. The "sacred egoism" and the "privileged relations," which French leaders always liked to cite to justify the claim of not being subject to the pressures afflicting other nations, had not protected the country from the oil crisis, the recession, the fears of war in Europe. The old industries—steel, automobiles, coal, textiles, ships—were badly hit, as elsewhere. Centuries of direct or hidden subsidies, a national reflex of looking to the government to bolster weak links in the economy, the new nationalizations and the left's unfulfillable promises of full employment added to the strains of readjustment. When the right came back in 1986, its rallying cry was free enterprise, less government interference.

Areas of the economy had been prepared for the shift, however, making a splotchy pattern, with some places flourishing and others in distress. The corseted towers of nuclear power plants had already sprouted all over the country, holding a pledge of industrial revival because France has no oil. The antinuclear movement was weak and sporadic compared to those in other countries, surprising to outsiders because the French are never loath to protest. There wasn't even an obvious explanation, but the rallying cry of energy independence, awareness of the need for a new industrial energy base and acceptance of the atom as the guarantee of security had their effect. Mitterrand put great emphasis on research and the new electronics and information industries. In the longer term, France had the resources and the capacity to surge forward again, but it had staved off the impact of the world recession with costly measures, and had to pay for them before joining the recovery. Ingenuity was not undermined—as the ability to create an important market in the United States for French bottled water and to sell refrigeration plants to Alaska bore witness. But there was a period of great malaise as the French looked ahead without intellectual marching orders.

A census in 1982 added both solidity to the French identikit and the impression of drastic change. The flood to the cities and towns has stopped. The average citizen is now a "rurbanite," owning a house on the outskirts of a city in an area where town and countryside have fused into TV-land. The family, once the fortress of French self-consciousness, has been divided, though not conquered. One in four households is solitary. The birthrate, though not as low as Germany's, has fallen below the population replacement rate of two for each woman of child-bearing age, at 1.8. Children, considered a resource in old agricultural France, are now a burden when so many women go out to work; women are 40 percent of the labor force. Besides the car, TV and the telephone, which was something of a luxury a generation ago but now is everywhere, loneliness in suddenly constricted households is eased with pets. There are 17 million, compared to 12 million children under age fourteen. The old right to obtain a certificate of "concubinage," recognizing cohabitation without marriage, is exercised as never before. The mayor of Montpellier said he issued three times as many as five years earlier in 1978.

Women still earn less and have more trouble advancing in careers than men, but the old discriminatory laws have been swept away, and along with them some small measure of what are acknowledged as "phallocratic" attitudes. Two familiar types have all but disappeared from the leisurely towns of the south: the *frotadou*, or rubber, who insistently rubs up against females in the vicinity, and the *pistachier*, or pistachio-cracker, who endlessly twists ears at the corner bar with accounts of romantic exploits. That kind of boasting no longer wins applause. The bars and cafés are still there, but the crowd that used to pop in for a brandy or a big balloon of cheap red wine at breakfast has thinned out. The talk at noon and in the evening is likely to be about sports and taxes. People still carry long, crunchy loaves of unwrapped bread through the streets two or three times a day. But it is rare to see a beret except on the head of an elderly man or a tourist; women in traditional weave skirt and coif are doubtless participating in a folklore festival, not peasants dressed for church.

One in every 12.8 inhabitants works for the government, fewer than in Denmark (one in 8.2) or Britain (one in 10.5) but a lot more than in Germany (one in 17.4), Holland (one in 21.2) or Italy (one in 22). Though he swears by his dogged individualism, the Frenchman maintains a great respect for authority, especially for the signs that mark the status of a dignitary, and he is transported at the thought of being entitled to a sash or a decoration. When anything goes wrong, even the weather, he blames the state and looks to it for compensation. Parents still aspire to government jobs for their children, though the entrepreneurs are becoming the new ideal. The state looks after almost everyone's medical bills, and guarantees paid holidays twice a year. And woe to the politician who launches controversy or allows strikes or other inconveniences during summer, winter and spring holidays. There are demonstration seasons, with enthusiastic attendance, but these are definitely not at the sacrosanct times that are reserved for vacations.

One commentator projected the demographic trends and foresaw a France made up of "the old, the Arab and the 'creatician,' " a neologism designating the computer-wise professional or businessman to whom the future has been assigned. It came as a shock to realize that France is as exposed as the next country to the great social and economic winds buffeting the world. The French think of "the Hexagon," as they call continental France without Corsica and overseas territories, as a walled domain, a place where they are masters of their fate and "have no lessons to take from anyone," in their common phrase. There is a deep sense of being special, separate, indeed superior, which is part of even the least chauvinistic Frenchman's identity. It is based not only on the glorious period of French history, remembered and memorialized in the lavish national monuments, but also on the culture. The country has become European-minded; participation in the European Community is a basic given of French life now. But it is also taken for granted that the quintessence of Europe is, above all, French. Others are expected to recognize that and to cooperate in making sure that this fact of European nature will endure.

For a century, the French had worried about German militarism. Their sense of security after World War II came not so much from participation in the Western alliance as from the constraints that Allied occupation and later membership in that alliance placed on Germany. Signals of pacifism in Germany raised the old fear of threat from the East but in a new way. A neutral Germany would no longer be a buffer. The line of defense could be moved back once more to the Rhine. Talk revived of the need for a common European defense, not to push back an American effort at hegemony as it was conceived a generation earlier, but to compensate for the waning credibility of American protection and envelop the Germans more tightly. But the obstacles appeared insuperable, above all France's own refusal to integrate defense responsibilities.

Unlike the Germans, the French have no problems of identity. They know who they are and can't imagine wanting to be like anybody else. Unlike the British, they are not tempted to withdraw into themselves and let the troublesome world go by. They are determined to remain a presence on the world scene. But the material means are lacking, and the world has become negligent in paying what France considers due deference to its moral and intellectual weight. It lives with its contradictions, its image of radiance and importance, and it never stops seeking ways to make its mark. The Gallic cock is sprightly, feisty. Its cry resounds and it wakes people up when they aren't expecting it.

IBERIA
Spain and Portugal
Return to Europe

I BERIA IS A TERM of geography. To the extent that it is a state of mind, it represents the view from outside. To the people who live in the Iberian Peninsula, the differences between Spain and Portugal are much more important than what they have in common.

Yet they do have a lot in common. Their Latin-based languages are quite similar, laced with many derivatives from Arabic words. (Practically any word that starts with "al"—*alcohol, alcove, alfalfa, algebra, alkali*—has come to English from Arabic via Spanish.) They are deeply Catholic countries that underwent centuries of Islamic rule in large parts of their territories, and it left a pervasive influence. Both produced extraordinary explorers, sparked perhaps by the richness of Arab science and learning which brightened the long occupation. They burst forth onto the seas, in what now seem ridiculously fragile barks, and brought Europe its first contact with lands beyond the oceans, discovering a "new world" named America (for Amerigo Vespucci, an Italian who followed Columbus) in the search for a sailing route to the fabulous Orient, which Marco Polo had reached by land. In less than a century, Spanish and Portuguese adventurers had so overrun the globe beyond Christendom that Pope Alexander VI, in a papal bull issued in May 1493, imposed a partition to prevent war between them. In the Americas, Portugal took Brazil and Spain the rest. A line was drawn in the Atlantic 370 leagues west of Cape Verde Islands, running from the Arctic to the Antarctic.

The homelands prospered with the loot, bringing a golden age literally as well as culturally. Then other Europeans, rising to the temptation with fresh vigor, set out to compete. There was resistance from rivals, and rebellion in the colonies. The empires tired and dwindled. By the time Europe was really coming to rule the world, with an explosion of commerce and industry, Spain and Portugal were virtually exhausted. They retained feudal structures longer than other Europeans, though under central monarchies, and it drained their energies. They sank into lethargy, like their earlier Arab rulers, as more northerly Europeans surged around the world.

Now they share the relatively small southwestern stump of Europe that juts into the Atlantic, an area smaller than Texas, the size of New Mexico and Arizona combined. Cut off from the rest of the continent by the daunting Pyrenees, the Spaniards and the Portuguese live back to back, but they do not like each other. The excitable Spaniards consider the Portuguese dull, plodding, lacking verve. The stoic, melancholy Portuguese consider the Spaniards overbearing, unsound, lacking patience.

As it happened, they emerged from long dictatorships only a year apart, painfully conscious of trailing modern Europe and eager to catch up. Portugal had a remarkably bloodless though passionate revolution, symbolized by red carnations. Spain's transformation was achieved through an even more remarkable, unspectacular series of elections. Their politics are not so different from each other. Both emerged from long isolation to become peaceable, firmly democratic countries, though the radicalized army which had made the Portuguese revolution maintained a critical role for the first decade. The Spanish army was the heir of Francisco Franco's victory in the Civil War, a bastion of conservatism. Spain had come a long way in economic and social development in the last two generations. Portugal had barely budged. The two countries joined the European Communities at the same time, January 1, 1986, a step both saw as the gateway back to the mainstream and the modern world. But their people remain deeply conscious of the things that divide them from each other.

SPAIN
Nation and Regions

GENERALISSIMO FRANCISCO FRANCO took a long time dying. There were morbid jokes and grisly predictions as he lay critically ill for over a month. Europe watched uneasily. The Spanish Civil War, which brought him to power in 1936, had turned out to be the rehearsal for World War II. It was particularly ferocious, but more than that it had deeply marked the ideas and ideals of a generation far beyond Spain's borders. Italian soldiers practiced landings. Hitler's Luftwaffe pilots practiced dive-bombing. Russian commissars practiced purging. Franco won with the support of the fascist powers preparing for bigger campaigns, while the democracies clucked idly. Moscow sent enough help to keep the Republicans—with their assortment of anarchists, Communists, socialists, Loyalists—fighting for three years, but not enough to save them from defeat. Then, surprisingly, Spain stayed neutral as the rest of Europe succumbed to disaster. Many thought Franco would never outlast his Axis friends. He did, though Spain became a pariah in Allied Europe, blackballed from all the organizations established to bring a peaceful revival to the ravaged continent.

It was more than a generation before the exclusion imposed on Spain from outside, the silence imposed within, could at last be lifted. The country had suffered alone during its three years of fratricide, which pitted not only neighbors in virtually every town and village but members of the same family against each other. Its anguish affected the whole intellectual world. The emotions it evoked were so intense that

114

they marked for life those foreigners who were drawn into the struggle or who watched it from afar. The Spanish war incarnated the moral-political conflict of ideologies which was the central theme not only in Europe but in much of the world between the two great wars. In the United States, a kind of middle way was found between the radicalism of the right and of the left under the leadership of Franklin Delano Roosevelt. But many people were drawn into an ardent faith as though by a holy grail, and many who were not necessarily impressed by the Soviet Union became Communists as the way to oppose fascism. Some lost their conviction through what they actually saw on the Spanish battlefields—George Orwell, Stephen Spender, Arthur Koestler and André Malraux were noted examples.

Some were converted or confirmed in a lifelong involvement that led to treachery. Kim Philby, the high-ranking British intelligence officer who fled to Moscow just as his long record as a Soviet spy was discovered, had been in Spain. Others, who had volunteered from a sense of moral duty, were persecuted in the 1950s when the Cold War inspired leaders in East and West to suspect anyone who had been involved in Spain of sympathy for the other side. Americans with a Spanish record had a bad time during the era of Senator Joe McCarthy's Communist witch-hunt. Eastern Europeans—and even before World War II, Russians in the Soviet army—had it worse as Stalin purged those he considered tainted by contact with the hodgepodge of idealists in Spain. In the East, they were called "the .Spaniards." Yugoslavia's Tito was among them. Few were aware in the 1950s of the strange parallel that the legacy of the Spanish crusade imposed on its veterans on both sides of the Iron Curtain. By that time, Spain itself was mute, almost ignored as it lived on under Franco's repressive concept of military order and Catholic faith. For two generations, Spain was little more than a memory for the world it had stirred so deeply.

No one was sure what lay hidden beneath the country's opaque surface, or how the people would react when the dictator was replaced. Many, invoking the proverbial hot blood of the Spaniards and the bitter heritage of the war, forecast widespread civil disorder. The Falange, Franco's party, appeared intact. The military, pampered and arrogant, appeared to dominate, and it in turn was dominated by the Generalissimo's old comrades in arms and the successors whom he had carefully chosen to perpetuate his austere, authoritarian rule. In Franco's last years, clandestine unions, organized by the outlawed Communist

Party, prepared a challenge. Terrorists mounted more and more audacious attacks, including an elaborate sewer bombing in 1973 which blew
Luis Carrero Blanco and his car two stories into the air. Carrero
Blanco, the Premier, was Franco's choice for the succession. Fierce
repression followed the assassination, but no new heir was named.

Long before, the Caudillo ("leader," as Franco was styled in fascist
fashion) had decided on restoring the monarchy to maintain a continuing symbol of legitimacy and national unity after his mortal rule had
ended. He picked the then sixteen-year-old son of Don Juan, Count of
Barcelona, himself the second son of Alfonso XIII, who had been
forced to abdicate in 1931 in favor of a republic and who had died in
exile. There were rival contenders. Don Juan could have been a candidate, but he was rumored to be rather liberal, disdainful of Franco's
harsh methods. His son Juan Carlos was considered too young to have
formed firm opinions. Franco took charge of his education, largely in
military establishments, and placed the young man on the throne as a
figurehead in 1969. Little was known about his character or his intentions. He made no waves in Franco's lifetime, dutifully performing the
ceremonies required of him. He married the sister of King Constantine
of Greece, who fled his country after the colonels' revolt in 1967 and
was formally deposed in 1973. Blond, pretty Queen Sofia, and her children as they came, provided a pleasing relief for the populace from the
regime of the aging, stiff-backed generals. Juan Carlos' youth and taste
for sports, skiing, sailing, motorcycle riding, and Queen Sofia's graceful
elegance seemed to promise some contemporary style at the formal
head of state. His background appeared, at least to his mentors, to
assure that the substance of the regime would not be greatly changed
in the future. His powers were ritual, but to become important later. It
was for the King to name the man who would organize the government
when Franco disappeared and thus set the course of Spain's future.
There was much gossip about his plans, much maneuvering for position. Many prepared to press or to challenge what he might decide, so
that his choices were far from unlimited. Maintenance of the monarchy
itself was considered a wide-open question. He kept his own counsel.

The Generalissimo's slow death was a time of great nervousness and
suspense, in Spain and about Spain. Madrid seemed stunned when at
last the official announcement was made on November 20, 1975,
though of course it was no surprise. People hung the red and yellow
striped national flag from their balconies, and not only in the fashion-

able neighborhoods. They gathered in the Puerta del Sol, the central square, but with closed, expressionless faces, saying nothing. It was impossible to tell if they were mourning or secretly rejoicing. Many were above all apprehensive. After thirty-nine years under Franco's heavy hand, it was hard to imagine Spain without him. Change meant the unknown. The funeral ceremonies were grandiose. There were official and religious rites in Madrid. Then a long cortège accompanied the body to the somber Valle de los Caídos, the enormous marble-lined mausoleum carved into the side of the Guadarrama mountains, where Civil War battles had been fought. Franco had ordered it built as a resting place for the fallen of both sides, proclaiming it the symbol of national reconciliation with the foes together in death.

But there was no sign of reconciliation as the coffin was carried in. Privately, many Spaniards brought out bottles of wine saved many years to celebrate the end of the dictator. Publicly, hundreds of buses brought the faithful from all over Spain to honor him, old men with the red beret of his forces, young toughs with bruised knuckles warily looking for a sign of opposition to justify a brawl. Some wore their old uniforms, some the blue shirt of the party. They gave the stiff-arm salute and sang, turning their faces to the sun as the words command, the Franco hymn "Cara al Sol." It all went just as he had ordered, without incident, with discipline. And yet there was the scent of bewilderment in the cold, clear air. The leader was gone. Where would the followers march?

The amazing thing was that Franco Spain died almost as imperceptibly, uneventfully, but just as definitely as the Caudillo. Eleven years later, after a new constitution and three completely free, well-run elections, the country had a government of young, democratic Socialists, a responsible and democratic-minded youthful king and a permissive society. It was as though the dictatorship had never been. The transformation had been peaceful but thorough. From the bloody augur of a world plunging into darkness in the 1930s, Spain had become a model of successful emergence from totalitarian rule to freedom. The controversies and social tensions remained, but there had been a national vaccination. Civil war had been too terrible to risk again. Tolerance, never considered a notably Spanish trait, had been won by necessity.

A few months after the stunningly handsome, forty-year-old Sevillian Felipe González first became Premier in 1982, the French pro-Socialist magazine Le Nouvel Observateur could comment with raised eyebrows,

"Anything goes in Spain now. Catholic Spain, corseted by retrogressive principles, has transformed itself into a country which knows no other rule but liberty, sometimes confused with abandon." Use of soft drugs, but not trafficking, was legalized. Men and women sunbathed nude on beaches where not long before even men were arrested for wearing trunks without tops. Porn flooded the cinemas, to the point where a new Socialist minister, herself a film producer, ruled that no town could show X-rated films unless it had at least three other movie houses offering regular fare so that grandmothers and children could still go to the movies without gasping. Prostitutes openly plodded the streets of Madrid. Homosexuals, who had been liable to arrest under Franco on the charge of vagrancy, flocked to their favorite bars and restaurants without concern.

The country of *machismo* came to accept gays and transvestites as a natural part of the human scenery. Peddlers of "chocolate," street slang for hashish fresh from Morocco via Algeciras, and of "caballo," the surprisingly literal translation of the American street word *horse* for heroin, plied Madrid's most elegant avenues. There was what one French observer called "an orgy of freedom," but the inevitable reaction of distaste for the excess was slow to come in the excitement of throwing off the restraints. Much more impressive and encouraging, civil servants were made to work their full seven-hour day instead of slipping off to more lucrative jobs after checking in. A serious effort was made to stop corruption. Morality was redefined from prudery to honesty. Reorganization of the army was launched. The generation gap became absolute, sharply marked at age fifty. Old, moody Spain was determined to become a new country.

Of course, it was a transition. Dumping the past cannot in itself define the future, which remained hazy. Times were hard. Spain had the highest unemployment rate of Europe and the most protected industry, bracing for rough competition when the Common Market opened its doors. By 1987, a wave of strikes and student upheavals showed Spaniards were losing patience at the economy's failure to move forward as rapidly as the political transformation. But the democratic base held.

The Church had quietly supported reforms during the first stage of groping after Franco. But it stiffened when the government insisted on permitting divorce and abortion, though in very limited circumstances of threat to the mother's life or urgent therapeutic grounds. Half the country turned out to see John Paul II when he made the first papal visit to Spain since Benedict XIII in 1423, and the crowds were ecstatic. Perhaps a few cynics speculated that González's Socialists might not have won such a sweeping majority had the Pope come earlier, as scheduled, instead of diplomatically postponing his trip until after the elections. The wealthy complained about the lack of servants and the insolence of shopkeepers. The traditional-minded complained of decadence and disrespect. The secretary of the Catholic Parents' Confederation, denouncing the proposal to allow abortion for victims of rape, said, "It is unusual and very difficult for a woman to become pregnant as a result of rape; and even if she does, she has no right to sacrifice the life of the innocent offspring." But the small group of extreme rightists who had vowed to keep Franco's heritage supreme faded away in disgrace. They had been feared, and made a point of provoking fear with bicycle-chain beatings and threats. Now they were ignored and forgotten.

Whatever was to come when it settled down, Spain had changed profoundly. It had been an evolution, begun long before Franco died. Parts of the country had modernized pell-mell, with thriving industry, glass towers and atomic scientists, businessmen, scholars and politicians who traveled the world. Other parts remained scratch poor and almost feudal. But few Spaniards were still illiterate. Roads, TV and films had reached into remote villages previously untouched by the moving world since the Middle Ages. Some of the migrants who had gone to work abroad came home to the countryside and built good houses with plumbing where there had been adobe huts. Some only sent money back and visited on holidays, but they brought the goods and the news and the habits of another way of life. A middle class emerged, with an interest in both progress and stability. Spain hadn't really been asleep all those Franco years; it was just playing 'possum.

The country had paid for achieving glory early in Europe's development. Eight hundred years of Arab rule brought a flowering of science and art unrivaled in Europe at the time. Córdoba was the ancient Athens of that period. But it cut much of Spain off from the rest of Christendom and left a heavy hierarchical structure. The Catholic reconquest (or conquest, as some Andalusians have come to say in an attempt to invert the snobbish superiority other Spaniards show them) also brought the Inquisition, with its cruelty and dark suspicion. Then came the period of expansion. The colonies sent home great wealth, but it was consumed before the invention of machines and the idea of capitalism brought incentives for investment. Wars bled the people and the treasury. Defeat by Napoleon was such a humiliation that young Spaniards can still say they love to visit the Invalides in Paris because there, at last, they can look *down* on the emperor. Spain had little part in the flourishing nineteenth century. It was left behind in the stony, agrarian past with scarcely more than nostalgic grandeur for nourishment.

It is not a clement country, soft to life. The great central plateau of Castile looks like the tortured landscape of the American Southwest from the air, dark red, raw and dry. Bitterly cold winds drive across unhindered in the winter. A burning sun bakes it almost barren in the summer. In the hills above Madrid is the forbidding Escorial, the medieval royal palace is appropriate for Spain. Here there are no sculpted nymphs or stone-laced vaults or gilt-framed mirrors or garlanded frescoes with which the rulers of other Latin lands displayed their privilege and delighted their courtiers. The square halls soar dark and chill. They show power and willfulness without the flutes of merciful pleasure. The correct tones for a scene of noble Spanish life are black and gold, stern, dignified. And the people followed suit, dour and drab.

There are flowered chalets beside tinkling streams in the bright woods of the Basque country. In their mountains, a darker, more densely wooded reminder of Switzerland, the rural Basques are poor and picturesque. But their country also includes fashionable Bay of Biscay resorts such as San Sebastián and the thriving, if grubby, industrial port of Bilbao. Not far from San Sebastián is the mysterious cave of Altamira where people who hunted and fished took shelter in the limestone grottos some 25,000 years ago. Their remarkable art, bison and deer and other animals painted in red and black pigment, can still be seen on the low ceiling and walls of the cave. No one knows the meaning of the painting. The people were primitive and had only the simplest stone and bone tools, but they had a sophisticated eye.

Catalonia, to the east, is rolling terrain, rivers and rocky beaches like the western Mediterranean coast of France. Cut off from other parts of Spain by mountains and rivers, Catalonia had a longer association with southern France than with the lands of the Douro and Guadalquivir river basins. The Moors conquered the area in 712, but they were expelled before the end of the century. That left the Catalans in closer association with the Christian lands than with the occupied parts of Spain. The rulers were often independent counts. Catalonia was restored to Spain, except for brief periods of conquest, in 1659, but it continued to feel itself special and to maintain the commerce and industry that linked its lovely capital of Barcelona to the outside world.

Barcelona is a strange mixture of a city, prosperous, spanking new and medieval, bustling and leisurely all at once. There are cobbled streets so narrow a person in the middle can almost touch both walls, and there are the broad, tree-lined *ramblas* where everyone comes out to stroll and gossip in the evening cool. In the great red cathedral, there is a chapel by the entrance dedicated by King Ferdinand to celebrate the successful return of Christopher Columbus from the new world he discovered and claimed for Spain. A few blocks in one direction there are modern glass towers, and no farther in another the intricate *art nouveau* façades of the puckish architect Antonio Gaudí. Atop the revered mountain of Monserrat, linked to the city by a swaying cable car, there is a fort, an amusement park and a museum devoted to the modern painter Joan Miró.

In the southeast, parched, impoverished, whitewashed Andalusia is the source of the Spanish stereotype. There are the flounced coquettish beauties, the maddening gypsy rhythms, the joyous defiance of a nature grown stingy once its ore-filled veins were bled. The parts of Spain are diverse. It isn't surprising that travelers took away the gaudy colors of Andalusia as their main impression of the Spanish folk. They fill the eye. But the core of Spain, its specific gravity, its temper if it is to continue having a national temper, is on the rugged plains of Castile.

The nation is the issue now. Spain was rigidly centralized centuries before most of Europe, even before France. The Catholic sovereigns Ferdinand and Isabel tied the country together when they drove out the last of the Moors in 1492. But the provinces have long been restive. Poor inland transportation and natural trade routes over the seas turned heads in directions other than Madrid. All roads lead to Rome, say the Italians. To cross France you must cross Paris, say the French. But to Spaniards, Madrid is the city of authority, not the beacon of irresistible light. The question of centralism was much magnified by Franco's rule. His theme was patriotism, a mystic Spanish essence in whose name all malcontents and opposers smacked of treachery. A dictator cannot scatter his power to local iconoclasts or even satraps unless they acknowledge the full supremacy of the center. So regionalism became identified with resistance to the dictatorship.

The Franco regime suppressed it energetically. It was a crime to display the old Basque or Catalonian flag. Canteens in Basque villages had signs announcing that it was forbidden to sing. The owners had been through too much trouble when young men, enjoying a little wine and song, would sooner or later switch from popular tunes to a Basque song, perhaps even a militant Basque song. The police would come because the language was not allowed. There would be a fight, things would be smashed, people would be arrested, perhaps including the owner. That might lead to demonstrations. The "gray mice," the contemptuous local name for the gray-uniformed national police always recruited from distant parts of the country, would swoop down with their sticks and rubber bullets. So the signs said "Singing Forbidden."

Regionalism is endemic throughout Europe, the remains of the old fiefdoms before the rise of nation-states and the reminder that borders now so firmly fixed were long contested. Its strength varies widely, a factor of geography, history and the politics of the day. Such an eminent commentator as Walter Lippmann was convinced that the Germans would feel little more than a pinprick from partition because they still had their organized regions. In fact, it was surprising that West Germany and East Germany managed to coalesce as states. Hesse in the West and Thuringia in the East, Lower Saxony in the West and Saxony in the East, had stronger links between them than with areas to the north or south. For Germans now, the problems of nationhood override the centrifugal pull of region.

France, on the other hand, so totally centralized after the revolution, has felt a need to loosen the reins. Inevitably, though the old provinces were formally abolished and replaced with a multitude of departments almost two centuries ago, it is the old provinces which have reemerged as regions. Insular Corsica is the most adamant. Brittany, with its near dormant Celtic tongue, is clearly conscious of its own identity. Languedoc, in the southwest, still remembers the virulence of the early thirteenth-century Albigensian crusades when the northerners came to massacre the southerners. The French call themselves a Mediterranean nation, but the northern areas have been dominant ever since. Alsace and Lorraine, whose patois is a Low German, have the most immediate grounds for cultural separatism and, no doubt for the same reasons, feel the least incentive to express it. They were too pleased at being reincorporated into France after forced Germanization between the French defeat by Prussia in 1870 and the French victory in World War I.

Belgium is torn between Flemings and Walloons, so insistent on language rights that little more than Brussels, a deliberately drawn separate region, holds the country together. Even little Holland has regional strains. The Frisians in the north see themselves as a people apart. Switzerland was organized deliberately to accommodate regional separation. Two generations of peace in Europe and the organization of the European Community with its wider borders have tended to heighten the appeal of regionalism. It has also come to serve as a counterbalance to the inevitably centralizing effects of modern industry and modern communications. Homogenization has been the relentless rule of current European development, so regionalism has become the insistent, irresistible exception.

No country has felt it more than Spain. The very question of nationhood is not fully settled, and it is an inflammable question, going deeply to the sense of identity and destiny. One of the first liberalizations after the end of the Franco regime was to lift the ban on traditional local languages and flags. After all, in other solidly established countries people assert local pride with state and provincial flags alongside the national flag. But the Basques and the Catalans wanted much more.

During the short life of the republic in the 1930s, the Basques had almost complete autonomy. They had been the most persistent opponents of Franco's rebels and they had suffered more than most. Pablo Picasso's *Guernica*, painted to arouse the world to the horror of aerial bombardment, was a tribute to a Basque town. It wasn't clear how far Basque separatism was revulsion against the hated regime, how far it had a momentum of its own. Terrorist undergrounds, long financed by tribute exacted from more or less sympathetic Basque businessmen, demanded independence. The conservative Basque Nationalist Party stopped short of calling for total separation from Spain but argued for no more than minimal powers to be left to Madrid.

The Basques are a mysterious people with a special capacity for cultural survival. They are believed to have migrated from the mountains of the Caucasus sometime before the Christian era. Their language is unrelated to any other European tongue and its origins are unknown. Traditionally, they are shepherds, and their lively dances, their folk art, their bagpipes and their nimble games—jai alai is Basque—speak of a people used to clambering over difficult terrain. Many migrated, choosing destinations like Idaho and Montana favorable to sheep raising and the life of the herder.

The "Basque country," as they call it, spreads beyond northwestern Spain to southwestern France, a perennial political dilemma for the French, who tend to sympathize with critics of Madrid but are not about to condone separatist agitation in their own nation. Basques on both sides keep in touch, however, and help each other, often illicitly. Accidents of national history have created very different conditions for the French and Spanish Basques. The Spaniards prospered, developing the country's greatest industrial complex around the busy port of Bilbao. They acquired large fortunes, established banks and resented the claims of poorer parts of Spain for a share of their wealth, as the rich everywhere tend to dislike demands of community with the poor.

The Spanish economy really cannot do without the Basques. Their French cousins, on the other hand, inhabit one of the poorer regions of their country, living on a meager agriculture and tourism, which they have also come to resent as an invasion of "foreigners" from other parts of France. Their complaint is that the central government in Paris does not do enough for them, does not provide enough of the surplus of industrial regions to help them develop. They want more, not less, redistribution of the national wealth. French statistics are not organized to show the relative contribution of the 270,000 French Basques to the national product, but they play a minor role.

Catalans are not so belligerent about their separateness as are Basques, but they are no less adamant about their historic identity. They reject description of their goal as "regional autonomy," insisting on the phrase "national autonomy" to emphasize that Catalonia remains a cultural nation if not a sovereign state. They, too, were anti-Franco as an ethnic group, and they too are richer and more developed than much of Spain. But their social structure and political attitudes are different from the Basques'. Iron ore, which led to steel mills, gave a base of heavy industry to Basque development. That produced a pattern of wealthy oligarchy, sullen proletariat and drained rural areas, rather like England's early Industrial Revolution. The Catalans built textile mills and light industry, producing a more moderate bourgeoisie and developing better, more integrated exchanges with the countryside. Though their attitudes to Madrid are similar, the two groups tend to ignore each other and do not organize mutual support. Catalans note that the Basques escaped both Roman and Arab rule, and it adds to Catalonia's sense of cultural superiority. "In those days," said Juan Badoza, a young Barcelona economist and diplomat, "the Arabs were the civilized ones and the Christians were the barbarians."

Under the republic, Catalans had their Generalitat, a regional government that could guarantee both home rule and a chance to be a prime influence on Madrid, which they tend to disdain. There is an old history of self-rule when Catalonia was linked to the north while the Moorish kings governed from Granada. Their language is Latin-based, something between Spanish and French. Catalans do not seek independence but full autonomy. In a very short time after Franco, Catalan was imposed as the second official language of the province and a campaign was under way to exclude Spanish, although some proud Catalonians would probably settle for imposing Spanish and Catalan as equals throughout the nation. In Barcelona and the countryside, not only all direction signs put up by the government but also advertising billboards are bilingual.

Because of its enterprise and prosperity, Catalonia, like other areas farther north, sought outside labor in the period of rapid postwar growth. The landless peasants of Andalusia flocked to its factories and service industries. They constitute about a quarter of the population now, and they feel threatened by the emphasis on Catalan separation and the Catalan language, which they don't speak, as the way to get ahead. Jordi Pujol, president of the revived Generalitat, does not hide his distaste for them. He is a short, garrulous man, who uses an orator's voice even in conversation and has an intense sense of mission. He would rather speak French than Spanish with visitors who don't speak Catalan. He considers his homeland unique among the areas of Spain. When the Madrid government sought to resolve the regional issue by offering a degree of local power to all parts of the country, Pujol was incensed. It was intolerable, he argued, that Andalusia with its backwardness and history of subjugation should be given equal rights, put on an equal plane, with the historic nation of Catalonia. But others are not quite so assertive as Pujol. Narcís Serra, the former mayor of Barcelona who, at forty, became Defense Minister in the González government, could mock the excess, saying, "I am not one of those who are jealous of people who get a Mercedes-Benz so long as I have a Mercedes-Benz too." Ambitious Catalan politicians felt a strain in choosing whether to pursue their careers in the capital in competition with Spaniards from other parts of the country or to seek more concentrated but more limited local power.

The dilemma of Spain's structure is far from resolved. "We are evolving," said Serra, "toward a federal model of our own." National unity remains a key issue for the army, for the King, for the many Spaniards who are aware that fragmentation cannot serve to advance the society or help it win the secure place in the modern European mainstream which it seeks. Yet decentralization became an equally sensitive issue in the effort toward institutional reform to consolidate new democratic habits.

Galicia, whose capital is La Coruña but most famous site is the medieval shrine of Santiago de Compostela, has its own sense of deserving special treatment. Gallegos, as the people are called, have their own character, speak a dialect near to Portuguese and are the butt of many jokes about dourness, slyness, shrewdness, stinginess, conservatism. They are often almost word for word the same jokes that are told about Galitzianers, the people from the area of southeastern Poland once occupied by Austria that is also called Galicia, and about Scots and Bretons. They probably had common Celtic ancestors long ago.

The ethnic clusters of Europe are whorled and layered, far more complex than any map can display, sometimes almost forgotten. They lie below the surface of the nation-states, maintaining ancient links and an almost unconscious pull of kinship which strengthen the roots of the move for European unity. Modern borders haven't really sorted people out in hermetic nationalities; there has long been too much mixing, too much ebb and flow of conquest and settlement for that. But the mixtures are not homogenized, and they can also undermine the effort for unity because people tend to define themselves by their differences from their neighbors, within and outside their country.

In the face of so much self-assertion by other Spanish regions, Andalusians too have joined the chorus, calling attention to their long neglect and pressing demands on the capital. There is no separatist element in Andalusia's rapidly rising regional consciousness, because it depends too much on national support. So far, development has been helter-skelter, often botched and savage, as on the splendid Costa del Sol, now nicknamed the Costa Concreta for the ugly jungle of concrete hotels and apartments built in the rush for tourist gold along Spain's southern beaches. There is a parallel between southern Spain and southern Italy, left behind when other areas surged toward modernity and without the resources or even the cultural traditions to catch up on their own. They tend to be a drag on the nation, and yet they impose the most urgent need for national cohesion. A Catalan, put to the acid test of loyalty—whom would he cheer in an international soccer match between Spain and, say, Germany?—asked first whether the team would be from Barcelona or Madrid. Told Madrid, he hesitated before conceding he would root for Spain. For an Andalusian, there is no problem. The answer is a ringing "Viva España."

An irony in all this regionalism is the case of Castile. The *New York Times'* James Markham reported in 1981 on the establishment of a new administrative unit in the national system of autonomous regions to be called Castile-León, comprising nine depopulated provinces. "In Spanish history, Castile is a proud name," he wrote. "Today it is a lament. Castile once sallied out to conquer the world. Today, it is merely a region." The legislators from Old Castile chose the hill town of Tordesillas, population 8,000, as their capital because the representatives from Valladolid opposed Burgos and vice versa. Still, it had old claims to fame. It was in Tordesillas that Spanish and Portuguese envoys met in 1494 to sign the treaty dividing the world between them, and the place Queen Juana I chose to rest in 1509 after wandering around her kingdom with the calcified body of her husband. Her son Carlos decided she was crazy, pronounced himself King and locked her up until her death forty-six years later. The Spanish colonists and adventurers who took over the New World came mostly from Estremadura, the barren, desolate western region bordering Portugal. But they carried the flag of Castile, called the language they spread Castilian (which everyone else calls Spanish) and brought the riches and glory back to the central monarchy.

It is common now to blame the greed of the monarchs and the arrogance of the Castilians for the long decline of Spain. They were *hidalgos*, living grandly off their huge estates. They continued to reject commerce and manufacture as ignoble long after most of Europe marched on. There was little chance for emergence of a merchant class and with it the demands for limits on rulers and participation in economic decisions that were the seeds of democracy elsewhere. Still, at the heart of the peninsula, Castile remains the heart of Spain. No matter how vocal their regional boosterism, Spaniards are still proud of being Spanish, proud that even under Franco they began to build a modern economy, proud now that they are living in a free nation.

They are even proud of the contradictions, of the divisions and clashes of temperament to be overcome in maintaining their nationhood, of a Socialist government that has become a staunch supporter of the monarchy, of a king imposed by Franco who foiled a military coup made in his name. The coup, on February 23, 1981, was called the "Tejerazo" after Lieutenant Colonel Antonio Tejero Molina, who led armed men into the Cortés (parliament) and took the legislators hostage. He apparently had the support of some key army leaders who expected King Juan Carlos to welcome the overthrow of the government. But when he found out what was happening, the King proclaimed his full support of the constitution and ordered the troops to barracks. He has been a surprise to almost everybody. It is said that his queen has been an important, prudent counselor, and clearly, he learned a lot about how not to lose a throne from the hapless example of her brother King Constantine of Greece, which is now a republic.

After his success in quashing the Tejerazo, Juan Carlos confided that he felt his main opponents in reinforcing constitutional democracy were the aristocracy and the old privileged groups, the would-be courtiers for whom he refused to hold court. He is an impressive man, not for any intellectual dazzle or deep knowledge, but for a natural curiosity, an easy informality and an apparently instinctive grasp of the need to maintain contact with all levels of society in order to understand and guide his country's transition. He had secret meetings with Communist leaders while the party was still officially illegal, and quietly made clear that in the interest of reconciliation he did not support right-wing demands to continue the ban. He has regular, private reunions with his old classmates at the university and in armed forces units where he served, people now engaged in many walks of life whose memory of youthful camaraderie enables them to speak freely. Awe of position is deeply ingrained among Spaniards. He finds ways to get around it without display.

Reaction to the attempted coup worked to strengthen the fledgling democracy and, eventually, to consign the Franquistas to history. Two years later, there was no longer even concern about the monuments that memorialized the old regime. They were allowed to stand, "like the statues of Philip II and Carlos I, the dead past," said a pro-Socialist professor. A taxi driver in Santander shrugged as he passed a bronze Franco on horseback. "Let him sit, he can't do us any more harm," said the driver. Even the army had lost its aura of omnipotence. "They aren't proud anymore," said José Cedillo, a young geologist. "It used to be that every family was proud to have a son in the army. Now we see that the officers are inefficient, not well educated, lazy. The conscripts know better. We are proud that we are developing Spain. What does the army know how to do?"

The task of restructuring the military, the economy, the institutions, the laws, the very habits of mind that still mark traditional Spain, is vast. The Civil War left deep scars. But the balm that eases the pain is the growing recognition that the suffering was national, shared by all. In October 1980 there was an exhibition on the Civil War in the Crystal Palace, a charming glass pavilion in Madrid's El Retiro park. For the first time anywhere, it was organized to show how the war touched people on both sides, children, women, soldiers, the press and so on. There was no attribution of praise or blame. Long lines formed every day to gain admission, mostly young people. "But the slogans are almost the same," gasped a young teacher. "They both thought they were saving the country. And look what they did." Especially among the young, a new self-awareness, a sense of the need to question, to learn, to build instead of to boast and to trust in miracles or theories, has provided a combination of energy and balance that is moving Spain forward.

Political differences on foreign policy are shadings more than contrasts. Spain quite definitely means to be a part of Western Europe and the larger world in which Europe has a role. As it gains self-confidence, it is gaining interest in Latin America, where it has been so hard for countries to master the art of establishing and keeping democracy and organizing the power to govern without force. Perhaps Spain will again become a model for its former dependencies.

Spain joined NATO after the 1981 coup, partly as a way to ease reorganization of the army, expose its leaders to working with officers accustomed to civilian control, and give them tasks and preoccupations beyond their narrow, national horizons. But it remains a divisive issue. Franco had always wanted to take Spain into NATO, as proof of Western respectability, but the European members would not admit his country during his lifetime. When González took power shortly after the treaty was signed, he barred plans for military integration, putting Spain in the ambiguous position of France as a formal ally but not a military member of the pact. As Defense Minister Serra put it, the idea of full participation was a difficult one, especially for the Spanish left. "It will take time for attitudes to accept a co-responsibility for defense of the West. Spain was neutral in two world wars. We did a lot of killing of each other, but nobody came here to attack us and occupy us. It's hard to explain that we need that kind of security. It isn't a priority," he said.

American bases in Spain, established by special agreement in Franco's time, also provoke sharp argument. There is a strain of anti-Americanism, increased by the charge that the bases imply some special American paternalism when Spain is now a fully accepted participant in Europe. The status of Gibraltar is another unresolved problem, particularly since Spain's entry in NATO removed the argument that the strategic British enclave had to be kept in Allied hands. The problem exists in reverse concerning Ceuta and Melilla, Spanish enclaves on the Moroccan side of the straits. In both cases, the inhabitants prefer their foreign status, while the people around them insist they are an affront to coherent national sovereignty. Once these disputes might have provoked a call to arms. Nobody thinks of going to war about them anymore; they are part of the standing diplomatic agenda, knots in Spain's ties with other countries but not barriers.

The first big domestic issue after Franco was whether to legalize the Communist Party and how best to prevent its rise to power, by continued suppression or letting it operate openly where it could be watched. The legalizers won, with less resistance than expected. Then an even bigger surprise came in the first election, in 1977. The Communist Party, which had symbolized opposition to Franco and was believed to have by far the best clandestine organization when virtually all but the official Falangist party was banned, won a feeble 10 percent. The Socialists, much influenced by the evolution of the German Social Democrats, won 25 percent. They themselves had anticipated the reverse. The Communists did even worse in the next election. The reasons were hard to analyze. Dashing, appealing Felipe González, with his boyish grin and sporty, casually elegant wardrobe, no doubt was a personal asset for the Socialists. Blunt old Santiago Carrillo, despite his call for Eurocommunism and his sharp tilts with Moscow, was a reminder of the Civil War, in which he had played a bloody part. He was later ousted as party leader for still being too authoritarian, though some Barcelona Communists opposed him for being too anti-Soviet. In any case, the old Spanish polarization of politics had broken down. Unlike Italy's, Spain's Communists were relegated to the margin. There was still a left and a right, but the extremes were melting away, leaving a broad, pragmatic center.

The extent of the shift was tangible in the position of Manuel Fraga Iribarne. He had held a number of high posts under Franco, including Minister of Tourism and Ambassador to London. But as one of the

young men of the old team, he had urged modernization and liberalization, and passed for being on the left wing of the establishment. By
the time of the third free election, Fraga with his Alianza Popular was
the acknowledged leader of the right. There was no respectable party
beyond him. Indeed, he was a proper image of Spain's conservatives, a
tall, hulking man with an air of authority, carefully groomed, appreciative of traditional manners, business-minded, linked to conservative
leaders in other countries. The newspaper *El Alcazar* expressed what
remained of Franquista nostalgia, but that wasn't Fraga's voice. He was
simply the farthest right of effective politicians in the new Spain, so
even ultraconservatives had to support him. Later, he was overtaken by
a less conservative leader.

The official center, a hastily concocted party stitched together by
Adolfo Suárez, soon fell apart. Dapper, well connected among the
upper classes, articulate, Suárez had been chosen by the King as the
first Prime Minister after Franco died. He was forty-three at the time, a
little older than González, and represented a deliberate move away
from the older generation, which had expected to remain at the top
despite the new era. His party did well in getting a new constitution
adopted and in the first elections. But he proved too ineffective, too
slow in moving reforms along for the taste of both the King and much
of the public, and he was replaced. The Socialists won the 1982 elections massively. Suárez later formed a new party, with left-nationalist
undertones. Still, Spanish politics became essentially a face-off between
the center-left and center-right. Sooner or later, it was assumed, the
pendulum would swing again, but not too far.

Felipe, as people called González without ado, was a political natural, reassuring, knowledgeable, energetic, without complexes. Nobody
was worried about him. But there were important gaps in lower echelons. The Socialists were obliged to address the basic problems of the
country's structure, administration, organization, the problems of transition, when they had thought of themselves as the builders of democracy once the foundations had been laid. Responsibility brought
restraint. At least they were aware of the need for prudence and steadiness. Unlike French Socialists, who won power in 1981 and thought
they could apply their theories to transform the nation overnight, the
Spaniards eschewed dogma for practical development. They tried to
take the long view and plant deeply, if not so quickly as some would
have liked, so that this time democracy could take secure root.

Their aim was modernization, "normalcy," by which they meant converting Spain from a Latin American kind of country, either chaotic or stagnant, to a Western European kind of country, in which the basic requirements of both the individual and society could be taken for granted. Old attitudes mattered, but the key to evolution had to be the economy. The timing was unfavorable. Growth was essential to improve the standard of living, also to deal with the mental habits and backwardness that were the result of age-old poverty. But the world was in the slough of a recession. Unemployment in Spain was the highest in Europe, above 20 percent. Inflation was far above the European average. The Socialists had campaigned on a promise of modest reflation.

The problems were compounded because the conservatives had pursued an almost leftist economic policy, allowing wages to rise rapidly, profits to shrink, subsidies to persist, government to spend more lavishly than it could afford and less productively than it needed. Investment had stalled. Industry was overmanned. The market for old products was drying up, as in most of the developed world, where steel, shipyards, textiles were ailing, and technology lagged behind. Foreign debt mounted and the peseta weakened under heavy pressure. The economic moment required a degree of austerity for painful, far-reaching readjustment and renewal, just when the political moment called for expansion to enlarge the slice of a shrinking pie for the poor. It makes a vital difference if a damaged or underdeveloped country sets out to build its national economy at a time when the rest of the world is prospering or when all are tightening their belts. Had Spain been an open society allowed to participate in the postwar European prosperity even without large foreign aid, it probably would have reached general European levels by now. As it was, it not only had to catch up, but at a time when the wind had died, leaving all sails slack.

Large parts of the countryside, especially in Castile, were almost emptied by the trek to the cities, but agriculture was only spottily modernized. With some 13 percent of its labor force on the land, Spain is still well above the European average. Andalusia and Estremadura have large numbers of landless laborers, but their crops are not labor intensive, and mechanization means disaster when industry is already surfeited with workers. Florentino Pérez, president of the National Institute for Agricultural Reform and Development, said that practically all the farms of Andalusia were economically inefficient, either too large for their haphazard and sometimes absentee management, or too small. Spain has more land under cultivation than any other Western European country, and could multiply its acreage with irrigation and better management of water rights. But a bigger flood of Spanish produce is just what its Common Market partners most dread.

The Spanish identikit is a double image, reflecting rapid change and a generation gap which breaks sharply at about age fifty. Three-quarters of the people live in cities now, and women, whose status is changing drastically, make up 30 percent of university students. There are still older women who habitually dress all in black, but their younger compatriots wear jeans, miniskirts or whatever is the latest Eurofashion. In the villages, the women still tend to the traditional peasant life, working in the fields, waiting on their men, eating separately. But in the cities, they are beginning to get managerial as well as service and factory jobs. The Church is losing influence, with only 46 percent of the population describing themselves as practicing Catholics and 18 percent who attend Mass regularly, though 85 percent are christened Roman Catholics. There are fewer marriages than a generation ago, and the birthrate is declining, from an expansive 2.9 percent in the mid-1970s to 1.7 percent in the mid-1980s and still falling, well below the population replacement rate.

One Spaniard in ten has a car, compared to one in a hundred in the 1960s, and the bulk of the urban population live in dense, concrete apartment buildings. But the daily timetable hasn't changed much. Most shops close from 2 to 5 P.M. for the lunch hour and a siesta. The dinner crowd doesn't begin to fill the restaurants until after 10 P.M., and TV prime time starts at 10:30. The great goal is to participate in *la movida*, the ferment of fashion, art, architecture, modernity, international culture. Madrid gobbles up the foreign plays and books which were banned in the Franco era, but few Spaniards travel abroad on their vacations; most prefer to take holidays in their own coastal and mountain retreats. Polls measuring political values show 69 percent think democracy is best, 11 percent favor dictatorship "in certain circumstances," and another 11 percent don't think the alternatives make a difference in their own lives. On a comparative scale, Spaniards rate Britain, France, Germany and, to a fraction of a degree, Italy as more democratic than their own country, Greece and Portugal as less democratic. On the political spectrum, 6 percent put themselves on the extreme left, 29 percent on the left, 27 percent in the center, 10 percent on the right, and 3 percent on the extreme right.

There is a certain tug-of-war between the euphoria of democratic freedom in Spain and the disillusion in finding that it cannot ease the passage of economic transformation. The first came amazingly easily; the second is much harder than dauntless spirits had supposed. Still, the country is changing beyond recognition and will surely become an important, vital part of the complex that is modern Europe. Its difficult problem of regional autonomy versus national sovereignty is in a way a smaller version of the European problem itself. The regions, in Spain and elsewhere, provide a historic experience of pluralism converging into a higher unity, a precedent for accommodating the tremendous diversity of Europe in a larger, more rewarding context. The nation is still the gritty atom. But it must arrange its parts harmoniously to prevent disintegration.

If Spain manages to work out a new model of federation that visibly succeeds, it could eventually inspire another push to European unity. Meanwhile, stability and full rights of membership in the European and Atlantic communities have stirred a tempered optimism. Spain has its problems, but it is no longer an outcast, a problem for Europe. That was an enormous advance in a short time.

PORTUGAL
Leaping Half a Century

R ED CARNATIONS HAVE NO THORNS. So it seemed, in April 1974, when Portugal slid painlessly out of a half century of dictatorship to an unknown but joyously welcomed new era. A group of captains and majors proclaimed the end of the regime. Marcello Caetano, the then sixty-eight-year-old successor to António de Oliveira Salazar, was chased away. He fled to Brazil and died in exile six years later. The revolution came as a complete surprise. There had been a period of unrest in 1961–62, quickly squelched, and a promise of liberalization when Salazar retired in 1968 after forty-two years of repressive rule. But he had prepared carefully to prolong the regime. Caetano announced "renovation in continuity" and the machinery clanked on as before. Then, that bright spring Thursday, April 25, people awoke to be told freedom had arrived. They gathered armsful of red carnations, which became the symbol of the revolution, and stuffed them in the gun barrels of the troops who paraded through the streets in triumph. Only a few shots were fired. The mood was pure exuberance. All Europe looked with excited admiration at what appeared as the new, decent, *European* way to make a coup and leap the barricades to modern democracy, with flowers.

But flowers, which fade, are also timeless. The first surprise after the breathtaking upheaval itself was a realization of how easy it had been for the regime to stop the clock in Portugal and how well that had been achieved. Salazar wanted his people to live "habitually," that is to say,

135

as they had in the long past. He hated the impact of modernity. He had been distressed to hear of the discovery of new wealth in Portuguese Africa, which would attract foreign investment, outsiders, bustle and change. "Oil in Angola? That's all I need," he was alleged to have said in exasperation. Deeply conservative, ardently Catholic, he was determined to maintain order and faith.

Portugal had installed a republic in 1910, a few years before the European system broke down in World War I and before it became widely fashionable to toss royal crowns on the junk heap. But it failed to evolve an effective government. Even before the Great Depression and general disintegration of the old societies, but after Mussolini had marched on Rome to install a new order called Fascism, the chaos had become intolerable. Salazar took over in 1932. Two generations later, when the dictatorship was ousted, anything to do with it, anything defective, was called fascist.

But it wasn't, in the sense of Mussolini and Hitler. Political scientist Manuel de Lucena has written that Salazar ran a fascist state without a fascist movement. The trappings were there. He had a secret police, the notorious PIDE, which tortured and killed. He had censorship. There was a single party, opposition was banned, and there was a form of corporatism. But there was no militant ideology, no attempt to mobilize the masses to control the difficult new processes of industrialization and urbanization. On the contrary, Salazar's effort was to demobilize, to conserve the vast colonial empire without any effort at expansion by force or ideology. In effect, the regime was not totalitarian but an old-fashioned autocracy. Portugal had stood still since early in the century, and had no momentum. The point was simply order.

That was achieved. The regime managed to keep the country in an economic and social deep freeze with remarkably little effort. Portugal was not isolated in anathema, like Franco Spain. It had been neutral in World War II, but with its ancient (anti-Spanish) alliance with England, it tilted at least as much to the Allies as Spain leaned to the Axis. It was admitted as a founding member of the North Atlantic Treaty Organization, while Spain remained taboo until it proved its capacity for democracy. There was no particular effort to keep out foreign papers, books or broadcasts as in Eastern Europe. There was no bar to foreigners visiting or effective block to Portuguese emigration; one million emigrated in the postwar years of labor shortages in industrial Europe. There was nothing to block the emigrants returning on vacation or to reestablish themselves and tell their families about life in flourishing, democratic lands. And yet it was evident after the revolution that Portugal had been as cut off from all the intervening changes in Europe as if it had been enclosed by an iron curtain.

Nearly a third of the people were still illiterate, rising to half among the rural population. Even many educated people were unaware of the books, the ideas, the customs that had taken hold elsewhere. The economy had been utterly stagnant. Industry remained at an early level. Small farmers in the north, as they had for centuries, divided up their land by inheritance into skimpy plots which provided a bare subsistence. Seignorial landlords in the south held vast tracts which villagers cultivated in near serfdom, or sometimes were not allowed to cultivate at all because the estates were preserved for hunting by the absentee owners. As in the rest of Europe, there is a sharp contrast between the hardworking, thrifty northerners and the impoverished southerners in Portugal. But when the revolution came with its red carnations, the rejoicing broke out everywhere.

The revolution was not made by exiles, intellectuals, the tiny, harassed Communist underground, nor by the somnolent people. It was made by the armed forces. In 1961 India's Nehru occupied Portuguese Goa. Anticolonial insurrection broke out in Angola, spreading soon to Guinea-Bissau and Mozambique in Africa. Except for Brazil, which proclaimed independence in 1822 after Napoleon had driven the monarch into flight from Lisbon, and Formosa (Taiwan), which was retaken by China and then ceded to Japan in 1895, Portugal had managed to hold its old empire when all the others were crumbling. In part, this was because the lethargic homeland had not made very energetic efforts to exploit the tremendous resources of the colonies. In part, it was because poverty at home drove craftsmen, artisans and small farmers overseas, where they settled, mostly modestly, to ply their trade. They behaved differently from British, French, Dutch, or Belgian colonists, mixing with the indigenous populations without pretensions of grandeur.

Still, the "winds of change" which British Prime Minister Harold Macmillan saw sweeping away the European empires in the 1960s blew up storms in the Portuguese colonies too. Change was Salazar's nemesis. By 1964, he sent 150,000 men out of a total population of some 9 million to fight on three fronts in Africa, at a cost far beyond the means of Portugal in money and manpower. The wars lasted thirteen years, until the disgusted, frustrated young officers decided to put an end to them by ending the regime.

The rebels they had been fighting belonged to leftist movements, often supported by the Communist powers. To some of the Portuguese involved, they seemed admirable idealists, disciplined to their cause, models of honor compared to the fusty, apathetic, almost mindless society whose sovereignty and property they were defending. A kind of battlefield osmosis took place. Portuguese officers brought home the ideology of the guerrillas they pursued. Still, there was no real revolutionary program or organization. The regime had in fact collapsed of its own dead weight, rather than been defeated.

There were no plans ready for a new society. All had to be imagined from scratch, and the liveliest imaginations turned out to be the most radical. The officers formed a military Council of the Revolution in 1975. They had many rival notions. A tendency developed for several to organize their own regiments, their own services, in support of their own particular view of how to make the future bloom. The Communist Party surfaced, at first attracting great sympathy because it had been the one consistent, persecuted enemy of the dictatorship within the country. Its leader, Alvaro Cunhal, a highly intelligent but tough, ruthless old Stalinist, had learned clandestine organization the hard way, and he maintained it as a nuclear force within the huge, floating movement of the masses.

The international camp followers soon arrived. There is a kind of revolutionary hippiedom which coagulates like ants on honey whenever a new power of the left erupts. They attend the meetings, chant the slogans, intensify the excitement and inject, if they can, their own particular favorites of the many theories which proliferate in the world about how to create a perfect society. They are Americans, northern Europeans, stragglers from all over who cannot resist dropping in for a while at a revolutionary open house. They had been in Cuba. They came to Portugal. Later they turned up for a while in Spain, and then Nicaragua. Among the Portuguese, dozens of groups emerged—many of them armed—to lead their country to the promised land. The wonder of it was that there was so little violence in such a heady atmosphere. That must be attributed to the Portuguese character, stoic, impassive, unassuming. Pride is displayed by self-control, not by explosive behavior, as in Spain.

The frenetic honeymoon lasted through the summer. But joy was cooling into ambition and resentment, egalitarianism fermenting into disorder. By fall, the government of the elderly, monocled General António de Spínola, who had been chosen as President because he was one of the few well-known officers, began to crumble. It was inept, unable to organize the great spurt of energy that was being frittered away in covering Lisbon's blue and yellow tiled walls with graffiti, in marching, moving. Alvaro Cunhal, his taut face and shock of white hair radiating cool authority, launched a bid for power. Whether the Communists acted on Moscow's instructions or on Cunhal's own decision was never clear. Using their military sympathizers, they made what their officials later called "an escape forward," breaking out in front of the confused masses to pull them to the left. Peasants were urged to seize the lands they tilled, and in the south they did so on a wide scale. City dwellers were told to form block committees, to incite and keep tabs on their neighbors. Poor people were encouraged to take over houses and apartments in the well-to-do parts of town. Committees were organized in factories, banks, and businesses to establish "the people's power." Moderates took fright and began to wonder about a movement they had first greeted with enthusiasm.

On March 11, 1975, there was a clumsy aborted coup, blamed on right-wing plotters. General Spínola fled in professed and unseemly fear. Later, some said the bungled attempt was provoked by Soviet agents to discredit the moderates, but there was no doubt that Spínola had been involved and had greased his own skids. Then, in April, came the first free and fair elections, although Communists controlled all the national mass media except the dauntless weekly *Expresso*. But the non-Communist parties had agreed beforehand to leave decisive power in the hands of the military council. The Communists did poorly, to their surprise, so they renewed their agitating and organizing effort among the populace and tightened their links with military men who saw things their way. By July they seemed on the verge of seizing and consolidating power through their military alliances. Frightened, the centrists took to the streets, using the same tactics of seeking military supporters and calling endless demonstrations that had served the Communists.

Other members of NATO were deeply worried. Portugal was not excluded from its councils, but discreet measures were taken to keep the country's "Red admirals" and officers away from sensitive secrets. Henry Kissinger, then U.S. Secretary of State, grew annoyed with U.S. Embassy reports urging patience and quiet help for the moderates. He swept out the staff, sending a new team of diplomats he considered more hardheaded, and developed a theory of "vaccination." It amounted to standing aside to let Portugal go Communist, and then tightening the alliance with other Western Europeans in stern defense. But the Socialist government of West Germany and others angrily rejected this approach. They sent strong support to the Portuguese socialists and centrists, and the United States moved in the same direction the following year. By September 1975 another government was formed, the sixth since the revolution, and it reversed the trend of events.

By then the factions were feuding openly. Cunhal chose an equivocal course, clinging to membership in yet another government coalition but throwing Communist support to the volatile leftists who had outdistanced him on the extreme. The Communists swarmed into the streets again. "Portugal will not become the Chile of Europe," the crowds chanted in response to sloganeers with bullhorns. It was an invidious way of accusing the moderates of betraying the revolution and trying to force them out. At the same time, it sought to cloak the Communists in the electoral respectability of Chile's Salvador Allende, who had been murdered in a right-wing military coup. The Communists promoted themselves as the "real revolution" in an effort to consolidate the seething leftist groups, whom they despised as "romantics" and "adventurists."

Isabel do Carmo was the most flamboyant example among the extremists. Her small group, the most militant, called itself the Portuguese Proletarian Reformation Party—Revolutionary Brigades. She was thirty-five at the time, a medical doctor with a strong, bony face and long, dark hair worn loose. She boasted that the thousand or so members—the exact number was a strict secret—were well armed with weapons "diverted" from military stocks by her radical friends in the army. General Otelo Saraívo de Carvalho, head of revolutionary security forces, who had quickly promoted himself from major, said openly that he approved of the distribution of army automatics to the extreme left. He was a colorful, dashing, histrionic figure who made mysterious political leaps and twists. He exerted a powerful pull on fellow officers in the Council of the Revolution, and he was a friend of Isabel do Carmo.

The PRP-RB finances were collected by robbery, of people as well as banks. A small, lively woman, Ms. do Carmo received visitors in a ramshackle office "liberated" from someone, adorned with photos of her husband and her three-year-old daughter, also Isabel. There was scarcely any furniture. Little Isabel's tricycle stood in the corner and two of her plastic dolls were tossed on a crate. Ms. do Carmo had been a Communist in her teens, but in the revolutionary atmosphere the party had become too staid for her. Cunhal was a politician with long training in the theories of stepping to power by combining mass support, tactical alliances, zigs and zags. "The Communists talk about democratic and national revolution first," Ms. do Carmo said with disgust. "We want immediate socialist revolution. That means central planning and worker participation in decisions. That's socialism for us. The people are tired of controls and bossism. That's why so many are leaving the Communists." She claimed broad hidden support, and said that her militant revolutionaries and some military units were so fully integrated that "a part of the army is completely blurred with the militants and the armed and unarmed worker revolutionaries."

At about the same time, another Lisbon woman told how she had turned against the Communists and their military friends to fight the hard left. She had been a sympathizer, but now she was threatened with arrest for criticizing the revolution's leaders. Vera Lagoa, an elegant, strong-minded journalist, had called the new President, Francisco da Costa Gomes, "Mr. Cork" because "he bobs around on all sides of politics and has disappointed and deceived the country." When the police came, she happened to be away from her Lisbon home, visiting in Oporto. But it was typical of her that when she returned she put a lot of creams, eau de cologne and makeup in an overnight case, then called her hairdresser, her secretary and her friends to stand by to escort her to prison "in style." Her crime was cited as disrespect for the President, forbidden by a law still on the statute book from the time of the dictatorship. "I have to expect arrest," she said, "because I'm going to go on writing what I think. My next column, already done, will be called 'Weep, O My Beloved Country.'" Her friend Fernanda Leitaõ had also prepared a jail kit, though more modest. She too intended to continue sharp criticism of the leftist leaders and the Communists "because they duped us. I worked with them for a long, long time. That was the big trap of the antifascist front."

"I'm thirty-eight," Ms. Leitaõ said, "and I've never lived in freedom."

"My dear," said Ms. Lagoa, "I'm fifty-seven and I've never known it." But she was determined to make use of the chance. "Now they see.

The economy is collapsing. The press is being killed. The government will look so ridiculous if they arrest me. Everybody understands."

Most did. The police never returned. Gradually things settled down. The turning point was November 25, 1975, when an alliance of non-Communist democratic forces and non-Communist officers established supremacy over the Communists and radicals. One of the officers, General António Ramalho Eanes, later became the first elected President. In Spain, which began its own transformation from dictatorship soon after, people warned each other, "This is not Portugal. Things cannot go as in Portugal." The Portuguese example was sobering. The Socialists won the next election, and the extremists on right and left disappeared into the woodwork.

The Socialist leader, Mário Soares, had been in exile for many years. A rotund, warmhearted man with a sad smile, he had many friends in Portugal and in the Socialist parties of Europe who tried to help him patch things together after the two years of upheaval. But the revolutionary phase had devastated what was left of an archaic, underdeveloped economy. Soares wasn't much of a manager, either of his own party, which began to split, or of the government, which had to function under a new constitution enshrining supreme military power and certain "revolutionary gains," including nationalization of the banks and much of industry. There was a series of elections, all in good order. But the country still drooped from an overdose of extremism. A center-right coalition came to power for a while. It was little more effective or stable, but in 1982 it did change the constitution, providing for civilian control. When Soares was returned by the voters in 1983, he formed the fourteenth government since the revolution eight years earlier. Later, he was elected President. Political stability remained elusive.

Portugal was calm again, but not recovered, not yet on its feet. António Vasco de Mello, head of one of the old banking families, had said of the past, "We didn't know if we were a small European country with big African holdings or a big African country with a foothold in Europe." That was decided. Despite its weak industrial base and the competition of its agriculture with the wine, tomatoes and olives of Italy and Spain, Portugal determined to join the European Community. The revolution had given up all the colonies, though in conditions that proved as debilitating as Portugal's own travail. About 600,000 refugees, many of them of mixed blood, streamed back from Africa, leaving the newly independent countries almost totally devoid of craftsmen as well as managers.

An intricate international contest developed for control of Angola on independence day, November 11, 1975, obviously an important reason for the Portuguese Communist Party's attempt to hold power in Lisbon before that date. It lost, but the coalition settlement worked out by Lisbon for transfer of power to Angola broke down with rival Soviet and U.S. efforts to install their clients. About two months before the deadline, an injection of secret U.S. aid made it appear that the pro-American faction was winning. Moscow responded with a massive airlift of Cuban troops, which turned the tables. The transfer to independence was made smoothly in Mozambique, but the flight of the Portuguese colonists and their money left it a shambles. Less than a decade later, the newly Marxist countries were beginning to seek the return of Portuguese businessmen. Mozambique was fighting a rebellion of its own. The ex-guerrillas who had become the government began to study the old Portuguese army manuals for tips on counterinsurgency. Some fighting, and much despair, was still the fate of East Timor, which had been seized by Indonesia when the Portuguese pulled out. The war in Angola went on indefinitely, with Cuban troops supporting the Marxist government while South Africa, and later the U.S., helped the rebels.

But after four centuries Portuguese eyes were refocused on their own country, and the approach to Europe. Portugal is a land of stunning beauty, baked by the southern sun but freshened and greened by winds from the stormy Atlantic. Lisbon had been largely destroyed in an earthquake in 1755. The old Moorish fort remained, towering over the city. The rest was rebuilt with grace and artistry. Wide avenues converging on great plazas, sometimes marble paved, cross the center. The façades of many houses are covered with ceramic mosaics, an adornment to treat passersby with the aesthetic pleasures that the rich in other cities so often reserve for themselves behind high walls. There is a measured pace to the city, a leisurely ambiance that is soothing.

Sintra, in the hills above the capital where the well-to-do escape the summer heat, has always drawn British devotees. The poet Robert Southey wrote that "Sintra is too good a place for the Portuguese. It is only good for us Goths—for Germans or English." Byron, in *Childe Harold*, spoke of "Sintra's glorious Eden." A peculiarity of the topography dominating the westernmost point of the continent and the broad mouth of the Tagus River just below Lisbon brings cool mists damp enough to favor dense stands of pine and lush tropical plants. "I never beheld a view that so effectively checked the wish of wandering,"

Southey said. The place "wants only fresh butter and genial society to
make it an earthly paradise." The disdain of lordly English visitors for
the fleas and decorous protocol of Portuguese society was returned.
After some English crusaders from Suffolk helped free Lisbon from the
Moors in 1147 and happily proceeded to assault their own dignity with
huge quantities of the light green Portuguese wine, the phrase *bebado
inglés* ("English drunkard") entered the language to mean an alcoholic.
Spectacular castles and convents, stonily Gothic, rise above the crests
and cataracts around Sintra. Seteais, nearby, has one of the world's
most beautiful hotels, built as a palatial summer house in the eighteenth century by a Dutch consul and decorated with flowery Italian
frescoes and fine furniture of the period.

Near Sintra, the road from Lisbon meets the road to Estoril, a
nineteenth-century beach resort which became the refuge for Europe's
dispossessed royalty in the second part of the twentieth century. Salazar
assured them security, the amenities of the place gave comfort, and
they kept each other nostalgic company. Estoril has housed four exiled
emperors and eleven former kings. The Duke of Windsor sulked there
after he was forced, as Edward VIII, to abdicate the throne of England
because he insisted on marrying an American divorcee. King Carol of
Romania and his red-haired companion Magda Lupescu settled there.
King Umberto of Italy, the Count of Barcelona (whose son became
King Juan Carlos of Spain) and the Count of Paris, pretender to the
throne of France, established a shadowy remnant of courts swept away.

Below the Tagus lies the impoverished Alentejo, a parched land
where the peasant women still wear traditional dress with scarves
topped by a felt hat and where the revolutionary rage ran like a brush-
fire. But the southernmost province, the Algarve, which extends from
the Atlantic to the Spanish border, has been developed for tourism. In
the summer, its pastel houses and pleasant hotels facing long, shining
beaches are a European potpourri where every continental language
can be heard, though not much Portuguese. Fishing is the local industry. Out of season the Algarve has the wan charm of abandoned holiday
havens everywhere, places that are not part of the everyday world and
live only for transient pleasure.

Northern Portugal, with its solid old merchant city of Oporto, is the
down-to-earth, industrious part of the country. The wine trade, textiles
and light industries gave it bourgeois purpose and a sense of solidity.
The Moors never reached that far. Its buildings and forts are un-

touched by their influence but distill instead the inspiration of Christian Europe reviving from the Middle Ages. Portugal is no larger than Indiana, but its people are as clearly marked by the north-south contrast as are much bigger countries of the continent, as much as Italy and Spain, even more than France and Germany.

The Atlantic islands, the Azores and Madeira, were never considered colonies but part of the homeland. They were empty when the first Portuguese arrived, so there was never any question of cultural allegiance or division. During the revolution, however, when the Communists seemed about to dominate, there were rumbles of secession in the conservative Azores. There are three times as many Azoreans in the United States and Canada as on the windswept archipelago, where hydrangeas grow wild in thick clusters along the narrow roads. The huge American air base at Lajes on the island of Terceira is a vital link in the U.S. defense chain to Europe, Africa and the Middle East. During the 1973 Arab-Israeli war, the U.S. airlift which enabled Israel to overcome initial reverses would scarcely have been possible without Lajes. Caetano, who then headed the Portuguese regime, was reluctant to permit its use but finally acceded to a stern demand from President Richard Nixon. As far as possible, the United States has found it wise to be discreet about the importance of Lajes and its activities there, though there has been no challenge or restive opposition in recent years, as in many countries where American forces are installed. Once revolutionary fervor ebbed in Portugal, tension eased in the islands.

After all, volatility seems un-Portuguese. They are a quiet, dogged people with a self-deprecating humor and a sentimental acknowledgment of the sadness in life. The national music, *fado*, is a style of mournful ballad, haunting, touching, minor in key and gentle in rhythm, never frenetic. One verse, about the origins of the style, goes:

> Fado *was born on a day*
> *When the wind was so still*
> *And the sky seemed part of the sea*
> *In the belly of a sailboat*
> *In the breast of a sailor*
> *Who sang because he was sad.*

Another typical fragment: "Nostalgia, please go away from my tired breast and take this *fado* far away."

Herman José, who became the most admired TV star with his wry satire, told jokes about President Reagan promising he would "visit Portugal and then go on to Europe," and the American visitor who went home to report that "Lisbon is the nicest city in Spain." One of his characters, Tony Silva, the equivalent of the apocryphal Joe Doakes, caricatured the postrevolutionary Portuguese, who adopts all the new fads, uses foreign words he cannot pronounce and has an opinion—no matter how distorted—about everything. Caught between their old immobility and a desperate desire to catch up, José's countrymen were delighted to laugh at themselves through Tony Silva's mild irreverence, saying and doing what he pleases but never quite getting it right.

The Portuguese learned to take their politics seriously, once the floodgates were opened. But the economy was the insuperable problem, it was so far behind its prospective partners in the Common Market. An ambitious plan aimed at the development of "a new California" by modernizing agriculture and promoting quality tourism. But the means were not adequate, not only for investment but of human capacity. As a foreign newspaper pointed out, Portugal was geared to a society with many illiterates (25.6 percent in 1970, 17 percent in 1985). The obligatory identity cards use thumbprints—too many people cannot sign their name. Ballots are specially designed for voters who must rely on clearly distinct symbols because they cannot read.

There is a profession of form-fillers, people who earn their living by writing in answers on the endless forms devised by a cumbersome bureaucracy to impose modern controls and extract statistics from a preindustrial society. Before the revolution, there was no minimum wage. During the upheaval, the young air force captain Tomás Rosa, who became Minister of Labor, said disheartenedly, "People think revolution means higher wages and shorter hours." The gold reserves, carefully husbanded by the dictatorship, dropped in the flush of demands to improve everything at once. The inefficient, undercapitalized economy could not respond even to the most legitimate needs. A tremendous effort was made to expand the schools, but in the rush they were blown up like balloons, without effective substance. Portugal was moving again after its long slumber, but in frequently wasteful jerks. There was no magic way to leap the decades of steady renewal that most of Europe had already achieved.

The tensions undermined one government after another. And yet, a decade after the end of the dictatorship, the modern European sense of democracy had taken root. It had come to be seen as an essential characteristic of being a modern European. There had been coups and political violence in other countries after World War II. Charles de Gaulle returned to power in France in 1958 in an unconstitutional, essentially military coup, but he immediately proceeded to arrange for a new constitution and regular, free elections. Greece had spent seven years under its colonels' diktat. Italy and Germany had been subjected to terrorism meant to provoke collapse of the democratic system and its replacement by a different organization of power. Nonetheless, these were all considered aberrations, in no way acceptable alternatives any longer.

Portugal and Spain were the last countries of Western Europe to get rid of the old way of providing order from above. Government by consent of the governed had come to be the first requisite of Western European statehood. The shared values, the underlying philosophies, the culture which produced democracy had been flouted, indeed massacred, in Europe on more than one occasion. World War II had discredited right-wing dictatorships and removed all but the most constitutional, democratic-minded monarchs. Left-wing dictatorships, or more often oligarchies, remained in the East. But even there, as Poland came to demonstrate, the sense of being truly European had come to be tied to a form of democratic government. It was an outlook that enabled Europeans and their descendants elsewhere to sustain the imagination, the daring, the arts which kept them in the ascendancy.

The Iberian countries' determination to follow that path was confirmation that no other choice could be considered. It was an impressive historical advance for Europe, and a great victory. President Woodrow Wilson had sent American soldiers to war in Europe to "make the world safe for democracy," and a generation later they had to go back to help defeat new dictatorships more powerful than any before. East of truncated Germany, government continued to be imposed by force. In the West, that was over. Of course, external threat, social collapse or economic catastrophe can never be ruled out for certain in the unforeseeable future, and that means there can be no absolute guarantee that people will not turn again one day to place their fate in the hands of a master, to submit to his demands. But it does not seem likely. Democracy has been consolidated, for all its travail. Portugal, too, is becoming part of the new Europe which no longer rules vast parts of the globe, but governs itself.

ITALY
Victory Over Terror

APPROPRIATING THE CULTURAL SKILLS of Greece and sending them forth with the Roman legions, Italy spread civilization through Europe. After the fall of Rome and the spread of Christendom, which soon sank into the long, unproductive Dark Ages, it was again Italian artists and craftsmen, architects and scientists who carried the Renaissance across the continent from Blois in western France to Warsaw. Even the walls of the Kremlin and some buildings inside were the work of Italians. Yet with all their extraordinary creative vigor, the fantasy and joy in life of the mixture of peoples who inhabit the sunny peninsula, the Italians could not manage to produce an organization of society worthy of their talents. Some Italians celebrate the ideal of indolence, of *dolce far niente*, as a superior philosophy to glum striving. Affectionately, but with a tinge of apology, Luigi Barzini, author of *The Italians*, extolled the stubborn dedication to habit, to self-delusion, to keeping order at a minimum. The prize-winning Milan journalist Indro Montanelli calls it the "Italian disease" and believes it stems from the Counter-Reformation, which "cut off Italy and made it impermeable to that Protestant spirit in which the great industrial revolution of the West found its motive force and moral standards."

Long after other Europeans had collected themselves into nations with a sense of identity and common will, the Italians remained divided and often oppressed in a variety of principalities, dukedoms and papal states, with frequent and violent changes of rule. Only Germany also waited for the late nineteenth century to achieve unity, but Prussia had long been a great power. The Second Reich, created by Bismarck, absorbed the duchies and principalities of the Rhineland, the kingdoms of Saxony and Bavaria and the assorted members of the German Confederation into the well-developed Prussian state. (The First Reich was the Holy Roman Empire, the Third, Adolf Hitler's twelve-year monstrosity.) When it did pull itself together, Italy had no core, no established administration.

The Risorgimento, literally "resurgence," dedicated to building a nation out of the stew of more or less independent bits of nineteenth-century Italy, modeled the new state on the tightly centralized structure that Napoleon created for France. But Italy's new nationalists did not have Napoleon's social concern for schools, a civil service based on tested merit, a well-defined legal system with firm protection of citizens' rights. The south remained feudal, relying for patronage and protection on a harsh vigilante system which hardened into the Mafia in Sicily, the Camorra in Naples, similar bands elsewhere.

Africa begins just below Rome, the northerners say. Even in Lombardy and the Piedmont, whose capitals are Milan and Turin, where a more generous nature afforded an easier life and Austrian dominion in the eighteenth and most of the nineteenth century had left an administrative framework, the absence of an effective banking system hampered the rise of industry despite lively local enterprise. Credit was distributed so nearly on the pawnshop principle that few would trust their savings to such banks, preventing the accumulation of adequate capital. Montanelli says, "The dying warning given by my own grandfather, who called himself 'an enlightened liberal,' to his sons and grandsons was: 'A decent man can go with a whore, but never with a bank!' "

So it was not until 1892, when the ambitious Italian Prime Minister Francesco Crispi appealed to German Chancellor Bismarck for help in staving off economic collapse, that a modern bank was founded by two German-Jewish financiers. "Milan saw the birth of the firms of Pirelli and Edison and of the Falck steelworks, and Turin became the home of Fiat along with all its associated enterprises," thanks to the bank's financing, Montanelli writes. "This was the birth, or rather the explosion—with action delayed, but also with all the power of pent-up energies released—of Italian capitalism, cutthroat and lawless as young capitalisms always are." The same year also saw the birth of Italian

socialism. It was an offspring of the anarchist movement, led by the
Russian Mikhail Bakunin, who made his home in Naples. At a congress
in Genoa, one group of delegates rebelled against the romantic and
impotent extremism of the anarchists, who wanted to abolish government as the source of all evil. They argued instead that it was the
capitalist system which produced oppression and which could be
changed by organizing the workers. The socialists, seen as compromising heretics by the others, split off and founded their own party.

"In all the other Western societies, capitalism preceded socialism by
at least a century. Consequently it was able to fulfill its function, which
is the accumulation of wealth, without being conditioned by considerations of social justice. Socialism came in when this process was completed, and as a corrective of this process. In Italy, the contemporaneity
of their development ultimately led to two stillbirths, that of capitalism,
which did not have time to run its full course and to give Italy a European economic dimension, and that of socialism, which doesn't know
how to perform its task as a redistributor of wealth for the simple reason
that there is no wealth. . . . So we have the shoddy socialism that our
shoddy capitalism has merited."

This is Montanelli's explanation for the weakness in Italy of a democratic left and the strength of communism, which he calls the "socialism of the underdeveloped." There may be other reasons, but the result
is plain. Between them, the Communists and the ruling Christian Democrats tacitly conspire to prevent the emergence of an alternative. The
twin launch of capitalism and socialism at the end of the nineteenth
century was in an Italy of peasants and artisans, 80 percent of them
illiterate. Not Marx but the Russian anarchist Bakunin was the prophet
of revolutionary thought. "And this was not surprising," Montanelli
says. "In fact the south of Italy in particular, where Bakunin made most
of his converts, was no less underdeveloped than Russia; it was a region
populated by inert, illiterate and reactionary masses who still regretted
the loss of the old regime of the Popes and the Bourbon rulers of
France, driven out by national unity."

Further, Montanelli holds that the northerners who broke away at
Genoa to form the Socialist Party "did not manage to free themselves
from the guilt complex about their anarchist 'brothers.' And these same
brothers, in fact, from the pinnacle of their martyrology—since it was
they who had the monopoly of attempts to assassinate the King, as well
as of the sentences of hard labor for life—continued to accuse the
Socialists of treason. The guilt complex persists to this day, when the

terrorists of the Red Brigades, guilty of the murder of Prime Minister Aldo Moro, and disowned and denounced by the Communists, have found a rather uneasy moral collusion among Socialists who continue to see them as the 'betrayed brothers' of 1892."

It is upon this background of anarchism, extortionate vigilante clans and banditry, and an unripened, not fully accepted industrial capitalism that terrorism built to explosive force once Italy recovered from World War II and defeat. It is by no means the only European country to suffer the outrage of organized but often indiscriminate political violence. Germany had its spell of the plague. Spain still suffers, primarily from Basque groups. The Irish Republican Army also murdered in England. Moluccan islanders, given refuge in Holland, repaid the generous Dutch with terrorist violence. Arabs—Palestinians, Syrians, Iraquis, Libyans—have conducted their bloody feuds in Europe against bystanders as well as one another. Armenians have taken up the tactics, for no goal but revenge. Terrorism is as ancient as hatred. But in the modern West with its elaborate structure of political steam valves, it seems a particularly shocking anachronism.

Anachronism is one facet of the Italian paradox. Far more than most of Europe, Italy is a patchwork of classical, medieval and ultramodern achievements and attitudes. Rather than building smoothly on one another, the centuries have left rival claims, often conflicting within the heart and mind of single individuals. Visitors marvel at the ancient stones and breathtaking vistas. But the uniqueness of Italy is that it is a land so impregnated by people. Everything in the scenery is the result of human effort, human care, human skill. It is particularly striking at Lake Como. Mountain lakes in other countries tend to be preserves of nature, touched by man perhaps but still a reminder of the great, silent world that existed long before humans began to fiddle with it and bend it to their will. At Como, every tree, every flower, every rock, the dirt of the terraces, was put there by somebody to suit the eye of human artistry. The azure lake itself seems to have been created for the boats that dance across it. Behind the hills with their rosy villas and well-tended gardens, the snow-furred Alps rise without awe or chill, like theatrical flats deliberately drawn to complete the composition of the scene. There is perfect balance. And within the perfect balance of Italy, there is disorder, as though having rearranged nature so thoroughly, its people must cede to the irresistible forces that ordain that nothing may be static, nothing held still.

Italians joke that everything can be done in their country because

people are so used to nothing working properly that they have learned
to manage anyway. An average of one government a year has fallen
since the republic was installed in 1946, but it never falls on anyone, so
nobody feels affected. There are rules for everything, but nothing goes
by the rules. Everything is known, and nothing is said. There is a
profound awareness of the tragedy of life, and it makes people merry,
blithe, laughingly impervious to blows that would crush or madden
more sober spirits. Barzini approvingly quotes Giorgio Bocca, who concluded that what Italians believe in is "public lies and private truths.
Do they believe in public lies because they are really convinced that
other Italians believe them? Of course not. They think the only expe-
dient way to live in public is to lie or keep silent. They compensate for
this by preserving their own private truths. . . . The humble lie by necessity, the powerful by cunning and arrogance."

"However," Barzini goes on to say, "the Italians' public role is not
always entirely play-acting. Most of them are unaware of their double
life. They think it natural. They are sincere, or hope that what they
pretend to believe in public may be true. What they are really trying
surreptitiously to do is to preserve as much as possible their own private
beliefs and customs; behind the façade, to cling to what is left of their
ancient and well-tested ways of conducting their lives, dealing with
problems, and managing their affairs, ways that do not always coincide
with the approved official and legal codes of behavior." The author of
The Italians, whose maliciously fond study of his countrymen became
a monument itself, attributes this dual behavior to "forced modernization." He points out similar traits in certain Latin American countries,
in Turkey, in Japan, wherever "a well-meaning intellectual minority
manages somehow to seize power after a revolution, tries to get up an
instant utopia, and works hard to change human nature and the laws
of the economy overnight." But the Italians, having been obliged to
live through so many changes, have digested the tangle of values and
learned to make light of the inner tensions that result.

Their country, slightly larger than Arizona, with a population density
of 490 per square mile, thrusts down from Alpine fastnesses to the
torpid middle of the Mediterranean. The sea's name means "middle of
the earth," as it seemed to the ancients before the age of exploration
revealed it to be only a great inland pond connecting Europe, Africa
and Asia. Italy is a hilly country, often rocky, without long waterways,
the kind of land that tends to cut people off and to develop small, closed
groups who know each other so well they do not need explanations and

are suspicious of outsiders who do. Even widespread use of the national language is a recent innovation. Local dialects, impenetrable to people from other regions, are still widely spoken in virtually every area. Local customs are cherished and preserved. That heightens the contrasts.

Milan and Turin are the bustling industrial cities, happily and ingeniously modern. For all Barzini's gloom about the effects of pushing society along too fast, some Italians at least are as adept and eager as anyone at being up to date, excelling at fashion and industrial design, trying new ideas. Venice must be the original Disneyland, a glowing fairgrounds of a city originally built in a lagoon for safety from marauders, then adorned with all the colors and curlicues and indulgences of the Orient whose wares once made Venetians rich and powerful. Florence is the city of the Renaissance, the gentling of society after uncivilized waves of conquerors were absorbed or had receded. The explosion of art, of refinement, of invention that suddenly took place in the fifteenth century was like a butterfly emerging from the cocoon spun by a grubby worm.

Rome is the capital because Rome was the capital in the days of classical glory. It wears proudly the trophies of all the ages. But it is not a grandiose city like Paris, whose beauties are the great openings on monumental panoramas, designed by the relentless planner Baron Haussmann who razed what was in his way. The delights of Rome are more intimate, the little squares hidden around the corner, the shuttered palaces, the friendly fountains. Naples, with its placid bay and verdant offshore isles, is the scurrying den of poverty, guile, sticky sentiment and shrill wit which testifies to the ingenuity of people to survive in all the world's slums despite the perversity of things.

Palermo is falling apart from the depredations of organized crime, abetted by Sicily's inability to shake off the torpor imposed by centuries of Arab rule. It was said, not altogether as a joke, in Italy that the decision to install U.S. nuclear cruise missiles at Comiso, at the other end of Sicily from Palermo, was because the Mafia could be relied on to protect the site in return for the inevitable rakeoff it could exact on hundreds of millions of dollars in construction contracts for roads, housing and so on. Max Raab, the American Ambassador in 1983 when the site was being built, was said by aides to be philosophical about the situation, holding that the corruption was a problem for the Italian, not the U.S., government and that in any case the dollars would help stimulate the bedraggled Sicilian economy.

There are many Italys, all contradicting one another, and many ways to look at Italy. With its beauty and elaborate history, it has been a kind of cult for a long time. It is a non-proselytizing cult, but foreigners can convert and practice it with an ease rare in other lands. This is because Italian nationalism is so weak that it can be catholic in the literal sense of the word, universal, open to anybody. But Italian pride is strong, if often mocking, and it encourages extremism to flourish alongside cynicism. The epidemic of European terrorism took a particularly heavy toll on Italian society.

Not all came from the extreme left, usually educated, often middle-class romantics who dream of making a more perfect society by destroying the existing order. Particularly in Italy, but also in France, extremists of the right have sought to destabilize by terror. At times it is impossible to be sure which side is the perpetrator. The brotherhood of violence created some strangely mixed families as the gangs moved from theories to the expediencies of outlawry. There has been clear evidence of international collusion among them and of a degree, not really known, of indirect Soviet support.

Recent investigations have shown a surprisingly important involvement of Bulgarian agents in Italy. Western intelligence was long aware that the Eastern bloc's espionage was organized along a certain division of labor, specific countries or types of information being assigned to various national services. Soviet agents were said to engage in hard, technical espionage in Italy, seeking microfilms of military equipment plans, for example. The Bulgarians turned out to have the dirty-tricks jobs and subversive contacts. It was disclosed at the trial of a union official who worked as an agent that he passed along to Bulgarian services the information obtained about NATO from the terrorist "interrogation" of U.S. Brigadier General James L. Dozier when he was held by kidnappers for forty-two days in the winter of 1981–82. But the Bulgarian connections probably arose after the terrorist groups were well organized. The phenomenon of Italian terrorism erupted as a strange, indigenous ailment in a Europe of unprecedented affluence, peace and democracy.

Benito Mussolini, Italy's Fascist Duce, introduced official violence and virtually wiped out the private cliques. It is one of history's quirks that he nearly managed to liquidate the Mafia, jailing many. Since he did not conduct free elections, he had no use for their special capacity to deliver votes. But when the United States was preparing for the invasion of Sicily in World War II, there was a need for intelligence and an advance attempt to persuade the people not to resist. Wittingly or not, the United States used Mafia aid in the invasion and occupation of Sicily, and the relation helped the underworld in Italy to rebuild its smuggling organizations. Sometimes American officers looking for people to install in local governments who could be trusted as true anti-Fascists opened Mussolini's jails and appointed inmates to posts of responsibility. Being imprisoned seemed prima facie evidence of not having collaborated. Thus was the secret society reborn, even before the Italian state, and its connections with the United States reinforced.

After kidnapping and terrorism developed tidal dimensions in the 1970s, there were signs of occasional cooperation between the old gangs and the new groups. At times the criminals themselves seemed unclear whether they were collecting money for their political cause or taking up politics as an excuse to extort money. Illegal bands, whatever their initial pretext, tend to deteriorate into bandits.

Italian society became the main target and the main victim of the upsurge of terrorism throughout the West in the 1970s. It has been noted that the affliction was worst in the Axis countries defeated in World War II, Germany, Italy and Japan, where a "Red Army" group was formed, undertaking assignments for the Palestinian terror groups in Israel and Europe. Whether lingering totalitarian urges were responsible, or some flaw of patriotic cohesion in the generation after the debacle, can only be a matter of speculation. Unlike the other two, however, Italy has a weakly organized state and an intensely clannish society whose people do not easily identify national interest with their own. It was at first the least able to cope with terrorism.

The event recognized as the beginning of turbulence was the bombing of the Piazza Fontana in Milan in 1969. Sixteen people were killed. The immediate official reaction was to blame the left, but after months of dogged effort, an enterprising press established that the extreme right was responsible. What was seen as a deliberate attempt by the authorities to shift the blame had a part in the evolution of public attitudes. Ordinary people were reluctant to help in identifying or tracking down terrorists and their supporters. Many, including middle-class people who preached the need to obey the laws, had a sneaking admiration for the derring-do of those who defied the state and challenged its pretenses. Among the broad public, there was a general sense of impotence and indifference to the violence, which made it easier for the criminals to live underground. People felt the fight was between authority and its challengers and did not concern their everyday lives or their responsibility as citizens.

The director Michelangelo Antonioni had a character in one of his films say, "Corruption is the glue that holds Italian society together." There have been enough scandals, real plots and intrigues for Italians to see conspiracy in practically everything. The sense of dark deeds in high places, the lackadaisical official reaction to proven crime, encouraged the belief that a coup was being planned at the beginning of the 1970s. Already in 1968, when other Western countries were going through leftist student upheavals, extreme right-wing groups were appearing in Italy. They had links to the police, the army, military intelligence.

The Red Brigades originated in response to a perception of people in various social groups, some poor students, some middle-class, some upper-class intellectuals, that fascists were moving in again on the structure of power. But the plotters and supporters of right-wing violence pulled back quickly when influential people who had indulged them concluded it was to their own political disadvantage, and that it was more rewarding to appear respectable and constitutional as the Christian Democratic Party moved toward an understanding with the Communists. At the same time, the Communists' emphasis on legal politics, their leadership's moving toward what was to become the quest for a "historic compromise" in which they could enter the government, frustrated and disgusted the more radical left. It wasn't just that the Communist Party leader, Enrico Berlinguer, was an elegant, eloquent nobleman from Sardinia and his wife and children were known to attend Sunday Mass. The Communists were seeking votes and broad access to power, which had to mean acceptance by large numbers of people. The radicals were impatient for revolutionary action, spectacular deeds. They chafed at the discipline the Communists demanded.

Significantly, the two initial centers of terrorist activism were intensely Catholic Trento, in the northeast, particularly the new sociology department at the university, and "Red" Emilia-Romagna, the region around Bologna where pro-Communist partisans had been particularly active against the Mussolini regime. They had taken over before Allied troops arrived, and the Communists have run Bologna efficiently and unusually honestly ever since.

Renato Curcio, an impoverished student at Trento, became the "historic leader" of the Red Brigades. He and Margherita Cagol (who became his wife, known as "Mara") and their friends had been practicing Catholics. She married in white, bemoaned a medically ordered abortion, willingly prepared the pasta for the clique. But they were repelled by what seemed a frozen society where nothing could be budged.

Giorgio Bocca, who made a thoughtful study of the terrorist movement, attributed its roots to what he calls "Cathocommunism." Both movements, he says, have "resolutely antidemocratic" traditions and culture which mark youth with their belief in total, definitive solutions even as they provoke rebellion against the glaring failures of society. A French extreme leftist who met with Curcio and the German terrorist Andreas Baader in 1970 to discuss an international clandestine alliance is quoted as saying, "It was impossible to explain to Curcio and Baader that a country like ours which had seriously had a great revolution, and had known the Terror [Robespierre and the guillotine], couldn't go in for minor imitations." It is a telling comment. It turned out to be true for modern Italy and Germany as well, but the realization took many painful years and neither the young terrorists nor their victim governments were aware of the implications at first.

Rebels from Reggio Emilia committed the first leftist act of terrorism, setting fire to the car of the director of a local technical institute, and then distributed a leaflet explaining their revolutionary purposes. Their passion attracted sympathizers in many places. One of the best known, and most surprising, was Giangiacomo Feltrinelli, a millionaire Milan publisher. He had a high-society background and a taste for adventure. He had played a key role in smuggling the manuscript of Boris Pasternak's *Doctor Zhivago* from the Soviet Union to the West, mingled with the international "beautiful people" and established a façade of geniality and goodwill. He did other things, too. In May 1972 he accidentally blew himself up while laying a dynamite charge on a high-tension pylon near Milan. Giorgio Semeria, son of a director at Siemens, the German industrial giant, and a mother who was a professor, was an example of the wealthy, educated youth who took their guilt and identity crises to be absolved in the Red Brigades, as Americans go to psychiatrists. "He took everything he did terribly seriously," his mother said later.

It was a time of radical chic in many countries. The incidents multiplied, and the crimes, at first against property, escalated. The first kidnapping, of the Siemens director Idalgo Macchiarini, occurred in 1972. On April 18, 1974, a judge was kidnapped in Genoa to enforce a demand for release of militant prisoners he had sentenced. The local

prosecutor refused. But the police were impotent. They searched the
area where the victim was held for thirty-five days without finding a
trace. When the judge's family appealed to the terrorists, he was released, blindfolded, in a Milan garden.

"Class" was a slogan of the terrorists, but not a catalyst. Still, the
proletarian rhetoric was asserted and faith advanced that "the masses"
would arise to destroy their "capitalist oppressors" if only they could be
shocked to awareness of their latent power. Curcio was arrested in 1974,
informed on by a Franciscan priest named Silvano Girotto, alias Padre
Leone. The police were beginning to infiltrate. But the Red Brigades'
leader was so casually guarded that Mara and some friends had no
trouble freeing him. Mara died later in a shootout with police, and after
Curcio was rearrested, a new, more bloody-minded leadership began to
form.

Some of the recruits were trained at Karlovy Vary, in Czechoslovakia. Prague had long been the headquarters of the international Communist youth movement. Despite the unrelenting antiterrorist stand of
the Italian Communist Party, foreign Communist agents were evidently
not so finicky in choosing whom to aid and support. In addition to
judges, the new group targeted shop directors of major factories and
the press. Autonomia Operaia (Workers' Autonomy) made a point of
penetrating the great industrial establishments in an effort to organize
the labor force against its bosses from within.

The impact of terrorism on Italian society was dramatically displayed
when the Turin trial of the arrested Red Brigades leadership had to be
postponed. Six people, required by law for a jury, could not be found
who were willing to face the threat to anyone who served. Fear had
taken hold, but indifference had not been overcome. The well-liked
deputy editor of the local paper La Stampa, Carlo Casalegno, was shot
in the head. The unions at Fiat called the workers out to protest the
murders and demonstrate support for the rule of law. Only 20 percent
heeded the appeal. Gianpaolo Pansa of La Repubblica went to Fiat's
Mirafiori plant to report the men's views. Some approved of the killings.
Most said they weren't concerned. One told him, "Look, journalist,
why should I go on strike? If I were killed, would you journalists go on
strike for me?"

The terrorist aim of establishing their movement as a recognized
alternative thread in the social fabric made some headway. It attracted
some normally law-abiding people, and it blurred the line between dis-

sidence, as legitimately free expression, and support for illegal violence. Giovanni Senzani, who was arrested at the age of thirty-nine in 1982, was a particularly disturbing example of perverted loyalties. He was a criminologist. His professional associates were magistrates, police officials and prison authorities. He knew the details of penal administration, the layouts of the jails, the names and habits of the guards. He chose to become an informer for the terrorists in order, he claimed, to increase the authorities' concern for the plight of prisoners and other unfortunates at the margin of society. Three judges, whom he had accompanied as a colleague to an international conference in Lisbon, were murdered at his word. He organized the kidnapping of Judge Giovanni d'Urso, a stunning success for the terror campaign. Senzani moved on to copy Mafia habits of killing those who gave information, and then to direct complicity with the criminal underworld. After arranging with the Mafia to kidnap the Neapolitan DC leader Ciro Cirillo, ostensibly in the name of revenge for the unemployed and homeless, the Red Brigades and the gangsters shared the $3 million ransom that was paid.

There is a seamy underside to practically every institution in Italy, and there is also a dedicated, honest, courageous attachment to a system of democracy and human rights. The Italian judiciary and press, in particular, passed the trial by fire without ever lowering the colors of republican legality. Neither extremists of the left nor of the right could destabilize the country and make it cry for the order of the fist. The memory of Mussolini's twenty-one-year rule was certainly a factor. It had led to disaster for democrats and anti-democrats alike. Now when Italian children are asked what they know about Mussolini, they jut out their chin, arch their chest, wave a stiff right arm and roar with laughter. He is buried in ridicule. Something similar is happening to the fantasies of revolutionary terrorism. A joke that circulated when the years of dread seemed over went, "What was the main result of the Red Brigades?" Answer: "They finally brought Italy a good modern police force."

German schoolchildren do not learn a great deal more about the Nazis; it isn't until they are fifteen or sixteen that history classes reach the twentieth century. There are no common guidelines for teaching about the Hitler period; it is left to the state education ministries to draw up general suggestions and most of all to the teachers themselves. After President Reagan's controversial visit to the German military cemetery at Bitburg where some SS troops are buried, schoolteacher Bettina von Engel-Forster said she discussed the role of the SS with her pupils for five or six hours, but they weren't very interested. For them, the Nazi period was ancient history that they had heard too much about on television and in the press.

For Italians, too, the prewar Fascist period is almost beyond recall, while terrorism has been a modern issue. The turning point in public attitudes was the kidnapping of Premier Aldo Moro on March 16, 1978. A sense of deep crisis was already spreading through the land. The lira was sick. Unemployment was mounting. The revolving-door governments kept revolving but it was always the same old DC faces playing peekaboo.

Everything seemed to be falling apart. Businessmen organized private mail service because the post office didn't work. Hundreds of sacks of undelivered mail were found simply thrown away. Government offices were often empty because so many people worked in the "submerged economy," augmenting pitiful salaries (but which guaranteed job and social security) with unreported, untaxed employment. There was a general feeling of social decay. The Red Brigades found the most spectacular way possible to prove it. On that spring day, the Premier left his home and went to Mass as usual, and then headed for his office. He had a bodyguard and a chauffeur in his unarmored car, and three young policemen from the countryside assigned to guard him in a following car. They had not even been given special training or told of the risks. The kidnappers drove up, blocking Moro's car, and dragged him away. They killed all five of the guards.

Then began the trial of the whole country. Moro was an intelligent, shrewd politician, a DC veteran but one who was trying to infuse the tired party with some new spirit. He was a small, trim man, elegant, cultivated. Day after day, his captors sent pictures of him to the newspapers with their demands for recognition by the government and direct negotiation for his release. They showed him progressively wilting, shriveling. The hunted-animal look came into his downcast eyes. He was allowed to write letters to his wife, and they took on a pleading, groveling tone. The kidnappers published records of his "interrogation" and "people's trial," a defiant performance intended to humiliate the whole legal system and force the government to its knees.

A fierce debate racked Italy. Should Moro be saved? It was an excruciating dilemma on every level, moral, political, social, historic. The government concluded that it could not deal with the terrorists, which would make them equals with the state. Finally, after fifty-five days in captivity, Moro was murdered and his trussed body stuffed in the trunk of a car. Interior Minister Francesco Cossiga took political responsibility and resigned from the government. In 1985 that act of statesmanship was a major factor in his successful election to the Italian presidency.

At first, the reaction built slowly. Moro's family was bitter and felt he had been sacrificed by colleagues to preserve their own positions. But gradually feelings hardened against all the terrorists. The police were better equipped, organized and directed. The bands themselves began to realize that murder was not making them revolutionary heroes nor stirring the workers to anything but revulsion. Incidents of terror continued, but arrests multiplied. Some of the prisoners repented and provided information that helped break up underground cells and uncover weapons caches. The tide had turned. When the worst was over, it became evident that Italian society had weathered the challenge with unforeseen solidity. Democracy and the rule of law emerged unscathed, perhaps strengthened, with new confidence in its capacity to survive on Italian soil. "We thought terrorism had nothing to do with us," said a Roman journalist, wife of a senator. "But with the Moro case, we saw it was out to destroy the very fabric of society, that nobody could consider themselves immune or unaffected."

The Italian experience affected others. Germany had reacted sternly, some thought with too strong a fist, to suppress its own terrorist bands. Spain had become a democracy, removing the argument for terror to fight dictatorship. But, as happens with outlaws, some had become bandits, and the restoration of order did not come automatically. Particularly among the Basques, the cult of separatism had grown to the point where large numbers refused to oppose the terrorists, if they didn't actively sympathize. Until the mid-1980s, Basque gunmen and accomplices found refuge with their kin across the border in France, where they benefited from the old anti-Spanish feelings. The Spanish government went a long way to meet Basque desires for regional autonomy, but it was not enough for those who demanded independence and sought to maintain the climate of emotional crusade with assassinations. Even the Palestine Liberation Organization, whose initial successes in gaining recognition by terror had prompted many imitators, moved to focus more on international diplomacy and politics. Terrorism by no means disappeared, but its revolutionary pretensions in Europe were clearly demonstrated as a failure.

In the period between 1968 and 1982, 403 Italians were killed in terrorist attacks and 1,347 injured by shooting and bombing. More than 4,000 were arrested or convicted on charges of terrorism. (In the same period, 2,300 were killed in Northern Ireland.) The murders achieved nothing.

All the other problems sapping Italy remained. An early Red Brigades slogan was "The vote doesn't count, the rifle does." Nobody asked, count for what? It was understood that the central question was the incapacity of the political structure to deal satisfactorily with the society's needs. The terrorists had maintained that the only solution was armed struggle against the state. But they showed themselves even more incapable than the authorities at bringing desired change. When their movement was defeated, Italy turned back to politics as usual.

It is a peculiar game of shuffling. The same old parties, the same old faces keep presenting themselves to a remarkably loyal electorate. There is constant motion and little movement. In Germany, the brunt of the attack was against a complacent materialism and a vague sense that the divided nation had lost its soul, its essential ideals. For the most part, the European terrorists were romantics or fundamentalists. The two are linked in their vision of a world infested with cowardly evil and divested of spirit, and in their righteousness. There were collusion, corruption, shady and greedy exchanges of influence on high. But the gun and the bomb could not clear the musty air nor heal the sores. In the end, the tedious process of investigation, disclosure and prosecution was preferable for all its slow uncertainties.

The republic constructed after the fall of fascism and the referendum that abolished the monarchy is constitutionally irreproachable. A system of proportional representation produces two large parties and a handful of small parties capable of giving expression to a full spectrum of opinion. The problem has been that one of the major parties, the Communists, is considered too dangerous to admit in the national government and the other, the Christian Democrats, too stultified and corrupt to govern alone. The result has been coalitions, sturdier than their frequent collapse would make it appear because they are almost always composed of the same groups, and the DC is always the strongest.

Three unwritten rules have guided modern Italian politics. The first is that a bare majority is not enough to govern, even though the constitution permits it. The Communists publicly acknowledged this tribute to Italian diversity when they first proposed a "historic compromise" in

1976, an appeal for a coalition with the DC that would provide a substantial majority, though few can imagine how it could effectively govern. The second rule defeats the Communists' acceptance of the first, excluding them on the national level in any kind of coalition with or without the DC, though they are well established in a number of municipal and regional governments, often in coalition with the smaller Socialist Party. The third rule finally went by the board in 1981. It had assured that the DC, the largest party, headed the government.

The Christian Democratic Party has older roots, but it was brought to flower by Alcide de Gasperi, the grand architect of Italian reconstruction after World War II. He was a man of vision, a convinced European who was a partner with France's Robert Schuman and Germany's Konrad Adenauer in building a new concept of European unity. There was a period in the wake of the war when the fate of Italy appeared to rest on the outcome of a duel between Communists and Catholics, East and West. It was a duel Italian-style, with many little accommodations and behind-the-scenes maneuvers epitomized in the hilarious book *Don Camillo,* by Giovanni Guareschi, satirizing the struggle between a village priest and a village party secretary. The Vatican and the United States backed de Gasperi. Moscow backed Palmiro Togliatti, the clever Communist leader. The DC won the first suspenseful contest. It proceeded to consolidate its hold by distributing lavish patronage and by offering the only visible alternative to the Communists.

As perception of the Communist threat receded, both because the Italian party pulled further and further away from Moscow's tutelage and because the Soviet Union lost ideological appeal with disclosure of its grim realities, patronage became the DC's main support. De Gasperi died and the clique who carried his banners aged, trading cabinet jobs and seldom admitting fresh faces to the inner circle of power.

"Clientism," more than opinion, became the driving force of Italian politics. The Communists also practiced it. There was even a reasonable sharing of favors where necessary, at the state-owned radio-TV (RAI), for example. Job aspirants quickly learned that the useful way to apply wasn't to the prospective boss but through the sympathetic party. A quota system rationed out the jobs. Considering these circumstances, RAI is remarkably professional and efficient. A decision in 1976 to permit local private stations, which burgeoned into the thousands, helped keep it that way by competition.

But clientism did not do much to instill a sense of good government.

It fertilized the opportunity for corruption on every level and encouraged the growth of the "parallel economy," too widespread to be called a mere black market. Public-sector jobs, in the government, public services or nationalized industry, were considered a safe perch from which to move on after a few hours a day, or even a few a week, and do some enterprising, rewarding work on the side. As a result, of course, the public didn't get service. Again and again after each election, there were earnest pledges to reform the tired DC apparatus and revive its spirit. Finally, in 1981, some modest reforms were undertaken. They produced a new party secretary, Ciriaco de Mita. He actually set out to recruit new candidates with better reputations. But he did not get far, partly because of resistance and sabotage by the veterans and their clients, partly because Socialist leader Bettino Craxi provoked elections a year earlier than scheduled so as not to risk a more attractive rival.

The DC's retreat was foreshadowed earlier, when for the first time the party lost the presidency, a formal job with little power but the possibility of considerable personal influence. In 1978 President Giovanni Leone was forced out of office because of his part in the huge Lockheed bribery scandal. Abashed by the shocking sequence of Prime Minister Aldo Moro's murder and President Leone's greed, the politicians turned for dignity's sake to an eighty-two-year-old Socialist of impeccable personal reputation and democratic credentials. He was Alessandro Pertini, a frail, great-grandfatherly figure with a peppery personality and a staunch anti-fascist record. As the new chief of state, Pertini at least provided a sense of decency and honesty at the summit, though his figurehead office prevented his leading the renewal for which many yearned.

Still, Pertini broke the DC monopoly on state power. Then, in 1981, it was possible for Giovanni Spadolini, fifty-six at the time, to be accepted in a coalition as the second non–Christian Democratic head of government. He led the tiny Republican Party, much respected by enlightened businessmen and nonideological Italian modernizers. But with 3 percent of the vote, he represented essentially a technical elite rather than the broad public. Spadolini was a chunky, robust man with a fine sense of the possible as well as an appealing awareness of the desirable. He had been a professor of history and a newspaper editor for most of his career, so he did not have the overripe aroma of a lifelong professional politician. But Spadolini found that the ties between political parties and unions made the needed economic reforms virtually impossible. The habit of milking the state had become a cherished tradition, so that deficits could only soar, especially in a period of world recession. Inflation could only rise. He rued the advent of a "Swedish-type mentality and life-style widespread in this country. However, we lack the preconditions for a welfare state. The gap between aspirations and possibilities is increasing."

Socialist leader Bettino Craxi brought down the fragile coalition in 1982, sensing a swing of opinion in his favor. Craxi formed the government after forcing early legislative elections in June 1983. That brought the first real crack in the intricate political balance. Everyone, including the DC's rebuffed de Mita, took the results as a broad protest, a sign that the electorate was truly losing patience with the old game and the shopworn players. Italians had tolerated baroque politics for a long time. Without doing anything drastic, they seemed to be demanding at last a breakthrough to a more rational, healthier and competent system of government. Still, for lack of an attractive alternative and probably out of sheer fatigue with the game of juggling players in a familiar cast, the politicians left Craxi at the helm without serious challenge well beyond the momentary leadership which had been predicted. It turned out that nobody was in a hurry to bring down his coalition or force another early election.

Beneath the surface of an almost theatrical political repertory, the country had been slowly changing. The Church itself had changed. The Second Vatican Council and Pope John XXIII had legitimized more liberal social attitudes, not only in Italy. The Vatican had been obliged to take account of movements elsewhere in the Catholic world, of the once controversial worker-priests and left-wing Catholics in France, of the progressive and all but rebellious Dutch Catholics, of ardent demands for Church support of social justice in Latin America. Even the deeply conservative old Spanish hierarchy had moved from support of Franco to a cautious liberalism and endorsement of democracy. When the tradition of centuries was broken and a non-Italian became Pope, the Polish John Paul II, the Vatican's intense focus on Italian affairs was diluted. Meanwhile, the society was growing more secular. After bitter debate, divorce was made legal.

The question arose whether the DC was headed for a long decline, whether there was any way to achieve the full reform it needed. Some argued for further distance from the Church. Others insisted that trans-

formation into a conventional conservative party, like those in the
United States, Britain and Germany, was the path to extinction. Certainly the record was badly stained. The successive scandals reached
high and wide, involving billions of dollars. The collapse of the Banco
Ambrosiano and the death of financier Roberto Calvi, judged a suicide
by British authorities who found him hanging under Blackfriars Bridge
in London, directly implicated the Vatican in mysterious money matters. There was talk that Calvi had arranged to send money to the Polish
union Solidarity for John Paul II. Calvi had been involved with the
mysterious Licio Gelli, leader of a secret Masonic Lodge known as P-2.
P-2 appeared to be the base of a plot to *buy* control of Italy, as an
unscrupulous tycoon might buy out a company, by planting paid agents
in most of the parties who would subvert the republic at their masters'
command. The extraordinary collection of names on the list of P-2's
membership represented a powerful elite, close to the Vatican, the top
of industry, the police, army, banks and politics. Some theories saw in
the group a plot to overthrow the republic and substitute a new form of
dictatorship. Some saw it as sheer greed and corruption, undermining
the republic without regard for consequences. It was never even proved
that this surprising amalgam of influence actually worked as a power
bloc, though practically any suspicion seemed justified in the weird
circumstances. Gelli fled Italy when the revelations put the police on
his trail, and he was arrested in Switzerland for bank fraud.

But when the Italian government got around to asking for his extra-
dition, he escaped and disappeared. Rumor had it that he was flown to
a Mediterranean port, perhaps Monte Carlo, and smuggled onto a ship
to South America. Late in 1984 he was reported to be living comfortably
in one of the impenetrable areas of Paraguay or Argentina. There was
a disturbing lack of evidence that any country's police was trying to
catch the fugitive. It was as though Gelli's unavailability to appear and
stand for trial was a comfort to every country in which his immense
financial empire had an interest—and there were many, including not
only Britain, where his associate Roberto Calvi died, but also the
United States, where his associate Michele Sindona was indicted in
connection with the peculiar bankruptcy of the Franklin National Bank
in New York. The P-2 scandal revived old charges and countercharges
about the subversive role of Freemasonry in Italy, going back to Gari-
baldi's campaign to unite the country against the interests of the Vatican in the nineteenth century.

The better discipline and relative lack of corruption of the Italian Communist Party sharpened the contrast. Its first leader, Antonio Gramsci, was an intellectual, a philosopher whose thinking provided an early basis for questioning the Leninist-Stalinist model which the Soviet Union proclaimed as the one true face of communism. His thought remained an important element in the gradual loosening of ties between Western Communists and sympathizers and their would-be Moscow mentors. Mussolini banned the party and drove the Communists underground throughout his rule, which enhanced their claim to exemplary patriotism and dedicated resistance when the Allies defeated the Fascist regime. Nonetheless, Mussolini's Italy was one of the first states to recognize the Bolsheviks and establish diplomatic relations with the Soviet Union. The party's bitterness at having thus been betrayed by Moscow in the early 1920s strengthened the factions which argued for more independence.

As Allied forces advanced up the Italian peninsula late in World War II, the Communists' partisan organizations sprang into activity, emerging as a strong, effective force able to seize local power. Like the DC, they set up a patronage system which made them a society within a society. They got people jobs, building permits, even maids. They arranged admission to schools, roles in the theater and opera, holidays. In Bologna, which they made a showcase of reasonable administration, the Communist mayor encouraged small business despite Marxist prescriptions because it protected his constituents from the dramatic swings of boom and bust that afflicted other parts of the country.

That pragmatism, however, kept the Italian Communists on a fence they could not cross. They were torn between a strategy of seeking power as a normal Italian party with no outside allegiance, not even to the role of the Soviets as "first socialist country," and thus risking extinction through assimilation with other Italian movements, or clinging to Moscow and orthodoxy, which the bulk of their compatriots could never accept. After the death of the wartime and postwar leader Palmiro Togliatti, the party chose Enrico Berlinguer as leader and guide in its dilemma. He was of Sardinian aristocratic origin, small, handsome, self-assured, capable of fiery speeches but also of elegance and refinement. He tilted away from Moscow, advocating the "historic compromise" in which Italy's two biggest parties, the DC and the Communists, would share power. As a logical concomitant, Berlinguer launched the idea of "Eurocommunism," an alliance of the Western

European Communist parties which would reinforce them against Moscow's demands. It eventually failed, primarily because the French Communists backed out, but it made a difference in undermining and eventually almost wiping out Soviet influence on Western European politics.

By making common cause with the Spaniards, Yugoslavs and Romanians at the extraordinary East Berlin conference of European Communist parties in July 1976, the Italians forced something of a watershed. It was at that meeting that the crackly old Spanish Communist Santiago Carrillo, later ousted by his own comrades for being too authoritarian, stood up and told the Russians to their faces, "October [the Bolshevik Revolution] is not our Christmas and Moscow is not our Rome." The Soviets were never again able to organize a formal display of Communist solidarity and subservience outside their own sphere of influence.

In Italy, the Communists remained a powerful blocking force to political realignment, never a viable alternative government but in effect an assurance of continued DC supremacy. When Berlinguer died in 1984, he was given a national funeral attended by President Pertini, a whole spectrum of politicians and huge, sorrowful crowds. He had won respect among the great majority of his compatriots, though not their votes. His successor, Alessandro Natta, was a less impressive figure who maintained the same party line but gradually lost electoral appeal. The Communists slipped back to about 30 percent of the vote.

The gelid state of Italian politics, the melodramatic personal feuds which littered the stage but left the audience scarcely moved, led the real dynamos of the society to work outside the political arena. That too was a turnabout because there was little tradition of voluntary nonpartisan organizations, such as the peace movement or ecology movement in other countries. Such causes tended to be promoted through the political parties. Instead, individuals emerged, sometimes quixotic, sometimes powerful, sometimes just quietly stubborn and effective, but always representative of an underlying strength which kept the nation from capsizing in crisis after crisis.

Angelo Dalle Molle was an example, neither obscure nor famous, a practical man with grand ideas. He was born in Venice in 1906 to a middle-class family that dealt in food and drink, and he expanded the business successfully. In the postwar boom years, Dalle Molle made a fortune launching an unpleasant-tasting but medicinal apéritif based on artichokes, called Cynar. Apart from appealing to compulsive Italian concern with health, his success was due to his early grasp of the use of computers. It was too easy. He sold out because, he said, "it didn't amuse me anymore," and began to look for other ways to use his time and money.

The "Italian miracle" was in full swing at that period, and he was aware of the malaise it was engendering. Affluence was not enough. He began to look for something "beyond demand and supply," something that would explain "irrational ways of thinking that are right" and that were moving restive youth to protest. The left-wing cult heroes of the time, Marcuse, Adorno, Horkheimer, were "anti-science" to his mind, negative thinkers who had got hold of something but from the wrong side. Dalle Molle decided to experiment with "technical solutions subordinated to a humanistic approach."

"Whatever the system, productivity determines purchasing power," he liked to say. "That's why people get poorer when the left is in power. . . . The way to defend against demagogues is the language of facts." He bought a deteriorating Palladian villa in the Veneto, near Vicenza, restored it and opened an electric automobile factory in the large yard. He intended to show that: (1) Computers make big industrial complexes and dehumanizing assembly lines economically unnecessary. (2) Productivity improves dramatically when workers have variety in their jobs and the satisfaction of seeing completed results. (3) Modern techniques make it possible to reverse the stifling swelling of cities and to provide industrial jobs in the countryside without spoiling it. (4) Computers and automation can replace many skills so that a worker need not be particularly specialized and can avoid the monotony of a single task. (5) Since cities and gasoline engines are inherently incompatible and electric engines have limited range, a different organization of transport could combine the benefits and eliminate the disadvantage of each.

It was, of course, a staggering agenda. Dalle Molle started small, deliberately, to prove that small is better and, since he had no desire to launch another business career, he only wanted to build a model for others to copy. In 1980 the backyard plant was turning out a simple electric automobile every day or two, with a dozen workers. It cost a few thousand dollars. The design wasn't much more impressive than a golf cart, but the car was complete, could go up to forty miles an hour, do forty-five miles of city driving without a recharge and had quick acceleration. The key to exploitation was rentals. Dalle Molle's idea was to establish centrally located garages not more than half a mile apart in a city, so that no point would be farther than a quarter mile from a station. He represented the constructive, modern and yet humane side of Italian creativity.

Judge Ilario Martella was a different example of the underlying solidity of Italy. Investigation of the attempted assassination of the Pope by Mehmet Ali Ağça fell to him. He was a close-mouthed man and dogged. There were tremendous pressures to whisk through the case and close the dossiers. Neither Italy nor the United States, nor many others, were eager for a serious probe of the suspected "Bulgarian connection" with its likely lead to then KGB chief Yuri Andropov, later to become Soviet party leader and President. The international implications were unforeseeable and frightening should convincing evidence emerge. Like Judge Joseph Sirica, who presided over the trial of Washington's Watergate burglars, Martella refused to bend his judicial responsibility for unearthing truth to any consideration of consequences. He plodded on, aware of the personal risk, waiting for Ağça to realize there would be no rescue by co-conspirators, as he had been rescued from a Turkish jail after he murdered a Turkish editor. Finally, the prisoner began to talk.

In October 1984, Judge Martella delivered a 1,243-page indictment against three Bulgarians and four Turks in the alleged plot to kill the Pope. A fresh-cheeked, round-faced man of fifty with an engaging smile, he had worked diligently and almost silently for three years. His straightforward, honest but shy manner, utterly devoid of any sign of ambition or self-importance, made a remarkable contrast with the sinister forces and dark intrigues that swirled around him for so long. Even a high-ranking official of the Communist Party, which could not have been pleased with his conclusion pointing to Moscow, said of Martella when the indictment was released that he was "totally incorruptible." After a trial in which Ağça claimed to be Christ, his alleged Bulgarian co-conspirators were acquitted for lack of evidence.

There was nothing typical about Susanna Agnelli, and yet she too represented the kind of public-spirited, modernizing Italians who knew what ailed their country and were prepared to make an intense personal effort to help it fulfill its capacity. Called Suni by everyone, she was born very rich, one of the seven children of the great Turin industrialist who launched the firm of Fiat. In a wry memoir called *We Always Wore Sailor Suits*, she told of growing up with British governesses who imposed a totally un-Italian discipline and responsibility in an atmosphere of luxury. In 1983, aged sixty-one, she said she still felt at a certain disadvantage with her lifelong compulsion to be punctual. By then, she had six children, nine grandchildren, three public jobs as mayor of Monte Argentario (near Santo Stefano), senator and Undersecretary of Foreign Affairs with responsibility for North and South America. She wrote a weekly advice column for the popular magazine *Oggi*, as well as making frequent TV appearances and campaign tours for her Republican Party. She chose the small Republicans, though her brother Umberto was long a Christian Democratic senator, because, she said, "it's neither right nor left, it's honest, it considers that running a country means running it in the best way for all and not just collecting votes with favors." In a way, she found it a political advantage to be an Agnelli "because people say she doesn't need the money, so she won't steal." In another way, it was a handicap because "the Republicans consider themselves progressive, it isn't the image they wanted. But they accepted me because I'm a worker. I really am."

Tall, very attractive, self-confident, she could intimidate in a society where public discourse is so often to adorn or to dissemble. She called her approach being "brief and very down to earth." She bemoaned the dearth of Italian women in politics, calling them "lazy." Once, addressing a feminist meeting, she was told, "You're not a real feminist, you're a capitalist."

"Oh, yes, I am," she answered. "I've been discriminated against too. I own just as many shares of Fiat as my brother, but nobody would ever think of making me president of the company, because I'm a woman."

Her bluntness, and even more her air of self-assurance and command, give her an insidious kind of influence. Italy is not ready to accept women as leaders, but women cannot be ignored any longer. Suni Agnelli is one of those who have opened a breach.

There isn't an Italian identikit. For one thing, the people don't have much confidence in statistics. For another, they are more curious about what others think than what the average is (the private truth?), so polls tend to concentrate on attitudes. Not surprisingly, they show passionate dedication to both tradition and change. "La mamma" reigns but doesn't rule. Italian feminists (they call themselves *streghe*, "witches") formed the most militant and widespread of all the European women's movements, reaching even into villages, factories, and slums as well as more educated, modern levels of society. The movement is not well organized, except at the lowest levels of neighborhood, school and such. Yet it can bring tens of thousands into the streets to demonstrate for vigorous prosecution of rape and for laws to punish sexual molestation or to legalize divorce and abortion. Once the laws were passed, prophets of moral turpitude were amazed to see how little use was made of the new rights.

A survey by political scientist Gabriella Calvi showed that 86 percent of adults felt family unity "must be defended at all costs," 76 percent considered children "too much of a responsibility," and 57 percent pronounced "family honor" as coming before the rights and interests of its individual members. Sixty-seven percent wanted the police to intervene more forcefully against crime and fraud, and admitted they made ends meet by some kind of cheating or illegality.

Twenty percent scarcely bought anything, rejecting or never entering the consumer society, and the next largest group, 15 percent, never stopped buying and showing off. Despite the proliferation of supermarkets, most people did their shopping at the first store they came across and did not bother to compare prices or quality—what sociologist Giuseppe De Rita calls the old habits of the big village. Asked to rate their confidence in a list of eighteen institutions or establishments, over 80 percent listed family, scientific research and medicine at the top, in that order, and big business, the lira and the political parties (26.6 percent expressed trust) at the bottom, in that order. The army, the judicial system and the laws were in the middle, winning the faith of half or a little more. The list of activities or ideas in which people had faith started with work, 85 percent, and ran with descending appeal through progress, friendship, study, marriage, loyalty, equality, patriotism, religion and reform, next to last with 58.6 percent. The very last, much lower but nonetheless a startling 26.2 percent, was revolution.

As in northern Europe, Italy's birthrate is falling, half of what it was in 1931, and the death rate has been stable for a generation. The population is aging. People say they are paying more attention to personal grooming and how they dress, and strive for individualism with less concern for political and social issues. Yet 91 percent surveyed by Calvi said they wanted "more energetic and decisive political figures." Perhaps Italian leaders, treading water with so much splashing, represent their people's ambivalent feelings about politics. There is a lively revival of interest in traditional cooking, and yet an assertion that there is no nostalgia for the past. Clearly, Italy has been going through a widespread transition that it both welcomes and fears.

The economy is the key. It has changed dramatically, forcing everything else either to adapt or suffer decline. De Rita argues that the
"Italian disease" is really hypochondria, a phantasmagoric reaction to
the strains of solid growth. The organism is functioning, though the
metabolism is uneven and the head and the body often pull in different
directions. After the problems from outside, the energy crisis and the
years of domestic terrorism, it is the old internal problems rooted in the
country's history which matter now—the Mafia, corruption, selfishness, financial crime. None of these words ends in "ism," De Rita notes,
meaning they are not rooted in intellectual concepts but habits which
sprang from the old way of life.

Like everything else, the economy is a study in contrasts. In the 1970s
an extraordinary 500,000 houses were built each year in a country that
always suffered from lack of adequate shelter. Three hundred thousand
new businesses were established in a decade (of course not all of them
were well managed and viable enough to survive). But the nonproductive "head" on the economic body, the government and public administration, was growing just as fast. Its personnel increased by 31.6
percent in the decade, a vast drain on the economy. The government's
budget deficit soared to absorb 17 percent of the gross national product,
compared to 2 or 3 percent in other parts of Europe. Such borrowing
and spending kept interest rates and inflation high.

Nobody quite knows the unemployment figures, because great numbers of people have both a registered and unregistered job, so many
who are receiving unemployment and disability benefits are actually
working unreported. In 1983, 40 percent of the labor force of the region
of Basilicata were listed as invalided pensioners. Naples is the world's
largest producer of leather gloves, but not a single glove factory is listed
among Neapolitan businesses. The determined small entrepreneurs of
Brescia in the north made so much specialty steel in small, unrecorded
mills, therefore without the burden of taxes and social security costs,
that Italy's Common Market partners complained angrily about the
flood of unfair competition with their vast, ailing steel industries. It was
as though the Bresciani with their backyard furnaces had figured out
how to succeed in making Mao Tse-tung's "great leap forward," which
was so disastrous for Communist China. In 1987, Italy changed its
statistics to include estimates of the unreported "parallel economy,"
putting it ahead of Britain as an industrial power, and fifth in the non-
communist world.

Everybody knew what was needed in theory, but practice was much harder. Government spending had to be cut on nonproductive projects. Companies had to become more competitive by cutting back on excess work force and imposing penalties for absenteeism. Favoritism and clientism had to be ended. The indexation of wages had to be reduced to lower automatic inflation. Agriculture, left to seed in the years of the "Italian miracle" when peasants streamed to city jobs, had to be revived. In short, austerity, productivity, and efficiency had to be imposed to cure the bloat of years of indulgence which had kept the DC in power by providing something for everyone. The Organization for Economic Cooperation and Development reported in 1982 that "Italy has an ungovernable public system and therefore an unforeseeable budget deficit. But its income and living standard are steadily progressing." The "seven plagues" of Italy were listed as unemployment, bankruptcy of public services, near bankruptcy of big firms in both public and private sectors, galloping inflation, excessive public spending, tight money and high interest rates, and a surfeit of scandals.

There were still pockets of intense poverty, but Italy prospered as never before and the problem was to digest it and achieve a steadier, more balanced base. There were still flagrant, wanton inequities with displays of wealth that would make a robber baron blush. But many millions of Italians had moved from the subsistence level to participation in the productive process and were ready and eager to keep on moving up. Literacy was almost complete. The universities were burgeoning—too much for some, who worried about lowered standards. But for the first time in the country's long history, education was no longer the preserve of a small elite. The Mezzogiorno, the impoverished, backward south, was still far behind, but it had thriving new industrial centers at Taranto and Pomigliano d'Arco near Naples.

Masses of southerners who had flocked to work in the north were beginning to be integrated. In the 1960s, when all of northern Europe was recruiting foreigners from southern Europe to man newly throbbing industries and expanding services, northern Italy recruited from southern Italy. The problems were similar at first. Uneducated, disoriented newcomers, with bundles and cardboard suitcases bound with twine, packed the second-class compartments of express trains to seek work. They crowded into unfriendly hostels, or built new slums where at least there was some sense of neighborhood among strangers. Ghettos are not only the result of discrimination, social or economic. They also spring from an attempt to maintain a minimum of familiarity, of social life, where everything outside is alien.

But gradually the strangeness wore off. Some went home with their nest egg, others settled in. Their dialects were different, and the southerners were usually smaller and darker than the people of the plains and Alpine approaches. Yet they were all Italians after all. There is an important difference for Italy in the mass migrations, an easier future than for countries like Britain, France and Germany, where the immigrants' race and totally different culture portend a dilemma of national identity for coming generations. The ironic, in a sense cruel, measure of the Mezzogiorno's advance was that after being a source of emigration for centuries, it was in turn attracting poor immigrants from beyond the sea. Nearly half a million Tunisians and other Africans moved in to do the low-paid, backbreaking jobs left behind by Italians.

Italians say the north produces the wealth and Rome spends it, mainly on the south. It is a grievance, but not really a source of friction. Nationhood has progressed enough to provide an awareness of urgent national interest in advancing the poor regions too. Comparison with the European Community's pious but ineffective regional development programs makes the contrast clear. European visionaries understood that to make a real community, member nations would have to accept a redistribution process to help less favored areas, as states in the United States receive federal funds according to perceived need. But the European vision was never realized.

More perhaps than any Western European country, Italy demonstrates the inseparable linkage of culture, politics and economics. For political reasons, the south has to be developed or it will drag the whole country down. For economic reasons, the state has to take responsibility with government projects and subsidies because the market structure will not support adequate investment in the area. For cultural reasons, the money flows as though through a seine into the sea because the long-victimized south has no tradition of enterprise, an extraordinary resilience but little productive vitality. Italy's ambition now is to become a fully valid, effective partner of its co-members of the European Community. All sense of imperial posturing was strung upside down along with Mussolini. Italy, like West Germany, has an emotional and psychological as well as a practical need to belong to a consciously European family.

Italy turned inward during the decade of terrorism and the energy crisis, which brought marvels of output to make up for the unavoidable leap in imported-oil bills. But as the 1980s began to pass, the country took an interest again in playing a foreign policy role commensurate with its station in Europe. Italian soldiers joined French and American troops in trying to pacify Beirut after the Israeli invasion of Lebanon in 1982. Italy joined Germany, Britain and more reluctant Holland and Belgium in accepting American nuclear missiles capable of reaching the Soviet Union so as to offset and, if possible, force away the new arsenal of Soviet missiles targeted on Western Europe. Early in the 1980s, Italian Foreign Minister Emilio Colombo teamed with German Foreign Minister Hans-Dietrich Genscher to press for a new momentum toward European unity.

Once again, the Italians have a keen sense of Europe as the heart of civilization and of their role in its defense. They are accustomed to variety, diversity, family quarrels. Knowing their own faults, they are not such stern judges that they have trouble accommodating the failings of others. They make good Europeans.

GREECE
Glorious Legend, Turbulent Country

GREECE IS A LEGEND AND A COUNTRY. The two meet, mingle, but do not merge. The legend is the fount of humanist history and an unsurpassed aesthetic of naturalism. This heritage was lost until the late Renaissance and the Enlightenment in Western Europe rediscovered the classics, and it was not restored to the Greeks until the early nineteenth century when they struggled to throw off their Turkish overlords. Nonetheless, it is right to consider Greece the birthplace of European civilization with its focus on human individuality. No other civilization celebrated the human condition—its tragic and comic dimensions, its unbridled passions and capacity for reason, its ability to create and to destroy—as the ancient Greeks did. Death, or rather the presumed life after death, was the centerpiece of Egyptian culture. Other early civilizations seemed to fear nature and concentrate on trying to appease it.

The earliest known European art, the cave murals which survive in France and Spain, show that as long as 25,000 years ago men had developed the refinement of eye and the skill of hand to produce artistic marvels. But they portrayed the animal world, never showing human beings, although they must have been able if they chose. Only the Greeks confronted nature with exuberance and joyous confidence in being human, reveling in the challenge of adventure, honoring this life on earth and determined to make the most of it. Their gods were immortal, but they were as fallible and unpredictable as human beings.

177

Modern Greece draws deep pride from this heritage and reflects a little, but not much, of its inspiration. It shows in the intensity of emotions, the delight in the pleasures of life and the rage at its frustrations. But it is an essentially Levantine society, permeated with mystique rather than classical rationalism. Eleni Vlachou, a firm-willed, outspoken editor, insists, "We don't belong to the West, we don't belong to anybody. We *are* European." The Greeks insist too much on what others take for granted because, in candor, they suspect what a distinguished, highly cultivated doctor said of his compatriots, "We are all a bit immature, a bit Middle Eastern, not fully European." A Western diplomat metaphorically placed Greece "somewhere between the Balkan Peninsula and the Middle East." There is among the people a sense of backwardness, of impotence and a certain incompetence in dealing with the countries which drew on the legacy of Greece and went on to become great powers. The Greeks look to shrewd maneuver to make up for what they feel they lack. "We are quick, charming, agile," Mrs. Vlachou added, "but we're not clever in the northern sense, the sense of having solid judgment."

The ancient history, like its monuments, adorns the daily scene but does not live in it. The past that weighs on Greece is that of the Orthodox Christian empire ruled from Constantinople and then the four centuries of Turkish rule. Modern Greek history began in 1830 when at last independence was achieved. But the country is only emerging from a rural, village society where the family and the Church provided the social services expected nowadays from the state. Greece is still far behind industrialized Europe, struggling with the old problems of development and urbanization when most of Western Europe is facing the problems of a new era of high technology, decentralization and awakened concern for the environment.

The ugly blanket of pollution over Athens is visible from the neighboring hills as a sharp line across the ardent blue sky. Greek politics are tinged with archaic, almost tribal dogmas and traditions. A third of the population now live in Athens, Piraeus and Salonika, but most Greeks retain close ties with the countryside. An Athenian woman whose parents fled from Smyrna (now Turkish Izmir) after World War I bemoaned her "homelessness" because, unlike all her friends, she could not cultivate her roots in an old family village. The economy produces poorly, straining to compete. Greek officials argue fervently that the Common Market should adjust more generously to their exports, that it is absurd for the Dutch to grow fruits and vegetables in hothouses when they might be bought from Greece. But the French point out that Greek oranges, for example, are too unevenly selected, too small and dry and spotty to capture the choosy, well-supplied French market.

Yet the country still produces great artists, especially in the cinema and theater, world-class traders, resorts in the most refined modern taste. Greeks are in love with their landscape, their language, one another, even as they quarrel and complain. "Did you ever see such a sun? Nowhere in the world is there such a beautiful golden sun, such a beautiful country," Eleni Bistika, an intense, aggressive journalist, pronounced proudly as the sun sank into a green sea off the Peloponnesus. There is a special Greek scenery, craggy and sere, harsh to an eye accustomed to more gentle climates but whose beauty lies in its forbidding austerity, the restraint of its color to endless nuances of gray-green and ocher. Like the Greek ideal of beauty, which prizes strong, noble line and eschews prettiness and frills, the landscape demands to be taken on its own dramatic terms. Though millions of tourists flock to Greece each year to warm their chilled northern bones and bronze their pale skins, it is not a clement land. It can be penetratingly cold in winter and stifling hot in summer, but there is always something lovely to look upon. The climate and the terrain help to explain the extravagance of the Greek temperament and its embrace of rapture.

Mainland Greece is mostly mountainous, dotted with inaccessible villages clinging to the rocks. The Peloponnesus, really a huge island cut from the rest of the country by the narrow gorge of the Corinth canal, is greener, more serene, with fertile fields edged with stands of pine, cypress and olive trees, perfumed with jasmine. The third part of the country is the islands, two thousand of them strewn across the Aegean Sea in the east and the Ionian Sea in the west. Greece is not large, 51,000 square miles, the size of New York State. But it has 8,000 miles of coastline, full of bays and beaches. The Greeks have always been seafarers; they think of the water as part of their land and of themselves as a nation more than as a state. The population is 10 million, but people speak of 18 million Greeks, laying claim to the emigrant diaspora as though they were wanderers temporarily away from home.

Ethniki, the origin of the word *ethnic*, also means "national" in Greek. The demotic language, the contemporary tongue, has many words derived from ancient Greek, but it has changed to the point where it is not easily comprehensible to those who learned from the classics. Still, it is part of the Greeks' pride that their ancestors gave not only a culture but the source of so much of the Western world's vocabulary. It gives them a sense of being more articulate than others.

With such a long history of habitation and so many invasions, Greece has produced a mixture of peoples who tend to be dark, curly-haired and often handsome. It is said that in the isolated valleys of Epirus, in the mountainous northwest, the people are nearest to the old stock, tall, often fair and blue-eyed. But the crowds in the cities look and behave like Levantines, sipping endless cups of coffee, eating crunchy salads with white feta cheese and lamb kebab or succulent fresh grilled fish. When the weather is fine, the restaurants and cafés spill out of doors, sidewalks and even streets jammed with tables. The Greeks are gregarious, talkative, gesticulating people, quick to enjoy life and quick to grieve. The heavily resinated wine known as retsina and the national anise-flavored drink, ouzo, are heady, but Greeks are so naturally lively that they seldom seem intoxicated. The tavernas, which stay open very late, resound with the shrill whine of the bouzouki and the thump of traditional dances, usually performed in a circle and often only by men.

Athens is a city of hills, with a few large squares and a lot of steep, winding streets. The oldest quarter, the Plaka, has narrow, cobbled paths impassable to automobiles, and it has become the center of a noisy, rather bohemian, strictly informal nightlife. In front of the yellow-stuccoed parliament building, formerly the royal palace, the guards strut in the old costume of Greek soldiery, a tasseled red hat, a bolero jacket, a short, pleated and widely flared white skirt, long white woolen stockings and slippers with pointy toes and pompons. They are a symbol of patriotism and virile manhood. Shops display the bright village embroideries, but only tourists buy them. Greek women wear modern European clothing, or dusty black. Jewelers still turn out the traditional pieces in gold and silver filigree, essentially an Oriental style, but a few have become world-famous with modern designs inspired by the classical displays in museums.

Men finger short strings of worry beads, of silver or amber or agate, as they talk, even in up-to-date computerized offices, and they smoke the local black tobacco. Relatively few women have broken out from traditional segregation and reserve, whether in the hard drudgery of the villages or the pampered, over-adorned life of high society. They are meant to be domestic or decorative, not to involve themselves in business, professions or public affairs. The exceptions tend to be extraordinarily talented and energetic, like the indefatigable newspaperwoman Eleni Bistika or the actress-turned-politician Melina Mercouri. A warm, confident, overwhelming woman, Mercouri is aware of her beauty but determined to make the most of her great intelligence. She became Minister of Culture in the Papandreou government and used the job to organize festivals, revivals of the classical theater, folk music concerts and exhibits to enhance national pride. Being Greek can be something of a profession in itself.

The early history of the Aegean world focused on the islands. They were open to the influence of Asia Minor in the Neolithic Age, and it was with the arrival of unidentified Asian invaders by sea that the Bronze Age began, about 2600 B.C. They brought new techniques, better ceramics as well as bronze, the cart and new crops of wine grapes and olives. This infusion led to a flourishing pre-Hellenic civilization in Crete, which also drew on its exchanges with Egypt and Phoenicia—a connection that profoundly influenced the first Hellenic civilization, which appeared in the early Bronze Age when the Mycenaeans emerged, mingling Hellenic and Cretan influence. The wars of the many small monarchic states based on a largely maritime economy are recounted in *The Iliad*.

The expedition against Troy is dated at about 1230 B.C., and the story gave rise to the Greek pantheon and the heroic tradition. There was a dark period after the last great Indo-European invasion at the end of the twelfth century B.C., with a regression in culture and taste and the rise of a military aristocracy. The unconquered peoples moved toward Asia Minor, which became the center of Hellenism. Attica, with its capital of Athens, was the preserve of Ionians from the west, people who had moved down from the Danube lands in the previous millennium.

The Greek golden age began at the end of the ninth century B.C. Homer's saga developed a sense of Greek religious and cultural patrimony, and pan-Hellenism was celebrated at the Olympic games, held in 776 B.C. for the first time. Olympia, located in cool groves beneath ruddy hills, was not a city but a special site reserved for the contests of strength, speed and skill and for the religious ceremonies that intermittently brought the warring Greeks together. It is on the northwestern side of the Peloponnesus, closer to Sparta in the south than to Athens

on the southeastern tip of the mainland. The games developed a community of language and culture, but not of politics.

Sparta was an austere, ostensibly egalitarian society based on military
power. Athens developed an aristocracy and a mercantile economy,
sending its younger sons to found colonies farther and farther away as
its population grew and its land lost fertility. Thriving trade led to the
creation of money, about 680 B.C. Other cities also sent colonists, to
the Nile, to Asia Minor, to Italy, to northern Burgundy and southern
Gaul, to Spain, and the colonies spun off new colonies so that the
Mediterranean became a "Greek lake."

The rising wealth and importance of the merchants and artisans, and
the greed of the aristocracy, which drove their peasants to revolt,
brought political instability. War leaders, supported by the bourgeoisie,
who demanded reforms and the abolition of debts, were elevated to
power by the angry populace. They ruled as "tyrants," that is to say
without the legitimacy of birthright, but it was an age of prosperity and
great cultural development for many cities, Athens, Argos, Corinth,
Lesbos, Miletus, Syracuse, Ephesus and others. Many of the new rulers
were builders and patrons of the arts, and their cities flourished. But
some established hereditary and repressive dynasties, and they gave the
word *tyrant* its modern meaning.

Power struggles brought a need for mediation in Athens, and people
turned to a man reputed for his wisdom, the merchant Solon. He
brought important reforms, including breaking up the biggest estates,
ending enslavement for debt and framing a constitution assuring direct
political participation to all free adult male citizens. Thus was democracy born with the advent of Solon in 594 B.C. But a new danger came
from the East in the middle of that century with mounting Persian
expansionism. The Persian king Darius was defeated at the Battle of
Marathon in 490 B.C. His successor, Xerxes I, sent a vast expedition of
men and ships to renew the campaign against Greece. Athens, under
Themistocles, had built a major fleet but it was unable to save the
capital, which was emptied of its people and burned to the ground. The
Persians defeated Sparta, but the Athenian fleet struck back and routed
the Persians at Salamis.

Flushed with victory and with the largest surviving fleet, the Athe-
nians converted the Delian League, organized for defense in the Persian Wars, into an Athenian empire. Victory revived prosperity, and
the ruler, Pericles, made further major reforms that consolidated Athe-

nian democracy, literally rule by the people. It nourished a creative explosion of art and thought, the golden age of Socrates, Anaxagoras, Plato, Aristotle, Aeschylus, Sophocles, Euripides, Aristophanes, Thucydides, Xenophon, Phidias. The great, enduring contribution of Greece to Western civilization came in a remarkably short time, and it came mostly from Athens.

Athenian imperial preeminence was so strong that it angered allies and frightened other maritime cities. The challenge came with the very achievement of glory. Sparta was the leader against Athens, even seeking help from the King of Persia, Artaxerxes II, in return for the cession of its holdings in Asia Minor. The Peloponnesian War lasted from 431 to 404 B.C., but fighting among the Greeks, with constantly shifting alliances, continued until the Roman conquest in the second century B.C. The warfare prevented economic, political and institutional consolidation. The cities were too small to continue as effective centers of administration, and the fragmentation and hostility of the states too great to achieve a decisive result. Macedonia in the north had been unified into a monarchy and grown wealthy with its gold. Its ambitious and skillful King Philip II set out to expand his realm. After his decisive victory over Athens and its ally Thebes in 338 B.C., he became the acknowledged master of Greece. But he allowed the Greek cities to retain their political independence in the Corinthian League, which they formed with the exception of Sparta, holding for himself the role of supreme military commander. He encouraged Hellenic unity and a new drive eastward, backed by the economic advantages of pacification within his domain.

Philip's son Alexander III, who had studied under Aristotle, took up the campaign with a burst of energy and extraordinary success. When he died, aged thirty-three in 323 B.C., the Greek empire had been established in the Greek lands and extended into Egypt and eastward to Persia and the Indian subcontinent all the way to the Indus River in the heart of what is now Pakistan. He became known as Alexander the Great and it is said that he wept at his last victory because there were no more worlds to conquer. His lieutenants fought over the young ruler's enormous heritage. After forty years, it was divided into three large kingdoms, Greece, Macedonia, and Egypt and the Asian provinces under Seleucus, son of Antioch. Important new cities were founded as centers of Hellenism in the conquered lands, among them Alexandria, Antioch and Pergamon, and the sciences developed, the discoveries of Archimedes, Euclid and Hippocrates broadening the radiation of Greek culture.

This time the rising counterpower was in the West. Rome had taken Macedonia, and in 146 B.C. Greece became a Roman province under the Macedonian proconsul. During the first century before Christ, the Greek cities and Ptolemaic Egypt submitted one after another to Roman suzerainty. But the Pax Romana encouraged the spread of Greek civilization, supporting its luster with Roman feats of engineering and administration, advancing its aesthetic in the realms of art, philosophy, history and literature. Hellenism had become dependent on Rome, and the decline of the Roman Empire brought it down. Emperor Theodosius outlawed paganism in A.D. 381. The last Olympic games, held in A.D. 393, and the closing of the great academies founded by Plato and Aristotle symbolized the end of ancient Greece.

The split of the Roman Empire into eastern and western domains, the Byzantine and the Roman, left Greece as part of Byzantium. It suffered repeated waves of invasion, Slavic, Albanian, then Arabs in the ninth century, Bulgarians in the tenth, Normans and Venetians in the eleventh and twelfth. At the end of the Fourth Crusade in 1204, Venice dominated the islands. Continental Greece was divided into feudal vassaldoms subject to Constantinople. The capital fell to the Turks in 1453, completing the destruction of the Byzantine Empire and its submission.

Islamic law recognized the religious and communal autonomy of Turkey's subject people, so the Greeks continued to take spiritual guidance from the patriarchate at Constantinople. The people were reduced to serfdom. Periodic revolts erupted whenever the Turks were busy at war with European powers, but they were repressed and the country slumped into a long stupor of poverty and ignorance. A small group of clergy, landowners and traders in Constantinople prospered by cooperating with the Turks. An even smaller closed caste of Greek aristocrats in Phanar, a section of Constantinople, offered their services to the Ottoman Empire and went out to help rule the provinces, more or less as viceroys. Corrupt, oppressive and, worst of all, considered traitors to their kind and agents of the enemy, the Phanariots were deeply hated, though they won concessions from the sultan which helped prepare the Greeks for struggle.

Because the Turks used the Greek church as an institution of rule, the priests became political as well as spiritual leaders. The fight for independence was launched from the monastery of Aghia Lavra, where Archbishop Germanos of Patras blessed the insurgents' banner, bearing the cross, in 1821. Intellectual revival and national awakening had developed as the impact of the eighteenth-century Enlightenment and the French Revolution spread to the Greeks. The Ottoman Empire had begun to decay, and while Greece was ravaged by occupying forces, the sympathies of Western Europe were aroused. More knowledgeable and more stirred by the cultural debt to the ancients than contemporary Greeks themselves, romantics came to help the small nation. England's Lord Byron died in 1824 during the long siege of Missolonghi, which ended only when the defenders blew themselves up along with their arsenal.

Finally, Greek independence was formally recognized by the European powers in the London Protocol of 1830. But the country was obliged to rely on a protector, necessarily a naval power. Sir Edmund Lyons, the British Minister to Athens, said bluntly that Greek independence was inevitably a myth. The Mediterranean sea powers in those days were Britain and Russia, and, he proclaimed, "since Greece can't be Russian, it must be British."

Like so many other new states in the nineteenth century, Greece chose a German princeling for its king because Germany was not yet a nation-state, and so not a power to threaten the cherished ideal of independence. Otto Wittelsbach of Bavaria mounted the throne in 1833 at Nauplia. The capital was moved to Athens the following year. Reigning as King Othon, he entered into constant disputes with his subjects who sought foreign patronage for their various factions. He courted popular support with his expansionist view that his kingdom was only part of Greece, and that true nationhood required restoration of the Byzantine Empire, with Constantinople as its capital.

But the powers of Europe opposed Greek campaigns of conquest, and the country was too weak to pursue its ambitions. After the Crimean War, the foreign-backed parties dissolved in the general disgust of Greeks for their having failed to exploit the situation. The King was also blamed. A new generation had arisen, influenced by the liberal ideas gaining in other parts of Europe, and by the upheavals of 1848. These factors, and the lack of a royal successor professing the Orthodox religion, led to a coup which deposed the King in 1862.

The European powers, who were determined to pick the new king and agreed he should not be from a reigning dynasty, chose the seventeen-year-old Danish prince William George, of the Glucksburg dynasty. He became King George I. The British backed him and returned the Ionian islands to Greece on condition they be neutralized. George also established a tie to Russia by marrying the Grand Duchess Olga in 1866.

A constitution, based on the liberal Belgian charter of 1831, firmly limited the rights of the monarchy. But again, turbulent Greek politics did not really change. Corruption remained the rule of the game. Emigration soared. The army sulked. It could not get the funds to strengthen Macedonia and worried about the forces of Serbia and Bulgaria. In 1909 there was another military coup. The officers had no political program, and called on the Cretan liberal Eleutherios Venizelos, the outstanding Greek statesman of the modern era, for guidance. He accepted on condition that the officers dissolve their Military League and leave politics. The new constitution brought no basic reforms in the system but permitted improved administration, the spread of education and strong leadership. Venizelos continued to dominate Greek politics almost until his death in 1936, though he was controversial.

Greece was on the winning side in World War I, but it suffered heavy losses. Venizelos, backed by Britain and France, had taken the country into the war against the opposition of King Constantine I, the successor to King George. Partisans of the exiled King resented it, as did many people who objected to continued foreign dictation. But Venizelos was dreaming of a Greece "on two continents and five seas," and he directed all his military and diplomatic efforts to achieve it. In two years at the postwar negotiating table in Paris, Venizelos gained much territory, but the Greek people were tired of war and wanted demobilization. He did not receive the hero's welcome he expected on his return to Athens, and instead, the new elections which he called turned on the issue of Constantine's return to the throne. Venizelos lost and himself went into exile.

Meanwhile, a nationalist regime had taken over from the collapsed Ottoman dynasty in Turkey. In July 1921 a Greek army of 100,000 was sent to attack the forces of Kemal Atatürk, and after false reports of victories joyously received in Greece, it was ordered to push on to the new Turkish headquarters, and later the capital, at Ankara. After a long stalemate, it led to a rout. The Greeks had vastly overreached and were forced to flee for their lives, civilians whose ancestors had lived in Anatolia for 2,500 years as well as soldiers.

It was another national disaster, and brought another change of monarch and government. King Constantine abdicated in favor of his son, George II, and the military gained strong influence in politics. A new treaty wiped out major Greek gains, to the bitter disappointment of the people, who felt they had been encouraged by their allies to attack and then had been abandoned to defeat. There was a massive, brutal exchange of populations, with 1.3 million Greeks moved west and 380,000 Turks moved east. Venizelos regained the premiership in 1924; altogether he was in and out of office eight times and frequently in exile. It was a period of turmoil which brought a series of military dictatorships. The terrible problem of resettling the refugees, the effects of the Great Depression, and the incapacity of the country to develop economically prolonged the instability.

New elections in 1935 produced no majority and no solution. Greece turned again to the military, in the person of General Ioannis Metaxas, who had been Minister of War. He moved swiftly to establish a dictatorship, outlawing strikes and proclaiming a state of emergency. He even took the title "Archigos," which like Hitler's "Führer," Mussolini's "Duce" and Franco's "Caudillo," means leader. His ultraconservative, nationalistic regime resembled those of Spain and Italy, with special uniforms and patriotic songs.

However, Greece steered away from the Axis powers. Italy was seen as the great danger, along with pro-German Bulgaria and Yugoslavia. So Metaxas looked to Britain's Mediterranean naval power for protection, while pronouncing neutrality. On April 27, 1939, Italy invaded Greece's northwestern neighbor, Albania, or, rather, walked in, and then in late 1940 invaded Greece. The Greeks put up a strenuous resistance, moving to the rugged mountains. The Italians were stalled. Metaxas maneuvered to hold off Hitler, but he died in January 1941. The new Premier, Alexander Koryzis, welcomed direct British intervention. Only about half the promised force of 100,000 troops arrived, however, and only part of the supplies. From the German point of view, it was nonetheless a strategic danger because from Greek bases the British could bomb the Romanian oil fields at Ploesti and interrupt supply lines. The German forces responded massively. The Greek armies were forced to surrender and King George II fled, to establish a government-in-exile in Cairo.

The Germans occupied Athens and other major cities, the Bulgarians moved into Thrace and part of Greek Macedonia, and the Italians held other regions. But the occupiers did not try to administer the entire country, leaving two-thirds of the territory and half the population outside their effective authority. There was no organized royalist resistance, as in Yugoslavia with General Draža Mihajlović, and the strongest insurgent forces came under Communist leadership after the German attack on the Soviet Union in 1941 drew the Communists into the resistance.

The situation was chaotic. The British imposed a blockade, and as Greece had been importing nearly half its wheat, many people starved during the winter of 1941–42. The resistance operated mostly in the mountainous areas, drawing support not only from leftists but also from republicans and former opponents of the Metaxas dictatorship. The Communist leader was Nikos Zachariadis, soon captured and held in the German concentration camp at Dachau throughout the war. Before the war the party had been feeble. But once it took a strong nationalist position against the Axis, it could appeal to Greek patriotism. George Siantos led the party during the war years until Zachariadis returned after liberation.

The British were determined to remain the leading Mediterranean power after the war and therefore to head off the rise of a pro-Soviet base for the future regime. So they continued to support the exiled King and government, but their political and military needs were in conflict because the Communist guerrillas were a stronger resistance force than their non-Communist rivals. The situation worsened when the Communists (EAM) managed to seize quantities of Italian army equipment after Italy's surrender in 1943. They quickly launched an offensive against the rest of the resistance, the start of the civil war which lasted until 1949, well after the Allied victory in 1945. The internecine war was of immense brutality, with the partisans driven to recruiting by intimidation and terror, as happens in guerrilla wars.

Behind the fierce Greek quarrels, however, big-power politics were operating to change the situation. Even before the famous October 1944 agreement between Churchill and Stalin on dividing influence in the postwar Balkans, Moscow apparently decided to concede British dominance in Greece. A Soviet emissary, Colonel Gregory Popov, was sent to meet with the EAM in July 1944. They agreed to put all partisan groups under a new government-in-exile headed by George Papandreou, which meant under the direct command of British General Sir Ronald Scobie, the senior Allied commander in the area.

The British hurried in troops, their own and emigré units. A mass demonstration took place in Athens' main square on December 3; the police fired and fifteen people were killed. Fighting broke out in almost all parts of the country. Partisan forces controlled the rural areas, isolating the government and its British supporters in the major cities. Churchill ordered General Scobie not to "hesitate to act as if you were in a conquered city where a local rebellion is in progress." Although they were undefeated, the Communists realized they lacked necessary Soviet support and agreed to an armistice, signed in February 1945. The first phase of the civil war took some twenty thousand lives.

There were eight governments between January 1945 and April 1946, all manipulated, even chosen, by the British, who determined policy. Parties, once again clustered around personalities clubhouse-style, formed shifting coalitions. All kinds of factions maintained armed bands. Banditry, an old Greek plague, spread again. People sought vengeance for the atrocities committed in the civil war. Food was short, inflation rampant, wages low. The country was racked with misery and bitterness. Elections were held in March 1946, and after a plebiscite King George II returned. Disaffection remained high and sporadic violence continued, especially in the mountains. Gradually it escalated and by the spring of 1947 the rebels under the command of Markos Vafiadis held an important strip of the countryside. The civil war was raging again. The rebels had ties with the new Communist regimes of Yugoslavia, Albania and Bulgaria and received help.

The Cold War had begun. Exhausted themselves, the British found they could no longer provide the aid needed to prop up the Greek government against the insurgents and turned to the United States. Washington was increasingly worried by Stalin's expansionism, shown on all fronts. In February 1947 the American ambassador in Athens, Lincoln MacVeagh, wrote to the State Department, "If Greece falls to communism, the whole Near East and part of North Africa as well are certain to pass under Soviet influence." President Harry Truman acted decisively. He asked Congress for an unprecedented $400 million to help Greece and Turkey. His speech on March 12, 1947, explained his reasons, in what came to be known as the Truman Doctrine. "I believe that it must be the policy of the United States to support free peoples who are resisting attempted subjugation by armed minorities or by outside pressures." This was the forerunner of the much larger Marshall Plan for aid to Europe, announced that June.

One result was that the United States supplanted the British as the protecting power and major influence on Greece. But change came only step by step as U.S. supplies arrived to build up Greek forces, as well as aid for the economy. Vafiadis found it harder and harder to fight back, using force for 90 percent of his recruitment. The peasants were turning against his bands, who infuriated them all the more by carrying off their children in hopes of growing new rebels. The Yugoslav dissident Milovan Djilas said in his *Conversations with Stalin* that in April 1948 Stalin told Yugoslav and Bulgarian leaders that the Greek insurrection was hopeless and "must be stopped, as quickly as possible." After his break with Stalin, Tito closed his border with Greece in June 1949, cutting off supplies and sanctuaries for the rebels, and the fighting ended in September.

The civil war was a greater catastrophe for Greece than defeat by the Axis had been. In addition to the toll in casualties, devastation and displacement of population, there was a legacy of outrage and hatred which still remains a factor in Greek politics. There had been many atrocities, and the people did not forget.

When the war was over, politics again focused almost exclusively on the center and the right, but in the usual fragmentary Greek fashion. The Americans took up where the British had left off, but they too were unable to solder together a stable, solid government. In disappointment, they moved their support further to the right. Meanwhile, Greece joined NATO in 1952 and made an agreement for the establishment of U.S. air and naval bases, which became strategically important for the Middle East as well as the immediate region. The conservatives at last managed consistent government under Premier Alexander Papagos, a military man who had spent most of World War II in German prison camps and disdained the usual political maneuvers. The central issue shifted to economic recovery, and important gains were made. By 1957 Greece was producing all the wheat it needed, though at the cost of reducing the traditional export crops of tobacco, cotton and fruit.

When Papagos died, Constantine Karamanlis became Premier, a controversial choice at first, but Karamanlis was a strong figure who was to endure in Greek politics. He was born in 1907, the son of a village schoolteacher. He managed to complete his education as a lawyer and then rose through the government to become Minister of Public Works. A straightforward man who won respect, he was reelected several times. His worst problem became the issue of Cyprus, which Britain had taken from the Ottoman Turks and annexed during World War I. Most of the population was Greek, the minority Turkish. The Greek Cypriots, with Athens' support, yearned to expel the British and rejoin the motherland in *enosis*, or union. Cyprus's Archbishop Makarios, a cunning, strong-willed man, became the dominant leader and kept in touch with island guerrillas trying to force the British out by terror.

There was no way the Turks would accept *enosis*, and no way the Greeks would accept the Turkish proposal to partition the island. Finally, after many conferences, there was agreement on giving Cyprus independence, which it achieved in 1960, with Makarios as President and Fazil Kücück, leader of the Turkish Cypriots, as Vice President. Britain, Greece and Turkey guaranteed independence, with each having the right to intervene unilaterally. Nobody was satisfied, and Cyprus became a roiling issue in both Greek and Turkish internal politics. Makarios, who leaned left, joined the nonaligned movement, which reinforced anti-NATO feeling in Greece.

The monarchy also remained a subject of irritable controversy, and the ambitions and hauteur of the royal family in a very poor country did not help them. The economy had improved, but to many it seemed that all the benefits were going to foreign capitalists and the new Greek millionaires. The spoils system was unchanged, and the left could argue that foreign exploiters colluding with a corrupt government were still keeping Greece down.

George Papandreou, a Social Democrat, made the argument up and down the country. He was a compelling orator with a knack for reaching simple people and a willingness to travel to the impoverished dusty villages. He had a simple message—the need for social justice. His call for pensions for old peasants, higher prices for their produce, and free health care and education touched the people's hearts, and no one disturbed the harmony by asking how he proposed to finance such programs. He won in 1964 and instituted a number of reforms in education, helping to modernize it and make it more accessible, raised the minimum price for wheat and released political prisoners. He could not possibly deliver all he promised, Greece could not afford it. Even his modest changes led to rising inflation and balance-of-payments troubles.

Fighting broke out again in Cyprus, where Makarios was impatient

for full authority. The British called in United Nations forces to separate the Greeks and Turks. Then a scandal broke about an underground group in Cyprus plotting with a group of Greek army officers to
overthrow the government in Athens and replace it with a socialist,
neutralist regime. Papandreou's son Andreas was accused of being implicated. He had lived for twenty years in the United States, becoming
an American citizen and marrying an American woman. Andreas was
a professor of economics who could use Marxist rhetoric and appeal to
the educated young and intellectuals as a new managerial type, far from
the old pattern of intriguing, greedy, backbiting politicians. George
Papandreou was seventy-six, and seemed to have made Andreas his
crown prince, vaulting him into parliament when he returned from
America and making him a deputy minister. Andreas had enemies as
well as supporters, and the opposition saw the scandal as an opportunity
to bring down George Papandreou.

This crisis bubbled for a year and broke in July 1965. All the old
arguments about the monarchy, the Americans, the corruption resur-
faced, and there was a rash of strikes and demonstrations in support of
the elder Papandreou, who again campaigned energetically. Elections
were scheduled for May 28, 1967, and the country was restive. Papandreou was expected to win, and many believed his son would soon take
over from him to turn the country sharply to the left. There were also
widespread rumors of a military plot to prevent the elections.

The generals had a contingency plan code-named Prometheus to
proclaim martial law under the King's authority in the event of armed
revolt or invasion, a plan known to NATO and the United States. This
was considered normal for a country with such a record of instability,
and similar plans existed elsewhere. On April 21, 1967, it was put into
effect, but by a small group of colonels acting on their own. Suddenly
there were tanks rumbling down the streets of major cities and troops
occupying public buildings and strategic rooftops and sealing the frontiers and the airports.

A distinguished Greek doctor, a close friend of the King, told later
how he was awakened by noises in the street in Salonika, where he
happened to be visiting. He and his wife jumped up to look out of their
hotel room window. Then they heard the soldiers singing. It was a
patriotic song of the right. "That was a tremendous relief," he said. "We
thought it might be the left, but [the song] meant it was the generals'
plan, our side." He and most people were mistaken. The colonels had

acted independently, using the King's name without his permission or that of the military chief of staff. The bewilderment lasted several days, enabling the colonels to seize power before people knew what had really happened. It also instilled a lasting belief among many Greeks that the coup had been instigated by the U.S. Ambassador.

King Constantine II, who had succeeded his father and his uncle, reluctantly resigned himself to the fait accompli. So did the generals, but they did not like the new regime and its strong man, George Papadopoulos. Papadopoulos and his handful of co-conspirators were typical of men who rose through the ranks of the Greek army. They came from poor families in small villages who found the military their only chance for social advancement. They retained the ideas of the Metaxas dictatorship absorbed in their school days, claiming they had saved the country from a Communist takeover in order to preserve religion, nationalism and morality. They knew next to nothing about government, the outside world or the economy, but they believed in order and had learned in the civil war how to use force to keep it. Greece was a creaky, disorganized juggernaut stopped by a few hands because it was on the point of running down. It was known as the cradle of democracy, true, but Greek democracy had never matured.

The colonels ordered many people imprisoned, took over the press and the radio, and dismissed judges, teachers and government officials whom they suspected of opposition. They had some initial support, particularly in the countryside, where people had always distrusted the politicians and nursed traditional, conservative values. To win peasant backing, the colonels wiped out agricultural debts, forgave loans and opened markets. But they behaved as modern fascists, enforcing petty symbols of their hatred for nonconformists, intellectuals and the educated elite. Papadopoulos was a crude stump of a man, not particularly articulate. The Greek government became an international pariah in intellectual circles.

But foreign countries did not, and could not, do anything decisive. The royal family left the country in December 1967, and the King tried to run a countercoup from Rome. It was clumsy, woefully unprepared, this time with evident CIA involvement, and it collapsed immediately. It left Papadopoulos stronger than ever, in a position to fill all major posts with his own men. Six years later, in 1973, Papadopoulos formally abolished the monarchy and had himself elected President. In the colonels' police state, he achieved it with ease.

In July 1974 events in Cyprus again provoked upheaval in Greece. The colonels backed a coup against Archbishop Makarios by the Cypriot terrorist Nikos Sampson. The idea was that Sampson would take power and then ask for union with Greece, abandoning the independence of Cyprus which the flamboyant Makarios had come to prize. Of course Turkey reacted, sending troops to protect the Turkish minority. The Greek government ordered mobilization, and there was imminent danger of war between Greece and Turkey, which would have meant another catastrophe for the ill-prepared Greeks. Commanders in the field, who would have had to face the far stronger Turkish forces, refused to obey, and the seven-year colonels' regime was deposed. Constantine Karamanlis was called back from exile in Paris to organize a new government and restore democracy.

He was received deliriously, and the rest of the world cheered. Greece was returned to honorable standing in the international community. But there was still a crisis over Cyprus. The Turks advanced to occupy over a third of the island, driving 170,000 Greek Cypriots to flee from their homes. Despite the sequence of events triggered by the defunct Greek military regime, many Greeks again blamed the United States, this time for not stopping the Turkish invasion. NATO became increasingly unpopular in Greece because people saw the major threat as coming not from the Soviet bloc but from the NATO ally Turkey. To the question of whether Greece, with its population of 10 million, would feel safer facing Turkey alone, with its population of 50 million and its large, well-equipped army, or preferred the protection of allies, the actress-politician Melina Mercouri replied, "What use were allies when the Turks invaded us?" She meant the invasion of Cyprus, but Greeks still consider it an errant part of their nation.

During the seven years of the colonels, Andreas Papandreou, in exile, had been building up a party, which he called PASOK, the Panhellenic Socialist Movement. There had never been a real socialist tradition in Greece, based on a workers' movement as in countries of Western Europe. Personality and patronage politics as usual had returned along with Karamanlis and democracy. Papandreou took the model of the Swedish Social Democrats and sought to combine it with Greek habits. He had his father's capacity for spellbinding oratory and appeal to deep yearnings for social justice and nationalism. And he had the aura of the New World, a technocrat who would know how to leapfrog Greece from its old doldrums into a modern state. He campaigned steadily and increased PASOK's vote in each succeeding election. In the assembly elections of October 1981, PASOK won enough to put Papandreou in power as Premier and head of government. His campaign attacks against both NATO and the Common Market, which Greece had joined in January 1981, caused apprehension among Greece's partners. But he did not carry out his threats to withdraw. Instead, he used them to extract ever more concessions, taking over from France the dubious distinction of being the most volatile, peevish, unpredictable member of both organizations.

Heading Greece's first Socialist government, Andreas Papandreou did make important domestic changes, though more in social than in economic affairs, and, like his father, dramatically less than he had advertised. He turned out to be something of a maverick, more moderate than he sounded, more traditional than he looked, more devious than he admitted. Businessmen said his labor laws and nationalization of banks made investment unreasonable and prevented industry from being competitive. Farmers were delighted with new support prices, almost entirely financed by $2 billion in subsidies from the Common Market. Isolated villages were given a start on new roads. Peasant women got their own pensions, instead of having to ask their husbands for money when they went to church. But politics remained bitter.

Andreas, as everyone called Papandreou, engineered a curious reversal of the usual political landscape, bringing the rural and intensely nationalist vote, normally conservative, into his leftist camp and driving many intellectuals, city people and workers toward the moderate right. And he stressed nationalism, usually the answer of the right to leftist internationalism. The polarization grew acute and angry.

The economy ran sharply downhill, with continued inflation, soaring debt and balance-of-payments problems. When an austerity program could no longer be avoided, there was a wave of strikes. Splits developed in Papandreou's party—between the dogmatic left, whom he tried to placate with Marxist noises, and the technocrats, whom he needed to make things work. No one was quite sure where he really stood, or rather, he said so many things that there was no resolution of the contradictions. The increased politicization of the administration and the economy and the renewed left-right hostility aggravated traditional inefficiency, with no effort to develop the consensus necessary for a spurt of energy and renewal.

Still, Greece was gradually changing. It had always been a contradictory country. As a French diplomat said, "Nothing is ever true and nothing is ever false in Greece." Papandreou's success was in large measure due to the country's thirst for change, but it could not be worked as quickly or as painlessly as people believed they wanted, and they did not want to give up old privileges and customs which stood in the way of modernization. The dream of most parents for their children was to get a government job, which guaranteed security and a measure of status. The country had missed the Renaissance, the Industrial Revolution, the vibrant recovery which Western Europe experienced after World War II and the 1968 student upheavals in revulsion at too much materialism. It left a certain naïve susceptibility to the kind of slogans popular in even less advanced third world countries, on top of the old Oriental cynicism. Emotion rules politics, with logic far behind, and even though they criticize themselves for it, Greeks like it that way.

The Orthodox Church, to which 98 percent of Greeks belong, is losing its grip, which was based on a static, village population. It is still deeply conservative, but even people far on the left would not dream of being married or having a funeral anywhere else. The vocabulary of both Church and state is paternalistic. Politicians talk of the schools and roads they "gave" to voters, as though they were patrons distributing largesse, not representatives. But per capita national income rose dramatically, from $300 in 1950 at the end of the civil war to $4,470 in 1980, though it has since been declining, to $3,700 in 1985, with high inflation. That is far behind Western Europe, but far ahead of all of Greece's neighbors. There are still old women who deliver milk in the villages by leading a goat from door to door and letting housewives milk it, and there are some very modern enterprises. The family structure has been kept strong despite urbanization, and as a result there is a low crime rate, though there have been episodes of urban terrorism. Superstition, pride and sensitivity mark the Greek temperament, but charm is the highest value. *Charisma* is an old Greek word which never depreciated.

So long as they do not get carried away with new nationalist adventures, the Greeks are bound to continue advancing toward the level of Western Europe. They live in the awesome shadow of their classical history, give their children the old names of legend and swell with pleasure at the thought that theirs are the ancestors of all Western civilization. But they had dropped out of it for five hundred years. The gap was too long for real continuity, for a living heritage to flower amid the sensuous marbles and glorious temples remaining from antiquity. It brings an instant sense of humiliation alongside the pride, a capacity for passionate grief alongside a joyous celebration of life. Greeks live with tremendous intensity, but not with confidence.

SCANDINAVIA
The Taming of the North

THE PEOPLE OF THE NORTH, nowadays among the most vociferous in movements for peace and disarmament, lived for thousands of years by the spear and the sword. They were inveterate fighters. They had migrated to the thawing, and later well-forested peninsulas as the last Ice Age receded, perhaps as late as 6000 B.C., when the first civilizations based on agriculture were already appearing in Mesopotamia. When they first reached the Baltic, it was still a great freshwater lake. Not until the ice pack melted further and the sea level rose did the ocean waters pour in. Theirs was a primitive fishing and hunting life. But already, more than two thousand years before Christ, they had become farmers and vigorous traders, seeking metal from distant lands for their weapons and ornaments. Their languages belonged to the Teutonic family, untouched by the Roman conquest. Until the collapse of the Roman Empire, they busied themselves raiding each other. Then they fanned out, as pirates, traders and colonizers. They moved into almost every corner of Europe and reached Asia Minor and North Africa. Their sturdy little warships were so well made that they carried the Norsemen over fierce seas to discover Iceland, Greenland and North America.

It is commonplace to believe that the rigors of the northern climate and the difficulty of survival made the people especially robust, adventurous and productive, compared to southerners grown languid with an easier life. But there is no decisive evidence. The story of mankind is a repetition of sudden explosions of energy in unlikely places, leading to expansion and the amassing of power, and then receding as others move to the forefront. The origins of civilization were in the Middle East, in Mesopotamia and Egypt. Distant China began to flourish over four thousand years ago. In the millennium before the Christian era, the dry hills of Greece supported a time of glory, followed by the emergence of civil and military genius from the swamps of Rome. The Arabs broke out of their deserts to dominate vast lands in the second half of the first millennium. The Vikings' turn came after that, in the first half of the second millennium. The focus shifted again, with the Renaissance spreading out from Italy, the reinvigoration of northern Europe, the rise of the New World in the Americas. Rigors or comfort of latitude cannot account for these waves of strength and achievement. They have never been well explained.

The large lands on the northern rim of Europe were vital centers in some periods, then lapsed into backwaters, then transformed themselves again into vanguards of a new kind of social development which radiated through much of the world. They form an integral part of the idea Europe has of itself, particularly of the idea of European modernism, with its clean design, its sense of what is harmonious and just in both the materials of life and the social order. The Scandinavian countries are peripheral to tense issues of international politics, and their art and music have seldom reached dominant influence. But they remain strong threads in the variegated European tapestry, and they left their mark on many lands.

The men of the north began to move out in the ninth and tenth centuries. Vikings traveled down the Volga and the Dnieper, founding strongholds at Polotsk, Vitebsk, Smolensk, Novgorod, Kiev, and on the Black Sea. They made their way to the rich silver mine at Menjohir in Afghanistan and to Sicily. They developed a fine craftsmanship in the metals they brought back to their lands of stone and wood. But the remains show little skill in the domestic arts, nor interest in the painting and sculpture and architecture of classical Europe. When they were at home, they spent the long winters roistering in bouts of drinking ale, telling stories and playing games, as the sagas recount. Their gods were lusty and fierce. They struck terror among the settled peoples whose lands they overran. But gradually those who stayed merged with their subjects and lost their distinctiveness. There are still many traces of the Danes in England, the Norsemen in Normandy and even of the Swedish Rus in Russia. But they are no longer links to the people living in Scandinavia, whose countries have a special sense of kinship among themselves.

Separation into distinct kingdoms came gradually, with an unending series of wars. Denmark was the first to unify its clans in defense against hostile neighbors. Norway, with its long, indented coast, was more difficult to unite. The Swedes did not develop a central power, although the most populated province of Skåne, now in southern Sweden but formerly Danish, is the origin of the name Scandinavia.

Danish poet Erik Knudsen says, "We were the last to come to Christianity and the first to leave it." He says it with a twinkle in his sky-blue eyes, explaining that he is a Marxist, not a Communist—a utopian Marxist, as he puts it. He represents both the complete transformation of Viking manhood from the cult of war and pillage and the continuity of its restiveness and love of the rugged outdoors. He retains both the feeling of a Nordic identity, which sets the Scandinavian off, and the feeling of rivalry and mild contempt which they hold for one another.

There is a love-envy among the countries. Sweden, with 8 million people, is the richest and weightiest. Swedes consider Norwegians big and rather dumb. But a Norwegian husband is a catch for a Swedish woman because he is likely to be handsome, considerate, hardworking and easy to live with. They consider Danes a bit flighty and frivolous, not really dependable. But Swedes flock to Denmark for weekends to escape the constraints of their intensely ordered lives and to bask in the sounds of laughter and spontaneous gaiety. They admire the Finns for their endurance and courage before the double rigors of the cold, dark north and the shadow of the Soviet colossus. But they look down on them as less civilized, closer to their Asiatic origins, tough, uncomplaining aliens whom they have often exploited as a source of unskilled labor. The others, especially the Danes, look up to Sweden for its skillful use of resources, its smooth organization and efficiency, its steadiness of mood. But the very stability of Swedish society, its earnestness and lack of whimsy, gives them a slight shiver. Danes go to Sweden for a tranquil holiday, and then hurry home. A permanent sense of their diversity is at the base of Scandinavian cohesion.

It was only after the first millennium A.D., more than a century later than Denmark, that the Swedish fiefdoms were united into a single kingdom under Olof Skotkonung. Becoming Christian, the realm established its first archbishopric at Uppsala in 1164. Later, Sweden absorbed Finland. At the end of the fourteenth century, Queen Margaret of Denmark united the Nordic lands in the Kalmar Union, but it could not hold them together.

Ravaging wars broke out frequently among the Scandinavians and with their neighbors until, with the fall of Napoleon, they renounced expansionism and chose neutrality. Norway, Denmark and Sweden managed to stay out of World War I; Finland was a part of Russia at the time and only gained independence after the Bolshevik Revolution. In World War II, only Sweden escaped invasion.

Despite their different experiences, and because of shared aspirations, the contemporary constellation of Scandinavia emerged from the two world wars. As a cultural, though scarcely a geographical concept, it includes Iceland, which established final independence from Denmark in 1944, and Greenland and the Faroe Islands, which remain under Danish sovereignty with local autonomy. It isn't a union, nor an alliance, nor even a common market, but it is a strongly felt association of mutual support with more intimate cooperation in many fields than the European Community provides. Perhaps its most tangible expression is SAS, the Scandinavian Airline System, which serves as the national airline of Denmark, Sweden and Norway. Its most important reflection now is an unwritten, vague understanding on security called the "Nordic balance."

When World War II ended, there was an effort to organize and seek international recognition for common defense in a "Nordic Pact." But the Norwegians and Swedes could not agree. Norway wanted to obtain Western security guarantees, and Sweden insisted on a neutral alliance. Finland did not take part in the negotiations since the Russians would have objected vigorously. They were prepared to accept Finnish independence, but on their own terms and only with the provision that Finland would aid the Soviet Union if it were attacked by the West. They wanted no joint obligations. They were so overwhelming in the area at the end of the war that they had no trouble extracting these conditions from Finland, without sending the Red Army to impose them. In the circumstances, with the Cold War intensifying, Denmark, Norway and Iceland decided to join the North Atlantic Treaty Organization. Sweden renewed its policy of heavily armed neutrality. The whole makes an intricate equation upon which all rely. The "Nordic balance" came to mean that Swedish neutrality helps protect Finland by reassuring the Russians, while Denmark and Norway, with American guarantees inside NATO, help buttress Sweden. But it is only a tacit arrangement.

These peoples who were once among the world's most bellicose are now among the leading pacifists. It is a demonstration that mentalities can change. The Scandinavians feel their own conversion as a responsibility and a mission to preach to the new barbarians who have not, in their view, yet learned the folly of war. That sense of duty stems in part from their Lutheranism, though the churches do not play a major role in the peace movements, as they do in other countries. It also stems from the modern evolution of their societies, egalitarian, welfare oriented, anti-ostentatious. They all have strong Socialist parties and an intense attachment to democracy even in its inconvenient, disruptive manifestations. In Copenhagen, a newspaper editor must debate and compromise with his subordinates before writing his editorial, with which he may not really agree. It would be "undemocratic" to impose his view. A theater director must win his cast's approval of a play he wants to do, and of his interpretation. Along with privilege and authority, individuality is leveled in the process. That produces its own form of frustration with the blandness of the societies, which have certainly produced common good, but little excitement.

In the lowering 1930s, when the rival claims of fascism and communism seemed to leave no room for liberty or justice, the American columnist Marquis Childs visited Sweden and announced with enthusiastic admiration that it had found the "middle way." It was by and large the Scandinavian way, a recognition that there was a need for the dignity of freedom and for order, for compassion and for discipline, for welfare and for enterprise. It was difficult to press for these competing goals at the same time, so there was a certain ebb and flow as the countries moved in one direction and then felt obliged to correct course when they had exaggerated. But there was a gradual advance beneath the flux, a taming and a gentling of harsh human impulses. The climate and difficult geography did not change, though modern lighting and heating and communications made them far easier to bear. The old Norsemen would not recognize the peaceable, humanistic temperament of their descendants.

It is not always easy to sort out what is basically Scandinavian and what is specific to the nations of the region. Except for Finland, their languages are virtually the same, they stem from the same Teutonic tribes, and they had the same primitive Viking past. They were late to enter Christendom; great cathedrals were being built in Italy and France when they were being converted. Lutheranism is important to them all; it brought their independence, which is why it still matters so much even though church attendance has fallen significantly. Except for Norway, they are all on the Baltic. They are all conscious, in varying degrees, of their dangerous big neighbor, the Soviets, and they all have egalitarian-minded welfare states. But Denmark, closer to the heart of the continent, is more sophisticated and concerned not to be absorbed by Germany. Sweden is in the middle, richer, and more inclined to remember its once great power. Norway looks westward, to the open sea. Finland lives in the immediate shadow of the Soviets.

All of them have accepted modern ideas about the standards of fairness, of social obligation, of how to live in a crowded world without being master or subject. Perhaps their homogeneity and their peripheral position in the great quarrels of the times have made it easier for the Scandinavians to work out new ways of organizing society, while continuing to be productive and generous. Each country went about it in its own way, at its own pace, with its own mistakes. But the paths have been parallel, certainly a contribution to the civilization of the unruly earth and to the aspirations of a divided Europe.

SWEDEN
Secure in the Nest

DESPITE SHAKESPEARE'S EVOCATION of the "melancholy Dane," it is the Swedes who tend to be mournful, as their brilliant film director Ingmar Bergman often showed. Young Swedes, gathered for a birthday party with a feast of many kinds of herring and aquavit, reacted typically when they were asked for Stockholm's current jokes. "There's nothing to laugh at," said one. "What can be funny?" said another. On that they agreed, and turned back to their food and their arguments with gusto. Swedes tend to be earnest people. They work hard, play hard, like to drink hard (though there are strict liquor laws and penalties for driving after even one drink), and they are harsh judges of human foibles. They do believe people can be improved through social effort, and their dominant Socialist Party keeps trying.

The editor of the Socialist women's magazine was campaigning at one point for a law to establish a six-hour work day. "When you consider how far people have to travel now from their home to their job, and how many women work, eight hours doesn't leave them enough time for other things, seeing friends, going to political meetings and so on," she said. "But of course, the thirty-hour week has to be spread over five days. Otherwise, most people would just work harder for four days and rush off to their country cottage for a three-day instead of a two-day weekend." But even if they had to stay in town five days, what was to prevent people from preferring a football game or extra TV time to political meetings and concerts in the two additional hours of leisure?

She accepted the question as a political problem to be tackled. "We'll have to persuade them and educate them to better habits," she said, without a moment's doubt of her own rightness.

Deteriorating economic conditions blocked the thirty-hour week, and the issue never came to a head. But the sense of almost unlimited social responsibility for individual lives did not change. There is both an enormous generosity and a nannyish quality in Sweden's approach to modern problems. Frenzy is frowned upon. Stockholm tolerates its traffic jams with patience and discipline, drivers carefully and courteously observing each detail of the law. People surge through the central city with its bright new buildings and its lovely old monuments, but they don't jostle.

Swedes talk of their sense of teamwork and their search for consensus, which implies self-restraint in order to get along. It is not so much conformity as a strong feeling of community and national identity, a willingness to make adjustments which others might consider a sacrifice of individuality so as to preserve the texture of social justice they have chosen for their society. The state is highly centralized, the legacy of an absolute monarchy which was flipped almost without transition into a determinedly democratic egalitarianism.

That heritage is quite different from Denmark's. The Swedes never had serfs after the thirteenth century. There is a landed aristocracy, a few of whom still have large estates. Titles command respect and are used without embarrassment. But most Swedes were small farmers eking a difficult living from a strikingly beautiful but reluctant land. There was massive emigration to North America in the middle and late nineteenth century, when population pressure or crop failures drove people off the land before industrial jobs were available, as was the case in other parts of Europe. The Scandinavians largely sought out similar rugged climates, settling in places like Minnesota, the Dakotas and Montana.

Compulsory education was proclaimed quite early, in 1842. It led to a proliferation of organizations, cooperatives, unions, without particularly harsh struggle, and a democracy which seemed to burgeon naturally instead of being wrested through conflict. Until recently, Sweden was the most homogeneous of European countries, all Protestant with only the Lapps in the far north and some Finns as ethnic minorities. That has changed drastically with the arrival of immigrant labor. It poses perplexing new problems for people who thought they were by their very nature above racism, and must now wonder whether the purity of attitude wasn't simply because they had never lived alongside different people. Only 5 percent of working Swedes still earn their living on the land; 83 percent of the population of 8.3 million live in and around the cities, clustered in the relatively temperate south.

The country is somewhat larger than California, only 250 miles wide but 1,000 miles long. It is as far from the northern tip to Stockholm as it is from Stockholm to Rome. Fifteen percent of the land is above the Arctic Circle. Rugged mountains cover the northeast, representing a quarter of the land area, and one-tenth more is under the lakes of the rolling southern and central plains. The warm North Atlantic current eases the climate, though the country is on the same latitude as Alaska and southern Greenland. The current makes for bright, brisk air, vivid flowers and dark greenery, but it doesn't do anything for the earth's tilt. Winters are long, with a bare glimpse of light in the north. In Stockholm, winter days last six hours and there are times when the full moon shines well above the horizon in midmorning, a strangely poetic sight. In midsummer, it is eighteen and a half hours from sunrise to sunset. Most people have some kind of country home, if only a tiny bungalow in the woods or on one of the many islands dotting the approach to Stockholm's harbor, and they flee to their gardens and boats with religious regularity.

Lutheranism with its lack of pomp and adornment suits the Swedes. But it has easily accommodated the old pagan festivals of the solstices, still celebrated with raucous joy. Midsummer Night is a time for huge parties where fresh shrimp cooked with dill are eaten after a precise ritual for peeling them, and schnapps may be drunk only after ceremonial songs and toasts with the glass held exactly at the level of the third shirt button. Everybody toasts everybody, so as to keep the party going. Buses are hired to return the guests home since no one dares to drive afterward. The winter feast is in honor of St. Lucia, the transmogrification of the goddess of light. Girls wear crowns with lighted candles. Torches and braziers set the dark streets aglow with ruddy flames, tinting the glistening snow.

There is a certain awe in the south of the small number of Swedes who still brave life in the far north and of the stubby, Asian Lapps who drive their reindeer across almost barren plains. They do not mix much. Trekking north is an adventure, not a national hobby. Swedes work in their cities and rest and play in the nearby countryside. Stockholm,

ultramodern in many ways, still has the grandeur of the capital of a
once great power. It is built along the water, in the imposing and yet
graceful Austrian style which characterizes important public buildings
all through northern and central Europe. There are narrow cobbled
streets, grand prospects, huge shopping malls. The Swedes are no
longer seafarers, but their cities embrace the ports and the inland waterways are avenues of recreation. It is now virtually impossible to become
rich in Sweden, the taxes are so high and the income differentials so
low. Yet there is no discomfort at the remaining signs of old wealth, the
royal castles and the stately banks and mansions. They are considered
part of the national heritage.

The King, Carl XVI Gustav, is powerless, his functions mainly symbolic, and he is popular. He was twenty-seven when he inherited the
throne in 1973 from his grandfather, King Gustav VI Adolph, whose
father, Gustav V, was one of the stalwart wonders of Europe who
played tennis and gadded about almost until his death at the age of
ninety-one. Carl Gustav's official portraits show him standing in stiff
protocol, sword at his side. In public, he gives an impression of slightly
awkward timidity, not a bit regal but not folksy either. He is a sports-
man, resolutely modern and informal. The personal slogan he has
taken is "For Sweden, with the times." His annual TV broadcasts from
the palace with his children and his German-born Queen Silvia are
among his countrymen's favorite shows.

Although the couple's second child was a boy, Prince Carl Philip,
born in 1979, his older sister, Princess Victoria, born in 1977, is first in
line for the throne. (A third child, Princess Madeleine, was born in
1982.) A law passed in 1980 gave women equal right of accession. When
Victoria is crowned, she will be Sweden's first reigning queen since the
dauntless seventeenth-century Queen Christina (who was not an ancestor despite the numerals in Carl Gustav's title which would make his
line appear to be ancient). The current royal line descends from Napoleon's Marshal Charles-Jean Bernadotte, who was offered the throne
and became King of Sweden in 1818. Another member of the family
was Count Bernadotte, assassinated by the Stern Gang in Jerusalem
when he was on a United Nations mission to Palestine in 1948. As a
neutral, Sweden has played an active U.N. peacekeeping role, but since
then the King's family has not been involved.

For most of its history, Sweden was embroiled in almost continuous
war. The first recorded mention of the Swedes was by Tacitus in his

Germania, but they remained almost unknown on the far fringes of European civilization. It was not until the ninth century that the Viking tribes moved east and south through the Baltic lands and Russia, raiding and trading over great distances, and still fighting among themselves in Scandinavia. In 1020, King Canute, a Dane whose father, Swejn Forkbeard, conquered England, sent the missionary St. Sigfrid of York to Christianize the Swedes.

The hardships of war and invasion provoked a sense of national resistance to other Norsemen, leading to the first Riksdag (parliament) in 1435 and an attempt to develop the country administratively and culturally. Uppsala, the ancient capital, became the site of Sweden's first university in 1477. The basic organization of the kingdom developed in response to harsh Danish rule.

For over three hundred years, the traditional enemy was Denmark. Gustavas Vasa, a young Swedish nobleman, managed to escape the Danish massacre of Swedish nationalist leaders in 1520 and returned with an army to take Stockholm and be elected King. But the cost of the campaign forced him to impose high taxes, provoking peasants and miners to rise against him. To appease the nobles, he promised them monastic fiefdoms and thus gained their support for his confiscation of Church property, the largest concentration of wealth in Sweden at the time. Denmark broke with Rome and adopted Protestantism in 1536, but Sweden moved gradually in its rejection of Catholicism, formally establishing the Lutheran Church only in 1576. The slower transition, compared with the abrupt break in Denmark, left the Swedish church with more of the medieval tradition.

Meanwhile, the decline of the Teutonic Knights left a vacuum on the southeastern side of the Baltic. The Knights had been formed as a hospital order during the Third Crusade, but they developed into a military club of German noblemen with administrative capacity. Called to subdue the heathens of Prussia in the thirteenth century, the order became a frontier government on the east, with rights of sovereignty, pushing relentlessly to enlarge its realm. Resistance arose in Poland, whose King Ladislas defeated the Knights and braked their expansion at the Battle of Tannenberg in 1410. Then the rise of the Prussian League undermined the Knights and they lost most of their lands, although it was not until the Napoleonic Wars that the order was dissolved.

As the order weakened, Swedish and Polish forces moved to seize its territory and soon confronted each other. The Swedes were victorious and continued pushing east, marching into Moscow and Novgorod at the end of the sixteenth century. They became the great regional power, stopped in Poland finally in 1655 at the Battle of Częstochowa.

Though his troops were few, drawn from a population of little more than a million, Sweden's King Gustavus Adolphus was so astute a warrior and his soldiers so skilled that he was able to hold court in Mainz and Frankfurt and saunter into Munich during the long, devastating conflict of power and religion which was the Thirty Years War.

Sweden's fortunes waxed and waned during the endless wars which enriched the nobility and ruined the peasants. At the end of the eighteenth century, it lost domination of the Baltic primarily to England and Russia, but it was not until the end of the Napoleonic Wars in 1815 that the country finally settled down to peace and the beginning of industrial development. Social strife led to parliamentary reforms and the emergence of strong labor unions in the mid- and late nineteenth century. By the outbreak of World War I, neutrality had become well-established policy and a democracy based on universal suffrage was firmly rooted.

Sweden was well endowed for the industrial age, with rich deposits of iron and other metals, hydroelectricity and forest products. The renunciation of expansionist ambitions, the country's domestic stability and avoidance of war for well over a century provided an affluent base for the welfare state it constructed when Europe's other industrial countries were torn by rival totalitarian ideologies in the 1930s.

There was a price: extremely high taxes and a bland leveling of life which dulled the prospects of excitement and adventure. But most Swedes pay it gladly, conscious of the benefits won by their transformation from a warrior nation into a modern, free but disciplined society. They have no nostalgia for lost grandeur and tend to disdain the frenetic striving of societies trying to prove themselves bigger or better or stronger or richer. They often sound smug and preachy. In any case, their own conscience is clear.

The Socialists have been in power since 1932, with the exception of the six years from 1976 to 1982 when a center-right government was in office, but that government did not change much, did not dismantle the welfare state, did not demonstrate greater vigor or efficiency. The country returned its scrappy Socialist Prime Minister Olof Palme to office in 1982. Palme was slim, rather small for a Swede, full of exuberance and concern for the world. He traveled widely, involving himself in practically everybody's quarrels and sustaining a lively interest in third world problems. In early 1986, he was assassinated on the street, walking home with his wife from an evening movie. Swedes were stunned and baffled; they had thought their moderate society was immune from the sudden, crazy violence which besets so many other countries. Failure to solve the crime, or even to establish a motive, caused upheavals in the leadership of the police and became a brooding source of self-doubt. Richard Reeves, an American journalist who looked into the totally unsuccessful investigation a year later, came to the conclusion that Swedes really did not want to know because revelations might touch off further scandals and that they preferred to put the mystery behind them.

The party's deputy leader, Ingvar Carlsson, took over the government when Palme died, and there was no change in policy or course. Sweden's keen attention to the third world may be because the Socialists have nearly run out of reform programs to introduce at home. They have reached the stage of reforming their reforms, trying to decentralize a bit and correct the excesses of past regulatory zeal. The most far-reaching, radical and controversial scheme is the Workers' Fund, which will gradually give the unions ownership control of major enterprises. This is in place of nationalizations, which Socialists elsewhere insisted upon as the antidote to raw capitalism. The Workers' Fund is to be used to buy stock. Nobody can really foresee how it will affect management, industry and the economy when it reaches the critical point of union responsibility for business decisions in a decade or so, providing there is not a reversal in the meantime. Critics fear drastic change and loss of effective enterprise. Sponsors argue that it will give workers a greater stake in productivity, as well as the right to protect their jobs.

It is an original social experiment, responding in a unique way to the old industrial relations problem of capitalism, but it is taking place at a time when industry itself has to face fundamental transformation. No society has begun to address the real problems of sustaining a labor force in the computer-robot age. Work itself, the role of a job in defining personal identity, dignity, fulfillment, will have to be reconsidered. It seems likely that unions will be a conservative drag on this vast new human task confronting a bewildered, frightened generation of youth for whom there will be many fewer jobs in manufacturing and low-skill services. Nothing in the old doctrines of socialism, nothing in Marx or

Adam Smith, offers insights into what can be expected to become a philosophical as well as an economic and social revolution. It may be that the Swedish Socialists are producing their innovation for a dying era, not for the future, as they imagine. In any event, they are proceeding gingerly, the Swedish way, in small incremental steps without dramatic upheaval. The results probably will not be apparent for many years.

The international recession in the early 1980s affected Sweden's exports, made even less competitive by high wages. The standard of living sagged, but it was still one of the world's highest, maintained by the complex series of government benefits, while the budget deficit rose to 13 percent of GNP. Ulf Adelsohn, former leader of the Moderates, which is the largest non-Socialist party, said, "Things are pretty crazy if a man is taxed so much that he can't pay his rent but the government is willing to pay him a rent subsidy to make up the difference."

There are complaints about the enormous bureaucracy. One in three Swedish workers has a government job of some kind, though only 10 percent of industry is nationalized. (Landsorganisationen), the big labor federation, has vast power, and the unions jealously guard their privileges, occasionally to the point of absurdity. A dozen teachers were once excluded from their union for taking summer courses to enhance their qualifications. They should have studied during working hours, with union approval, the leaders said. Parents who wanted to volunteer at day-care centers so as to reduce their monthly bill were not allowed to do it, on the grounds that all work must be properly paid in accordance with contracts. People chafe at the welter of rules, and they pay taxes that amount to half of the gross national product, but in return they enjoy excellent services, social harmony and a sense of fairness. Sweden has the world's lowest rate of infant mortality, but also an aging population which puts a strain on the social security system. A fifth of the population is under fourteen and another fifth is over sixty, so more than 40 percent of the people must be supported by the rest.

There is an industrial bias in the state's redistribution of wealth, however, that has so far supported entrepreneurial vigor. An individual's income can be taxed as high as 84 percent, but businessmen say Sweden is a "fiscal paradise" for their companies, which encourages investment and modernization of firms. Sweden is third in the world in the use of robots. But some small, fast-growing firms with high profits and little capital have begun to flee because of the new taxes to establish the Workers' Fund and the prospect of union domination in the future. One example was Datatronic, a computer software producer, which moved to the United States. A massive 16 percent devaluation in 1983, which infuriated Sweden's neighbors and competitors, gave an important boost to trade, which had been declining for a decade.

During the boom years of the 1960s and early 1970s Sweden imported migrant labor on a large scale, Finns but also many Turks, Greeks and other southerners. From almost complete homogeneity, Sweden suddenly became a country where one out of eight people was from another culture. To their shocked surprise, Swedes, who had so long righteously condemned racial discrimination in America and Africa, found that they were racists when it came to intermingling at home. They called the migrants "the dark-haired" and blamed them for crime, unemployment, disorder. Some landlords refused to rent to them. Some people pushed them to the back of bus queues. Ghettos formed in the dense suburban apartment complexes. The government set up administrative machinery to deal with complaints of discrimination; officials and editors thundered at the blotch on Sweden's image as a warm, humane society.

But attitudes scarcely changed. Migrants were given the right to vote in some local elections, and may be put on the national rolls for the next legislative elections as a way of giving them the power to compel acceptance. It was also, the Socialists calculated, a way to assure an important new base of votes for the left. There was a bright side to the ugly problem. Cities became much more cosmopolitan, with pizza parlors and tavernas and exotic shops to spice the familiar sameness. Reformers could only hope that eventually the Swedes will come to welcome the variety introduced to their society, since it can never return to its old monochrome existence. Simply confronting the fact has been salutary, provoking a bit more tolerance for the idea that there are troubles in the world which cannot just be legislated or organized away.

Another problem beyond their control began to weigh on Swedes as Western Europe moved to enhance its nuclear defenses. After an intense, passionate debate, Sweden voted to ban nuclear energy after the year 2010, but the 1986 Chernobyl reactor blowout in the Soviet Union buttressed demands for an earlier stoppage. There had long been ardent campaigns to establish a nuclear-free zone in Scandinavia, despite huge Soviet missile installations across the border from Finland. Peace and disarmament movements are a major Swedish occupation.

On October 27, 1981, the Soviet presence in the region surfaced dramatically on a rock not far from Sweden's main naval base, in the form of a Soviet Whisky-class submarine. Frogmen ascertained that it carried nuclear weapons, probably torpedoes. Then Prime Minister Thorbjorn Falldin called it "the most flagrant violation of Sweden's territorial integrity since the Second World War." After a humiliating ten days, the Swedes let the Russians rescue the sub. They could have folded their arms until the submariners were hungry and thirsty enough to accept the request for inspection of their craft in return for supplies. That they didn't, a Swedish ambassador said at the time, was "the inevitable response of a country of 8 million to a power of 267 million." The country looked to its defenses, but there was no question of compromising its determined nonalignment and neutrality.

The Swedish identikit is a picture of a man and a woman in their middle years, Lutheran but not churchgoers, who had lived together for a number of years before marrying, and who both work, though her job may be part-time. If they have children, they own their home. Otherwise, they have equal chances of being owners or tenants. In addition to the living room and bath, they have a room each, hot and cold water, sewers, central heating and a kitchen with modern appliances. That was not true less than a generation ago; housing has improved dramatically, from 24 percent not completely modern in 1968 to 5 percent in the mid–1980s. They are almost certain to vote in legislative elections (90 percent), and one in three has spoken up at an organization meeting, one in four has taken part in a demonstration. Though they work well while they are at it, at jobs which allow them to set their own pace and are seldom monotonously repetitive, they have a lot of free time. If a child under twelve is sick, they can take sixty days off per child per year at 90 percent pay. When a child is born, they have a choice of a year's maternity or paternity leave at 90 percent pay for nine months and then with a daily stipend of about $7. She does most of the household chores (domestic help is very rare), but he is more willing to do a share than his father was.

In their time off, they read a lot of books (78 percent of the population) and magazines (69 percent), go for a drive, work in their garden or make do-it-yourself things. Only one in three participates in some kind of sport, but nearly half the people go dancing or to the cinema. But it makes a big difference where they live, as distances are huge and the overall population density is low (20 people per square kilometer), so that city people have many advantages unavailable in rural areas.

There is agitation for some kind of law or regulation to equalize this gap as well.

The identikit couple live in a suburban apartment complex and have a cottage in the countryside which they work hard at maintaining every weekend. There is a sense of class, inherited from the old days along with property, but not much difference in the way people live because there is not much difference in spendable income. The couple talk about anonymity, dullness, emptiness of life in their comfortable society, but the statistics do not show the apathy and passivity which intellectuals decry. And despite the high divorce rate, the number of children born out of wedlock (35 percent) and the shifting relationships, the number of people who live alone with little contact with family or friends is low (2 percent) and isolation has not increased over the years.

To the extent that an organization, a rule, a law can shelter the individual from the vicissitudes of life, Sweden has adopted it. Its idea of welfare goes far beyond the provision of money and health and education benefits. Scarcely any convention is taboo to challenge. The divorce law now requires no grounds and imputes no blame. The divorce rate has soared. In one seventh grade class in Stockholm, only five out of the twenty-seven children lived with both parents. On the other hand, the courts can give joint custody to unwed parents living together in what is called an unregistered marriage. There is no such thing as illegitimacy. Birth certificates do not give the marital status of parents. Women are so equal, at least in theory, that men are equal too. In divorce, the judge can award guardianship of a minor to whichever parent he considers better for the child. Fathers are entitled to up to a year of paternity leave, the same amount of time granted the mother, so that the couple can take turns minding the baby and the house or staying on a job. Despite the government's energetic promotion, not many men take off more than a couple of weeks, though most women work.

The old tradition of ombudsman is kept very much alive. It is a recognition that law and administration do not guarantee justice, and provides a channel of direct appeal to a person specifically named to hear complaints about the failings or errors of the authorities. The ombudsman does not have the power to act on his own decision, but can publicize the case or pass along his recommendation and it provokes serious attention. This is a version of the ancient practice of a monarch's open court to hear his subjects' grievances or needs, as exemplified by France's Louis XI (St. Louis), who sat under a tree once a week accepting petitions from anyone who came, or by certain contemporary Arab sheikdoms where the custom persists. The idea arose well before the notion of democracy, but it remains an important and useful tool in dealing with bureaucracy.

In addition to the traditional justice ombudsman, Sweden has a special children's ombudsman, an energetic grandmother who campaigned for a law prohibiting any kind of physical punishment of children, even by their parents. Social workers are so zealous in what they consider their duty to children that a parents' movement arose to protest forced removal of their offspring on grounds of neglect, a decision left to municipal boards. Special provisions and subsidies exist to encourage the employment of the handicapped and mentally retarded.

Prisoners also have benefited from Swedish liberal activism. Sentences are short, which keeps the prison population low. Each inmate has a single room (the word *cell* is frowned upon). Most are in minimum-security or even completely open institutions. Guards are unarmed. But the ambitious rehabilitation program was a disappointment. The rate of recidivism remained at 75 percent, as high as in unregenerate penal systems elsewhere. Serious crimes of violence are rare. In a 1978 survey, only 6 percent of those questioned said they had ever been victims of violence or the threat of violence. In 1980, crime reports showed 3 cases of assault per 1,000 people, one shoplifting per shop.

Still, in the years since 1950 there has been a fourfold increase in the total number of crimes, especially in the urban areas and particularly in drug-related crime. Most convicted criminals, three out of four, are only fined, and those sentenced to more than three months' imprisonment rarely serve the full term. They are paroled after a half to two-thirds of their sentence. Compared to the rest of Scandinavia, Sweden has the highest crime rate and Norway has the lowest. There are more thefts in Sweden and Denmark than in Finland and Norway, and more crimes of violence in Sweden and Finland than in Denmark and Norway. Finland sends more people to jail and imposes longer sentences than any of the others. Taken together, the statistics seem to show that the temper of the people and the fabric of society make more difference than the penal system in determining the amount of crime.

The result of all this effort and determined goodwill is no Garden of

Eden, but it is a widely contented land. Swedes grumble, but they feel far more comfortable in their web of security than when they venture into the uncertainties of less ordered societies. Others might find so many rules and so much conformity an irritating constraint. Swedes feel free in their nest. Prime Minister Ingvar Carlsson says sternly, "A poor person, an unemployed person isn't free."

NORWAY
Somber Turned Bright

NORWAY IS A YOUNG-OLD COUNTRY, with tremendous gaps in its conscious history and culture. It leaped almost from the mythic, rampaging past of the Norse, recounted vividly in the *Eddas*, to modernism, without much role in the world between. A brooding, watery, Sleeping Beauty of a land, the terrain more rugged even than Sweden's, it suddenly stirred again in the late nineteenth century. It sent its sturdy young men to America in such numbers that the depleted labor force was able to wrest far-reaching reforms which produced a freehold agriculture. It sent its freighters tramping around the world, forming a great merchant fleet quite out of proportion to its own commerce. It sent the spruce and pine from its great dark forests tumbling down rapids to lumber and pulp mills. And now it sends oil and gas pumped by the rigs afloat on its cold, stormy waters to fuel the industries of Europe. It is on the rim of the continent, psychologically as well as geographically cut off, and yet it keeps carefully up to date.

King Olav V's silver jubilee was celebrated in 1982 in Oslo's austerely modern concert hall with folk dances, folk songs, country music and the archi-Norwegian Hardanger fiddle. The bright, embroidered traditional costumes are worn not as relics but as a sign of festivity, as they always were. Ancient rites are observed on Midsummer Night and at weddings with no sense of anachronism in a fully advanced welfare state with an officially established Lutheran Church. It was one of the first countries to give women the vote, in 1907 (after New Zealand and

Finland), and one of the last to define its language, still something of a compromise between tradition and education. The spoken language, a medley of dialects, is the closest of the Scandinavian tongues to Old Norse. For centuries, while Norway was a Danish province from 1380 to 1814, the language of literature and government was Danish. A mixture, called Norwego-Danish, is now the common official language, though it still depends on place and occasion, temperament and aspiration, whether one or another form is preferred. The sense of nationhood is relatively new.

On the map, the country looks like a jagged noodle, or a fringe pasted onto the Scandinavian peninsula by the rise and fall of the sea level over ages and the relentless thrust of glaciers. It is 1,100 miles long, 260 miles at the widest but with an average width of 60 miles, narrowing to 5 miles at one point. For most of its length, it clings to Sweden. Stretching farther north, it borders Finland and at the very tip shares a short frontier with the Soviet Union. The coastline is counted as 1,650 miles if a crow kept flying along it from cliff to cliff, but the actual shore is some 13,265 miles, veering in and out of the long, steep fjords. The mountains appear to plunge abruptly into the sea, but they pop up again in chains of islands which screen a placid coastal passage against the heaving Atlantic.

Norway has 150,000 islands, many of them bare rock. The ocean currents warm the air, protecting the country from the bitter cold of other lands at the same latitude but bringing frequent rains and fogs and what are called "smoking fogs," actually fine snow. This is a land where nature shows its untempered power and grandeur, demanding awe, not gentle lilts of flattery. The greens are deep and shadowed. The water's blue is darkest sapphire, except where glacier-fed streams spread a milky layer on the surface. It is a place to contemplate the mysteries in silence and to feel the movements of the earth and the smallness of the human scale. There are "giants' kettles" below high tide, great bowls scooped out by glaciers on their way to the sea when its level was much lower. And there are ridges on the cliff sides, sometimes one after another, ledges which marked the shore when the sea was much higher.

The rivers run swiftly westward from the Kjølen, "the Keel," the long north-south Scandinavian watershed, providing Norway's bountiful and far from fully developed "white coal" of hydroelectric power. They flow more slowly eastward, on the Swedish side. These are Norway's resources, some minerals but mostly the energy, the trees, the fish, the furs and, above all, the beauty. The salmon leap up breathtaking streams. Ski trails, once simply winter transport, flash across broad slopes. In the north, the sun never sets from mid-May to the end of July. Even in the south, there is no dark in this period, only a long, opalescent twilight. In winter, the sun disappears or is at best a pale, timid alien. Norwegians are sportsmen, enamored of their outdoors, and they do not try to compete with its majestic decor in their modest houses, traditionally of wood. They live long; the death rate is particularly low. But they scarcely multiply, due in the past to massive emigration, late marriage and perhaps a self-containment that comes from isolation and an austere religion. The 4.1 million Norwegians, on a land space slightly larger than New Mexico, are Europe's most sparsely spread population.

Oslo, the capital and largest city, with 455,000 people, has a homey, provincial air. There is a Viking ship in the museum, but it is not easy to imagine these upright, pleasant townsmen as the descendants of marauding pirates. Drunkenness was a great public issue in the late nineteenth and early twentieth century. Prohibition was sternly enforced at times, somewhat eased at others. The state retains a monopoly of beverage alcohol, and there are strict controls on sales. Inevitably, the oil boom of the 1970s, with the sudden influx of money and foreigners, who worked hard on the offshore rigs and wanted to play hard when they landed, brought a loosening of customs. The small coastal towns resented their transformation into frontier outposts at first. But there was an adjustment on both sides, a Norwegian prudence and adaptation to prosperity, a careful pacing of exploitation and investment, so that a balance was maintained.

Its history hardly suggests the emergence of such a responsible nation. The earliest reference to the area is in the Old English poem *Beowulf*, which speaks of "Finnaland," now believed to have been southern Norway. Norwegians still call the Asiatic Lapps who live in the far north "Finns," and there is record of ancient laws which forbade consulting Finnish seers about the future. The organization of society beyond clans headed by chieftains or jarls (the origin of the title "earl") is traced to 866. Harald Haarfager, son of Halfdan the Black, sought to subdue independent feudal lords and establish himself as king. By 872, he had overcome his rivals and extended his realm to include the Orkneys and the Shetlands, off Scotland. But his son, Erik Blödox (Bloody Axe), could not hold the supremacy. There were constant battles.

At the end of the tenth century, King Olaf brought missionaries from

England and proclaimed the kingdom Christian. There are still traces of English architecture in cathedrals and medieval churches, but not much remains because most of the structures were wood. Christian or pagan, the leaders' struggle for dominance and the resulting civil wars seldom stopped. In the thirteenth century, King Magnus established a more centralized power, partly because the baronial class lost its monopoly of trade to the Russians and Germans, and its slaves (thralls) to the wars. Seeking more popular support against them, Magnus enlarged the king's council on occasion into what was called "palliment," or parliament, but it was not institutionalized. In the fifteenth century, King Christian I raised money by pawning the Orkneys and Shetlands to the King of Scotland. So it went, mostly under Danish rule and largely in violence, until the end of the Napoleonic Wars. Sweden was forced to cede Finland to Russia in the settlement, but it was compensated in the Treaty of Kiel in 1814 with the award of Norway.

The Swedes and the Norwegians have different versions of their relations after that. To the Swedes, they simply acquired a former Danish province. To the Norwegians, the Treaty of Kiel was abrogated and Norway agreed to form a union under the Swedish crown but with its own government, administration and armed forces. The Norwegians wrote a constitution and declared independence on May 17, 1814. Sweden attacked, and after a short war Norway entered the union on condition that the Swedish king recognize its constitution and its own defense. Sweden was in charge of foreign affairs. The constitution was very liberal for its time. It guaranteed human rights and established the principle of popular sovereignty and political equality. Half the adult males were eligible to vote, including farmers, which was unusual then. Titles and privileges of the aristocracy were abolished, despite the Swedish king's objections. The Norwegians insisted that the remaining nobility were all Danish and that the real Norwegian nobility were peasants descended from the old jarls and chiefs.

Nationalism was rising throughout the nineteenth century, often led by poets and playwrights. Ibsen followed a movement already established in his pressure for social and political reform. As in parts of the Austro-Hungarian Empire, particularly Bohemia, the nationalist impulse was advanced by the introduction of literature in the rustic, spoken language instead of the educated speech used at royal courts. There was friction, and at times upheaval. The growing reform movement brought constitutional change in 1884, introducing parliamentary dominance.

The 150-member Storting is elected for four years. After each election, the Storting chooses a quarter of its members to serve in the upper house, the Lagting, while the remainder form the assembly, the Odelsting. The King names the Prime Minister, who then forms a government, but it is totally subject to the Storting and cannot dissolve the parliament to call new elections. This system has created persistent cabinet crises.

The dominant issue throughout the nineteenth century was the tie to Sweden, at times bringing the two countries to the verge of war. But finally, in 1905, Norway's complete independence from Sweden was negotiated peacefully. The Norwegians chose Prince Carl of Denmark as their King. He was the second son of King Frederick VIII and brother of Christian X, King of Denmark from 1912 to 1947. Before accepting, Carl insisted there be a referendum on the monarchy. Then, with his wife, Queen Maud, youngest daughter of England's Edward VII, he mounted the throne as King Haakon VII. He reigned for fifty-two years, through two world wars and the rise of socialism and an egalitarian, welfare state. His dedication to the constitution and democracy was never doubted. He was succeeded on his death in 1957 by his fifty-four-year-old son, King Olav V, the second monarch of the independent Norwegian state.

By the time of Europe's climactic wars, Norway, like the rest of Scandinavia, had lost its taste for expanding power in favor of addressing internal problems. It succeeded in remaining neutral during World War I, a stance which brought some hardships but even more rewards. The policy had not changed at the outbreak of World War II. In 1939, the Western allies (but not the United States, still neutral until 1941) asked passage for troops to go to the aid of Finland, fighting off the Soviets after the Stalin-Hitler pact. Norway, in hopes of staying out of the spreading war, refused. The Germans were buying vital iron through the port of Narvik. The British were doing their best to keep the sea-lanes open. There seemed a chance of repeating the World War I escape. But in April 1940, Britain mined Norwegian territorial waters to block supplies to Nazi Germany. Almost before the Norwegian government could formulate a protest, Hitler's forces invaded and overran the country.

Norway presented difficult terrain to a conqueror. But it had known 150 years of peace. All its army divisions were understrength, poorly equipped and weakened by decades of neglect and inactivity. The peasantry as well as the intellectuals were antimilitary pacifists. During the

Depression years, there had been open hostility between left-wing workers' groups and members of the military establishment, denounced for their elitist and conservative views. This army, without experience and scorned by a substantial part of the population, had to try to organize the defense of the country against the mighty German war machine. The confusion and its consequences are discussed in Richard Petrow's *The Bitter Years*.

D-day for the Germans was April 9. It was only at one o'clock that morning that the Norwegian navy issued orders to activate mines planted at the mouth of the fjord approaching Oslo, the capital. But it was too late; the German ships had already entered. Their troops landed simultaneously at Narvik, Trondheim, Bergen and Stavanger as well, the key ports from north to south. Weserübung, code name of the operation, was a triumph for the Nazis from the start, except for Oslo, where the German navy did badly and the air force not much better.

If Oslo, the transportation center of the country, had held, Norway might have been able to resist long enough for the confused British and French efforts to send reinforcements. But the information available to the government and senior command was spotty; the situation looked hopeless to them. The army command moved out of the capital, and shortly afterward King Haakon, the government, and members of parliament fled inland by train. A fleet of twenty-three trucks followed them, carrying the Bank of Norway's stock of gold and sensitive government papers. By 8 A.M. on invasion day, the capital was without a government or an organized defense, its residents frightened and bewildered, its remaining army units without leadership. But Norway did not capitulate. King Haakon rejected the German demands and escaped with key ministers and advisers to England, where they formed a government-in-exile.

Hitler sent forty-one-year-old Joseph Terboven as Reichskommissar to arrange an administration under occupation. He understood the structure of the country well, and exploited it to put local Nazis in crucial positions. Almost every Norwegian belonged to one or more national organizations representing professions, businesses, unions, social and athletic groups, which Terboven moved to infiltrate and put under pro-Nazi leadership. Most of the older organizations re-formed as underground groups, but their resistance was political, psychological and emotional, not military. Quisling, whose name has since become a synonym for traitor, was made Minister President of a puppet government in 1942. His willingness to govern as a Nazi surrogate was an enormous shock to waverers and pacifists.

The London government became a full member of the Allied coalition, and at the end of the war there was no question of Norway's position. It was liberated, its independence restored and its strategic alliance alongside Britain confirmed. The experience left little allure in neutrality, to which the Swedes, who escaped the war, continued to cling afterward.

When the North Atlantic Treaty Organization was formed in 1949 to defend the West against what was perceived as a grave new Soviet menace, Norway joined immediately. Its border with the Soviet Union is short and far from population centers. But it faces the heavily armed Kola Peninsula, and the Nazi invasion had shown how easily the country could be overrun by a modern war machine without guaranteed outside defense. Over the years, new military technology has greatly increased Norway's strategic importance to North Atlantic defenses. Murmansk, the only Russian ice-free port with open access to the Atlantic, is on Kola, not far from Norway. The peninsula is home-port area for 65 percent of the Soviets' nuclear missile-carrying submarines, 60 percent of its nuclear-powered attack submarines and its Northern Fleet, strongest of the global Soviet navy's four fleets. It bristles with early warning and air defense installations.

The area is so sensitive to both sides that certain tacit rules of mutual restraint have been accepted. Neither NATO nor the Soviet Union maintains permanent naval combat patrols in the Norwegian Sea to the west. Allied maneuvers never take place in the neighboring Norwegian county of Finnmark, leaving five hundred miles between maneuver regions and the Norwegian-Soviet border. No American planes patrol the Barents Sea to the northeast, leaving it to Norwegian aircraft to keep NATO informed of any ominous activity in the area of the Soviet bases. But the ability to monitor Soviet fleet and submarine operations from the Arctic into the North Atlantic is absolutely crucial to the West. The air and sea space off northern Norway and what NATO calls the Greenland–Iceland–United Kingdom gap is vital to both East and West against surprise attack.

Though it cooperates fully in these defenses, Norway has imposed certain limits so as to make clear it would not serve as an offensive base. No nuclear weapons may be stocked or deployed on Norwegian soil in peacetime, and there are no agreements or training for Norwegian forces to join in their use in wartime. (Some continental European countries have such agreements with the United States.) No foreign troops may be stationed in Norway. But after intense internal debate, Norway agreed to store equipment for U.S. air, marine and naval reinforcements. This activity is in central and southern Norway, not in the north, which would have been the more logical site militarily but might also have been considered by the Soviets to be a threat calling for retaliation.

Norwegian analysts speak of a need for a Nordpolitik, a search for regional understandings and stability in relations with the Soviets that would have some parallel to West Germany's Ostpolitik. Norway is keenly interested in East-West nuclear arms control and an agreed military balance which could ease its front-line vulnerability. Meanwhile, in the words of Defense Minister Johan Jürgen Holst, it feels it has contributed to "the maintenance of a state of low tension in the northern corner of Europe in spite of the competing strategic interests of the great powers in the region."

In contrast to this active participation in the military alliance, Norway has snubbed the European Economic Community. Its entry into the Common Market had been negotiated and was scheduled for 1972, when Britain, Ireland and Denmark joined. But in a national referendum, the voters rejected membership by a small majority. The main reason at the time was the problem of fisheries. The oil and gas bonanza has spared Norway any serious regrets. Still, the briny black gold has been a mixed blessing. The government foresaw the wrenching distortions that a sudden gush of money could impose on the society and planned what was called a "get-rich-slow scheme," limiting production. But OPEC rocketed world prices to a level that brought inflation and an overvalued currency.

The temptation to boost wages and welfare spending was irresistible, making the traditional export industries noncompetitive and adding to pressures for government subsidies to flagging enterprises instead of investment in new fields. When the oil market softened, surpluses turned into deficits and debts. Petroleum is a peculiar product economically, based almost entirely on capital and little on labor and materials. By 1981, it accounted for a third of Norway's exports, employing directly and indirectly only 2 percent of the labor force but providing 20 percent of national tax revenue. The tensions brought unaccustomed labor conflict in a country where union representatives were used to saying, "Our employers are progressives," and management would reply, "Our unions are responsible." The comfortable consensus on social justice and egalitarianism was skewed, though not destroyed.

Norwegian politics are based on a special combination of fragmentation and consensus. Long before real political parties emerged, opposing groups developed in the Storting, with the conservative bureaucrats on one side (Hoyre) and their critics (Venstre) on the other. After the reform in 1884, the rise of the middle class and the workers' movement brought the critics, who had formed a Liberal Party, to power. Its right wing split off on one side, and the workers on the other to form a Labor Party on socialist principles. Industrialization began in earnest around 1900, shortly before independence was achieved in 1905. The Labor Party became the main challengers to the Liberals, and the middle class became more conservative.

The depression of the 1930s hit Norway very hard, polarizing the society in a way which laid some basis for the emergence of collaborationists after the Nazi invasion. A third of the union members were unemployed and some 50,000 farmers were driven into bankruptcy. There was a rash of strikes and a countervailing lockout in 1931, which lasted five months. The Labor Party moved toward reformism and away from its revolutionary demands, but right-wingers moved away from the traditional conservative and liberal parties and joined fascist organizations. The National Socialist Party (Nazi) was formed in 1933.

When the government-in-exile returned and held elections in 1945, Labor proved strongest with 41 percent of the vote. It led the government for two generations.

Norway's Conservatives came to power under Kaare Willoch in 1981, interrupting the long socialist rule. A smooth-faced man with a well-clipped circle of white hair around his eminently respectable pate, he replaced the Labor Party's Mrs. Gro Harlem Brundtland. She had been made Premier shortly before the elections in hopes of bolstering her sagging party. She was forty-one at the time, daughter of a former cabinet minister who had herself been Minister for the Environment, and she was popular for her forthright, strong-minded leadership. Norwegians took the advent of a woman head of government in comfortable stride. She had a master's degree in public health from Harvard, and she was married to an employee of the Conservative Party, Arne Olav. Clearly, it was neither her sex nor her views which lost her the election but the swing of the long-stalled pendulum, and she remained a forceful leader of the opposition.

After all, it did not make a drastic difference. There was no question

of dismantling any part of the welfare state, which was too solidly entrenched. Nor was it possible to reduce the enormous rate of taxation
—at 48.5 percent of GNP the industrial world's highest after Sweden's
—but only to prevent its rising further. Even the nationalized Statoil,
which dominates the petroleum industry, was seen as a useful protection for Norway's interests in the world of giant oil companies, and not
just the bureaucratic monster which the conservatives had considered
it when they were out of office. Willoch formed a coalition with two
other non-socialist parties in 1983, giving Norway its first majority government in twelve years. But by 1985, its strength had eroded; the
country was shifting left again. The Socialists won a majority of the
votes, but not quite a majority of the Storting seats, which left Willoch
in power but "hanging by a thread," as Norwegians put it, until Mrs.
Brundtland and her party regained power in 1986.

"My God, How Well They Behave!" *Le Monde* of Paris headlined its
dispatch on the election campaign, comparing the "amiable conversations among well-brought-up persons" to the French political discourse
of gibes and insults. It quoted Henry Valen of Oslo's Institute of Political Studies as saying, "Here, politicians enjoy a great capital of confidence. Our studies show this confidence is steadily increasing,
doubtless because we haven't had any corruption scandals. Norwegians
don't like technocratic politicians. We prefer those who are calm, sincere (or at least appear to be), who come from an ordinary background
and don't try to overwhelm their opponents. Sweden's Olof Palme, who
was a cynic and a demagogue, could never have become Prime Minister
of Norway. To succeed in Norwegian politics, you have to be tough
and firm on principles but soft in the way you present your ideas, and a
touch of humor doesn't hurt."

The wars of ideology had pretty well worn away over the years. Despite the old partisan names, practically everyone had become a moderate. The differences were more in attitude and nuance, an attempt to
have a little less bureaucracy, a little more encouragement for the
private sector.

Above all, the shifts in government and the responses to mistakes
induced by the oil vertigo served to confirm Norway's underlying political and social stability. It has its problems, but like the other countries
of Scandinavia, it has developed a solid, reliable and, on the whole,
contented society. The values of individual freedom and compassionate
community, so often pitted in opposition elsewhere, have been fused

to the general satisfaction. Norwegians are no longer the gloomy, angry, taut-nerved people of the great playwrights. After she slammed the door of her Doll's House, Ibsen's Nora went on to become an amiable prime minister.

DENMARK
Small Is Cheerful

T HE LITTLE BRONZE MERMAID smiling seductively from the jetty at the entrance to the harbor is Copenhagen's symbol. The Danes like to think of their capital and their country in her image, friendly, unpretentious, charming, and enduring. The American comedian Danny Kaye sang of "wonderful, wonderful Copenhagen," and of course they loved it, with the reference to the fairy-tale land of Hans Christian Andersen and its buttery tranquility. There is indeed a quaintness about the place. There was scarcely any damage during World War II, leaving centuries-old buildings and squares intact, and scarcely any temptation to build high-rises afterward. The outskirts of the city are full of dull, boxy apartment buildings and endless rows of little houses to take advantage of the tax benefits of home ownership. But the downtown streets are narrow, the uniformly four- or five-story buildings highly ornate with gables, bow windows and stone garlands.

Medieval palaces and warehouses still serve everyday life. The Tivoli Gardens amusement park hasn't moved out of the nineteenth century, with its sideshows and stalls. There is not much neon or garish advertising of the kind that makes so many modern cities shoddy, and world-famed Danish pornography is sold discreetly behind prim storefronts. When they launched their sexual revolution, the Danes insisted on the same democratic right of choice which they applied to almost everything else. People were entitled to shed their inhibitions if they wished, but those who did not were entitled not to be accosted by offensive displays. When the weather is good, the sky and the sea sparkle. The atmosphere is crisply bright with cleanliness and the radiance of health. It does seem a bit archaic, "a land set apart from the rest of the world, where the pace is slower, the air fresher," as the Board of Tourism's brochure says.

But it is a paradox. Modernism is a Danish mania, in design, in dress, in industrial and agricultural techniques, above all in social welfare and organization. The Danes are acutely conscious of being a small country, though perhaps they speak of it so often in suppressed memory of ancient times when Denmark was a great power. They have a need to feel up to date, in step with the world or even a few steps ahead when it comes to political moralizing. Their romanticism sounds stodgy with echoes of Jean-Jacques Rousseau's eighteenth-century school, which thought of nature as unfailingly gentle and kind, the savage as noble and civilization as the source of all evil.

The land, though not much of the history, gives some support to the idea. Composed of a peninsula jutting up from the north German plain to separate the North Sea from the Baltic, two large and many small islands, Denmark is a low, softly rolling country the size of Massachusetts and New Hampshire. No place is more than forty miles from the open sea, making the climate milder than other regions at the same latitude. The fertile soil and the warm, moist breezes from the Gulf Stream support a flourishing agriculture; the rich land is almost its only natural resource. Endless white sand dunes in the west, a horizon of beech and pine woods, cornfields and meadows filled with browsing cows make the landscape idyllic. The tourist brochure announces confidently that "you may travel to other countries with more dramatic landscapes than Denmark, but you'll never find a place with so peaceful a countryside where calm reigns supreme." Tourist brochures, like nineteenth-century landscape painters, tend to overlook the gnarled, muddy, hungry, sweaty side of nature.

But the history is all the opposite of serenity, full of wars and disasters, riches and rags. Modern Danes like to idealize their Viking ancestors as rough but just and honest men, blond adventurers in horned helmets who rejected hierarchy and privilege for the fellowship of the open sea and the lure of exploration. In fact, they were cruel plunderers. They held slaves (thralls) to work their lands while they set off on conquest. They emerge from legend only in 985, when Gorm the Old founded the Danish monarchy, now the oldest in Europe. The Angles, or Anglians, who gave their name to England, were early invaders from Denmark. Little is known about them beyond the accounts of their life in the fifth and sixth centuries in the Old English poem *Beowulf*. Gorm's great-grandson, known as King Canute to the English and Knut the Great to the Danes, made his country a dual kingdom of Denmark and England in 1016, only half a century before the Normans who had settled in France wrested England away.

The Valdemar dynasty brought the Danish kingdom into Christendom in the twelfth and thirteenth centuries, though the religion was first introduced by King Harold Bluetooth, who died in 988. The kingdom was rich, its trade based on herring from the sea and horses and cattle raised on the grasslands. The kings' need for money to support their endless wars and the landowning nobles' resistance led to disorders. In 1282 the nobles forced signature of a royal charter, similar to the English barons' Magna Carta, but it did not last as a foundation for Danish democracy.

There was a continuous struggle between the merchant shipowners, who tried to hold a monopoly of trade, and the landowners, who wanted to retain the profits from export of their peasants' produce. The king was supported, or imposed, sometimes by one side, sometimes by the other. Sometimes his powers were constrained by rich, lordly families, such as the fifteenth-century Guildensterns and Rosencranzes, whose scions Shakespeare placed in the coterie of the rebellious Prince Hamlet. After the alliance in 1660 between the king and the burghers, the king was made an absolute monarch to repress the ambitions of the landowners.

The royal search for revenue led to construction of a fort to enforce collection of a ship transit tax called sound dues in the narrow passage of the Øresund between the Kattegat leading to the North Sea in the west and the Baltic in the east. This strategic position both propelled Denmark into wars and protected it as other maritime powers developed. There was always an outside power to help Denmark resist the dominant regional power of the day, so as to keep the passage open. Admiral Sven Thiede, Chief of Defense in the early 1980s, believed this geography accounted for the survival of Danish independence. First Holland, later Britain, and then America intervened to prevent the greatest Baltic power, Sweden, Germany and Russia in turn, from overwhelming Denmark and controlling the straits.

Trade and the wars it provoked always determined Danish fortunes.

There were periods of misery when commerce was blocked or prices fell because of rising competition, such as English wheat exports in the sixteenth century. There were periods of great prosperity when trade revived, as in the eighteenth century with the arrival of sugar, coffee and tobacco from the West Indies and spices and silk from the East. Although Denmark took the Virgin Islands in this period (sold to the United States for $25 million in 1917), it was neutral in the great English-French colonial wars and benefited grandly, as it did from the Napoleonic Wars.

A system of semi-serfdom had been imposed after the great plagues killed off much of the yeomanry and left farms untilled. The prosperity of the eighteenth century led Denmark to abolish it and to carry out Europe's first great land reform in 1788, establishing a system of small freeholdings which led to the rise of cooperatives. That remains the structural foundation of Danish agriculture to this day. It did not bring simultaneous political liberalization. Small-holders' agriculture did permit Denmark to adjust with relative ease, however, when mounting American and Russian wheat exports in the late nineteenth century threatened its market for grain. The farmers switched to concentrate on production of butter, eggs and pork, marketing through co-ops. "We thus became dependent on the peculiar breakfast habits of the British," Søren Nielsen, a Copenhagen journalist, pointed out. The Danes, like the rest of the continentals, eat bread with jam or cheese for breakfast, often combined in a pastry. Only the English eat bacon and eggs.

Political demands to match agrarian reforms only began to take effect toward the end of the nineteenth century. Acceptance spread of the concept of public responsibility for health care, pensions for the old and all kinds of social benefits and workers' rights. Long before the word entered the political vocabulary, Denmark was becoming a welfare state. As World War I approached, the dominant argument was whether more public money should be spent on social needs or defense. The Danes managed to stay neutral, though they were compelled by the Germans to mine their own waters so as to prevent the British from using them in attempts to bottle up the German navy. However, the pressures of war were felt in the political debate on extending democracy. Universal suffrage, including women, was achieved in 1915. Iceland was granted independence, though under a joint sovereign, in November 1918. It was not until 1944, during the German occupation of Denmark in World War II, that it broke away completely. Greenland was incorporated as a province with standing equal to those at home in 1953, and granted home rule in 1978.

The Danes reacted to the crises between the wars with what by then had become their characteristic liberalism. At the worst of the Depression in 1933, Denmark introduced its great social reform, one of the world's most advanced. It provided generous medical care, welfare, aid for children and accident and unemployment insurance, going far beyond President Franklin D. Roosevelt's New Deal. It established a social texture which won such wide consensus that it was never eroded, no matter which party came to power.

After the outbreak of World War II, the Danes hoped to go their way undisturbed. But on April 9, 1940, the Germans occupied the country. Berlin claimed it was not an invasion, only a means to prevent Denmark from letting the British turn it into a battlefield. Being overrun by foreign troops is nonetheless being overrun by foreign troops. King Christian X was allowed to remain at liberty. Defiantly, he rode his horse around the streets to show his compatriots that if he could not resist the Nazis, neither did he submit.

There is a story that he wore the yellow Star of David on his jacket to show his solidarity with Jews, and another that he told the Germans if they did impose the infamous badge on Danish Jews, "I and my whole family will wear it as a sign of the highest distinction." It wasn't true; the Germans never introduced the star in Denmark. The legend seems to have been a bit of Allied propaganda invented to give some cheering contrast to the tales of horror and atrocity coming out of occupied Europe. The truth did not need such embellishment. When the Germans started capturing Jews, the Danes organized secret escapes to Sweden. They helped 7,220 flee safely after 284 Jews had been rounded up by the Germans in raids on October 1 and 2, 1943. Another 275 people were caught during the rest of the month, 85 of them half-Jewish who were later released, and only then did the Germans realize what had happened. When the rescue was announced, it created tremendous excitement after so much bad news for the Allies.

Denmark's agriculture continued to prosper, so that its people were the best fed on the war-torn continent, and food was exported to Germany. In late 1942, Hitler tried to tighten up, ordering that no democratically run country be allowed to exist in German-occupied Europe. But there was disagreement between the tough new German commander and the Nazi plenipotentiary, Dr. Werner Best, who believed that the Danes could be persuaded to collaborate if they were not mistreated. He succeeded in holding off the new policy for a time. After the Battle of Stalingrad showed that Germany might not win the war, resistance groups began to act. When the British air force raided a Copenhagen shipyard that manufactured engines for German submarines, the underground press said there was a lesson to be drawn: there would either be more bombing, with civilian casualties, or the Danes would have to increase sabotage on their own. They became increasingly daring.

At the end of August 1943, the Germans reacted, taking over key public buildings, arresting people of influence and attacking Danish army garrisons. Martial law was proclaimed. The soldiers had been ordered to surrender under protest, so there was scarcely any fighting. The navy, which had been even more humiliated than the army for not fighting at the time of the invasion, carried out its standing orders to flee to Sweden or scuttle its ships in case of attack, despite the government's call for surrender. A total of twenty-nine ships were sunk and many more heavily damaged. By the end of the war, Denmark was considered an Ally in good standing after having been criticized for collaboration at the start. Compared to most of Europe, the Danes did not have a devastating war and were in a position to revive quickly after liberation.

The country hoped after the war to base its security on the United Nations but was soon disillusioned. Then it sought a defense community with Sweden and Norway, but Norway wanted it to be closely associated with the Western alliance then being formed and Sweden refused to dilute its neutrality. So Denmark, along with Norway, joined the North Atlantic Treaty Organization from the start. This was a sharp turn away from traditional Danish attitudes, which had relied for more than a century on maintaining security through neutrality and keeping out of international conflicts. But the old feelings linger, making Denmark a recalcitrant ally at times.

King Frederick, Christian's son, beloved for his courage, his dignity and his determination to share in his countrymen's ordeals, died in 1972 at age seventy-three. His eldest daughter, Margrethe II, named for the queen who had tried to unify Scandinavia five hundred years earlier, came to the throne. She was thirty-two, a pretty, graceful woman. Margrethe had studied at Cambridge and had wanted to be an archeologist, but she accepted her role without complaint. After her marriage to a French count, Henri de Monpezat, renamed Prince Henrik, she called herself a "working wife" and wore her tiara, jewels and fashionable gowns on state occasions as nurses wear uniforms. Despite claims of a Danish "fairy-tale land," she was not in the least a fairy-tale queen. She and her handsome, sports-loving husband lived simply with their two sons in the rather stolid old Amalienborg Palace in the center of Copenhagen. There was little court protocol or fanfare, though the red-coated palace guard matches the Garde Républicaine of Paris for elegant splendor. The royal couple never joined the international jet set, and there was never a hint of scandal about their quiet, demure life.

In law, the Queen is more powerful than most modern constitutional monarchs. She shares legislative powers with the parliament and has full executive power through the government ministers. But in hallowed practice, her role is utterly neutral and symbolic, embodying the continuity of the nation and the stability which underlies its quirky politics. The Danes tend to produce quixotic politicians. "Remember," said a Liberal professor of history, "you are in the land of Hamlet." There tends to be a gentle oscillation of power between the center-right and center-left, with smaller, usually inconsequential factions at each margin. But within the power blocs, and sometimes between them as coalitions shift, there is an intricate proliferation of groups and splinters which makes the political scene utterly confusing. Nobody really questions the welfare state. But there are sharp confrontations about cultural affairs, such as pornography and abortion, about taxes, the Common Market, NATO, the economy and aid to the third world which cut across the usual right-left lines. How the sides draw up depends on the issue.

A system of proportional representation and a habit of factionalism fragment Danish politics, making it impossible for any party to win an absolute majority and imposing tenuous coalitions.

By far the strongest of the parties is the Social Democratic Party, major heirs of a century's steady progress in reform. It was founded in 1871, at the time of the Paris Commune and dawning revolt across Europe against inhuman conditions of industrialization. Thorwald Stauning, a cigar factory worker born in 1873, became the historic leader of the Social Democrats. He died in 1942. He did not follow the Marxist thesis of class struggle but fought to establish a consensus on welfare and the protection of workers. It was an essentially moderate position which did not challenge the right of proprietors to own and manage the means of production, but obliged them to recognize that labor also had its rights. The role of the state, in this view, which gradually gained ascendance, was not only to assure the security of property but also to assure the economic and social security of wage earners. The Social Democrats have been Denmark's biggest party since 1924, and have usually provided its prime minister. They established the country's basic political climate.

The Socialist People's Party was an offshoot of the Communist Party. It broke away after Khrushchev's revelations of Stalin's terror and the Hungarian revolution of 1956. The issue was democracy and refusal of continued allegiance to the Soviets. They preach communism without Leninism, nonviolent ballot-box revolution, with an acceptance of reversal and counterrevolution by election if the voters change their mind. They advocate Yugoslavian-type workers' management of industry, but are against the one-party state. Their leader, Gert Petersen, is a stocky man in his fifties with a slightly battered face. He wears a cloth cap and looks as though he stepped out of a cartoon of life on the barricades. In fact, he has a sprightly intelligence and a keen sense of political strategy, and keeps better informed on the affairs of the rest of the world than most Danish leftists. He is a fiery orator. The Left Socialists, in turn, broke away from Petersen's party on the grounds that its willingness to contemplate democratic rejection constituted "elevator socialism," which could go down as well as up at the electorate's choice.

The parties on the other side of the line are all known as "bourgeois," though some have names such as Radical Left, Venstre (which means left), Justice Party and Progress Party. It takes a scorecard to follow Danish politics. The Social Liberals are somewhere in the middle of the Danish spectrum, originally a small-holders' party which split off from the Liberals in 1905, primarily over the issue of defense. They favor neutrality. The traditional Liberals, also known as Venstre, are liberal in the European nineteenth-century sense of free market, free enterprise and minimal government interference with citizens' liberties. They scoff at the Social Liberals' pacifism and support NATO. The largest party on the right, counterweight to the Social Democrats but never up to its popularity at the polls, is the Conservative Party, business-minded and concerned with efficiency and individual rights. It is only conservative in the Danish context, seeking to curb extravagance but without challenging the principle of the welfare state.

A new party with the most eccentric politician of all is Mogens Glistrup's Progress Party, which burst on the scene in 1971. It quickly gathered a following of 12–14 percent of irate voters, fed up with the heavy taxes needed to support public spending in excess of 60 percent of the gross domestic product. Glistrup is a nearly bald man with a big grin and uneven teeth who takes gleeful pleasure in defying authority and upsetting the public composure. He is against taxes, for any purpose. His solution to the argument on the defense budget was to provide the army with a tape-recorded message in the languages of all possible and even improbable invaders, saying, "Don't shoot, Denmark surrenders." He claimed that his refusal to pay a penny in tax was completely legal because he had found loopholes in the intricate law, which he delighted in sharing with the public. He was jailed for tax evasion nonetheless, and went off trumpeting that he was a prisoner of conscience entitled to sympathetic exertions from Amnesty International. Then he faded from view and his party lost support.

The Danish politicians seem remarkably eccentric to the other, more stolid Scandinavians. Jens Otto Krag, who was the Social Democratic Prime Minister from 1962 to 1968 and again from 1971 to 1972, was a melancholy man who wrote essays and dawdled as long as he could in cafés to put off obligatory attendance at formal ceremonies.

Krag designated Anker Jørgensen as his successor. The loyal, well-disciplined Social Democratic Party accepted him without a murmur, though he too was known for being odd. A short, stubby man with a little Mephistophelian beard and brooding eyes, Jørgensen was given to inconsistencies, which he defended with haughty adamancy. He watched over Denmark's slump into debt and deficit in the recession of the late 1970s and early 1980s, and then resigned rather than accept responsibility for unpleasant measures.

As a result, Poul Schlüter became the first Conservative Prime Minister in nearly a century, presiding, as usual in Denmark, over a weak coalition. In fact, his government was regularly in the minority on important foreign affairs and defense issues, particularly the issue of deploying American missiles in Western Europe. There was never any question of stationing missiles in Denmark. Like Norway, the other Nordic member of NATO, the country determinedly bars any nuclear weapons on its soil in peacetime.

But the Danish opposition considered it had the right and the duty to take an antinuclear position for Europe and to seek to influence the defense policies of the British, the Germans and the Dutch. None of the Danish parties wanted the Schlüter government to fall on the NATO issue, however, because that would mean having to accept the onus for the drastic economic cure which any government would have had to impose. So Denmark became what its urbane Foreign Minister Uffe Ellemann-Jensen wryly called a "footnote country." Each time there was a NATO decision or communiqué, though the Danish government itself agreed, it was obliged to insert a footnote reserving the country's position in deference to the parliament. The Danes simply lived with the contradiction.

Political proliferation and volatility do not have their usual disruptive effect in Denmark because the society has a very solid underpinning of political associations and local government. There have been as many as four parties in the coalition cabinet at times, and many more in the parliament, and few governments last long before collapsing. But it doesn't matter a great deal. The affairs of the country proceed without undue disorder. One in every five Danes is a member of the powerful Landsorganisationen (LO), which means virtually everyone who earns a salary. Eight out of ten Danes tell pollsters they are content with their lives. Whatever the arguments of the moment, there is a strong sense of national community. The politicians are close to the people, who address them informally and see no reason for deference. The people are proud of their country's achievement of social justice, with a decent standard of living for all and no flagrant preserves of privilege. In fact, the main problem of the Social Democrats is that they have just about run out of wrongs to right at home, more or less as in Sweden and Norway.

Denmark is considered a nation of farmers, though in fact only 7 percent of the working population lives off agriculture, forestry and fishing, which together account for one-third of the exports. Denmark exports as much electronics per capita as Japan, though mostly in components, so that Danish brand names are not well known. Industrial enterprises are small and highly flexible, able to adjust quickly to changing market and technological demands. Few employ more than a hundred workers. This eliminates the temptation for radicals to press for nationalization since there are scarcely any suitable targets. Those that might have existed have long since disowned and disarmed themselves, so to speak.

The owner of the famous Carlsberg brewery, which also makes Tuborg beer and owns the Tivoli Gardens, established a foundation for research in science and natural history in 1876. His will made the Carls-berg Foundation full owner of the breweries, and his son added a new foundation devoted to the arts. The board of directors of the founda-tions, which receive all the profits of the enterprises, is made up of professors, artists, philanthropists, former civil servants and the like, but no businessmen. Yet Carlsberg does a highly successful export business throughout the world, using profits to stock museums and subsidize artists to adorn public buildings. Another major exporter is a fertilizer company, which imports phosphates from Morocco and ni-trates from the United States and sells its product competitively as far away as China. Tourism has been developed into a major money earner. The Danes, who tend to travel only to stretch out in the sun somewhere, marvel at the hardiness and good humor of their visitors regardless of the weather, and treat them appreciatively. When he was Prime Minister of Sweden, Tage Erlander told a Danish audience, "We are rich because we have resources. But you are so resourceful at business that you're almost as rich as we are."

Their comfort and resilience weigh on the Danish conscience. The Danes are not smug, as Swedes sometimes are. They feel a kind of Sunday school obligation to pay for their contentment in an unhappy world, and their intellectuals do their best to stir them up and goad them. Erik Knudsen is a flamboyant example. He has given up writing poetry and plays "because I don't have to anymore." He is one of the writers, painters and musicians accorded special state support in rec-ognition of eminence. Does that mean the government subsidizes him not to write? "Yes," he says with a laugh, "I guess that's what it amounts to. Anyway, I'm too busy now. I'm a prisoner of the peace movement. I'm always having to make speeches, organize demonstrations and so on." Does that mean the government subsidizes him to attack and harass the government? He is delighted with the question. "Yes, ex-actly, because that's what we need. This country is so petit bourgeois. It's the worst of anything. I'd hate to be petit bourgeois; I'd do anything, even insanity, to escape being petit bourgeois."

There was a huge old barracks called Christiania in Copenhagen that the army no longer used. In 1968–69 squatters quickly moved in and established a sort of indoor village. There are now about a thousand of them, more in the summer, when wanderers arrive. They have opened arts and crafts shops and even restaurants. They pay no rent, and the city supplies electricity, water and maintenance, though not eagerly.

But people in the capital point out that otherwise most of the residents would be on welfare and it would cost the taxpayers a good deal more. In 1973 the government gave Christiania the status of a "social experiment." One day the food critic of *Politiken,* a major newspaper, decided to try one of the restaurants and found it extremely good. The review attracted businessmen, who began to make a habit of taking foreign customers to lunch in the barracks as an out-of-the-ordinary treat. Soon the place was regularly overcrowded. Solid citizens complained that they could never get a table in the hippies' house, which served meals more cheaply than normal restaurants because it didn't add the tax it never paid. But nobody suggested doing anything. Danes were rather pleased with the anomaly. It showed their indulgent good humor.

FINLAND
Life in the Soviet Shadow

THE FINNS AND HUNGARIANS tell opposite versions of the same joke. An Asian tribe wandered into Europe and came to a crossroads. The Hungarians say those who could read followed the sign north to Finland and the others trudged on into Hungary. The Finns say those who had some sense about the weather settled in the Danube plains and the foolish ones kept going as far north as they could. The languages are related, both of them members of the Finno-Ugric group, which seems to have developed in the lands around the Urals. They are not mutually comprehensible. Some scholars consider the difference about the same as that between English and Persian.

Whether the people are actually related is more of a question. Certainly, they are not descendants of Slavonic, Teutonic or Viking tribes. Their emergence from Central Asia is lost in misty time. Most Finns are blue-eyed blonds, but others are short and dark-haired, with high cheekbones, oblique eyes and straight or flat noses, a slightly Oriental look that is quite different from their Scandinavian neighbors. And their temperament is different, more passive, simpler, more defensive.

In 1155, the newly Christianized kingdom of Sweden launched a crusade to convert the pagan nomads in the marshes to the east and absorb them into the realm. The Swedes called them Finns, presumably "the people of the fens," and the country Finnmark. The Finns call themselves Suomi, which in their own language means "the people of the marshes." The language and the character persisted, despite pervasive Swedish overlordship.

The language is spoken also by the Lapps of northern Sweden and Norway, though they are a quite different people, also of Asian origin, who seem to have something in common with the Eskimos of North America. There are groups of people who speak Finnish in Russian Karelia, the eastern half of the great inverted V which juts out from the Eurasian land mass into the Arctic. (The western side comprises Norway and Sweden.) And there are groups in the Volga basin and the Urals whose language is related. History offers no guide, but some common traditions have been handed down through legends of nature worship, ancestor worship, a belief in magical spells and great skill at hunting. The Finns' cultural survival attests to a deep, stubborn clannishness, since there were no records, no monuments, no important urban centers to sustain it.

Finland itself is a daunting country of brooding, rugged beauty, but it is not bountiful. It is shaped like a torso, with only 3 percent of the land arable and another 5 percent grassland. The rest is forests, lakes and swamps. Publicists call it the "land of a thousand lakes." Actually, there are 60,000, many connected by canals forming great inland waterways to make up for the shortage of land transport. The climate is harsh, except in the south and southwest, where it is moderated by warming winds from the sea. The population of nearly 5 million is gradually becoming urbanized. Living standards have risen dramatically in recent years, but a hard peasant life with little to relieve the drudgery is not far in the past.

Helsinki, the capital, is a quiet provincial-looking city in the midst of birch woods. But it has endowed itself with some of the world's loveliest modern architecture, clean, bare surfaces of wood, glass and marble carefully set to harmonize with surroundings for scenic harmony. The great Finnish architect Eero Saarinen was the leader of a school of modern design which springs from the sweep and simplicity of the countryside, exalting the natural texture of materials, especially wood, and the open plane of the pale sky. Foreigners in Moscow flock to Stockman's, the major department store in Helsinki, to buy all the Western comforts and provisions they cannot get in the Soviet Union. Stockman's has the biggest bookstore in the world. Finns flock to Leningrad by boat or by train for weekend vodka binges because of the extremely high prices the temperance movement has imposed on alcohol at home.

Their glum history has not been kind to the Finns, but they have made the best of minimal opportunity. Long a backwater of Sweden, which introduced Lutherism in 1528, Finland was embroiled in repeated Swedish wars and sent men to fight with Swedish armies in Germany and elsewhere. From 1710, when Peter the Great set out to conquer the land, it was recurrently contested by the Russians and the Swedes, suffering the famine and pestilence which are the ghoulish companions of war. The Tsar won in the war with Sweden of 1808–09, transferring Finland to his empire but as an autonomous grand duchy with special rights.

Alexander I granted a constitution, and in 1863 Alexander II convoked the Diet, which had not been allowed to meet for fifty-six years. It was a period when cultural nationalism was stirring throughout the empires of Europe. The national saga *Kalevala* by Elias Lonnrott, called the Finnish Homer, was the first major work to establish a literary language; until then, Swedish had dominated among the educated. The tale became a much loved and important base of national identity. The first Finnish novel, *The Seven Brothers* by Aleksis Kivi, paid tribute to the Finnish soul, the woods, the land, and so helped define the Finns for themselves.

But there was also a move toward Russification in the late ninteenth century. Tsarist officials adopted the motto "One law, one church, one tongue" to combat both Swedish influence and rising Finnish national consciousness. At the end of the century, Nicholas II took matters brutally in hand. He wiped out Finland's semi-independence in a series of measures which culminated with the Russian governor, General Nikolai Bobrikov, assuming dictatorial power. Helsinki was subjected to the St. Petersburg system of spies, police raids, illegal arrests, banishment and suppression of newspapers. The Finns put up dogged resistance. In November 1905, they added a national strike to the Tsar's other problems—the attempted revolution at home and defeat in the war with Japan.

St. Petersburg hastily restored the Finnish duchy's privileges, and a new constitution was drawn up with universal suffrage and freedom of the press, speech and association. But the respite was short-lived. Russification began again in 1908. The Finnish Diet was twice dissolved, killing its social reforms, including child welfare, state insurance, old-age pensions, provisions for landless workers and prohibition of alcohol. When war broke out in 1914, Russia made some concessions in an attempt to appease the Finns and persuade them to volunteer for the Russian armies. But the Finns feared a Russian victory would bring renewed oppression. Only two thousand offered to fight for the Tsar, no more than those who fled and enlisted to fight against him on the German side.

Finland itself was spared the carnage. But the Allied blockade caused suffering to those who were not involved in military supply industries, which prospered hugely. After Nicholas II was forced to abdicate in the Kerensky revolution of 1917, the Russian Provisional Government quickly restored representative government to Finland. There was a split in the Diet, with the Social Democrats prepared to accept an autonomy that would leave defense and foreign policy in Russian hands, while others sought complete independence. It was a time of turmoil, with many strikes, food shortages and outbreaks of rioting. The Bolshevik Revolution in October 1917 sharpened the division of sympathies.

Finally, that December, the Finns declared independence, recognized by the new Bolshevik government and confirmed by the Treaty of Brest-Litovsk, which took Russia out of the war against Germany in March 1918. But it did not shield Finland against the Russian civil war which followed. Starving Red Guards, reinforced by rebellious Russian troops, began to overrun the country. Baron Carl Gustav Emil Mannerheim quickly organized a White army to oppose them. It was not enough to restore order. Sweden was asked for help and refused, so the government turned to Germany, which sent 12,000 troops. The Whites and Germans defeated the Reds and drove out the Russians, proceeding to a counterterror which cost thousands more lives. A Finnish throne was offered to Prince Frederick Charles of Hesse, brother-in-law of Kaiser Wilhelm II. He never went north to be crowned. Germany's defeat in November 1918 turned Finnish aspirations away from the quarrel between sympathizers of the Bolsheviks and the Kaiser. They looked then to the British-American model of constitutional government. Mannerheim was still keen to intervene on the White side in the Russian civil war, but neither the Allies nor Finnish moderates offered support.

A republic was established on June 17, 1919, with a new constitution. A peace treaty was signed with Russia in 1920. The experience left a strong strain of pro-German sentiment, especially among conservatives. It flared up again after the Stalin-Hitler pact and the outbreak of World War II. Stalin took half of Poland and the Baltic states in agreement with Hitler, and then sought to press the advantage by demanding territorial concessions from Finland. The Finns refused.

In November, the Soviets launched the "winter war" of 1939–40. The

Finnish defense was vigorous and determined, despite the greatly superior strength of the Soviet forces. Britain and France, at war with
Germany and fearful that the Finns might call Nazi troops to their aid,
offered help. Sweden gave assistance, but it and Norway would not
allow passage of foreign troops for fear of being drawn into the war,
and Helsinki refrained from the public appeal for an expeditionary force
which the Allies considered necessary. On March 13, 1940, the Finns
signed a treaty in Moscow ceding 10 percent of their territory in return
for peace. But when the Germans invaded the Soviet Union a year
later, Finns went to the front to fight the Russians again.

The Allied victory in World War II not only confirmed Soviet territorial gains, it established a tacit but firm new Soviet right of surveillance in Finnish affairs. But the Red Army attempt to occupy Finland
in 1944 was stopped short of the 1940 border, so there was room for a
kind of diplomatic maneuvering that became impossible for the countries of Eastern Europe as the wartime Allied agreements hardened into
hostile Cold War. The Finnish statesmen who found the way to appease
the Soviets without surrendering basic national rights were the conservative President, Juho Kusti Paasikivi, and his cautious but clever successor, Urho Kekkonen. They devised a policy of bear-soothing which
consisted of assurances that Finland would never be an invasion route
into Soviet territory nor the ally of an invader, but a friendly outsider
with the right to be different. They called it the "new realism." It has
never been seriously challenged within the country, though people in
the West came to call the arrangement "Finlandization." The Finns
find the term offensive because of its failure to recognize their remarkable achievement of maintaining freedom under the Soviet shadow.
For people in Eastern Europe, it represents a dream far beyond their
horizon as they struggle to maintain a national existence under Soviet
weight.

To show its willingness to be considerate of Soviet interests, Finland
followed Stalin's lead in rejecting the Marshall Plan of American aid for
European reconstruction in 1947. In 1948, the year of the Communist
takeover of Czechoslovakia, Finland obtained a treaty of friendship and
cooperation with the Soviets which stopped short of initial Soviet demands. It was not in the pattern of the pacts Moscow signed with the
countries absorbed into the Soviet bloc, though it obliged Finland to
help the Soviet Union "with all the forces at its disposal in the event of
aggression by West Germany or any of its allies" and to hold "consul-

tations" in case of danger. But its preamble also recognized "Finland's aspiration to remain outside great-power conflicts," and the Soviets gained no right to station troops within the new Finnish borders.

More important than the formal agreements, however, was the intricate way the new relationship evolved. Finnish diplomats point out that, although the country was deeply disturbed, Finland did not vote for the United Nations resolution condemning the Soviet invasion of Afghanistan. Neutral Sweden and Austria did. But then, neither did Finland condemn the United States during the Vietnam War, as Sweden did. "Our idea of neutrality," an official said, "is never to take sides." Juridically, Finland is not absolutely neutral, because of its obligation to come to the aid of the Soviet Union. But though it carefully sets a line that never goes beyond what the Russians are likely to consider provocative, Finland still tilts toward the democratic countries whenever that is possible. With quiet diplomacy, President Kekkonen provided important support for Austria when the Soviets sought to block its membership in the British-sponsored European Free Trade Association in the 1960s. Finland was a member. Later, it was able to sign a trade agreement with the European Common Market, balanced by a similar agreement with the Soviet-led Comecon, though two-thirds of Finland's trade remains with EEC and EFTA countries.

The constitution of 1919 was maintained, with its religious rights and its requirement for a five-sixths legislative vote to prevent restriction on the right to private property. There is no censorship, but self-censorship is practiced widely and rigorously as a requirement of "responsible patriotism." When pressure does come, it is accommodated as reservedly as possible, resisted when that seems feasible.

There are Finns who resent the need to bow this much, but there is no alternative and they recognize that. The Soviet treaty was extended for twenty years in 1970. There is already concern about renewal in 1990, lest Moscow make new demands when the time comes for renegotiation. Looking ahead, the Finns made in 1974 what many consider a shameful understanding to return any defectors who escape from the Soviet Union into their territory. Looking away, they have managed not to notice those refugees who make their way all across Finland to asylum in Sweden.

The Russians got on well with Kekkonen, an important reason why he remained at the helm for twenty-five years. When he retired in 1981 at the age of eighty-one, the Finns proceeded to the choice of a new leader with great delicacy. They did not pick the Soviet favorite, Ahti Karjalainen, who like Kekkonen was a member of the Center Party but unlike Kekkonen was not very popular. Instead, in early 1982 they picked Mauno Koivisto, a stocky, rock-faced Social Democrat who had been Prime Minister. He had already signaled his determination to hold Finland's foreign policy steady, and Moscow made no objection. He was the first foreign head of state received after Yuri Andropov's accession to power in Moscow, a reminder that Andropov's own climb to the top began in Soviet Karelia as a protégé of the veteran Finnish Communist Otto Kuusinen.

The Soviets interfere with a heavier hand in the politics of Finland's Communists, members of the inevitable coalition government, than in other areas of Finland's political life. There is a minority pro-Soviet faction and a majority nationalist faction, whose retiring chairman, Aarne Saarinen, attacked the minority in 1982 for relying on Moscow support instead of on Finnish workers. The Russians publicly came out for the minority leader, accusing his rivals of deviationism and anti-Soviet tendencies, a thorough whacking in Soviet jargon. The Communist party congress chose a young man in the middle of the split, the thirty-nine-year-old Minister of Labor, Jouko Kajanoja. But on his way out, Saarinen openly accused the Russians of "provocative activity" and, in an unprecedented tongue-lashing, said, "The Soviet Communist Party can sometimes be in error. We are now faced with one such error." This kind of blunt exchange delights Finns with its fresh air of freedom, but also worries them lest it bring a Soviet crackdown. They are always attentive to the straw in the wind. But the party has been steadily declining of late and no longer is significant to Finnish politics.

The Helsinki negotiations, concluded with a summit conference of European, Canadian and American leaders in 1975, was a reinforcement of Finland's position. It was an acknowledgment that the West as well as East accepts Finland's position outside their rivalry, allowing it to be a little more neutral than the treaty with the Soviets suggests. From Moscow's point of view, the main significance of the Helsinki accords was that it ratified postwar borders in Europe in the absence of a German peace treaty. This seemed to imply that the special Finnish role and Finnish borders were also ratified by all the signatories.

In one of the rare Soviet territorial retreats, Nikita Khrushchev had returned the Porkkala Peninsula in 1956 when he was seeking to ease international tensions. It was in the same post-Stalinist period that he approved the Austrian State Treaty, withdrawing Soviet troops from their occupation zone in Austria and making Austrian neutrality an international obligation, and made his remarkable trip to Belgrade for a reconciliation with Marshal Tito. No such Soviet withdrawals have taken place since, not even from the four small northern Japanese islands whose disputed ownership has prevented a Soviet-Japanese peace treaty and encouraged Japanese friendship with China, to Moscow's unease. In comparison with others who fought the Soviets and lost, the Finns did well. On balance, Moscow has endorsed the Kekkonen line that if Finland maintains friendly relations with the Soviet Union, it will be free to govern itself and develop economic relations with the West.

The military-political issue is the central one, but Finland also has serious economic interests in the East. Soviet orders have kept its specialized shipyards—mainly icebreakers—busy when shipbuilders elsewhere were having to shut down. The Soviets provide a guaranteed supply of petroleum at world market prices and buy Finnish machinery, which would have trouble finding other markets. The decline of oil prices in the mid-1980s left Finland with a huge trade surplus with the Soviets, beneficial in terms of jobs but worrisome in terms of dependence. It tries to keep at least three-fourths of its trade directed westward, but the competition is tight with other Scandinavian countries. By far the largest export is wood and wood products, including paper, which account for 60 percent of hard-currency earnings. It is a very modern industry, with new equipment and high productivity. But there is a conflict with farmers who own those forests that have not been nationalized and drive up the price of wood.

Still, life has improved so dramatically in a generation that Finland is no longer one of the countries which send a high proportion of their youth abroad in search of a living. There is social welfare, without the astringency of Swedish socialism, and encouragement to enterprise. Young people travel, mostly in search of the sun during the dark winter, and return home with a new pride in their quiet, unpolluted, uncrowded, very clean country. Happiness is tranquil solitude beside a shimmering lake.

The Finns are dedicated sports fans and they read a lot, winter nights are so long. They worry when world tensions rise—it could easily affect them—but the trouble spots are usually far away. From what seemed an extremely precarious situation, they have built a sense of security and optimism in a young, future-looking society. People in other countries sometimes warn of the risk of being "Finlandized" and of the need to face down the Soviets, but the essentially moderate Finns tried that and failed. They are aware that the guarantee of their success in finding a tolerable balance depends on the existence of strong defenses in the West. But they are pleased with themselves. Matti Virtanen, a young clerk in an export company who likes to drink beer in an English-style pub, and who jogs, plays darts and follows the news of disasters around the world, summed it up, "Being born in this country is like winning the lottery of life."

THE LOW COUNTRIES
The Bourgeois Monarchies

T HE ROMANS CREATED the first sense of a European entity with roads, flung out to link their conquests from the British Isles to Romania on the shores of the Black Sea. But it was by waterways that Europe began to flourish. The great rivers were its arteries, and the great cities, Paris, Vienna, London, were built on their banks. The low-lying lands around the mouth of the Rhine and its subsidiaries were the vital portal to much of the continent, a strategic prize to contending powers. The area in general was referred to as the Netherlands, a name now reserved for Holland alone, and the Low Countries now comprise Holland, Belgium and Luxembourg.

When Julius Caesar reached the region in 57 B.C., it was inhabited partly by Gallo-Celtic tribes who had been pushed westward by advancing tribes of Germanic stock, partly by Germanic peoples who had reached the Rhine. The Gallo-Celts were called the Belgae; farther north were the Batavi, and between the Rhine and the Ems were the Frisians. There was intense resistance to the Roman invasion, but by 15 B.C., under Augustus, the territory was formed into an imperial province, Gallia Belgica, and the frontier was fortified. The Batavi, not absorbed but ranked as allies, revolted in A.D. 69, then associated themselves once again with Rome. But by the late fifth century the empire had disintegrated, and the advantages as gateway to the world were eclipsed.

Charlemagne, whose parents came from Belgium and northern

France, was crowned Holy Roman Emperor by the Pope in 800. But with his death, what remained of the old imperial unity fell apart again into a mosaic of feudal and ecclesiastic domains. It was the Dark Ages; there was little commerce, and access to the old trade routes had no great importance. The Norsemen raided the Low Countries repeatedly in the ninth and tenth centuries, strengthening the rise of feudalism in defense. But land holdings and manpower mattered most. The House of Burgundy grew to strength and splendor. When Philip the Bold, Duke of Burgundy, married Margaret de Male of Flanders and Brabant in 1384, her heritage was added to his domain.

Burgundian power was consolidated by his grandson, Philip the Good, during his well-fortuned forty-eight-year reign from 1419 to 1467. By marriage, purchase and force of arms, he established strong authority over most of the territory. His courts at Dijon, on the Saône, and at Brussels were the most splendid and luxurious of the time. Philip's granddaughter Mary married Archduke Maximilian of Austria, later to become Emperor, transferring her inheritance to the House of Habsburg and launching its long rule of the Low Countries. Their son Philip married into the Spanish succession, and when he died soon after reaching the throne, his six-year-old son became Charles V, Holy Roman Emperor and Habsburg monarch of Spain and the Netherlands. Marriages affected sovereign allegiance of the lands more than the recurrent wars.

By then, the advance of navigation and shipbuilding had changed the outlook of Europeans with access to the sea, and was changing the sources of wealth. The lands along the North Sea were not particularly favored with resources, but their ports became the great trading centers of the continent. Water brought them danger, open as they were to the sea, and the low terrain offered them little defense against invaders. They resented the demands of their Spanish overlords, and as the Reformation spread rapidly among the Dutch-speaking peoples, they resented the ardently Catholic Spaniards' attempt to hold them submissive to the Roman church. It was the time of the Inquisition in Spain, the period after the expulsion of the Moors when no torture was too brutal to serve the cause of imposing the faith. Sometimes the lowlanders used the water as a weapon against the Spaniards, opening their dikes to flood the countryside. The Spanish siege of Alkmaar was thus broken in 1573, and of Leiden in 1574, though at the cost of the lives of many peasants who could not find refuge in the towns.

The religious differences tended to crystallize between the northern and southern areas, with the south remaining Catholic, loyal to Spain, and alarmed at the spread of militant Calvinism among their northern neighbors. There were repeated battles and numerous massacres. Three southern provinces formed a league for defense of the Catholic religion, quickly countered by the Protestant Union of Utrecht in 1579, which established an independent confederation and proclaimed itself a republic. Habsburg Spain recognized it in 1609, and from then on the northern and southern areas developed separately, looking in different directions.

But even during all the quarrels of politics and religion, there was a great opportunity for enrichment in trading with the vast, newly opened world, and the Dutch became its masters. They turned their backs then on the endless continental wars of territory, succession and religion. Despite the rigid strictures of their Calvinist morality, the prosperous burghers supported not only adventurous captains on long trading voyages, but slavers who plied the seas between Africa and the Americas and pirates who preyed where the booty was rich. Commerce was their king. When Spanish warships needed vinegar to cool their cannons and renew the battle, Dutch merchants sold it to the enemy. There was a saying that "the Dutch would trade with the devil in hell if they weren't afraid their sails would burn."

With their wealth and their refusal to take sides in the great conflicts which roiled the larger powers, the people of the Low Countries developed to an unprecedented degree a society of towns, in contrast to the traditional rural society of lords and peasants. Unlike the flourishing city-states of Italy—Venice, Genoa and Florence—their prosperity and power depended on merchants and guilds instead of on aristocrats and soldiers. They became patrons of artists and architects. Their commissions reflected their homely concerns, in contrast with the religious, mythological and neoclassical art ordered by church and palace. They built town houses, bought portraits of themselves or depictions of household goods or lively scenes of revelry or bucolic delights. They inspired a new earthy aesthetic celebrating everyday things and ordinary people, and they produced great masters.

The seventeenth century was Holland's golden age. It could afford all that was new and luxurious and tasty from wherever it was available in Europe or overseas. Rembrandt van Rijn enriched his great canvases, ordered by the municipal corporations, with the technique of chiaroscuro, which had just come from Italy. The palace at Dam Square in Amsterdam, which served as the town hall, was designed in fanciful Palladian style with marble floors and Corinthian columns. Kings traveled to Delft to peer through the wondrous microscope of Anton van Leeuwenhoek, which could magnify a drop of water 270 times. In Leyden, Hugo de Groot (Grotius) wrote his great treatise on war and peace, the beginning of international law and law of the sea. Baruch Spinoza, grinding lenses for a living because his works challenging articles of faith of his Orthodox Jewish community were banned, extolled the wisdom of tolerance and proclaimed, "The real purpose of the state is freedom."

The Dutch sage and priest Erasmus of Rotterdam, who left for Oxford and roamed his world in the late fifteenth and sixteenth century, was the greatest humanist of the Renaissance, a man of learning and moderation. He disliked the dank, ascetic life of his Dutch monastery and never returned, but he spread his ideas and respect for knowledge throughout Christendom. Erasmus felt the need for reform in a Roman church grown corrupt, authoritarian and closed in on itself. He argued against dogma and ceremony and for a return to the simplicity of early Christianity. In the house of his friend Thomas More, in England, he wrote *The Praise of Folly*, a fierce satire on the pretensions and prejudices of the time. Kenneth Clark, in his book *Civilisation*, called it a "dam-burst" of frustrated intelligence. Erasmus was above all a rationalist arguing for common sense, not a metaphysician. But he refused to join Luther and forsake the Catholic Church, foreseeing the hysteria and violence that the great split among the faithful would unleash to ravage Europe for more than a century.

For a long time, however, he also refused to oppose Luther, occupying himself with literature. When pressures grew strong, he chose the central point at issue between them, explaining in *De libero arbitrio (Of Free Will)* in 1524 why the dignity and liberty of the human spirit could not be reconciled with Lutheran determinism. He spent his last years in Basel, Switzerland, where he died at age seventy in 1536. It is said that not long before his death, the Vatican made a last attempt to induce him to denounce the Reformation with promises of a substantial income and perhaps a cardinal's hat. Erasmus was not interested. He lived by his principles.

It can be argued that the Dutch interest in peace was above all to protect their trade, that their interest in law was not just because of

Calvinist doctrine but the natural search of the weak for a defense against might. That may be, but it led to a society which offered haven to refugees, including the English Pilgrims who later went on to America and landed at Plymouth Rock, to freethinkers and to the enterprising. This hub became so important that once again the powers pressed to force it into one of their rival spheres. France was determined to dominate these lands so as to confront England. England could not afford to leave them in French hands. The Dutch managed to balance them off most of the time.

But the French Revolution sparked new pressures among these independent-minded lowlanders for reform. The southern provinces, in part French-speaking and still Catholic—essentially modern Belgium —were incorporated into the first French republic in 1796. It brought extended civil rights and reopened the port of Antwerp, closed by the wars. But it also brought conscription and a campaign against the refractory clergy which infuriated the peasantry. In the north, the Dutch revolted with Napoleon's help, proclaiming the Batavian revolution (after the Batavi tribe which had rebelled against the Romans). But Napoleon was no democrat. He suppressed the republic and named his brother Louis as King of Holland in 1806.

The Dutch ports were vital in Napoleon's scheme to deny England all trade with the continent by boycott. Louis Bonaparte sympathized, however, with his stubborn, antiwar subjects, who busied themselves with smuggling through the French blockade. Napoleon wrote Louis contemptuously, "You have neither army nor navy yet you pretend to be a free and independent state," and threw him off the throne, integrating the whole kingdom into the French empire in 1810.

Napoleon's defeat at Leipzig in 1813 was followed by a general uprising in the Low Countries that ended French dominance. The issue became the future of an independent kingdom of the Netherlands and its territory. Conditions for full union were even less favorable than they had been in the sixteenth century. The Belgians outnumbered the Dutch by 3.25 million to 2 million, and the Dutch worried about their winning preeminence, about their Roman Catholicism, about the economic rivalry between their great ports. At that time, the Belgians had a flourishing industry of textiles, coal, munitions and shipping, and the Dutch feared being overwhelmed.

The Belgians were even more opposed to union, particularly their clergy and nobility. Still, up to 1828, the Belgians were divided, with the professional and commercial bourgeoisie opposing the recalcitrant clergy and aristocracy. Then they united on the issues of freedom of education (from state control) and freedom of the press, and when they rose in insurrection in 1829, the workers joined them and brought victory.

The revolution of 1830 established the independent kingdom of Belgium under Leopold I, and from then on, the Netherlands meant only what is now called Holland. Luxembourg was partitioned, with part incorporated in Belgium and the remainder comprising what is now the grand duchy. The settlement of the Napoleonic Wars confirmed the region's determined neutrality, with the approval of the major powers. For once, the people's deep inclination and European geopolitics converged.

The three countries did manage to stay out of war for a century, though both Belgium and Holland were active imperialists overseas. Holland's most important colonies were Indonesia and Dutch Guiana, now Suriname. It retains only the Netherlands Antilles in the Caribbean. Belgium's were the Belgian Congo, now Zaïre, and Ruanda-Burundi, now separated as independent African states. In World War I, Holland's neutrality was respected. It had strengthened defenses and mobilized just before the war, which persuaded the German general staff to skirt Holland and attack France through neutral Belgium. That reinforced Britain's decision to enter the conflict. Vastly exaggerated propaganda atrocity tales, about Belgian babies tossed on bayonets, mobilized the already enthusiastic British public's support for sending troops to the continent to kill the Kaiser. The Dutch took their escape from the murderous fighting as an immunity on which they could rely. They were quite unprepared and easily overrun when the Nazis launched their western offensive in 1940.

The disaster of isolated defenselessness and devastation for both countries in World War II revived the old ideas of union. Belgium had an economic and currency union with Luxembourg, and during the war negotiations began in London to join the three in a unit called Benelux. It never fully matured. The three countries were delighted to be absorbed in the larger European Community in 1957 and became the most ardent advocates for transforming it into the core of a historic United States of Europe. That was not to be, in part because the British clung to their old opposition to any continental coalition for nearly a generation longer, in part because France insisted on preserving national prerogatives.

The failure of the European Community to develop cohesion reinforced the differences among the Low Countries as they moved on in
the succeeding generation. Once again, they went different ways. Holland discovered a bonanza of natural gas in the northern part of the
country. Belgium and Luxembourg sagged when coal and steel were
deposed as the sovereigns of industry. Language differences and politics
were again sharply divisive, with Holland moving much farther to the
left than essentially conservative Belgium. They reacted differently to
decolonization, Holland negotiating its way out of empire on ultimately
generous terms, Belgium abruptly pulling up stakes and leaving chaos.

In many ways, the people have more in common than in contrast.
They are beer drinkers (though Luxembourg produces an excellent
Moselle) with the stolid joviality, the dislike for fanciful extravagance,
the prudence of populations who prefer the hops to the grape. The
Belgians have grown ever more bourgeois, the Dutch ever more tolerant. Both are very much a part of the north as the European Community balance swings with the addition of more Mediterranean countries.
But they are on separate paths, economically and socially, and there is
no more talk of union.

Acutely aware of being small and vulnerable after World War II, the
three countries produced some of the most effective and intelligent
statesmanship in the creation of a new international system. Their
leaders, such as the cultivated Paul-Henri Spaak of Belgium and Luxembourg's witty Joseph Bech, were able to take a large, cooperative
view exactly because their own countries' political weight was too slight
to provoke resistance or tilt the balance. They made important contributions to the development of the United Nations, the North Atlantic
alliance, the vision of a united Europe. They were more sensitive to
the gains from integration than were some of the leaders from countries
still focused on strictly national goals, and they helped ease the necessary compromises. But the new system did not go far enough to absorb
their countries' energies. The time came when a focus on local politics
overtook the larger issues. The next generation of politicians was
obliged to concentrate on domestic disputes, the language problems of
Belgium and the extent of the welfare state in Holland. They could no
longer command an international audience. It was a loss for Europe.

NETHERLANDS
Dear Father State

I<small>T SEEMED TO HAVE HAPPENED OVERNIGHT.</small> In the 1970s Holland, the merchant monarchy par excellence, whose stolid, conservative values had been taken for granted, emerged as Europe's most socialist country. The proud, satisfied old burghers, luxuriating in their satins and stiff, finely pleated ruffs, still looked down from the walls of the many museums celebrating the glories of old Dutch painting. The gabled town houses of Amsterdam still had hooks and pulleys under the eaves used for centuries to haul up supplies from barges on the canals below. Rotterdam, almost leveled by German bombing early in World War II, was flourishing again, the world's biggest, busiest port. There were a few glass skyscrapers and new suburbs with rows of brick houses not so different from the old towns. But the look of the country had not really changed. It was still clean, neat, flaunting thrift and modest diligence, intensely independent-minded and individualistic. It was the last place where socialist theories for transforming society through government power might have been expected to take hold. And yet, by any measure *except* Marx's public ownership of the means of production, Holland had become broadly socialized.

Through a combination of heavy taxes and generous welfare, there was a dramatic redistribution of income. The difference in income between the richest and poorest 10 percent of the population was reduced to less than 5:1. Egalitarianism was expressed not only in material goods. People living on welfare or unemployment insurance—80 percent of their previous salary for six months, then 75 percent for two years—also received an extra month's allocation for holidays. Dutch officials explained that everybody had a right to an annual vacation and it would be unjust to exclude the poor.

Artists, with minimal requirements of proof of talent beyond their own declaration that they considered themselves artists, were guaranteed government commissions for painting and sculpture. The thesis was that they had an equal right to choose their profession and receive recognition. Squatters organized themselves with remarkable efficiency and, with the approval of a large number of compatriots, enforced their right to live where they found space regardless of property rules. On October 13, 1980, Bergerhoff Mulder, president of the Amsterdam court, upheld a squatter's appeal against police harassment. They were disturbing the peace of his household, the petitioner said, at the behest of the owner, who was trying to evict him from a basement, which had been used as a garage. The court ruled that the owner would have to park his car in the street. Some called it "established disorder," but many considered it reasonable that society should provide according to need, not wealth or status. There came a point, before the recession forced some austerity and spending cuts, where one-third of the national income was spent on social welfare. The bonanza of natural gas, discovered at Groningen not long after the war and enormously increased in value by the oil crisis, made such generosity possible. But it was a social consensus, a special national attitude which made it desirable for the Dutch.

Along with the concern for welfare, there was a social permissiveness, an insistent tolerance, a strong wave of pacifism, an internationalism which gave ardent support to the United Nations and foreign aid to third world countries, to a degree that was unique. Holland had not become pro-Soviet or anticapitalist. It proclaimed no ideology. But it revised its way of life to its own ideals and hoped that the example would spread.

The youth mood of the late 1960s was more cheeky than angry in Holland, and there was a new sense that well-being was a right, not a privilege. The Socialists won the government and the unions won strength in this period of reform and demand for welfare.

Policemen and soldiers—conscription was maintained without serious challenge—were allowed to wear their hair as long and lanky as they wished, and after all it didn't turn out to hurt efficiency or discipline. Amsterdam's "Provos" (for provocateurs) were not really rebellious, just trying to stir things up. They camped in the parks and bathed in the fountains. They painted bicycles white and left them on the streets for communal use, an experiment in public transport intended to reduce traffic jams by eliminating the need for everybody to ride and park his own vehicle. It didn't work, but it was an exhilarating notion. They proclaimed the sexual revolution and entered the drug culture. That didn't work so well either. Entrepreneurs moved in, adorning the red-light district with lots of garish red lights, which soon enough turned exuberance to tawdriness. Finally, the Dutch cracked down on heroin traffickers. But the indulgence of youth and the rejection of stuffiness remained.

Surprisingly, the Catholic Church had a lot to do with the demand for liberalization and social change. The Catholics had long been a minority in Holland. But in the prosperous postwar years, they began to outbreed the Protestants. Those who professed their faith, about 80 percent, were almost equally divided between the two religions in 1950. Of the 14 million Dutch in 1980, nearly 40 percent said they were Catholics and 30 percent Protestant, leaving a sharp drop in religious affiliation. Perhaps it was the austere Calvinism of the long-dominant Protestants which turned Catholics in a new direction, perhaps the feeling of breaking out into majority status. The Church developed a social vigor, a liberalism, a new sense of mission which put it at odds with Rome for many years. The main issues were the increasing role of laymen in religious work and priests who married but wanted to continue their vocation. All but one of the Dutch bishops defended the married priests against Vatican strictures. Gradually, the controversy expanded to a demand for the right to develop new structures. The Protestants made an effort to keep up. Their churches too became intensely involved in the peace and third world movements. Dutch society is intensely compartmentalized by religion. Rivalry between the churches tends to make them compete for avant-garde position.

The transformation of the country and its habits took Dutch conservatives and many moderates by surprise. Holland had seemed such a stolid, businesslike place. But once it happened, people began to probe and reconsider their traditions. They found the roots of the change deep in their history and culture. Under the monarchy as well as under the republic, the dominant social class had been the merchants, not a landed aristocracy. Neutrality had been the normal policy, not an interlude between alliances. Seafaring and a sense of mission had long taken the Dutch to the farthest corners of the world and pushed their thoughts far beyond the horizons of their little country. Missionary zeal was so prevalent that at one time half the Dutch clergy had become foreign missionaries and a tenth of all the missionaries in the world were Dutch.

At home, the democratic outlook was ingrained, a dimension of everyday life to be taken for granted. Tolerance did not have to be won and defended; it was an integral part of the national heritage. Aberrations were not taken as an improper but understandable reversion to an unreconstructed past. There was a race riot against Turkish workers in Rotterdam in 1972, and later, with the increase of the foreign-born and non-Europeans to 5.7 percent of the population, an anti-foreigners party went on the ballot. Most people considered such developments profoundly un-Dutch, and were shocked and shamed when the anti-foreigners list of candidates polled 1 percent.

The wartime experience had strengthened the sense of community and the commitment to social justice. The failure of a British commando team to take a bridge on the lower Rhine during the large battle at Arnhem in September 1944 delayed the full liberation of the country until May 5, 1945, just before the German surrender. Meanwhile, the Allies were fighting across France and Belgium and the Germans removed all transport and fuel supplies from occupied Holland to impede their advance. The result was very nearly mass starvation in the hard winter of 1944. Rich and poor suffered alike from hunger and cold. Fifteen thousand died. Many subsisted on tulip bulbs. The underground sent word of the catastrophe to Queen Wilhelmina in London. There were three weeks' rations left for the 3.5 million people in western Holland. After that, nothing. In response to her urgent pleas, some food stocks were air-dropped to her countrymen. Otherwise, there would not have been much of the population to welcome her back when liberation finally came. The country was drained and exhausted, but the ordeal had annealed the solidarity of its people.

Wilhelmina was a monarch in the late Victorian style, a stalwart *grande dame* of mettle and manners. She had come to the throne in 1890, the first eight years under a regent until she reached the age of eighteen. In 1948 she decided that fifty years was long enough to rule and, firm-willed as ever, abdicated in favor of her daughter, Juliana.

Queen Juliana once told a visitor to her country palace at Soestdijk, where she moved to get away from the courtly royal seat at The Hague, that each generation is a reaction to the one before, even in a monarchy. Her reaction, she said, was against the stately, circumscribed half-century of her mother's reign. She sent her four daughters to progressive schools in the village, as different as possible from her own private education. They studied with the baker's and the butcher's children, rode their bicycles through the streets and dressed like everyone else.

Juliana personalized her speeches and chose her own husband, Prince Bernhard of Lippe-Biesterfeld, a German whom she met in Austria during the 1936 winter Olympic Games. (King Carl XVI Gustav of Sweden also found his queen at a German Olympics, in 1972 in Munich, where Silvia Renate Sommerlath was working as a guide. Royal marriage-makers could not compete with sports.) Juliana and Bernhard were immensely popular with their informality. She did away with the curtsy. There was a dark period after the birth of her last daughter, Maria Christina, congenitally near blind. The Queen called in a faith healer, Greet Hofman, and rumors spread that the woman had achieved a Rasputin-like influence on Juliana. They were hushed for a time. But when Hofman began to insist that there were evil influences in the palace that must be cast out and naming Prince Bernhard as the main one, he succeeded in throwing her out. "The Queen is boss of the country. I am boss in the home," he said.

The Dutch were discreet about the couple's personal relations, but it was noticed that the Prince made a lot of trips alone to Paris. He apparently was having money troubles in connection with his private life. That, at least, was the gossiped explanation when it was revealed in 1976 that Bernhard had accepted $1 million from Lockheed as part of its attempt to win the lucrative European market for a new NATO fighter plane. (Investigations showed that Lockheed had also paid off the President of Italy and the Premier of Japan, which led to a U.S. law on corrupt business practices by American firms overseas.) But while he was censured by a special commission and forced to resign from a number of honorific posts, including the presidency of the World Wildlife Fund, Bernhard was forgiven by the people for the Queen's sake. In 1977 the government increased his pay by 16 percent, to $335,000 a year. Juliana's salary was raised to $1.7 million.

The Dutch were startled and saddened when, on her seventy-first birthday, April 30, 1980, the Queen followed her mother's precedent and abdicated in favor of her eldest daughter, Princess Beatrix. It was soon after Beatrix's forty-second birthday. Juliana had been on the throne for thirty-one years, not so long compared to her mother, and she was still in good health. There was fighting in the streets when Queen Beatrix was invested as the country's sixth sovereign. Some resentment lingered over her marriage to Claus von Amsberg, a German diplomat who had served in the wartime German army, though much was dispelled when her firstborn was a son, Prince Willem-Alexander. He was twelve when his mother rose to the throne, and when he succeeds he will be the first Dutch king since his great-great-grandfather Willem III died in 1890.

Blue-eyed, dimpled Beatrix had her escapades as a girl. Once she ran away from school, and at age ten she and her sister were reportedly arrested for stealing some papers from a cart. At the University of Leyden, where she studied, she had a romance with an impoverished fellow student. The royal family intervened. But by the time of her accession, she was a stocky matron with a sure sense of dignity and more concern for protocol than Juliana had. She had said several years before, "My mother taught me that being queen is a position that you carry around with you day and night. You can never forget it, not for a moment."

Aside from the traditional origins of liberal Dutch attitudes, the conversion of society was also impelled by the shock of decolonization. The Dutch had been among the earliest European explorers and overseas settlers. Like the other European countries which were occupied in World War II, they fully intended to restore their empire when the war was won.

Dutch colonies in North America, South Africa and the Caribbean had been lost in the wars and colonial rivalries of earlier centuries. But the vast Dutch East Indies remained the imperial jewel. Indonesian nationalists, however, had different ideas when the Japanese surrendered. There was bitter fighting for four years as the Dutch sought to reimpose control. Finally, in the fall of 1949, the Dutch accepted the futility of attempting to reimpose colonial rule and sat down to negotiate at what was called the Round Table Conference in The Hague. It resulted in Dutch recognition of Indonesian sovereignty on December 27, 1949.

The Dutch repatriated their own emigrants and descendants, Eurasians who chose Dutch nationality and Moluccan Islanders who fled centralized Javanese control. The transition went surprisingly smoothly

in Holland. It came at the time of reconstruction and revival of the
Dutch economy, so that fears of a painful readjustment never materi-
alized. That was the beginning of important new perceptions about the
meaning of empire, the role of the colonizer, the burden of absorbing
immigrants rather than exporting emigrants. The first sense of a huge
loss was transformed into a sense of shedding responsibility, of being
freed to concentrate more on the needs of the homeland and discovering that the newcomers were a welcome source of labor and skills. In
1975 Suriname, formerly Dutch Guiana, was declared independent.
Although the country, on the north coast of South America, was four
and a half times larger than Holland, it had a population of only
400,000. Most of it was jungle, and most of the population was black,
the descendants of slaves. Some 100,000 people, almost one in four,
took advantage of Holland's offer of free immigration. Along with the
Moluccans and others from the East Indies and, later, Turkish migrant
workers, they established their own, less than neat, neighborhoods
around Dutch cities. For the first time the Dutch became a multiracial
society.

The break in intimate ties with distant lands and races also brought
the outward-looking Dutch a new sense of smallness, to be overcome
by deliberate involvement with the third world. From tough-minded
colonists, they turned into enthusiastic patrons of the underdeveloped
countries' efforts to enter the international community as equals. Guilt
played a part. So did Calvinist morality and the old missionary impulse.
While it was never so vast as the British or French empire, the Dutch
empire had been far-flung and it gave the people of a little country a
feeling of presence in the world. They did not retreat with decolonization into a sense of isolation, impotence, uninvolvement—like Switzerland, for example—but sought to replace the direct responsibilities and
privileges of empire with moral and political activity.

In the social climate of Holland, causes proliferated. Permissiveness
and social justice at home, environmentalism, development aid and
support for the third world, antinuclear campaigns, disarmament, pacifism—all found fervent support. They were part of the restive youth
culture of the 1960s and early 1970s, but in Holland they caught up all
kinds of people, Protestants as well as Catholics, the sober bourgeoisie
as well as the industrious workers. Walter Laqueur sought to explain
and identify the spread of European neutralism in a 1981 essay entitled
"Hollanditis," a name quickly taken up to describe a general shift of

attitudes long after the hippies had settled in the suburbs and donned business suits.

The "troops," the followers of various militant movements that would have no importance without the ability to attract much larger numbers, consisted, according to Laqueur, of "idealists in search of a cause, ecologists fearful of irreversible changes on earth and in the atmosphere, churchmen in pursuit of a new faith, young people bored by the absence of genuine challenges and attracted by any movement promising action. They are the products of the permissive age, repelled by sundry trashy subcultures yet also decisively formed by them."

The Dutch have had to struggle not only against their political geography in the path of often bellicose neighbors, but against nature itself. Their success in wresting their land from the sea may have something to do with their conviction that effort and right thinking can overcome all obstacles. They were already building dikes to reclaim lake bottoms and swampland in the thirteenth century. Now 27 percent of the country is below sea level and two-thirds of the 14.5 million people reside on land so low that it is vulnerable to flooding. There is little hinterland.

Even with its vast reclamation projects, Holland is Europe's most densely populated country, with 912.4 people per square mile. It is all flat. Where the land does undulate, occasionally producing little hills, they are called mountains. Vaalser Mountain, the country's highest point, is 200 feet high, one-fifth the height of the Empire State Building. From the top of a windmill one can see almost as far as from its observation tower. The early works of Piet Mondrian show clearly that the painter developed his characteristic style of colored rectangles from this view of the Dutch landscape. From above, the countryside is a neatly divided, two-dimensional canvas of varying tones. Mondrian's black and white lines of separation are the canals and roads. There are scarcely any indisciplined wriggles and blobs of feckless nature's design. Holland is a cultivated country, in every sense, tangibly the work of man and his intelligence.

The climate has the moods of the open sea, sparkling bright, choked with fog, glum-gray, but always fresh with a scent of salt. Wooden shoes still make sense on the wet cobbles and muddy fields, though they once were the footwear of poverty when stout boots were a luxury. The Dutch rely on flowers to break the monotony of the horizon. There are window boxes everywhere and, in the spring, vast fields of brilliance. Tulips were an aristocratic rarity in the seventeenth century, a prized badge of elegance which came originally from Constantinople and the Levant and caught the fancy of the enterprising Dutch. Now Holland is one of the world's largest exporters of flowers and bulbs. At some Dutch embassies around the world, instead of inviting dignitaries on the national holiday an annual reception is held on Tulip Day. In Holland, there are fairs and parades with floats. When the moment comes to cut the heads of the flowers so that the bulbs can be dug up in full vigor, the petals are strewn in the roads to form mosaic pictures, huge fragile postcards honoring Dutchdom.

Officially, the name of the country is the Netherlands. Holland is the name of an old province, now divided in two, North and South Holland, but foreigners use it to mean the whole country. *Dutch* is an English corruption of *Deutsch*, "German," apparently stemming from an early confusion about the two peoples. Amsterdam, the largest city, is formally the national capital, but the seat of the government is in The Hague, which is capital only of the province of South Holland. Altogether, there are eleven provinces, soon to be twelve with new lands reclaimed from the Zuyder Zee. Small as the country is, there are sharp local divisions and a profusion of spoken dialects to which people still cling. When separatism was surging in many European countries in the 1970s, the Frisians in the north sent delegates to conferences with Basques, Bretons, Welsh and others who were campaigning against their national governments for cultural recognition and special autonomy rights.

Yet to others, the Dutch seem remarkably homogeneous, easy to identify. They aren't all blond, blue-eyed and husky, but enough of them are to make the appearance characteristic. They dislike pretension. Even the wealthy are likely to live in unimposing brick houses with small gardens and fill their living rooms with knickknacks collected on trips, pieces of pewter and painted faience. They do not seem to feel a need for space and protected privacy. Windows seldom have their curtains drawn. Instead, a row of potted plants and a small embroidered screen or a lacy half-curtain are all that shield an interior from the gaze of passersby in the street.

Everything works so well, grievances and aspirations are so routinely accepted with a sympathetic response, decency is so commonplace, that the prime Dutch complaint is boredom. Franz Peeters, young editor of the radical weekly *Vrij Nederland (Free Netherlands)*, complained that "there are no poor people in the country anymore, and really no very rich. The intellectuals are looking for the last taboo [to challenge]. It's all too dull here." He considered himself a revolutionary, by definition an adventurous profession. But he was at a loss for goals, he told an interviewer. "That's the trouble. I don't want a revolution now. We have a totally free press, and there are no good papers, nobody really digging up hidden facts and attacking. I would be content with the American political system where a senator can really show up some scandals."

Amsterdam's Provos had a fine time in the mid-1960s, gathering on Saturday nights to shock the citizenry with "happenings" and provoking the police. They won a seat on the Municipal Council with the slogan "Vote Provo for a Laugh." The movement was built around the use of marijuana, but by the early 1970s that was no longer an issue. Fully co-opted, the movement collapsed in frustration at success. One disillusioned member said after the Provos' election victory, "No matter whom you vote for, the government always gets in."

The capacity of Dutch politics to co-opt challengers is matched only by the irrelevance of its intricate rivalries to the exercise of power. At one point, after the government had fallen, negotiations for a new coalition dragged on for nearly a year. Asked how it felt to endure such a long political crisis, Dutch banker-professor Ernst van der Beugel shrugged and said, "The country is so well run it can do without a government." In a sense, it usually does, because the permanent need for coalitions produces such a patchwork that no single group can dominate and no leader can impose a program without endless compromise. The national system of proportional representation fragments the political fabric and assures that no majority can emerge from the polls. At last count there were nineteen parties, with eleven represented in parliament. There is no threshold for eligibility, unlike Germany, which requires 5 percent of the vote for a seat, or Sweden, which requires 4 percent, so new parties with a catchy appeal or a popular prejudice can easily break through. They are born and die in a natural rhythm. Some political scientists consider the system a formula for remarkable stability in a pluralistic society with deep cleavages, imposing a search for psychological consensus. Others see it as a guarantor of unstable, hamstrung government. Both are right. It can please practically everybody in good times, but is woefully unequipped to make painful decisions.

The unique feature of the Dutch political and social scene, underlying everything else, is the *zuilen* ("pillars"), which stand separately but together uphold the national roof. They developed as political parties in the nineteenth century, but they stem from the old wars of religion and compromise confirming national independence in the 1648 Treaty of Westphalia. The anticlerical Socialists repelled workers who remained pious, and the churches set out to build their own organizations, discouraging the faithful from also joining class-based, functional or even merged Catholic-Protestant associations as the modern society took shape. Separate groups were organized at every level and for practically every activity—employment, unemployment compensation offices, schools, hospitals, unions, newspapers, funeral societies and recreational fraternities. People did not cross these lines, and intermarriage was a scandal.

The underground press argued against this divisive structure during World War II, and there was some relaxation afterward as people ventured to associate more freely with those from other groups. But the tradition was deeply entrenched. Intermarriage across religious, political or sheer traditional barriers increased for a time after the liberation, and then declined again as people cuddled around their own *zuil*. When television came, channels were reserved for each major group. People tend to switch from one to another, and now with cable TV they can also tune in directly to the BBC, German, Belgian and other stations. But they retain a very clear sense of "us"—in our group—and "them"—everybody else. Such clannishness, based on religion, ideology, life-style, to some extent but not primarily based on class, and not on family, could result in a closed, highly conflictual society. But the Dutch developed early a strong feeling for rationalism, and reason drove them to conclude that, with so many divisions, they must be especially accommodating to get along.

The welfare state has been an expression of that accommodation even more than of a political or ideological orientation. The Dutch call it *Vadertje Staat*, an affectionate diminutive which author Helen Colijn translates as "Dear Father State" in her sympathetic study *Of Dutch Ways*. It also multiplies bureaucracy. The state is prepared to provide subsidies for so many things, she says, from an esoteric book on baroque pipe organs to installing central heating and a bathroom in a structurally sound old house, that a new profession has arisen. The person who can guide an applicant through the maze of regulation is a "subsidiologist."

Despite all this paternalism, the Dutch economy has remained vig-

orous and essentially capitalist. Four of the world's leading multinational firms are Dutch—Shell, Phillips, Unilever and Akso. While
young leftists throughout Europe denounce multinationals as the bane
of the third world and the source of all social evils, the Dutch companies spread and flourish without undue restraint. The government is
prepared to spur the private sector. Profit, so long as it moves on into
investment and not conspicuous consumption, is not a dirty word.
Dutch agriculture has benefited from Common Market price supports,
contributing massively to the milk lake and butter and meat mountains
of surplus. Productivity and per capita gross national product register
among the highest in the world, although barely over half the population between the ages of fifteen and sixty-five is in the labor force,
compared to 65–70 percent in other industrial countries. When they
are at work, the Dutch work conscientiously, though Holland has also
been hit by the world recession and the challenge of newly developed
countries to traditional industry. The guilder, pegged to the deutsche
mark in the European Monetary Union, is one of the world's stronger
currencies.

"Hollanditis" has come to mean protesting—against American missiles, against atomic weapons, against police, against pollution, against
war. A young schoolteacher selling protest paraphernalia at the open
market in the town of Alkmaar said proudly, "There is a whole network
of people ready to act on short notice to organize demonstrations, with
buttons, posters and so on. It's Hollanditis." But Holland remains a
merchant monarchy, stolid even in its sin, tolerant even in its righteousness, good-humored in its sobriety, chafing but, after all, well at
ease in its order. Others may mouth the sentiment, but the Dutch do
believe that small is beautiful.

BELGIUM
Divided by Language

I T IS ONLY HALF IN JEST that the question of whether Belgium is a country keeps coming up. To the French, being Belgian is such a ridiculous joke that considerate Frenchmen feel they should apologize for noticing. They look down on the French-speaking Walloons in the south as people who lack refinement, whose diction is inelegant, who gorge on *frites* (French fries to us). The Dutch waste little sympathy on the Flemings in the north, whose written language is the same as their own although spoken dialects differ, considering them bumptious country cousins, industrious but greedy, deprived of higher moral values. The hostility and petty rivalry between Belgium's two language communities has become so intense that national fission is predicted repeatedly. But it hasn't happened and probably won't.

Their quarrels keep the Belgians together, a problem so specific to the country and such a nuisance to outsiders that they reinforce the national identity. They have divided themselves into three major areas, with 57 percent of the population living where Flemish is compulsory, 32 percent where French is compulsory and 10 percent in the capital area of Brussels, which is officially bilingual. Every Brussels street sign and public facility has to be designated in both languages. At times the language issue is carried to such extremes that it has contributed true stories to France's stock of derisory Belgian jokes. Paris's *Le Monde* reported in 1984 that French- and Flemish-speaking farmers in one region were embattled over regulations on whether artificial insemination of their cows had to come from bulls of the same language area or not.

The language border sprang up in the fifth century along the line where the Frankish tribes split into those influenced by the Roman heritage, who adopted a Latin-based language, and those who clung to their Germanic origins. But by the time of the Renaissance, the use of French had spread throughout the upper classes and the bourgeoisie. Flemish was the language of the uneducated peasantry. As the French state consolidated in the seventeenth and eighteenth centuries, there were repeated efforts to recapture the Low Countries, which had once belonged to Burgundy but had been lost to the Habsburgs, ruling from Spain. England always considered French control of the lowlands ports a direct threat. For centuries, it was vital to English strategy to keep them out of French hands by diplomacy if possible, by war if not. As early as the thirteenth century, close ties were formed between England and the growing lowlands cities which flourished as the crossroads of trade with the continent. Powerful and prosperous cities grew, based especially on the manufacture of weapons and cloth woven with wool imported from England. Among the most famous were Bruges, Ghent, Ypres, Antwerp and Brussels. Their lace, linen and woollens were prized, and their burghers developed habits of autonomy long before the end of feudalism.

But after the Reformation, the loyally Catholic Belgians were ill at ease with the dominant Protestantism of their Dutch neighbors in the north. Even before Napoleon, the revolutionary French Convention had annexed Belgium in 1795 with local compliance. Sympathy for the revolution waned quickly, however, as the Church was persecuted, the government centralized and conscription introduced. In 1804, under Napoleon, French laws and the Napoleonic judicial system were introduced, the metric system imposed and prefects appointed as the basis of administration. England considered this absorption a disaster. The Belgians would have liked independence when Napoleon fell, but London was convinced they would be too weak on their own to resist renewed French attempts at dominion.

So, for "the convenience of Europe," as diplomats put it at the time, the Belgian provinces were incorporated in the Kingdom of the Netherlands under William I of Orange in the grand postwar settlement of 1815. William spoke French and paid special attention to the industrial development of coal-rich Wallonia, neglecting development in Flanders. Most of the Belgians resented William and chafed at the imposed union. But it was not until 1828 that the rival Catholic and Liberal parties composed their differences, briefly, in common hostility to the Dutch throne. The French revolution of 1830 sparked the Belgian tinder, and a few weeks later came the Belgian revolution. Independence was proclaimed along with perpetual exclusion of the House of Orange from the Belgian throne. It was not a republican revolution, nor really a social revolution in the French sense, but it was a defiance of the 1815 decision by the powers of Europe as well as of the sovereign.

The powers agreed to recognize Belgian independence and neutrality as a compromise of their own ambitions. An uncle of Queen Victoria, Prince Leopold of Saxe-Coburg, was sent to launch the Belgian dynasty, with powers strictly limited under the constitution drawn up by a revolutionary congress. It was the most liberal charter in continental Europe. At that time, French was still the language of government, business and education. After the period of crisis, new energies were released by the spread of democracy and a determined effort of the young state to industrialize. Belgium built some of the first railways on the continent. A fresh spurt of prosperity and its liberalized institutions enabled the country to escape the wave of unrest that swept the continent in 1848. During most of the nineteenth century the country was relatively calm and stable. The issues, as in Holland, were slowly rising demands for social reform, education and, at the end of the century, workers' rights.

Leopold I was a strong ruler who busied himself with the development of industry, moderating the perennial quarrels over church versus public education and strengthening the national defense. His death after a long reign in 1865 provoked alarms about the future, until the Prussian defeat of Napoleon III definitively balked French ambitions. His son Leopold II was a vigorous economic promoter and an ardent colonialist. As a personal enterprise, he created a state eighty times the size of Belgium in central Africa, a land of fabulous mineral, timber and other resources. His monopoly was contested, and in 1908 he ceded the territory to the Belgian state as the Belgian Congo. By then, he was an awesome old man with a long white beard, one of the richest anywhere. Tensions were mounting in Europe over colonial rivalries and mounting nationalism. War was on the horizon. Just before he died in 1909, Leopold II was able to sign the law instituting conscription which he had been urging for years.

The throne passed to his nephew Prince Albert, son of Leopold's younger brother the Count of Flanders. Albert had married Princess Elizabeth, Duchess of Bavaria, a *grande dame* who lived to be eighty-nine and to become a world-famous patron of music. When Germany violated the solemn treaties of Belgian neutrality in World War I, they led the nation at war and kept it fighting on at least a small front until the Allied victory in 1918.

The language issue took on new abrasiveness during the war. Flemish-speakers were already a majority at the time of independence. But they were mostly poor small-holders, with farms among the smallest in Western Europe. They spoke a variety of subdialects, and it was not until the 1880s that a few intellectuals sought to promote a cultural self-awareness, which had long since developed in Holland. One was Hendrik Conscience, whose book *The Lion of Flanders* (1838) called for a national awakening. The inscription on his monument says, "He taught his people to read."

Flemish nationalism arose in the last decades of the nineteenth century, along with the rise of the workers' movement. The latter was more social Christian than Marxist, supported by progressive elements in the Church. The propertied class was French-speaking, and social mobility depended on language. The first demands of the Flemings were for an administration and judiciary in their own language, and for the opening of a Flemish university so that a knowledge of French would no longer be the key to entry into the professions.

As World War I occupiers, the Germans granted language rights which the French-speaking ruling circles had long denied. Some Flemish-speaking conscripts at the Yser battlefield created the Front Movement, protesting that 80 percent of the troops were Flemish but few of the French-speaking officers knew their soldiers' tongue. Some soldiers were punished for failing to obey commands they could not understand. After the war, the reforms granted by the Germans were revoked. Flemish nationalists were judged "traitors to the Belgian motherland" and their movement was effectively repressed for almost a generation. It was revived again in the 1930s, reinforced by the grievances produced during the Great Depression. This time, there was greater acceptance of the demands. A series of laws was passed permitting the use of Flemish in administration, education, the courts and the army, in the areas where it was the mother tongue. The university of Ghent was converted to Flemish. But economic power remained with the French-speakers.

The Germans invaded a second time in World War II. In ideological terms, Léon Degrelle's Rex Movement in Wallonia was closer to the Nazis than were the Flemish nationalists. But, inspired by revulsion against French-speakers' dominance of the state and encouraged by Hitler, who found them "sympathetic," some of the nationalists once again collaborated with the occupier in the belief that Germany was sure to win. And again, after the war, there was widespread and severe punishment. More than three times as many Flemings as Walloons were sentenced for collaboration. There were 242 executions, compared to 88 in Holland, and thousands in France. This was the beginning of the intense strains which persist in dividing the country and paralyzing its politics.

The behavior of King Leopold III during World War II exacerbated the emotional friction. The Dutch had complained at first when their Queen Wilhelmina fled the Nazi invasion and took refuge with her family in Canada. But the vigorous government-in-exile which she headed and its active participation in the Allied effort soon reconciled them to the justice of her decision to symbolize resistance from abroad. In contrast, Leopold's decision to remain with his countrymen seemed heroic at first. But he surrendered to the overwhelming force of the blitzkrieg after eighteen days. The Germans kept him a prisoner in his palace at Laeken, and he played no part in opposition to the occupation. Some saw him as a collaborator. A government-in-exile was established in London without him. After D-Day, the Nazis moved him to a fortress in Germany and then to Austria, where he was liberated by American forces in 1945.

The London-based government returned to Brussels, and Leopold's brother, Prince Charles, was elected regent while controversy raged over whether the King should be allowed to return. The death of his first wife, the beloved Queen Astrid, in an automobile accident in 1935 had deeply grieved the Belgians. Walloons resented his second marriage to Liliane Baels, a commoner, and felt that she influenced the King to tolerate the Nazis because she was pro-Flemish.

Leopold III was a cold, haughty man who did not inspire popular affection. The charge of collaboration inflamed passions because it implicitly judged the behavior of every Belgian. The French-speaking population, whose sympathies had been with France, considered him a traitor. Flemings supported him and considered the charge a reproach for their own easier passage through the war, because they were farmers with better access to food and fuel and because Hitler had ordered less harsh treatment of the Flemings, whose language is so near to German.

The royal issue provoked demonstrations and riots. Finally, a referendum was held in 1949, with results sharply split along regional-language lines. While the King's return was endorsed by 57 percent of the overall vote, a majority of Walloons had been opposed and argued that he would only be "King of the Flemings." He accepted their rejection and returned to pass the crown on to his son Baudouin, then twenty. Baudouin mounted the throne in 1951 and has reigned without controversy since. Timid, with an air of fragility and seeming to squint through his glasses, he keeps carefully apart from politics. His marriage to the pretty Spanish aristocrat Fabiola de Mora y Aragon in 1960 was accepted without great ado. The monarchy survived as one of the few symbols of nationhood in a divided land, but without the powerful unifying appeal of the British royal family or the ability to inspire fresh national effort, like King Juan Carlos of Spain.

In addition to their history, modern social and economic tensions reinforced the dispute between Flemings and Walloons. Wallonia, the southern part of the country bordering France and Luxembourg and reaching almost to Germany, was the prime industrial region. It thrived in the nineteenth and first half of the twentieth century when steel mills and big factories were the signs of wealth and the trade of the old merchant cities was being bypassed. The agricultural Flemings, mostly in the north but with pockets in other parts of the country, with their big, placid dray horses and their fat cows, were left far behind, neglected and disdained. They were efficient, industrious farmers, but they could not rival the riches produced by manufacturing and far-flung investment. They resented the realm's failure to develop their lands and the sense of social slight. In the 1960s, the imbalance was taken into account and there was a conscious effort to invest in their areas. By then, new light industries were coming to the forefront—electrical goods, appliances, chemicals, pharmaceuticals—and Flanders leap-frogged ahead. The prosperity of grimy Wallonia began to blow away through the big old smokestacks of Liège, Namur, Charleroi. Flanders emerged as the favored region in the shifting economy, benefiting as well from the Common Market's increasing subsidies to agriculture.

Its people determined to get their own back and to make the most of the ironic reversal of fortune. Economic improvement brought greater political power. They insisted on exercising it in their mother tongue to prove that Flemish was just as good a voice of government as French, Flemings just as worthy of prominence as Walloons. The Belgian political parties, long organized throughout the country on traditional lines of socialists, conservatives, Catholics, broke up in the 1960s into two sections each, one for each language. It became almost impossible for truly national figures to emerge, or to deal with national issues except through debilitating compromises putting the language question ahead of other pressures. Coalition governments, unavoidable given the fragmentation of parties, struggling to make difficult decisions on problems of inflation, investment or defense, were brought down by the disputes over language.

Not only have the Flemings been the majority since independence, though long silent; their birthrate has been increasing relative to the Walloons'. Of the country's 10 million people, the count is 5.5 million Flemish-speakers, 4 million French-speakers and half a million of foreign nationality, though there has not been a census for a long time. Henri Simonet, a dynamic, worldly Socialist, said Belgium had become a country intelligent enough to analyze its ills but not wise enough to cure them. Paul van den Boeynants, a Social Christian (conservative) who served for a time as Premier, said that they could only be solved by a national leader respected by both communities. The Walloon politician and the Flemish politician agreed on what was wrong and what was needed, but the country has yet to produce a leader with broad enough appeal to achieve it. Belgium has developed into a prize example of the dangers of allowing a society to divide against itself in the name of bilingualism.

The rules have become so complicated about how a postman, a policeman or a court clerk may be addressed in any given place that no one can be sure of exact legal rights. At the ancient Catholic university of Louvain, one of Europe's oldest and long a bastion of French, bilingualism was introduced, but then, in 1968, the French section was expelled on the grounds that courses in French could no longer be tolerated on Flemish soil. It was resettled as a new university in Wallonia and the library of the old institution was shared out—books with even reference numbers remaining at Louvain and books with odd numbers being sent to the new campus.

Language and social disputes had become intertwined in a way that aggravated both. After the issue of the monarch was settled with King Baudouin on the throne, the old question of Church versus state education reached a point of anger in 1955 called the "school war." That too was handled by a national vote, which showed the majority of the

Flemings favoring Church control and the Walloons, with more of a socialist, lay tradition as a result of nineteenth-century industrialization, preferring state schools. There was a general strike in 1960–61. Belgian workers are prone to strikes, though their productivity is high. It was nationwide, but the Flemings gave in quickly while the Walloons held out to the bitter end. They felt they had been let down by the Flemish workers. The union leader André Renard of Liège founded a radical new federalist movement as a result, heightening separatist demands.

The idea of federalism gained support and, inevitably, opposition. Regional governments are not linked to the central government, have elections on different dates, and often different majorities. It took an intervention from King Baudouin to block an attempt by some regions to establish their own diplomatic representations abroad. Brussels successfully fought off federalist pressures, arguing that it would "downgrade" the capital to a mere Washington, D.C., instead of a dominant national seat of government and undermine its ability to compete with other continental cities as a great international center of commerce and finance. The tens of thousands of foreigners who live in Brussels seldom speak Flemish and favor the efforts to limit constricting language rules and the city's key position.

The decision to establish the headquarters of the European Communities in Brussels was natural enough. It had to be in a small country so as not to confer privilege on one of the large ones against the others, and it had to have good communications. The results have changed the city. The Berlaymont, a chunky arc of glass and concrete which houses the European Economic Community, is more than a landmark. It is the capital of Europe. There are some 13,500 "Eurocrats," international civil servants, and most of them are in Brussels. NATO also moved "temporarily" to Belgium, with its political headquarters in Brussels and its military command headquarters in Casteau, near Mons, forty-three miles to the southwest, when General de Gaulle threw it out of France in 1966. It is still there and not likely to move again. All this makes protocol problems for the Belgian authorities, since many countries send three ambassadors, one to EEC, one to NATO and, lowest on the totem pole, one to the government of Belgium.

Brussels has also drawn a bustling new international set. Businessmen, labor and farm representatives, politicians, scientists, economists from all parts of the world conduct affairs in the capital, many of them establishing residence. They participate very little in Belgian life. The lines between Belgians and internationals are almost as tautly drawn as those which make the United Nations a lesser island on the island of Manhattan. But, by being there, these people have given Brussels a tangible new look. Hotels, office buildings and housing developments have gone up to accommodate them. There are also large communities of Turks and Yugoslavs, drawn north in the period of great southern worker migrations. They have opened little restaurants. They drive taxis and work in shops. As a result, old Franco-Flemish Brussels acquired an unpremeditated cosmopolitan side, though its business is still business.

Belgium's geography, which gave it great advantage for trade and produce, has also been its undoing. Though it is only the size of Maryland, its flat fields and thinly wooded forests made it one of Europe's natural battlefields for centuries. Sooner or later, almost every army marched through, laying waste to towns and villages, destroying much of a rich monumental heritage. The wonder is that so much of the old splendor survived, in the flamboyant cathedral of Antwerp, the pastry-icing houses along the tranquil canals of Bruges, the Old Town Square of Brussels. The heavily decorated houses around the huge, cobbled square give a lively sense of what it meant to be a wealthy burgher when Europe was taking over the world. Their façades exude well-being, satisfaction, a confident sense of knowing how to turn a profit and how to spend it on the good life. There is no soaring grandeur, nor any humility, but enjoyment of the comforts and the ornaments that enterprise could bring. There are fine restaurants in the neighborhood. Other parts of the capital are mostly drab and tacky, or gleaming glass, depending on whether they are pre- or post-Community.

Given its history of invasions, belligerent or peaceful, it is surprising that Belgium has not produced the kind of militant peace movement, assertive hippiedom, people who protest for the joy of protest, attitudes and ways of life which the Dutch have come to call "Hollanditis." It has something to do with the Church. Belgium is almost totally Catholic. Though some of its bishops were active in the liberal coalition at Vatican II, allied with Dutch and German bishops pressing for reforms, on the whole the Church has remained traditional. There is no strong Protestant rival, as in Holland, leaving less incentive for the Church to plunge into the intense push for social and theological reform which seized the Dutch Catholics as they emerged into demographic majority status. The lack of activism also has something to do with the language feud, which absorbs so much energy. And it has something to do with national self-image. Belgians are more concerned with making the best of whatever is offered or has to be endured.

The Belgians were diffident, disengaged colonists. When the time came to pull out of the Belgian Congo, now Zaïre, a vast country with three times Belgium's population of 10 million, they simply went home. They left behind no more than a handful of indigenous university graduates, doctors, trained administrators. They had never felt what the English poet of imperialism Rudyard Kipling called, with arrogance but still a certain compassion, "the white man's burden." Zaïre's capital, now Kinshasa, was Leopoldville until independence. Brussels businessmen are still intimately involved with Zaïre, but take no responsibility for its backwardness and corruption.

Unlike the Belgians, the Dutch feel an obligation to act on the world, to nudge it and nip at its heels. They decolonized reluctantly at first, but in the end more generously. They preach, and they are usually prepared to practice what they preach. They tend to be more righteous, more openhearted and more adventurous than their Belgian neighbors, and less indulgent. The Belgians, less inhibited by a sense of moral duty, have more respect for pleasure, more exuberance and style. They still mount uproarious village festivities, with the excuse of honoring Brueghel or tradition, or without excuse. Rather than resenting clumsy jokes at their expense, they make fun of themselves and do what appeals to them, often superbly. They are not terribly self-important and see no reason not to enjoy life.

André de Staercke, a retired diplomat of the old school, is a model of Belgian worldliness and charm. He worked with Allied leaders during the war, meeting Roosevelt and Churchill and coming to intimate terms with the establishments of the West. For over a quarter of a century he represented his country at NATO, a sturdy advocate of alliance solidarity and dean of its diplomats. He is full of cheer and bounce, appreciative of all that is erudite, beautiful, intriguing, well done. (When boring official meetings dragged on, he surreptitiously exchanged limericks in Latin with John Foster Dulles, Eisenhower's Secretary of State.) As a lifelong civil servant, he was never rich but liked to say when others complained of the recession and lowered living standards in the 1980s that he was the master of ninety servants. He had only one, a faithful, aged housekeeper. But he calculated how many people it would have taken to provide horse-and-carriage transport equivalent to the little car he drove himself; how many people to cut and deliver the ice he got out of the refrigerator; how many people to keep stoves and chimneys going for the heat he got from the radiator; how many people caring for lamps and candles to give the light he produced by flicking a switch. He concluded that he lived like a Roman emperor.

Belgium is a small pond, and it takes an effort for its people to make a splash in the big world. But the Belgians are proud of those who manage. Ensor, Magritte, Maeterlinck and Simenon are Belgian names known to the world of arts and letters, not to speak of Flemish masters from the earlier period of a united Low Countries. Christine Ockrent is a star of French television. She leaped the dual barrier of being a woman and a Belgian to become France's most popular and respected newscaster by sheer professional preeminence, bringing a larger view to the national-minded French audience. The inevitable parochialism of a small, long-subjected country makes it harder to achieve wide recognition, but it adds depth to the internationalism of those who transcend the bounds. Paul-Henri Spaak, Belgium's Foreign Minister in the postwar years, had an outsized part far beyond the weight of his country in the diplomacy of restoring a world order, in creating the United Nations, Benelux, NATO and the European Communities. He won deference as a sage who could see far beyond narrow national interests.

"It is an old country but a young state," de Staercke said of his homeland. "The state could disappear, but the country would remain." Belgium has the lowest proportion of its people in the labor force of any country in Europe, 3.6 million who must support the population of 10 million. In hard times, it has one of the highest rates of chronic unemployment. Leo Tindemans, the tall, able leader of the Flemish Social Christian Party who was Premier for a time, summarized the politics of his country almost hopelessly. "Belgians love freedom, liberty and human rights," he said. "But they are difficult to govern. That is the synthesis of Belgium."

The sense of national solidarity rises high when a Belgian triumphs abroad, when the national football team does well or when Eddy Merckx, the champion cyclist or one of his successors, wins another Tour de France. But that isn't enough to rally unity in everyday life or modernize the economy. Bickering and grumbling, the country manages to go on, hoping for a revival of the momentum toward European integration to spark new energy. In the once flourishing Low Countries of monarchs and merchants, late twentieth-century Belgium is falling behind, in political disorder. But like Italy, it has no tradition of a strong central government and its people manage well enough without attending to politicians.

LUXEMBOURG
A Simple Grand Duchy

THE SMALLEST OF EUROPE'S NATIONS or its largest ministate, Luxembourg is big enough to have its own language and to participate actively in international affairs. Yet it is a cozy place. Once during a visit, I mentioned to the Foreign Minister that I would like to do a wine-tasting tour of the Moselle Valley. He looked at his watch—it was nearly 5 P.M.—and told me to hurry around to the Ministry of Viticulture before it closed. In an old palace, behind a massive wooden door, the ministry's director received me graciously. He made a telephone call, and the tour was arranged to start at nine the next morning. No fuss, no protocol, a family kind of hospitality.

Like the rest of Western Europe during the years of rapid economic growth and labor shortages, Luxembourg drew a flood of migrants. They came mostly from Portugal and Italy, some from neighboring France and Germany, and some from Yugoslavia and Eastern Europe during the brief periods, such as the Hungarian revolution, when refugees could stream out. Now one in every four of the country's 368,000 population is a foreigner. But because of their origins, the influx scarcely dented Luxembourg's homogeneity of religion. The percentage of Catholics in the total population dropped from 99.5 percent in 1871 to 96.9 percent in 1970, although church attendance has dropped more noticeably. In old-fashioned, country-style welcome, the newcomers are accepted more easily, often treated more considerately than elsewhere. Without them, the country might have been headed toward extinction, because it has the world's lowest birthrate, 1.3 per woman, just under half what is needed to maintain population stability.

It's not that people leave. Life is just so tranquil, so well ordered and so comfortable that they do not seem to feel much urge for the effort of bringing up large families. Luxembourg is smaller than Rhode Island. The countryside in this 1,000-square-mile, pear-shaped land squeezed between Belgium, France and Germany is all rolling woods and valleys, nothing dramatic, ideal for bicycle tours and a jovial outdoors life. In a way, it's a very modern land, with the most automobiles, telephones and hospital beds and the highest domestic electricity consumption per capita in Europe. Yet it remains romantically picturesque.

The skyline of the capital, also called Luxembourg, is battlements and bridges, spires and mansards, perched across two ravines. Streets in the center are stone. People greet each other as they walk along, Premier and bank clerk. They probably went to school together, and they know who everyone is. The government statistical office has a hard time calculating an index for rents, needed for Common Market cost-of-living comparisons, because almost four out of five families own their houses, including the immigrants. Few are pretentious, almost none are slummy. Everyone is middle class, even the well-liked Grand Duke Jean and his wife, Princess Josephine Charlotte, daughter of Belgium's late King Leopold III.

The Grand Duchy has a long, embattled history, roiled in the tides of European sovereignties, often tributary to foreign crowns but managing to keep its special character nonetheless. The people came with the early westward Germanic waves. As a political entity, Luxembourg was a product of the feudal system which arose after the decline of Charlemagne's empire. In 953, Sigefroi, Count of Ardennes, exchanged his Abbey of St. Maximin at Trèves for a rocky promontory called Licilinburhuc where he wanted to build a castle. It became the base for a future fortress, later the city of Luxembourg.

Half a millennium later, Philip the Good, Duke of Burgundy, captured the fortress, ending Luxembourg's feudal autonomy. He established French as the main language of government and administration, but Burgundy was the enemy of France. Philip was adept at diplomacy by royal marriage and assured support against France through alliance with the Habsburgs. That brought Luxembourg under the Habsburg crown of Spain for almost two centuries, from 1506 to 1684. Staunch

Catholics, the Luxembourgers were loyal to their Spanish king during the wars of the Reformation and Counter-Reformation, which devastated the country. In the eighteenth century, sovereignty of the Spanish-ruled Low Countries reverted to the Habsburgs in Vienna. After the Napoleonic Wars, Luxembourg was elevated to a grand duchy under the Dutch crown but lost territory in a series of partitions. Independence was achieved only in 1867, with a guarantee of neutrality in a compromise which delayed but did not prevent the war between France and Prussia in 1870.

At Prussia's insistence, Luxembourg had joined the customs union of the German lands, the Zollverein, which increased dependence on its German neighbor but laid the foundation for development and wealth. German capital, manpower and markets were the base for the creation of Luxembourg's great steel industry in the last quarter of the nineteenth century. In the absence of a suitable heir, the title of Grand Duke went in 1890 to Adolf of the German duchy of Nassau, who had lost his lands to Prussia. The new dynasty, Nassau-Weilburg, was the first to rule only over Luxembourg. His daughter Charlotte ascended the throne in 1919, after the abdication of her elder sister Marie-Adelaide, and reigned for forty-five years, winning great popular affection.

Grand Duchess Charlotte, who had come to seem an imperishable institution, stepped down in 1964, leaving the throne to her son Jean. He had married the sister of Belgium's King Baudouin, Princess Josephine Charlotte, which reinforced the old ties with Belgium. By then, Luxembourg was economically linked to Belgium by the postwar Benelux agreements and membership in the Common Market, but it did not diminish the country's independence. The heir is now Jean's son Henry, who married a Swiss citizen of Cuban origin, and they have three sons, so the dynasty seems assured for a long time ahead. Like other modern European sovereigns, Luxembourg's grand dukes or duchesses reign but do not rule, providing a symbol of national unity and identity above a fully democratic government headed by an elected premier.

Despite the history of foreign sovereigns and shifts of tutelary allegiance, the people of the grand duchy always stubbornly refused to change. They were loyal to the line in their national anthem which says, "We want to stay what we are." Among themselves, they speak Luxembourgisch, a dialect closer to German than to Dutch or Flemish, and use both German and French for official purposes, sometimes mixing all three. They are aware that their country was once much larger, gnawed away by neighbors over the centuries, but they get along with them without resentment. There is a currency and economic union with Belgium, formed after World War I, when Luxembourg left the German customs union. It has had unforeseen advantages beyond trade, providing double access to international exchange markets now that the country has become a world banking center.

From the late nineteenth century until the great shifts of the global economy and industrial base of the late twentieth century, Luxembourg's wealth and prosperity rested mainly on steel. Arbed, the giant firm which was to Luxembourg what the United Fruit Company was to a banana republic, was Europe's fourth biggest producer, a multinational with only a fifth of its work force in Europe. At its peak, it had 100,000 employees in plants in Europe, Asia and America. From 1975 on, steel was a crisis industry and there were massive cutbacks by all European producers. But even after five years of retrenchment, in 1980 steel still accounted for 15.5 percent of the country's gross national product, half of its industrial output, nearly half of its industrial work force and over half of its exports. Arbed, though heavily in debt, managed to remain highly efficient. The government, in agreements with the management and unions, worked out provisions to absorb the unneeded labor. The "Luxembourg model" for cushioning the impact of recession and distributing the social cost was widely admired. It buttressed social stability, easing the pain of readjustment. But no one expects steel to recover its old prominence. Even before the crisis, Luxembourg began to find other economic outlets.

It is a determinedly liberal country, in the nineteenth-century European sense of free enterprise, free movement of capital and minimal regulation, so it became a magnet for international finance. Luxembourg is not a tax haven. But it respects money. Discretion, political stability, good communications and noninterference with banks have turned its Boulevard Royal, circling the city center atop the old city walls, into a Wall Street with 112 banks from around the world. The same kind of indulgence for commercialism has made it a major European radio and TV center, broadcasting primarily into France, where the state monopoly controls airwave advertising. Its passenger airline, Luxair, and its air freight line, Cargolux, developed into powerful international companies by cutting overseas rates so that it was cheaper to make a detour through Luxembourg than to fly directly to the big markets.

Luxembourg's role as a good-tempered political dwarf among much bigger rivals enabled it to attract an outsized share of Common Market institutions, including the European Court of Justice, the European Investment Bank, the European Publications Office and until 1984 the European Parliament half-time. Now the Parliament sits full time on the French side of the Rhine, in Strasbourg. Rotation imposed an expensive and irritating trek several times a year, with all the people and truckloads of files and equipment moving back and forth in long convoys. Luxembourg is still fighting to retain the three thousand parliamentary secretariat jobs, of immense importance to the city with its steel industry on the wane. But France is likely to win. In compensation, Luxembourg officials want more freedom for broadcasting facilities to other countries and the seat of the European Monetary System, which could make the claim to being a capital of Europe even more effective than does being the transient seat of the powerless Parliament.

A large complex to house Common Market institutions was built at Kirchberg, a plateau some two miles outside the capital and linked to the city by a bridge and fast highway. Modern and imposing, the buildings make a sharp contrast with the fairy-tale gables and cobbles of the old town, but an appropriate one, because Luxembourg functions as a modern cosmopolitan society in a traditional, provincial setting. With their families, the foreign employees of the various European institutions headquartered in Luxembourg number ten thousand, a privileged group who live tax-free.

With its history, its languages, its deep folk roots and open spirit, its attachment to old styles and readiness for modern methods, Luxembourg is at once a conglomeration of Europeanness and a unique, landlocked island. Gaston and Liliane Thorn are perfect examples. The Thorns are an old family, probably descended from people who came from Torun in Poland in the Middle Ages. Short but slim, athletic, crackling with energy and humor, Gaston Thorn went into politics almost as soon as he could vote and zoomed upward. He belongs to the Liberal Party, a centrist group between Conservatives and Socialists. At forty-one, he became Foreign Minister.

Liliane, his college sweetheart, had already launched her own career as a journalist and by then was local correspondent for Associated Press, the American news agency. She is an independent-minded woman,

attractive, chic, warmly unselfconscious. While she was proud of her
husband, she saw no reason why his rise should confine her to the
drawing room and the kitchen. When he became Premier, she conceded that there could be a conflict if she continued reporting on politics. So she switched to writing articles and broadcasts about artists.
But she never stopped doing her own job, even when Gaston Thorn
became President of the European Commission, as near as there is to
a president of Europe, and they had to leave their rambling old house
in Luxembourg and move to Brussels. They became one of the world's
most traveled and most popular couples. It was typical of Liliane that
when she was told at the last minute to appear at a royal wedding in
London, she tossed an evening gown in her tote bag and changed in a
toilet on the plane. Of course, it was a couturier gown from Paris and
she knew how to curtsy to the Queen.

Luxembourgers tend to find ways to cope, and not to have complexes. They speak several languages—nobody else speaks theirs—and
they have little trouble feeling at home in the world despite the seeming
insignificance of their homeland. They are among the most ardent of
European unifiers; membership in the big club balances their own lack
of weight. They are at ease with the times.

SWITZERLAND
The Quiet Cuckoo

T HE SWISS ARE NOT NOTED for effervescent humor or tart jokes.
But they do have jokes considered revealing of their basic view of the
world. One explains the origin of Switzerland as the result of God's
compassion when He realized He had made a country in the middle of
quarrelsome Europe with no resources of its own. So He made towering, awe-striking mountains. The Swiss thanked Him politely, but
pointed out it would be hard to live off the Alps alone. He understood,
and made magnificent lakes. Still they complained. He made lush,
nourishing pastures. They shrugged; they would need more than that.
He filled the pastures with herds of fat cows which would produce rich
milk and fine cheese. They were pleased. By then God was tired and
thirsty from His labor. Wiping His brow, He asked for a glass of milk.
"Of course, God," came the hospitable answer, "here it is, fresh and
creamy. That will be two francs, please."

Another is a line Orson Welles spoke in Sir Carol Reed's film *The
Third Man*, with screenplay by Graham Greene. "In Italy for thirty
years under the Borgias they had terror, murder, bloodshed—but they
produced Michelangelo, Leonardo da Vinci and the Renaissance. In
Switzerland, they have brotherly love, five hundred years of peace and
democracy, and what did they produce? The cuckoo clock."

The myths are as much a part of the country as the mountains and
the banks. They are cherished as a bulwark, a stronghold against the
turbulent, foolish, often profligate outside world—but a world whose
people can be coaxed into providing a good Swiss life and a serene

286

Swiss conscience. At home, when they are among themselves, the Swiss scarcely feel they are a nation. The village of the father's birth is the source of identity, registered on passports. Aliens are people from a different valley, even the next one. They cling together as Swiss because they are convinced that being anything else is much worse. But the official name of the country isn't even Switzerland. It is Confederatia Helvetica, the confederation of the mountain-dwelling tribes whom the Romans called Helvetii, and that designation, abbreviated CH, is used on Swiss coins and license plates for foreign travel.

Though their image now is prosperous, they were poor tribes who had to scrape a living from their mountainous land. They were so scrappy that for centuries a major export was their brawny young men, to serve as mercenaries in the armies of foreign lords. But as a nation, they opted out of Europe's wars and proclaimed their state neutral after a defeat by Burgundy in 1515. From time to time after that, they were subjected to incursions by their bellicose neighbors until the Congress of Vienna gave formal recognition to Swiss neutrality in 1815. In the intervening years the Swiss had come near fighting each other more than once. But they avoided the murderous wars of religion by standoff compromise, made possible by fragmentation and local option, having little to do with tolerance and brotherly love. They were farmers and cowherds, not among Europe's venturesome merchants and traders except for the dispatch of soldiers. It was the romantic, restless English who spread the idea that scrambling up snowy peaks and boating on glacial lakes was a tourist's paradise. Lord Byron, who celebrated in melancholy verse the dank Château de Chillon, near Montreux, called Switzerland "a curst, selfish, swinish country, placed in the most romantic region in the world." His compatriots flocked to see for themselves, and the Swiss cleaned up their chalets and opened hotels for their strange, insistent visitors.

The folds of the Swiss Alps are Europe's central watershed, draining the land to the North Sea through the Rhine, to the Mediterranean through the Rhone, to the Adriatic through the Ticino-Po connection and to the Black Sea through the Inn and the Danube. There is an area called Konkordiaplatz (ironically translated as Place de la Concorde Suisse by author John McPhee) where ice streams from half a dozen directions feed the greatest remaining glacier, Grosser Aletsch, a reminder that geologically it has not been long since much of Europe was frozen and that it is still warming up.

Some see it as a symbol of a congealed society, which seems to move only at glacial speed along the paths of social and economic change. Others infer the Swiss temperament from the national flower, the edelweiss. It is a small white blossom with no scent and no pretension beyond growing only at the highest altitudes. Swiss geography has deeply marked the people's character, locking them not only inside the continent with no natural gateways to the larger world save down the rivers, but also into narrow valleys. The Alpine sky is vast, of that bright, crisp blue that opens the heart, and the horizon of sharply formed peaks is the very shape of splendor. It is possible to breathe the crackling air and feel on top of the world, limitless, in Switzerland. But it isn't really the Swiss view, for all its intoxicating beauty. There is a sense of being hemmed in, overwhelmed by an immensity that makes people small and vulnerable, obliged to live prudently in a setting so far beyond the human scale. It is a challenge to be faced with caution.

The history is defensive, originating with the collapse of the Holy Roman Empire and the gathering of remnants to resist the expansionist rise of the Habsburgs. The story of William Tell is a feat of resistance against Austrian overlordship. Tell was from Uri, a forest district belonging to the Holy Roman Empire whose lands had been granted to the stewardship of the convent in Zurich. Gessler, the local Austrian bailiff, demanded that he doff his hat and salute as he was passing by, but Tell refused. So Gessler condemned him to shoot an apple off his son's head as a nerve-racking punishment. Tell was such a fine archer that he succeeded without touching his son, and then he took to the mountains in rebellion. That was supposed to have happened on November 18, 1307.

But the Swiss celebrate their national holiday on August 1 in memory of the meeting of men from Uri, Unterwald and Schwyz (from which the name Switzerland derives) on that date in 1291. They formed an "Everlasting League" for common defense against all comers and signaled their agreement with bonfires on the mountains to those who waited apprehensively below. Schwyz, which had belonged to various nobles before, was granted freedom from its lords and from direct dependence on the Austrian king in 1240. Unterwald had a more complicated history, disputed between the emperor and the pope. But after the three initial cantons sealed their confederation, they all became anti-Habsburg.

Zurich tried to establish feudal rights with the support of Austria, and there were continuous struggles between the rural people and the town. In 1315, the confederates defeated Habsburg forces sent against them and consolidated their union. The Austrians continued to mount intermittent campaigns to regain their dominion, and in 1492 the Confederation made its first alliance with France. By then, it had been enlarged and had attracted various towns and districts, some independent and others under an assortment of feudal rulers. There were various categories of affiliation in the Confederation—members, associates and more loosely bound protected areas. They quarreled at times among themselves, but when Maximilian sought to revive the authority of the Holy Roman Empire at Worms in 1495 and assert its sovereign rights over them, the Confederates resisted. Thus they established their practical independence. Twenty years later, after the Swiss attempt to expand farther into Italy was defeated by France's King Francis I at Marignan, near Milan, the Swiss made their first treaty of neutrality.

The Reformation spread unevenly in the cantons. Ulrich Zwingli, more a humanist than a strict disciple of Martin Luther, brought Protestantism to Zurich in 1519, and again in 1536. In Geneva, the French-born John Calvin established his views of man's direct relation to God. The Swiss were divided by religion, but took sides in the quarrels as much on political grounds as on points of theology, joining with French Catholics to support Protestant forces against those of the Habsburg Counter-Reformation. But they were spared the worst of the fratricidal ravages and managed to ward off invasion. It was not until 1798, inspired by the Directory established after the French Revolution, that the Confederation provided itself with a formal constitution. And only after the fall of Napoleon were the borders assured. The Congress of Vienna, in 1815, recognized Switzerland's "perpetual neutrality," which has never since been actually challenged, though there were times of serious threat.

In 1848, a year of revolutionary upheaval in much of Europe, the Swiss proclaimed a new constitution and winnowed their way through the international problems created by the flood of refugees which was said to compromise their neutrality. They have ever since been nervous about granting asylum to any large numbers, particularly from the neighboring powers. Giving expression to the moral aspect of neutrality and the preference for providing humanitarian service afield rather than gathering in the afflicted, the International Red Cross was founded in Geneva in 1864. Its symbol is an inverted Swiss flag, which is a white cross on a red ground.

The circumstances of its acknowledged neutrality made Switzerland a natural home for governmental international organizations as well. The oldest still functioning, the International Postal Union, was established in the Swiss capital of Bern in 1874. And in the euphoria of internationalism that flared and quickly faded after World War I, Geneva seemed the obvious, serenely neutral place for the League of Nations. The frustrating and finally tragic failure of the League was an important reason why Geneva was rejected as the site of the successor United Nations after World War II, though another weighty consideration in favor of New York was to bind the United States in close participation.

Many other international bodies made their headquarters in Geneva, however, and the U.N. itself opened its European seat in the rambling old Palais des Nations perched above Geneva's lake. Built in monumental style to match the idealistic ambitions that surged after the "war to end war," the building opened only in 1937, a bare two years before Europe was drowned in war again. But the peacocks, set out to parade in its park in accompaniment to, some said in mockery of, the puffy orators, were not disturbed. Geneva is still a city of diplomacy, international protocol and intrigue, and the peacocks are still there.

Switzerland's grandiose topography, in the heart of the continent, has paradoxically assured the nation only a modest role in Europe's history, providing a natural defense once the Swiss learned to take the precaution of staying out of other people's quarrels. The benefits they derived, and the towering mountain barriers between valleys, also taught them to apply the lesson of accommodation among themselves. Each canton took to concentrating on its own problems, letting its neighbors alone in the understanding that none was really in a position to overwhelm and dominate the others.

Curled around the southern end of Lake Geneva (which the Swiss call Lake Leman) where the Rhone rises, Geneva is not a large city but it has two quite distinct lives. One belongs to the international set, who fill the grand hotels, interrupt their year-round cocktail party with conferences and saunter along the neatly flower-bordered lakeside promenades. The other belongs to Calvin's Geneva, a tradition-bound city of merchants and functionaries, meticulous in dress and manner. Geneva's Protestantism and staid society led to the development of boarding schools as an important Swiss enterprise. It was a place where children could be sent for a non-Catholic education in French. The local pecking order is vigorously maintained, with status set precisely by the family address. The best people live in the dark bourgeois houses along the Rue des Granges, the largest street winding through the hilly, medieval Old City. But the ones who live on the even-numbered side of the street consider themselves so much better than the ones who live on the other side that they mix stiffly. With others, they scarcely mix at all. There is a hot damp wind, the foehn, at times and a nasty cold one, the bise, to tighten people's faces all the more in winter. But in the spring and summer, a great water jet splashes bathers in the dancing lake, sailboats festoon the view, and visitors lolling in the outdoor restaurants wonder why Geneva is called dull.

Zurich, Switzerland's largest city, takes its stodginess more earnestly, making and spending money with determined regard for good sense, good art, good music, good food, good comfort. It is the haunt of the legendary "gnomes of Zurich"—the imperturbable bankers who guard, cultivate, sprinkle and multiply the world's spare cash in their prosaic office burrows. It has complexes. Rich people hang their stunning collections of paintings in dark corners or behind doors so as not to appear to flaunt their wealth. Apartment windows are not curtained; if they were, neighbors would whisper suspiciously about what must there be to hide. Zurich is also at the foot of a lake and the rise of a river, but it spreads more than Geneva and its old sections have a livelier, better-preserved look. Guildhalls with elaborately adorned wooden interiors are lovingly maintained and displayed.

Basel, where Germany, France and Switzerland meet on the Rhine, is the city of trade and manufacture, headquarters of the great Swiss pharmaceutical and chemical companies. Basel the trade city, Zurich the bank city and Geneva the hotel city have disputes because national economic policies that may favor one, with a strong franc, constrain another, where business would be better with a softer currency. But Bern, the capital, is not the point of discord. It is a sleepy, low-storied town, set amid rolling hills, and doesn't bustle. The Confederal government sits there and the Confederal parliament meets there, but the most notable sight in Bern is the municipal bear pits. The animals, symbol of the canton, stand to beg for carrots, making their appeal with a lumbering dance.

The Swiss government is not so awesome as the bears. The current constitution, proclaimed in 1874, zealously preserves the rights of the cantons, cities and communes against any central encroachment. There is a president, but few know his name because the office is rotated every year among the members of the Federal Council. It isn't unusual for him to take a streetcar to work without being recognized. The right of initiative covers almost any subject, and the referendum requirement applies to practically any bill of importance. Swiss citizens are called to the polls more often than those of any other country, and likely as not vote no, although women still cannot vote in three cantons. Politicians complain that it is excruciatingly difficult to put through reforms. It cannot be said that the Swiss have less government than other countries; they have it in many active layers. But they keep it on a tight rein.

With gradual enlargement and change of status, Switzerland is now composed of twenty-three cantons. The majority (70 percent) speak German, or rather various forms of a dialect called Svitzerdutsch (it isn't written, so it is spelled here phonetically). North Germans do not find it easy to understand. Six cantons speak French. The language of Ticino, on Lake Lugano, is Italian, and in part of the Grisons the people speak Romansch, a language left behind by the Roman legionnaires and said to be the closest now spoken to the ancient Latin vulgate. All four are official, printed on the currency, but the country is not comfortably multilingual, or even widely bilingual. Each canton insists on using its own language and dislikes accommodating to the tongue of visitors from another, although many people are glad to learn English to accommodate tourists and businessmen. The proliferation has not been culturally fruitful.

Some say there is no Swiss culture, which is not true, but its segments are more a part of German or French, or to a slight degree Italian, culture than of an identifiable whole. Still, there is something special which might be called Swissness to the plays of Max Frisch or Friedrich Dürrenmatt, the paintings of Paul Klee, the sculptures of Alberto Giacometti, the movies of the young Geneva filmmakers. It is an acid quality, a stab of mockery or exaggeration, to take the edge off the cloying self-satisfaction of idyllic calendar landscapes, velvet vests thickly embroidered with flowers, and chunky wood carvings, which represent the folk art. There is a felt yearning for sophistication in the Swiss cities, but it doesn't come naturally.

People in each of the three main language areas look abroad, to the country of their mother tongue, for their cultural mecca. Nor have the famous dissidents and conspirators who sought refuge in Switzerland at various times, such as Rousseau, Voltaire and Lenin, left any mark on the society. Millions of visitors go through Switzerland, even make their residence there, but very few enter the country in more than the simplest physical sense. When it is in the news, it is almost always as the site of some tense international gathering or some scandal among foreigners. Seldom does anyone else notice Swiss affairs, and seldom is there anything to compel attention. No doubt that was why the brief disorders provoked by rebellious youths in Zurich in 1980, demanding that the city provide them with a recreation center instead of spending more money on its impressive opera house, seemed so startling. The events were minor compared to youthful upheavals elsewhere. But Switzerland is supposed to be the country where people go to get away from trouble, not where they find it.

For the most part, however, the Swiss observe what is going on out in the world and take pains to be up to date in technology, marketing, style and trends. They know that complacency can be costly. The watchmaking industry was nearly destroyed because leaders at the manufacturing center at La Chaux-de-Fonds, in the canton of Neuchâtel, were smugly convinced that Swiss timepieces were the best in the world and always would be. They failed to notice that their venerable little ruby-studded cogwheels had been overtaken by oscillating quartz until the Japanese captured most of their markets. Based largely on light industries, the economy has proved essentially stable in a time when the great heavy industries of Europe and America were going limp before the competitive onslaught from newly industrializing countries. But Switzerland has become sensitive to the general economic climate. It cannot avoid a chill when the winds of recession blow around the world.

On the surface, Switzerland and Holland have so much in common that it seems an enigma why their politics are so different. Both are small countries, about evenly divided between Protestants and Catholics, compulsively neat and thrifty, strong on moral certitude. But Switzerland is the most conservative country in Europe, and Holland can be called the most socialist of the democracies in terms of generous welfare, concern for social justice, egalitarianism and workers' rights, if not in nationalized ownership of industry.

Of course, one faces the sea and the other clings to the mountains, but with modern transportation and communications that does not seem enough to explain the contrast. Holland is a member of the Atlantic alliance, but it has a highly influential pacifist movement and con-

stant disputes about defense efforts. Switzerland is determinedly
neutral, but it is not pacifist at all. For defense, it is not frugal. The
largely citizen army requires a period of annual service from every male
up to the age of fifty (fifty-five for officers), after the completion of
seventeen weeks' conscription duties. If they are nurses, women are
included in the reserves and must report every second year for refresher
training.

Perhaps the difference comes from living on flat land, constantly
aware of neighbors and of a larger community, and living in isolated
valleys with little expectation of outside support or obligation. Certainly, social attitudes are opposite. For example, the Dutch worry
about assimilating their immigrant laborers and protecting them with
political rights, and the Swiss simply expel theirs when the supply of
jobs drops, making it as difficult as possible to earn the right to remain.

The Swiss writer Hugh Loetscher has diagnosed the Swiss unwillingness to contemplate social change or agitate for causes as "premature
reconciliation." After the 1980 youth riot in the Bahnhofstrasse which
so shocked orderly Zurich, quite unused to demonstrations and certainly not ones that bring property damage, the president of the central
bank, Fritz Leutwiler, offered to spend $20,000 to clean up and repair
broken windows. That would be a lot cheaper, he said, than having to
intervene on foreign currency markets to protect the Swiss franc from
loss of confidence at such upheaval. On another occasion, restive youth
looking for a rallying cry to express their frustrations could find nothing
more audacious than a demand to "flatten the Alps so we can see the
sea."

There is a particular balance to the Swiss temperament which often
goes unnoticed amid the contradictory, stubbornly persistent myths.
The people have the vices of their virtues. They are economical, hardworking, self-reliant, reflexively disdainful of self-indulgence and osten-
tation. They hold their country open to the world, but keep themselves
apart. They refuse to be involved in other people's quarrels and self-
destruction. They are peaceful for their own purposes, not as a moral
crusade. Their society is heavily militarized, and they are eager merchants of arms.

They have developed a very clear idea of how to live as a small
country divided by language, culture and religion, without any ambition of influencing the world. Their intricate system of accommodation
really could not serve as a model for peace among nations, as is some-

times suggested, or within a warring society such as Lebanon. It is arranged to serve their inward-looking needs of comfort and security, not to light a beacon. In return for this withdrawal from larger human causes, whether evangelical, social or political, they are prepared to offer dispassionate services that quarrelsome international society truly needs. They do make cuckoo clocks and hold yodeling contests. That isn't a vision of heaven on earth to fulfill utopian illusions, but nobody is the worse for it. Between the idyll and the insensitive stereotype, theirs is a solid country.

AUSTRIA
Small Can Suffice

AUSTRIA REVERSES PHYLOGENY. It was once a giant frog, its pads splayed at various times in distant corners of Europe from Spain to Galicia (now in Poland) and Ruthenia (now in the Soviet Union), from Sicily and Sardinia (Italy) to Flanders (Belgium and Holland). Now it is a pollywog, mostly head with a squiggle of tail. It has adapted with *gemütlichkeit*, the untranslatable state of mental and physical comfort which is the ultimate in cheerful, small-scale aspiration. But it hasn't forgotten grandeur. Playing with the acerb title of a memoir by French actress Simone Signoret called *Nostalgia Ain't What It Used to Be*, Austrian writer Peter Henisch characterized Vienna as the place where "nostalgia *is* what it used to be."

The splendid imperial capital, adorned with the palaces that great power builds, was one of only six cities in the world with a population over 2 million in 1910. Now it is fifty-eighth of the world's cities, with 1.53 million and going down, in a national population of 7.5 million. Vienna is the metropolis which has probably changed least in this century, not so much because of reverence for the past as by accreted habit. It never quite got around to removing streetcars and building expressways, though that was the intention. It turned out to be a boon when the energy crisis arrived in the mid-1970s. Victor Gruen, an Austrian architect and city planner who invented the shopping center when he was a refugee in America, has said, "Austrian slowness has been our best guarantee of progress. Many things done in haste all over the world will have to be torn down."

But thanks to convention and tradition, the Austrians have spared themselves much of this. Tenancy laws remaining from the turbulent 1920s make it almost impossible to sell buildings or land, except for bombed-out sites, so the high-rise developers never got a foot on the ground. The long, square-windowed façades of the glory days, when Vienna set the style for much of Europe, are still intact, if a bit cracked and grimy here and there. The parks and the woods are sacrosanct. *Schmalz* (literally chicken or duck fat but extended by usage to oozing sentimentality) and *Kitsch* (glittery or elaborate junk) bear Austrian trademarks, offered without apology but with a twinkling eye that invites complicity in amusement. The Merry Widow lives on beside the brown and rather muddy Danube, but in her heart it's adamantly blue. The legend is what counts and merits tender care. Reality can fend for itself.

Gentlemen still take a lady's hand, incline their head a little and say "Küss die Hand," but never touch it with their lips. The Vienna Opera House, handsomely restored after wartime destruction in a tasteful combination of the old baroque and shining modern styles, is still the scene of a gigantic annual ball—white tie, evening gowns and waltzes *de rigueur*. The ball season begins in January, and by Ash Wednesday the city normally holds over two hundred major balls, each attended by more than a thousand people and sponsored by all manner of groups and associations, and some five hundred smaller ones. The social cream floats ostentatiously at the top; Vienna is still acutely conscious of which are the "good" families. But practically everybody goes to a dance somewhere.

The breeding stock of the hefty white Lipizzaner horses was hidden and saved during the war, and they still prance and cabriole in elegant unison at the Spanish Riding School in the Hofburg. Not a thread nor a tint of the riders' courtly costumes has been changed. Originally brought from Spain in the sixteenth century, the breed of huge but surprisingly graceful animals has been kept pure. They perform in a great baroque hall completed in 1735, and on their way in, the riders still observe the rule requiring them to salute the equestrian statue of Emperor Charles VI which stands across from the main entrance.

The Vienna Boys Choir, founded in 1498 by Emperor Maximilian, still sings its celestial soprano in the chapel of the Hofburg Palace, though the boys' uniforms were "modernized" after World War II, to the sailor suits worn by upper-class children at the turn of the century. Potted flowers line the steps and candles sparkle in the magnificent gardens of Schönbrunn Palace when there is a state reception, whatever the season. On the terrace at teatime, Sacher's Hotel serves its rich chocolate torte made from the original recipe. At Demel's, the most fashionable pastry shop, the portrait of Emperor Franz Josef, who died in 1916, presides with solemn approval over the display of strudels and cakes. The sugary manners and adornments of bygone stately days are cherished and preserved. So are the dreary concrete boxes which were the pride of "Red Vienna's" progress in housing for workers in the 1930s. But the theme of politics now is "social partnership," compromise and cooperation instead of class struggle. Patronage is meticulously regulated by *proporz*, doling out jobs in the administration, the state-owned radio and television, the public enterprises, in strict proportion to party strength.

There is an unending argument about whether Austrians are just a variety of Germans, cut off from their linguistic brothers by the misfortunes of history, or a separate people who happen to use the same tongue. It swings with circumstance. Scholarship and emotion can be summoned to testify either way. The predominantly Alpine lands of Austria, Switzerland and the German state of Bavaria have many similarities, in custom as well as topography. People sing raucously, slap and stomp in heavy-booted dances, put flowers in their windows and on their lampposts. But while the Bavarians consider themselves special, they never doubt their Germanness and wouldn't dream of joining Austria. Contemplating their massive peaks, the Swiss have always considered themselves small and apart. The Austrians have only recently got used to the idea of being a little country. Their landlocked republic is the size of Maine, 70 percent of it mountainous. Austrians see definite advantages in their reduced status, but they smile with misty appreciation and a moth-eaten pride when they hear that Italians have taken to buying souvenir busts of old Emperor Franz Josef in Trieste or that Czechs complain because Central Europe, once dominated by Austria, has been squeezed between East and West.

Austria was at the center of much of the violent history of Europe, especially modern Europe. From its now placid face, it is hard to believe that so much has happened in less than a century. Austria's was the most spectacular crash in the fall of empires. It reached nation-statehood only a generation before the once progressive idea of nation-states began to pall and seem reactionary. It was the battleground of socialism and clericalism in the 1920s. It was absorbed by Hitler's Third

Reich in 1938, with the enthusiastic cooperation of home-grown Nazis who proceeded to apply Hitler's laws, including persecution of Jews, with a ferocity that the Germans had not yet shown. It was occupied by Russians, Americans, British and French after the war. And then, in the Soviets' only postwar retreat, it was freed of foreign troops by the State Treaty of 1955 and committed itself to permanent neutrality, a protected perch between East and West. There could be no more dream of the old multinational Austro-Hungarian Empire, sheltering or lording it over the lands between Prussia and Russia, depending on one's vantage point. So the Austrians set out to try to become an isthmus that could serve as a passage between East and West on a divided continent.

The idea of connections, instead of exclusion, goes back through all of Austrian history. It has always been a crossroads, a place whose people tried to reach out and assemble all they could around themselves rather than defining themselves as distinct and separate. When they were overlords, the Austrians sought to dominate variety rather than try to homogenize it in their image. Left to themselves, they still try to reach out to the neighborhood.

The original inhabitants of the region were Celtic tribes, an Indo-European people who early settled in what became Germanic lands. They established themselves along the amber route, from the Baltic through the Alpine Brenner Pass to the Mediterranean. From the early Iron Age, they quarried iron, other metals and salt, that once precious necessity. They were colonized and Romanized early in the Christian era. Vindobona was the Roman name for Vienna, already a place of strategic importance in those days. The Huns and the Ostrogoths pushed into the area in the fifth century, but the Germanic tribes which felled Rome and organized the Holy Roman Empire remained dominant.

By the tenth century, the land had become the empire's Ostmark, its eastern line of defense against the pressing Slavs of Bohemia and the Magyars of the Hungarian plains. (In 1938, after proclaiming the Anschluss uniting Austria with Germany, Hitler restored the regional name of Ostmark.) It was fear of growing eastern influence, particularly from Ottocar, King of Bohemia and son of Wenceslaus I, which led the imperial electors in the Rhineland to crown Count Rudolf of Habsburg as King of the Germans on August 24, 1273. His house had modest possessions in Switzerland and Alsace, and the electors considered him safely unprepossessing in the interminable rivalries of the time. The scramble for lands and fortune, for privilege and the right to tax, spread growing misery. It was aggravated by the fourteenth century's terrible waves of plague. The once robust peasantry was pressed into serfdom. Times were very bad.

In the fifteenth century, Rudolf's descendant Maximilian I sought to restore the earlier imperial order, to the benefit of the Habsburgs, of course. It was achieved less by combat than by marriage. He lived from 1455 to 1519 and came to be called "the last of the knights." His own marriage, to Mary of Burgundy, brought Burgundy and Flanders to his realm. He married off his son Philip to Juana of Spain in 1496, which put Burgundy and Flanders under the Spanish crown but added Spain with its enlarged possessions to imperial sovereignty. His daughter Margaret married John of Aragon in 1497, consolidating the new power of Spain and adding it to the legitimate Habsburg heritage. He arranged marriages of his grandchildren, though they actually took place after his death, to the heirs of Vladislav III, King of Bohemia and Hungary. Maximilian reigned as the Renaissance was developing, and he made his court a center of learning and art. When he died in 1519, he had opened the way for Austria to become a great power in the world. So successful was the dynasty that from 1438 to 1804, when the title was abolished, all but one of the Holy Roman Emperors was Austrian, though the distinction had been emptied of power and meaning long before.

A quarrel over the succession in Hungary helped the advance of the Turks, who first laid siege to Vienna in 1529 and pressed intermittently on Austrian lands. The capital was saved from the great siege of 1683 by Poland's King Jan III Sobieski. Coming to the aid of the embattled Christians, he descended so suddenly on the Turkish camps that the soldiers fled from their evening fires. They left behind their fresh bread, baked in the national symbol of the crescent, and the pots and beans used to make their dark tasty brew. Thus were croissants and coffee introduced to Europe. Vienna acquired the levantine habit of gathering and dawdling in cafés, one it still indulges with melancholy but assiduous pleasure.

Lifting the siege was a turning point in the long Turkish-Christian struggle, but the victories came just as Christendom itself was split by new furies over religious reform. Protestantism had spread through the Austrian lands, provoking the Counter-Reformation, which was led by the Jesuits from their headquarters in Graz, Austria. There had been a briefly successful rising in favor of the Reformation in Prague, led by Bohemian nobles and savagely put down by the Emperor's forces in 1620. It marked the start of the Thirty Years War. Austria emerged as the great Catholic power, against Protestant Prussia. This sealed the division of the German-speaking peoples. There were occasional alliances in which power struggles overrode religious allegiance, but it was a time when loyalties were not to a state but to a sovereign.

Gradually the Danubian monarchy developed cohesion, much advanced by the reforms of Empress Maria Theresa in the eighteenth century but also by the loss of more distant dominions. Maria Theresa, who reigned from 1740 to 1780, was one of the outstanding women of world history. She had sixteen children with her husband, Francis Stephen, Duke of Lorraine and Emperor Francis I, but her main energies went into statesmanship. She turned a feudal agglomeration of states into a centralized empire, modernized its financial system, promoted trade and industry, established a new legal system abolishing torture and reformed education, making the universities independent of the Church. But Austrian power invited competition. Napoleon's successful campaigns against Austria and Prussia at the beginning of the nineteenth century definitively ended Vienna's eroding position as head of the empire. The Habsburg dynasty remained, buttressed by Prince Metternich's cleverly agile but cautious diplomacy in the face of defeat, and by his prudence in victory when the Holy Alliance of Austria, Russia and Britain brought Napoleon down.

The Congress of Vienna in 1815 fixed most of the borders of Europe for a century, ending the interminable continental wars and enabling the powers to shift their ambitions to acquiring territory overseas. There were limited wars in Europe, as Prussia unified Germany and then fought France, but they did not engulf the continent. Austria did not participate in the race for colonies, continuing to confront the Turks for primacy in the Balkans.

By the middle of the nineteenth century, nationalist and liberal forces within the Austro-Hungarian Empire as well as in other countries arose to challenge what had come to be seen as obsolete, barnacled obstacles to progress and social reform. The year 1848 brought an eruption of upheavals across Europe, in a chain reaction similar to the antiestablishment outbreaks around the world in 1968. With hindsight, they can be seen as early warning signals that the whole system was breaking down and needed thorough overhaul. But the rebellions were suppressed.

Europe tottered on complacently into the abyss of World War I. It has become fashionable to see the start of war in 1914 as a colossal miscalculation, a string of explosive errors triggered by overrigid planning and stupid arrogance. Certainly, the war ought to have been avoidable, but it would have taken much more than subtler diplomats and wiser strategists. An old structure, riddled with rot, was collapsing. It could not have been saved. The question is whether the decay could have been recognized and replaced with fresher, more democratic supports in time to prevent the terrible conflict, whether it is within the nature of nations to perceive the danger of their ways before it overwhelms them. The continental empires were doomed. But even had they known it, they didn't know what to do about it.

The first casualty in World War I was Archduke Franz Ferdinand, heir to the Austrian throne. He was murdered at Sarajevo on June 26, 1914, by a South Slav nationalist. One after the other, the nations were drawn into the war. The cataclysm went on for over four years, leaving 8.57 million dead, 20.5 million wounded and 7.7 million prisoner. Civilian deaths were estimated at 13 million, including 1.5 million massacred Armenians, 6 million dead from famine and deportation, 800,000 killed in bombing and combat and 4.7 million victims of the influenza epidemic which swept Europe in the closing years of the war.

After the armistice was signed on November 11, 1918, the monarchies in Austria, Germany, Russia and Turkey were demolished. In Russia, the revolutionary Bolsheviks preached "proletarian internationalism" and retained what they could of the multinational tsarist dominion. But elsewhere nationalism was elevated to a first principle and a whole series of nation-states emerged from the wreckage of empire. Finland, Poland, Latvia, Lithuania, Estonia, Czechoslovakia, Hungary and Yugoslavia achieved independence. At the time, the new arrangements seemed liberal and pacifying, likely to ease the tensions that foreign rule had provoked. But the redrawn map inevitably left pockets of disgruntled minorities who resented the denial of President Woodrow Wilson's promise of "self-determination" for themselves. Various nationalities were so intermingled in much of Central Europe that there was no "clearly reasonable line," as Wilson had urged, to divide them into new states. Before the war there were some 60 million people who felt themselves under alien rule. Afterward, there were still 30 million outside what they considered their own ethnic state. The seeds of World War II were planted on the green baize conference tables where Europe was remade.

From a great, multinational empire, Austria became a small Central European republic. It had a population of 6.4 million on 32,376 square miles, compared to a population of 52.8 million on 261,241 square miles before the war. What had been parts of Austro-Hungary became the territory of seven states, three of them—Czechoslovakia, Yugoslavia and Poland—new sovereignties. Hungary gained complete independence, and Romania and Italy were given former Austrian lands. And what was left of Austria was torn by ideological violence made worse by the economic effects of amputation. Tremendous inflation starved the workers and fattened the conservative peasants, whose debts evaporated. Hungary went Bolshevik in March 1919 for a tumultuous 133 days, and then exchanged Communist rule for a right-wing dictatorship.

In Austria, private armies were organized by political parties on the left and right, and they battled in the streets of Vienna. The Great Depression, which began with the stock market crash in New York on Black Tuesday, October 24, 1929, spread via Vienna's Kredit-Anstalt, Austria's biggest bank, which collapsed in May 1931, followed by a series of bankruptcies across Europe. Country after country plunged into trade protectionism, trying to save itself by beggaring its neighbors. The Austrian National Socialists—Nazis—made big gains in the 1930 elections. An attempted Nazi coup in 1934 failed to seize power, but the right-wing Social Christian Chancellor, Engelbert Dollfuss, was assassinated. His successor, Kurt von Schuschnigg, appealed to Italy's dictator, Benito Mussolini, to help protect Austrian independence against the campaign for union with Nazi Germany.

With a combination of threats and subversion, and in the face of paralyzed indecision from the rest of Europe, the Führer forced his way. Hitler had been born in Austria, but his ambitions were to lead a greater Germany to rule Europe and the world. His first grab for power, which failed, was the Munich beer-hall putsch in the postwar distress in 1923. In 1933, at the bottom of the Depression, he succeeded.

When he marched into Vienna in March 1938, there wasn't any active resistance, though the Anschluss (union) of the two countries was in violation of World War I treaties. Hitler proclaimed the absorption of Austria into the new German Reich, which he said would last one thousand years. Many Austrians rejoiced, though there was also opposition and much emigration. There were sympathizers in Western Europe, some because they saw Hitler as a bulwark against communism and more because they felt that Austria was a natural part of Germany. The *Encyclopaedia Britannica* of 1945 commented that Austria had been united with Germany in the Holy Roman Empire for nine hundred years and was only expelled from the German Confederation when Bismarck determined to enlarge the Prussian kingdom into a single German state in 1866. The implication was that it was only reasonable for Berlin to end a historical aberration. Hitler and Mussolini met on the Austrian-Italian border at the Brenner Pass and formed the Axis alliance, later joined by Japan. World War II was on its way.

The twenty years between wars had been traumatic for Austria. It was a period of impotence, upheaval and bitter domestic strife. Once the Germans took over, the local Nazis enthusiastically persecuted Jews and applied the rules of the dictatorship. But Austria was not a major battlefield until nearly the end of the war, and escaped much of the devastation visited on Hitler's enemies and then on Germany. Hitler had prepared an Alpine redoubt to hold out after the Allies began pouring into Germany from east and west, but in the end he stayed in Berlin and committed suicide in his bunker. There was destruction in Vienna and industrial areas from Allied bombing and combat as the Red Army approached and fought in the streets of the capital for twenty-seven days in April 1945. The opera house was left in rubble, the famous Burgtheater was a burned-out shell, and the magnificent St. Stephen's Cathedral was badly damaged by a fire caused when a German incendiary shell hit its wooden roof supports.

Roosevelt, Churchill and Stalin had agreed in 1943 in Moscow on a special postwar status for Austria, in hopes of discouraging support for Nazi forces. Considering the Anschluss an act of German aggression and Austria as Hitler's first victim, they announced that Austria would not be considered an enemy belligerent. But, of course, neither was it a liberated ally. Zones of occupation were allocated, as in Germany, with an added zone for France.

Unlike Berlin, however, Vienna was not divided. The symbol of a supposedly united administration by the occupiers became the "four men in a jeep," military police patrols composed of one American, one Briton, one Frenchman and one Russian. The capital quickly became a haven for spies and black marketeers, a sinister island in the mounting storms of the Cold War. British film director Sir Carol Reed caught the strange, tense atmosphere in *The Third Man*, a classic of shadowy suspense. The Café Mozart, near the opera house, and the "Harry Lime theme," played on a zither, represented Austria's period of postwar corruption and limbo.

The 1945 Yalta agreements dealing with Eastern Europe and Greece, which also affected Austria, were meant to be temporary measures until new governments could be organized, formal peace negotiated and foreign troops withdrawn. But within a year after the end of the war, East-West antagonism had reached a point where the provisional arrangements were congealing into the partition of Europe. The Big Four, as the occupation powers were called, negotiated desultorily on Austria for years without any progress. Only in 1955, when Nikita Khrushchev had won out in the struggle for succession to Stalin and felt strong enough in the Kremlin to launch new policies, was there a sudden breakthrough.

Agreement was reached on a peace treaty, called the Austrian State Treaty, providing for the end of the occupation and withdrawal of all forces, which led to permanent neutrality. In 1960 the Soviet leader paid a state visit to Austria, confirming its position between East and West. The following year Vienna, as a neutral capital, was chosen for Khrushchev's meeting with President John F. Kennedy. By then, Soviet-American relations were strained again. The summit was a disaster. The aftermath heightened confrontation, provoking fears that led to a torrent of refugees from East Germany into West Berlin and, in August 1961, the erection of the Berlin Wall. But Austria managed to escape renewed troubles, reinforcing its conviction of the advantages of neutrality.

Vienna provides a meeting place, an observation post, even at times an escape hatch. But the new idea of bridge building never got very far. Superpowers have little use for bridges. They deal with each other or they don't. Nonetheless, Bruno Kreisky, Foreign Minister from 1959 to 1966 and Chancellor from 1970 to 1983, was a diplomatic activist who enjoyed seeking a role in the world well beyond Austria's limited interests. A Social Democrat, he had no inhibitions about dealing with Communist and conservative leaders. A Jew, he cultivated Arab leaders and even gave quasi-diplomatic recognition to Yasir Arafat's Palestine Liberation Organization in an attempt to find some grounds for mediation with Israel. A chunky man with reddish hair, an Austrian taste for irony and a large portion of undoubting self-esteem, he gave his country a sense of stability and tranquility which it had not known for generations. Prudent investment and careful management of the budget and the money supply strengthened the economy. For a number of years, when other countries were hurting with inflation and then unemployment, Austria was held up as a model of sound economic policy.

Inevitably, it suffered from the recession of the early 1980s with all of Europe. But the shocks were buffered. The time of terrible turmoil between the wars had receded into the past, remembered as an ugly passage from grandeur to modest self-satisfaction. The Austrians came to enjoy their neutral status. Because of their ticklish international position, they could not join the Common Market, something of an exclusion from the Western European club, but they made accommodating agreements and accepted gratefully their new position as a small country with special status after the terrible years.

Believing the world had taken them to heart as the good-humored, capable, innocent people they had come to consider themselves, Austrians were shocked and resentful at the international outcry when Kurt Waldheim was nominated and then elected President in 1986. Tall, stiff, entranced with pomp and protocol (he has been called the epitome of the Viennese headwaiter), Waldheim had served as Secretary-General of the United Nations for ten years. It came out during the campaign that he had also served as a German army officer in Greece and Yugoslavia when some of the worst wartime atrocities were committed. He had conveniently "forgotten" his presence in these areas in his autobiography, and claimed that he was unaware of war crimes committed by his unit. The dominant Austrian reaction was to support him against "foreign interference" in local politics, and he won easily. Even his opponents found it hard to understand why Austria was suddenly being criticized abroad, and many blamed it on some Jewish or foreign media "plot." Endemic anti-Semitism surfaced, though the Jewish community had dwindled to a few thousand from its thriving prewar 300,000.

After so much conflict during the interwar years, Austrians and especially Viennese had taken up the habit of avoiding argument, nodding and smiling and brushing aside the unpleasant. "Why are you foreigners taking the dirt out from under the rug and putting it on the table?" a participant in a TV debate asked after the election. They had chosen to ignore the dirt, and thought it a breach of amity to be reminded. But the dark side was still there. Austria had gone through little of the repentance and soul-searching of West Germany after the war, and most people did not see why they should.

In a way, the dark side had always been there, even in the times of splendor. In the mid-1980s, an exhibition called "Vienna: Dream and Reality" was shown in Vienna, then Paris and New York. Devoted to the early part of the century, it was a dazzling reflection of how brilliant, how original, how creative Vienna's cultural life had been. Freud, Musil, Wittgenstein, Klimt, Schiele, Schoenberg, Mahler—there had been a proliferation of riches. But the exhibit also showed an obsession with sex, veiled with flowers as in Klimt or almost pornographic as in Schiele, and with Jews, fixations which came to characterize Hitler and his Nazis. There was a warning of coming putrescence, shiny and perfumed, ostensibly frivolous. It was in clear contrast to the fiercely satirical, hard-edged, black humor with which Berlin's intellectuals foresaw impending disaster a little later. The Austrian art pointed to hidden corruption beneath the surface of well-regulated formality and indulgent fantasy. The social criticism implicit in the works of the artists, philosophers and scientists who had made Vienna so much more than the handsome capital of a crumbling empire was largely missing after World War II. The exhibit was a mute reminder of how large a role Jews had played in providing the city's intellectual sparkle, but they are gone, killed or driven into emigration.

What remains is pretty, hearty, imposing or picturesque, but scarcely stimulating. Like the green May wine served with slabs of pork, coils of blood sausage and hunks of roasted chicken in the vast, rustic garden restaurants of Grinzing, on the edge of the Vienna Woods, the city's flavor has become pleasant but flat. There is still music, great torrents and tinkling springs of music in all sizes of halls and churches, but most of it familiar, little new. Older people still wear dirndls with aprons and laced bodices or heavy loden coats with a tufted hunter's hat as though they had just descended from a mountain village. The old ghetto has become a garish nightlife district, well policed since a terrorist attack on the main synagogue, but the city is safe from the street crime which plagues more up-to-date urban centers. People tend to live quietly in well-ordered routines, and the press focuses on cheesecake, petty scandals and local politics.

Once again there are signs in the streets of Vienna pointing to the roads to Budapest, Bratislava and Prague. Austrians can cross to the

East for weekends, to hear a Mozart opera or visit the castles once owned by their aristocracy. Hungary's passport regulations, the most lenient in the Soviet bloc, make it relatively easy for Hungarians to resume the old custom of a trip up the Danube or a drive to visit Vienna. The city no longer feels so isolated from its traditional hinterland as it did after World War I and in the early Cold War, though its traditional supply of Czech tailors and Hungarian musicians has been cut off. The influence is essentially one-way only, from Austria eastward.

There are no longer outside political or even cultural tugs in all directions, which reduces Vienna's once glamorously cosmopolitan appeal. But the city does radiate its news and views and standards across the East-West frontiers. Radio and television programs are closely followed in the neighboring countries, so regularly and unpreventably that Hungarian papers stopped trying to ignore Vienna broadcasts and took to printing the schedules. That was a major concession for a Communist state. Austria necessarily has an interest in détente to ease all kinds of contacts in what it still sees as Central Europe, and shudders when barriers are tightened. But it has adjusted. It did not choose to be either small or neutral. Austrians will smile at the thought, something mildly humorous, and remind you that they have always known how to accommodate to circumstance.

WEST GERMANY
The Phoenix of Industry

T HE STOCK STORY of how Bonn came to be the capital of the Federal Republic of Germany in 1949 is that Konrad Adenauer admitted his home village of Rhöndorf really was too small. The old man never moved from his comfortable but unpretentious village house with the rose garden he loved to tend, but every day he crossed the Rhine to Bonn, where he launched a new German state and governed it for fourteen years. The Federal Republic (Bundesrepublik Deutschland) was forged from the American, British and French zones of occupation in the defeated Third Reich. On the other side of the electrified barbed wire and plowed strip of minefields which Winston Churchill had called the "iron curtain," another German state was formed in what had been the Soviet occupation zone. Its capital was in East Berlin, formerly the Soviet sector. There was no question of establishing West Germany's government in West Berlin, where the three Western powers had occupation sectors. It was an enclave, cut off from West Germany by the surrounding Red Army, and had been forced to withstand a Soviet blockade for over a year.

Virtually all the major cities of southern and western Germany had been ravaged in the war—Frankfurt, Düsseldorf, Hamburg, Munich, even Cologne a few miles down the Rhine from Bonn. But people were beginning to sweep away the rubble and start reconstruction. Any one of the big cities could have been chosen as a capital. Adenauer insisted on Bonn; it was his own neighborhood. He had been mayor of Cologne immediately after the war, but the British authorities who had installed him soon deposed him for being uncooperative. Bonn was a completely unlikely capital.

The small university town had suffered little damage and bore no symbolism. It was Beethoven's birthplace. Hitler had stayed in the riverside Dreesen Hotel in neighboring Bad Godesberg when Britain's Prime Minister Neville Chamberlain came to appease him shortly before World War II. The Drachenfels (Dragon's Cliff), a ruined tower on a hill across the Rhine, figures in the mythology of Siegfried and the Nibelungen. From there, you can see the rocks and meanders in the broad river where the plaintive song of the siren Lorelei, celebrated by the poet Heinrich Heine, was said to lure boatmen to their doom. But Bonn had played no special role in German history. If it represented anything, it was minor provincial enlightenment. So there was little thought that it would ever be more than a temporary capital, a place from which to start organizing a future united German government, which would certainly have its seat in a reunited Berlin.

For many years, under the first postwar Chancellor, Adenauer, and his successors Ludwig Erhard and Kurt Georg Kiesinger, the insistence that Bonn was only a provisional capital was implemented by a refusal to put up solid buildings or construct highways and bridges to bypass the railway tracks through the center of town or the ferry across the river. Bonn was deliberately left sleepy and makeshift. It would have been considered a whiff of treason to introduce the glass towers and modern throughways that were beginning to transform the big cities recovering from the war. That would have implied accepting the partition of Germany. Besides, practically everyone expected to move away to Berlin one day, so there seemed no point to investing in Bonn.

Still, as the government grew and the Federal Republic took on solidity, people and ministries had to be housed. When Willy Brandt became the first Social Democratic Chancellor in 1969, he launched a new policy of reconciliation with the East, Ostpolitik, to balance Adenauer's reconciliation with France and ties with the European Community. It was a recognition that divided Germany would not soon be reunited. Then the pretense of Bonn's transience was finally set aside. Office skyscrapers were put up for the Bundestag (parliament) beside its rambling chambers. A squat but monumental modern building was erected for the chancellory. There was a rush of construction to catch up with the cities. But Bonn remained the capital only of politics and bureaucracy, like Washington, D.C. Düsseldorf was the center for industry, Frankfurt for finance, Hamburg for trade, Munich for films and much of the arts. West Berlin, despite conscious effort to maintain its sense of importance, faded into lesser significance. It became a city of the aged and the rambunctious young, lured by the exemption of its residents from the West German draft and the atmosphere of bohemian irresponsibility they re-created in its grubbier quarters.

The first German revival, directed from Bonn but scarcely reflected there, was strictly material. The "economic miracle" of the 1950s and early 1960s produced new millionaires, scandals, "manager's disease" (ulcers), floods of German tourists in Spain and Italy, everywhere attractive, working-class comforts never dreamt of before—and eventually student protest and a literature and art of dissent. People spoke of *Bundesgesellschaft*, Germany, Inc. They felt they were members of a company, not a country, and complained that they had no central, all-important city, no London, Paris, Rome or Vienna. Bonn remained a dull joke, pleasant enough with its tree-lined streets and riverside parks, but without sparkle. And so at last it did become a symbol, the nerve center of an economically powerful democracy with increasing political weight in the world, remarkably stable, but emotionally and intellectually unfulfilled.

The question of identity came to focus the feelings of truncated nationhood, of incompleteness and dissatisfaction. In many ways, it was an old German problem, the result of continued fragmentation long after other European tribes had coalesced into nation-states. There had seldom been as clear an answer to just what it meant to be a German as there was to the identity of a Frenchman, or an Englishman, or a Swede. But the issue carried new undertones of self-doubt and self-assertion entangled together, of a sense of impotence despite demonstrable power, of having become a passive object of history determined by others, yet not really knowing what active role might be desirable.

Citizenship in the Federal Republic was well and good. It conferred many privileges, a fine standard of living, as much personal freedom as any country. Two generations after the war, Germans were once again proud to say they were Germans. But they were not sure what they expected it to mean. The notion of identity implied a firm connection with roots, a clearly defined community to be taken for granted, symbols available to all who belonged and not shared with anyone else. But even the flags of the two German states were the same, the black-red-gold of the interwar Weimar Republic, with the sheaves of wheat and tools representing a Communist state on the East German flag making the only difference.

The fact that for most of its history Germany was a loose collection of princely states and duchies, that Prussia, Bavaria, Saxony and the Hanseatic cities had a far longer record of quarrels and rivalry than of the unity imposed by Bismarck in 1871, scarcely eased the sense of amputation. In response came old romantic notions of a "German soul," a "German mythos," a special German personality that was being denied its full expression. The last quarter of the twentieth century brought a certain rejection of rationalism and materialistic science in many countries. It reflected a psychic search for something that modern industrial society had failed to provide. In West Germany, it took the form of a restless quest for "identity" and, especially among the young, the demand for an "alternative," another vague but compelling idea that something else must be better.

The extraordinary success of the fifteen-part television series *Heimat* in 1984 revealed the tremendous yearning for a specific sense of belonging to something beyond the bustling cities. *Heimat* means home, hometown, the place of origin, but in a sentimental sense, misted with memories of old stories and nostalgia for bygone scenes. Set in the tiny village of Hunsrück in the Rhineland, the long film was a cavalcade of German history from 1919 to 1982. Edgar Reitz, who made it, said he was trying at last to face the past but in its own terms, its own atmosphere and feelings, and not through history books. Ten million Germans watched it. The news magazine *Der Spiegel* said, "It is no longer the exaltation of progress, but a return to the country, the rediscovery of the country, the defense of the country. It's the return to a concept long disdained, towards new feelings which have been stirring in these recent years." In effect, the film revalidated romanticism, rural life, modesty of manner, little gestures and small pleasures that seemed more human, more authentic, than the blaring, glaring modernity which Germans had embraced so eagerly as they emerged from total catastrophe. It wasn't just "back to nature," but it seemed to say identity was to be found in a simpler, more traditional life.

Adenauer had foreseen his countrymen's eventual need for a satisfying image of themselves, a psychological category into which they could fit in comfort and safety once the shame and trauma of the war receded. Germany had not only been defeated, it had outraged the world. When the war ended, feelings were strong that it must be punished, quarantined and strictly controlled. In the name of national and racial supremacy with the claim of an inherent right to rule the world, Hitler had unleashed a cold-blooded, cruel and murderous campaign beyond imagination. Not only had a people capable of producing the highest achievements of culture and civilization practiced the utmost barbarism, they had carefully used their advanced skills in science and organization to massacre efficiently.

The victors generally rejected the idea of "collective guilt"—it was too much like Hitler's ideas of superior and inferior "races" to be tolerable. But they were determined to render the German nation incapable of launching a third world war. President Reagan spoke of "one man's totalitarian dictatorship" at the Bitburg military cemetery where he laid a wreath on the fortieth anniversary of the end of World War II, creating great controversy. Nobody would have said that earlier. Such a statement cannot be made with any historical honesty. Most of German society had supported Hitler, and many thousands of individuals had participated in mass murder.

No one has yet been able to explain from what demonic springs Germany's frenzy welled, whether the source of such evil taints all humankind or has some special link to flaws in the national character. What happened has been well documented and need not be repeated here. One sheet of paper alongside many unbearable photographs in a museum display case gives the unique texture of the horror. The museum was established in the former concentration camp of Ravensbrück in Brandenburg, now in East Germany. It was a camp reserved for women, especially political prisoners, many of whom, but far from all, were Jewish. Unlike Auschwitz, it was intended as a detention, not a liquidation, center. The paper was a leaf from an accountant's fine-lined ledger, written in the neat, flowery hand that well-trained German schoolchildren were required to develop. Prisoners were sent out to work at factories in the area, from which the S.S. collected wages. The average life span of a prisoner was calculated at nine months. The cost, income and net profit were listed as follows:

Daily wages	6.	Reichsmarks
Deduct food	.60	
Deduct amortization of clothes	.10	
On an average life span of 9 months, amounting to 270 times 5.30 RM	1431.	
Add a rationalized valorization of corpses: tooth gold, clothes, valuables, money, deducting the cost of incineration, 2 RM		
Average net profit	200.	
Total net profit after 9 months (per person)	1631.	

A book published on Ravensbrück after the war in East Germany noted that in 1943 and 1944 daily transports carried prisoners from the camp to the munitions factories and that almost every week transports brought the most exhausted prisoners back to die in the camp. It cited a report from an S.S. official who wrote: "Prisoners are cheaper than horses. First, you don't have to buy them, they are delivered to the camp gratis. Secondly, turnips are cheaper than hay, and thirdly, their ashes make good manure."

The Third Reich ended in flames and rubble. For a few years, bare survival was the preoccupation of the Germans. But once they had begun to build a material base, there were bound to be questions of how to restore society, how the children, and the unborn, and the surviving victims, and even, too, the people who had gone along with the Nazis but still had to keep on going, could find a way to lift their heads and live as Germans.

A Rhinelander and a Catholic, Adenauer felt some new base was needed to restore the civilizing impulse of the German temper and to regain the confidence and respect of the world. He knew it would take time, and he looked to the vision of Europe to provide it. By locking West Germany into a European house built with France, Italy, the Benelux countries and eventually others, he had thought a sense of family would grow so that his people could come to consider themselves primarily Europeans, subdivision Germany, as U.S. citizens consider themselves Americans, subdivision Texas, or Oregon, or Georgia. In this way, the identity of the Germans would take on a new significance and the past would be allowed to merge into the larger past of a troubled continent.

But the realization of a united Europe never got beyond halfway. It stalled with walls and no roof. France's Charles de Gaulle, convinced that his own feverishly dispirited country could only be cured with an intense dose of nationalism, blocked supranational power for the institutions of the European Community. In Germany, postwar generations felt no responsibility for their elders' behavior. In fact, rebellious youth expressed doubt at their parents' arguments that they could not have resisted Hitler. But neither did many of them feel well implanted in the Federal Republic, at the dangerous front line of a divided, superarmed continent torn between East and West. The psychological burden was never well defined. The past, the present and the future all contributed. *Sturm und Drang* ("storm and stress"), the historical poetic vision of the inner torment of Germanness, did not disappear when most of the external landmarks of the old Germany were leveled. In the middle of Europe between rival cultures and hostile powers, the Germans were still pulled in two directions.

The Federal Republic's eastern border is the Elbe River, along a line drawn at Yalta in early 1945 for purely military, supposedly temporary, convenience to avoid clashes when at last the American armies met the Soviet armies to complete the defeat of Germany on the battlefield. Historically and culturally, it was an artificial division of Germany. Germany, like most European countries, developed more differences between north and south than between east and west over the centuries. Hesse in the center-west had more in common with Thuringia across the border than it did with Schleswig-Holstein in the northwest. Bavaria in the south had more in common with Saxony in the southeast than either had with Prussia, split on both sides of the new frontier. There was no basis for the postwar political geography beyond the outcome of the war itself. But then, there had seldom been clear lines to mark the German homelands. A series of maps in the Bundeshaus in Bonn, the seat of the legislature, shows the fluctuating territory claimed by the Germans over the centuries, sometimes vast areas spreading across most of Europe, sometimes condensed in the center. Even they are misleading, because Germany did not constitute a state in the modern sense until 1871.

It is a clement land, brisk but bright along the North Sea coast, heaving gently above green valleys to the majestic Bavarian Alps. The mighty Rhine, one of Europe's oldest, most traveled highways, is still a great commercial lifeline. There is nothing forbidding, stern or harsh in the topography. Neither daunting nor dreary, the land is one of nature's moderations. And if civilization came later to the area settled by Teutonic tribes than to Mediterranean Europe, when it did come it brought a flowering of art and architecture, crafts and music which remain among the greatest European treasures. The coal-veined Ruhr valley had been Germany's industrial heartland, and the plains in the east had been its bread basket. Once economic activity revived in earnest, West Germany had the production base and the skills to regain commercial power.

The coast is divided between the North Sea and the Baltic by Schleswig-Holstein, at the base of the narrow peninsula tipped by Denmark. These are mainly windswept flatlands, leveled by Ice Age glaciers. Dunes and grassy marshes stretch along the shores and the many islands, which became popular vacation resorts after the war for the hardier types who made it a matter of pride not to join the annual exodus to the Mediterranean sun. It is a fertile area, its resources enriched by the great trading traditions, shipbuilding and seafaring. The capital is Kiel, on the Baltic and the North seas, the busiest waterway in the world. The city-states of Hamburg on the Elbe and Bremen on the Weser retain their flavor of flourishing merchant centers, looking out to the markets of the world, stolid, a touch smug, steeped in their own special histories. Hamburg was almost totally destroyed in a huge wartime bombing fire and was rebuilt as a modern city. Bremen still boasts the cobbles and gables which usually appear in illustrations of the old fairy tale about the four "musicians," a donkey, a dog, a cat and a cock who frightened the town with their serenade.

The whole of West Germany's territory tilts upward from the lowlands on the coast to the Bavarian plateau and the Alps, so that the major rivers flow north. The exception is the Danube, which rises in Bavaria and flows east and south into the Black Sea. It was the great river systems and their tributaries, interspersed with forests rich in game, which made the country so central to the development of European settlement and commerce in early ages. The eleven *Länder* (states) of the Federal Republic vary widely in size and importance, though they have legal equality. Three are simply cities, Hamburg, Bremen and West Berlin, the latter still formally under the occupation powers and allowed only limited participation in the federation.

South of Schleswig-Holstein, in some epochs part of Denmark, is Lower Saxony, previously a part of Prussia. The capital, Hannover, is famous for its industrial fairs, and various cities in Lower Saxony are

important centers specializing in petroleum refining, automobile production and assembly, fish and food processing. But this area, leading
to the central uplands, also has great agricultural importance, producing cereals, sugar beets, corn and potatoes. It is rolling country, with a
temperate climate and stretches of heath and mountain which provide
variety but little natural defense. This is part of the "north-central
plain" which NATO scenarios predict might succumb within a matter
of days to an offensive of massed tanks from the East.

North Rhine–Westphalia, to the southwest, is the most powerful
state, the center of the coal and steel industry, the richest and by far
most populous part of West Germany. Its capital is Düsseldorf, a city
of skyscrapers and tycoons, an overwhelming contrast to Bonn, some
fifty miles south and also a part of the state but with no special status in
terms of local or *Land* government. Unlike Washington, D.C., Bonn is
just another town in its state.

The Ruhr valley, which conjures up the image of a soot-blackened,
smokestack landscape, is surprisingly green and bucolic in many parts,
the river meandering between steep, grassy banks. But the cities of
North Rhine–Westphalia form a formidable list of German industrial
might—Essen, Dortmund, Duisburg, Bochum, Wuppertal, Bielefeld,
Gelsenkirchen, Solingen, Leverkusen, Paderborn and Cologne among
them. Because of their vital production, they were the targets of heavy
air raids in the war and were rebuilt in modern style. The towering old
twin-spired cathedral of Cologne, symbol of the city, was damaged, but
miraculously enough of the structure survived to make its full restoration possible. That was a pet project of Adenauer's.

Hesse lies to the east, with a long border with East Germany. It is in
the center of the Federal Republic, and the bustling but uninspiring
city of Frankfurt, near the confluence of the Rhine and Main rivers,
became the country's financial capital and transportation hub. Its annual book fair put Frankfurt on the world publishing map, but it is
more conducive to the promotion than the creation of literary works.
Wiesbaden, a quieter town nearby surrounded by famed vineyards, is
the capital of Hesse and one of the main bases of the United States Air
Force in Europe. Although the Hessians were known for their role as
British mercenaries in the American Revolution, the state as such had
little importance in German history and was almost always divided into
dukedoms and principalities with their own special traditions. Mineral
springs arising in several spots on the approaches to the Taunus Mountains were converted into fashionable, sometimes dazzlingly elegant

spas where the socialites of nineteenth-century Europe gathered to gossip and gamble.

There is more ancient splendor in the Rhineland-Palatinate (Rheinland-Pfalz) to the southwest, which grows most of Germany's wine grapes on the terraced slopes of the Rhine and Mosel valleys. It is hilly country, dotted with ruined castles and pretty villages. Many of its towns date from Roman times—Koblenz, Trier, Mainz and Worms— and contain the stony vestiges of a long and active history. But the *Land* was a postwar contrivance, patched together from territories which had belonged to Bavaria, Hesse and Prussia. The people are Catholic and conservative, with something of the south Germans' more easygoing approach to life than that of the crisp, energetic northerners.

Saarland, virtually an enclave on the border with France, was the smallest and last *Land* to join the Federal Republic. It was detached from Germany at French insistence after World War I and put under League of Nations administration, in an attempt to assure French access to its coal to fuel the steel industry of neighboring Lorraine. In 1935, Hitler forced through a referendum which brought the Saar's reincorporation into Germany, an ominous step followed by remilitarization of the Rhineland the following year. After World War II, the Saar was again broken off and there was a creeping attempt at French annexation. But the political climate had changed. In 1957, the same year that the Common Market treaty was signed, Saarland was again returned to Germany to be one of the federal states. It was an important milestone in Franco-German reconciliation. The capital, Saarbrücken, is highly industrialized, but the countryside has the wooded charm of the rest of the area between the Rhine and the Mosel.

The Black Forest, thatch roof and cuckoo clock country, is in the state of Baden-Württemberg in the southwest, bordering France and Switzerland. There are still large areas of dense woods, favorite retreats for camping and hunting. But the beloved forests of Germany are dying, apparently from acid rain. One estimate said a third of all Germany's trees had been afflicted. It is an awesome sight in midsummer, when all should be deep green, to see from the highways long stretches of leafless brown trees. They look as though they were in mourning, refusing to emerge from winter because of some secret grief. *Waldsterben* ("dying forests") is an intense political issue throughout West Germany, a major reason for the strength of the antipolitical "Greens," whose causes include general environmental concerns, pacifism, a cer-

tain antimodernism and a militant attitude against the whole establishment and its views. Baden-Württemberg also has thriving industrial
centers, including Mannheim, where Mercedes cars are made, Karls-
ruhe, Pforzheim, Ulm and Stuttgart, the state capital. Medieval architecture survived better in this area than in the parts of Germany that
were the main military fronts. Some small towns have been preserved
intact from the fifteenth and sixteenth centuries, and Stuttgart itself
still has a handsome old-city area dominated by a castle.

Bavaria in the southeast, bordering Austria, Czechoslovakia and East
Germany, is by far the largest state in area and the only one with its
own independent tradition. For over seven hundred years, it was the
kingdom of the Wittelsbach dynasty and feels itself special, different
from its new-drawn partners in the Federal Republic. Native Bavarians
do not really share the identity problem of other West Germans; they
consider themselves Bavarians above all. This was recognized in the
organization of the Christian Democratic Union, the party which Adenauer created to surmount old political fights between Catholics and
Protestants.

Fiercely Catholic Bavaria has its own regional party, the Christian
Social Union, affiliated with the CDU but careful to draw distinctions.
In the Bonn parliament, deputies of the CSU join CDU members from
all the rest of Germany in a single caucus, which they call the Union,
but they exact a price for their support. The northern part of the state
is fairly industrialized, but the south is mainly lake and mountain country. Men still wear leather shorts and felt hats with a feather and dance
the stomping, thigh-slapping *Schuhplatter* to whet their thirst for huge
mugs of the local beer. Augsburg, the old imperial city, Nuremberg,
home of an old university and a world-famed annual toy fair, Bayreuth
with its Wagnerian festivals, and Berchtesgaden, the steep peak where
Hitler built his "Eagle's Nest," are among the attractions of Bavaria.

But its capital, Munich, is a major national city, center of filmmaking
and the arts, bohemian nightclubs and beer gardens. With West Berlin
isolated, Munich has become Germany's cosmopolitan cultural capital.
It was badly destroyed in the war and still has large sections of dull
concrete apartment houses thrown up quickly afterward to shelter the
homeless. But a great effort was made to restore some of the most
handsome monuments, including the delicious little Cuvilliés theater
in the Prinzregenten Palace. Then, in preparation for the 1972 Olympics, the whole downtown area had a drastic facelift, deliberately

baroque-picturesque in architecture but decidedly modern in transportation and convenience. Domes, houses painted pink, pistachio and lemon and huge flower boxes in the streets dominate the scene. A large part of the central city was made into pedestrian malls forbidden to traffic. There is a strong contrast between the sprightly, lighthearted air of Munich and the hearty, heavy, beery temperament of Bavaria, but it is the contrast between city and countryside, the imposing town house and the chalet.

The legendary founder of Germany was Prince Arminius of the Cherusci tribe, who defeated three Roman legions in the Teutoburg Forest, near modern Bielefeld, in A.D. 9. In the nineteenth century, when ancestral origins and romantic nationalism captured the public's interest, a huge monument was built to him in a forest clearing. People still go to visit it, though more for the excursion in the woods than to pay homage to an otherwise unknown hero. Many Teutonic tribes pushed into Europe in the first millennium, but they were loosely organized. Historians say the word Deutsch ("German") probably came into use in the eighth century but only to identify the language used in the eastern part of the Frankish realm.

Charlemagne imposed an imperial order on a variety of distinct tribes, primarily the Bavarians, the Swabians, the Saxons and the Franks. But it fell apart after his death in 814. After that, the western groups, whose Latin-based language developed into French, organized separately from those in the east, called Tudesci in Latin. It meant "ordinary people," those who did not speak Latin. The modern Italian word for German is Tedeschi. Only in the tenth century did "Deutsch" come to mean the territory of the German-speakers as well as their language family.

The first German king, Conrad I of Franconia, was elected by the nobles in 911. With the coming of Christianity, the title changed and the realm was called the Holy Roman Empire. It was the first great successor to ancient Rome's vast domain, but it had none of the administrative, engineering and organizational talents of Rome. There was no capital and there were no taxes. In theory, the Emperor was the temporal ruler of all western Christendom while the Pope held supreme religious authority.

But the vast dimensions of the realm and its weak central authority encouraged feudal dukes and princes to proclaim their local sovereignties, with only limited acknowledgment of imperial rights. As other lands were being gathered into national states, the German-speakers were fragmenting. The Habsburgs, who rose to dominance in Vienna, were the first to create a dynasty, but they lost control of much of the lands to the north and the west. As commerce developed, merchant towns established their independence and economic strength, which they reinforced with trading leagues. In the fourteenth century, the Hanseatic League dominated the Baltic region and had ties as far as Cracow, in Poland.

The long series of wars with the Turks diverted the Habsburgs from imposing their imperial rights. It was not until 1806, during the Napoleonic Wars, that the Holy Roman Empire, the First Reich, was formally dissolved. But it had disintegrated long before. There was a generic sense of people who were Germanic, but not a German nation, when other parts of Europe had moved from feudalism to organized statehood. Identity had to do with the local sovereign, with religion, not with ethnic community.

The Renaissance and the rise of humanism focused the grievances of the people on the abuses of the clergy, who had been the representatives of a unifying faith. After the proclamation of protest by Martin Luther in 1517, the Reformation spread quickly through much of the German-speaking lands, sparking the Peasants' War in 1525. That contributed to the divisions. Princes were entitled to choose the religion of their subjects. Their rivalries, inflamed by religious zeal, led to the Thirty Years War from 1618 to 1648, a devastating conflagration which depopulated much of German territory and ended with the cession of huge areas to neighbors. Catholic Austria and Protestant Prussia were the major, usually hostile, powers.

The French Revolution provoked an opposing coalition of powers whose sovereigns based their claim on divine right. But Napoleon's armies found allies among subjects and princelings who resented subordination. The influence of France did not bring revolution in the German lands, but it brought further changes in the political geography and sparked new nationalism and movements for reform. Finally, as industrialization developed, Prussia's Chancellor Otto von Bismarck made the decisive choice to re-create a "smaller" German empire, leaving out Austria and its dominions, the Netherlands and German-speaking Switzerland, but incorporating the rest of the areas inhabited by the descendants of the eastern Germanic tribes (not those who had long before become Latinized in Italy, France and Spain). The provinces of Alsace and Lorraine (Elsass and Lothringen in German), wrested from France in the Franco-Prussian War of 1870, were included, but had to be returned after Germany's defeat in World War I.

King Wilhelm of Prussia was crowned Emperor Wilhelm I of Germany on January 18, 1871. That was the Second Reich, the beginning of the modern German state. Except for the reappearance of Poland, which had been wiped off the map in the eighteenth-century partitions among Prussia, Russia and Austria, it was essentially the same territory which comprised Germany down to World War II. Shortly before the war, Hitler annexed Austria and seized mountainous Czech borderlands inhabited largely by the German-speaking Sudetens. After the war, most of the German minorities in Eastern Europe were summarily expelled. The sizable communities remaining are in Russia and Romania.

Coming late to national unity and the power it brought, Germany then scrambled to catch up with the European countries busily carving up other continents, especially Africa. All its colonies were stripped away after 1918 and eastern borders were somewhat changed to accommodate the restoration of Polish independence. But essentially, Germany remained intact. The most important change was the abolition of the monarchy and the proclamation of a republic, based on a new constitution drawn up in the town of Weimar in 1919. There was little sympathy lost on the deposed Emperor, Wilhelm II, who lived out his life in exile in the Dutch town of Doorn. But Weimar came to be called the "republic without republicans," so stormy was its existence. The aftermath of war, aggravated by heavy reparations and French occupation of the industrial Saarland, inflation and massive unemployment as the Great Depression engulfed Europe, brought intense social unrest. Gangs of Communists and the new extreme-right National Socialist (Nazi) Party fought in the streets.

It was against this background of turmoil that Adolf Hitler and his Nazis, promising to restore order and discipline, won a plurality of votes in the 1933 election. Hitler, born in Austria, was obsessed by a vision of the ancient German empire, which he was determined to restore in domination of all Europe. He proclaimed the Third Reich and said it would last a thousand years. It collapsed twelve years later with the total defeat, destruction and occupation of Germany.

The way Germany was treated after the 1914–18 war and the frontiers drawn on the ruins of empire, leaving restive minorities in many lands, were widely recognized as a major cause of World War II only a generation later. While the fighting was still going on, the Allies began to plan how they would deal with Germany this time. They agreed on "unconditional surrender" so there could be no new version of the myth Hitler used for propaganda purposes, claiming that Germany had not really been defeated in 1918 but was "stabbed in the back" by traitors.

President Franklin Roosevelt's Secretary of the Treasury, Henry Morgenthau, put forward a scheme to reduce Germany to a pastoral society of loosely confederated states, an attempt to guarantee total sterilization of nationhood as well as of economic and military power. Roosevelt never approved it. But, with Stalin and Churchill, he agreed on occupation zones (later assigning part of the U.S. zone to France), reparations and border changes. The eastern territories of Pomerania and Silesia were assigned only to Polish "administration," awaiting definite settlement in the peace treaty which has never been written. But Poland, which had lost its eastern half to Russia, took the lands as compensation with Soviet approval. Some 3 to 4 million Germans were expelled from their homes by Poland and Czechoslovakia in circumstances of great distress, but no worse than the Nazis had inflicted on populations they had temporarily conquered. Most fled to West Germany.

The Roosevelt-Churchill-Stalin Yalta plan of 1945 established the Allied Control Council to coordinate the occupation, with a separate four-power council for Berlin. There were disagreements from the start. Reparations to the lands Germany had ravaged were ordered to be paid with dismantled factory equipment, rather than production, so as not to repeat the economic distortion of markets that World War I reparations had imposed on the victors as well as the vanquished. The Russians helped themselves in their Eastern zone. In the Western zone, the authorities stopped dismantling industry fairly quickly, partly because they no longer wanted to ship equipment to the Soviets as East-West tension increased, even more because they realized they would have to feed and support the people for whom they were responsible if the population was not put back to work. To facilitate revival of production and food distribution, the British and American zones were combined in an economic unit, Bizonia, later expanded to include the French zone.

In 1948, with the Cold War developing in earnest, the economy was still stagnant and living conditions scarcely better than at the end of the war. Money was worthless, but the powers could not agree on how much to print. Exasperated, the American commander, General Lucius Clay, ordered a currency reform (discreetly through Ludwig Erhard), which was suddenly announced for all three Western zones in June 1948. It was magic. In response to the new money, peasants abandoned barter with urban dwellers for cigarettes they often wouldn't smoke and heirlooms they didn't particularly want, and at last brought food to sell in the markets. With provisions reappearing to be bought, workers looked for jobs to earn the wherewithal. It had scarcely been worth looking for work before, except on the black market where goods were traded, because the pay bought practically nothing. With effective money in circulation, there was incentive to launch construction, hire people, open shops, offer services. Almost overnight, economic life began again. But the Soviets did not accept the currency reform for their zone. The partition of Germany had begun. It congealed the following year with the drafting of a constitution and establishment of a government in the West, followed a few months later by a government in the East. Since 1949, there have been two German states.

The Federal Republic wound up with 52 percent of the territory which had belonged to the Second Reich, the Democratic Republic with 22 percent (Poland and the Soviet Union took the rest). But West Germany alone now has a population of some 61 million, including about 4.5 million foreigners, three times as many as all who lived in Kaiser Wilhelm's empire. Most of those expelled from the lost areas in the East and another 3 million from East Germany resettled in the West during the early postwar days when vast population movements remained possible.

West Germany, about the size of Oregon or Wyoming, is the third most densely populated country in Europe, after Holland and Belgium. But after a brief postwar baby boom, its numbers have been declining; its birthrate is below replacement level. Protestants predominate in the north, Catholics in the south and west. Their old frictions have been surmounted, and the importance of the different churches' role as a pillar of community has been renewed by cooperation on many issues, including the peace movement. But the old regionalism remains strong, reinforced by the federal system and the artificiality of Bonn as a capital city. The division of power between the federal and state (*Land*) governments is somewhat similar to the U.S. system, making West Germany the most decentralized European government after Switzerland. For the most part, the *Länder* correspond to traditional regions and even once independent states and cities (Bavaria and Hamburg, for example). The use of local dialects is waning. Yet differences in accent and idiom still mark many people's place of birth and education. There is still an intense sense of the particularisms which marked Germany's historical development.

The constitution written in Bonn in 1949 brought together the diverse, disjointed bits of Germany west of the Elbe left in the wreckage of war. As in buildings, political architecture comes before usage and often decides how the people who will inhabit it behave. The architects of the Federal Republic built prudently and solidly, keenly aware of the flaws that had undermined the Weimar Republic. The federal system, preventing revival of a centralized power at the insistence of occupation authorities, also eased the merger of the parts into a new state. An ingenious electoral system was devised to ward off the fragmenting effect of proportional representation and a tendency to proliferation of parties, yet assure pluralism and the chance for change. The result has usually been a two-and-a-half-party system, sometimes two major and two minor parties, excluding extremists of both right and left and leaving little room for spoilers.

The other crucial constitutional provision that completed West Germany's guarantee against the revolving-door governments which plague countries such as Italy and Holland and doomed France's Fourth Republic (1944–58) is the vote of "constructive no confidence." A government cannot be turned out by a simple majority vote against it. A majority vote for a new government is required. Thus deputies are held to strict responsibility. It isn't enough to oppose. An alternative must be accepted.

The occupation powers, especially the Americans, paid the closest attention at each step in constructing the foundations and political framework of the new state to make sure it went in the desired direction. It was no secret that General Clay, the U.S. commander and the real ruler of Germany in the immediate postwar years, favored the devoutly Catholic, conservative Adenauer and his CDU when the first federal elections were held in 1949. Adenauer was stubborn, he could be difficult. But he was shrewdly political and thoroughly dedicated to the idea of integrating the new Germany in the West.

Adenauer's main rival was Kurt Schumacher, leader of the old Socialist Party, which was able to renew its once strong bases in urban and industrial areas. Schumacher was younger but as wizened as Adenauer after years in Nazi prisons and wounds which had cost him his right arm in World War I and his left leg in World War II. Instead of striking out with new ideas, his program was to leap back over the Third Reich and revive a workers' party of proud tradition. The elderly conservative who rejected the past and the socialist who sought roots in it made an odd contrast. Schumacher was bitter, a thin, bony, scowling man toughened beyond malleability by the sheer effort to survive great suffering. He was anti-Communist, but he was more susceptible than Adenauer to the Soviet argument that the Germans' only chance of restoring united nationhood was by rejecting the United States.

The elections, supervised in their respective zones by the Americans, French and British (then under a Labour government at home), were scrupulously fair. What voters wanted most, it turned out, was stability, security and Western support against repeated cycles of threats and blandishments from Moscow. Adenauer provided it all, winning election after election with the pledge of "no experiments." The experience of the early postwar years put a premium on reliability, respectability, pragmatic caution. The message sank in for the heirs of Kurt Schumacher, who died in 1957. The Socialist Party, the SPD, was repeatedly excluded from power by its failure to overcome the threshold of a third of the vote, though Socialists did enter some state governments.

The evolution of German politics came logically from the opposed views of Adenauer and Schumacher. Herbert Wehner, a former Communist who was expelled from the party during his war years in Sweden and had turned Social Democrat, was a key influence in moderating the left. He was originally from Dresden, in the East, and he dreamed of reuniting Germany as a parliamentary democracy with a strong SPD. A bluff, practical man, he soon realized his vision was doomed to failure and turned instead to a program abandoning Marxist doctrine and supporting the NATO alliance and the new European Community. It was accepted by the SPD at its Bad Godesberg conference in 1959, a watershed which enabled the party within a decade to grow to the point of heading the government.

The first successful candidate, on the new, Wehner-inspired model, was Willy Brandt, a convivial, hopeful new face. He was born an illegitimate child in a working-class district of Lübeck in December 1913. He had fought in the street battles against Nazi ruffians, and when the opponents of Hitler were forced underground, he escaped to Norway and then Sweden, where he married. He could have remained there comfortably, but he chose to return to famished, devastated Berlin soon after the war, and became a rising star in the city's politics during the period of confrontation with the Soviets in the Eastern sector. He was mayor when the Berlin Wall was built in 1961, a moment of great danger because the unarmed West Berliners wanted to march east to prevent the sealing of their city. Single-handedly he dissuaded the population from such a reckless move, but he was deeply disappointed at the American government's lack of understanding and unwillingness to react quickly. The message from Hyannisport, where President Kennedy was vacationing, was that the Wall represented "a great propaganda victory" for the West.

Brandt never forgot what seemed at best indifference, at worst a betrayal by the American protector. It rankled long afterward, and played a part in turning him in his later years to a third world outlook, not exactly equating the superpowers but not seeing them as the poles of good and evil either. That brought him closer to the leftist youth movements which arose in the late 1960s than were other leaders of his party, and defined an important, continuing strongly left current in the SPD. But it was not clearly visible at first. As Foreign Minister, he took the SPD into a "grand coalition" with the CDU in 1966. The demonstration that the party could be trusted in government broke the taboo which had kept it below the threshold of needed votes. In 1969, Brandt became Chancellor, proving for the first time that the Federal Republic was capable of an orderly transfer of power between democratic parties. The German Socialists, inspired by the Scandinavians, became an important influence on other parts of Western Europe and more distant lands, including Latin America, promoting a mixed economy with a predominance of private enterprise, social justice and the cooperation of labor and capital.

By then, West Germany was firmly anchored in the West, militarily in NATO, economically in the Common Market, politically in the grand treaty of reconciliation with France which Adenauer had signed with de Gaulle. Brandt turned to reconciliation with the East, Ostpolitik. Step by step, he negotiated treaties with Poland, the Soviet Union and other Eastern bloc countries, and lastly with East Germany. In 1971, the four occupying powers signed an agreement on Berlin which left the western part of the city an island in the middle of the continent but buttressed its status and guaranteed access to and from West Germany. The long festering East-West Berlin crisis was laid to rest. It was an important precondition for President Nixon's détente negotiated in Moscow in 1972.

A spy scandal and moral and political fatigue from his extraordinary adventures in war and peace wore Brandt down and he suddenly resigned in 1974, leaving the leadership to the sharp-tongued, hard-headed Helmut Schmidt, whom he admired but did not like. After the sentimentalist came the political economist. The policies did not change, but the tone did. Schmidt represented the other current in the SPD, staunchly pro-American (though he could not abide President Jimmy Carter), convinced that the key to political stability was sound economic management. His cool efficiency won him great popularity. With West Germany's prosperity established and Schmidt's own self-confidence unbudgeable, the country began to flex its political muscle. No longer, as people had been used to saying, was the Federal Republic an economic giant and a political dwarf. "We are somebody again," *Der Spiegel* crowed on its cover.

But the public's contentment wore off, and the idea of alternating ins and outs was no longer frightening. There were strains between Schmidt and Brandt, who had kept the party leadership and become head of the Socialist International, marking the divisions in the SPD. The CDU, Adenauer's old party, regained power in 1982 after Schmidt's coalition partner, the small Liberal Party (FDP), changed sides.

The central, highly emotional issue in the next elections, in 1983, was the deployment of medium-range American missiles. Helmut Kohl, the first of the post-Nazi generation to come to the top, led the CDU in a successful demonstration that West Germans had not veered from their basic choice of close alliance with the West. His rise was due more to the tug-of-war between other ambitious CDU figures and the CSU's Franz-Joseph Strauss, the bull from Bavaria, than to any compelling qualities of his own. Kohl was seen as an amiable if lackluster bumbler; "a little bit Adenauer, a little bit old country watchtower," was the way one journal described him. Tall, heavy and stolid, but even-tempered and imperturbable, he was proud of his deep-rooted provincialism. Kohl could hardly be called the latest model German politician, but he showed his electorate's continued preference for reassuring sturdiness at the helm. In his shadow, the CDU produced a string of livelier, more interesting men, but they had to wait him out.

Meanwhile, the SPD moved leftward, in the Brandt vein, seeking openings to the East, flirting with antimissile, antinuclear programs which had an element of anti-Americanism. In part, this was an attempt to co-opt the more rebellious left which had emerged outside the party ranks in the new generation. The main new force was the "Greens," an assortment of idealists, bohemians, pacifists, environmentalists and counterculture devotees who were the heirs of the West German student revolt of 1968. They won seats in a number of state parliaments and in the Bundestag, but this presented a problem for them. Since they were against the political system, should they join it and share power? Since they were against parties, should they behave like one? They argued these points, but nevertheless established a solid if marginal place for themselves on the political scene, rivaling the centrist Liberals for the power to decide which of the major parties should head the government. They were not strong enough to force real changes, but they remained a spicy, unpredictable irritant in West German politics, keeping alive the question of whither Germany.

All Europe had recovered and achieved a general living standard well above anything known before, but West Germany's "economic miracle" was the most unexpected, the most dramatic, and so the most visible. It was only one part of an unprecedented quarter-century of growth. At first, the United States had seen Europe's need as "relief and rehabilitation." Food was the first problem, and agriculture was encouraged. Soon the expert talk was of the "dollar gap." Europe had nothing to sell to earn the dollars it needed to re-equip industry, rebuild cities, buy raw materials and begin to export. The amounts each country needed seemed staggering, with the United States as the only possible source of aid. Yet restoration of industry was urgent.

Perhaps too much has been made of the fear that without quick economic progress the countries west of the Red Army's high-tide mark on the Elbe would have fallen to communism through internal disorder. That was the main grounds given the U.S. Congress and public for appropriating funds for the Marshall Plan. There was also the memory, always acute among the leadership of the period, of the terrible consequences of the attempt simply to take the world "back to normalcy" (in President Warren Harding's phrase) after World War I. And there was the realization that smooth transition from America's wartime economy required huge civilian orders which the Europeans could only place if they were given the purchasing power.

In sober generosity and enlightened self-interest, the United States offered nearly $16 billion in aid over four years, nearly $5 billion of it in the first year alone, a sum worth many times more at inflated current prices. All the Allies were invited to participate. The Soviet Union, though it was tentatively offered an additional $10 billion for itself, refused. Stalin smelled a capitalist trick to gain leverage in the East, just as he was setting out on vast new purges to get rid of any trace of Western influence acquired from wartime comrades in arms. Czechoslovakia hesitated, wanting to join. But Moscow was sternly forbidding.

So it turned out that the Marshall Plan was a purely Western organization, the economic basis for the Atlantic alliance and the foundation for what later became the Common Market and the Organization for Economic Cooperation and Development (OECD). Suspicious, Stalin missed his greatest opportunity to weaken the West. The plan was named for General George Catlett Marshall, who was Army Chief of Staff during the war and in 1947 was appointed Secretary of State by President Harry Truman. Though his background was entirely military, he became one of the most effective, farsighted statesmen the country ever had. Aware of Europe's postwar ordeal and the dangers it could create, he proposed in a speech at Harvard to provide America's support for a European recovery plan if one could be worked out jointly. Britain's Foreign Minister Ernest Bevin, a lumbering, bluff ex-dockworker, answered publicly and almost immediately that the Europeans would get together. It wasn't a blueprint stamped "Made in America." Even the concept arose from cooperation.

The genius of the Marshall Plan was that it not only provided seed money, it sowed a pattern. The United States put up the dollars, but all recipients joined with America in planning how to spend it to maximum common benefit. That meant avoiding duplication of effort, agreeing on division of investment, encouraging trade. Of course there was some competition and bickering, but there had never before been such an international enterprise. It paid off handsomely. There were no losers, except those who turned their backs.

Headquarters were in the ornate Hotel Talleyrand, previously a Rothschild residence just off Paris's Place de la Concorde, now the U.S. Consulate. W. Averell Harriman, who had been ambassador in Moscow, and David Bruce, director of the European theater of operations for the Office of Strategic Services (OSS) during the war and then Assistant Secretary of Commerce in 1947–48, presided successively. They were a special breed of Americans—rich, experienced in business, accustomed to and therefore unimpressed by the respect accorded to power, enamored of statecraft, members of the Eastern establishment with a strong attachment to Europe. Committee after committee was set up, to get the coal dug, the freight cars to carry it to the furnaces, the steel mills to produce the materials to make more railway cars, factories, generating plants, houses. New industries, new entrepreneurs and, most important, new trading habits sprang up to build an industrial web that spanned national borders.

While this was going on, a stubborn man from Cognac was drawing up plans to make it last. Jean Monnet had served on the Franco-British purchasing board in World War I and helped establish the League of Nations. That experience, not only of what was achieved but of the disintegration that set in when peace removed the pressure to cooperate, convinced him that the lessons people learn from their mistakes can only be preserved through institutions. Otherwise, societies are doomed to repeat their tragic errors. Monnet was a short, mild-mannered man who preferred the wings to the stage, avoided confrontation but never relented in his attempts at persuasion, and believed passionately in the supremacy of the fact. He was the opposite of Charles de Gaulle.

Nevertheless, or perhaps because of this, de Gaulle had charged him with preparing a recovery plan for France. It was a model of perspicacity, and gave him a chance to assemble some old ideas on correcting what he felt was the source of Germany's military advantage in the 1930s. Unlike de Gaulle, the cavalry colonel who had grasped the meaning of tanks while his countrymen blindly insisted on building forts against the last war's artillery, Monnet attributed Germany's successful amassing of power between the wars to the fact that its coal and steel industries were integrated while French steel mills had to rely on buying energy on the international market. Monnet developed plans for the European Coal and Steel Community, which would assure fair access on both sides of the border. He was one of the first Frenchmen to see his country's future safety not in keeping Germany down, but in tying it into a partnership for recovery. He had spent much time in Washington organizing Allied procurements during the war and, as France's postwar economic architect, had intimate knowledge of the links forged through the Marshall Plan. He was farsighted. His ultimate goal was really a united Europe. But he proceeded step by step as far and as fast as governments would go.

Jean Monnet was also the force behind what was called the Pleven Plan, after French Defense Minister René Pleven, for a European Defense Community that would encompass America's insistence on rearming Germany to bolster Western forces. It would have gone well beyond NATO in integrating a European army, and therefore might have been the base for a nascent European political structure. But Britain, still clinging to the old policy against continental coalitions, refused to join. Eventually, worried about facing renewed German militarism without British help, the French Assembly rejected the idea as too dangerous. On the other hand, atomic energy was a brand-new field unmined by vested interests, and Monnet succeeded in creating a community to deal with it, Euratom. To balance the basic industrial community, he began work on the Green Plan, for agricultural policy. That went slowly, confronting the most ingrained opposition.

But the postwar boom was gathering speed, and it made possible the far-reaching negotiations which were to culminate in the 1957 Treaty of Rome establishing the European Economic Communities. Jean Monnet's dream of European unity was never fulfilled. But the institutions he built were sturdy enough to support a steady economic expansion which lasted until the 1973 oil crisis. All the Common Market countries prospered, at different moments and in different measures, but in a way which convinced them, and doubting outsiders, that something new and enduring had happened to European industry. Britain lagged behind, perhaps for reasons that would have sapped it even if it had become a founding member of the EEC. The Germans, who flourished spectacularly, never doubted that the EEC had hastened and enlarged their success. The vision of Europe was of tremendous importance to them in regaining psychological and emotional health. They were the most enthusiastic supporters of the new idea of looking for a role beyond nationalism.

The expanded market soon enabled the Europeans to compete with new products that had become the symbols of the American standard of living—automobiles, household appliances, office machines. The U.S. economy was the inspiration. American marketing techniques became the fashion. Housewives began ignoring the neighborhood shops in favor of supermarkets. Office workers took to fast-food outlets instead of two-hour breaks to go home for lunch. Traditionalists on both right and left complained of "coca-colonization," a creeping American takeover of their habits of thinking and behaving. Gradually, the trend was understood as modernization. Reformers then urged more rapid steps to meet the "American challenge," felt especially after U.S. firms organized subsidiaries and multinationals to leap the Common Market tariff wall and benefit from the new continental-sized economy. While consumers reveled, the newly affluent, newly secure young discovered the grubby clay feet of glittering consumerism. Oil was cheap, wonderfully clean compared to coal, humane to produce and seemingly limitless. Europe's first Industrial Revolution had taken over a century. The second was nearly complete in a generation.

West Germany became the industrial star of a Western Europe that was again a world economic power only a score of years after the war had left it prostrate. Again, people began to ask whether there was something special about Germans that made them different from everybody else. East Germany did relatively well too, once the Soviets stopped stripping it and urged it to produce. "The Germans work so well they even make communism turn out goods," said the West Germans. The myth spread that nothing could keep the Germans down, that they laid golden eggs with or without a goose.

But there was no secret formula. A combination of circumstance, aid, desperation and the old religion-based work ethic underlay the phenomenon. The most important element was people. That hadn't quite been understood until students of development started trying to figure out why big injections of capital could not begin to transform third world countries the way Germany had risen from its ashes. Buildings and machines might have been smashed, but the skilled labor force was still there and so were the businessmen. Some firms revived as organized units, despite Allied efforts to break the structures which had armed the Nazis, often with slave labor.

There was even an advantage in having to start over. It meant getting all new equipment while rivals abroad were using old machinery. And it forced some new flexibility and room for fresh ideas in the rigid old economic hierarchy. "Denazification," the process by which the Allies sought to exclude Hitler's main supporters from recapturing economic power, and "deconcentration," the attempt to break up the Ruhr industrial baronies, were something of a charade. The strong and the wily got around both.

Management and *manager* became German words, implying modern, computer-oriented, international-minded businessmen, ready and eager to compete anywhere, disdainful of plodding old habits and conventions. Heinz Nordhoff, an engineer who had worked for General Motors' German subsidiary and spent time in Detroit learning assembly-line techniques before the war, was named by the British to organize Volkswagen. Hitler had announced plans to build a "people's car," cheap and easy to maintain, in 1938, but actual production had never started. After the war, operating mostly by will and wit, Nordhoff made Volkswagen the world's third largest automotive firm and Germany's foremost company in gross income. He had neither tradition nor stockholders to guide him, which, he said in 1953, "was a blessing for us. We didn't have people looking over our shoulders and saying, 'You can't do this, because we never did it that way.' We solved our problems as we encountered them, in our own way, not by what the book told us, but usually by improvisation. It is a very educational experience."

The other factor in the emergence of German industry was labor. Before the currency reform, there were scarcely any jobs, except working for the occupation authorities. Then people were glad to take what work they could get. The British authorities rationalized the union structure, based on the key Ruhr industrial areas they occupied, with a clear insight into how their own complex, querulous system served to block productivity. Mistakes made over a century during the slow, painful transformation from the traditional farm and trading culture of preindustrial Europe could be corrected at a swoop, putting the new Germany ahead of others. It was an irony recognized by both Germans and British that the changes helped Germany flourish while Britain, mired in custom, vested interests and politics, could not apply them. Its industry languished.

But even more important to the smooth surge of production was the labor docility that came of need. The incentives grew rapidly, and the market was insatiable. Large numbers of refugees poured into West Germany from the East. At first, they were considered a burden. But as industry revived, they proved to be a stimulus, an ever expanding pool of workers and consumers. When that migration ended, West Germany began to recruit abroad in the poorer countries around the Mediterranean. The new migrants were called "guest workers," and the assumption was that when their contracts ended, they would go home.

The import of labor spread throughout industrial Europe during the long period of expansion. It was in a way the other side of decolonization. Instead of exporting capital to the south, where labor was cheap, workers were brought to man the factories and services of the north. It was one of the greatest peacetime displacements of people since the populating of America. And in the same way, regional concentrations of migrants developed as newcomers followed relatives and neighbors. They went in waves, along beaten paths. Italians and Spaniards moved practically everywhere. Portuguese went to France, Greeks to England, and Yugoslavs to Germany. That was still not enough, and the siphoning went farther. West Indians, Pakistanis and Indians began pouring into Britain. Algerians, Moroccans and later black Africans flocked to France. Turks moved to Germany.

The look of every major European city changed. All industrial countries were touched. Dark faces, once a rarity, became commonplace in streets and subways. Shops and restaurants opened, first to serve the new communities, gradually introducing new products and food and clothes into everyday life. There was no melting pot American-style, because the migrants were moving into established, deeply nationalist societies. But they added a cosmopolitan flavor that had not existed before. As in New York, ethnic neighborhoods sprang up, and even though there was little mixing, they became a familiar part of the city scene.

At first, the newcomers were welcomed. They kept to themselves and did the dirty jobs that affluence led the local populations to disdain. Before the war, their role had been performed by the rural population moving off the overcrowded land into the towns. But the farm people were of the same nationality, the same language, the same culture as those who had gone to the cities in earlier generations. The newcomers were aliens moving into nonabsorptive, essentially xenophobic societies, and they were never expected to assimilate.

Of course, there were problems. If the workers were allowed to bring their families, they would have to be housed more reasonably than in dormitories. Children would have to be schooled. And if the men came without women, they became troublesome. Attempts to be enlightened, tolerant and compassionate were punctured with outbursts of resentment, bigotry and downright meanness among the most self-assertedly decent of people. Determinedly liberal Holland was shocked to have a race riot against Turks in the working-class district of Rotterdam. French Communists, whose party proclaimed itself the defender of the poorest and the foreign, bulldozed shut the entrance to a workers' hostel in the Paris suburb of Ivry to force its African residents to move to another town. Britain came to expect "long hot summers" in the slums where frustrated young West Indians vented their anger. Racism, which had been considered an American and colonial phenomenon, reached everyday Europe.

History and circumstance dictated ironically contrasting responses. Traditions of the British Empire, transformed by Prime Minister Harold Macmillan's ultimate bow to decolonizing "winds of change" into a multiracial Commonwealth, provided access to passports and citizenship to immigrants from the former colonies. That didn't ease social and cultural problems of integration, and it sharpened political issues as new ghettos grew. Switzerland, jealous of its small but carefully preserved identity and long unwilling to grant citizenship to Swiss-born children of aliens, interpreted its democratic tradition to mean foreign workers had only the right to leave when they were no longer wanted. Recession, unemployment and a staggering welfare burden, which had been expanded when the economic pie was growing steadily, hardened hearts against the foreigners everywhere. (It did not apply, of course, to rich Arabs and Latin Americans, whose new money also transformed certain aspects of European cities. But as much as their lavish spending was welcome, they too were kept in a margin of social disdain.)

The oil shocks of the 1970s spurred inflation and distorted the patterns of investment and growth. Unemployment spread and the battered economy sank into recession, more severe than any shock since the war but cushioned by the extensive welfare provisions built up in the period of growth and labor shortage. Across Europe, governments were switched between left and right, ins put out, as they grappled between the opposing pressures to pare welfare spending and government subsidies so as to stabilize the value of money, and to maintain basic welfare gains so as to protect social stability. Memories of the collapse of the Weimar Republic's currency had made the Germans acutely sensitive to the dangers of inflation, while others, such as Britain and later France, struggled unavailingly against unemployment.

The West Germans did relatively well, though their caution about expanding once the worst of the crisis had passed irritated their trading partners and cost them sympathy. Nonetheless, unemployment rose, to 2.5 million at its peak in June 1985, and labor unrest increased. At first, the dominant view was that the problem was cyclical, that the pause in growth was only a temporary adjustment soon to be followed by a "normal" spurt of renewed prosperity. But the world had acquired a whole new set of economic tools and analysts since the 1930s depression and its catastrophic theories of how to cure capitalism. The diagnosis this time was "structural" obsolescence. The old industries—steel, coal, ships, textiles—could no longer provide a solid foundation for economic health.

Some developing countries had actually developed a good deal, especially in turning out the products with which Europe had initially industrialized. With their newer plant and their cheaper labor, they became almost unsurpassable competitors. Europe had to constrict the old labor-intensive industries or undermine the whole economic fabric with subsidies and protection. It was a painful process, made possible only by the existence of the Common Market to help distribute the burden equitably and force observance of the trading rules.

New jobs and new output had to be sought in higher-value manufacturing, using automation, robotization and other advanced technology to reduce costs. It was the onset of the third Industrial Revolution, a quantum leap for which the Europeans, and the Germans in particular, had some of the capacities but not all. The skills for research and production were available, but the Common Market hadn't become common enough for the consolidation of companies and purchasers to achieve adequate economies of scale. Germany remained on the lower end of the Community's chronic unemployment rate, which reached 10 to 15 percent, though German unemployment was still unacceptably high for the expectations generated. Guarantees easily won by labor in the expansive period worked as barriers to a switch to new industries and new deployment of available capital.

The combination of high unemployment and emphasis on high technology wiped out openings for unskilled labor, which had provoked the great migrations. The human problems became intense. Most countries were required by law to give citizenship to children born on their soil, but they could not bring themselves to think of them as part of their established nation. And yet the children, as they grew up, knew no other homeland. Even the parents had come too far from their torpid villages to go back. The countries of Europe have barely begun the experience of assimilation that America, a nation of immigrants, knew was painful. Future storms were gathering.

When the one-millionth "guest" worker, Armando Sa Rodrigues, a carpenter from the northern Portuguese village of Vale de Madeiros, arrived at the Cologne-Deutz railway station, he was welcomed with ceremony. He was given a motorbike to symbolize Germany's gratitude to the people who had left their homes, crowded into dreary hostels, slogged with picks and axes at the hardest jobs to build an alien country's fortune and a modest nest egg of their own. A generation later, with recession deepening, four Germans out of five felt there were too many foreigners in the country. New laws, passed to keep them out, and even out of work, were overwhelmingly popular. By 1982, there were 4.5 million foreigners in Germany, of whom 2 million were workers. That represented 10 percent of the total work force because of pressures to leave generally large families behind. Chancellor Helmut Schmidt declared that the saturation point had been reached.

German xenophobia was not indiscriminate. Austrians were welcome enough and so were Poles, "because they're willing, work cheap, and they're not Pakistanis," a Hamburg electrician said bluntly. Racial hostility was directed mostly against Turks, however, because they had become so numerous, 1.5 million, a third of all the foreigners. Their children were nearly half of all the foreigners in schools. Hamburg, Frankfurt, Munich, but especially Berlin, had "Little Turkeys," whole districts run down into slums, as packed, odorous and alien but nothing like as picturesque as the back streets German tourists enjoyed visiting in exotic lands.

The economy redoubled the issue of German self-awareness. At first, the German "miracle" had sufficed to give people a sense of what their country stood for—high production and a good standard of living. But mere materialism became unsatisfying in less than a generation. Especially those too young to remember the time of terrible hardship had come to take prosperity for granted and they looked for something else, something more inspiring that "being German" could mean for them. Later, the recession made people uncomfortably aware of the flood of migrants who weren't German and challenged them once again to consider rights and duties in a national sense. What did they owe to others in their midst by virtue of being a democratic, liberal society? What demands could they make by virtue of themselves being German? Two generations after the war, people no longer felt responsible for the Nazis or thought they should apologize for being German, and were more than ever frustrated by the existence of two Germanys.

The problem of conscience posed by the migrants in turn aggravated the nagging question of identity. What is a German? Who is a German? There was no difficulty in accommodating *Auslandsdeutsche*, ethnic Germans living in other lands. After the expulsions and flow of refugees from the East, there were still an estimated 14 million remaining. They continue to be an issue in German politics and their right to emigrate a major goal of German foreign policy. Those who took refuge in West Germany and their descendants became a recurrent focus of controversy after the Federal Republic moved toward reconciliation with Eastern as well as Western Europe. Most Germans accepted the postwar borders, even if the issue of a divided Germany was hard to swallow. But there were obstreperous hard-core groups who continued to feed the East's charges of German "revanchism" with their claims for recovery of Silesia and other lands transferred to Poland. Bonn's insistence that its formal recognition of international frontiers (by definition not what is called the "inner-German" border) cannot bind a hypothetical united German government of the future has been a factor in convincing its neighbors of the wisdom of partition.

The identikit of the modern West German can be drawn from the probing polls, tirelessly examining the mirror of opinion for self-definition. She (there are nearly 5 percent more women than men) is married, forty years old (the average male is thirty-six), lives in a town of under 100,000, doesn't work, and doesn't belong to a political party although she professes interest in politics and considers voting a duty. The family owns its home, participates little in sports, loves to travel on vacations, watches color TV a lot and seldom goes to the movies. Less than half the population have a job, and half of those who do are white-collar workers in the service sector. Family is important, but few have more than two children. Most claim they would rather have more spare time than more money. What neighbors think and being liked come high on the list of values. The average German says he finds less need for more authority to be exercised by social leaders than does the average American (53 percent to 89 percent), is less impressed by the importance of technical progress (48 percent to 75 percent) and would like to see less emphasis placed on work (38 percent to 25 percent). But there is a pervading malaise, almost a cult of anxiety, more about the world getting too complicated and too technological than about specific dangers of war or unemployment or crime or illness. Angst is approved —in sharp contrast with the past, when Germans were brought up to be ashamed of showing fear. Songwriter Gunther Kunert put the new consciousness succinctly. "Anyone who isn't scared, who isn't a coward, is a psychological cripple," he said. The world looks hostile; satisfaction is sought in private life.

Patriotism is acceptable again, though people dislike being asked, and the young, aged sixteen to twenty-nine, have a strikingly different attitude from their elders. In 1981, 61 percent of the rising generation told pollsters they considered "the notion of Fatherland obsolete." Men have changed their attitudes toward women. Now more than half consider their wives their closest confidant. But while the emancipation of women and their increased self-confidence have been a major social change, the women do not find their husbands more interesting than before. Only half as many as a generation ago think it necessary or even desirable for a man and wife to agree on everything, and couples argue more often, though about the same things as before—friends, how to raise the children, money. Terrorism is widely condemned, but among known terrorists and their sympathizers, women predominate (60 percent).

The generation gap remains stark. On anticonformism, disrespect for authority, putting happiness first, seeing the world, rejecting America and what they think it means, distaste for the work ethic and craving for leisure, the young part company with their parents. The 1968 syndrome, the student revolts which affected virtually all the industrialized world, seemed to go deeper and last longer in West Germany than in other countries. Like all stereotypes, the German image of a dutiful, stolid, efficient, insensitive, beer-swilling creature of order is made of reality as well as myth. It comes distorted in peculiar shapes now. Germans take more time off, on supposed sick leave, often with visits to a spa, and on holidays, than any other Europeans. But the counterculture group in Berlin is so efficiently organized that they have a network of alarms to warn squatters of impending police raids and what amounts to a medical corps to look after their injured when they stage a riot. They publish manuals on what to do against teargas and how to make effective firebombs. Their defiance is highly disciplined. The young tend to disbelieve their elders' claim that they could do little to resist the Nazi dictatorship, and yet they feel impotent about their own society.

National character is an elusive concept, turning up when you aren't looking for it, disintegrating like atoms when you try to identify its elementary particles. Language, however, does have patterns which impose themselves on habits of thought, and it is the foundation stone of community. The discipline, the careful building-block construction of the German language, its ponderous order, weigh alike on the iconoclast and the unquestioning loyalist. Ideas are expressed by combining ordinary words into longer and longer strings, so that complexity and abstraction reign as the highest forms. It is the opposite of the Platonic notion of essences from which all that is concrete derives, but provides the precision that made German so well suited for science and philosophic speculation. The character of the language may also account for the German respect for theories and the elaborate pecking order of titles in virtually every profession. The British are more class conscious. But the notion of status is far more refined and developed in Germany, even when rebels turn the scales upside down.

Two generations after the war, the Germans had risen again. They had shucked off the reality, and then the lingering feeling, of being outcasts on the international scene. But they remained torn, not so much among as within themselves, trying to figure out what they wanted, what they wanted to be. Their own efforts symbolized the achievement of European prosperity, yet the material success for which they had worked so hard did not satisfy them. They felt an urge to influence the world again because, in the center of epic pressures, they felt acutely aware of the dangers ahead. The historic Teutonic expansionism, tugging sometimes east and sometimes west, was transformed into discomfiture at being caught in the center. With the sense of guilt left behind in time, there was a sense of being the victim of overwhelming outside forces which they ought to be able to transcend, but could not for lack of the voice of confident identity. The Federal Republic restored pride and substance, but the Germans still weren't happy with themselves. They felt something beyond reach was still missing. They had always been stuck in the middle of the continent, losing their way in tragic explosions of arrogance and ambition or, when sternly contained as now, feeling lost.

But should the dreams of a vigorous new European renaissance be fulfilled someday, which can only come through an effective union, then the Germans would partake in it fully and contribute enormously. They have reason to be the most eager Europeans.

PART II

EASTERN

EUROPE

THE NOTION OF EASTERN EUROPE is little more than contemporary politics, certainly not geography. The ancient east-west division was between Rome and Byzantium, with Russia, Romania, Bulgaria, Greece and Serbia looking eastward to Constantinople, the rest looking west. Then came the Turks, and the division was between the lands they conquered and those they never reached. After the expulsion of the Turkish rulers, the East was Russia and the rest of the area was Central Europe and the Balkans. Like Western Europe, the countries to the east were querulous, bellicose societies, forever disputing dominance and territory, but through their quarrels building strong attachments to a great diversity of national cultures.

It was only in 1945, when Soviet and Western armies met in conquered Germany, that the old divisions were overwhelmed by a new fact marking East and West. The new line was drawn simply as a rendezvous for the wartime Allies. But it soon hardened. Ever since, it has been the front line between the troops of adversaries. Even so, the Eastern Europe which emerged from the ravages of war is a political-military concept, not a simple map. Greece, on the southern end of the Balkan Peninsula, is a part of the West, an eastern Mediterranean member of the Atlantic alliance. Albania, on the same peninsula's Adriatic shore, is a maverick, a sullen, isolated enclave with a Communist regime which broke away from Soviet tutelage, tried an outlandish link to distant China that couldn't last, then slumped into self-quarantine.

Yugoslavia, which stretches up the northwestern side of the Balkans to the Hungarian and Romanian plains, is Communist but nonaligned. Yugoslavs share the social system of the East, with modifications, but they sharply resent being lumped with Eastern Europe and insist that they float free in political space. Austria, once the heart of a vast Central European domain, is a small, neutral country but fully absorbed in the West.

The difficulty in making the line clear is precisely because the East-West division of Europe is unnatural, unhistoric, unacceptable to its people and therefore ultimately unstable. But it cannot be changed or dismantled without provoking great conflict, possibly cataclysmic nuclear war.

This scar on the map, and the soul, of Europe is commonly ascribed to the Yalta Conference, the meeting of Russia's Stalin, Britain's Churchill and America's Roosevelt in the Crimean seaside resort on February 4–11, 1945. The war against Germany was drawing to a close. The Allies needed to arrange for the encounter of their troops since it had been decided that whenever Germany finally accepted their terms of unconditional surrender, it must be totally occupied to eliminate all vestiges of Nazi power. And they needed to plan for the restoration of peaceful rule, the construction of new regimes to replace those which had been destroyed by the Nazis or had collaborated with them.

There was no glimpse, at that point, of the end of the war against Japan. The Soviet Union had been preoccupied with the German war and had maintained nonbelligerency with Japan. The ultrasecret U.S. Manhattan Project to make the world's first atom bomb had not yet achieved success. The test, at Alamagordo, New Mexico, came at 5:30 A.M. on July 16, 1945. No one could know beforehand if the awesome new weapon would actually work. No one could know if its use would suffice to make the Japanese surrender. The United States was planning a million-man invasion of Japan as soon as victory in Europe permitted the transfer of troops and the assemblage of ships and equipment. In Washington's eyes, it was essential to persuade Stalin to join a common campaign against Japan, which still held vast areas on the Asian mainland. Hundreds of thousands of lives were at stake.

These were the great issues to be decided at Yalta. Stalin did not hide his expansionist ambitions. To protect Russia, and in compensation for the enormous suffering wreaked by the German invasion, he determined to change the map. East Prussia was to be taken from Germany and divided between Poland and the Soviet Union, which had already absorbed the Baltic states of Latvia, Estonia and Lithuania. Poland was to be shoved westward, ceding its eastern territories. The border between Poland and Russia on the Bug River, which Stalin insisted upon, was not very different from the old tsarist frontier; the Soviets were reclaiming territories Lenin had given up in the 1918 Treaty of Brest-Litovsk with Germany when revolutionary Russia negotiated its way out of World War I, before Poland regained independence.

Pomerania and Silesia were to be detached from Germany and awarded to Poland in compensation, putting its new frontier along the line of the Oder and Neisse rivers and eliminating the need for the awkward, contentious Polish Corridor to the Baltic invented by post–World War I mapmakers. Ruthenia, or Transcarpathia, was to be detached from Czechoslovakia and incorporated in the Soviet Ukraine. Romania's province of Bessarabia and northern Bukovina were also transferred to the Soviets, as part of the greatly enlarged Ukraine. Not all the changes were decided at Yalta; some were settled later in the year.

Churchill had long argued that the Western Allies should open their second front in 1943 for the reconquest of Europe against the "soft underbelly" of the Balkans, but he failed to convince Roosevelt. Accepting what he could not change, Churchill then sought in 1944 a compromise in plans for the future of the East, an attempt to preserve at least a degree of British influence. That was the origin of the notorious slip of paper on which he wrote in Moscow in October 1944 the formula for sharing out percentages of British and Soviet spheres: Greece 80–20, Romania 20–80, Hungary 50–50, Yugoslavia 50–50.

While the United States was to occupy zones in Germany and Austria, it planned to withdraw from Europe once the transition to peace and establishment of new governments had been completed. Roosevelt did not seek a sphere of American influence, nor, apparently, was he aware of the Churchill-Stalin informal deal. He told startled Allies at Yalta that American troops would stay in Germany "about two years," according to an account by his interpreter.

The Yalta agreements provided for Allied representatives in the states allied with Germany—Hungary, Romania and Bulgaria—who were to supervise free elections for new civilian governments. But the Americans and British had great difficulty getting into the capitals, where the Red Army was imposing the appointment of Communists to key ministries and arresting politicians considered unsympathetic. Austria, though divided into zones of occupation, was to be restored to independence and given special status as neither an enemy nor an ally. Czechoslovakia, Yugoslavia and Poland all had governments-in-exile with Allied status. There were arguments about how they would be returned to power and their future composition. In the end, each case was handled differently. But the professed purpose of the Yalta accords was in all cases to provide interim rule until free elections could be held for the choice of new, independent national regimes.

Stalin violated all his commitments, in some cases quickly and roughly, in others gradually and deviously. In 1946, in a speech at Fulton, Missouri, Churchill said that "from Stettin on the Baltic to Trieste on the Adriatic, an iron curtain has descended across the continent," as the Soviets moved to cut off from the West the lands their forces had reached. By 1948, when Communists seized power in Czechoslovakia by coup d'état, the Stalinist takeover was complete.

Many people, especially in the East, blame the Western wartime leaders for failing to foresee and prevent the Sovietization of Eastern Europe. Some Western revisionists believe that Western anticommunism was equally responsible with Moscow for provoking the Cold War and the continental cleft. This will long remain an argument among politicians and historians of differing outlook. What did happen in the immediate postwar years was the monopolization of power by Communists throughout the area and the imposition of a Soviet-style system. The East indeed became a Soviet empire in the sense that central power was decisive, tribute was exacted, and secession was not to be tolerated. In the Western vocabulary, the Eastern countries were transformed into "satellites," fixed in orbit around the Soviet Union with nothing to say about their own lives.

In the early years, there was an attempt at homogenization. Distinct nationalities and cultures were to be allowed no more room for separate development than is allowed to the various nationalities in the Soviet Union. Histories were rewritten to cast Russia in a favorable light, and efforts were made to extinguish national traditions and memories, especially since the Bolshevik revolution but also going well back into tsarist times. In the name of "proletarian internationalism," first allegiance was owed to the Soviet Union, the "socialist motherland." Patriotism that was not redefined as remodeling the nation in the Soviet image was a crime. The people of the countries concerned went through a period of great distress and terror.

Inside each country, a combination of police informer systems, censorship, arbitrary arrests and persecutions was established to break down the sense of community and to make people feel helpless and isolated. After a time, it was possible to identify the line of partition from high in the air, even where the fortifications blended into the countryside. Suddenly, the checkerboard of farms typical of Western Europe gave way to huge fields as the plane crossed into the East. There were hardly any farmhouses; they had been replaced by clusters of buildings which housed the new collectives and their machine stations.

Even the land showed the drastic changes imposed by the regimes in the name of creating "a new socialist society." Collectivization and farm policy led to a serious failure of agriculture almost everywhere. But it was years before the authorities stopped blaming the war, enemies of socialism, the climate, essential demands of industry and plain bloody-mindedness of the peasants and conceded any need for reform. When they began to admit some changes were essential, they reacted in different ways in different countries according to specific local problems. By then, so much had been invested in ideological righteousness and bureaucratic privilege, it seemed almost impossible for the authorities to undo the damage without risking their power.

In the 1950s, America's Secretary of State, John Foster Dulles, had talked of "rollback liberation" of the Eastern lands. It was a delusion. There were uprisings and revolts, in East Berlin in 1953, in Poland and Hungary in 1956, in Czechoslovakia in 1968. The Soviets were strong, and the West challenged their determination only with words. The desperate Hungarian revolutionaries of 1956 made repeated, poignant appeals to the West for help. None came. The Czech dissident writer Milan Kundera recalls that the last message sent to the world by telex from the director of the Hungarian press agency just before Soviet artillery demolished his office was, "We are dying for Hungary and for Europe." What did that mean, Kundera asks. And he answers that it had to mean Hungarians were prepared to die to keep their country Hungarian and European, not to disappear without resistance behind the electrified wire barricades and mined frontier strips.

It is hard to grasp now the pervasive intent of Stalin's effort, truly totalitarian because it aimed at controlling the totality of human thought as well as action. The case of the Soviet biologist Trofim Lysenko is a spectacular example, but only one of an endless number in every field. Not even science could escape from Stalin's dictate that everything had to conform to his vision of "Soviet reality." Lysenko claimed to have changed the genetic properties of wheat plants in his laboratory by controlling the way they were grown. That appeared to confirm Stalin's theory that the very nature of man could be changed by his environment, by the way he was made to behave, without regard to origins natural or divine. Therefore, Lysenko's theory was proclaimed official and any criticism or contradiction banned, on pain of punishment. It was a fraud, and Lysenko's experiments were later proven to be unscientific. But in those days, what pleased Stalin was right and what displeased him was wrong, with no appeal. Soviet biology was set back a generation, but more important to the Eastern Europeans was the concept that they were to be made over into a new kind of people, with a new identity, without any right of choice.

Every major city in the bloc was ordered to rename its main street for Stalin, and others that had old sentimental or historical associations were to be renamed for revolutionary events and Soviet heroes. Each capital was ordered to erect a huge statue of Stalin. Only Warsaw dawdled and never quite got around to it. Steel, in the Stalinist concept, was the basis for creating a modern, industrial society, and the countries were obliged to found or enlarge steel production on a gigantic, uneconomic scale. The requirement that a city in each country be named for Stalin was, preferably, imposed on the steel-making town. Monumental new buildings had to mimic Stalin's favored wedding-cake style, epitomized by Moscow University. Poles used to say the best view of Warsaw was from the huge Soviet-style Palace of Culture in the center of the capital, because it was the only place you could look out and not see the Palace of Culture.

Communism still had a certain ethos in that period, however; there were people who believed that all the tribulations were the birth pains of a new world. In Western Europe, sympathizers could be found among intellectuals and the many who had fought fascism in the name of remaking society. "You can't make an omelet without breaking eggs," they would assure critics who pointed to the fear and misery imposed. They had seen the faults of capitalism and its initial failure in resisting Hitler. They wanted to believe that with Marx as applied by Lenin they had found the secret of happiness for the mute masses, though of course they refused to listen to anyone who dared to speak out.

With no hope of relief from the West, and no visible recourse at home, most people in Eastern Europe slumped into bitter silence. They had been exhausted by the war. Gradually, they more or less accepted their incapacity to change the regime under which they lived and sought to limit the worst of things. They learned to give lip service and keep their real thoughts to themselves.

The theories of communism, of a classless society for the benefit of workers and peasants, were endlessly extolled, and required at least the appearance of producing "a better, just society." Social services were expanded, in countries where they had scarcely existed. Education, health care and employment were guaranteed, except for "class enemies" and their children, which could mean anything from former aristocrats to hapless ex-merchants to people who had somehow provoked the authorities. It was only when the prisons and the labor camps began to disgorge their inmates after the start of de-Stalinization in 1956 that there was even a vague idea of how many had been arrested. There is still no reliable figure, but it was certainly extremely high.

In 1949, as the Marshall Plan was reviving Western Europe, an economic organization called Comecon (Council for Mutual Economic Assistance) was created to reinforce bloc ties, impose Moscow's pricing system and enmesh the other countries' livelihood with Soviet needs. Military ties were formalized in 1955, when the Western powers decided they needed to rearm Germany in order to face the still huge Soviet armies and to admit the Federal Republic to the NATO alliance. The Soviets called their alliance the Warsaw Pact because the documents were signed in an old palace just outside Warsaw. Eventually, the Soviets were obliged to make concessions to strengthen the economies of Eastern Europe. But in the early postwar years, the relationship was pure exploitation.

Later, living standards began to rise, but never anywhere near catching up with the West. A gap developed on the other side, between the reviving countries of Eastern Europe and the Soviet Union, a matter of resentment for Russians and one reason even their malcontents never had much sympathy for the grievances of Moscow's bloc dependents. Sometimes deliberately, as in Romania, sometimes by tacit bargain, as in Hungary, sometimes by the force of popular insistence, as in Poland, the old nationalisms revived.

By the middle of the 1980s, national feelings were once again strong throughout the area. The monolith had cracked, though it was still bolted together with Soviet power. The border changes and vast displacement of populations after the war had made most of the countries more homogeneous than they had been during the interwar period of ferment over ethnic minorities. But unlike the new approach of cooperation by consent in the West, Soviet tutelage did not solve any of the problems of nationalism and irredentism.

The result is that the map of Europe, built on a balance of power, still swings on that uncertain balance. It has not put down roots. The East-West divide has been eroded by the renewal of many contacts, explicit efforts to circumvent the partition. Western policy has always been of two minds about it. On one hand, a loosening of bolts in the East and a greater independence of its people from Soviet control can only be in Western interests, emotional, cultural and economic as well as security. On the other, an attempted breakaway in the East could provoke a new war.

Détente seemed to offer an opportunity for relief from the dilemma. At the least, it did ease some of the pressures on the Eastern Europeans, who were the main beneficiaries of reduced East-West tensions during the 1970s and the main advocates afterward of renewed détente. But it also created concern in the West that a false sense of lowered danger would demobilize the Western alliance and leave Moscow relatively stronger.

Meanwhile, the East-West line has become a blur etched in arms. Each Eastern country has renewed a sense of its distinct past and special identity and evolved in a somewhat different way. They are not drastically different, because that is not permitted, but neither can they be lumped together any longer as a bowl of dull, consistent porridge. Each has its special flavor, its own calculations and interests. The dominant theme to be drawn from each is how it goes about living in the shadow of the Soviet Union, in a system of monopolized power. There is a single question, but as many variations in the answer as there are countries in the East.

THE SOVIET UNION
A Continental Weight

T HE SOVIET UNION IS TOO VAST, too continental, too diverse to be considered fully a part of Europe. The ethnic Russians dominate, though the Soviet state structure of separate republics was devised expressly by the revolutionaries to meet the grievances of other nationalities against the tsarist policy of Russification. In deference to the idea of equality, observed no more than other principles of law, justice and democracy embodied in the constitution, Soviet official forms have separate entries for citizenship (Soviet) and nationality, which may be Russian, or Ukrainian, or Uzbek, or Jewish, or another.

The number of Soviet republics has changed over the years, and each is in theory, but only in theory, sovereign, with a constitutional right of secession, the right to have relations with foreign countries and the right to complete national autonomy. In 1945, shortly before the founding of the United Nations, Stalin drew on this theory, which he compared with the structure of the British Commonwealth, to demand sixteen seats in the U.N. General Assembly, one for each republic of the time. He settled for three, one for the Soviet Union as a whole and one each for Byelorussia and the Ukraine. This was a concession granted by President Roosevelt to balance the overwhelming pro-American majority in the world organization, which was then founded with fifty-one initial members. There are now a total of fifteen Soviet Socialist Republics, including the colossal Russian Soviet Federated Socialist Republic (RSFSR), which itself contains sixteen autonomous republics and a number of autonomous regions and districts. The others, in alphabetical order, are Armenia, Azerbaidzhan, Byelorussia, Estonia, Georgia, Kazakhstan, Kirghizia, Latvia, Lithuania, Moldavia, Tadzhikistan, Turkmenistan, Ukraine and Uzbekistan, and some of them contain associated republics and autonomous districts. Some but not all of the RSFSR, the Ukraine, Byelorussia and the three Baltic republics are certainly European. The southern republics of Georgia (Stalin's birthplace), Armenia and Azerbaidzhan in the Caucasus between Europe and Asia are considered European more by tradition than by geography. A generation ago, when official U.S. forms put the question of race, "Caucasian" was the answer expected from people of European origin. The supposition was that the white race originated somewhere in the Caucasus, though Hitler pushed the source farther to the east, proclaiming "Aryan" (actually the ancestors of the Persians) as the pure wellspring of whiteness.

The Soviet Union is much more than European, so it will not be considered here in its entirety, far beyond the scope of this effort, but in terms of its weight on the other European states. It is a giant shadow on Europe's many-colored window.

Until the 1917 Bolshevik revolution, almost all the lines of influence went in one direction, west to east. The very idea of social revolution came from the West, primarily from France and Germany. Russian aristocrats dawdled in the fashionable Western European spas and took home governesses to teach their children languages. Russian merchants collected paintings and furniture to adorn their Austrian-style, ice-cream-hued mansions in St. Petersburg and Moscow. Russian intellectuals gobbled books forbidden by the censors and argued endlessly about how to save the Russian soul with Western ideas. To Westernize meant to liberalize, they thought.

The political and social program that the Germans Karl Marx and Friedrich Engels had drawn up in their *Communist Manifesto* in 1848 inspired the fervor of Western intellectuals and workers' movements in the late nineteenth and early twentieth centuries, as the pains of growing industrialization spread. But when it echoed back from Russia after the Bolshevik victory had brought a new Soviet state, it had a totally different impact. The Russians seemed to have proved that the workers' state was possible, that society could be turned upside down, and they did it with traditional Russian ferocity on both sides, the revolutionaries and the defenders of the old order. There was an explosion of wild hopes and fears. Now that the Soviet Union is in its seventies, moving on from a gerontocratic leadership to a generation of hard-minded technicians and *apparatchiki* (functionaries), it is hard to understand the hypnotic, overwhelming appeal that its promises once held for Western idealists. They desperately wanted to believe that a new society and a new, purer, better kind of human being had been born.

Beatrice and Sidney Webb, the nonrevolutionary British socialists, went to the Soviet Union to look at the model kindergartens and the model chocolate factories and the model collective farms in the early 1930s and echoed the earlier statement of American journalist Lincoln Steffens, "We have been over into the future and it works." The ardent sincerely felt they had witnessed the dawn of a happy world, all the more so because the establishments in their own countries, the moguls of money and privilege who in their view had deformed nature's state of grace, were just as fervently opposed to the Bolsheviks.

Lenin justified his "dictatorship of the proletariat" and his "democratic centralism," which meant absolute rule from the top, with the need to mobilize effectively against enemies who were visibly, tangibly present. Stalin, who won the first succession, justified his increasing tyranny with the argument that consolidation of the revolution also intensified the enemy's effort to overthrow it and therefore the faithful must sacrifice more. Even as word of his atrocities and deliberate starvation began to spread, it strengthened the faith of Western believers in the Soviet experience because the reports did seem too horrible to be true. It wasn't hard to discount them as the outrageous counter-revolutionary propaganda that Moscow denounced. For the more sophisticated, another argument became compelling with the rise of fascism. It was that any criticism of the Soviets, any derogatory facts, could only serve a vicious enemy and obscure the higher truth of ideology.

The passion of the battle of ideologies, Communist versus anti-Communist, fascist versus Communist, even before the outbreak of war, should not be underestimated with cooler hindsight. It is a mistake to compare Hitler and Stalin or to draw up a grisly balance sheet of terror. Both were monstrous in their way; both were totalitarian tyrants, Hitler more cold-blooded and calculating, Stalin more paranoid. But as a theory, Hitler's fascism promised domination and the maintenance of a stern order by what he considered his "master race," which had a right to liquidate or enslave all others. As a theory, Marxism-Leninism

offered egalitarianism, self-rule and rescue of the poor from the power
of the rich. Hitler wanted war so as to bring the triumph of his Third
Reich. Stalin did not want war but was determined to exploit the Soviets' costly victory.

After the conquest of Western Europe, Nazi Germany turned on the
Soviet Union, in June 1941, putting Britain and the Soviets on the same
side in a war which the United States did not enter until the Japanese
attack on Pearl Harbor in December of that year. For many Europeans,
the choice had not been for some time between supporting or opposing
communism; it was between the fascists and the Communists, who
were fighting back. Hitler Germany was very arrogant, but particularly
toward the Slavs on the eastern front. They were not marked for total
genocide, a "final solution," as were Jews and Gypsies, but they were
classed as *Untermenschen*, subhumans to be treated with less than the
minimum regard for other enemies. Not all the Soviet people felt initial
hostility to the invading German forces, particularly those in the
Ukraine, which had suffered atrociously during Stalin's collectivization
campaign and where regional nationalism made a strong distinction
between Ukrainian and Russian. But the Germans were so deliberately
brutal that Stalin could make a successful appeal to patriotism. The
Ukrainians rallied and fought bravely alongside the Russians and other
Soviet citizens, and went through terrible ordeals.

The figure of 20 million Soviet citizens who died in the war does not
begin to evoke the dimensions of the national catastrophe. It has seared
the people's consciousness. It is foolish to believe, as Alexander Haig
said when he was U.S. Secretary of State, that the bellicosity of the
coming generation of Soviet leadership was to be feared because they
had not felt the war on their own skins and thought of the Battle of
Stalingrad "as a movie." No country remembers and memorializes its
experience of World War II more vividly than the Soviet Union. Children are taught about it when they are toddlers. It is called the "Great
Patriotic War," and that is the way people think of it, a tragic but finally
victorious defense of the homeland. Military planners continue to
brood over its lessons. Michel Tatu, a French expert on Soviet affairs,
says their conclusion is two "never agains." The Soviet Union must
never again be taken by surprise in war; and war must never again be
fought on its territory. "The trouble for us Westerners," Tatu points
out wryly, "is that means if war comes, we are the ones to be taken by
surprise and the fighting is to be done on our soil."

Certainly, the war greatly increased the Soviet obsession with security, already well developed after foreign interventions (including American troops sent to fight with the Whites in the 1918–21 revolutionary war) and the European diplomatic attempt to build a *cordon sanitaire* against the Soviet Union by agreements among its Western neighbors between the two world wars. Historians and politicians argue whether the border changes imposed by Stalin after World War II and Moscow's insistent hegemony over Eastern Europe reflect primarily expansionist ambition or an urge for the safety of ever more depth, pushing the front ever farther from the heartland. It makes little difference. As strategists note, a demand for total security by one side means total insecurity for the other side.

For the foreseeable future, the Red Army has everything in Eastern Europe pinned down tightly. Not only were the countries obliged to reproduce the Soviet system, but Russians were sent to supervise the police and sensitive ministries. In Poland, the Minister of Defense from 1949 until the upheaval in 1956 was a Soviet marshal who happened to have a Polish-sounding name. May Day parades, slogans, architecture, statues and giant posters of the leaders had to conform to the Soviet model. When the Czech Communist leader Klement Gottwald died in 1953, a week after Stalin's death, he was embalmed and enshrined in a huge mausoleum, Red Square style, on a Prague hill. There is a chicken-and-egg question of whether Moscow was so determined to Sovietize its neighbors in order to make sure their regimes would always be friendly and cooperative, or whether the Kremlin needed clones to reinforce the legitimacy of its own system, based on belief in the "inevitable triumph of the revolution." The requirements of security and ideology reinforced each other, producing a drab, imitative sameness that chafed the Eastern Europeans as much as the prescribed allegiance to Soviet interests.

And for the Russian people, dominion over their allies is also a double issue. They are proud and reassured by the proof that their state is a great power, an acknowledged leader of nations. But there is also a combination of envy and disdain at the way their minions have wriggled around the precepts of communism to assert their own national and cultural identities, improve their living conditions and find means to tweak and challenge their ideological "brother." The Eastern Europeans feel exploited by the Russians, but the Russians find their allies ungrateful and greedy since they are so much better off and complain nonetheless.

A recent production of *Boris Godunov* at the Bolshoi Theater gave a startling glimpse of how the Russians view themselves and their Polish neighbors. As usual, the staging was magnificent. The set showing old Moscow was solidly impressive, evoking a city of historic substance. The tsar and his court were costumed in rich, jewel-toned velvets and furs, a luxury of warmth and girth. They moved with assured majesty. Some of the peasants were poverty-stricken, in gray sackcloth, others bright with layers of skirts and scarves, all very real, fleshly people with outsized, full-throated passions. When the scene switched to a palace near Warsaw, everything was pale blue and silver, airy, diaphanous. It was enchanting, the people flitting gracefully and singing tinkling sentiments. But they could hardly be counted as souls. The Poles were shown fairylike in a fairyland. The director seemed to be telling his audience that such people with their fragile elegance were all very well as a brief distraction from real life, but they couldn't reach the earthy depths and the pulsing human drama that Russians knew in their bones.

The exiled Czech writer Milan Kundera mocks the idea of the "great Russian (or Slav) soul," and he cites Central Europeans speaking long before the Soviet revolution. In 1844, he says, Karel Havlíček warned his Czech compatriots against the vogue of pan-Slavism and admiration for Russian emotions which they had developed in cultural opposition to their Austrian overlords. "The Russians like to say everything Russian is Slav so that later they can claim that everything Slav is Russian," Havlíček said. The Polish-born writer Joseph Conrad protested in irritation when critics attributed his talent to a "Slav soul," saying nothing "is more alien to the Polish temperament with its chivalrous feeling of moral constraints and its exaggerated respect for individual rights."

"How I understand him," Kundera comments. "I, too, I know nothing more ridiculous than this cult of obscure depths, this sentimentality as noisy as it is empty that is called the Slav soul." Kundera's point is to emphasize the difference between the Russians, whom he considers outsiders in Europe, and the neighbors they dominate. He pays tribute to the great Russian novelists and musicians who did become a part of European culture. But he sees them as exceptions among a people belonging to another world, with another history and mentality that have nothing to do with the essence Europeans share. He revives the idea of Central Europe, the nations between Germany and Russia, as the easternmost part but still definitely in the West, definitely European despite the political-military divide imposed by the Red Army through the middle of Germany.

The West, in the deepest cultural and emotional sense, Kundera says, extends as far as the lands which look to the Roman Catholic Church and use the Latin alphabet. The East begins with the Orthodox Church and the Cyrillic alphabet. Bulgaria, so long ruled by the Turks, always looked to the Russians for support, so they do not suffer from the cultural deformation of Moscow's dominion in the way the other Eastern Europeans do, he says. Naturally, Kundera's view is greatly influenced by his country's oppression and, if he had thought about it, of course he would not have defined the West in a way that leaves out Serbia, Romania and Greece. Nonetheless, Kundera represents the real feeling of the Europeans on the Soviet borders, a feeling rooted firmly in their history.

"On the eastern frontier of the west which is Central Europe, people have always been sensitive to the danger of Russian power," he writes. "And not only the Poles. František Palacký, the great historian and the most representative personality of Czech politics in the 19th century, wrote a famous letter in 1848 to the revolutionary parliament in Frankfurt justifying the existence of the Habsburg [Austro-Hungarian] Empire as the only possible bastion against Russia, 'this power which, with its current enormous size, increases its force more than any other western country could do.' Palacký warns against Russia's imperial ambitions, its seeking to become 'a universal monarchy,' that is to say, seeking world domination. 'A Russian universal monarchy,' says Palacký, 'would be an immense, indescribable misery without measure and limit.' "

There is a continuity in Russian history and Soviet policy that goes beyond the issue of expansionist ambitions. Kundera addresses the question of whether the distress Eastern Europeans feel comes from being under communism or being under Russia. He contrasts the European "passion for diversity" with "Russia, uniform, uniformizing, centralizing." And he asks whether communism is "the negation of Russian history or its fulfillment." It is "certainly both the negation [of its religiosity, for example] and its fulfillment [of centralizing tendencies and imperial dreams]. Seen from inside Russia, the first aspect, that of discontinuity, is most striking. But from the point of view of the countries forced to submit, it is the second aspect, the continuity, which is most strongly felt."

An important element of that continuity lies in the notion of a special "Russian soul." It is the concept of suffering, a virtual exaltation and pride in the capacity to suffer. Russian dissidents who are totally anti-

Communist reflect it as much as ordinary people who never think of challenging the regime. Kundera repeats with wonder a story told by the Polish author Kasimierz Brandys about another Polish writer who met the great Russian poet Anna Akhmatova and complained to her that the censor had banned all his works. "Have you been imprisoned?" she asked. He said no. "At least have you been thrown out of the Writers' Union?" No. "Then what are you complaining about?" And Brandys commented, "Such are Russian consolations. Nothing seems horrible to them in comparison to the fate of Russia. But these consolations are senseless. The fate of Russia isn't part of our conscience; it's foreign to us; we are not responsible. It weighs on us but it is not our heritage."

There are many other examples. The most striking is Alexander Solzhenitsyn, reviler of the Soviet system and all its works in prose that sears with passion and integrity, but advocate of a return to Russian "purity," that is to say, to the old, anti-Western, closed mind of the Russian ensconced in vast forests and steppes. Obviously, those Europeans under Soviet sway have nothing in common with Solzhenitsyn's idealization of a brutal tsarist system which their ancestors fought.

Among the new wave of Russian emigrants, whose writings are beginning to appear, one finds a similar attitude to suffering as an ennobling Russian trait, even if they disagree flatly with Solzhenitsyn's nostalgia for a past untouched by Western "decadence." There is a certain boastfulness about how bad things are, how patiently but slyly the people endure their rulers, as if to say Russians are better than others because nobody else could stand what they go through as a matter of course. There is never any suggestion of rebellion. Disgust is worn as a badge of honor.

Revolution really isn't a Russian idea. It is a European idea, an idea that sprang up in France, Germany, Poland, Hungary, Italy and even England, at the time of Cromwell, and in the American colonies. The notions behind all the stirrings and conspirings that finally overthrew imperial Russia came from Western thinkers and were absorbed and given new shape by Russians. Perhaps that underlies Solzhenitsyn's rejection of all that is Western. It helps to explain the deep conservatism of the Communist regime and its resistance to internal change.

Rudolf Slansky, son of the Czechoslovak Communist leader Rudolf Slansky who was executed after a Stalinist purge trial in 1952, and a much-harassed dissident himself in Prague, believes the Soviet leaders

can never tolerate dissent or challenge because they know what horrors
they committed and cannot allow a whisper of what might lead to a
renewal of revolutionary turmoil. They find it hard to imagine that in
their own country change could come in any other way, Slansky thinks,
and they are determined that there must never be another civil war.
But there are probably more profound sources for Russian conservatism that lie far back in a history of tyranny and a vast geography of
danger. Only endurance and a stubborn will to survive overcame the
constant threats, not insubordinate challenge.

The whole Soviet system is built to prevent important change, an
irony considering the old slogans about remaking the world, remaking
society, fashioning a "new Soviet man." People rise by co-optation from
above, not by a display of merit or talent or ingenuity, unless it can win
them a sponsor. The rewards are for submission and complaisance to
superiors, and they include the right to vent inevitable frustration by
trampling on inferiors. Yet there has been some change. Nikita Khrushchev ended the bloodiness of the Stalinist years and tried to innovate.
But he was too sporadic, experimental and eccentric for Russian tastes.

His successor, Leonid Brezhnev, ruled by immobility. It was a great
relief for the establishment, the bureaucracy which rules the Soviet
Union, to feel securely that nothing new would happen. But the law of
entropy works in the Soviet Union too. Without the addition of new
effort and new ideas, things deteriorate. The regime is ambitious and
the people sullen in their deprivation. There is a great desire to build
and to achieve better living conditions, and growing awareness that it
cannot be done without reform. But reform immediately implies risk.
It wasn't until 1985, after three old men at the top had died within two
years, that power was passed on to the next generation in the person of
Mikhail Gorbachev, who had just turned fifty-four when he took over.

Gorbachev moved swiftly after his accession to demonstrate a new
style, a new vigor, a new demand for efficient work and a more modern
approach. He took draconian measures against alcoholism, which had
become such a plague that Russian male life expectancy was declining.
He proclaimed a campaign against corruption. A stocky man, with a
large wine-red birthmark on his balding head and an agreeable manner
in public, he traveled about to show himself to the people and appeared
on television, quite novel behavior for a Soviet leader. Usually he was
accompanied by his comely wife, Raisa, and sometimes a daughter or a
grandchild, showing as the rulers never had before that he too was a

normal man with a family life. They dressed well and smiled, something in the style of Western politicians seeking personal popularity. Andrei Gromyko, the dour old Foreign Minister whom Gorbachev soon pushed upstairs into the Soviet presidency so he could take control of foreign affairs himself, said of the new leader, "He has a nice smile, but he has teeth of steel."

Gorbachev's clear priority was to galvanize the Soviet economy and move it forward. He did not make extravagant promises, as Khrushchev had done when he pledged in the 1950s to "catch up with the West by 1980," but he showed his determination to develop a production system to match the Soviet Union's vast resources. To begin with, the changes were in personnel, in manner, in discipline. It was impossible to tell at the start how much he really wanted to reform, or how much the hidden forces sustaining the Soviet system would permit him to reform. But Gorbachev was also clearly determined to keep the Soviet Union in its superpower position, clinging to the catchphrase of the Brezhnev period for foreign negotiations that it must have "equality and equal security." That seemed to mean not only parity of arms with the United States but recognition of equal standing in the world, an illusion so long as the Soviets remained economically weak, politically unappealing and unable to offer a desirable quality of life. Gorbachev's ambitions for his country were great, but the question was whether the Soviet system could generate the enormous human energy required to attain them.

There has long been a debate in the West over whether the threat it feels from the Soviet Union stems primarily from a crusading ideology which proclaims it will inevitably conquer the world or from historical Russian expansionism. In the postrevolutionary days, proselytizing communism was felt as the main challenge. The Soviet Union was weak as a power, but the liturgy of its faith in a new social system for all mankind stirred millions. There was no real hesitation in the West to welcome and support the Soviets as an ally in World War II, because Nazism as an ideology and Germany as a power were seen as a far greater menace to survival and liberty.

After the war, perceptions were reversed. The extent can be measured in the way U.S. presidents court China, certainly a great Communist state, and warn against the danger of Soviet-backed communism in Grenada and Nicaragua. They are really talking about the possibility of the extension of Russian state power into the western hemisphere. Communism as an ideal or a diabolic theory has become a marginal matter.

In Stalin's time, there did seem to be a "Soviet man." The citizens one met abroad, at least, seemed monolithic, closed, wooden, like the monumental statues and the Socialist Realist pictures where the boy in overalls and the girl in pigtails appeared to be moved above all by love for their tractor. It was a mystery. Were all those crooning balalaika players and tea-drinking gossips living in exile only a thin, unrepresentative layer of Russian society which had been siphoned off after the revolution, leaving solid stone? Were the great Russian writers—Tolstoy, Dostoievski, Chekhov, Gogol—describing only exceptional people who agonized about love and life and moral values while all the rest of the nation was silent? Or had communism really changed the character and the nature of the people?

After Khrushchev's de-Stalinization speech in 1956, the mask began to drop. The people hadn't changed. They had been congealed and paralyzed with fear. When it eased, they were recognizable again from the old books and the old tales. The ideology of "building communism" had rejected and denounced the Russian past and its traditions as the remains of tsarism, reaction and primitive conditions. But during World War II, Stalin's appeal to patriotism in order to mobilize the people for war led him to revive the past and many of its symbols. Nationalism continues to thrive, with official encouragement, and it has again grown very strong, as it had been through the ages. There is also a certain revival of religion and of old customs, such as having special cakes blessed at Easter and putting them on the graves of loved ones. Setting out food on graves goes back to pagan times, but old habits were incorporated into Russian Christianity. The rise in religious observance is certainly not encouraged, but neither is it persecuted as it was in Stalin's day. Communist propaganda manages to ignore it.

Nationalism serves the rulers, making sacrifice more acceptable as patriotic duty. But it is a problem for the centralizing state. The Ukrainians, the Balts and the Georgians are asserting their own national feelings too, and historically they are antagonistic to the Russians. It is not clear how much all-Soviet nationalism, as contrasted with ethnic assertiveness, Moscow has been able to inculcate. From the reaction of Russians to the growing Central Asian population of their country, it would appear to be minimal. Russians talk openly of the "yellow peril" in reference to China, but they imply they are also thinking of the

EUROPE

Asians east of the Urals who are Soviet citizens. Demography is one of the changes that the system cannot control, especially as birthrates stay high in the east and decline in the western Soviet lands. The last available figure for ethnic Russians in the Soviet population dates from 1979, when they numbered 137.4 million, 52.4 percent of the 277.4 million total. In another generation, all the Europeans in the Soviet Union taken together will probably be a minority. Changing ethnic proportions have always been a difficulty of empire, since it raises the issue of sharing power or increasing repression to muzzle the claims of rising groups.

The French writer Hélène Carrère d'Encausse has made a careful study of Soviet trends and predicts that the Soviet Union will shatter into fragments under the pressure of these forces. That doesn't seem likely. The countervailing centralizing force does not depend only on ideology but also on the need for development and on the concern for security.

The other Europeans, coming at last to absorb the meaning of the loss of empire and economic dominance, tend to feel increasingly squeezed between two continental powers, the Soviet Union and the United States. Western Europeans are tied to America in outlook, but they must share their continent with the Soviets. They tend to like the Russian people and sympathize with them, unlike Eastern Europeans, who want to turn their backs. There is a cultural appeal in these stocky people with their gusto, their mournful and frenetic songs, their lilting, gliding language. But so long as politics overrule culture, the Elbe, where Europe is now divided East from West, is a wider gap than the Atlantic. Russia is in Europe, but not of it at this stage in history.

EAST GERMANY
State Behind a Wall

O N JUNE 17, 1953, the workers of East Berlin suddenly threw down their tools and swarmed into the streets. It was the first massive demonstration against the new Communist regimes anywhere in what had come to be known as Eastern Europe. The upheaval, which spread to many cities in East Germany, was quickly suppressed by Soviet armor. The playwright Bertolt Brecht, a Communist with a sense of humor, was working in his Theater am Schiffbauerdamm near the dividing line with the Western sectors of Berlin. He was at first startled and appalled as the proletarians burst in to tell him they were rising against the proletarian state. But when he collected himself soon after, he delivered a classic line: "The leaders have lost confidence in the people. Wouldn't it be simpler to dissolve the people and elect another?"

In a sense, that is what happened in East Germany over the years. The leaders remained, no matter what. The people sorted themselves out one way or another. Many fled to the West. Those who stayed behind found ways to accommodate themselves to a regime which had learned on June 17 that it too had to make a basic accommodation, that of providing tolerable living standards. Propaganda and police were not enough to create a rump Communist state out of the part of Germany that had been occupied by Soviet forces at the end of World War II by agreement among the Allies. A tacit social compact was established. The workers would rebuild their land in whatever system the regime required, and the regime would make sure they were fed. That was the turning point, and the rule was never again seriously challenged. It assured that the new state would arise from the rubble and ashes of defeat to become the second biggest economic power of the East, after the Soviet Union. And it assured a peculiar combination of strict Communist orthodoxy alongside a certain tolerance in such things as religion and eventually nationalism, as the state evolved. In this way the temporary partition of Germany settled into concrete and the German Democratic Republic, the state's official name, became a fact of European life.

There are many parallels between the circumstances of the two Germanys which emerged from World War II, though they are at opposite poles of the East-West contrast. Facing each other, they grew in opposite directions and yet to a degree in mirror image, linked like Siamese twins by a common origin but nurtured to be different. From the start, the Communist regime rejected the German heritage except for historic revolts by peasants and workers, and particularly refused any responsibility for Hitler's Third Reich. Since Communists had been victims of the Nazis, the regime held that the state, which was proclaimed on October 7, 1949 (shortly after the formation of the Federal Republic in Bonn), was innocent of German history, a revolutionary infant with no parents but the Communist tradition and its heroes. The sponsor and mentor was, of course, the Soviet Union, on which everything was modeled, including the Stalinist-style buildings erected on the main avenues of East Berlin once reconstruction started. The sins of the Nazis were presented to public memory as above all their persecution of "progressives," especially Communists.

Even concentration camps on the territory that had become East Germany, such as the camp for women at Ravensbrück, were made into monuments to the Communist resistance, overlooking of course the Hitler-Stalin pact which immediately preceded the outbreak of war. There was scarcely an indication in the museum at Ravensbrück, or at Buchenwald for another example, that Jews were the primary targets of Hitler's genocidal racism. Unlike West Germany, the regime in the East never acknowledged any debt to the victims or to the state of Israel, insisting that the Hitler era was the natural outcome of capitalism and imperialism in the "bad" part of Germany and had nothing to do with the East German government. Nonetheless, it was reported after his death that Nahum Goldman, longtime president of the World Jewish Congress, had once been approached by East German officials who offered to deposit $1 million to his account as "settlement in full" of Jewish claims. Goldman had, of course, dismissed it with contempt.

The Soviet occupation forces made their headquarters in Potsdam, just outside Berlin, observing for a time the formal requirements of the wartime decision that the German capital was to be jointly ruled by the four leading Allied powers. Unlike Vienna, however, the city was divided into four separate sectors and each occupier took charge of its own. Also unlike Vienna, Berlin was not a point of convergence of occupation zones but deep inside the area assigned to the Soviets. All this had been settled during the war, when it was arranged that the Elbe River would be the meeting point of Soviet armies driving into Germany from the east and the other Allied forces pushing from the west. It had not been foreseen that the Soviets would keep the Western Allies out of Berlin for two months after the final victory, which gave them time to round up people and Nazi archives of great political importance without any interference. Nor was it foreseen by the West that there would be any problems with the agreed access routes to Berlin from the American occupation zone in the south and the British zone in the northwest. (The French zone in the southwest was carved out of what was to have been a larger American zone. The French were only admitted as an equal occupying power at the end of the war. They were given a sector in Berlin, but no special route to reach it.)

The Allied Kommandatura in Berlin continued to exist for three months after the overall Allied Control Council, which was supposed to govern defeated Germany as a unit, had broken down. Then the Western currency reform, which provoked the split in the rest of the country, was extended to the Western sectors of Berlin. The Russians boycotted the Kommandatura meetings, completed the political and economic partition of the city and cut its land and waterway links to West Germany by a blockade. But people continued to circulate freely within the former capital.

The Russians had planned carefully, and secretly, during the war for the immediate establishment of Communist rule in their part of Germany. A troika of leaders was prepared among the German Communists who had spent the Hitler years in exile in the Soviet Union. They were Walter Ulbricht, to be head of the party, Wilhelm Pieck, who became East Germany's first President, and Otto Grotewohl, its first Prime Minister. Ulbricht was dispatched to Berlin with a handpicked team as soon as the Red Army took over. He had detailed instructions on what to do, including making sure to seize Gestapo records so that new police spies could be quickly recruited by blackmailing those who had served before and were vulnerable because of their Nazi past. A fascinating account of this period was eventually published by Wolfgang Leonhard, a young aide who accompanied Ulbricht but later defected to Yugoslavia and then, in complete disillusion with his Communist faith, to West Germany. He called his book *Child of the Revolution*. It shed new light on Stalin's hidden intentions even as he was professing to agree with Roosevelt and Churchill on the fate of Germany.

There is historical controversy over just what started the Cold War and when, but Germany was certainly the focus. By the fall of 1946, it was clear that the wartime Allies were moving toward confrontation. Hostility mounted by degrees, reflected in a series of sometimes small and sometimes openly provocative steps. The crisis broke on June 25, 1948, when the Soviet army began the blockade of West Berlin. That too came in steps, cutting off road, railroad and river traffic to the Western zones. Some in Washington thought of putting troops on a train and forcing a way through, daring the Russians to back down or risk what could have been the start of another war. But Washington did not realize, as the American commander in Germany did, that the trains from the West were hooked onto the East's locomotives at the zonal border and could not have proceeded on their own. On April 5, 1948, a British military plane flying in the air safety zone of the British airfield in Berlin was harassed and made to crash by a Soviet fighter. All fourteen passengers, including two Americans, were killed. It was a moment of terrible tension. The air lanes were the only Western transport left to Berlin. The land blockade had cut off the flow of food, coal and other essential supplies. The city seemed doomed to be starved into total submission to the Soviets, with the small Western garrisons unable even to support themselves.

General Lucius D. Clay, the American commander and head of the military government, decided on a daring but well-calculated plan. As a test of both Soviet intentions and Allied capacity to supply West Berlin by air, he collected all the transport planes available to the three Western commands in Germany and started an airlift. After forty-eight hours had shown that an incredible number of planes could land one after another at the city's two poorly equipped airports, unload and take off, he went to Washington. Later he told how he appealed to President

Truman for the equipment to mount a massive jump over the blockade by air. Truman called a cabinet meeting and asked each member for advice. One by one, they opposed the idea because it would strip American air capability worldwide. Clay, a tall, trim man of very military bearing, slumped farther and farther down in his chair. When the cabinet had filed out, he faced Truman dejectedly, deeply disappointed but willing as a good soldier to take orders without argument. "I guess that's the end of it," he said. But the President asked him if he was certain an airlift could be made to work. Clay assured him and Truman replied, "You will get your planes."

It was a huge scramble to work out the logistics of the operation, but the result was a masterful, unprecedented organization, which at its peak succeeded in bringing the surrounded city 12,940.9 tons of cargo in 1,398 flights in 24 hours, with a plane landing every 61.8 seconds. The total airlift carried 2.2 million tons of cargo on 274,418 flights. West Berliners went short on food and shivered through the winter with little coal and almost no light. But they took comfort from the continuous buzz of planes overhead all through the night as well as the day. Some patronized a black market that sprang up in the Eastern sector, for there was no attempt to keep them out. On the contrary, the Soviet aim was to draw them into its orbit in despair. That was when the two-dog joke first appeared. An East Berlin dog and a West Berlin dog met at the sector line, each going to the other side. "Why are you crossing?" asked the East dog. "I'm hungry," said the West dog. "I want to eat. But why are you going over? There's nothing there." The East dog answered, "I want to bark." There was a tremendous surge of stubborn spirit among the West Berliners, still living in the rubble of their devastated city. It brought a new sense of comradeship between the defeated people and their American conquerors, who had previously been under strict orders not to "fraternize" with Germans at all. The British and French also participated in the airlift, but their nations too had barely begun to recover from the war. The operation was overwhelmingly American.

After 328 days, Stalin backed down and lifted the blockade. The first cars and trains from the West arrived during the night of May 12, 1949. The Federal Republic had been proclaimed in Bonn on May 8 of that year, despite a fierce Soviet propaganda campaign warning that a move to legalize the union of the three Western zones of Germany and provide self-government would bring dire results. The end of the blockade was a thrilling moment, not only for Berlin. That was the turning point of the expansion of Soviet hegemony in Europe. West Berlin survived as the symbol of peaceful but unyielding Western resolve. The East-West lines were drawn then, and they have never been moved. Several times again, Berlin became the center of East-West crisis, but it did not succumb. The sturdy allegiance of the West Berliners to the Western camp despite their hardships sparked the friendship that began to evolve between the Western Allies and their former enemies.

In the period that followed, the Marshall Plan was organized and American policy shifted to an active effort for Europe's revival. West Berlin was also a beneficiary, and life gradually eased. In the East, it was the period of forced collectivization of the farms and nationalization of industry. *Volkseigen Betriebe* ("people's own enterprises"), run by the state apparatus, took over almost everything. A little over 50 percent of the shops were still in private hands in 1950, but the number declined to under 5 percent within a few years. Ulbricht was unrelenting. The difference in living standards between East and West Berlin, definitely in East Berlin's favor during the blockade, shifted markedly.

In June 1953, the East German regime proclaimed a 10 percent rise in work norms, without a rise in pay, in order to force an increase in the rate of production. Some masons and carpenters engaged in reconstruction in East Berlin laid down their tools and started a march to party headquarters to protest. Soon they were joined by hundreds. The next day, after the radio in the American sector had broadcast the news and urged support, hundreds of thousands turned out in the streets. Strikes and protests spread to major cities throughout East Germany. The slogans shouted by the workers escalated rapidly from cancellation of the new norms, in effect a pay cut, to demands for the ouster of Ulbricht and free elections. Soviet tanks came out to quell the uprising. People in the West held their breath, but no one intervened. Afterward, East Berlin said twenty-nine had died, but others reported deaths in the hundreds. Some 1,500 were imprisoned, and a vast purge removed the wobblers and the doubters from the regime, leaving proven hardliners. The upshot of the revolt was a tightening of Ulbricht's stern control.

As reconstruction and recovery continued, West Berlin became the portal for East Germans who turned their back on the Communist regime and sought another life in West Germany. And it became the lively, glowing "showcase," as politicians put it, of the difference between the West and the East, the one place where it was easy to visit both sides and see the contrast. Berliners were the same people, with the same history and same language, living in the same city. As the years went by and the "iron curtain" along the East-West German border became more impenetrable, more and more East Germans fled through Berlin. It was a costly and humiliating drain for the East German regime.

Suddenly, in 1961, the mounting stream rose to a flood. President John F. Kennedy and First Secretary Nikita Khrushchev met in Vienna on June 3–4 of that year. Their encounter was stormy, and when they went home they began to exchange public threats and insults. To prove he could not be bullied, Kennedy called for an additional $3.5 billion in defense spending and an increase of about 15 percent in military manpower, to be ready for mobilization if necessary. The prospect of a Soviet-American confrontation on the ground decided many more East Germans to leave while it was still possible. By August 1961 nearly 2,000 a day were arriving to seek refuge in West Berlin. From 1949, the year of the airlift, to 1961, 2.7 million people had passed into West Berlin, of the total of 4 million Germans who moved West after the war. From January 1, 1961, until the Berlin escape hatch was slammed shut that August, the total was 150,000.

On the night of Sunday, August 13, 1961, East German troops began to stretch barricades of barbed wire along the sector border. Most crossing points were closed. The regime announced that it was cutting off all but a trickle of traffic across the city to protect its people from "imperialist" designs. But everybody knew it was to hold them in. That was the start of the Berlin Wall, another major East-West crisis. Taken by surprise, President Kennedy let it be known that he considered the Communist action a "propaganda victory" for the West. He seemed to be relieved that tensions over Berlin, building up since Khrushchev had announced in 1958 that the city was a "cancer in our throat" and should be turned over officially to East Germany, were to be resolved by total and permanent partition. Cowed by a show of force, East Berliners did not openly react. But West Berliners were outraged. As days went by and the West did nothing while the wall was built, their anger mounted. On Thursday, August 17, a quarter of a million irate people gathered in front of the City Hall. They wanted to march to the Brandenburg Gate on the East-West dividing line and by their sheer unarmed numbers force open again the connecting links of their city.

Willy Brandt was mayor of West Berlin. He understood that there was an imminent danger of massacre, with unforeseeable consequences for the city, for the whole of Germany, perhaps for the world. Passionately but skillfully, he harangued the crowd, persuading them to return to their homes without acting provocatively. President Kennedy was jolted into awareness that the Berlin crisis had not been eased but exacerbated. General Clay, the retired hero of the airlift, was sent back to Berlin with a reinforcement brigade to show that America was still determined to protect the Western sectors. The incident left a deep mark on Brandt, who would become Chancellor in 1969. It was one of the factors that decided him to seek reconciliation with the Eastern bloc, including East Germany. He never again had the same full trust in the dedication and wisdom of American governments, and although he never put the alliance in doubt, he looked to the East as well as to the West for equilibrium.

The ugly wall, some twenty-seven miles of concrete and another seventy-five miles of barbed wire and minefields through the surrounding countryside, became an enduring part of the divided city. People resigned themselves, but the drama lasted for years, with sensational escapes from East to West by tunnel, tragic killings at the border and another direct Soviet-American military showdown. The two sides' tanks met on October 27 a hundred yards apart at the two approaches to Checkpoint Charlie, the one crossing point left open for Allied officials. The issue was an intricate point of occupation protocol, but significant in its symbolism for the status of Berlin. Once again, the Soviets backed down without violence, as they had done during the airlift.

It was not until 1971, during President Richard Nixon's policy of détente, that the four occupation powers reached a new Berlin agreement. It confirmed their respective responsibilities for the city and provided guarantees for Western access to West Berlin, recognized as closely tied to the Federal Republic but not an integral part of it. When the Western powers sent envoys to East Germany, they stationed their ambassadors in East Berlin but continued to refuse formal acceptance of its status as the capital of East Germany and insisted on maintaining their occupation rights to send in military patrols. From time to time after that, there was harassment on the access routes and minor quarrels over Berlin. But the endemic crisis, which had festered since the end of the war because of the peculiar, badly defined status reserved for Hitler's capital, was ended. It cannot be considered solved. Berlin remains an anomaly in a divided Germany and a divided Europe which the West accepted but never endorsed.

The development of East Germany proceeded behind the lines. Walter Ulbricht, a raspy-voiced Saxon with a comic-opera goatee, was a devoted Stalinist, always attentive to Moscow's needs. He was one of the last in the Eastern bloc to remove the monument to Stalin from his capital after Khrushchev's 1956 de-Stalinization speech, and he fashioned his new state as closely as possible to the Soviet model. It had been a predominantly agricultural, predominantly Protestant part of Germany with some light industry (porcelain in Dresden and Meissen, optics and photography in Lena) but little of the heavy-industry base of the western part, concentrated in the Ruhr Valley. The eastern parts of Prussia (minus areas incorporated into the Soviet Union and Poland), Thuringia and Saxony formed the new state, less than a quarter the size of the prewar German Reich and about two-fifths the size of the postwar Federal Republic. It is for the most part a flat land, with many historic and impressive sites but little natural beauty. The population was 16.7 million in 1981 (down from 18.8 million in 1949), compared to West Germany's 61.7 million.

The regime set out to integrate East Germany into the Soviet bloc economy, bit by bit becoming the major industrial power after the Soviets and the main source of technology. Its prime resource was the proverbial German capacity for work and acceptance of discipline. Until the 1980s, reconstruction focused on developing production and changing the face of the country to coincide with the theory that it was created brand new, in communism, in 1949.

Ulbricht revised the state's 1949 constitution in 1968, ostensibly bringing it "up to date." It omitted the long-ignored clauses on the right to strike and the right to emigrate, and provided that the basis of government was "socialist ownership of the means of production." But he also responded, evidently reluctantly, to Brandt's overtures, partly because it was a way of gaining wider recognition and partly because Moscow was moving toward better relations with Bonn and détente with the United States. The West German Chancellor was received in East Germany in March 1970. His visit, to Erfurt, produced a mass outpouring of excited welcome and affection. Ulbricht was naturally displeased. Such scenes were never allowed to be repeated. And when the East German Prime Minister, Willi Stoph, returned the visit to

Kassel in West Germany, there were protests. But meanwhile, Brandt had signed treaties normalizing relations with other Eastern bloc countries and pressures were building for some flexibility in East Berlin. Without advance notice, on May 3, 1971, Ulbricht stepped down as party leader, though he remained until his death in 1973, at age eighty, in the largely honorific post of President. Soviet leader Brezhnev did not attend his state funeral.

His successor was Erich Honecker, a gray-faced man with a wooden oratorical style but a sharp mind, more interested in organization than in cultivating his personality. He was born in 1912 in the Saarland, which borders France, to a family of coal miners. As soon as he was eligible, at age seventeen, he joined the Communist Youth Movement and shortly after was accepted for training at a party school in Moscow. Returning to Germany in 1931, he worked as a party official, continuing clandestinely after Hitler took power in 1933 and outlawed the Communists. In 1935 he was arrested in Berlin and spent the war years in a Nazi jail. As soon as he was freed by the Red Army at the end of the war, he rejoined the Communist Party, which was converted in 1946 into the Socialist Unity Party (*Sozialistiche Einheitspartei Deutschland*) in the pattern of all the Eastern countries. He returned to the Soviet Union for further training in 1956–57, and then moved from youth work to internal security responsibilities. In 1958 he joined the Politburo. A man of the prewar generation, he was immune from suspicion of having become a Communist through opportunism. Rather, he was convinced that the Nazi epoch was a direct, natural consequence of the evils of capitalism and that, despite its flaws, the Soviet system represented a historic advance.

Honecker's wife, Margot, born in Halle in 1927, was the daughter of a shoemaker who was a Communist activist. She too entered the Communist Youth Movement and had her turn at school in Moscow. The couple met in the Party and lived in it, climbing up the hierarchy together. Mrs. Honecker wound up as a member of the Central Committee. They lived fairly modestly, in contrast to other important people in the regime who developed the Eastern bloc *apparatchik* habit of indulging in luxuriously appointed villas behind high walls. Like Ulbricht before him, Honecker took care to develop an heir apparent so as to ensure continuity in the regime. But this time it was a much younger man, of the postwar generation.

Honecker's choice was Egon Krenz, born in Kolberg in 1937 and thus only eight years old when the Hitler years ended in Germany's collapse. He was one of the first to volunteer when East Germany established its new army, and he led the Communist Youth Movement until, at age thirty-nine, he could no longer claim boyish zeal. Tough, disciplined, Krenz represented the special flavor of East Germany, which combines the efficiency, the habits of command and obedience, the insistence on precision of the German tradition with the Communist style of heavy bureaucracy, repression and the demand of the state's priority above the individual.

Since Honecker's family background was socialist, he was presumably not baptized. But growing up in the intensely Catholic Saarland, he was not ill at ease with churchmen, which made an important difference from Ulbricht's stern antireligious policy. It also mattered that he had never fled the country, but spent the war in jail along with non-Communists in the anti-Hitler resistance. That enhanced his feeling of Germanness and gave him a sense of solidarity with all who fought fascism from inside the country, in contrast with the Communist "internationalists" who had gone to the Soviet Union. West Germans who dealt with him regularly felt that his ambition was to win acceptance of the German Democratic Republic as a valid state, not just a satellite held in place by the 400,000 Soviet troops regularly stationed on its territory and the might behind them.

Honecker realized that little progress had been made over the years in converting the people of East Germany to a new nationality, as citizens of a country alien to the Germans of the West. Ideology was not enough to win their consent and loyalty. Hungarians, Czechs and Poles might flee their country, but a nation remained on the lands they left. Honecker understood that two factors were essential to make East Germans consider the state a country in its own right. They were history and the Protestant Church, intertwined over the centuries.

The Federal Republic never abandoned its aspiration for the reunification of Germany, nor its insistence that German was the common nationality of all on both sides. Though it developed many official ties with the Eastern regime, on those grounds it refused to exchange ambassadors, naming Bonn's chief envoy a "special representative" instead, and it granted immediate citizenship to any East German who crossed the line and requested it. Bonn considered the East-West border not as a frontier but as an intra-German division, and extended the logic to its trade. That brought enormous gains to East Germany, including access to the European Common Market without any of the obligations of membership.

Jettisoning the dogma that the past was blank, belonging only to the West, Honecker set out to recapture German history and establish a relation of mutual respect with the Church. There were certain advantages available. The eastern part of the German lands had been the breeding ground of Protestantism. Much of the south and the west had remained Catholic, but the east could claim prime possession of the Protestant tradition. The five hundredth anniversary of the birth of Martin Luther in 1983 was used to dramatize this claim. It was celebrated with tremendous, year-long fanfare. Honecker, the atheist Communist, proclaimed Luther "one of the greatest sons of the German people."

Prussia had been the base for the nineteenth-century unification of the German lands, the foundation for German nationalism. Reviving Prussian history could make the East seem more truly national, more German than the lesser fiefdoms and city-states that had once existed on West German soil. The Federal Republic had become more Westernized, some said more Americanized, over the years as it grew to prosperity and power. But the German Democratic Republic, for all its intimate absorption into the Soviet sphere, never became at all Russified. The old German culture remained with little change, and it gave the East a certain nostalgic appeal for West Germans when they felt soul-sick with consumerism and modernity. In their hearts, East Germans could feel superior to their Russian overlords, but West Germans had something of an inferiority complex toward Americans. Oddly, some West Germans came to look on the East as more independent, more neutral than their own country, with its ties to Western Europe and America. They blocked from their minds the total Soviet domination of East Germany, just as the Soviet presence was blocked from everyday view in the East. The Russians kept out of sight, in their encampments, and did not mix with the local population as Americans often did in West Germany. Occasionally, a few Soviet officers might be seen in a museum or on the street, but no one talked to them; they never colored the social and cultural scene.

The German left had a long literary tradition, and Communist writers flourished in exile during the Hitler years—Bertolt Brecht and Anna Seghers were examples with which the new regime launched its own "progressive" cultural standards. But it left little room for individuality, and the requirements set by politics were at least as strict as those in Moscow during Stalin's time. One after another, the creative talents wandered or were hounded off to the West. Music, with its private, uncensorable messages, was acceptable and became important again. Theater flourished, but limiting innovation to production of old plays that could not be controversial. East Germany did well in that.

But literature necessarily foundered in the severe requirements of ideology. One of the few East German writers whose work won acceptance in the West was Christa Wolf, a Communist who was able to create without a steel mold in the place of imagination. She had a deeper sensitivity, and her eminence provided room to express it. "What is past is not dead," she said. "It is not even past. We cut ourselves off from it. We pretend to be strangers." Another success was Stefan Heym, but he was considered a dissident and was not allowed to publish in East Germany. His books were smuggled back from West Germany and circulated clandestinely. But he refused to emigrate even though the regime would probably have been pleased to be rid of him. He argued that he wanted to stay in the Communist society in hopes that his books could "contribute to the evolution of 'real' socialism into a more attractive socialism that will make it possible to tear down the Wall."

Constant exposure through TV and radio, though not through movies or the printed word, to Western life made it impossible for East Germany to prevent the emergence of new styles. When they were too challenging, however, solutions were found. Wolf Biermann, a popular singer with a talent for satire, was expelled to West Germany in 1976. That caused a period of ferment among intellectuals, but it ebbed away without aftermath. Small numbers of punks, resentful dropouts and determined nonconformists appeared in the major cities after their peers became noticeable in the West. Learning that it could not deal with them effectively with its usual measures, the regime came to tolerate them and even take a certain pride in what it considered evidence of its willingness to accept a bit of pluralism. But this was hypocrisy. These young people were few and too troubled with themselves to be troublesome.

There did emerge a certain pride in the country's economic progress. Of course, East Germany never began to fulfill Ulbricht's promise in 1961 that it would overtake West Germany's standard of living, even

taking into account heavily subsidized prices for basic needs such as
food and housing, generous social services and acceptance by many
that a quiet, orderly life without competitive pressures was worth a lot
in material goods. But the country did live better than any other in the
Eastern bloc. People felt it showed that Germans, East or West, know
how to produce and organize, and congratulated themselves. During
the period of Solidarity's success in Poland, the authorities were extremely nervous lest the agitation and resistance to officialdom spread
to East Germany, and rules were made reducing contacts to a minimum. But they needn't have bothered. The general attitude was the
historic German contempt for the Poles, not sympathy for fellow workers struggling against an oppressive regime. "If they'd do a real day's
work, the Poles could eat," one East German laborer said, and it reflected the country's view at the time.

But that wasn't enough to develop the sense of legitimacy of the East
German state which Honecker and his comrades craved. Accepting
that identity required deeper roots than living memory, they moved in
the 1980s to make the past visible, a renewed part of everyday life. East
Berlin's monuments, which had been left as blackened skeletons from
the war, were faithfully restored. One by one, the majestic complex of
the National Theater and the twin German and French cathedrals on
either side were put back as nearly as possible to their original condition. The statue of Frederick the Great of Prussia, which had been
banished to obscurity near his Versailles-model palace at Potsdam, was
returned to a place of honor on Unter den Linden, East Berlin's main
thoroughfare. It was not far from the spot where Stalin's statue had
stood during the period when the street was renamed Stalinallee.
Nearby, the statues of four famous Prussian generals were installed in
a shady little park, part of the rehabilitation of Berlin's Prussian past.

A stamp was issued in 1980 commemorating Karl von Clausewitz, the
eighteenth-century general whose treatise *On War* became a bible for
the world's military strategists. By then, the regime no longer found it
useful to indulge in its customary denunciations of Prussian militarism
because it was taking far-reaching measures to rear its youth in familiarity with and admiration for the military life. Volker Voigt, the Communist Youth Movement's secretary in Magdeburg, gave the tone
when he said, "We must educate the young in love for the DDR [Ger-
man Democratic Republic] and hatred for the BRD [Federal Republic
of Germany]."

Even Otto von Bismarck was accorded new respect. He was Wilhelm I's "Iron Chancellor" who re-created the German empire (the Second Reich) in 1871 out of Prussia, Saxony, Bavaria and the multitude of German-speaking kingdoms and fiefdoms left from the collapse of the Holy Roman Empire (the First Reich). Only Austria, then a great Central European empire itself, and multilingual, determinedly independent Switzerland remained outside. Bismarck had made Prussia the first industrial country to adopt social legislation, but until the change of policy the official East German line reviled him as a reactionary Prussian Junker, a representative of the monied classes. His role as unifier might have provoked undesired notions about an all-German future. But the new line stressed the argument that East Germany, and its capital in the old Prussian capital of Berlin, was the legitimate heir to all that was good in the German past, and that the synthetic German state now was the Western one, risen from the debris of Hitler's Third Reich.

The charming little town of Weimar, where a constitution was written for the ill-fated republic established when the Kaiser was forced into exile after World War I, was refurbished and garnished as an island of the idyllic past amid the gray, cement-block landscape of most East German cities. Goethe and Schiller had lived there, and the town was their monument. The famous old Hotel Elephant was reopened in late eighteenth-century elegance, although the cuisine was never restored and offered "chickenbunnypork," as travelers called the unidentifiable meat dish they were served. Leipzig had partly escaped the uniform drabness of East German reconstruction up until the 1980s because of its semiannual trade fair.

Saxony also made grandiose efforts to restore the visible glories of the past. The kingdom had often been an enemy of Prussia before Bismarck, and was as proud of its artistic and architectural achievements as Prussia was of its military record. Dresden, the Saxon capital, had been nearly obliterated in the enormous Anglo-American air raid on February 13, 1945, less than three months before the end of the war. Local officials say 35,000 were killed, though some accounts say the figure may have been as high as 135,000. Most of the people, including vast numbers of refugees fleeing before the advancing Red Army, were left homeless. Just before the Russians arrived, the retreating German forces blew up all the bridges which linked the two sides of the city across the broad Elbe, completing the destruction. Dresden had been rebuilt at first in dull, communist-color concrete. Its palaces and monuments were left in ruins as a symbol of the official theme that the Western Allies had been the destroyers and the Soviets the liberator of the German nation.

The statue of King Augustus II, called Augustus the Strong, had been allowed to remain in the proletarian era at the entrance to what was renamed Liberation Street, but like everything else, it looked tacky and charred. For the resurrection of history, the king and his prancing horse were completely re-covered in gleaming gilt. The Zwinger palace and museum, a huge complex of gardens and baroque galleries where the courtiers once promenaded, was reopened in early 1985 with a gala production of Carl Maria von Weber's *Freischütz*, the last opera performed before the house was destroyed. Ordinary residents in old parts of the city were allowed to form cooperatives to return the façades to their eighteenth-century brightness and delightful variety. Both Dresden and Berlin began to look like fine capital cities again, though there was no shortage of dreary back streets.

Dresden had been one of Europe's richest cities, based on silver mines in the area. And Augustus II had acquired a taste for finery and flamboyance, traveling around Europe in his late teens. When he was elected to the throne of Poland as well in 1697, he was obliged to renounce his Protestant faith and convert to Catholicism. But he didn't mind because he had concluded from his tours that Catholics lived with more beautiful things and had more fun, while Protestants were more austere and narrow-minded. He built an elaborate church next to his palace and connected them with an exquisite little bronze bridge modeled on the Bridge of Sighs in Venice. Italian artists were summoned in droves to make Dresden baroque. The people were pleased and considered him tolerant, because he did not impose his conversion upon them and permitted a choice of religion.

But he could be tough when it came to his treasury. He got word that an alchemist named Johann Friedrich Böttger, son of a metallurgist who minted Prussian coins, had fled from servitude at the Prussian court. Augustus ordered him kidnapped and imprisoned in the battlements of his palace. Böttger was told to produce gold from base metal within a year or he would lose his head. Afraid to admit the impossibility, he set about using his knowledge to seek the secret of porcelain. It was then a Chinese monopoly, so highly prized in Europe that it was imitated in cups made of enamel laid on gold. The Zwinger museum displays a service made before Böttger's discovery. He did find the formula and baked Europe's first china in the ovens of his dungeon in less than a year. It was not white at first, but he learned to refine it. That meant vast new riches for the Saxon court, and for Böttger himself, who was then offered his freedom but preferred to stay safely in his battlement. Ever since, Dresden and the smaller town of Meissen nearby have been famed for fine porcelain. The story is once again told with pride, though the tale hardly offers the previously required proletarian moral.

There was an ironic consequence of all this rehabilitation of the past. Instead of legitimizing the German Democratic Republic as the appropriate successor of an old nation, for many of its citizens it revived their sense of identity as Prussians or as Saxons, who had always disliked each other. East Germans had learned the hard way to keep unauthorized thoughts to themselves and to understand that the only place for democracy in their state was in its formal name. It will be difficult to know whether Honecker's efforts to implant an East German patriotism took life at all until the people have a choice. Their greatest grievance, after tolerable if far from prosperous material living standards, history and the right to religion were restored, was that they were not allowed to travel.

It was possible to visit countries in Eastern Europe, of course, except for Poland, whose border was closed by East Germany after the rise of the Solidarity movement in 1980. That was partly to keep out Polish shoppers who emptied German stores near the border when practically everything became unavailable in Poland, and partly to isolate East Germans from what was considered infectious Polish ideas about free trade unions. But usually travel had to be in groups; Hungary was expensive for East Germans, and the countries with Black Sea coasts not easy to reach. East Germans felt unreasonably shut in.

Only the elderly could easily obtain permission to visit West Germany. In 1985, twin brothers who had been separated by the wall were allowed their first reunion in West Berlin to celebrate their sixtieth birthday. The one from the East broke down in tears. "To think," he said, "that now I can see the Kurfürstendamm and the Wannsee again, and even go to the Bavarian Alps and the Rhine." Many must feel the same. Most of the East Germans who are allowed to visit the West, for family emergencies or on reaching pensionable age, do return to their

382   EUROPE

homes. Bonn officials believe this would probably be true if the East's restrictions on travel were lifted for all. But East Berlin has not been willing to test that, fearing particularly that young, educated people at the start of their careers would pour out as they had done in the early years of the state.

For many years, the Federal Republic interpreted its constitutional provision that it represented the whole of Germany as requiring anathema against the DDR. But the eastern regime took hold nonetheless. Its first international goal was to seek prestige that would demonstrate foreign acceptance and thus command acknowledgment from its own people. Prestige was a prime policy. Sports seemed to offer the best opportunity, since they did not depend on politics abroad or invite a challenge to politics at home, as art and literature might have done. With determination, East Germany launched a wide-ranging program to develop champions in every possible sport. It succeeded, as its eventual harvest of international medals demonstrated, doubtless the highest yield of Olympic gold per head of population in the world.

The time came when Bonn felt obliged to admit that reunification of Germany remained far beyond the horizon. It saw little choice but to make the existing situation less painful and to ease relations with all the countries of the Soviet bloc. The grand culmination of Chancellor Willy Brandt's Ostpolitik came with his spectacular visit to East Germany in 1970. East Berlin never permitted another occasion for such a mass outpouring of emotion to welcome a West German leader. But Bonn developed a new policy of doing whatever it could to help people in East Germany and to maintain contacts between the two populations.

This presented something of a dilemma for East Berlin, whose purpose was precisely the opposite one of cultivating separate German identities. The pressures and the lures of easing relations between the peoples were irresistible, however. As television spread to practically every household, it became impossible for East Berlin to impose its ban on watching Western TV and therefore to keep its people uninformed about life in the Federal Republic. Four out of five East Germans regularly switched on Western broadcasts by the 1980s. There were rumors that, in resignation, the regime planned to make the programs available by relay to the area around Dresden, where reception was impossible, as a concession to the public. It did not happen. Nonetheless, East Berlin found more people asking for emigration permits in the area and had to conclude that reception of Western airwaves had an appeasing and normalizing effect on the population. Isolation was further reduced by making it easy for West Germans to visit the East, where many had family ties. Bonn used its economic prowess to extract more and more scope for its people-to-people campaign, offering East Germany a vast source of hard currency available to no other country in the Soviet bloc.

It is impossible to know how much of East Germany's economic success was due to what was, in effect, a multifaceted subsidy from Bonn. There were many forms of payment, and no one could be sure of the total amount. By the mid-1980s, it was almost surely over $5 billion a year, and perhaps as high as $10 billion. There was an annual direct payment of nearly $1 billion that the East claimed as compensation for the use of roads and communications linking West Germany to West Berlin. There were rollover interest-free trade credits. Westerners going to East Germany had to exchange a minimum of about $10 a day at the official rate of parity between East and West marks, though unofficially the West mark was worth four times more. Beyond that, they could take in as much money as they wished and give it to relatives and friends. Special state stores were opened all through East Germany where goods otherwise unobtainable could be bought for hard currency, with no questions asked about how it was obtained. And there were state distributing agencies to which Westerners could send money and order deliveries to East German citizens. Automobiles, pleasure boats, even houses, could be provided in this way by people who had made good in the West and wanted to help those they had left behind. In addition, there was open access for East German exports to the Common Market through West Germany, classified as "intra-German trade."

An ugly human traffic developed. West Germany tried almost as hard to keep it secret as did East Germany, but for each side the results were believed to justify the shame. Political prisoners—though not all—could be ransomed by Bonn for what was reported to be an average $20,000 a head. On the argument that the state should be reimbursed for what it had invested in the upbringing and education of emigrants, East Germany exacted an average fee of $5,000 for others to whom it decided to grant exit permits. That brought East Berlin not only income but a convenient escape valve for malcontents and irreconcilables who might otherwise have spread ferment. Special details were negotiated separately, usually through Wolfgang Vogel, a secretive East Berlin lawyer who also maintained offices in West Berlin and had rare permission to come and go at will. It was said—such things were never officially confirmed—that Bonn paid $180,000 for a niece of East German Prime Minister Willi Stoph who had taken refuge in the West German Embassy in Prague. A whopping $1.8 million was reportedly paid for the exit of fifty-five East Germans who managed to storm the West Berlin Mission in East Berlin and refused to leave until they were assured the right to emigrate.

These incidents embarrassed both governments and led to much stricter control of entry to diplomatic premises. Sometimes West Germans admitted the shamefulness of the trade, but they accepted without grumbling that it represented a higher moral obligation to their isolated compatriots. Uta Giersch, an East German who spent seven years in jail for trying to leave the country illegally before she was "sold" to West Germany, became the leader of such former prisoners in the Federal Republic. "We are blackmailed on humanitarian grounds," she said. "It's macabre." But having been rescued herself, she felt the same opportunity was due to others.

All this contributed to East Germany's achievement of the highest living standard in the Soviet bloc, without the necessity of diluting its extremely strict socialist marketing system, as Hungary had found desirable. But it brought a curious two-tier economy, with problematic social and political implications for the future. West marks began to circulate freely in East Germany, almost as legal tender, not on the black market basis common in the rest of the bloc. Before West marks were presented to make purchases in the state-owned special shops, they had often been used in a whole series of transactions for services that were hard to obtain otherwise. People who had access to West marks became a privileged group. They were the ones with friends and relatives in the West, or the plumbers and carpenters and doctors and inspectors or whoever had something useful to offer.

By definition, however, such people were not the stalwarts of the regime, the ones on whom it relied to maintain ideological fervor and rigid loyalty. Party workers, bureaucrats, the cadres of the system, had less opportunity to acquire West marks, which put them at a disadvantage when they were disposed to consider themselves the class with a right to be favored. A joke circulated in 1984 when Erich Honecker was

scheduled to make the first visit by the East German Party leader to
West Germany. The trip was put off at Soviet demand, made so publicly
and insistently that it was evident that East Berlin chafed at the constraint. But the joke assumed that he did go, and came back to answer
excited questions about what things were really like across the line. He
brushed them aside with disdain. "Really, it's no different from here.
For East marks, you get nothing, but for West marks, you can have
anything you want."

Of course, satire exaggerated. But the second economy did become
important, and it did enable the state to resist making concessions in
the first economy. Only the most meager forms of private enterprise
were permitted; a few bakeries and cafés operated under trying conditions. The lovely old marketplaces in small towns were restored archi-
tecturally, but rarely was a farmer allowed to set up a stall and sell the
produce from his little private plot or the fruit tree outside the collective
orchard. Permits to hawk flowers in the street were doled out meanly,
usually to aged women with very small pensions. Ordinary vendors
were not allowed.

Like the rest of the industrial world, East Germany felt the recession
at the end of the 1970s. It had piled up huge Western debts in a crash
attempt to modernize its economy with Western technology. The Soviets raised oil prices to their allies, who had been insulated previously
from the soaring petroleum market. It was necessary to declare a period
of austerity, which made West German credits and the maintenance of
reasonable relations with Bonn all the more important. In the 1960s
there had been an economic reform providing somewhat more autonomy to industrial managers, a degree of decentralization, but which
was then offset by the vertical organization of the economy into 157
giant trusts. No further reforms or concessions in the way of incentive
pay or a little more scope for private initiative were contemplated. According to Western analysts, industry was drastically overmanned, East
Germans achieving only 70 percent of West German workers' productivity per capita, 43 percent per working hour. In East Germany, the
working year was 2,100 hours, compared to 1,700 in West Germany.
Ninety percent of the women between the ages of sixteen and sixty
were in the labor force, a world record.

The one noticeable change in the scene brought by TV familiarity
with the West was a bow to advertising. Some big buildings had illuminated rooftop signs, which did brighten the gray streets, although they

only promoted technically named state industries such as Elektrokom-
binat or Robotron. Shops, unnamed because they all belonged to state
distribution services and were numbered, had signs saying "Groceries,"
"Women's Clothes," "Meat," "Toys," "Musical Instruments," but many
had added colored lights and some were even animated. It livened up
drab city centers. There were no graffiti, of course. Private initiative
was even less tolerated on the walls than in the economy. But except
for special occasions, there were fewer of the once ubiquitous hortatory
red banners, which had taken the place of public display in the early
days with such proclamations as "Socialism for the good of the people"
or "We work for peace and security" or "Long live German-Soviet
friendship."

In the glum, but not penurious, circumstances, people turned inward
and focused on family life. They called it *Nischengesellschaft*, a society
where each looks for a cozy niche to install himself and let the world
go by. That had its personal rewards, and was one of the aspects of East
German life that seemed more "authentic" to some West Germans,
more truly in tune with idealized old tradition. Leisure was used for
family outings to the countryside, or the parks, or the newly reopened
monuments. Insulated from regime propaganda and exhortation to
ever more effort by the mental earplugs they had fashioned in fatigue
and boredom, people attended to their personal relations. It meant a
calm, unexciting life, constricting for energetic and adventurous souls,
but undemanding of great effort and without tension so long as the
rulers were obeyed.

Relaxation of strictures on the Church also brought an important
change in East Germany. Including only those who are active in
church life, the Protestants count their flock as two-thirds of the population. Only 12.9 percent are Catholic. An accord on "peaceful coexis-
tence" concluded between the state and Evangelical churches in 1978
made the Church the only legally accepted institution not controlled
by the Communist Party, so it was appealing to the young and to those
seeking surcease from the regime's litany. The Church also became the
center of the unofficial peace movement and of protest against the
broad militarization of East German society. The army, including ready
reserves, numbers 260,000, but there are several other special armed
services. It is estimated that East Germany keeps one out of twelve of
its eligible citizens at arms, a staggering number for a country the size
of Virginia and with a population of 17 million. Military drill is obliga-

tory in the schools, and adults must participate in regular civil defense drills.

The official boast that there is no unemployment in East Germany is perfectly true. The country has the world's highest proportion of its total population working, 54.5 percent. In the West, it is said that this shows lower efficiency than that of Western workers. But in the years of rapid expansion, East Germany never took in many foreign laborers, as West Germany and other countries of Europe did. As a result, it has a much more homogeneous population than West Germany. On the other hand, there is a controlled flow of East Germans to exotic lands, where they perform as "Europe's Cubans." They are sent to places like Ethiopia, Libya, Guinea, South Yemen and Nicaragua, often with a primary responsibility to train security police and to organize a Communist party structure where requested.

Except for Slavic Bulgaria, which has deep and ancient affinities with Russia, East Germany became the country most thoroughly integrated into the Soviet bloc despite the absence of cultural influence. Not only the regime but the state itself could hardly expect to survive otherwise. Economically, East Berlin favored Soviet policies of dividing up fields of prime investment among its dependents in the bloc, resisting urges of national autarky. The others disliked the effect of limiting the directions of growth, but East Germany got the lion's share of advanced manufacture and technology. Its economists boasted that the United States had helped too, by putting an embargo on high-performance pump compressors when the Soviets were building big gas and oil pipelines to Western Europe. A crash order was diverted to East Germany, which managed to do the job and thus develop a new and valuable type of export machinery. The Soviet Union is by far East Germany's largest customer, taking 40 percent of its exports. Altogether, the Eastern bloc absorbs two-thirds of DDR foreign sales. Making purchases in West Germany, which has become important for some segments of the Federal Republic's economy, the East Germans have functioned as a transmission belt for technology transfer from West to East. There is a vast espionage net in West Germany to pierce barriers imposed on this trade for security reasons.

But there are strains in the intimate East German–Soviet relationship. Like the Federal Republic in the West, the German Democratic Republic has become a power in the East. The motor was economic strength, but that necessarily led to assertions of political interest. The

EUROPE

forced cancellation of Honecker's trip to the West in 1984 was a sign. On their side, the Russians scarcely hid their dislike for the rehabilitation of pre-twentieth-century German history, particularly the history of Prussia. While Moscow certainly was determined to maintain a Communist state in Germany, it did not appreciate its being too emphatically German. Soviet Ambassador Piotr Abrassimov once complained that eventually the Germans might be justified in restoring their sense of themselves, but they were doing "too much, too fast."

Nobody in the West, at least, foresaw the creation of two German states at the end of World War II. Presumably, neither did anyone in the East. As late as 1949, when the decision to form separate governments was made on both sides, Stalin wrote, "The existence of a peaceful and democratic Germany beside the peaceful Soviet Union eliminates the possibility of new wars in Europe and makes impossible the subjection of the European countries by world imperialism." He expected all of Germany to become Communist and thereby, with the Soviet Union, to assure Communist dominion in Europe. The clear purpose of the Berlin blockade was to demoralize West Germans through the fall of the national capital and, to advance that aim, provoke the departure of American forces. But it didn't work.

Ever since, West Germans have talked from time to time of reunification, meaning in freedom, but the hope has receded into the distant future. Others, particularly the French and the Poles, fear that one day Moscow might offer some kind of German unity, perhaps in confederation, in return for the neutralization of West Germany and the rupture of ties with the United States. That would be another, veiled, form of the extension of Soviet influence continent-wide. But it is most improbable. The love-hate relation between Russians and Germans is too old and too deep to suppose that Moscow would willingly risk the re-emergence of a consolidated German nation in the center of Europe, or that it would trust even a neutralized and disarmed Germany not to regain strength and burst its bonds. Any attempt to solve this "German problem" against Moscow's will would surely provoke cataclysmic war.

So the modest hope in West Germany has to be that the East German system will mellow a bit, that maximum contacts will make life easier for Germans on the other side and that both will find a way to live with their predicament until the world changes once again. Meanwhile, the two states are growing apart. Austria and part of Switzerland are Germanic lands too, but developed separate nationhoods. The East German regime, with new self-confidence, is looking to find its place in the sun with other relatively small countries, though it remains too fearful of its fragility to remove the wall. How long it will last and where it will lead cannot be guessed. So far, the two Germanys have proved the old French proverb that "nothing is so enduring as the temporary."

POLAND
The Malady Is Geography

IN THE MID-1980s:
Teacher: What is abundance?
Boy: It's a pile of potatoes that reaches heaven.
Teacher: Nonsense, there's no such thing as heaven.
Boy: And there's no such thing as potatoes.

In the late 1970s:
Man in a queue: This is it. I just can't stand queueing up for everything all the time. I'm going down the street to the Central Committee building and punch the leader in the nose. Will you hold my place for me?
Neighbor, thirty minutes later: You're back already? Nothing has moved here. How did you manage to do it so quickly?
First man: It's hopeless. The queue there is even longer than here.

During the Chinese Cultural Revolution:
How lucky we are to have a buffer state between Poland and China.

Question: What is an optimist?
Answer: Somebody who is learning to eat caviar with chopsticks.

In the 1930s:
Students at a university were asked to prepare a dissertation on the elephant.

The German spent six months in the library and produced "The Origin of the Elephant and Its Culture." The Englishman went on safari and wrote: "Elephants and How to Hunt Them." The Frenchman went to the zoo and composed: "How to Make Love to an Elephant." The American went to an expert and delivered: "Bigger and Better Elephants and How to Grow Them." The Pole went on holiday until the day before the theme was due and then handed in: "The Elephant and the Polish Corridor."

The Polish joke is no accident. Disaster, fear, stubborn perseverance, willful rejection of a reality which can be neither accepted nor changed, and with it all an endless hope, have crafted a wry, self-deprecating wit. No other people but the Jews turn so much of their experience into jokes. In Warsaw, people flock to the cafés to see their friends—few have room or resources to entertain at home—and to sample the fresh-baked supply of jokes which arrive, mysteriously, every day. Who thinks them up? Nobody knows. Who tells them? Everybody, even the members of the regime against whom they are usually aimed. The jokes give a special quality to Polish life and make it considerably harder for the rulers to intimidate the ruled. The Church is the symbol of the nation. But the joke is its pulse, proof that, however wan and sickly it appears, there is still a throbbing life.

That has repeatedly been put in question, and the answer has always been affirmative. The national anthem is imbued with the tragic sense that underlies the humor. It begins, "Poland is not yet lost . . ." The reference is to the Napoleonic Wars. The words are an expression of will intended to defy the evidence. Other nations have succumbed to defeat, been overrun, even wiped off the map and forgotten. But defiance became a particularly Polish trait, a matter of pride even when the odds were overwhelming. Of course it isn't true that Poles cannot be cowed, that they are habitually and wildly reckless in response to threat. But they like to think of themselves that way and to show themselves as brave as possible.

Despite martial law at the time, forbidden demonstrations were held in Warsaw in 1982 to commemorate the second anniversary of the agreement which the government had made with the independent union Solidarity, and had quickly broken. The police warned that people would be driven off the streets. Units armed with explosive teargas launchers and huge water cannon patrolled up and down to scatter the crowds. I ducked behind the low wall of a subway entrance when the

jets were aimed my way. The Polish journalist next to me, no opponent
of the regime, stood tall and glared. He was nearly toppled by the force
of the stream, but he didn't buckle. The motorized units moved on.

There is a great deal of mythology and caricature in the idea of
national traits, of characteristics which almost inevitably mark the individuals who spring from a particular society. The Poles are closer to
their stereotype than most, deliberately, it seems, cultivating their sense
of what it means to be a Pole in order to make sure that Polishness is a
well-defined, unmistakable identity. It isn't a comfortable one—it seldom has been—but that makes people cling to it all the more. The
Europeans with whom Poles feel the most affinity are not other Slavs
at all, but the Hungarians and the French. There are firm historical
reasons. But it is also a matter of temperament, of impulsiveness,
quirkiness, dogged insistence on being different. Poles do feel profoundly European, an integral part of the great kaleidoscope of culture
which the continent developed. It never led them to like any of their
neighbors. They find it easier to sympathize with people who live farther away, perhaps not only because of the suffering imposed on them
by neighbors but also to assert their separateness.

Many years of subjection had left Poland a desperately poor and
largely illiterate country when independence was regained at last after
World War I. Peasants used to walk barefoot along the roads to church
on Sunday, carrying their boots so as not to wear them out. They split
matches in four. One generation later, World War II started in Poland
and the state was again snuffed out. No country suffered more from
the war. Six million Poles were killed, half of them Jews, and 2 million
were deported to work as slave labor. Only the medieval city of Cracow
escaped almost total devastation. The Germans deliberately set out to
flatten Warsaw. When they were forced into retreat, a map left behind
showed plans for modest, completely changed rebuilding. It was titled
Warschau, Eine Neue Deutsche Stadt ("Warsaw, a New German
Town"). The Nazis considered Poles racially inferior, to be excluded
from cultured life.

At Stalin's demand, the postwar borders were drastically shifted,
leaving eastern Poland to the Soviet Union and in the west incorporating territories emptied of their German inhabitants. The population
then was 24 million. By the mid-1980s, it had risen again to 35 million.
Wartime deaths and a postwar baby boom made Poles one of Europe's
most youthful populations, with a third under age fifteen and half

under age thirty. The new frontiers enclosed a rectangular land the size of New Mexico, with a 328-mile coastline on the Baltic replacing the narrow, extremely vulnerable prewar corridor through German territory to the sea at Gdynia, next to the then Free City of Danzig (now Gdańsk). The borders are no more strategic than before, running along the line of the Bug River, facing the Soviet Union, and the Oder and Neisse rivers, facing East Germany. The broad Polish plains have always offered an unimpeded invasion route from east or west. The worst Polish joke of all, people say, is Poland's geography. But the redrawn map, and population transfers in which 8 million Germans were expelled, did leave a much more homogeneous society with no significant ethnic or religious minorities. There were no basic divisions that could be played upon for ulterior political purposes. That was a factor in the strong social cohesion which eventually developed, pitting the people against the regime in adamant confrontation.

The land itself varies at the edges of the country, though most of it stretches flat and open under a pale sky. The northeast is lake and forest country and includes half of former East Prussia, where the stern Junkers ruled over vast estates. It was never well developed, and remains a favorite recreation area for hunters and fishermen. The Baltic coast has long bright beaches, big ports and shipyards. Pomerania in the northwest and, even more, Silesia in the southwest have important industrial centers, based on the big coal mines which have long provided a major export. The southern part of the country climbs up the Tatra and Karkonoski mountains, not towering but steep enough to break the usual straight horizon. The southeast leads to the Carpathians, rugged country which was left behind when other areas were developed. Everywhere, except where the sea warms the air, it is cold and damp in winter. The land is exposed to the chilling winds off the Russian steppes. But summers are warm and verdant. The favorite season is fall, "golden October," when the woods display their utmost finery before retiring for the dead of winter. The rigors of the climate have made the people hardy.

Tadeusz Konwicki, a writer with a dagger-sharp pen for satire, has bemoaned the cultural impact of the loss to the Soviet Union of the eastern territories with their varied population. They had a "magnetic force, a metaphysical radiation," he said, and gave the world many artists, Polish, Lithuanian, Byelorussian, Ukrainian and Jewish. "It was the land of poetry, from Adam Mickiewicz [Poland's revered

nineteenth-century master] to Czesław Milosz," who won the Nobel
Prize for Literature in 1980. But the loss of diversity has been compensated by an intense sense of unity, which supports the nation.

Polish is a purely Slavic language, with many roots similar to Russian.
But because Poland has looked to the Roman church for a thousand
years, it uses the Latin alphabet with special groups of consonants to
represent Slavonic sounds. The spelling looks bewildering. In fact, it is
completely and regularly phonetic. Polish words are easy to pronounce,
once the sounds are recognized and it is understood that the accent
always falls on the penultimate syllable. An example of letters whose
pronunciation differs from English may be useful. Some of them represent common English sounds, but where they are Slavic sounds, the
common English rendering of the equivalent Russian sound is given.

Some names: Zbigniew Brzezinski = Z-big-nyev B-zheh-zhin-ski.
Lech Wałęsa = Lekh Vah-wen-sa. Tadeusz Szulc = Ta-day-ush
Shultz. Wojciech Jaruzelski = Voy-chekh Yah-ru-zel-ski. Karol
Wojtyła = Ka-rol Voy-tih-wa. Some cities: Kraków = Krah-kuv. Lódź
= Wudge. Szczecin = Shche-chin. Warszawa (Warsaw) = Var-shah-
vah. Wrocław = Vrots-wav. Katowice = Kah-toh-vee-tseh.

As in other Slavic countries, the arrival of the initial population is
lost in prehistory. Poles date their state to 966, when Duke Mieszko I
converted himself and his people to the Roman church to help
strengthen them against the pressure of German feudalists. But Ro-
manesque ruins and objects, and vestiges of monumental palaces dating from about the same time, indicate that an organized society existed
long before. Amber from the Baltic, prized in trade, has been found in
Mediterranean ruins from a much earlier date, so there were probably
Polish merchants well before the tenth century. The dominant tribe,
the Polanie, gave their name to the land. There were already towns in
Mieszko's time, including Cracow and Gniezno, still the see of the
Polish Cardinal Primate. But the feudal lords were strong and the
crown was weak, unable to prevent the nobles from arrogating ever
more privileges to themselves and dividing the kingdom into fiefdoms.

Tatars, Lithuanians, Germans and Prussians were constantly attacking. Konrad, Prince of Mazovia, called in the German Order of the
Teutonic Knights to defend his lands against the pagan Prussians. But
when the Knights were victorious, they founded their own state on the
territory, seizing Pomerania and Gdańsk in 1308. Casimir the Great
finally made peace with the Knights in 1343 and then turned to consol-

idating the Polish state. He founded the University of Cracow in 1364, and codified the law. Cracow, his handsome capital, became one of the richest cities in Europe, center of a vast system of trade. He was the last of the first Polish dynasty, the Piasts. On his death, the crown passed to Louis I of Hungary and then to his daughter Jadwiga. The nobles arranged her marriage in 1386 to Wladyslaw Jagiello, the Grand Duke of Lithuania. He took the title King of Poland, forming a dynastic union of the two lands. In 1410, the Poles achieved a great victory over the warring Teutonic Knights at the Battle of Grünwald (Tannenberg), a date still celebrated as a turning point of Polish history and cited as justification for the absorption of German territory in the west after World War II.

There was a period of flourishing, in the arts and sciences, the economy and political influence. The achievements of the Renaissance flowed into Poland. The nobles built fine palaces and mansions; the towns thrived on crafts and trade. In Toruń, the astronomer Copernicus pronounced in the mid-sixteenth century his revolutionary observation that the earth was not the center of the universe but revolved around the sun. (A century later when Galileo came to the same conclusion, the leaders of the Roman church felt threatened in their authority and condemned him.) The Polish flowering also sowed seeds of decay, however. The assertive nobles gained important rights which constrained the monarchy and squeezed the peasants and the townspeople. The nobles' Diet (Sejm) limited the powers of the king, and they extracted ever more feudal privileges and exemptions, increasing the burden on the peasantry. The Jagellonian dynasty was extinguished in 1572, and the custom of electing kings was instituted. This provoked repeated quarrels and intrigue.

In the sixteenth century, Protestantism made important headway in Poland, but only among the bickering gentry, who turned to fighting each other. Campaigns from Protestant Prussia and Eastern Orthodox Russia renewed the identification of the Catholic Church with Polish nationalism. Full union was achieved with Lithuania, and the capital was moved from Cracow to Warsaw. Stephen Báthory, a Transylvanian prince, was elected King on the insistence of the "gentry democracy," the lower-level aristocracy, and their effective leader, Jan Zamojski. Báthory was a consummate statesman and brought Poland to the peak of its international power. His broadly based army pushed Ivan the Terrible's Russia entirely away from the Baltic. He conciliated the Cos-

sacks and protected the Jews, who had fled to Poland from persecution
in England, France, Germany and Austria, and his grandiose plan was
to expand his realm all the way to the Black Sea. But he died in 1586,
before he could launch his next campaign.

Historians say the next king, Sigismund III, presided over Poland's
"last and lost chance" to make the country the dominant power in the
whole region, instead of being squeezed between Russians and Germans as it has been ever since. But he yearned for his father's Swedish
crown, and the gentry was more concerned with its own rights and
liberties than with imperial ambitions. In 1606, the gentry revolted
against his attempts to destroy the constitution; by doing so, they established the right of subjects to depose their king but weakened the state.
The Cossacks were mistreated by their Polish landlords and transferred
allegiance to the Tsar, leading to a brutal war with Russia which lasted
thirteen years. Then Sweden invaded in 1655, capturing the capital and
the best half of the land. The successful defense of the monastery at
Częstochowa, in the south, turned the tide and the Swedes were driven
out. The "Black Madonna," a small, dark painting at the monastery,
was credited with the miraculous victory and became the national
shrine. (Over a million Poles gathered there in 1979 to pray with John
Paul II, the first Polish pope, for the well-being of their country.)

The diplomacy of Europe was changing even as Poland revived. In
the second half of the seventeenth century, the rivalry between the
French Bourbons and Austrian Habsburgs led to a vast and intricate
system of patronage, in fact bribery, to extend influence beyond what
could be achieved by royal marriage and alliance. Poland, with its
elected monarchs, was ripe for such intrigue. Foreign meddling was all
the easier because the gentry, to perfect its limited democracy, had
proclaimed the absolute political equality of every Polish gentleman.
That meant Diet resolutions had to be unanimous, for anyone who
disapproved could prevent a decision. This right of "liberum veto" was
further extended to the right to dissolve the Diet, annulling all measures passed. Foreign ambassadors had only to buy one vote to assure
the fall of the legislature and paralyze the state's affairs.

In 1674, a military commander of growing fame who had ties with
France was elected King, Jan III Sobieski. He became a historical hero
in all of central Europe for his daring rescue of besieged Vienna in
1683, marching on the encamped Turks from the rear and routing
them. It was, said one historian, "the last noble reflex of the great

crusading impulse of the middle ages; it was a unique service, rendered in the old chivalrous spirit by one nation to another in the age of Machiavellian diplomacy and growing national selfishness." All the European powers expressed gratitude to Poland, but it gained nothing more from Sobieski's gallantry.

The other monarchs intrigued incessantly to determine who would wear the Polish crown. Frederick Augustus, Elector of Saxony, was the successful contender out of eighteen candidates who presented themselves in 1697 because he arrived in Warsaw last, with fresh funds, when the agents of his rivals had exhausted their resources. He renounced his Lutheranism without a qualm to become Poland's King Augustus II. He had already entered a plot with Frederick of Denmark and Peter of Russia to overturn the young Charles XII of Sweden. The attempt dragged Poland into a war on its soil that lasted twenty years, with Swedes, Saxons and Russians systematically plundering the country as the tides of battle shifted. When the war ended in 1720, Poland was again devastated.

The following period brought increasing quarrels among the great Polish princely families for ascendance. They did not hesitate to invoke foreign support. The Czartoryskis sent their handsome, charming nephew Stanislaw Poniatowski to the court of Russia. He won the heart of the Empress Catherine. She had already agreed with Frederick of Prussia, however, that the chaotic situation in Poland must be maintained so that it could not threaten either one of their lands again. Thus, Poniatowski was elected and crowned Stanislaw August in 1764, with the support of St. Petersburg and Potsdam. But plans had been laid to create internal upheaval and undermine the Polish state. Prussia and Russia signed a treaty at St. Petersburg in 1772, dividing parts of Poland between them. The same year, a second treaty allocated another part of the country to Austria. Poland lost a fifth of its population and a quarter of its territory in the first partition.

Stanislaw August tried to reform the constitution to enhance his authority and defend what was left. Three aristocrats hurried to enlist Catherine's aid against him. Ironically, the autocratic Empress pledged her support in the name of resisting tyranny. Backed by Russian troops, the conspirators returned, coordinating their plans in the small eastern town of Targowica, still a name for treachery to Poles. Russia declared war. A small Polish army, led by Tadeusz Kosciuszko, fought desperately but the country was demoralized. Kosciuszko had led a band of volunteers to fight for the cause of liberty in the American Revolution. His compatriot Casimir Pulaski had died in that distant war. Though in the service of a king, the cause he was defending in Poland was the same in Kosciuszko's eyes. When the Russians poured in from the east, Frederick the Great feared that Catherine would swallow the whole country and confront him on the Prussian border. So he moved forward from the west. The second partition of Poland was affirmed by treaty in 1793, reducing the state to one-third of its earlier territory and a population of 3.5 million. Kosciuszko fled west, to Leipzig and then to Paris, which was then in the hands of the revolutionary Jacobins, to seek support for an insurrectionary army. He returned to Cracow, called the peasants to arms and gave them complete freedom. At first, he had successes, but the country had fallen into anarchy and defeat was inevitable.

Treaties in 1795 and 1796 proclaimed the third partition of Poland, completely gobbling it up. Austria took southern Masovia and western Galicia, including Cracow. Prussia took western Masovia, including Warsaw. Russia took all the rest, including Lwów. The name of Poland was erased from the map of Europe for over a century, and the Poles became a subject people. Officers and soldiers of Kosciuszko's army made their way to Italy, where they formed Polish Legions to fight for the French republic and for Napoleon against the autocratic powers. Kosciuszko himself did not trust Napoleon. But one of his best generals, Jan Henryk Dąbrowski, commanded the Poles in the French campaigns. He is the hero of the national anthem because he bore the nation's hopes of revival.

Indeed, after Napoleon defeated Prussia, Polish forces returned to Poland. But the French leader's diplomacy did not envisage reestablishment of a full Polish state. Out of the central provinces of the lands Prussia had seized, he created the Grand Duchy of Warsaw in 1807, adding Cracow and western Galicia in 1809 after his war with Austria. He provided a constitution, on the new French model, with equality, religious tolerance and an effective administration. The King of Saxony was made Grand Duke, with the initiative for legislation. When Napoleon set out to march on Moscow in 1812, the Poles made an enormous effort in raising an army of 80,000 to follow him. They suffered the same disaster as the French troops. The victorious Russians seized the grand duchy, ending the brief restoration of independence for a small part of the country. It had lasted only eight years.

Maria Walewska, the beautiful wife of a Polish nobleman, had been chosen to intercede with Napoleon on behalf of her country. They fell in love and she left her husband to go with him. When he was finally defeated at Waterloo, she went into exile with the deposed Emperor on the distant, barren island of St. Helena, and died there. It is a favorite story of the romantic Poles. Walewska is honored as a patriotic heroine and a loyal mistress. Her husband is considered something of a bore. The Napoleonic interlude cemented Poland's ties of sympathy with France. They are so strong that a Polish student, visiting London for the first time, exclaimed in amazement that the peculiar English would name a bridge and a railway station for a tragic defeat. This was after World War II. The student had to be reminded that the Battle of Waterloo was not a defeat for all Europeans. For the British, it was a great victory.

The fate of Poland was an important issue at the Congress of Vienna. Tsar Alexander I agreed to reconstituting a kingdom of Poland out of part of the duchy of Warsaw, but under Russian authority. "Congress Poland," as it was called, became the center of secret societies plotting for full liberation. After revolutions in France and Belgium in 1830, young Polish officers rebelled and called for a national uprising. It collapsed in 1831.

Russia then determined to wipe out Polishness. The universities were closed. If they wanted to study, Poles had to go to St. Petersburg or Kiev. An attempt was made to undermine the Catholic Church. Russification extended to barring the use of the Polish language so far as possible, certainly in official usage. The nobles, however, were left in charge of much of the civil administration with power over the peasants, whom they abused as before. Again in 1848, a wave of revolution swept across Europe. That time, the peasants also played an important part in Poland. But the forces of counterrevolution were once more triumphant. With a more moderate Tsar, Alexander II, the Poles under Russian rule regained some privileges. But the reforms were instituted by Count Alexander Wielopolski, who stood for loyal union with Russia, and thus he inflamed young patriots while his harsh temper alienated the gentry. A guerrilla war broke out in 1863. Religious ceremonies became occasions for liberation demonstrations. The fighting lasted nearly two years. Then there was total repression, with mass executions, confiscations and deportations.

The Polish tradition of rejection of authority, on the one hand, and harsh feudal rule, on the other, had developed in a centuries-old cycle of upheaval and suppression. In the last half of the nineteenth century, it seemed to have been broken. Poles under Prussia, Austria and Russia went their separate ways. The towns grew, swollen by the landed gentry ruined from so much fighting, and the peasants became more self-reliant. Prussia sought to Germanize its Polish subjects, particularly under Bismarck. But it was also industrializing, drawing people off the land into factories, creating a new bourgeoisie and a proletariat, which meant a spread of education. Austria, at first fiercely repressive, began to liberalize after its defeat by Prussia in 1866. It did not try to force its culture on the Poles. Cracow thrived again as a Polish literary, artistic and cultural center, keeping the language vital. But the relative indulgence of the Austrians, leaving local administration and the schools in Polish hands, blocked economic development. The Polish landlords, who were dominant, were not interested in industry. Russian policy was exactly the opposite, forbidding education in Polish, denying official posts to Poles, imposing censorship and a stultifying police regime, but encouraging economic enterprise.

When Russia lost its war with Japan in 1905, there was another surge of hope in Poland. One group sought reform and accommodation through the Duma, the Russian parliament. Joseph Pilsudski led an opposing revolutionary movement. He was obliged to flee to Cracow, where the Austrians didn't mind his anti-Russian activities. When World War I broke out, Pilsudski led a small armed group against the Russians in the name of an independent and united Poland. The powers again competed for the support of Poles on their side in the war, promising the restoration of a free and independent Poland. America entered the war in 1917, and revolution changed the position of Russia. The famed pianist Ignace Paderewski, who rallied 4 million Poles in the United States, prevailed on President Wilson to support the Polish cause. At the Treaty of Brest-Litovsk, signed on March 3, 1918, Soviet Russia renounced all claim to Poland. On November 7, 1918, Polish independence was proclaimed. Pilsudski reached Warsaw on November 10, took over command of all Polish forces and became the nation's leader.

But the new state had undefined borders, a backward economy and a heritage of internal dispute. Pilsudski raised an army of 800,000 to press territorial claims while Paderewski, as Prime Minister, went to argue for them at the peace conference in Paris. With great difficulty, agreements were made or imposed on the western and southern frontiers. To give Poland access to the sea, across the lands which Prussia had occupied and where many Germans lived, a corridor some thirty to fifty miles wide was drawn. It became a source of permanent contention and strategic vulnerability. The German-speaking city of Danzig was declared a free port under the League of Nations, but with Polish responsibility. On the eastern border, however, the Allied powers at Versailles could make no effective ruling. Poland went to war, attracting great sympathy from the West in its campaigns against the Bolsheviks' Red Army, but little help. In 1920, the Soviet forces neared Warsaw. Alarmed, France sent General Maxime Weygand to help the Polish general staff. In a battle which came to be called "the miracle on the Vistula," Pilsudski succeeded in launching a counteroffensive which pushed the Russians back. A peace treaty was finally signed at Riga in 1921, awarding Poland roughly the eastern frontier which had been left after the second partition in 1793.

The new Poland had enemies on all sides—the border dispute over Teschen prevented alliance with Czechoslovakia to the south—and strong minorities within, nearly a third of the population. Minority rights were protected by the Versailles Treaty. Property rights were more difficult to handle. Forests were nationalized and a land reform proclaimed, but not widely implemented. The first President was elected at the end of 1922. Pilsudski refused to stand for the office. His favored candidate won, but Polish nationalists were furious that the President had been chosen by a margin due to the votes of the minorities, including the Jews, and he was assassinated within a few weeks. Under a series of short-lived governments, turbulence increased and the economy foundered.

Pilsudski, who had been allied with the socialists before the war and was considered a man of the left, returned from his retreat to head a coup d'état in 1926. The government he overthrew had been the fourteenth in eight years. After three days of street fighting in Warsaw, he won power but in circumstances that left his position permanently ambiguous. He detested the splintered, quarrelsome parties which had undermined the young republic, but he was eager to respect the letter, if not the spirit, of the constitution. He was determined to exercise unchallenged authority, but he did not want to be an overt dictator. The result was a regime capable of brutality, but not of orderly construction. He began to lose support on all sides. When the terrible strains of the Depression hit Poland in 1930, he turned for major support to the "colonels" who had campaigned with him in the war and instituted an even tougher regime, called the *sanacja* ("sanitation"). After his death on May 12, 1935, several groups vied for influence. The nationalist right imposed extensive discrimination against minorities and increasingly violent persecution of Jews. There had long been a vicious streak of anti-Semitism in Poland, and it was used as a political weapon.

Meanwhile, Hitler had come to power, intensifying German revisionist claims on Poland. There was tension on every border, and Warsaw felt increasingly isolated. Though Poland had signed an alliance with France in 1934, a ten-year nonaggression pact was also signed with Germany following a similar pact with the Soviet Union. At the very start of 1939, however, Hitler began making demands, which Warsaw refused. On August 23, Hitler made what was advertised as a nonaggression treaty with Stalin, a mere cover for secret clauses providing for a fourth, and complete, partition of Poland between Germany and the Soviet Union. The Soviets also prepared to swallow the Baltic states of Lithuania, Latvia and Estonia. They had been part of the tsarist empire before the 1917 revolution. In the brief period between the wars, the three were independent.

Poland assured itself of British as well as French support, but it had no time to mobilize. After a staged uprising of Germans in Danzig provided the pretext for a call for assistance, Germany invaded on September 1, 1939. Britain and France declared war, as they had pledged. But it was no help to the unprepared Poles, who sent a cavalry charge against tanks and watched dive-bombers attack the defenseless cities. On September 17, the Soviets moved from the east to the line secretly agreed upon with Berlin. Warsaw and other pockets kept up resistance for another two weeks. There was no hope. Soviet Foreign Minister Vyacheslav Molotov hailed the fall of Warsaw as the disappearance of the "monstrous fetus of the Versailles Treaty." A government-in-exile was formed, led by General Władysław Sikorski. He had been Prime Minister briefly in the early 1920s, and became commander-in-chief of the reorganized Polish army. The first refuge was Angers, in France, and in half a year a Polish force of 100,000 was created from Polish emigrants and troops who had escaped through Hungary and Romania. Some of them had already fought beside the Allies in Norway. Upon the fall of France, the exiled government moved to Britain.

Throughout the war, Poles fought in almost every theater. They organized an air unit which operated with Britain's Royal Air Force. A Polish army unit was so badly mauled in the bloody battle at Monte Cassino, in Italy, that a song called "Red Poppies of Monte Cassino" became a national ballad. A resistance group was formed at home called Armia Krajowa (A.K.—Army of the Country). Later, the Communist leadership formed another resistance group called Armia Ludowa (A.L. —Army of the People), about one-twentieth the strength of the Home Army, as the A.K. was called in English. After the war, the new Communist regime claimed that only the A.L. had defended the country and virtually denied the existence of the A.K. Wartime events mattered enormously in the postwar period, as they were distorted or denied for the regime's political purposes. They added another stratum to the layers of historic Polish grievances against Russia.

Katyn was the most shocking. German troops had advanced eastward to attack Russia in 1941, and in 1943 mass graves found to contain 4,143 Polish dead were discovered in the Katyn Forest near the Soviet border. The Nazis said they were Polish officers who had been killed by the Russians in the period of the Stalin-Hitler pact. Moscow denounced the report as outrageous Nazi propaganda. There were fully convincing indications later, however, that the massacres did take place during the 1939–41 Soviet occupation of the area, and men who were listed as missing then never turned up in anybody's prison camps.

After the German invasion of the Soviet Union, General Sikorski, in London, established relations with Moscow and negotiated the release (through Iran) of the Polish forces who had been interned by the Soviets. But when revelations about the Katyn atrocities came out in the middle of the war, he called for an investigation by the International Red Cross and Stalin angrily broke off ties with the London Poles. He had formed the Polish Committee of National Liberation in Moscow, but it fell completely under Soviet control.

The Communists were weak, but the Socialists were lively and important. There was also a Jewish Socialist Party, the Bund. Its leaders had escaped from the Nazis to Russia, but Stalin did not trust them. He had the two top Bund men, Henryk Ehrlich and Viktor Alter, murdered in Moscow. The Polish Committee of National Liberation, which Stalin advanced as the rival to the London government-in-exile, was itself a deformed, patched-together offspring of the prewar Polish Communist Party. In connection with the great Moscow purges in the late 1930s, before the war, Stalin had dissolved the Polish party in 1938, killing its whole leadership, sending activist Polish refugees to labor camps and creating a new, subservient Polish Communist organization. Those Communists who stayed behind in Poland to organize the A.L. underground after the Nazi attack on the Soviets were subjected to discrimination after the war on Moscow's orders, though they suffered nothing like the persecution of A.K. resistance veterans.

In occupied Poland, the Nazis were organizing their death machines. Auschwitz, the German name for the Polish town of Oświęcim in the south of the country, was built as a "final solution" camp, the major place to put to death the millions of Jews whom the Germans were rounding up across Europe. Polish anti-Semitism was traditionally more virulent than was the German brand before Hitler. While some courageous Poles tried to help their Jewish compatriots, most turned their backs and some even helped the Nazis catch them for dispatch to the camps. In Warsaw, Jews were hounded into the old ghetto in the central part of the city and forced to build a wall to cut themselves off from everybody else. Conditions were desperate, with almost no food, medicine or other necessities.

By April 1943, word was spreading about the death camps, and some of the leaders in the ghetto came to understand why the Nazis had concentrated them in isolation. They made a despairing decision to die fighting instead of in a gas chamber, and launched an uprising. There were 70,000 left in the ghetto when the insurrection began. Some 430,000 had been shipped out to death camps. The fighting lasted twenty-one days, from April 19 to May 10, 1943, and only a handful escaped. When the uprising was crushed and nothing but rats were left alive in the area, the Germans razed the ghetto. They left a flat sea of bricks, about ten feet tall, with only the occasional tip of a crazily tilted lamppost rising above to show there had once been streets, and houses, and many people there. Poland's prewar Jewish population had been 3.5 million. Now there are only a few thousand.

The rest of Warsaw was subjected to a similar fate the following year. When the advancing Red Army approached Praga, a suburb on the opposite side of the Vistula from Warsaw, an insurrection broke out in the capital on August 1, 1944, to drive out the Germans. The Russians charged that it was a maneuver by the A.K., under orders of the London government-in-exile, to take control of the city before the Soviet forces arrived. Desperate couriers swam the Vistula to beg for munitions, medicine and food from the Soviet forces. But they refused. As the dreadful fighting wore on, America planned to parachute supplies from its air bases in Italy. But the planes did not have the range for a round trip. Permission was asked for them to land in Russia to refuel. It was denied, and Stalin called the insurgents "criminals."

After sixty-three days, the Germans completely crushed the Warsaw fighters. They marched the few survivors, mostly women and children, off to the countryside and announced that Warsaw would be razed. Methodically, they planted dynamite in the monuments and set about destroying buildings street by street. They had come a long way toward completing the task when the Red Army decided it was ready to move again, and crossed the river to liberate the depopulated ruins of Warsaw. The Soviet behavior reinforced Polish suspicions that Stalin deliberately sought to destroy those who asserted Polish hopes for independence and Poland's patriotic youth in preparation for a regime of his own preference after the war.

Stalin had moved the Polish Committee from Moscow to Lublin, in eastern Poland, as soon as the Red Army crossed the frontier earlier in 1944, and once it was on Polish soil he recognized it as the provisional government of Poland. Churchill was quick to realize that the installation of a postwar Polish regime would be a matter of serious dispute with Stalin. Poland's eastern borders had already been discussed at the Roosevelt-Churchill-Stalin meeting in Teheran in 1943. It soon became obvious that the Soviet leader was intent on reacquiring all the territories he had claimed in his secret pact with Hitler on the eve of World War II.

Meanwhile, the Polish government in London was weakened by the death of General Sikorski. Returning from an inspection trip of Polish forces in the Middle East in 1943, he made an overnight stop at Gibraltar. Almost immediately after takeoff the next day, his plane crashed, killing almost everyone aboard. There were rumors of sabotage. There were even rumors that Churchill had knowledge that the Germans planned to kill Sikorski on that trip, but that he gave no warning so as not to alert Berlin that its code had been broken. Much later, it was learned that Kim Philby had been the resident British secret service agent in Gibraltar at the time. Philby was the Soviet mole who had infiltrated almost to the top of British intelligence. He escaped from Beirut to Moscow in 1963 when the British had finally learned enough about his activities to be on the point of confronting him. When Philby's presence in Gibraltar at the time of the "accident" happened to come to light after he had fled to the Soviet Union, it raised entirely new questions about Sikorski's death.

In any event, powerless to block Stalin's demands on Poland, Churchill and Roosevelt accepted the eastern border changes. Stalin acceded to their insistence that the provisional Polish government be composed of a fusion of the London and Lublin groups. It was then to conduct free and democratic elections as soon as possible after the liberation. But Stalin continued to back the Communist group. Just a month after Yalta, Churchill wrote to Roosevelt, "Poland has lost its border. Must it also lose its freedom? We are faced with a tremendous failure, a total collapse of what had been agreed at Yalta." Roosevelt cabled Stalin on April 1 that renewal of the Warsaw government was unacceptable, that it would bring the United States to conclude that the Yalta agreement was a failure—an implied threat to withdraw recognition of the border and possibly of other concessions made. After Roosevelt's death, President Truman maintained the pressure. Stalin then reassured Truman that so long as Poland was "friendly" to the Soviet Union, it would live under a "parliamentary regime similar to that of Czechoslovakia, Belgium and Holland."

In the spring of 1945, sixteen Poles had been flown from London to Moscow to negotiate the future coalition government. Word later reached San Francisco, where the first constituent conference of the United Nations was taking place, that all sixteen had been arrested. Outraged, Truman demanded their release. The issue almost broke up the conference, which would have aborted the U.N. before its charter was written. Negotiations were allowed to resume with another group of Poles, and a new government was formed. But with the Red Army at hand, and the measures taken by Communists in the government, the elections were anything but free. Once they had served their sentences, those of the sixteen Poles who were released were immediately re-arrested in Poland and condemned to new sentences by the Communist government, which had consolidated its power. The President of Poland was Bolesław Bierut, a man presented as an independent who had good relations with the Russians. Only after he suddenly took over leadership of the Communist Party in 1948 was it revealed that he had been a lifelong secret Communist and Comintern agent. He died in Moscow in 1956.

Young Poles now tend to blame the United States and Britain for "giving away" their country at Yalta. That was certainly not the Western intention, though Churchill said afterward that they had been mistaken to trust Stalin's promises. But the war was still going on, and the Western leaders were particularly eager to get a Soviet commitment to move forces east and to enter the war with Japan after victory over Germany. Stalin did keep that promise. It was meaningless, or even counterproductive, because in the meantime the atom bomb was tested successfully. The vast invasion of Japan which had been planned was not necessary after all, and the Soviets took new territory in Asia.

Poland's western borders remained at issue throughout the wartime negotiations. Stalin's proposal was to compensate the Poles for loss of territory at Germany's expense. They were awarded half of East Prussia —the Soviets took the northern, more valuable half with the main city of Königsberg, now Kaliningrad. And Stalin argued for moving Germany's eastern border back to the Oder-Neisse line, awarding Poland the rest of Pomerania and industrial Silesia. By the time of the Potsdam Conference in July, the Red Army had imposed Stalin's new map on the terrain. Britain and the United States resigned themselves to the *fait accompli*, though it was nearly a generation later before they officially recognized the new frontier. But the Polish forces immediately set about expelling the Germans who lived in the areas. They revived the ancient name of Breslau, Wrocław, and sent the Poles who had fled from the lost territories in the east to be resettled in the devastated new "western territories."

Stalin's purpose was not so much to make up to the Poles for what he took from them as it was to enforce a geopolitical guarantee of Poland's dependence on the Soviets. He understood that sooner or later the Germans were likely to demand restoration of their lost land. The Poles could then look only to Moscow to assure defense of the new border. It served to put an additional leash on Poland's "loyalty" to its Soviet "protector." The Federal Republic of Germany finally recognized the Oder-Neisse line in its 1970 treaty with Poland, but with the reservation that a new united Germany which might one day emerge would be free to settle the issue for itself. If the post-Yalta division of Europe and the partition of Germany were ever abrogated, as so many wish, there would be the surviving irritant of the German-Polish border. It is a land mine Stalin planted deliberately to prevent removal of his iron curtain ever coming about except under Moscow's aegis, in other words, with the communization of West Germany and a Soviet decision to unify the German states.

As in the former enemy countries of Eastern Europe occupied by the Red Army, the Sovietization of Poland proceeded in jerky but rapid steps after the war. There were not only massive confiscations of property and widespread arrests of the aristocracy and bourgeoisie, but anyone who had anything to do with the A.K. or London government was put under a shadow. Stanislaw Mikołajczyk, the leader of the Peasant Party, who had been in London, managed to escape in 1947. Land reform, distributing the old estates to peasants, was soon abandoned and replaced by forced collectivization. A campaign of progressive intensity was launched against the Church, culminating in the arrest of Stefan Cardinal Wyszynski in 1953. During the anti-Titoist campaign, the Communist Party leader Władysław Gomułka was also arrested. He had spent the war years in the Polish Communist underground and was therefore suspect in Stalin's eyes. He was never actually tried, however. Stalin died in March 1953, before the Polish regime completed its show trial plans.

Exhaustion from the war, disappointment at the aftermath of Yalta and bitter hardship well after hostilities had ended finally subdued the Poles, or so it seemed. A guerrilla war of resistance continued for a couple of years in the southern mountains, then petered out. The dank gray conformity which had descended over the rest of Eastern Europe also seemed to have blotted out Poland. The winter of 1946–47 was phenomenally cold, the coldest in nearly a century. The Oder froze. People were still living in rubble, in wrecked houses sometimes without windows, sometimes with a whole wall missing. There was scarcely any coal or electricity. Food was extremely short. Few had warm clothes; the Germans had scavenged everything worth taking. People who agreed to work for the regime, especially in the police, received extra rations and were entitled to buy in special shops, their windows shielded with yellow curtains, where unavailable necessities and some meager luxuries were stocked.

The regime appeared in firm control, although there were small signs of mounting resentment from youth, from writers, even from some intellectuals within the party apparatus: things could not go on indefinitely in this painful way. But nobody was prepared for the shock of the sudden uprising in Poznań in 1956. There was a trade fair going on, and there were Westerners in the city who reported what happened. Young workers, disgruntled under a regime which never ceased boasting that it was the vanguard of the working class, organized a demonstration. Some soldiers joined the protesters and gave them weapons to defend themselves. When the uprising was put down, more than seventy people had been killed and a great many were arrested. Attitudes were changing, and they brought a crisis within the Party.

Nikita Khrushchev, who had contributed to the new spirit with his secret speech denouncing Stalin, was furious when the Polish Communists decided in October to reinstate Władysław Gomułka as their leader. They had released him from prison not long before. Khrushchev flew to Warsaw to demand his removal. When the Poles refused, he threatened to use Soviet tanks. The Polish leadership said they would order their army to resist. It was the first time there had ever been a direct threat of confrontation between two Communist armies. And it turned out to be the first time that Moscow backed down. The Polish leadership made a point of informing the public what had happened. The people were jubilant. When the news reached Budapest, students marched to a statue honoring the Polish hero Joseph Bem. That was the start of the Hungarian revolution.

Gomułka, who was immensely popular, threw out Marshal Konstantin Rokossovsky, the Red Army officer who had been imposed as Minister of Defense, and the other Russians who had been put in the government, especially in the police. Hard-liners were removed from top posts. Censorship was drastically eased. An effort was made to improve relations with the Church, and Cardinal Wyszynski was freed from the monastery where he had been detained. Collectivization was abandoned. Within two months, almost all the peasants established themselves on the plots which had been taken from them. There had been 10,600 collective farms in October. At the end of the year, only 1,700 remained.

But the euphoria of 1956 soon waned. Gomułka was not the eager reformer that he had appeared. Discontent returned as Gomułka made his peace with the Soviets and tightened controls. The next outburst was in 1968, essentially from students and intellectuals, who were harshly repressed. In 1970, it was the workers' turn again. The uprising came at the Lenin Shipyard in Gdańsk, and Gomułka fell in the aftermath. At least forty-five workers were killed. One of the first demands of the workers who launched the Solidarity independent union at the same shipyard in 1980 was to build a monument to those who had died there ten years earlier.

The new party leader, Edward Gierek, followed a similar course of initial accommodation followed by renewed repression, but people were no longer so easily intimidated. Workers' revolts in 1976 over price increases were again quelled. But they brought together a small committee of dissident intellectuals and the families of workers who had been killed or imprisoned. It was the nucleus of an alliance that was to swell and unite the whole nation when Solidarity was born four years later. In place of needed reform, the regime accelerated its crash program of economic development with huge Western bank loans. The theory was that foreign capital would permit rapid improvement of living standards, satisfying the workers and thus bringing an end to political agitation. It was doomed from the start. The underlying problem of the Polish economy was the rigid, inefficient system and the lack of incentives.

Living standards deteriorated. Polish agriculture, once an important supplier to Europe, could not feed the country's own people. This too was largely of the regime's making. The private farmers were a good deal more productive than the collective and state farms. But the party had never really given up its aim of corraling them back into "socialized" agriculture. It could no longer use force, but it did everything else possible to discourage private farmers. The quarter of the land under state control got more than half the supplies of seed and fertilizer. Prices were skewed so that it was often cheaper for peasants to buy bread to feed their animals than to buy feed. The only tractors produced in the country were huge, heavy ones suitable for vast "socialized" tracts, but the private farmers were seldom allowed more than a few acres. So they continued, as in ages past, to rely on horses, clumsy old wooden carts and inadequate plows and equipment. The regime was willing to spite the anticollectivist farmers at whatever cost to the country.

In the circumstances, food was short. At the beginning of July 1980 the government announced a sharp rise in food prices in an attempt to regulate distribution. The workers protested. At the Lenin Shipyard in Gdańsk, an unknown worker with a stubby face and a big ginger moustache organized a strike. Each time there had been an upheaval, there had been a new leader, someone unknown who suddenly emerged from the ranks and became a heroic symbol. In 1956, it had been Leszek Gozdzik from the Zeran car factory near Warsaw. In 1980, it was Lech Wałęsa, who won the Nobel Peace Prize in 1983 for the persistent, always nonviolent way he led the nation to demand economic reform and a degree of freedom. Within a month of the decision to strike in Gdańsk, the whole country had mobilized into a network of independent unions named Solidarity. The Polish flag became their banner, the Polish church their refuge and inspiration. Peasants organized rural auxiliaries. The frightened regime dithered and wavered, torn between arguments for repression and accommodation. There could be no doubt that this was a workers' and peasants' revolt in a self-proclaimed workers' and peasants' state. Students and intellectuals gave full support.

Unlike Hungary's revolution in 1956, there was no fighting. But it was clear that a general strike would bring the country to complete paralysis. Reluctantly, grudgingly, the regime compromised and signed an agreement on August 31, 1980, recognizing Solidarity and promising reforms. Those were heady days. There was a tremendous surge of hope that, at last, a middle way had been found to correct the worst flaws of the Communist state, revive the economy and the people's sense of dignity, and yet not go so far in defiance of the Communist establishment as to provoke Soviet armed intervention. One small scene at the entrance to the Lenin Shipyard epitomized the pride, discipline and spirit of national renewal that coursed through the country. The strike leaders had forbidden any consumption of vodka during their well-organized sit-in. Alcoholism, especially among workers, had become a national scourge. In response to their call, vodka virtually disappeared from Gdańsk in that period. But one day, among the parcels which families passed through the iron gates to the men barricading themselves inside, some were found to contain vodka. It was immediately seen as a police provocation. Strikers waved the bottles in the air and then smashed them to the ground as the crowd cheered. That was a phenomenal sign of determination in Poland, and the leaders and police understood it.

The Communist Party reeled at the shock. There were massive defections. Its reliance on opportunism, corruption, patronage and careerism had long made it a particularly clumsy, incompetent organization. The leadership was changed again, and there were attempts to introduce some responsibility toward ordinary members. They foundered on the wooden-headed, self-protective resistance of the very apparatus which had run the country down and whose presence blocked renewal. The impasse between the people and the regime continued. The tattered economy declined further. Foreign currency

was so short that export orders could not be filled for lack of minor
needed imports. A ship built for Sweden, for example, had to be sailed
away unpainted at a substantial discount because there was no money
to buy the right kind of paint to finish it. It was a drastic sign of the
Party's incapacity to pull itself together—either to deal straightfor-
wardly with Solidarity or to launch a new tack—that in 1981 it had to
turn to the army for leadership. General Wojciech Jaruzelski, Minister
of Defense, was named Prime Minister and then also First Secretary of
the Party. Never before had a Communist Party put itself in military
hands. That was a taboo which the Soviets called "Bonapartism," an
old fear that the military would take over the revolution from the revolutionaries and install its own authority, as Napoleon had done in
France.

Thinly veiled threats of Soviet intervention recurred. They were met
with repeated warnings of sharp but undefined Western reaction if that
should happen. The Soviets had been surprised at the reaction to their
invasion of Afghanistan in 1979, and at the Afghan resistance, which
embroiled a part of their forces. Moscow could not have doubted that
Polish resistance would be at least as furious, quite possibly involving
much of the Polish army. It may be that Afghanistan deterred a march
on Poland, or it may have been simply the lessons of history.

The Western powers were unprepared for the decision that was
made. On December 13, 1981, General Jaruzelski proclaimed martial
law and put the administration of the country and key economic installations under the army. The operation was stunningly efficient. All
civilian communications within the country and outside were totally
cut off. Most of the Solidarity leaders were arrested and thousands were
interned. Poles and their sympathizers abroad were numbed. Jaruzelski's argument was that his resort to force had saved the country from
disintegration into chaos and armed Soviet repression, which undoubtedly would have been at least as brutal as the nineteenth-century experience. Nominally, Poland was still independent. Soviet troops had
been stationed in the country since the end of the war. Warsaw Pact
headquarters were in western Poland, at Legnica. But the Red Army
did not move. Poland was desperately unhappy, but still Polish.

Gradually, the sternest measures were eased. A certain cooperation
with the Church, on which the regime had come to rely as a moderator,
was maintained. A lively, prolific underground press sprang up. People
plodded back to work, heavy-hearted and totally disillusioned. The new

policy was called "normalization," a deadening attempt to achieve a new social contract by relaxing repression in return for docility. It succeeded to the extent that strikes and demonstrations tapered off and a certain everyday calm returned. But it was a sullen standoff. Never had the gap between Polish rulers and the ruled been so broad and deep, between "them" and "us," as practically everyone put it. As after each previous outburst, cynicism and resentment mounted. These things are cumulative in Poland. New faces, new names are thrust forward each time the coiled pressures spring up for release, but what went before is not forgotten. Bitter memories are nursed.

General Jaruzelski became an ambiguous figure, a symbol of Poland's frustration. Tall and ramrod stiff because of a back brace he wore, his pale, almost expressionless face all the more enigmatic because his sensitive eyes required dark glasses, he maintained an almost impenetrable reserve. He usually appeared in uniform, with his four stars and eleven rows of campaign ribbons. Nothing irritated him more than when U.S. Defense Secretary Caspar Weinberger called him "a Russian in a Polish uniform." He complained privately, saying, "My father and my grandfather were killed by Russians. I am a Polish officer." He was the son of minor nobles who had joined a Soviet-commanded Polish force in World War II to fight the Germans. It became the nucleus of the postwar Polish army.

Jaruzelski was sent to the Soviet Union for training after the war, where he also was taught to be a political commissar, and he rose rapidly on his return. Whether he was more a soldier, acting strategically to prevent the occupation of his country, or more a Communist, acting ideologically to preserve the tenets of the regime, was a question for Poles. Typically, they put it in terms of history. Was he a Janissary, one of the Europeans forced to serve the old Ottoman Empire against its European subjects? Or was he a Wallenrod, a fifteenth-century hero immortalized by the poet Mickiewicz? Wallenrod was kidnapped by Teutonic Knights who killed his parents and brought him up in their order. He came to be a leader, and deliberately took his forces into a Polish trap, dying on the battlefield but avenging his family and his nation. Aloof, ascetic General Jaruzelski provided no answer. But history's answer would not really be a matter of his choosing. It would depend on the ever resilient forces of Polish nationalism and the powerful currents that divide Europe.

Meanwhile, a kind of manic despair seized the country. Alcoholism soared again. The lobbies of certain Warsaw hotels filled with "arabesques," the name given Polish girls who prostituted themselves to dark-skinned migrant workers come from various parts of Europe to trade little Western luxuries for sex with pink-skinned blondes. When the curfew was lifted, teenagers thronged to halls to dance a jerky "Martial Law Hop." One town organized a dance marathon, which continued until all but one couple had collapsed in brutalized exhaustion. The Poles did not shut up and withdraw as the Czechs had done when they were "normalized." They went on talking, with the fury of futility, and teaching their children what not to believe. Instead of the Czechs' mute "internal emigration," withdrawing into private life and trying to ignore the regime, the Polish response to repression and hardship was a form of trench warfare without battles. Both sides made occasional forays and observed occasional truces. But neither ceded. People tried as best they could to follow writer Adam Michnik's recommendation, "We must live as if we were free."

There was no visible way to break the deadlock, no opening for the national "renewal" for which the people yearned and which the regime knew it had to seek, but wanted on its own terms. Even the Russians appeared flummoxed, unwilling to leave enough room for the concessions that might at least launch a search for national reconciliation, yet unable to think of any other way to resolve the dilemma. The explosive potential remained high, the foreign debt overwhelming, the economy limp. The one glimmer on the horizon was Mikhail Gorbachev's program for reform in the Soviet Union. The farther the Russians moved, the more space the Poles could claim for change. Gorbachev seemed to accept Jaruzelski as a junior partner in his campaign, valuing his support against evident opposition from East German, Czechoslovak and possibly other Eastern leaders who agreed with Soviet critics that he was going too far, too fast.

As always, the Church played a crucial role in the Polish impasse. Most Poles are devout, but it is not so much their piety which makes the Church important as its tradition of symbolizing the nation for a thousand years. Cardinal Wyszynski died in 1981, after thirty-two years as Primate. He was a man of great political skill and vision, aristocratic, awesome, a figure of authority. The regime which had imprisoned him and fought the Church mourned him almost as much as the people did because, toward the end of his life, the party leadership came to value his moderating influence. His successor as Primate, Archbishop Jozef

Glemp, was not as intellectually agile and sure of his instincts. The son of a salt miner, Glemp had done forced farm labor under the German occupation. He was a stocky, informal, homespun kind of man, essentially modest. Many Poles felt he resisted the regime too weakly.

But by then the Church had other heroes. One was a young parish priest, Father Jerzy Popiełuszko, who openly supported the banned Solidarity movement. He was kidnapped and murdered by the security police in 1984. That was not a unique incident in the Communist countries. But its remarkable aftermath was a reflection of the unusual and ambivalent state of Poland. The people immediately established the priest as their martyr. In an attempt to appease them, the regime put the policemen directly involved on public trial and sentenced them to prison. But it could not resist using the trial to attack Church activists and try to sully Popietuszko's memory, so the unheard-of retribution for secret police crime did not win the leadership any gratitude or indulgence.

The other unexpected, and joyously celebrated, Church hero was Pope John Paul II, formerly Cardinal Karol Wojtyła of Cracow, the first Polish pope in the history of Rome. His election in 1979, when he was fifty-eight, solidified the unity of the people and the sense that whatever happened in the big marble block that is the Central Committee building in Warsaw, seat of the regime's power, the expression of the nation was in its Catholic churches.

Warsaw is a city of scars. It would have been easier to build an entirely new capital after the war than to clear and reconstruct from the crazy quilt of rubble that was left. But for emotional and symbolic reasons, the phoenix was summoned from the ashes. Apart from tacky housing, hurriedly thrown together for emergency needs, the early rebuilding was made to conform to Stalin's pervasive orders. But other parts of Warsaw were lovingly restored to their Renaissance or baroque beauty, especially the Old City. Most of the architectural documentation had been destroyed, so the paintings of Canaletto were used as the model. Alone among cities, Warsaw was designed to its portrait instead of vice versa.

Cracow, the ancient capital, remains a medieval city. It escaped the devastation of World War II. The city was once a flourishing member of the Hanseatic League, the association of independent merchant towns in the late Middle Ages. The huge sprawl of covered markets still stands in the central square, dominated by a tower from which a broken tune still rings out at night. The story is that a boy assigned to keep watch for the invading Tatars in the thirteenth century was felled by an arrow in his throat as he was trumpeting out the signal. But he had managed to sound the alarm, and the city was saved. Cracow is more sedate, more gracious, less irritable than bustling, lively, politically minded Warsaw. Gdańsk has some areas of charming old gabled Baltic housing, but it was largely destroyed and rebuilding was mostly in grubby Eastern European modern. Wrocław was an almost total ruin and was reconstructed from its German past to its Polish present without affection.

Poles are obliged to think of their history to keep the roots of identity alive, because the ravages of wars left so little standing to bear tangible witness. Apart from the Church, the monument of nationhood is their culture, especially literature. That may be surprising in a country that reached full literacy only after the mid-twentieth century, and where traditional rural life was isolated, without access to the world of intellect. But the poets and writers form a special kind of aristocracy, greatly respected. In return for this recognition, they feel a special responsibility to express not only their personal feelings but those of the nation.

The late Antoni Stonimski, a beloved poet known to all as simply Pan Antoni (Mr. Anthony), worried continuously about the difficulties and harassments endured by writers not subservient to the regime. He was not thinking only in terms of offering support to professional colleagues or of abstract principles of free expression. "This is very serious," he used to say. "The spirit of Poland is at stake." Long experience of censorship over the centuries, combined with the wry Polish temperament, produced a talent for subtle allusion, for the metaphorical wink and stabbing satire. After martial law, many intellectuals who refused to bow to the regime were fired from their jobs, a severe punishment in a Communist regime where there is scarcely any way to earn a living except as an employee of a state-run enterprise. Those who were spared retaliated with a boycott, refusing to write for the legal press, to appear on TV, to act in officially sponsored films. This was the Polish form of "internal emigration," an active protest. Parents who were tempted to compromise, to spare their families the hardship, were often faced with the choice of breaking with their children. The young were the toughest, their new flame of hate inextinguishable. The regime worried about the youth, in which it once hoped to see its future, "a new socialist man," but all communication was cut by youth's total rejection.

So Poland lived on, in anger and sly humor, unwilling to work in what Tadeusz Konwicki called "an atmosphere of occupation," unable to grasp the renewal its people craved. In the period before Solidarity, as the urges that created it were building up, one gesture of the censors toward an increasingly demanding public was to allow publication in Polish of the works of Joseph Conrad as a set. But his essays, which touched too closely on Russian sensitivities, were discreetly excluded, though they referred to prerevolutionary Russia. Just as discreetly, Polish expatriates arranged for a London printer to add them in a volume with just the same binding, just the same paper, as the official set. It was smuggled into Poland so people could have the complete works on their bookshelves without giving themselves away. And when the workers in Gdańsk rose in protest, one of their demands to the state was to permit publication of the complete works of Witold Gombrowicz.

Konwicki's *Minor Apocalypse*, written in 1978, came to be taken as the valid reflection of modern Poland. It is a surrealistic work, describing one summer's day in Warsaw when the First Secretary of the Soviet Union was coming to pay an official visit. Two dissidents wake up the story's narrator at dawn to tell him he has been chosen for the honor of symbolizing the nation's protest by public self-immolation on that day. He sets out running through the town to find a jerry can of gasoline, a rarity, and a box of Swedish matches, since the current Polish product is too unreliable for such an important event. His experiences form a hilarious nightmare, revealing the secret idiocies of the system and the impossibility of achieving anything, even an act of desperation. Toward the end of the book, Konwicki quotes four lines from Stonimski (freely translated):

> *If at the end of this life of labor*
> *I have the right to ask for a favor*
> *Be sure that my coffin is held by the hand*
> *Only of those whom I could stand.*

Konwicki, who had been one of the bearers at Stonimski's funeral, said a few years after martial law had come and gone and the impasse remained that he had become an optimist because at last the nation had awakened. The point of Polish jokes is that you never know whether they are for laughing or for crying.

CZECHOSLOVAKIA
A Sullen Quiet

C ZECHOSLOVAKIA, like Yugoslavia, was a creation of the powers who refashioned Europe from the debris of the Austro-Hungarian Empire, which crumbled in World War I. But its people were much better prepared for independent nationhood and more accustomed to cooperation. Prague has one of Europe's oldest universities, founded in the fourteenth century by King Charles of Bohemia, and it was long a flourishing center of artistic and intellectual life. The extravagance of its stones, a full-scale architectural museum on steep, narrow streets and large, cobbled squares, reflects centuries of prosperous, settled comfort. It is one of the best preserved of Europe's cities. Somehow it was spared in the wars which ravaged so many others. The people, unhappily, are mute now, like the stone, testimony to a history which has repeatedly muzzled them.

The Czechs are the westernmost of the Slavs, poking out into Germanic lands. The neighborhood, as well as a highly diverse ethnic mixture until 1945, has affected their temperament. The Czechs are more stolid, cautious and practical than other Slavs, without the streak of wild passion, gaiety and cruelty. Most of Czechoslovakia's lands and its climate are gentler, tamer. (Historically, the country was divided into three regions, Bohemia and Moravia, inhabited by Czechs, and the Slovak lands of Slovakia. But in modern parlance, it is common to refer to the population generally as Czechs.) Their forests are neater, more orderly, without underbrush, and their mountains, while high in

418

some places, are not forbidding. There is a sense of measure about almost everything, which can be considered stodgy or admirably rational according to the point of view, but it doesn't provoke strong feeling.

In the brief twenty years of independence between the two world wars, Czechoslovakia was a model of stability, democracy and balance in the midst of a turbulent continent. Of course, it wasn't the perfect little state that nostalgia pictures. It was an exception to the general rule of violence and dictatorship which marked the states created after World War I from fallen empires. But the country had its seamy side and underlying tensions, which exploded as Europe went back to war. The combination of ethnic antagonisms within its borders and disgruntled, ambitious neighbors outside brought it to its knees. Czechoslovakia provided the occasion for Soviet leader Leonid Brezhnev to pronounce the doctrine named for him in 1968, asserting Moscow's right to intervene by force if a Communist regime appeared in danger of being overthrown by its own people.

So while it remains formally an independent country, independence is limited to acquiescence to Soviet demands. That is more or less true in all the lands that fell under Soviet dominion. But it is particularly noticeable in Czechoslovakia because there is a Westernness, a profound Europeanness about the country, because the people bear the burden in such glum resignation, and especially because it is not at all clear that their fate was unavoidable. The Red Army did not stay after World War II. There was no excuse, as in Bulgaria, Romania, Hungary and Austria, which had fought on the enemy side. Nor, unlike Poland, was Czechoslovakia a strategically vital path to the Soviet forces in Germany. As an occupied, Allied state with a government-in-exile in London, Czechoslovakia was not a subject of the Yalta agreements beyond the general provision that liberated territories were to reestablish self-government in free elections. Unlike Poland, Czechoslovakia had a tradition of sympathy for Russia and a strong Communist Party, which had never been made illegal and driven underground. Moscow was not worried about a hostile population. It had seemed, for a couple of years after the war, that Czechoslovakia could achieve its leaders' proclaimed desire to be neutral, a bridge between East and West, friendly and on good terms with both sides, minding its own modest business.

But in 1948, the Communists took power in a coup d'état and rapidly

Stalinized the country. Though Soviet agents were doubtless involved, the takeover was achieved by Czechoslovak Communists without any Soviet military support. Some historians contend that they were more rigidly, eagerly pro-Soviet than Moscow sought, and that their subsequent subservience to the Soviets went even beyond Moscow's requirements. In the aftermath of the coup, which was made to appear as a response to a massive popular demand, Czechs had an explanation for the sudden claim to love communism by so many compatriots. There were some beets, they said, people who were red all through, and some turnips, who were white all through but were quickly and thoroughly repressed by the well-entrenched Communist police. But many people had conveniently become radishes, red on the outside only, to make the best they could of the bad times.

That pretense eventually wore off into a sullen, shriveled grayness, which they came to call "internal emigration." It meant withdrawal into an intensely private life, without much communication, each family indifferent to the society around it and shielded by passivity. In the circumstances, the economy and living standards declined, though they remained higher than in much of Eastern Europe because Czechoslovakia had been far more developed before the war and did not suffer great destruction. In the early 1980s, Prime Minister Lubomir Strougal was quoted as saying sarcastically, "We should put up a new sign at the border, to read: Welcome to Czechoslovakia, a former industrial country."

Historically, there was no tradition of unified nationhood. The Czechs of Bohemia and Moravia and the Slovaks speak almost the same language. It is not identical, but they can understand each other. For a thousand years they had been separated, with the Slovaks under Hungarian rule and the Czechs under Germanic influence. The oldest known inhabitants of the region were a Celtic tribe called the Boii, hence the name Bohemia. The Slavs arrived from the east in the sixth and seventh centuries. According to legend, there was a Princess Libuše who stood on the hills above the steep valley of the serene Vltava (Moldau) River. Flinging her arms wide with pleasure at the majestic scene, she proclaimed, "I see a great city, whose glory will touch the stars. The town you will build here will be called Praha [threshold]. Honor and praise shall be given to it, and it shall then be renowned throughout the world." She sent her white horse off to find a consort, and he returned with a sturdy farmer named Přemysl. So was founded the Přemyslid dynasty and the kingdom of Bohemia, with its capital at Prague.

Germans as well as Slavs migrated into the area and the adjoining fertile land of Moravia. In 873, King Borivoj was baptized by the monk Methodius, whom he called from Byzantium to convert his people. But shortly afterward, in 880, Prince Mojmer I of Moravia chose instead to turn to Rome, which brought the lands definitively into the western empire and the Latin rites. The people of Slovakia, at the eastern end of what is now a pollywog-shaped country, were not distinct at that period. But in the tenth century, their lands were conquered by Hungary and they remained under Hungarian rule, cut off from their Slav brethren, until the twentieth century. They were neglected, left largely illiterate when education began to spread, mostly an underclass of downtrodden peasants.

The Czechs fared better. The Good King Wenceslas of the Christmas carol was King Vaclav, a moderate monarch who sought accommodation with the Germanic tribes. His brother Boleslav, more ambitious and bellicose, murdered him in 929, an important date to Czechs, for Vaclav became their national saint. There were periods when the dynasty shifted to the houses of Luxembourg or Poland, at one point expanding the kingdom to the shores of the Adriatic.

The rise of the Habsburgs and the Holy Roman Empire cemented the ties of the Czechs with the Germanic lands. In 1273, Rudolf of Habsburg as Holy Roman Emperor proclaimed his suzerainty. The golden age of Prague and of Bohemia began with Charles IV, who reached the imperial throne in 1341. His father, John, had fought with the French against the English at Crécy. Charles moved the capital of the empire to Prague and began to build fitting monuments, including the Charles Bridge, which connects the low-lying old city with the great Hradčany Castle on the opposing hill. The bridge still stands, a span of solid, blackened stone adorned every few paces with vivid sculptures of saints and sages. Charles traveled to Rome for his coronation, in 1355, but his great memorial is the city of Prague.

Christendom was soon stirring, however, with complaints at the corruption and mendacity of the powerful clergy. The son of Bohemian peasants, a man named Jan Hus, who had studied at Prague University and was chosen to preach in the local language at the Bethlehem Chapel, began to attack these abuses. He was influenced by the writings of the Englishman John Wyclif, some of which he translated into

Czech. It won Hus great popularity in the town and at the court, but it also earned him the fury of the Church establishment. He was excommunicated and forbidden to continue preaching. He ignored the ban. The populace made him their hero. The Council of Constance commanded him to appear to explain his conduct and hear its judgment. Hus realized the danger, but King Sigismund of Bohemia gave him safe conduct, which was supposed to mean a guarantee of a safe return. It was a deception. On July 6, 1415, Hus was burned at the stake. He was forty-six, "a pale, thin man in mean attire" who, the history says, recited the Kyrie Eleison as the flames engulfed him. His ashes and even the earth on which they lay were collected and thrown in the water. He was not a formal Protestant and did not renounce Rome, but the issues he raised were those which Martin Luther elaborated later.

A Hussite movement developed, preparing the Czechs for the Reformation. It was more about Church reform and justice than about theology, an uprising of peasants against landowners when a third of the land belonged to the clergy. There was also a nationalist element. Germans held the most important ecclesiastical appointments, which was much resented by the Slav Bohemians. The King sought to put the Hussites down, which led to prolonged upheaval and the first of the famous Prague defenestrations. The burgomeister and some town councillors threw stones at a Hussite demonstration in the New Town Square. Enraged, the people stormed the town hall and threw them from the windows. They were killed by the crowd. The Hussites formed armies and a new settlement, called by the biblical name Tabor, where they established a puritanical and fully democratic administration. The struggle, with intermittent battles and negotiations, continued until an agreement was sealed a generation later at Iglau, in Moravia, in 1436. As was to be the case in the later wars of religion, questions of misrule, of peasants' rights, of privilege and of ethnic rivalries underlay the churchly arguments. They left strong traces on the Czechs. There is now a large monument to Hus in Prague's Old Town Square. Many consider him the nation's first democrat.

The date most deeply engraved in the national consciousness, however, is 1620, when the Czechs were defeated in the Battle of White Mountain. Protestantism had developed and made broad advances. It drew more German immigrants into the Czech lands, but also strengthened the resolve of the Catholic Habsburgs to tighten their grip on the empire. In 1618, two lieutenants of the imperial crown, Martinic and

Slavata, were sent to make demands on Prague. They were received at the castle and thrown out a window. They landed in the moat and were not gravely injured, but the insult was intolerable to Vienna. An expedition was sent to punish the Bohemians. The Bohemian king asked for help from his relative James I of England, who only offered to mediate.

On November 8, 1620, at White Mountain, not far from Prague, the Austrians won an overwhelming victory. They proceeded to take devastating revenge. Twenty-seven nobles, who were considered the leaders of the insurrection, were executed in Prague's Old Town Square. Twenty-seven crosses, made of white stones set in dark cobbles, still mark the spot. All but a quarter of the land, that belonging to the King and the Church, was confiscated and given over to new landlords, who flocked not only from Austria but many parts of Europe to reap the bonanza. The Czech gentry was wiped out. It was a precursor of a Wild West homestead rush, except that the hapless peasants were left to the will of their greedy new masters. A quarter of the townsmen and nobility emigrated, some thirty thousand families. The population was reduced by half. In 1670, the last of the notable Bohemian intellectuals of the time, Comenius (Jan Komenský), died in exile in Holland. The language survived in the illiterate villages, but manor and town and court life were fully Germanized. Only in the folk memory did the idea of a Czech nation remain. The defeat and its long-lasting tragic aftermath affected the Czech character, leaving a lack of self-confidence, a sense of historic victimization and of a need to seek accommodation.

Vienna put responsibility for the Counter-Reformation in the hands of the Jesuits, and they undertook it with unbrookable zeal. The new, mostly Austrian aristocracy brightened the atmosphere, though only for themselves, with a splurge of luxurious buildings. Great baroque palaces, lavishly bejeweled shrines, sprang up among the narrow streets, especially in the Mala Strana (Small Side) district near the Gothic castle and cathedral. Terraced gardens were laid out on the steep hills, to take advantage of the tender spring breezes and the panoramic view. Prague became an even more beautiful city, but as the capital of an Austrian province. Cultural life flourished, in German. When the delectable Tyl Theater was built, Mozart came himself in 1787 to conduct the premiere of his *Don Giovanni* in its gold and scarlet decor. So fully had the Austrian empire consolidated its mastery that when industrialization began in the nineteenth century, there was no hesitation at investing in Bohemia and Moravia.

It was only in the nineteenth century that Czech national consciousness began to stir again, especially after the revolutionary year of 1848.
It came, above all, from intellectuals, who addressed themselves to the
peasantry and the lower bourgeoisie, excluded from the refinements of
German culture. Music—which speaks in every tongue—was very important. Bedřich Smetana wove folk melodies into his scores, and
showed cosmetic scenes of village life on the operatic stage. They were
fully sanitized, in the sentimental fashion of the time, but they gave a
new sense of legitimacy and dignity. His *Ma Vlast (My Fatherland)*
symphony played to rapturous audiences at the new National Theater
by the Vltava, which is still considered a monument to the campaign
for nationhood. Leoš Janaček and Antonin Dvořák, by their themes
and by their names, moved dormant spirits. Literature appeared in
Czech. Imperial rule had mellowed somewhat. Czechs had been allowed to send deputies to the parliament in Vienna since 1880, and by
1907 they had universal suffrage, though the Slovaks did not. Austria
was especially indulgent of the arts. As a result, Czech intellectuals
have felt a special responsibility ever since to maintain their role as
guardians of the national spirit. They served the national mobilizing
purpose performed by the gentry in Poland, Hungary and Serbia. They
are still the focus of resistance to alien dictates, and that is why they
are still persecuted as the major threat to the regime.

By the twentieth century, industrialization was well advanced. There
were big metallurgical and arms factories in Plzeň, the railroads were
spreading, and coal was a major export. It was from Bohemian pitch-
blende, shipped to them in Paris, that Pierre and Marie Curie discovered radium, and the mines were expanded to produce the valuable
new element. Czech crystal and porcelain were prized. It has been
estimated that when the Czechoslovak state was created in 1918, its
territory held two-thirds of Austro-Hungary's industry. Along with that
development came education and a new cosmopolitanism. The favorite
musicians and most elegant tailors of Vienna were Czech. The Bohemian spas, built in the nineteenth century when the waters were believed to be medicinal, attracted the crowned heads of Europe. People
still go to Karlovy Vary (Karlsbad) and Mariánské Lázně (Marienbad)
to take "the cure," but now the spas are sanitariums set in the charming
parks and pavilions which once served as more of an excuse for leisure
and dalliance than for a regimen of health.

Jaroslav Hašek's *The Good Soldier Schweik* gives the most incisive picture of how the Czechs felt about the state of their affairs and their Austrian overlords as World War I approached. It is a devastating book, hilarious and cruel, ironic and sly, self-deprecating and warily aggressive. Schweik is a wangler and finagler whose ambition is food and drink, surcease from work and punishment, and every crumb of enjoyment he can extract from a harsh life. He is a good-humored lout with the unabashed philosophy that if the people on the bottom squirm and wriggle enough, without actually being provocative, the people on the top will fall on their faces. And he is a national symbol, celebrated by a Prague café named in his honor, complete with an impertinently fly-specked portrait of Emperor Franz Joseph. It says something about the Czechs that they prefer to see themselves symbolically through Schweik's sardonic antics than through some dashing, romantic figure. Franz Kafka caught another side of life in Prague with his haunting surrealism, his nightmares of stuffy little bureaucrats obsessed with meaningless routine, his terrible judgment for unnamed crime. But Kafka wrote in German, and he was romantic.

The city commingled attitudes as well as cultures, but it didn't fuse them. In the Parisian sense of *la vie de Bohème*, there was a busy, carefree, almost insolent artistic life in deliberate defiance of the sober bourgeoisie and their layers upon layers of snobbery. But *bohemian*, in current usage, has nothing at all to do with the character or history of the Czech province of Bohemia. Gypsies came into France from the east, and since many of them had lived in the Czech lands, the French thought they were Bohemians. English came nearer the mark in calling them by a corruption of the name of EGYPT, their presumed origin. Actually, the wandering tribes of tinkers and singers, who astonish, enchant and frighten settled peoples with their refusal to join established societies, have been traced to northern India. They were no more assimilated in Czechoslovakia or neighboring Hungary, where they were also an important minority, than in other countries, but they added a bright jangle to the cultural scene.

The Jewish minority, in contrast, had become an integral part of society. They were leaders in the arts and in commerce, accepted as in few other parts of Europe except perhaps in Germany. One of Europe's oldest Jewish quarters, dating back at least to the tenth century, was in Prague. In the thirteenth century, a separate district was created and called the Jewish Town. It became a center for Jewish culture throughout middle Europe.

The story of Golem, the artificial servant-turned-monster, reflected
the importance of Prague Jews in the sixteenth and seventeenth centuries. Legend ascribes the creation of the automaton to Rabbi Jehudah
Loeb, a kabbalist born in Poland but who was the Great Rabbi of Prague
until his death at age ninety in 1609. It was a time of great discoveries,
scientific curiosity and belief in mysteries. There is still a street of odd
little houses in the Prague castle complex where alchemists once
worked to find the secret of transmuting lead into gold—a delusion, of
course, but a remarkable early forerunner of the atomic periodic tables,
just as the idea of Golem was a preconception of the robot. Rabbi Loeb
was in touch with the great Danish astronomer Tycho Brahe and his
eminent student Johannes Kepler, and he is said to have been received
at the castle to discuss mysteries with Emperor Rudolf II. Scientists,
kabbalists and spiritualists were part of the rich mixture of Prague's
cosmopolitan influence of the period.

Segregation of the Jews was legally abolished in 1848, ending the
ghetto's separate existence, but the community continued to thrive.
The Old-New Synagogue, built about 1270 with later additions, is a
superb example of early Gothic architecture, with elaborate sculptural
elements presaging the ornamentation of High Gothic. It has wood-
screened balconies for women, in the old tradition which forbade them
to mingle or be seen by men at prayer lest their presence distract from
piety. In the Old Jewish Cemetery nearby, tombstones tumbling over
each other date from 1439. Because of lack of space, graves were piled
atop each other, up to twelve layers deep. There may be as many as
twelve thousand. The inscriptions give a glimpse of the community's
history up to 1787, when a new burial ground was established. Medieval
Jewish art, religious objects richly embossed in silver, and masses of
books are preserved in the State Jewish Museum. The people, the Jews
and Gypsies of Czechoslovakia, were all but wiped out in the Nazi
holocaust. That contributed to the change of the texture of life after
World War II.

World War I came as a time of opportunity, not tragedy, for the
Czechs. Many fled abroad to avoid serving in the Austrian army, and
eventually a Czechoslovak émigré army was formed to fight with the
Allies. Thomas G. Masaryk, a professor of philosophy and sociology
who had developed a passionate interest in politics and a determination
that a union of Czechs and Slovaks should be formed into an independent state, made his way to Paris. There, with Eduard Beneš, who had
been a Czech deputy in Vienna, he proclaimed a Czechoslovak

government-in-exile in 1915. Masaryk's vision was based on Hussitism and democracy, on the model of England and the United States, and his thesis was humanism. He was married to an American, Charlotte Garrigue. Traveling widely, including a trip to Russia after the outbreak of the revolution, where a Czech legion was formed and proceeded to harass the Bolsheviks, he raised funds and support for the Czechoslovak cause. The Allies were slow to recognize the demand for a new republic, but émigrés, particularly in the United States, were enthusiastic. On October 18, 1918, Czechoslovak independence was proclaimed in Washington, D.C. It was announced again in Prague on October 28, and the Slovaks formally added their voice on October 30, a week before the armistice.

There remained a lot of wrangling at the Paris Peace Conference to settle the new state's frontiers. Masaryk and Beneš argued what have since been pointed to as conflicting principles: on the one hand, geographic security with solid mountain borders whenever possible, and on the other, Czech-Slovak ethnic unity. They were skillful diplomats, and they got their way. The result was the inclusion of the largely German-speaking Sudetenland, in the western mountains; Teschen, on the slopes of the Tatras to the northwest, inhabited largely by Poles; and sub-Carpathian Ruthenia at the pollywog's tail to the east, with a heavily Ukrainian population. The state was a complete ethnic mix, despite its name. In addition to the Czechs, it included more Germans than Slovaks and a large Hungarian minority.

Even before the treaties were signed, the turbulent Slovak leader Monsignor Andrej Hlinka made it clear that the Czech diplomats had exaggerated Slovakia's enthusiasm for absorption and that it had national demands of its own. Masaryk and Beneš prevailed by persistence and persuasion in Allied chancelleries and conference rooms. But the historian Joseph Rothschild later surmised that the effort left the new government, particularly Beneš, with "a heavy psychological mortgage," and "an exaggerated sense of dependence on the west and inadequate confidence in the nation's own resources . . . Beneš' conviction, born of his own diplomatic experience, [was] that ultimately Czechoslovakia's fate and salvation rested less with her own forces than with her powerful patrons."

Masaryk, the father of his country, was its revered President until December 1935, when he resigned at age eighty-five. Then Beneš became President. Masaryk died in 1937.

Their new state was landlocked, but the mountains surrounding most

of it provided natural frontiers. The Danube, which enters at Bratislava, just below Vienna, and flows through to Hungary, gave access to
the Black Sea. It has the same area as New York State. The population
is now 15 million, Czechs and Slovaks. Almost all the Germans were
expelled after 1945; the Ukrainians were absorbed when the Soviet
Union annexed Ruthenia, and most of the Jews and the Gypsies were
killed or fled. Hungarian and Polish minorities remain, but the country
is now largely homogeneous. Lying on a west-east axis, the landscape
moves from the rolling Bohemian plain, where the climate is mild and
the fields are fertile, to the snowy High Tatras of eastern Slovakia.

In the summer, the Czech countryside is strung with what look like
giant clotheslines, where hops are hung to dry. Beer is the Czech drink,
and the Plzeň breweries are world famous. It's understandable; it takes
quantities to wash down the heavy *knedliky* (bread dumplings) which
invariably accompany the favorite dishes of pork and goose. Often the
villages are operetta sets, with flower boxes and maypoles. But there are
grimy industrial towns and bleak rows of little concrete houses near the
mines and the steel mills. Wine is the Slovak drink. The countryside is
less manicured and the people are merrier, more impulsive and more
Slavonic than the Czechs. Slovak Protestants, less than 20 percent, get
on better with their Czech compatriots than the dominant Catholics.
In the Czech lands, about half the people are Catholics and the Church
has less influence.

Despite Prague's importance, the capital does not overshadow the
other cities to the same extent as in some European countries. Brno,
the capital of Moravia, has a full sense of itself, and Bratislava, formerly
Pressburg, considers itself virtually a rival to Prague as the capital of
Slovakia. It looks more to Vienna, or would if the watchtowers, the
mined strips and the barbed wire symbolizing the East-West divide did
not block the way. But Prague is unique, with its exuberant mixture of
buildings from many ages. In the winter, coal smoke settles down in its
sharp valley, leaving a gritty patina on everything, new or old. Spring,
summer and fall are brightened by the city gardens and the flowers on
the river island where people go to stroll and drink coffee. But the city
is best by night, when the streets are empty and the lovely little fountains and weathered stones stand out from the dark arcades in serene
solitude. Gaslight has been restored to the Old Town Square and the
neighboring area, bathing it in warm, golden tones that chase away
desolate thought. For Czech thought has grown desolate.

The euphoria of independence was not allowed to last long. There was full political freedom, which permitted the mushrooming of twenty-nine parties by 1925. But they were all ethnic and fragmentary. Only the Communists were able to unite in a single party for the whole republic, in 1921. Czechoslovakia was the richest successor state of the Austro-Hungarian Empire, with only a quarter of its population and one-fifth of its area but most of its industry as well as a vigorous agriculture. The rise of tariff barriers and national rivalries cut it off from traditional markets, however. The balanced economy staved off the impact of the Great Depression a year or two longer than in neighboring countries, but when it hit, it hit even harder. Unemployment was catastrophic and exacerbated ethnic tensions.

All around, dictatorships were digging in. The ethnic Germans, concentrated in the Sudetenland along the German border, flocked to the banner of the local Nazi leader, Konrad Henlein, who not only proclaimed his admiration for Adolf Hitler but his ambition to include in the Greater Reich the territories where German-speakers predominated. The Slovaks, cut off from their traditional access to the Hungarian economy, also had grievances. The central government provided heavy subsidies to develop roads, railroads and electric power in Slovakia, but the gap with Czech living standards widened. By 1937, per capita income in Slovakia was half that in the Czech lands.

The war dogs were growling in Europe. In 1935, Beneš entered into an alliance with the Soviet Union as a protection against Hitler. He had also turned to France, joining the Little Entente. But frenzied diplomacy could not muffle the increasingly raucous demands from Berlin for the "return of the Sudetenland," supported by menacing demonstrations of Henlein's multitudes. In 1938, in response to Hitler's threats, the powers met in Munich to deal with the issue. Italy's Benito Mussolini, France's Edouard Daladier and Britain's Neville Chamberlain joined Hitler at the conference table. The Soviet Union, backing the Czech stand, was not invited. But neither was Beneš. His country's dismemberment was to be decided without its representation. On September 29, 1938, the four powers agreed to award the area, which contained all of Czechoslovakia's western defenses, to Germany. The Nazi Brown Shirts and the German army proceeded to take occupation. Waving his furled black umbrella, Chamberlain returned jubilantly to London proclaiming that war had been averted at Munich and he had brought back "peace in our time." He described Czechoslovakia as "a faraway little land that few of us know anything about."

Hitler waited just seven months to violate his pledge and take advan-

tage of the open door to overrun the country. The German invasion of
what remained of Czechoslovakia began on March 15, 1939. There was
little resistance. There scarcely could have been. Bohemia-Moravia was
proclaimed a German protectorate. Slovakia became a puppet state,
ostensibly independent but allied to the Nazis, under Father Jozef Tiso,
an agitating nationalist. His regime persecuted Czechs as well as Jews
and Gypsies. Even before World War II began, with the invasion of
Poland that September, Czechoslovakia had been wiped out. There
was deep bitterness at what people considered betrayal by the democracies. It was not forgotten later when the Soviets, who had played no
role in surrendering the country, returned in triumph, and it had a lot
to do with the strength of the Communist Party after the liberation.

In his book *The Unbearable Lightness of Being*, Milan Kundera, the
Czech expatriate writer, takes up the problem of big decisions. Since
there is only one life, and no previous experience to offer guidance,
how is one to know, he asks, which is the right choice and which is
wrong? What is a person confronted by crisis to do? The question is put
in human, novelistic terms, and the characters' choices end badly. But
would the opposite choice have made any difference, been any better?
Kundera makes it clear that his story is a metaphor for his country. He
writes:

In 1618, the Czech estates took courage and vented their ire on
the emperor reigning in Vienna by pitching two of his high officials out of a window in the Prague Castle. Their defiance led to
the Thirty Years War, which in turn led to the almost complete
destruction of the Czech nation. Should the Czechs have shown
more caution than courage? The answer may seem simple; it is
not.

Three hundred and twenty years later, after the Munich conference of 1938, the entire world decided to sacrifice the Czechs'
country to Hitler. Should the Czechs have tried to stand up to a
power eight times their size? In contrast to 1618, they opted for
caution. Their capitulation led to the Second World War, which
in turn led to the forfeit of their nation's freedom for many decades or even centuries. Should they have shown more courage
than caution? What should they have done?

If Czech history could be repeated, we should of course find it
desirable to test the other possibility each time and compare the
results. Without such an experiment, all considerations of this
kind remain a game of hypotheses.

Einmal ist keinmal. What happens but once might as well not have happened at all. The history of the Czechs will not be repeated, nor will the history of Europe.

Kundera's book appeared in 1984, after two more fateful moments of choice for Czechoslovakia, both greeted by caution and then despair. That is the great burden smothering his compatriots.

During World War II, there was no widely organized resistance in the Czech lands. Beneš led a government-in-exile in London, joined by Jan Masaryk, the son of Thomas, as Foreign Minister. Once again, many Czechs who managed to escape joined Allied forces in the fight, and did what they could to organize an underground from abroad. Their most spectacular exploit led to a disaster. On May 27, 1942, an underground unit led by Czechs parachuted in by the British ambushed and killed the German governor, Reinhard Heydrich, as he was speeding along a country road. In retaliation, the Germans razed the nearby village of Lidice, killing 184 and deporting 235. Partisans set off an uprising against the Germans in Slovakia in August 1944 and were brutally suppressed, but they tied down eight German divisions. Otherwise, resistance was mainly passive.

As Soviet troops, joined by Czech troops, moved westward in 1945, a provisional government dominated by Communists was being formed in Košiče, in eastern Slovakia. Beneš, who had signed a treaty with the Soviets in Moscow in 1943, decided it was time to go back. Representatives of the four major parties agreed on a program for the revived state on March 27. It would be reorganized on the basis of two Slav nations, with considerable autonomy for Slovakia. Germans were to be expelled, there was to be extensive land reform, major industries were to be nationalized, and foreign policy was to be based on friendship with the Soviets and good relations with the West. This was offered as a compromise between the liberalism of Beneš and the demands of Klement Gottwald, the tough Communist leader. They were meeting, after all, under the auspices of the Red Army, and Beneš had already made sweeping promises to Moscow.

The people of Prague rose against the retreating Germans on May 5, fighting in the streets. The U.S. Third Army under General George Patton had reached Plzeň in western Bohemia by then, and Patton wanted to rush ahead to save the capital forty miles away, as U.S. forces had done the year before in Paris. Supreme Allied Commander Dwight D. Eisenhower ordered him not to move and, when the Russians arrived at his lines, to withdraw from Czechoslovakia completely, to the German border. Eisenhower was determined to stick precisely to the agreements which had been made for the meeting of the Western and Soviet troops at the end of the war. So it was that Marshal Ivan Konev's tanks, red flags flying, liberated Prague on May 9. The provisional government arrived from the east a few days later. Gottwald, who was named a Vice Prime Minister along with the Slovak Communist Viliam Široký, made a speech announcing "a new type of democratic regime."

Although they held only eight out of twenty-five cabinet posts, the Communists had the key Interior Ministry (police), along with Agriculture, Information, Education, and Social Affairs. Vladimir Clementis, a Slovak Communist, was put in the Foreign Ministry as deputy to Jan Masaryk. The Communists moved quietly, without provocation. The first clash came in 1947, when the Marshall Plan was offered. Eighty percent of Czechoslovakia's trade was with the West, and the cabinet accepted. Moscow roared. Gottwald, Masaryk and another minister were summoned to the Kremlin. After a few days, Prague announced that it rejected the American aid plan after all because it might harm relations with the Soviets. Beneš said there was no choice. Masaryk, despondent, was said to have told a friend, "We are now nothing but vassals."

He sensed what was coming. Jan Masaryk was a *bon vivant*, a musician, a man who would much rather have spent his life as a cultured playboy. But he had accepted that, as his father's son, he must serve his country. As Foreign Minister in the government-in-exile, he had been active in wartime diplomacy and postwar planning. He had many friends in Britain and America. There came a time when some of them urged him to leave Prague and move back to the West, as he had no doubt that a complete Communist takeover was in the offing. But he replied that he had already gone through the distress of flight and exile and could not face it again. He would simply stay, whatever happened.

It happened in February 1948. The Communist Party called for the creation of revolutionary action committees everywhere and armed a "workers' militia." Gottwald went to Beneš and demanded cabinet changes expelling "reactionaries." Former Premier Zdeněk Fierlinger, supposedly a Social Democrat but thought by many to have long been a secret Communist, came out in support of Gottwald. Fearing civil war, Beneš accepted, too readily and spinelessly, many thought. The coup d'état succeeded. Wide-scale purges and drastic measures to Stal-inize the country were launched. On March 3, Masaryk was found dead on the stony ground below the window of his apartment in Hrad-čany Castle. He was pronounced a suicide by the authorities. Most believed he had been murdered, one more defenestration. But it was never proved, and given his mood and his foreboding, it is not impos-sible that he chose death rather than lend his name and authority to liquidate his friends and repudiate the West, or to try to escape.

Starting late, the Czechoslovak Communists moved very quickly to catch up with their mentors, as the Austrian Nazis had done after the Anschluss with Germany in 1938. Virtually all private property was confiscated. Those deemed "bourgeois," whether they said or did any-thing against the new regime or not, were expelled from their city homes and obliged to find menial labor and housing, sometimes in hastily mended garden sheds, in the countryside. University admissions were limited to children of workers and peasants, unless the parents were Communists, and "reactionary influence" was relentlessly combed out of the faculties. Tens of thousands were arrested.

By November 1952, the regime was ready for the next step, the show-trial purge of its own ranks, which Stalin had ordered. There had al-ready been similar postwar trials in Bulgaria and Hungary. It was the familiar, sinister pattern of forced, wildly fabricated confessions which, in turn, provided the secret police who had composed and extorted the "revelations" with an excuse to persecute whole classes of people, most of whom were never tried. The themes were similar to those at the trial of Laszlo Rajk in Hungary: being Jewish, sympathy for Yugoslavia's Tito, nationalism. Under Stalin, the old Communist slogan of "prole-tarian internationalism" meant accepting absolute allegiance to Mos-cow regardless of one's own country's needs and agreeing to impose the "Soviet model" in all details laid down by Soviet advisers.

The star defendant of the Prague trial was Rudolf Slansky, a lifelong Communist. There were fourteen defendants, eleven of them, includ-ing Slansky, Jewish, which the party paper *Rude Pravo* pointedly noted in proclaiming Zionism as the main enemy. All but three were executed on December 3, 1952. The survivors, Eugen Löbl, Arthur London and Vavro Hajdu, were sentenced to life imprisonment. After de-Stalinization, which the Czech regime applied late and with evident reluctance, they were released. The dead were rehabilitated posthu-mously. Not surprisingly, Slansky's son, also named Rudolf, became a dissident in later years, but he showed remarkably little bitterness, more a tragic insight into the nature of the system. "The reason it can't be reformed is that these people," meaning the Soviet as well as Czechoslovak rulers, "know what they did to others. They are afraid that if they ease controls even a little, others may wrest away power and do the same to them," he said. In 1968, during the brief "Prague Spring" when it was possible to talk about such things, it was estimated that during the 1952–54 purges 136,000 people were killed, jailed or interned in camps. Many prisoners were forced to work in the coal mines.

Klement Gottwald, the leader, died a few months after the Slansky execution, on March 14, 1953. It was just a week after Stalin's death. According to the historian François Fejtö, he was a broken man after signing the death warrant for so many of his closest comrades. He became a drunkard, a blithering wreck. But the secret was closely held. In a final act of mimicry, he was embalmed and enshrined in a huge white mausoleum on a Prague hill. Czechs were paraded past the mummy to do homage to the "great man," as Russians filed past the remains of Lenin and Stalin in Moscow's Red Square. A gigantic statue of Stalin dominating another hill, which the Czechs only got around to erecting in 1955, was also taken away in 1962.

There was a period of "collective leadership" after Gottwald, but Antonin Novotný, a shrewd, tenacious authoritarian, soon emerged as dominant. He had joined the Communist Party in 1921 at the age of seventeen and spent part of the 1930s in Moscow at the Comintern. During the occupation, he was one of the clandestine leaders and was caught by the Germans in 1941. He spent the rest of the war in Mauthausen, a Nazi concentration camp in Austria. Only forty-nine years old when he reached the top, he was ousted in January 1968 by the reformist wave which came to overwhelm the party.

There had been a workers' upheaval in 1953, mainly at Plzeň but also with some echoes in Prague and Ostrava. It was fiercely repressed. In the following decade, the demands for reform and liberalization came from a quite different source, inside the party hierarchy. Novotný had maneuvered skillfully to hold the reins. Watching Poland and then Hungary explode with anger in 1956, the Czech party was wary of giving even the slightest ground. The people did not push. During the Hungarian revolution, a mechanic in Prague said, "You've no idea what a strain we're all under these days. I scarcely sleep. Every time I hear a noise in the street, I run to the window to see whether demonstrations have started so I can join if there's a big crowd. But it's always just a car backfiring, or some drunks."

But by the early 1960s, Hungary was recovering and its reforms were bringing visible economic advance. The Czech economy was slumping badly. There was a shortage of food, caused by collectivization and bad weather. Industry was stagnating. The Slovaks in particular, Communist or not, were growing restive at the loss of remnants of autonomy after the Slansky trial and the anti-Tito campaign. Official economists led by Ota Sik began to press more and more insistently for changes in the system, to provide more incentive and managerial discretion. Little sparks of audacity showed up in the arts and music, and especially in films. In January 1968, Novotný was forced to compromise, ceding party leadership to the rising Slovak leader Alexander Dubček but retaining the presidency of the republic. To celebrate, Prague students made a pilgrimage to the little, out-of-the-way churchyard at Lany, some fifty miles from the capital. Thomas and Jan Masaryk were buried there, side by side. The students held a small but defiant memorial ceremony in honor of their nation's now unmentionable but never forgotten first family.

Suddenly, there was a burst of talk, of articles, plays, proposals. As spring arrived, Prague and Bratislava were in ferment. Communists began to argue about building "socialism with a human face." Official crimes and incompetence, long denied, were exposed as a vaccination against their repetition. The general public watched, warily, but with fresh hope. Moscow watched too. There were Warsaw Pact maneuvers in Czechoslovakia that spring, which justified the presence of large Soviet forces in the country. Repeatedly, it was announced that the maneuvers had to be prolonged. The Russians did not leave, as they should legally have done. There was no direct explanation, but increasing Soviet irritation with the way things were going was made clear. The Czechoslovak press, radio and TV became more and more outspoken. There were meetings to discuss reform inside the party to make it function more democratically. There was an atmosphere of exhilaration, especially among intellectuals, but there were no disorders.

There were differences within the Czech leadership, but Dubček clearly had broad and enthusiastic support for his new line. He was not, he insisted, challenging the Soviets or undermining the party's control. On the contrary, an approach had finally been found that might win the Communist regime the popularity to which it had vainly pretended.

The sincerity of the reformers, who did believe they had discovered a way to combine what they considered the benefits of socialism with the values of Western humanism, should not be doubted. Nor should their continued dedication to the idea of communism.

It was with some trepidation, but also considerable optimism, that the Czechoslovak leadership accepted Moscow's convocation to a top-level meeting at the border. At Soviet request, each side came in a special train to Cierna, a little town of 2,500 inhabitants on the Czech-Soviet frontier. Jana Neumannova, who served as Dubček's interpreter, later recorded her memory of the dramatic encounter. On July 29, 1968, the Soviet train pulled in silently. The station personnel did not know where it would stop so as to lay down the red carpet, and they miscalculated. Leonid Brezhnev waited politely for them to move it to the door of his parlor car, and then descended, expressionless, on Czech soil.

At their meeting in the Soviet car, Brezhnev sternly lectured the Czech Communists. Dubček explained that it was impossible to go backward to the situation before January, but that "our policy is fundamentally socialist and friendship with the Soviet Union is indestructible," Neumannova relates. But as the meetings progressed and the participants took their turns to speak, the Soviet tone grew nastier. They charged counterrevolution and loss of party control. Soviet Prime Minister Alexei Kosygin said the border with West Germany was not properly defended, adding, "The western border is not your border. It is our border and we will not abandon it. We will defend it victoriously." The Russians provided a long list of people whom they considered "revisionist" or "counterrevolutionary." (Neumannova said they were all arrested after the Soviet invasion.) The session broke up without a conclusion. The Russians pulled back across the border for the night. They never shared a meal with the Czech hosts. Each day was worse. But on the fourth day, August 1, Dubček agreed to a Soviet-drafted communiqué. It seemed to represent a compromise, in which he gave up his objections to a Warsaw Pact summit to consider the situation in Czechoslovakia, and Brezhnev did not press the demand for arrests.

That was a deception. On the night of August 21, 1968, Soviet tanks rolled into Prague. An uninterrupted airlift into Prague's Ruzyne airport, which special Soviet forces speedily secured, brought vast reinforcements. Moscow took no chances. It sent half a million troops to cow the bewildered Czechs, telling the soldiers they were going to a friendly country to help its people fend off imperialists. The Czechs took down road and street signs all across the country, to confuse the invaders. But it did not make much difference. In Prague, girls in miniskirts taunted the men in tanks, kissing local passersby at random to show the Russians that Czech affections were not for them. The Red Army men were puzzled, but followed their orders. A young man, Jan Palach, set himself on fire in the middle of Václavské Náměstí, Prague's central avenue, as a sacrifice for his country. The spot was covered with flowers and surrounded by candles for some weeks. The West made a lot of sympathetic noises, but did nothing more. From a strictly military point of view, the Soviet operation was exemplary, well planned, organized and executed. It had evidently been decided upon well before the meeting at Cierna. It was a complete success within a few days, with only a few casualties.

In response to outrage in the rest of the world, including a muted but disgusted reaction among many Communists both East and West, Moscow announced that it had an inalienable right to protect and preserve "the revolution" wherever it had succeeded and was threatened with being overthrown. That came to be known as the Brezhnev Doctrine. It was a proclamation that ostensibly put the full might of Soviet armed forces at the service of the tenet that the revolution was irreversible. But like all doctrines, it had to face the test of circumstances. In places like Grenada in the Caribbean, Somalia, Guinea and to some extent Mozambique in Africa, Moscow allowed it to lapse for lack of means.

Later, the Czech writer Pavel Tigrid wrote in a Western paper, "The fate reserved for Czechs makes it possible to demonstrate fairly convincingly that capitulation as a doctrine, as the *raison d'état*, finally leads to the destruction of practically all civic virtue, to a national decline." Saving lives and cities, he said, "is too high a price when it means the destruction of other values, less tangible, but all the same absolutely necessary for a people which seeks to live in freedom, and to a certain extent, in dignity." He speaks of a feeling of "collective guilt" which then saps the society. Kundera found the issue of choice impossible to solve in good conscience. Tigrid chose an answer. Which attitude is preferable is the question which haunts Czechs, mutely within their country, sometimes vociferously abroad. The results of 1938, 1948 and 1968, they feel, do not leave much room for pride.

The aftermath of 1968 was devastating, more immediately dramatic than 1948. Some compared it to 1620 and the Thirty Years War, but it was more sophisticated. There were no massacres, but a sweeping, generalized repression which brought a sense of total impotence and futility. The universities were more thoroughly swept out than after 1948, expelling students and faculty suspected of antagonism to what the regime announced as "normalization." Since the economy was totally state-run and the records of all citizens fully documented, it meant that all affected were doomed to eking out their living at the most menial jobs with no prospects ever for advance short of actively serving the regime's purpose. Half a million members of the party were expelled, losing all privileges.

The massive purge lasted about two years. The country was paralyzed. People turned up at their workplaces, but nothing was done. Production sagged. Then after 1970 a new phase began. Gustáv Husák, the Slovak who had replaced Dubček as the leader with Soviet approval, had suffered in the purges of the 1950s, like the Hungarian postrevolutionary leader János Kádár. But unlike Kádár, he did not evolve a policy of reconciliation with his people on the thesis of "he who is not against us is with us." Instead, he used the technique that Kádár's predecessor, the brutal Mátyás Rákosi, had once called "goulash communism." It meant: if you stuff the people's mouths, they won't complain about the rest. The economy could not provide the resources for consumerism. But in a crash effort, the regime mobilized all its hard currency and, apparently with special one-time access to Soviet reserves, filled the shops with Western goods. There were French cheeses, Italian shoes, English sweaters on the once bare shelves, offered at astronomical prices, and household appliances, even cars. It drove workers to make an extra effort. Passing a Prague store window with Italian shoes selling for the equivalent of two weeks' to a month's pay, I asked a Czech secretary who would buy them. They were of better quality and more stylish than Czech shoes, famous before the war, but they cost ten times more. She laughed. "We know how we work," she said, "so we never buy Czech goods if we can help it."

The trick succeeded, for a while. During the first half of the decade, production grew at an encouraging rate of 5 to 6 percent a year. At the same time, the policy of repression was shifted from all-encompassing to selective. At first the focus was on former Communists, people who might still harbor the illusion of finding a way to make "socialism with a human face." Then it shifted to what remained of the intellectual dissidents, who hoped that the Helsinki accords could be applied at least partially and would provide some protection, a group which sought to organize university instruction in fly-by-night classes in tiny apartments and participated in the "parallel culture"—underground theater, clandestinely circulated literature, and so on. Finally, as each succeeding target group was more or less eliminated, sometimes with political trials to prove the point, the campaign turned against workers and Catholics who dared to be aroused by the rise of the Solidarity movement in Poland.

For the most part, it did not take a vast machinery of cruelty to keep people in line. Those who remembered 1938, those who remembered 1948, had no expectations of outside help and little confidence in themselves. Those who had allowed themselves euphoric hopes in 1968, essentially people who believed enough in communism to feel they could make it work, crashed in disillusion. Reminders of police power were enough to keep their spirits low. People were summoned for interrogation, their apartments searched and thrown in disorder, and jailed for shorter or longer periods without any explanation or charges. Sometimes they were beaten. Or the electricity was cut. Harassment, quite arbitrary and at odd, disconcerting times, was enough to make it clear that all authority lay with the authorities. Sheer fatigue counseled submission.

Slovakia, concerned with national equality with Czechs, was more easily pacified than Bohemia and Moravia. The one reform from 1968 which was retained was the establishment of a regional government in Bratislava, providing a large new range of bureaucratic jobs previously reserved for Prague. Slovaks also were given about a half of the top jobs in the capital, well beyond their share of the population. In addition to Husák, the Minister of Defense, Martin Dzúr, and the Foreign Minister, Bohuslav Chňoupek, were Slovaks.

Gradually, the economy declined again. Trade was diverted back from the West to the East. Industry, which represented two-thirds of the GNP, fell behind for lack of investment. There was no attempt, as in several Eastern countries, to leap ahead on the basis of huge credits from the West. Vasil Biľak, the guardian of orthodoxy who had supported the Soviets at the fateful Dubček-Brezhnev meeting, said, "He who borrows from the West is the same as the Christian who sells his soul to the devil." As a result, Czechoslovakia avoided the crisis of debt which hit Poland, Hungary and Yugoslavia in the recession of the early 1980s. It simply slumped more and more downhill. Trade was 77 percent with the Eastern bloc countries, 45 percent of it with the Soviet Union. Then it didn't matter so much that official statistics showed only 2 percent of industrial output at world-quality level, in a country which had had a reputation for first-rate machine tools. One ton of Czech steel was produced at seven times the cost of a ton of Japanese steel. The result of this decline came to be known as "demoderniza-tion," at a time when other industrial countries were straining to catch up with the third Industrial Revolution.

Considering their wages almost worthless, people resorted to barter. Swindling the state, the only employer, "is the only way not to harm your family," a whispered maxim went. A traditionally energetic, disci-plined population forgot about civic standards and turned exclusively to material concerns.

The national obsession became a cottage in the country, a place to go and putter in privacy. Practically everybody had one. People also managed to buy little cars to get them back and forth. A philosopher who went to work in a factory told a Western visitor, "The energy of the people is used in scheming against society more than on behalf of society. People are allowed to better their living standards in illegal ways. Everybody does it, so nobody is clean. This is a more cohesive factor than the secret police—this spread of corruption that unites all Czechs." The scaffolding of Prague has become a symbol of the mal-ady. Everywhere, the beautiful old buildings are flanked with wood and steel put up at some point to make repairs that never get finished. It has something to do with the plan, some people say, which counts erecting facilities for maintenance as fulfillment of the ubiquitous norms but does not check up on jobs completed. No, say others, it's just that things are so run down there's a danger of stones falling and hitting pedes-trians.

No one is sure; no one asks questions. People don't talk on the street. The country runs behind its people's backs. As in all the rest of Eastern Europe, the structure of power was established after World War II and modeled closely on the Soviet Union's. There are differences due to history and national temperament, and to the personalities who man-aged to emerge above their rivals and establish leadership. But the system functions on the same principles in each country, and because of the failure of even limited attempts at reform, Czechoslovakia offers a pristine example of its anatomy. The two key points are the Leninist dicta that "the [Communist] party is the leading force in state and

society" and that the party should operate by "democratic centralism."
This means that no opposition can be tolerated from outside the single,
dominant, organized party, because any challenge to the party of the
revolution is by definition counterrevolutionary. Democratic centralism has come to mean a tight hierarchy within the party so that decisions flow from the top down and disagreement cannot spread from the
bottom up, because any challenge to the leadership is by definition
threatening to the requirement of party unity.

All the trappings of the state exist alongside the party, but its function
is to give legal standing to party decisions and to put them into effect.
The party has been called the "supreme political and moral arbiter."
The number of Communists in the Czechoslovak party has varied from
30,000 in 1929 to 2.5 million after the 1948 coup made obvious the
privileges that were to be won by joining and the penalties to be suffered
by resisting. Now the total membership runs between 8 and 10 percent
of the population, about 1.7 million, not so many as to be unwieldy and
dilute the party's "vanguard" status, not too few to do the jobs of control
and administration.

Law, both in terms of legislation and the administration of justice,
represents in Lenin's phrase the "state will of the proletariat," that is to
say, of the proletariat's only acceptable expression, which is the party,
and that is to say, law is arbitrary, without reference to popular consent,
regardless of constitutions. In Czechoslovakia, as in most of Eastern
Europe, there is a "National Front" composed of non-Communist
groups as well as Communist, organized in the early postwar period
when the Communists were working at gradual absorption of other
social forces. Now the Front is entirely subservient to the party, serves
as the umbrella for all mass organizations—unions, youth, women,
music lovers, athletic clubs, chess players—and names all candidates
for elections. There may at times be a second candidate for an office,
but he or she must also be nominated by the Front. Because the police
and informers' system make it risky to fail to vote or to cast a blank
ballot, Front candidates regularly receive around 99 percent of the vote.

One special feature of Czechoslovakia is the existence of a separate
Communist Party of Slovakia as an entity within the overall Czechoslovak Communist Party, because of historical reasons and a continuing
Slovak sense of different identity. There is no parallel Czech Communist Party. But the government has been declared a federal republic,
with a Czech Socialist Republic established in Prague and a Slovak

Socialist Republic in Bratislava. Both come under the central government in Prague, though they do have some autonomy over such affairs as education, health, culture and construction and share some powers with the federal republic in the management of industry and agriculture.

As people outside the ruling apparatus have nothing to say about what is done, they pay little attention to the political organization and functioning of the state. Ideological education is compulsory, in the schools, the army and other organizations, and propaganda is all-pervasive, but its very omnipresence makes it a white noise that serves as mere background to the sounds people really hear.

Of course, life goes on. There are sports, and food, and gardening, and repairing the car, and family, above all family, to think and talk about. By the middle of the 1980s the economy was able to support a consumerism that no longer compared too unfavorably with East Germany's or Hungary's. As in East Germany, there was a tacit social compact that the regime would provide a tolerable material life and the people would keep their mouths shut, except to consume. In 1986 the U.S. Ambassador in Prague, William H. Luers, pointed out that the bargain was being kept by both sides. "There is now much more open and interesting debate and discussion going on in the Soviet Union than in Czechoslovakia," he said.

There was even something of a religious revival, especially among young people. The government keeps strict control of Church activities and has abrasive relations with the Vatican. One priest, Vaclav Maly, had his official license canceled and took a job as stoker in the boiler room of a small hotel. He faced a two-year prison sentence if he wore clerical garb or served communion. His crime was that he met with young people outside the church and did not isolate himself inside the parish house. The licensing of priests in Czechoslovakia goes back to the Thirty Years War in the seventeenth century, but the regime has used the system to curb the spread of religious discussion, arguing that it is only another professional rule similar to the one that requires a surgeon to perform operations only in a hospital. There is a great shortage of priests; only one in three Prague parishes has a local priest assigned.

Father Maly said people's attitudes were different, however. "When I was in high school in 1968, I was the only practicing Christian. My friends would always tease me for my beliefs. Now things are changing.

No, it is not Poland. Religious feeling is not strong, but no one now laughs at religious feelings. They may not share them, but they respect them." With the country's Hussite tradition and widespread secularism in the interwar years, mounting Catholicism seems an anomaly in Czechoslovakia, especially in Bohemia and Moravia. It is attributed to the search for something beyond the frantic materialism of the years since 1970, and the regime's bleak ideology.

The moans of the intellectuals, always the nation's conscience, and the wide awareness of the loss of vitality are signs that spirit still slumbers somewhere beneath the bland surface. The flowers bloom in spring and the deer dart through the forests. The charm of the countryside gives heart. Czechoslovakia is quiet now, but it is not serene.

HUNGARY
The Most Amusing Barracks

EVERY HUNGARIAN SCHOOLCHILD is taught a song for the annual
April 4 celebration of the country's "liberation" by Soviet troops in 1945.
It goes, loosely translated: "Depart on the road, and don't look back.
Your past is a sorrowful thousand years." But, of course, Hungarians
do look back, and with pride, for all the turbulence and suffering of
their history. The national anthem, written in the early nineteenth
century, begins, "God bless Hungary . . ." Regimes have changed, revolutions have come and gone. But the anthem has not changed, even
under a professedly atheist, "proletarian internationalist" Communist
rule.

Hungary is a unique country in many ways. The language, from the
Finno-Ugric group, has nothing to do with the Slavic and Germanic
cultures surrounding it. It was brought by the Magyars (pronounced
Mud-yars), a tribe from east of the Urals who arrived on the Danubian
plains in the centuries after Attila, who died in 455, had opened the
route at the head of the fierce Huns. The start of the thousand years in
the song refers to the reign of Magyar king Stephen I, from 997 to 1038.
He converted the country to Roman Catholicism, preferred to the Eastern rite because the Byzantine emperor was nearer and stronger, so
more to be feared. Stephen established the Church and the state. Despite endless wars and long occupations, the people retained their special identity. It sets them apart from other Europeans, who absorbed
wave after wave of conquerors. That is a matter of both vanity and

sensitivity, if anyone should suggest that Hungarians are therefore somewhat less European than their neighbors. They feel themselves the quintessential continentals.

Nobody else knows Hungarian, so they learn many languages when they can. Before World War II, a travel agent's representative at an Italian train station replied to a compliment on his fluent English, "Madam, I am Hungarian. I speak seventeen languages." Their difficult tongue, unrelated to the major European groups, has both cut Hungarians off from easy access to the great cultural currents and spurred them to special communicating skills. The urge to vault the barrier of cultural isolation produces an enormous effort of translation to comprehend other mentalities. It has a subtle political effect. In *Culture and National Identity*, Béla Köpeczi argued the need for "cultural pluralism" without falling into the forbidden trap of advocating political pluralism in an officially Communist country. In such intricate ways, Hungarian intellectuals can keep up a European debate without running afoul of the official line.

Half the people still live in villages and small, rural towns, but the ambition of Budapest is to be as cosmopolitan as possible. It had been a glittering, frivolous capital, naughty and reckless, swooning to the frenzy of gypsy violins, caroming between delight and despair. There was a story about the wild, dark streak in the Hungarian temperament which shocked and titillated the capitals of Europe in the 1930s. It was said that a song called "Sad Sunday" so deeply moved otherwise normal people that whenever it was played, they would rush to commit suicide by jumping off a Danube bridge. Years later, a French journalist stationed in Budapest admitted he had made it up on a day when there wasn't any other good story, and kept it going for months when it attracted attention. But it was widely believed, because Hungarians traditionally have had an extraordinarily high rate of suicide; they are considered an extremely moody people, and the song was mournful.

The capital is still a city of many charms and memories. Until a little over a hundred years ago, it was two separate cities, Buda on the hills overlooking the broad Danube, Pest on the opposite, flat side. Buda was the ancient town. There are bits of Roman ruins lying in what is now the garden of the Hilton Hotel. But the great fortress which crests the hill dates from the medieval kings. It was completely destroyed during the long battle for the city in World War II, along with all the bridges. The area has been lovingly restored. Little restaurants along the narrow, cobbled streets seek to recapture the carefree Middle European atmosphere of imperial days and the hearty, spicy cuisine. The splendor of the St. Stephen's Cathedral spires dominates the skyline. All around, on the steep slopes, are villas and gardens built in the late nineteenth and early twentieth centuries by the well-to-do. Living in Buda still carries prestige, though housing is usually assigned by Communist authorities. Pest, across the Danube, was a commercial town, built to serve the dignitaries of the court and church. It still has the fashionable shopping streets, the parks and broad squares, the nightclubs and big outdoor restaurants where white wine and goulash are served in summer.

The people make natural hosts, with a manner disdainfully described by some of their intellectuals as smarmy servility but which can just as well be considered extravagant courtesy. It seemed typical that a hotelkeeper, waving goodbye to departing guests, suddenly grabbed some little bottles and ran to present them so the visitors would not go away empty-handed. "It's barack," he said, the powerful apricot brandy which is the national tipple. "It was the Duke of Windsor's favorite drink. It will keep the flavor of Budapest on your tongue a little longer."

Hungarians tell lots of jokes against themselves, which make a gleeful point of boasting about a reputation for being sly, unreliable, good at wriggling out of the snares they get into. One is about the time the leader of the Soviet Union convoked a Communist summit and put a thumbtack on each delegate's chair to test his responses. The Czech sat down and winced, but held his tongue. The Pole sat down and jumped up with a scream. The Hungarian, never trusting, looked first, discreetly brushed off the tack, sat down and then let out a yell. Another, older joke asks the difference between a Hungarian and a Romanian. The answer is that both will sell you their grandmother, but the Romanian will deliver.

Hungarian nostalgia is more brash, swashbuckling, than the sentimentality that glazes Viennese eyes. But people do look back warmly on the old relation with imperial Austria and cultivate close ties when possible. There is an apparently apocryphal story about a post–World War II visit of Otto von Habsburg, son of the last Emperor, Charles, who reigned for only two years before defeat in World War I changed all the maps. Otto was told, with some excitement, that he had arrived just in time for the Austria-Hungary football game the next day, the match of the year. "Excuse me," he inquired, "but against whom are we playing?"

Though the government provides a loyal echo of Soviet positions in the international arena, internally Hungary has managed to achieve the most relaxed, most liberalized society within the Soviet bloc. It has a relatively high standard of living and a relatively low quotient of the alienation or "internal emigration" which afflicts countries like Poland, Czechoslovakia and Romania. The Soviets do not complain as much about economic and social experiments in Hungary that deviate from their own model of Communist society as they do about reform attempts in other Eastern countries, perhaps because the Hungarians inched along with their changes instead of proclaiming spectacular policy turns, but more likely because their fierce revolution in 1956 showed they required more leeway if they were to be kept calm.

Hungary is one of the European countries which have had rubber-band borders; it has stretched over huge territories at some periods, snapping back to the flatlands between the eastern Alps and the Carpathians at others. On the losing side in the two world wars, Hungary is now a small country, not quite as large as Indiana. Many ethnic Hungarians were left outside when the frontiers were redrawn after the collapse of the Austro-Hungarian Empire at the end of World War I, some 3.5 to 4 million, compared to the 10.7 million within the country. The largest group left under alien sovereignty was the 1.7 million in Transylvania, now the westernmost region of Romania. Another 600,000 are now in eastern Czechoslovakia, 477,000 in northern Yugoslavia and 200,000 under Soviet rule in the Carpatho-Ukraine, all areas which had been under Hungarian rule at one time or another but which have been detached. In addition, over a million Hungarian emigrants have settled in Western Europe, the United States and Canada. Successive waves of refugees fleeing political persecution in the nineteenth and twentieth centuries have spread this small, tenacious and homogeneous ethnic group around the world. Sturdy and resourceful, they usually do well.

The country is divided by the Danube, which forms the border with Czechoslovakia beginning at Bratislava, where Hungary, Czechoslovakia and Austria meet, flowing east until it makes a right-angle turn above Budapest and then south through Yugoslavia and Romania to the Black Sea. The great river is Hungary's only access to open water. To the west, the "Little Plain" (Kis-Alföld), the land is undulating, with small hills and highlands. The region's lovely Lake Balaton is a popular summer resort. To the east is a vast flat stretch, a natural breadbasket like Kansas or Iowa but also a natural battlefield. Geography provides

Hungary no protection against the momentum of sweeping armies, which its agricultural advantages incessantly lured. It was not an easy land to settle and to hold.

The Huns and the Magyars after them were vigorous, warring Central Asian tribes who drove into Central Europe. By the end of the first millennium, however, they found themselves under constant attack from their better-organized neighbors. That is why King Stephen, later beatified, and honored still as the national saint, chose to join the Holy Roman Empire system of Christendom and to form a state. His crown, the most revered national relic, was moved to the West for safekeeping during World War II and fell into American hands. Not until 1978 was it returned, when at last Hungarian-American relations had improved after the Cold War and the consequences of the 1956 revolution. Secretary of State Cyrus Vance took it to Budapest as a gesture of reconciliation and recognition, a moment of great joy for Hungarians. Stephen's Arpad dynasty was replaced by a descendant of the French house of Anjou in the fourteenth century, and through marriages and alliances the Hungarian crown was linked with Poland and the West Slavs. But by the sixteenth century, the increasingly mighty Ottoman Turks had overrun the central part of the country. Budapest fell in 1541.

For nearly 150 years, Hungary was under Turkish sovereignty, though the Magyar nobles exercised direct rule. Ottoman overlordship spared the country from the wars of religion as Turkish tolerance, or indifference, permitted the spread of Protestantism, particularly among the feudal lords, who had differences with the landowning Catholic clergy. Nonetheless, Christian Hungary made constant efforts to enlist Western support—from Austria, from France, from England's Cromwell—to expel the Turks. But as a hedge, Hungarian envoys to the Sultan's court continued to practice the outrageous flattery and intrigue required to stay on good terms there.

The period left strains of both cruelty and devious grandeur in Hungarian manners, which kept reappearing. In 1655, the nobles elected the Habsburg Archduke Leopold as King of Hungary in the hope that he would send his armies to drive out the Turks. Hungarian historian Agnes Varkonyi attributes the Turkish siege of Vienna in 1683 to the Sultan's awareness that the powers of Europe were looking to Leopold, by then Emperor, to lead them in reconquering Christian lands. Poland's King Jan III Sobieski came to the relief of Vienna and reversed the tide of battle. For that he is also a Hungarian hero. The Austrians then led the counteroffensive. In 1686, the Austrians succeeded in taking the great red stone fortress of Buda, built atop the steep hill above the Danube. But with their administrative reforms, their Counter-Reformation, their insistence on centralizing and restraining feudal rights over the miserable peasants, the Austrians soon irritated the Magyar lords. For eight years, from 1703 to 1711, the Hungarians fought a war of independence, with some aid from the Habsburgs' long-standing enemy, France. But they were no match for the much better organized, better trained Austrian troops.

The terms of the monarchy then installed, with a degree of autonomy for Hungary, worked to shield it from the evolution away from feudalism as the more western European lands advanced. The nobles grew richer and more flamboyant, their dependents impotent. But their intense nationalism never ebbed, nor the stubborn resistance to Austrian cultural assimilation. By the middle of the nineteenth century, when ferment was spreading across newly industrializing Europe, nationalist demands for political reform would not be stilled. In 1848, the year of revolts, Lajos Kossuth led an uprising in the Hungarian capital and succeeded in establishing a parliamentary democracy. The nobility's exemption from taxes was rescinded and their feudal obligations to the King and Emperor annulled. Kossuth was a dashing, romantic figure. He became an idol. In the tradition of the Holy Alliance formed to save thrones and privileges against Napoleon earlier in the century, Russia intervened in 1849 to help the Austrian emperor quell the revolution. Thus was Hungary's second war of independence lost. Defeat was followed by a generation of bloody, merciless repression.

Kossuth, like all the leaders of the period, was of the nobility. But he was not just a flaming patriot. He was a great statesman, born before his time. His vision is stunning in hindsight. He realized that the empire was crumbling, that the many national minorities under Vienna's rule were growing restive. Later, Austria was weakened in defeat by Prussia and loss of its Italian lands to the new Italian nation-state. Vienna at last ceased its persecution of the Hungarian nationalists and offered reconciliation. Kossuth, from exile, argued against it. It would preserve the privileges of the Hungarian lords and gentry, but at the price of making them Vienna's policemen to repress all the other national minorities in the empire. Instead, he urged the establishment of a great Danube Confederation, including Hungary, Austria, Bohemia, Mora-

via, Serbia and Romania, a great Central European power based not
on national domination but on something like the ties that held the
Swiss together.

Kossuth traveled to England, America and many other countries,
seeking to raise support for Hungary and his anti-imperial idea. He
failed. He died in exile in Italy in 1894, only twenty years before the
outbreak of the war which destroyed the whole existing power system.
Had he succeeded in provoking a transformation of relations among
the empire's minorities, Austria might not have felt obliged to declare
war on Serbia in 1914. There might not have been a first world war.
Doubtless the Russian tsars were due to fall, but without the aggrava-
tion and miseries of war, the Bolsheviks might not have taken over
Russia's revolution. Stalin might have remained a marginal revolutionary terrorist. Adolf Hitler might have completed his life as a minor
Austrian painter. And without all those upheavals, contemporary Europe would not have been partitioned between rival Communist and
non-Communist worlds. Kossuth's vision merits contemplation not just
as a tragically missed alternative of history but as an inspiration for a
distant future. If ever the line now dividing Europe can be overcome,
his idea offers one way of organizing a new continental power balance
with stability based on consent instead of fear and force. Reveries on
what might have been may not be fruitless.

But Europe was shortsighted. When Austria went to war in 1914,
Hungary followed the banner of its King and Emperor to another defeat. The Bolshevik revolution broke out a year before the end of
World War I, electrifying the subject peoples of Europe. As the Austro-
Hungarian regime came crashing down, an attempt was made to establish an independent liberal republic in Budapest. But the weak,
indecisive leader, Mihály Károlyi, resigned when his efforts to form a
Czechoslovak-type democracy were blocked by a combination of monarchists, ultraconservatives and revolutionaries. In the chaos of the
times, a Red Army led by Hungarian Communist Béla Kun seized
power. His soviet lasted 133 turbulent, murderous days in 1919. Romanian troops, with the support of France, which had become the dominant power in the area, led the initial phase of the counterrevolution.
Béla Kun fled, first to Germany and then to the Soviet Union, where
Stalin had him killed in the great purges of the 1930s.

An admiral, the victor of a 1916 battle between the fleets of Austro-
Hungary and Italy in the Adriatic, emerged as the conservative leader.

Miklós Horthy was fifty-one years old at the time, a stolid, hulking member of the country gentry. Since the fall of the republic had led to the brief soviet, he obliged the parliament to name him regent of a nonexistent royal government, instead of founding another republic. He had to preside over dismemberment of the old kingdom's domains, dictated by the victorious Allies in accordance with President Woodrow Wilson's vision of independent nations and fixed by the Treaty of Trianon in 1920.

The treaty was a disaster for Hungary. It lost three-fourths of its historical territory, two-fifths of its prewar population and two-thirds of the Magyar people, including those who had been living as minorities in various other parts of the empire. The area lost to Romania alone was larger than what was left as the Hungarian state; Croatia and Bacska went to Yugoslavia, and Slovakia and Carpatho-Ruthenia to Czechoslovakia, without counting Croatia-Slavonia, which had a medieval union with the kingdom of Hungary but was not always considered an integral, legal part of it. Economic resources were dramatically reduced. Hungary lost 58 percent of its railroad and 60 percent of its road mileage, 84 percent of timber resources, 43 percent of arable land, 83 percent of its iron ore, 29 percent of lignite and 27 percent of bituminous coal deposits. Furthermore, the new borders were hard to defend.

With no fleet and no monarchy, Hungary was ruled by a regent-admiral throughout the interwar years. Horthy led a bloody counter-revolution, but even Hungarian Communists would say later that he was not a fascist or an anti-Semite. He had a passion for bridge, and his favorite partner was a wealthy Jewish industrialist. There were Jewish relatives in his wife's family. In fact, Hungary's fascists pressing for a pro-Nazi regime in the late 1930s and early 1940s sometimes whispered that Horthy resisted because he was part Jewish himself. It was not true, but he did seek to keep a tenuous balance, preserving a right-wing establishment, limiting rights of the Jewish community and promoting Hungary's national interests as he saw them. He had come to power to put down a Communist revolution, and he never forgot it. On ceremonial occasions, he wore his naval uniform, swaggering under yards of looped gold braid.

Hungarian nationalists were obsessed with their thirst for revenge after what they considered the punitive inequity of the Trianon provisions. They felt a natural common cause with Germany and Italy, the other two powers determined to overthrow the provisions of the World

War I settlement, and to shift the European power balance. The combination of a strong pro-German faction, Hitler's success in absorbing Austria and Czechoslovakia without resistance from Britain or France and his offer to restore lost Hungarian lands led Horthy to ally his country with Nazi Germany after an agreement in Vienna in November 1938. In stages, he took Ruthenia from Czechoslovakia, Transylvania from Romania and areas from Yugoslavia, revising the Trianon borders. When Germany attacked the Soviet Union in 1941, Hungary also declared war, and later against Britain and the United States as well.

During most of the war years, Hungary's adhesion to the Axis served as a shield against the raging storms around it. Units were sent to fight alongside German troops in the Soviet Union. But Germany needed Hungary's supplies of grain more than its soldiers. The thriving Jewish community in Budapest was protected from Nazi deportation, but not Jews elsewhere. Horthy's regime was no democracy, but it was not so severe as other dictatorships in the period. There was an opposition press, and opposition parties were represented in the parliament. Thousands of Allied prisoners of war who had managed to escape, especially Poles and Frenchmen, were given refuge. Hungary seemed almost an island of peace. By 1943, Horthy had come to realize that once again his country was on the losing side. In the old tradition of Hungarians who salaamed before Turkish sultans and secretly sought Western support against them, he began looking for a way to take the country out of the war. He hoped not only to avoid destructive battles, but to prevent a Soviet occupation and maintain Hungary's political institutions by agreement with the United States and Britain.

Envoys were sent rushing to the neutral capitals of Switzerland, Portugal and Turkey to make contact with the Allies. American and British bombers were allowed to overfly Hungary without hindrance on their way to German targets. Of course, all these frantic but supposedly secret efforts did not escape Hitler's spies. Berlin drew up a top-secret "Project Margarethe," apparently named for the Danube pleasure-park island just outside Budapest. In early March 1944 the Hungarian government learned that German troops were massing on the borders. Hitler summoned Horthy to a meeting at Klessheim, near Salzburg in Austria. Raging, the Führer accused the Hungarian leader of betrayal. He demanded dismissal of the Prime Minister and formation of a new, pro-German government, on the model of puppet regimes established in Nazi-occupied countries. While Horthy was still on the train riding home from the fierce encounter, German troops marched into Hungary at dawn on March 19, 1944. They met no resistance. It would have been useless. Opposition deputy Endré Bajcsy-Zsilinszky fired the only shots, at German agents sent to arrest him at his home.

The Gestapo with its long lists of suspects took over, sweeping up politicians, intellectuals and Jews for deportation. Premier Miklós Kállay was shipped to Dachau. Overnight, the illusion of serenity and having wangled safely through the abyss of war was destroyed. In the last year of the war, Hungary was plunged into Nazi terror, the mass murder of Jews and the full thrust of battle. There had never been any real chance that the Western Allies would arrive before the Soviets. That too had been an illusion. When the Soviet army arrived at the outskirts of Budapest in December 1944, the Germans had completely taken over. They were ordered to resist as long as possible. The destruction of Budapest was of no concern to them. The Russians and the Germans fought for two months, street by street. The old castle on the Buda hill had been transformed into a baroque château in the days of the dual monarchy, but it was still of strategic value as a fort. The Germans dug in, and the Soviets gradually demolished it. Admiral Horthy was whisked away to Germany, and was eventually captured by American troops. He was allowed to take up exile in Portugal, where he finished his days at Estoril in the company of deposed kings. The Red Army established itself in Hungary and never went home.

As a former enemy belligerent, Hungary was a subject for special agreement among the Big Three allies. The prewar borders were reimposed. The agreement provided for a control commission representing the three powers and, once calm was restored, elections under its supervision. A vote was held in November 1945. The result was a great shock to Stalin. Of course, everything had been done by the Soviet occupants to give all possible advantages to the Communists. Nonetheless, the elections were conducted fairly enough to produce a victory for the liberal-democratic Smallholders' Party. They won 57 percent. The Communist Party scored a meager 17 percent. Never again was a foreign-supervised election permitted in any of the countries or areas where Soviet troops held sway, despite the solemn wartime agreements.

There are many arguments about the origins of the Cold War and the transformation of the Yalta agreement, originally an accord to provide for transition from war to peace but which turned into a blueprint

for dividing Europe. They cannot be settled objectively. But certainly
the Hungarian elections played an important role. They reinforced
Stalin's determination to Sovietize the whole of the area his troops had
captured. What minimal risks he had been willing to take through diplomacy and persuasion were ruled out by the evidence that Soviet
"liberators" were not long welcome. From then until Stalin's death in
1953, the fate of Eastern European countries was homogenized.

Communist Hungary, like the others, was obliged to launch a purge.
The star victim of Budapest's show trial was Laszlo Rajk, Foreign Minister (his last post). But there were eight defendants, carefully assem-
bled to represent the various elements of existing Communist rule
which Stalin wanted to eliminate. They included Yugoslavs denounced
as Titoist agents, Jews, suspected nationalists, Social Democrats and
army officers. The major charge against Rajk was sympathy for the
Communist heretic Tito, who had been excommunicated from Stalin's
church for seeking to put his own country's interests ahead of the Soviet
Union's. The defendants were forced to confess to outrageous fictions.
Rajk and two others were hanged in 1949. The two military men were
shot. Many other Communists were arrested, often without benefit of
stage-managed trials. Among them were former Premier Imre Nagy and
János Kádár, who was brutally tortured. Kádár had replaced Rajk as
Interior Minister in 1948, in effect head of the police, including the
dreaded AVH, Hungary's version of the Soviets' KGB. But in 1951 he
too fell victim to the thugs he had commanded.

The leadership of the party, and thus the country, was taken over by
Mátyás Rákosi, a savage, arrogant man who was pleased to execute the
worst of Stalin's orders. The survivors began to be released in 1954, a
year after Stalin's death and the arrival of Nikita Khrushchev at the
apex of Soviet power. It had taken Khrushchev time to win the fight for
succession within the Kremlin, but once he felt secure he began moves
to prevent the recurrence of political cannibalism within the Communist hierarchies. Kádár and Nagy were readmitted to the party and given
important posts.

In February 1956, Khrushchev took a more decisive step to launch
what came to be called "de-Stalinization." At the Twentieth Congress
of the Soviet Communist Party that year, he delivered a secret speech
denouncing the man who had made himself the living god of the Communist world, attacking him for crimes against Communists (though
not against the other people who had been killed and persecuted) and

foreign policy errors, including the break with Yugoslavia. The speech stirred great ferment in the Eastern European Communist parties. It was taken to justify demands for release of people still imprisoned, for rehabilitation of purge victims and for various reforms. A workers' demonstration in Poland in June 1956, put down with fifty-four deaths and three hundred wounded, opened a period of gradually mounting turmoil in that country.

Intellectuals and students in Hungary followed Polish events closely. Rákosi was forced out of the leadership in July as discontent brewed among Hungarian Communists. He was replaced by Ernö Gerö, considered less of a monster, but little else changed. Then, in October, Polish Communists forced the ouster of their leader in favor of Wład-ysław Gomułka, defying Soviet threats. All of a sudden, the monolithic Stalinist empire seemed to be cracking apart. In Budapest, Hungarian students joyously organized a celebration march to the statue of Joseph Bem, a nineteenth-century Polish hero who had fought with Napoleon in Russia, with Polish insurgents in the 1830 revolution and with Hungarian rebels in 1848–49. The students prepared a list of demands for reform in Hungary to match the liberalizing aspirations of the Poles. A few thousand gathered at Bem's statue on October 23. That was enough to embolden the people, so long mute in repression. Someone suggested marching on to the parliament buildings. By the time the demonstrators reached the great open square beside the Danube, the crowd had swollen to hundreds of thousands. People began calling for Imre Nagy, considered the most reform-minded of the Communist leadership, and he made a brief speech. Part of the crowd went on to the huge statue of Stalin, which every Communist capital had been required to erect, and in their fury toppled it. The first shots were fired by the AVH secret police into a crowd in front of the Radio Building, where students were trying to get their petition broadcast. Soldiers joined the demonstrators and distributed arms to workers from the barracks and ordinary police stations. It was the start of a spontaneous national uprising.

The party leadership held an emergency meeting and decided on simultaneous measures of repression and concession. They co-opted Nagy into the Politburo, arranging to make him Premier once again. But they also asked Soviet armed forces stationed in Hungary to come to the capital to put down what they considered the start of a counter-revolution. The first tanks arrived at dawn on October 24. At noon,

Nagy addressed the country by radio, promising some democratization, higher living standards and the development of independent Hungarian communism. He appealed for an end to the fighting. But it spread, not only through Budapest but to other major cities. The next day, Ernö Gerö was replaced as First Secretary by János Kádár, who seemed to be in tune with Nagy. He promised to seek negotiations with the Soviets, including a request for withdrawal of the seventy thousand Soviet troops stationed in Hungary as part of the Warsaw Pact forces.

That afternoon, however, Soviet tank crews, who seemed to mistake fire from Hungarian police at the people in front of the parliament buildings as an attack on their unit, shot blindly into the unarmed crowd. There was a massacre. More fighting broke out around the country. The rebels took over a radio station in the town of Györ and began broadcasting what was happening, contradicting the lies and distortions of the official radio. By October 28 the movement had such momentum that the Communist Party paper *Szabad Nep* proclaimed it "a great national democratic movement, led by Communist and non-party intellectuals" and not a "counterrevolutionary fascist attempt at a coup d'état," which had been the official line. Important parts of the Communist Party itself were changing sides. Nagy promised to disband the secret police. The following day the Minister of Defense said Soviet troops would withdraw and maintenance of order would be left to the Hungarian army, largely in sympathy with the demonstrators. The Russians actually moved out of Budapest. The rebels seemed to have won.

The Kremlin appeared stunned. Moscow called a meeting with foreign Communist leaders, including China's. But something happened between October 30 and November 1. Some Hungarian Communist officials said later that China, which had been in sympathy with Polish reform demands and seemed to support the Hungarians, switched when Nagy appealed to the United Nations and proclaimed Hungarian neutrality. Massive Soviet intervention was endorsed. New Soviet troops began pouring into Hungary, some crossing Czechoslovakia from bases in the Ukraine. Nagy protested the Red Army's invasion to Soviet Ambassador Yuri Andropov, later to become head of the KGB and then briefly Soviet First Secretary. He told Andropov that Hungary was quitting the Warsaw Pact. That night, Kádár made a speech praising the "glorious uprising" which brought "freedom for the people and independence for the country" but warned against counterrevolution. Then he disappeared from Budapest. He is believed to have gone to the

Soviet Union to plan the overthrow of Nagy and the restoration of Communist monopoly power.

The borders with Austria had been thrown open by the people. Reporters and photographers flocked into the country so the whole world could know how Hungarians were fighting for their freedom. One famous picture showed a boy in embattled Budapest throwing a bottle with a wick—the "Molotov cocktail" which unarmed Russians had used in futile attempts to resist the advancing Nazis in World War II—at a Soviet tank. They were days of great drama. Urgent appeals were broadcast to the Western countries for help. None came, only encouraging commentaries telling the overwhelmed Hungarians to keep up their struggle.

By one of those tragic coincidences of history, Britain, France and Israel embarked at this time on a war against Egypt to force its leader, Gamal Abdel Nasser, to revoke his nationalization of the Suez Canal. It was a totally bungled, inefficient campaign. But when it seemed that Egypt would be defeated, Moscow threatened to intervene and dispatch troops to help Egypt. That sent shock waves throughout Eastern Europe. People in Poland, in Czechoslovakia, in Romania, had been deeply stirred by Hungary's heroic fight, which no amount of local censorship could prevent them from following minute by minute on foreign radio broadcasts. They began to ask themselves why their own countries were not joining the Hungarians in a great, mass breakout for freedom. They had been called the "captive nations" by the West. It was time to pull down the jail. The Soviet empire was threatened with collapse. But it was only eleven years after World War II. Memories were still vivid. When they heard the reports from Suez and the escalation of threats, people also began to ask whether they were witnessing the start of World War III. The possibility was so terrifying that it paralyzed those who would have liked to follow the Hungarian example. They waited, at the end of their nerves, for a sign of where the world was going and how Moscow and the West might react to a generalized uprising throughout the East.

In Budapest, Hungarian military leaders began negotiations with a Soviet delegation on withdrawal of the Red Army. Jozsef Cardinal Mindszenty, who had been arrested in December 1948 and then freed in the uprising, spoke on the radio on the night of November 3. He called for free elections with international supervision and peace without enmity toward any nation, in effect an offer to Moscow. But at midnight, the Hungarian delegation was arrested. By 4 A.M. on November 4, eight Soviet divisions had attacked Budapest and other key cities, occupying airfields, bridges, railway yards and all strategic points. Nagy made his last broadcast at 4:20 A.M., announcing the Soviet attack and the determination of the government and the army to resist.

But Kádár soon followed with a broadcast on a Soviet-controlled radio station announcing that he had formed a new "Hungarian Revolutionary Worker-Peasant government." The Russian blow was overwhelming. Nagy and some of his ministers took refuge in the Yugoslav Embassy. Cardinal Mindszenty fled to the American Embassy. Budapest's free radio was silenced. For several days, free-radio broadcasts from the countryside reported on the continued fierce fighting against Soviet forces and pleaded vainly for Western help. The Yugoslavs, claiming they had secured safe passage for Nagy and his group from the Russians, evacuated them, ostensibly on their way to exile in Yugoslavia. But it was a ruse. Once out of the embassy, they were seized and killed after a secret trial. Mindszenty lived in the American Embassy for fifteen years, until finally Pope Paul VI negotiated his release and expatriation.

Hungary's spectacular fight for freedom was crushed. The Soviet empire remained intact. There had been smaller-scale popular uprisings in Eastern Europe earlier, in Plzeň in Czechoslovakia in 1953, in East Berlin in 1953, in Poznań in Poland in the summer of 1956. But the collapse of the vast Hungarian effort was a watershed. That was what really sealed the Yalta partition of Europe, and implicitly assured the Soviets that their hegemony east of the Elbe River border between the two parts of Germany would not be challenged by the West. The Hungarian events amounted to a kind of international ratification of the lines drawn at the end of World War II. Things might have gone differently if it had not been for the Suez war, if people in other parts of the Soviet bloc had acted on their instincts to demand a new basis for relations with Moscow. As it was, the fate of Europe was fixed, probably for generations.

Hungary itself was traumatized. Everything afterward derived from what happened in 1956. Hundreds of thousands fled the country while the borders were still open and resettled in distant lands. The people who remained resigned themselves to the regime. There was a period of fierce repression and retribution. But the regime itself had been totally shaken. Napoleon said you can do anything with bayonets except sit on them. Still, while force had cowed the country, it could not revive its economy or productive capacity. It could not re-create the myth of Communist idealism, the pretense of legitimacy based on the support of workers and peasants for rule in their name. The Communist Party had had 900,000 members in September 1956. In December, it had 30,000. There were several years of bitter stagnation. National life was reduced to mere existence.

Then, in 1961, János Kádár made an audacious decision. He was hated as a Soviet puppet, the man who had betrayed Nagy and the nation. To reverse that, to revitalize the country, he would have to make some concession to the people. He offered a reconciliation, a tacit deal which would set limits on the people's aspirations in return for limits on the powers of the regime. The words he used were, "Whoever is not against us is with us." This was a startling change from the still prevailing Stalinist theme throughout Eastern Europe. It had been, in effect, "Whoever is not with us is against us," and that was the grounds for exacting obeisance, praise and unstinting lip service to the regimes. Kádár was saying that refraining from open opposition was now enough.

People were skeptical at first and cautious. They had been badly hurt. But they gradually realized this meant whole areas of life were to be freed from the deadly hand of all-pervasive ideology. Art, music, even literature, so long as it had no political content, were removed from strict party dictation. There was to be room for individual choice, initiative, techniques, a kind of pluralism so long as it did not spill over into politics. Nothing was institutionalized, no rights were explicitly granted. But the bargain began to have important effects. It is a peculiar kind of social contract, unwritten, without guarantees, but well understood by both the people and the regime.

The rules require acceptance of close ties with the Soviet Union and support of its foreign policy, in return for regime acceptance of limits on the dominating role of the Communist Party and its ideology. In 1968, a series of economic reforms were launched which bolstered the compact. Living standards improved dramatically. People began to breathe and to work. Kádár's image changed completely. He was seen as the architect of the best, or at any rate the least bad, compromise possible between the exigencies of belonging to the Soviet empire and sustaining satisfactory nationhood. His authority was confirmed on this basis, and he actually became popular.

But it was a very personal authority. The relative success of the Hungarian system rested upon his skills, his instincts, his unusual personality. His deeply lined face, with the sad eyes and drooping lips of a bloodhound, expressed the profoundly tragic experiences of his own and his country's life. But he reveals no sentiment. He is a very private man, austere, with none of the taste for adulation, pomp or extravagant indulgence of whims which has marked most Communist rulers. He is tough but restrained. He does not reveal himself, and not a great deal is known about him.

Kádár joined the clandestine Communist Party at age nineteen. Kádár may be the name he took at that time to give himself a new, independent identity, for he used the Slavic name Csermanek as a youth. He was often arrested, by the Hungarian police before World War II, by the Gestapo during the war and by his own Hungarian Communist police during the Stalin purges. He has never revealed his feelings about the treatment he received, except to say that he felt less hurt by the torture than by the accusation that he was not an honorable man and a good Communist.

Kádár's behavior was certainly that of a true believer, never shaken in his faith in communism, and that may be what eventually gave him the flexibility and suppleness to accept compromise and launch reform. After 1956 he rebuilt the utterly shattered Hungarian party with more concern for competence and ability than is the case in other Eastern European ruling parties, which are usually stuffed with opportunists, dunderheads and fawning, self-serving yes-men. He has been able to suppress corruption, rampant in most Communist countries, a factor in the approval he has won. He lives in a small, unpretentious house and seldom appears on social occasions, preferring to watch a movie or television at home for diversion.

The biggest question is whether the "Hungarian model" of more or less reform communism can be maintained without him. He is said to have wanted to retire in 1972, but changed his mind when he saw it would bring sharp factional infighting for the succession and endanger the balance he had achieved. The instruments of repression, the institutions of dictatorship, remain in place. A less talented successor might not manage to sustain stability without reverting to their use. But in the end, the fate of Hungary's experiment depends on what happens in the Soviet Union. Moscow's policy, domestic and foreign, places the real limits on both the Hungarian regime and the people who submit to it.

Ironically, however, just when leader Mikhail Gorbachev was moving to press important reforms somewhat similar to Hungary's on the Soviet bureaucracy, the Hungarian "model" showed signs of running out of steam. Discontent surged at the frenetic pace required to make the most of opportunities to work privately, and at the resulting inequalities and deprivations for those who could not or would not keep up. The economy began to stagnate again, and the hidden fight for the succession became more and more intense.

More than thirty years after their devastating upheaval, Hungarians say, "We are socialists in the morning and capitalists in the afternoon." It is a reference to the peculiar mix of the economy and the social system. The state runs the official economy, with the central planning that communism decrees, though with a good deal more leeway for industrial managers to direct their specific enterprises. Ede Horváth, general manager of the giant Rába engineering firm, explained his unprecedented decision to lay off workers in 1980, saying, "The constitution guarantees every citizen the right to a job, but it doesn't stipulate that it has to be here in my factories. . . . It isn't possible for Rába to pay for superfluous people." "Morning socialism" means working for the state, having to meet norms, but also the right to benefits of the state-administered health services, pension scheme, education and so on. The Hungarian reforms permit managers to adjust pay scales to productivity within certain limits, and in certain cases to have direct involvement in foreign trade instead of having to go through a centralized trade ministry. More than two-thirds of the national income depends on foreign trade, and half of the trade is with Western countries. There was a deliberate effort to reduce dependence on Soviet-bloc trading partners in the expansive 1970s, to force the better quality controls and competitive productivity that the Western market requires and to earn the hard currency needed for modern equipment and special materials.

The Ikarus bus factory in Budapest is an example of the odd result. There, an American reporter observed, the difference between the American and Soviet way of life comes down to a radiator. Ikarus produces over half of the Soviet Union's buses, which means they have to be turned out at the rate of seventy a day. When a radiator doesn't fit, a worker kicks it into the bus frame with his boot. But the same plant makes buses for Houston and several other U.S. and European cities. They are built in a separate shed, where the skilled workers call them-

selves the *haute couture* group. They spend a lot more time to make
sure the painting and welding are up to Western standards. And when
they install radiators, the reporter noted, "they gently nudge them into
place."

Hungary, like Poland, tried to make an economic leap forward after
the oil crisis with massive Western credits for modernization. But then
the recession at the beginning of the 1980s drastically shrank Western
markets, limiting exports with which the debts could be repaid. With
the added burden of increased interest rates, Hungary nearly went
bankrupt in 1982. The need to cajole more effort from workers, and the
rise of the Solidarity trade union in Poland, which Kádár watched
uneasily, led to some further reforms and relaxation. The official Hungarian labor union, modeled, like those in the rest of the bloc, on Soviet
authoritarian practice, was urged to be more alert to worker grievances
and provide a little more authentic representation. No free union
movement arose, but the regime bent a bit to make the union it runs
less irrelevant. It is symptomatic of Kádár's rule to prescribe an aspirin
at home when a fever of independence breaks out in another Communist society.

Alongside the essentially orthodox Communist economy, what is
called the secondary or parallel economy has been allowed to develop.
It is the steam valve which releases pressure on the regime. That is the
capitalist afternoon. Small shops, restaurants, repair businesses and the
like have been allowed to flourish as private enterprise. János Fekete,
the elegant president of the national bank, said, "Not everybody likes
what we are doing. They are afraid we are being capitalist. But I say
that it's logic." The private sector, he insisted, will never account for
more than 5 percent of the national income.

But others say the unofficial economy accounts for 30 percent of the
gross domestic product, and that eight out of ten Hungarians have
some kind of extra job or income. Two-thirds of the country's apartments are built completely or partly in the tolerated black market. State
construction firms often do not complete their buildings, and future
tenants must make an agreement with teams of workers for after-hours
jobs to make their new homes livable. Some forms of this kind of private
initiative have been legalized, and the workers are allowed to use their
firms' equipment on their own time. This shadow economy has indeed
provided Hungarians with some Western-style services that more rigidly
managed Communist systems simply fail to deliver. There is far more

choice of goods in the shops. Váci Utca, Budapest's Madison Avenue or Bond Street, is once again a row of high-fashion windows. Hungarian women, often stunning beauties, need not be ashamed of their home-bought outfits when they go on a trip to the West. With money to be made and things to buy, people work harder than in other bloc countries. They produce better. Hungarian goods have a high reputation in the East, even though the artificial pricing system for Eastern trade brings the kind of differentiated output of the Ikarus plant. In Moscow, when word gets around that a shop has received a new shipment of Hungarian cosmetics, a huge queue forms immediately.

But the "capitalist afternoon" also exacts its price. Most people have two or even three jobs, an official one to be eligible for benefits and a private one to make money. It has brought a peculiar distortion in wealth, since not everyone has the particular qualifications that the limited private sector prizes. A carpenter or a mason can make much more than an engineer, because housing is in short supply and there is a tremendous private demand for builders and remodelers. An estimated one-fifth to one-quarter of the population lives at the poverty line. One person in ten lives on less than half the average per capita income.

Kádár told the 1980 Communist Party Congress that "we should resolutely reject the appealing notion and easygoing practice of egalitarianism." But there isn't a lot else that communism has been able to offer its devotees. "We work like madmen to keep up our standards, and our standards are high," a Hungarian journalist said. The mortality rate of men between forty and sixty years of age is considerably higher than in other industrialized countries. Those who won't or can't keep up the frenzied race see their purchasing power constantly declining. It could be said that Hungarians wind up with the worst of both systems, the constraints of communism and the material obsessions of capitalism without much of the benefits. The strain and illogic of the limited secondary economy may be another source of eventual instability in Kádár's special system. George Schöpflin, an English academic specialist on Eastern Europe, has pointed out that the mix led to the socially damaging "emergence of two contradictory value systems—one private and one public."

Hungary's greatest success, which makes possible all the rest, has been in agriculture. It has the only collective farm system that works. After 1956, Poland abandoned the effort to force peasants into collectives, leaving them on tiny private plots which had been distributed by a misleading land reform right after the war, when the Communists were trying to win supporters.

Hungary maintained its collectives but instituted a number of incentives to improve output. The state made large-scale investments in agriculture and permitted private plots where farmers could grow food not only for themselves but to sell in town. They were allowed to use the collective's equipment and facilities for their own purposes when they had done their share of work for the state. Particularly important, as industrialization was pursued, processing plants and small factories were established on the collective farms with considerable latitude for management. Instead of driving farm boys into huge plants in the cities, Hungary kept them on the land by providing forms of industrial work that could be done alongside farm work. It developed a kind of agribusiness that is not much different from flourishing Western agriculture except for the fact of ownership.

There is an unending argument among specialists in the East and the West about whether the "Hungarian model" offers guidelines for reforming communism generally, or whether it is inimitable. Certainly, the implicit compact forged between the regime and the people after 1956 was the basis for it, and it may not be enduring. It remains to be seen what happens after Kádár. Nor have other Communist countries really tried Hungary's complex system of incentives and search for efficiency. China under Deng Xiaoping may be the exception, but the vastness and backwardness of China make it impossible to compare its modernization and reform program with other countries'.

For Hungarians, in any case, the result has made their country "the most amusing barracks in the camp," as a young punk with spiky hair and a safety-pin earring put it. The guitarist of the New Wave music group Lavina (Avalanche) told a visitor, "In Hungary, nothing is impossible and nothing is possible. Every day we come up against bureaucracy, skepticism, lies, pull, the mafia. Listen to the words of U.H.R. [U.H.R., slang meaning the police are driving up, is the name of another rock group.] 'This city is a prostitute. I hate her when she satisfies me.' " The youth subculture is restless but not defiant, because the youngsters in their outlandish garb are well aware that they have comparative privilege in terms of other Communist societies.

So long as the Soviet Union is determined to maintain its bloc as an ideological camp, accepting minor variations but no political challenge, it is hard to see how Hungary can evolve beyond its present precarious compromise. But so long as the people are determined to assert their own sense of themselves, it is hard to see how a straitjacket could be reimposed without provoking profound and possibly violent resistance. The country is obliged to live a kind of day-to-day existence, without asking too many questions of the future. The furious pace of work, the search for comfort and pleasure are in part a deliberate effort to drive out thoughts which cannot be expressed, hopes which cannot be answered. There isn't much point to looking ahead, so people look back, despite the official song. Meanwhile, they live on.

"You know," said a teenager named Tamas, "life isn't too hard here. And when you really want a breath of fresh air, you can get out of the country for a bit. We're resigned to living under the guardianship of Big Brother, but we still have our sense of humor. Everybody knows that the Soviet troops temporarily stationed on our territory have established permanent lodging in Hungary."

ROMANIA
The Lights Went Out

ROMANIA HAS LONG BEEN CALLED a maverick country, and it keeps finding new ways to prove that it is indeed different. It is the only Latin state in southeastern Europe, surrounded by Slavs and Magyars. But while many of its Slav neighbors are Roman Catholics with traditions looking to the West, Romanians received their religion from Byzantium via Bulgaria, though not their alphabet. They remain Orthodox Catholics but use Roman letters. Before World War II, Bucharest delighted in its sobriquet "Paris of the East," a frivolous, pleasure-loving capital, stylish, with grand tree-lined avenues and vast squares, places to promenade in finery. Cultural life was greatly influenced by France. But politics were tough, with a strong fascist movement and an affinity for Germany. Afterward, like all the rest of the area occupied by Soviet forces, Romania went Communist, something of a tour de force because the Romanian Communist Party had eight hundred members at the end of the war, of whom half were in exile and many were from ethnic minorities. The country managed to get rid of Soviet troops in 1957, the year after the invasion of Hungary, and to establish a foreign policy divergent from and sometimes openly contradictory to Moscow's.

Romania found a way to teeter between the Soviets and China when the two great Communist powers broke relations and all the rest of Eastern Europe had to follow Moscow's line. It helped to arrange Chinese-American contacts when President Richard Nixon was secretly planning his dramatic trip of reconciliation. It refused to follow the Soviet bloc in breaking relations with Israel after the Six Day War in 1967, and helped establish the contacts that led to Egyptian President Anwar Sadat's spectacular visit to Jerusalem. It was the only Warsaw Pact country which denounced the 1968 Soviet invasion of Czechoslovakia and did not participate with troops, and the only one to take part in the 1984 Olympics in Los Angeles.

But it was also the only Warsaw Pact member to make scarcely any effort to experiment with economic reform, maintaining a rigidly orthodox Stalinist system and a sycophantic "cult of personality" long after the others had backed away. It has a witty, saucy intellectual elite, almost totally silenced, and a glum, deeply depressed population, which has suffered far worse deprivations than those which drove Polish workers to create the Solidarity movement. There was scarcely more resistance than mutters of "Thank God it isn't worse." It ought to be the richest country in the region, with oil, minerals and unusually large resources of fertile land, and it became the poorest. Juliana G. Pilon, an academic who fled into exile, wrote of her benighted land that it had been turned "from the breadbasket of Europe into a basket case" where bread was rationed.

Nicolae Ceauşescu, the lifelong Communist who came to power in 1965, styled himself "Conducator," which means the leader, just as Der Führer and Il Duce do. His wife, Elena, took second place in the hierarchy, and some sixty members of his family manned the upper echelons in a fashion little short of imperial. Playing on Stalin's dictum of the 1920s that Soviet policy of that period should concentrate on "building socialism in one country," Romanians came to say that their state's contribution to ideology was "building socialism in one family." All the trappings of Marxist-Leninist theory were present, total state monopoly of the economy without even restaurants or taxis left to private enterprise, and a huge Communist Party of 3.5 million in 1985 (in a population of 23 million) with control of everything. An official claimed that a proof of Romania's "democratic" management was that in factories the head of the party unit was invariably the head of the workers' council, and the deputy head of the unit was the factory manager. A saddened, terribly hard-pressed but still spunky artist said, "We do have real equality here—at the very bottom and at the lowest possible level."

Somehow the texture of Romanian society doesn't seem to have much to do with communism at all, though the windy slogans express the conventional dogmas. It is much more reminiscent of the worst traditional Byzantine despotism, functioning by fear, venality, cultivation of deviousness to circumvent an unbudgeable, swollen bureaucracy, patronage and, above all, the unquestionable whim of one man, one family. Some say that one out of every four Romanians works directly or indirectly for the secret police. Others say no, it is one in three. It is hard to tell whether Romania's "difference" provoked what happened, or whether it was the result.

It is a relatively large country, twelfth in area in Europe, the size of Oregon. The climate runs to extremes; in a typical year the temperature in Bucharest descends to −11°F during the long, hard winter and up to 102° in summer. But nature favored it topographically, with a generous balance of plains, plateaus and mountains, rivers and woods and beaches. The scenery is awesome in parts, in the peaks of the Carpathians in Transylvania and the raw majesty of the Iron Gates, where the Danube flows through a deep gorge cut between rugged red cliffs. In other areas it is bucolic, bright fields rolling over gentle hills, wildflowers alongside the narrow roads. Peasant traditions are strong; villagers sing and dance and flaunt their brilliantly embroidered costumes as they have for centuries. But the lands they till no longer bear the name of an aristocratic proprietor, they have been turned into collectives with such names as "The New Life" or "In the Socialist Way." Over a quarter of the people still make their living in agriculture, though the men have been drained off to the factories and four out of five farm workers are women. The men send money home to help their families.

Like the rest of the Balkans, Romania was late in developing, cut off from the European mainstream by Turkish overlordship, with feudal habits and extremes of wealth and poverty. For all the cosmopolitan sophistication of the capital, the people were largely illiterate well into the twentieth century. In Western eyes, Romania was embodied in dazzling blond actresses such as Elvira Popescu or the ingeniously surrealistic dramatist Eugene Ionesco, exciting figures who were part of the general sparkle of European culture. There were writers and painters and professors who could be at home anywhere, and who contributed to the saying that "Romanian isn't a nationality, it's a profession."

As World War II approached, Bucharest was a fabled capital of intrigue, high life, refugees and espionage. The dowager Queen Marie, of royal British and Russian descent, was a breathtaking world figure who deliberately attracted attention with the extravagance of her wardrobe and her dalliances. Her biographer, Hannah Pakula, called her "the last romantic." The Athenée Palace Hotel was an international center for the people whose names provided the glitter of gossip columns and, no doubt, for many whose names fattened police dossiers. For some years afterward, it was still elegant but the comfortable chairs in the lobby and by the elevators on each floor were occupied by sharp-eyed, awkwardly dressed men who pretended to read the same newspaper all day long. Now the police are still there, but the hotel is dark and shabby, with miserable little refrigerators that never work in each room and cheap furniture with the veneer splitting off.

Romania has always been a land of great beauty and great hardship, a slow place moving no faster nor further with the centuries than a horse-drawn cart can move. The original inhabitants were Dacians, a people whom Herodotus described as "the most valiant and righteous of the Thracians." They had an advanced civilization with achievements in music, astronomy and medicine and wrote in both the Greek and Latin alphabets. Under Emperor Trajan, Rome conquered Dacia in A.D. 106 after long, stubborn campaigns spanning more than a generation. The conquest was followed by intensive colonization in which the populations merged, creating a new Daco-Roman ethnicity with strong roots and high culture. The Latin poet Ovid lived much of his life in exile at Tomis, near Constantsa, a subtropical city on the Black Sea whose languid climate and pleasant life encouraged thoughts of romantic love. Because of its prosperity, the province was known as Dacia Felix, one of the empire's most agreeable and civilized. In A.D. 271, Emperor Aurelian officially withdrew the Roman legions to tighten his embattled defenses. Historians disagree about the mixture of peoples after that. But the dominant view is that large numbers of the colonists had stayed on, and resisted assimilation by waves of invading Asian tribes who moved into Europe in the second half of the millennium. The language and the customs remained firmly based on Latin culture.

But the people were unable to organize their society in the face of succeeding onslaughts by Goths, Slavs, Avars, Bulgars and Magyars. After the conversion of the Bulgarian Tsar Boris in 864, during a period of Bulgarian dominion in Dacia, Christianity was brought to the region in its eastern, Byzantine form. That was the origin of Romania's Orthodox faith. It had lost all ties with Rome. Magyar advances drove the people into the Carpathians, where they became known as the Vlach tribes and established an independent kingdom in Transylvania in the second half of the tenth century. In the eleventh century, they were conquered by King Stephen and Transylvania was incorporated into his kingdom of Hungary.

The dispute persists today over whether Transylvania should be considered historically as a Romanian or Hungarian land. Romania's large Hungarian minority is concentrated there, and its treatment is a constant source of friction with Hungary because of attempts at forced assimilation. The capital of Transylvania, called Cluj in Romanian and Kolozsvár in Hungarian, is a large, handsome old city with proud traditions. Records of the area's early inhabitants were all destroyed during a Mongol invasion in 1241. It was not until the end of that century that existing documents confirm the development of two Romanian principalities, one south of the Carpathians, called Valachia, and the other to the east, called Moldavia. They remained separate until 1774, when their annals were combined under a uniform Turkish administration.

The Turkish advance had begun in the fifteenth century. Valachia sought help from the Bulgars and the Serbs, first against Hungary and then against the Turks, but all the sovereignties of the region were succumbing to the overwhelming Turkish expansion. Joint Christian forces, with expeditions from France and Burgundy, were defeated at the Battle of Nikopol in 1396. Valachia was finally forced to capitulate to Sultan Muhammad I in 1417, but in subjection was allowed to maintain its dynasty, territory and religion. Resistance continued under Hungarian leadership until the death of the unbelievably cruel local Romanian ruler Vlad IV. His full name was Vlad Dracul, but he was known as Vlad Tepes (Vlad the Impaler) because of his atrocities. He was the origin of the story of Dracula, the vampire. Some say the myth of his depraved rituals was deliberately spread to Western Europe by subjects who sought revenge by defaming him. But with or without satanic connotations, his behavior was monstrous enough to inspire the nineteenth-century novelist Bram Stoker's horror story. His supposed tomb lies in a little chapel on an island in Lake Snagov, not far from Bucharest. Romanians are of two minds about his memory, because for all his crimes he did mount an effective opposition to the Turks, but it collapsed after him.

Over the next two centuries, there were fitful but generally unsuccessful efforts to wrench free from Turkish suzerainty. At the start of the seventeenth century, Michael the Brave did amass enough support from Christian powers to win battles and establish a kingdom under the Habsburg emperor, although it was short-lived. Nonetheless, he is remembered as Romania's leading national hero because for the first time since the Roman period he brought the Romanians of Transylvania, Valachia and Moldavia under a single rule and established the goal of full national unity, which was not to be realized again until 1918. Michael's was the last stand against Turkish domination, which was exercised increasingly through Greek surrogates.

The Turks moved the capital to Bucharest in 1608, away from the frontier of restive Transylvania, and appointed a series of local rulers who both accepted and intrigued against their dominion. By the start of the eighteenth century, the Sultan's vast power had entered decline and reinforcement was sought by shifting to direct rule of the principalities. Greeks from the Phanar district of Constantinople were chosen as Turkey's agents. But these hospodars (princes) were given brief and uncertain tenure of their stewardship. Thus they felt obliged to extract as much as possible from their subjects as quickly as possible. The average reign was two and a half years. So the word *Phanariot* came to stand for bribery, exaction and corruption, though the hospodars themselves were said to have often been men of culture and intelligence.

Many peasants fled the oppressive regime, drastically reducing the population. Meanwhile, Russia was pressing hard against the Turks. After important victories, Empress Catherine demanded that Turkey recognize the independence of Valachia and Moldavia under Russian power. In the early nineteenth century, St. Petersburg's influence increased. To counter it, Napoleon urged the Sultan to dethrone the princes of Moldavia and Valachia in 1806. It led to a disastrous six-year Russian occupation of the principalities, with requisition of their produce, forced labor and deportation of resisters to Siberia. The Romanians never forgot. By their count, Russia invaded their country thirteen times, always bringing distress. Once Romania invaded Russia to recover lost territory, but it was a costly failure. Unlike the neighboring Bulgarians, who remember the Russians as Christian liberators from the Turks, Romanians feel a deep-rooted hostility and fear of Russia.

In the revolutionary year 1848 there were uprisings in several places. A national movement emerged, inspired by France, which had become a beacon for the Romanian intelligentsia. The Turks, at Russian insistence, put down the rebels. European influence was enhanced by the Treaty of Paris in 1856. An attempt to unite the principalities under the name of Romania and to proclaim neutrality was blocked, but a single prince was named as the ruler of both regions in 1859. He was Alexander Cuza, a man of progressive views but despotic ways whose agrarian reforms infuriated the landowners and the Church without going far enough to please the peasantry. He was deposed in 1866 and replaced, by general agreement, with a German princeling. The new ruler, accorded hereditary rights, was Charles, second son of Prince Charles Anthony of Hohenzollern-Sigmaringen. Before the unity of Germany, its noble houses were a desirable fount for countries in search of a ruler with legitimate claim to a title but without the power status which would provoke rivalry from the important European states.

Prince Charles, who romanized his name to Carol, accepted a new constitution based on the liberal Belgian constitution of 1831, after Belgian independence. The country remained nominally under the Turkish empire, but it developed autonomous government. When Russia and Turkey went to war again in 1877, however, Romania joined on Russia's side and was rewarded, by the Treaty of Berlin in 1878, with formal recognition of its full independence. Authority was restored over the province of Dobrudja. But Transylvania, part of the Austro-Hungarian Empire, remained outside the new state. Prince Carol was crowned King Carol in 1881. Having no heir, he arranged to have his nephew Prince Ferdinand of Hohenzollern named his rightful successor.

Political power was held tightly by Liberal Party leader Jon Bratianu and his Francophile supporters, whose policy was to encourage the development of a strong middle class. The opposition Conservatives were divided into the old nobility, who tended to favor Russia, and a younger pro-German group. The standing of Jews became an abrasive issue. There had been few in the country before independence, but they immigrated in large numbers afterward. Russia's failed 1905 revolution sparked a peasant uprising in Romania against the Jews, who were considered a cause of poverty because of their money-lending businesses, and against the large landowners.

The country was in social, political and financial trouble when King Carol died at the beginning of World War I. He had tried to bring Romania into the war as an ally of his relative the Kaiser. His nephew, who became King Ferdinand I, was less fervently pro-German, and Queen Marie, Ferdinand's wife, was adamantly anti-German. She had been born Princess Marie of Edinburgh, a granddaughter of Queen Victoria and of Tsar Alexander II, and her favors were firmly for England and Russia. (She died in 1938, as Romania again faced the choice of which side to join in the coming war.) The country stayed neutral for the first two years of World War I, courted by each side with an offer of territory from the other. The Central Powers promised to return Russian-held Bessarabia, and the Allies offered Transylvania, of much more emotional as well as economic importance to the Romanians.

So Romania declared war on Austro-Hungary on August 22, 1916. It was a disaster, bringing both Germans and Russians into the country and resulting in the fall of Bucharest. With the Bolshevik revolution in October 1917 and Russia's withdrawal from the war, the Russian forces in Romania broke down into scavenging bands. An armistice was signed with the Central Powers in December, taking Romania out of the war at great cost. By the terms of the Treaty of Bucharest, signed on May 7, 1918, half of Dobrudja was ceded to Bulgaria with only the pledge of a trade route to Constantsa affording access to the Black Sea. Hungary's Transylvanian border was advanced eastward, and far-reaching concessions had to be granted on Danube transport, the railroads and the oil fields. It was a national catastrophe. Then, on November 9, 1918, two days before Germany signed the armistice acknowledging its defeat, Romania again declared war on the Central Powers in another attempt to emerge on the winning side. On November 30, when German troops evacuated in accordance with the surrender terms in Western Europe, the King returned to Bucharest.

Romania then proceeded to proclaim the incorporation of Transylvania, fulfilling the old dream of national unity. But there remained the problem of obtaining Allied recognition, complicated by Romania's ambitious invasion of further Hungarian territory and occupation of Hungary's capital, Budapest, defenseless in the turmoil of Béla Kun's Communist revolution. The Treaties of Saint Germain, Trianon and Neuilly finally fixed internationally recognized borders, less than Romania had hoped to obtain by the initial 1916 agreement to enter the war but still satisfying major aspirations. They left an important Hungarian minority within Romania, a source of continuing irredentism, as well as the traditional ethnic minorities of Germans, Jews, Gypsies and others.

The internal political situation was unruly. The old Conservative Party collapsed because of its failed pro-German policy. Eighty percent of the population were peasants, leaving the Socialists and the Communists with little of their customary working-class base. They tried to make up for it by audacity; as a result, their leadership was arrested and in 1924 the Communist Party was outlawed. There was fierce controversy over a promised agrarian reform and expropriation, finally passed by the legislature but to no one's satisfaction. And there was trouble over the succession to the monarchy. Crown Prince Carol, King Ferdinand's son, was a notorious, extravagant playboy. In 1925, he was forced to renounce his right to the throne and his five-year-old son was recognized as next in line under a regency council. But two years later when King Ferdinand died, Carol plotted to return and take the throne back from his own son. He finally succeeded and was crowned King Carol II in 1930.

In this time of disorder, a right-wing terrorist organization rose to prominence. It used various names in various periods, but it was generally known as the Iron Guard. The government's foreign policy was opposed to the interwar fascist powers; Romania supported the Balkan Entente of 1934 and opposed Italy's invasion of Ethiopia and Hitler's occupation of the Rhineland and annexation of Austria. But, supported and financed by the Nazis, the Iron Guard and its death teams kept the country in chaos. In 1938, hoping to regain control, King Carol banned all political parties and proclaimed a royal dictatorship. When World War II began right after the Hitler-Stalin pact in 1939, the King tried to bargain with the belligerents as his father had done in World War I to see which side would pay the most for Romania's participation. He sought first to get promises of territorial expansion from Britain and France, but, dissatisfied with their offers, he then turned to Germany. Hitler offered economic aid but demanded inclusion of the Iron Guard in the cabinet. When the King refused, Hitler outmaneuvered him and made agreements with Romania's rivals which partly dismembered the country. The Soviets, still at peace with Germany, were awarded Bessarabia and northern Bukovina. Southern Dobrudja, twice taken from Bulgaria since 1913, was returned to Bulgaria again, and Transylvania was restored to Hungary. As a consequence, Carol was forced to abdicate in September 1940. His son Michael, by then twenty, once again was crowned King, but as a puppet in the hands of a military dictatorship backed by the Iron Guard.

The new leader was the pro-Nazi Marshal Ion Antonescu. Carol was packed off into exile, along with his flamboyant, redheaded Jewish mistress, Magda Lupescu. The new regime launched a reign of terror, but the Iron Guard still was not sated. It tried to oust Marshal Antonescu and seize power for itself alone in January 1941. But the army was opposed, rallying to the marshal, who proceeded to apply the terror to the Iron Guard in its turn, executing all of the leaders. Though he suppressed the Nazis' Romanian counterparts, Antonescu took the country into the war on Germany's side. Once again, Bucharest gambled on a German victory to gain territory. By February, there were 500,000 German troops in Romania, which declared war on the Soviet Union. Great Britain declared war on Romania, and after Pearl Harbor, Romania declared war on the United States. Joining the Nazis was popular at first because Romania was rewarded with Bessarabia, since the German invasion of Russia in May 1941 had overthrown the previous Hitler-Stalin agreement.

But when the casualty lists arrived from Stalingrad and it gradually became clear that Romania had again chosen the losing side, public discontent increased. The outlawed political parties had managed to keep their organizations. The four main ones were the National Peasants, the Liberals, the Social Democrats and the Communists, who had recruited Iron Guards eager for action but without direction after the execution of their leaders. The four joined to support a coup mounted by King Michael, which overthrew Antonescu and switched sides in the war on August 23, 1944. Soviet troops poured into the country even before the formal armistice, signed in Moscow on September 12, 1944. The reversal was in the nick of time to regain Transylvania but too late to prevent Soviet domination, despite wartime Allied agreements. Antonescu was tried and executed in 1946.

As in the other countries occupied by the Red Army, the Soviets at first accepted a coalition government and encouraged organization of a national bloc. There simply weren't enough Communists to be installed from the start, and Stalin was cautious about not being too flagrant in undermining the accords with Roosevelt and Churchill signed at Yalta in early 1945. The agreement was that postwar governments were to be democratic and antifascist. Nonetheless, he sent Soviet Deputy Foreign Minister Andrei Vishinsky, who had been the prosecutor at the prewar Moscow purge trials, to install Petru Groza as Premier. Groza was head of a splinter leftist peasants' party called the Ploughman's Front. Britain and the United States objected because the National Peasant Party and the Liberals, by far the most popular, were excluded.

In response to an appeal from King Michael, the Big Three agreed in Moscow in December 1945 on naming a broadly based government which would hold elections. They took place in November 1946. But by then, the Communists had established themselves in key ministries and put their candidates on a single government bloc list so that their strength could not be measured. In the Romanian peace treaty signed the next year, it was provided that Soviet forces could remain in the country until peace was concluded with Austria. That assured adequate time for Soviet influence to be firmly implanted.

Stalin never accepted an Austrian peace treaty. It was not until Nikita Khrushchev sought to relax tensions with the West that the Austrian treaty was signed, in 1955, providing the legal basis on which the Romanian government could secure Soviet withdrawal in 1957. The Romanian peace treaty ceded Bessarabia and northern Bukovina to the Soviets again, awarded southern Dobrudja to Bulgaria again, but returned northern Transylvania from Hungary, establishing the country's current frontiers.

After the 1946 elections, however, when Romanian Communists were still very close to Moscow, non-Communist politicians and their followers were imprisoned. The National Peasant Party, which had majority support, was outlawed. A split was maneuvered within the Social Democrats which led to a forced merger with the Communists, to create the Romanian Workers' Party. That pattern was followed in almost all of Eastern Europe. New elections were called in 1948 with a single list presented by the People's Democratic Front, which claimed 405 out of the 414 seats in the assembly. Shortly before the elections, a treaty of "friendship, collaboration and mutual assistance" was signed with the Soviet Union, firmly binding Romanian policy to Moscow. Then, with the other politicians out of the way, the internal Communist purges began. The party had been swollen by gorging all it could sweep into its ranks right after the war. In 1949, it threw out 18 percent of its membership, admitted new people more carefully vetted for reliability and by mid-1950 announced its strength at 720,000 card carriers.

The leader was Gheorge Gheorghiu-Dej, a dark-eyed, rather handsome man who had spent the war in prison and escaped just before the 1944 coup. He was the son of a laborer with only a few years of formal schooling, but a long experience of agitation, jail and labor camps. He had added "Dej" to his surname after he was interned in that town in the 1930s. After the arrival of the Soviets and his inclusion in the government as Minister of Communication, he went off to Moscow for a time, returning in January 1945. He was known as an ambitious, unscrupulous, subtly cunning man, skilled at outbidding his rivals for Soviet support whatever the Moscow line of the moment. He was secretive about his personal life, but his stolid, rustic figure was seen at times in Bucharest cafés. Gheorghiu-Dej was junior to others in the party. But he was an ethnic Romanian and he had been a worker, on the railroads, claims which few of his comrades could advance. In 1945 he became the party's First Secretary.

From outside, the most visible member of the leadership was Ana Pauker, a grim-faced, lumpy woman who kept her iron-gray hair in an awkward bob and wore ill-fitting mannish suits. There was no more telling image of what was happening in Romania than her arrival on an official visit to Warsaw in 1947. She went by train—air service was still uncertain—and used one of the luxurious old Orient Express specials, newly painted and polished. The Warsaw station had been totally destroyed in the war, made into a crater of twisted tracks. So Mrs. Pauker's train pulled up in an open clearing just outside the city, where the Polish dignitaries lined up to greet her. The contrast between her and her escort was even greater than that between the elegant cars and the devastation. At each window as the train slowed to a stop were the men of her honor guard, wearing extravagant red and blue uniforms with operetta decorations. Some were obviously corseted, their cheeks and lips rouged, their moustaches waxed and twirled. Then came Ana Pauker. She clomped to the ground, eyes steely and lips sternly set. She made no concessions. The men around her were nothing more than Romania's vanishing past.

She was born Ana Rabinsohn, daughter of a Moldavian Jewish butcher, and had taught Hebrew at a Bucharest synagogue school before going to Zurich to study medicine. There she met and married Marcel Pauker, a Romanian student whose father was a newspaper publisher. But she developed a consuming interest in Marxism, joined the Communist Party in 1921 and was elected to its Central Committee after only a year. She had the usual experiences of underground work, arrest, study in her filthy, solitary cell. The main difference in her career from those of her comrades was that during the late 1920s she had lived in the United States, where her husband represented the

Soviet trade organization. That was only an interlude, however. Back
in Romania, she landed in prison again. In 1940, there was a Soviet-
Romanian exchange of prisoners after the occupation of Bessarabia,
and she was released to Moscow. During the war, she helped organize
a special Red Army division of Romanian prisoners of war and marched
home with them in 1944, wearing the major's uniform of a political
commissar.

Ana Pauker's visit to Warsaw was for the meeting which drafted a
new manifesto reviving the official international Communist movement and establishing the Cominform. She was not to become Foreign
Minister until two months later, but she already ranked among the
world's top Communist figures, along with Yugoslavia's Tito and Bulgaria's Dimitrov. She was said to be the only Romanian with direct
access to Stalin. Along with Mrs. Pauker and Gheorghiu-Dej, Finance
Minister Vasile Luca (an ethnic Hungarian whose real name was Laszlo
Lukacs) appeared to compose a sturdy leadership troika that could not
be budged. But the Romanian Communists were having trouble. The
country had been plundered, had lost a fifth of its territory and, on top
of that, had had to pay heavy reparations to the Soviets. The peasants
resisted collectivization, which was imposed slowly but inexorably.
Over 12 percent of the population belonged to restive minorities. Turks
and Jews were allowed to emigrate in the early years, but Germans,
Serbs and, most of all, the large number of Hungarians were difficult
to deal with. Monetary reform, introduced suddenly, wiped out both
inflation and virtually all private savings. The Romanian leadership was
totally dependent on Moscow, and Moscow was not entirely pleased
with its results.

The break between Stalin and Tito gave Gheorghiu-Dej the arguments to eliminate first the "nationalists" among his Communist rivals
and then, in 1952, the "cosmopolites," which in the context meant
nonethnic Romanians and intellectuals, especially Mrs. Pauker and
Luca. With some shrewd detours, he continued to consolidate his
power. Later, Gheorghiu-Dej was to take credit for creating some distance from the Soviets on foreign policy. But at the time, he was always
in step, providing new headquarters for the Cominform in Bucharest
after it had to be moved from Belgrade. When Tito demonstrably succeeded in escaping from satellitedom, however, the Romanian leader
began to feel the attraction of more independence. He moved gradually, but the people noticed the growing coolness toward the Russians

and were delighted. Gheorghiu-Dej had found that nationalism was a more effective way to force down the pill of Stalinism. Besides, he was having increasing arguments with Khrushchev, who had observed the productive impulse that the Common Market was giving Western Europe. The Soviet leader determined to reverse the Eastern bloc's economic policy, built on trying to imitate the Soviet's heavy-industry model in each country, and to increase cooperation and trade by allocating each state a special task. East Germany and Czechoslovakia were pleased, anticipating benefits because of their industrial base. But Romania was sharply opposed. Bucharest was determined to continue its policy of self-sufficiency and grandiose projects.

Unaware of these underlying arguments and what they would mean to the development of Romania's economy, the public applauded any sign of defiance to Moscow. The Soviets were seen as the source of the worst difficulties, and people found ingenious ways to show general dissatisfaction with their rulers. In the summer of 1956 I asked a man standing in a packed truckload of workers, waiting to be taken to a "spontaneous demonstration" of approval for the government, a deliberately ambiguous, neutral question: "How are things here?" He shouted down a wily answer which revealed all: "We're not allowed to tell you." There were reports later of uprisings in Transylvania during the Hungarian revolution that fall. One rumor reaching other parts of Eastern Europe was that two Romanian army divisions had been disarmed. But it was never clear whether Soviet or other Romanian troops took the action and, although credible, the report was never documented. Undoubtedly, the uneasy situation precipitated the decision to demand removal of Soviet forces the following year, which Khrushchev accepted because he had larger concerns at the time.

Gheorghiu-Dej made the most of the people's joyous reaction for reviving nationalism. He had all the streets and cinemas, which had been given Russian names, rebaptized in Romanian. He had history rewritten to claim that the Romanians had "liberated" themselves, without the Red Army, an ironic assertion because in that case the Communists would never have had the slightest chance at power. He even re-explained the purges to pretend that he had shrewdly gotten rid of the pro-Moscow people in the leadership by the devious charges of "nationalism" and "cosmopolitanism." Romania remained in the Warsaw Pact, but as an increasingly obstreperous member. After 1962 it prohibited Pact maneuvers on its territory and began to diverge from

Soviet foreign policy. In principle, the Romanians have also refused transit rights to Soviet forces. In fact, however, Soviet units have been seen crossing to Bulgaria for exercises. Romania's military stand came to be compared with that of France in NATO, a prickly, uncooperative ally but an ally all the same. At the time of Tito's death in neighboring Yugoslavia, when there were fears of Soviet attempts to reestablish a pro-Moscow regime by force, Romania constituted a barrier on a vital invasion route.

By 1964 the schism reached a point of openly declared policy. The Romanian party proclaimed that "there cannot be a father party and a son party, a superior party and a subordinate party, only a great family of Communist and workers' parties with equal rights." It was called a Romanian declaration of independence, a claim to follow the party's "own road to socialism," as the Yugoslav and Italian Communists had done before. But unlike the other quarrels between Communist leaders and Moscow, it advanced no real issue of ideology, no departures in the theory or practice of "building socialism" and brought no internal innovations. Gheorghiu-Dej died on March 19, 1965, at the age of sixty-three, without having relinquished a jot of power.

Once again, there appeared to be a troika. There was Ion Maurer, an intelligent, educated man who was then Premier; Chivu Stoica, a party stalwart who had long done Gheorghiu-Dej's bidding and was elected President; and Nicolae Ceauşescu, only forty-seven at the time, who had had a meteoric climb through the party hierarchy, rising all the way to the Politburo in the decade 1945–55. Ceauşescu took over as First Secretary. He had the coveted credentials of being an ethnic Romanian, coming from a poor family, having been involved with the Communist movement from his early teens and being young and healthy. It soon became clear who was the absolute boss. Ceauşescu did not change the policies of his mentor, Gheorghiu-Dej, either in foreign affairs or internally. He reinforced them. Romania continued to straddle the Moscow-Peking divide and seek improved relations with the West, pursue extravagant development plans at the cost of living standards and clamp the tightest possible lid on any expression of complaint or even mild challenge.

Ceauşescu is a small man, which is seldom noted because he takes care to be photographed in the midst of children or standing above the people around him. His hair is curly, his eyes narrow, his nose sharp, and his portraits show him with a warm smile, though he holds himself with a cold, royal reserve. A comrade who served time with him in the severe Doftana prison in King Carol's days described him as "a skinny kid who rarely said a word. He didn't whine when they kicked him. He didn't smile when they fed him." As supreme leader, he took great pains to control his image. "Luminous beacon," "Helmsman who guides," "Our lay God," "Thinking polar star," "The first thinker of this earth," "The most eminent personality of international political and scientific life," "The earth lives today under the Sign of Ceauşescu"—the minions were made to gush geysers of adulation. Ceauşescu's imaginative scriptwriters even surpassed Stalin's commandeered hagiographers.

In 1980, he made his wife, Elena, his second-in-command, with the title of Vice Premier, and the key job of control of party personnel. She too was accorded the right to the most extravagant encomia. Her "good and tender smile replaces the sun on a gray day," read the officially published "Homage to Comrade Elena Ceauşescu" on the occasion of her promotion in the government. A poem offered by the Union of Romanian Writers said, "By your wisdom, you are our mother, a valiant woman who has conquered all the secrets of science, the worthy and proud companion of the Magnificent Man." The official biographies are as discreet about the facts of the reigning couple's lives before the ascent to glory as they are garrulous about the Ceauşescus' professed virtues. Elena was born the daughter of a landowner in a little southern Carpathian village and made her way as a girl to Bucharest, where she worked in a textile factory. The only claim made for early political activity was that she was chosen queen of the ball on May Day in 1939. But once installed in power beside her husband, she insisted on being treated not just as a consort, a first lady, but as a political and intellectual luminary in her own right.

Ceauşescu's method of rule was to rely on his family and to keep reshuffling the rest of the governing apparatus so that everyone owed position and privilege directly to him and could never forget it. The result was such a stifling, paralyzed hierarchy, with the most trivial decisions requiring a ruling from on high, that even Communist Chinese delegates told Westerners they disliked doing business with Romania because nothing could be moved through its bureaucracy.

Though their images were ubiquitous, the leading couple were so insulated, so distant from the everyday life of the country, that sometimes people wondered whether they actually knew what was going on. But there could be little doubt in a system of such stringent and centralized control. When food shortages became acute, Ceauşescu announced that 30 percent of illness throughout the country was due to gluttony. He prescribed a "scientific diet" for health purposes. It permitted, per month, 10 eggs, ¼ pound of butter, 2.2 pounds of cooking oil and 2.2 pounds of meat—though he did not say how these items were to be found in the empty markets. Sharp-tongued Romanians said it was a new contribution to historic ideology, "dietetic Marxism." Bread was rationed in 1981. One of the few known incidents of disorder came when Ceauşescu visited a mining town shortly afterward and was greeted with a hail of stones. He fled by helicopter.

Energy was also critically short. Because of Romania's rejection of integration in planning by Comecon, the Soviet economic bloc, the Soviets refused "ruble oil" and petroleum had to be bought with hard currency. Huge tubes of methane gas, which looked like crude rockets, were placed atop city buses for their fuel. The streets, and even the luxury hotels built for foreign tourists, were left in a dim gloom at night. Police had a right to enter anyone's home at any hour to see if they were using more than the ration of electricity. Light bulbs over 40 watts were no longer on sale. Refrigerators had to be unplugged in winter, and apartment dwellers caught using forbidden electric heaters risked penalties. Except for special occasions, such as celebration of a Ceauşescu birthday, TV stations broadcast only two hours a night. In any event, it was such dreary, propagandistic television that people took to watching Bulgarian broadcasts, which could be received in Bucharest and some other parts of the country. Bulgarian TV schedules circulated clandestinely. An underground Bulgarian-Romanian dictionary was compiled for viewers, but even without understanding the words, people felt the pictures were livelier, more interesting. And they could see that Bulgarians lived better. That hurt. Romanians were accustomed to looking down on Bulgarians as backward, crude, less European. "I never in my life would have imagined that the day would come when we would envy Bulgarians," said a famous painter's sister.

A new kind of personal solidarity arose among the people, exchanging little favors and services, getting up to queue in the middle of the night or passing on word about a country family who managed to hide from the authorities part of the goat cheese it produced and was willing to sell. A woman told about a friend who was ecstatic at having found a pair of stockings and added sadly, "It takes so little to make us happy now." But there was nothing like the social cohesion which developed into the Solidarity movement in Poland. People grumbled and cringed.

There seemed to be a degree of sadism and megalomania that went well beyond mere totalitarian mismanagement of the country. A large part of old Bucharest was razed to build another monumental forum and triumphal avenue. Some of the fine old villas were left, occupied often by foreign diplomats, but most people were jammed into jerry-built anthills of apartment blocks. Central heating and hot water were available only occasionally. People would get up at 3 or 4 A.M. to see if the two hours of hot water promised daily happened to be on. Kent cigarettes and small packets of coffee became a medium of exchange, needed to get quick attention from a doctor or to persuade a plumber to moonlight. The national currency, the lei, was not of great use, and it was dangerous to be caught with unauthorized foreign currency.

In the circumstances, foreign observers speculated about after-Ceauşescu. Nobody imagined that he might fall, but he was at least human enough to be mortal. Few supposed that his high-living, hot-tempered, self-indulgent son Nicu would really be able to hold the succession which his father was preparing for him. "I don't mind that he drinks, chases women, gets into fights," one official confided, "but he's incompetent." Yet nobody outside the family had been allowed to rise to a position where power might be transferred smoothly. Would there be a battle of factions or a great upheaval? It seemed that so much repression, so much deprivation, such concentration of power could bring an explosive relief when the dictator ultimately disappeared. But Romanians, asked what they expected, tended to furrow their brows in puzzlement. The editor of the Communist Party paper *Scinteia*, a position of high importance, said blandly, "Life always brings new problems." The regime did not show fears, and the people did not show hopes of change. It was as though the existing situation had become so pervasive, so embedded in the country's thought, that it was impossible for people even to imagine things might be different. They appeared to have renounced the future in the dogged effort to survive the present.

The basic resources of the country and its industrious, if exhausted and sullen, population should provide for a happier future for Romania if it can ever emerge from its political deadlock. But it has always had to squeeze by on wit and wishes, on ducking when possible and bowing when necessary, on evasion and ingratiation. It has escaped a measure of Soviet thralldom in international relations only to be hopelessly ensnared in its own, no longer a consolation. There is nothing different on the horizon.

BULGARIA
The Soviets' Most Loyal Ally

SOMEHOW, BULGARIA BECAME a funny word, signifying something strange and distant. George Bernard Shaw chose it as the setting for his satiric play about war, *Arms and the Man*, because in so improbable a place it seemed that anything could happen. There was a children's song in America years ago, one of those endless repetitive ballads that pass the time, about the deadly battle between Ivan Skvinsky Skvar, the pride of the Tsar, and Abdul the Bulbul Emir, an exotic legend about the period under Turkish rule. Bulgaria seems misty, farther distant and less substantial than Turkey, which abuts it at the eastern end of Europe. It has much in common with the other countries of the Balkan Peninsula: rugged mountains and fertile valleys, harsh winters and hot summers, a tough, stolid peasantry, a cuisine of spicy grilled meat and crunchy salads topped with goat cheese, crafts of wood carving and embroidery that speak of long, uneventful village days and nights.

But differences are sharply marked. The Bulgars were one of the Central Asian tribes which moved into Europe after the fall of Rome, but were absorbed by the Slavs whom they conquered. The Thracians, a Greek tribe, also lived in the region. Bulgarians claim Saints Cyril and Methodius, brothers in the ninth century who brought Christianity to the Eastern Slavs and devised the Cyrillic alphabet so they could read holy texts in their own language. Others say the brothers were Greeks, or Thessalonians, or Macedonians. They were missionaries of Byzantium, which, like the Roman church, embraced many peoples.

But now Bulgaria is a firmly Slavic country, its language so close to Russian that the two peoples can understand each other, its church Orthodox, its writing in the same Cyrillic alphabet Russians use. It is Russophile by virtue of a long tradition of looking to Muscovy for aid against the historic Turkish enemy, though, ironically, it was on Germany's side in the two world wars. It has never been a happy land, nor one that breeds exuberance. The people tend to be big and muscular, solemn, suspicious, resigned to the blows of untender fate. They have learned to survive by accommodation, by mere doggedness, by self-effacement when that is prudent and by tricks when they may work well. It is not surprising that after Soviet advances into Europe in World War II, Bulgaria became the Soviet Union's most reliable ally, the least discontented and least restive of its satrapies, the most willing to adapt to Communist rule as its people had adapted to other rules. Brutality and repressive authority have seldom been strangers to them. Democracy, the assertion of individuality and the pursuit of grace have seldom been at home in the country.

Yet, two generations after the war, Bulgaria too was stirring, not with dissidents—there was no such movement—but with an avid nationalism to set it apart from the Russians and an eagerness to shake off centuries of stagnation and plunge into modernity. The cities are largely new, peopled with peasants drawn recently off the land. Some of them work in computer factories, making what one Western resident of Sofia, the capital, derisively called "wood-burning computers," but nonetheless scheduled for use in stores that never even had cash registers. The latest buildings have Dallas-style tinted reflecting windows and show a concern for design far removed from the ubiquitous Stalinesque architecture once ordered to homogenize Eastern Europe. The Communist Party headquarters in Sofia was surmounted with a Moscow University–style tower topped with a big red star. But the newer local party building in Varna, on the Black Sea, is all coppery glass and pleasingly curved dark metal. Todor Zhivkov, the grandfatherly First Secretary, who reached power in 1954 and has held it serenely ever since, proclaimed that his aim was to make Bulgaria "the Japan of the Balkans." He meant industry and advanced technology, but the implication of a disciplined, docile society with a high awareness of its special culture was also evident.

Like the rest of the Balkans, where "nationality" has traditionally meant ethnic allegiance rather than citizenship, Bulgaria has stubborn

minorities. Most of the once flourishing Jewish community, largely
saved from Nazi murder by a wily pro-fascist government allied with
Hitler, was permitted to emigrate to Israel by the postwar Communist
regime. The minority Macedonians are considered full-fledged Bulgarians by the majority, and there is a long-standing bitter dispute with
Yugoslavia, which incorporates most of Macedonia but is claimed by
Bulgaria. That is one of the several disputed frontiers in Eastern Europe, muted by the overriding might of the Soviet Union but not resolved by acceptance as are the borders of Western Europe. The most
important minority, and the most politically sensitive, is the Turks, an
estimated 1 million out of the total population of 9 million.

In 1985, the regime sought to climax a long campaign of Bulgariza-
tion by forcing its Turkish citizens to change their names to Slavic ones.
The newspaper and the state radio broadcasts in Turkish had previously
been suppressed. Moslem religious schools had been shut down long
before, and Turkish was banned as a language of instruction in the
regular schools. Children overheard speaking Turkish to each other at
school were punished.

The regime was determined to create what Zhivkov called a "one-
nationality state" and "a single Bulgarian national consciousness." It
officially claimed "there are no Turks in Bulgaria," arguing that all the
people of truly Turkish origin had emigrated when that was permitted
for a few years under an agreement between Bulgaria and Turkey. The
rest were pronounced, by fiat, descendants of true Bulgarians who had
been obliged by force or opportunism to convert to Islam and adopt
Turkish language and customs during the five hundred years that Bulgaria was a province of the Ottoman Empire. The attempt to cow and
to absorb the minority was in the long Balkan tradition, part of the old
plague that had earned the region the epithet "the powder keg of
Europe" and that made it so difficult for the area to enter the system of
confident statehood.

Religion seemed to be more a tool than an object of these measures.
Atheism is, of course, a basic principle of the Communist regime.
Churchgoing is not encouraged, nor is there much latitude for the
clergy. But the dominant Orthodox Church fared much better than the
Moslems. Priests were allowed to be trained in seminary, and the metropolitan was treated as an honored figure with a place at state occasions. The Moslem clergy, the focus of Turkish ethnicity, had no such
privileges. At the time of the mass name changing, over half of the
Moslem clergy was over sixty. They were being left to die out. An

offshoot of Byzantium, the Bulgarian church was under the Greek Orthodox patriarchate during the long Turkish rule. But in the nineteenth century it separated and established itself as an independent body. As a result, when the Communists came to power they had to deal only with a national hierarchy without outside support or connections. A tacit understanding was reached. It permitted a degree of mutual support between the Communist state and the Church, which also contributed to strengthening the sense of nationalism.

There is a striking tapestry in the vast, lavish Palace of Culture in Sofia, named in honor of Lyudmila Zhivkova. She was the adored daughter of Zhivkov, an intense, dark-haired woman with a passion for reviving Bulgarian culture and tradition. She died in 1981, a few days before her thirty-ninth birthday, after an automobile accident. She had been taken to the Soviet Union for treatment, and rumor had it that Soviet police did away with her. That was probably nonsense. The suspicion fed on the fact that she had developed distinctly non-Marxist spiritual interests after visiting India, where she encountered Hindu mysticism, and Japan, where she was intrigued with Zen Buddhism. She also was influenced by the writings of a French Catholic. The tapestry, one of many which she commissioned, shows the historic heroes of Bulgaria, including Cyril and Methodius, on one side and recent cultural eminences on the other. Her own figure was inserted in the foreground after her death. In the center is a large Christlike figure, arms spread, body hanging, loins draped as in the customary depiction of the Crucifixion. The sharply planed face, however; looks more like the worker typified in "socialist realist" art, except for the haunted, sorrowful eyes. A guide explained blandly that the figure "represents sacrifice in the struggle for progress." It is a remarkable aberration from the norm of official Communist art, another hint that the Bulgarian Orthodox Church is not entirely anathema to the regime.

Another unique feature of Sofia is the equestrian statue of Tsar Alexander II. He is despised in the Soviet catechism, but revered in Bulgaria as the victor who drove out the Turks. Alexander is allowed to remain as a memorial of Bulgaria's historic gratitude to Russia. Nearby is another reminder of that friendship, the brightly colored, golden-domed Alexander Nevsky Cathedral, which has a superb collection of icons in its underground museum. Otherwise, the city lacks character. It grew from 20,000 to over a million in less than a century and has little to evoke the past.

Bulgaria is small, slightly larger than Tennessee. About a third of the country is mountainous, with plains to the north between the Danube and the Balkan chain and to the south between the Balkan and the Rhodope mountains. Sofia, 1,800 feet above sea level, is approximately in the center of the Balkan Peninsula, just below Mount Vitocha. It had long been a capital, but until independence only the Turkish province of Rumelia, a rundown oriental town whose churches had to squat half underground because their roofs were not allowed to be higher than a man on horseback. In antiquity, it had been the capital of Roman Dacia and Emperor Constantine spent time there. The invading Huns, led by Attila, destroyed it in the fifth century.

At the western end of Bulgaria, Sofia is near the Yugoslav border, dominating the routes to the Black Sea and the east. The central route passes through the Valley of the Roses, a sea of tender color in the late spring and the source of Bulgaria's oldest industry. The flowers are cultivated for their oil, a base for perfume. The petals have to be picked between dawn and about 8 A.M. because they dry when the sun rises high. It takes three tons to make a liter of oil, which is why scents based on rose attar are so expensive. But after it is extracted by heating in huge copper vats, there is still rosewater and residue for jam. Lavender, fruits and wine grapes also grow in the valley. The whole of the country is cheerily green in spring, a natural garden used to supply the Eastern bloc with coveted fruits and vegetables.

The old Bulgarian capital of Veliko Tŭrnovo in the north is being restored as part of the effort to revive a sense of national history, and the city of Plovdiv still boasts a central, medieval town. But most of the urban centers are recent, thrown up to accommodate the hasty transformation from a totally agricultural society to one with an industrial base. With long stretches of tawny beach on the Black Sea coast and lots of sun in summer, Bulgaria has made a special effort to develop a tourist industry. It is said to receive 6 million visitors a year, though most are Turks passing back and forth from their homeland to their jobs in Western Europe. Russians and Eastern Europeans, seldom permitted to travel to the West, flock to the Bulgarian resorts, usually in organized groups, for a change of landscape. There are leafy woods by the sea and long promenades between the large hotels, which have earned the area the sobriquet "the Red Riviera."

If the earlier movements of Central Asians into the region are hard to fix, Bulgaria has a firm date for the founding of the state, 681, when Khan Asparuhk and his tribe moved to the gates of Constantinople and

Salonika and won the province of Moesia from the eastern Roman emperor. The thirteen hundredth anniversary was celebrated with great fanfare in 1981, and the Palace of Culture in Sofia was built for the occasion. The early state, called Great or Black Bulgary, stretched along both sides of the Danube, now the border with Romania. But the northern lands were lost to new invaders in the ninth century. The Bulgars were more successful to the south. In 811, Khan Krum annihilated the army sent by Byzantium, slew the emperor Nicephoris and used his skull as a drinking goblet. He laid siege to Constantinople, but his sudden death saved the city. The center and the southwest of the Bulgarian state became the core of the nation, by then thoroughly Slavic. The original Asian language died without a trace. But the struggles with the Christian empires continued.

Like other pagan rulers on the margins of Christian Europe, the monarch decided it was better to join than to continue the ravaging fight. It was a period of great controversy between Rome and Byzantium. Khan Boris dickered with both. When the Roman pope refused to recognize his independent sovereignty in 870, he opted for the Eastern church ruled from Constantinople, a momentous turning point which affected all subsequent history. Bulgaria obtained its own patriarchate. The state flourished, reaching its grandest point under the reign of Simeon, 893 to 927. The lands on the northern side of the Danube were permanently lost, but he expanded the kingdom to the Adriatic in the southwest and dominated the lands of the Serbs. His power in Eastern Europe was so preeminent and his capital, Preslav, so much a rival to Constantinople that he took the title "Emperor and Autocrat of all the Bulgars and Greeks" and was recognized by Pope Formosus. But the state declined with his death.

Not until the thirteenth century, under what is called the second empire, did Bulgaria reassert itself in glory. Ivan Asen II, who ruled from 1218 to 1241, was the greatest Bulgarian leader, an enlightened man who presided over a flowering of civilization and a burst of previously unknown prosperity. He adorned his capital at Tŭrnovo. Many monasteries and churches that survived later depredations date from that period. He was also, of course, a warrior, the requirement for a successful ruler, and extended his sway over Albania, Epirus, Macedonia and Thrace. But the dynasty died out in 1280. Subsequent rulers failed to maintain strong central authority. Feudal anarchy weakened and constricted the state while invading Mongols ravaged its northern

regions. Half a century later, in 1330, the Serbs under Stephen Uros
III took their own back. He defeated the Bulgarians at the Battle of
Velbuzhd (Küstendil), and the Bulgarian rulers became subjects of the
Serbs. For a time, the Bulgarian lands formed part of the Serbian em-
pire of Stephen Dushan. These medieval tides of battle still underlie
endemic Bulgarian-Yugoslav hostility and rival border claims.

But both were soon overwhelmed by another invading force, the
Turks. In 1366 the last Bulgarian tsar of the second empire, Ivan Shish-
man III, was forced to declare himself the vassal of Sultan Murad I.
Sofia was captured in 1382. The Turkish rout of Serbians, Bosnians and
Croats at Kosovo Polje in 1389 decided the fate of the Balkan Peninsula.
The Bulgarian tsar perished, according to legend, in a battle near
Samokov in 1393. His brother Srazhimir fought on for a time from the
town of Vidin on the Danube, but it fell in 1396, and Bulgarian independence was completely extinguished. A Greek patriarch was named
by the sultanate to head the spiritual governance of subject Christians,
so the Bulgarian church was also subdued by foreign influence. The
conquerors laid waste to the land, ravaging whole districts. The plains
people fled to the mountains to eke out a precarious existence, or dispersed to more distant lands. Some adopted Islam at the victors' bidding, though the Pomaks of the Rhodope Mountains accepted
conversion only in the seventeenth century.

Many Turks were brought in and resettled on the emptied, fertile
lands. The country was divided administratively into sanjaks, and a new
feudal system, ruled by Turkish chiefs and renegade Bulgarian nobles,
was established. Some boys between the ages of ten and twelve were
requisitioned to become Janissaries, servant-warriors in the Turkish
forces, but otherwise the Christians were not forced into military service and no systematic effort was made to change their language or
religion. Once the conquerors had settled in, roads were constructed
and commerce prospered again. The people were left to get on with
their lives so long as they were docile.

Some of those who had taken to the mountains organized guerrilla
warfare. They were known as Haiduks, or outlaws, the heroes of many
Bulgarian legends. They were encouraged by Christian powers fighting
the Turks to the north and west, first the Austrians and later the Russians, who took on the role of protectors of the Balkan Orthodox Christians. The long years of repression and occasional audacious resistance
gave rise to Balkan traditions of both outlawry and terrorism, and of
resignation, a glum bending of the back at the sight of the whip.

When Turkish power began to wane after the failure of the siege of Vienna in 1683, however, anarchy spread. Turkish armies passing through to the wars with Austria wreaked havoc on the land. Toward the end of the eighteenth century, bands of soldiers who had thrown off imperial authority set about plundering and terrifying the people with the worst atrocities. Pascanoglu, one of the chiefs of these desperadoes, who were called Krdzalis, even routed three large Turkish armies sent to subdue him in 1794. He established himself as an independent sovereign at Vidin and maintained his own order for a time. As Turkish power declined and the empire fragmented into increasingly corrupt, vicious and decadent vassaldoms, the sufferings of subject peoples were greatest. Christendom was by no means always less cruel, but religion inspired added outrage at the atrocities of those who followed another faith.

All through this period, the Bulgarians were cut off from the rest of Europe, excluded from the advances of its civilization and its culture. The rest of Christendom scarcely knew of their existence in the early nineteenth century. They were too subdued by the failure of past revolts and too isolated to join the uprisings that brought the liberation of Serbia and Greece from Turkish rule at that time. Russian invasions in 1810 and 1828 did not ease their plight. But a literary revival began to stir the long-dormant national spirit. A monk of Mount Athos, Paisii, had written a history of Bulgarian tsars and saints in the eighteenth century, and as knowledge of it spread, it inspired a new school of modern Bulgarian literature and the opening of places of instruction in the language.

That in turn led to reaction against the authority of the Greek clergy, who had dominated the spiritual and what there was of cultural life in the land as much as the Turks had dominated the temporal power. Though the peasants spoke the vernacular Slavonic, they called themselves Greeks and the Slavonic liturgy was suppressed. The greedy, venal Greek priests were seen by Bulgarian patriots, who kept attempting abortive military revolts, as the main obstacle to their drive to reawaken the nation. Their goal then was to establish an autonomous Bulgarian church. With Russian support, the first Bulgarian exarch was chosen in 1872. He was immediately excommunicated by the Greek patriarch, but his authority was accepted as an emblem of nationalism.

The sap of nationalism was rising against empire in all parts of Europe. There were insurrections almost everywhere in the mid-nineteenth century. Bulgarians broke out in revolt in 1876, after the uprisings in Bosnia and Hercegovina the year before. They were suppressed with ferocity, by Pomaks (Bulgarian converts to Islam), Ottoman irregulars called *bashi-bazouks* and newly arrived Circassians and Tatars, determined to defend their own privileges as well as the Sultan's domain. Some fifteen thousand Bulgarians were massacred near Philippopolis (Plovdiv); many villages and monasteries were destroyed. Britain's Prime Minister Gladstone denounced the atrocities in a ringing broadside to provoke the indignation of Europe, but only Serbia took action, declaring war on the Turks. Bulgarian volunteers fled to join the Serbian army.

The following spring, April 1877, Russia went to war and won. Bulgaria was restored to independence by the Treaty of San Stefano in March 1878 with a population of 4 million and a territory stretching over three-fifths of the Balkan Peninsula. Russian troops occupied the country, and Russian officials took over its administration. This provoked the other European powers, who feared the new state would become a mere Russian dependency. By the Treaty of Berlin, in July 1878, they forced a drastic reduction of its size, dividing the country into two parts. The northeast part was granted independence, but the south, called Eastern or Oriental Rumelia, was restored to the sovereignty of the Sultan.

Most of the members elected to the first assembly of independent Bulgaria were peasants, with the Liberal Party well ahead of the Conservatives. They chose as head of state Prince Alexander of Battenberg, a member of the house of Hesse and a nephew of Tsar Alexander II. He had been Russia's candidate, not surprising in the circumstances. He was an autocrat and considered himself more a representative of his uncle than the guide of the new Bulgarian nation and quickly ran into trouble with the deputies, especially the Liberals led by Stefan Stambolov. The quarrels provoked a period of authoritarian rule and the arrival of Russian generals to strengthen the Crown's authority. Upheavals continued as the European powers grew concerned about the balance of power in the area and deviously intervened.

After the death of his uncle, Alexander fell into dispute with his Russian mentors and was forced to abdicate. Bulgarian delegates were sent out to tour the courts of Europe in search of a new monarch who would be acceptable both to the Russians and the other powers. Prince Ferdinand of Saxe-Coburg-Gotha was chosen, and took the throne in 1887. In 1893, he married Princess Marie Louise of Bourbon-Parma, a

Roman Catholic. However, their first son, Boris, was baptized in the Orthodox faith, which sealed the reconciliation with Russia.

But politics remained turbulent, with internal factions aligning themselves with rival foreign courts and ambitions mounting to expand the kingdom to its previous broader frontiers. Ethnic Bulgarians had been left under the rule of Romania, Serbia and Turkey. Macedonia, still under Turkish rule, was the prime candidate for incorporation. A Macedonian revolt in 1903 nearly led to war with Turkey. The Balkan fuse was burning short, with claims and counterclaims throughout the area. In 1908, immediately after the Austrian annexation of Bosnia and Herzegovina (now in Yugoslavia), Prince Ferdinand, taking the title of King, proclaimed the full independence of Bulgaria and the end of all vassalage to Turkey.

A network of crisscrossing secret alliances was woven in the following years. The stench of war was in the air. In 1912, Greece, Serbia and Bulgaria went to war against Turkey. The allies met quick success, and a conference was called in London to draw up peace terms. They could not agree. Hostilities resumed in February 1913, leading to a second peace conference, in which Turkey surrendered all its possessions in Europe to a line from Midia on the Black Sea to Enos on the Aegean, a mere bridgehead. Division of the spoils led to a second Balkan war the same year. This time Bulgaria attacked its erstwhile allies Greece and Serbia. The war was settled a few months later by the Treaty of Bucharest, a disaster for Bulgaria. Greece and Serbia shared out Macedonia. Romania, forced to cede Bessarabia to Russia, was compensated with the previously Bulgarian lands of southern Dobrudja.

This was the eve of World War I. The disconsolate Bulgarians failed to obtain an important loan they sought from France, Britain and Russia and had no chance of territorial concessions from the Entente, so they turned to Berlin. When war broke out in August 1914, the public desire for neutrality succumbed to public hopes that Germany and its allies would restore Macedonia to Bulgaria. The King was certain of German victory. The Entente powers tried to sway the Bulgarians into their camp, but Bulgaria's price was the cession of territory by Serbia and Greece, which was refused. In October 1915, Bulgaria declared war on Serbia. Honoring their alliances, Great Britain, France and Italy then immediately declared war on Bulgaria.

At first, the Bulgarian forces won victories and absorbed territory, but the triumph could not last. Bulgaria was invaded just before the end of the war in 1918. The King was forced to abdicate in favor of his son Boris and to leave the country. All the wartime gains were lost, including the Aegean coastline. Revolutionary feelings flared in reaction against the failed war policy. Alexander Stambolisky, the Agrarian Party leader, who had been imprisoned during the war for opposing the King's stand, became the popular hero. After winning the election of 1920, he proceeded to open communications with the Bolsheviks and to proclaim agrarian reform.

The impact of the 1919 Treaty of Neuilly, resulting from the lost war, caused profound disturbances in Bulgarian society. As many civilians had died of epidemics in the war years as soldiers on the battlefield, and now the country was shrunken and laden with debts and indemnities. "The harshness and vindictiveness of the Neuilly terms left Bulgaria not only an angrily revisionist state, isolated from and hostile toward her neighbors, but also a rancorous society," wrote historian Joseph Rothschild.

In structure, Bulgarian society between the wars was of the type that ought to have provided stability, according to conventional wisdom. It was relatively egalitarian, there was no nobility, opportunities existed for social mobility, and the distribution of property was not extravagantly out of kilter. But politics were conjugated by violence. The extremists, on right and left, were strong. Powerful anarchist and Communist movements sporadically indulged in assassinations, bombings, riots and attempted insurrections. The worst of the violence indulged by the frustrated nationalism of the general public came from the Macedonian minority in the 10 percent of Macedonia left within Bulgaria's borders, who wanted union with Macedonians in Serbia and Greece. "They exercised a degree of power far out of proportion to their numbers and came close to functioning as a state-within-the-state," writes Rothschild.

Their paramilitary arm, IMRO (Internal Macedonian Revolutionary Organization), somewhat similar to the contemporary Irish Republican Army, set out to terrorize Bulgarian leaders considered lax in pursuing irredentist claims. They launched cross-border raids and assassinations, increasing tensions between Bulgaria and its neighbors. The assassin of Yugoslavia's King Alexander and French Foreign Minister Louis Barthou, gunned down in Marseilles in 1934, was an IMRO member in the service of the Croatian Ustacha. During most of the two decades between the wars, IMRO imposed "intimidation and terror on a Bulgarian society that was both victim and collaborator," Rothschild notes.

The land reform had produced an agriculture based on small and medium holdings, with 98 percent of the farmers owning their own land. They lived on bread, potatoes, cheese, yogurt, onions and peppers, and only one village in nine had electricity on the eve of World War II. But they were diligent and industrious, open to improved techniques when those were available, and despite their poverty they had a sense of participation in the society. The achievement of independence in the nineteenth century had swept away the Turkish feudalism, so that the political, bureaucratic and military elites were recruited from the peasants and artisans. The educational system was open and more widespread than in other countries in the area. The literacy rate was the highest in the Balkans. Bulgarians were proud of their work ethic, which they compared with disdain to what they considered the Serbs' "haiduk-hero culture" or the Romanians' and Greeks' mercantile-ingenuity culture. Neither were they attracted by what they saw as the mysticism and romanticism of the Russians and other Slavs. They appreciated order, sobriety, practicality, innovation.

Rather than producing sturdy democrats like the Swiss and Swedes, however, stoicism and diligence in Bulgaria favored autocracy. Stambolisky, who dominated the initial phase of politics after World War I, was an intensely ideological and emotional man, an agrarian radical. He wanted to impose "the dictatorship of the village" on the society, denouncing the cities as "Sodoms" whose industrial, commercial and bureaucratic interests should be liquidated. Thus he underestimated the Communists with their urban, proletarian, industrializing ideology, and considered them "toothless bears," useful for frightening the middle classes. They in turn misjudged his essential radicalism. On June 9, 1923, conspiratorial army officers aided by IMRO mounted a coup which overthrew the demagogic, irrational Stambolisky regime. The Communists stood aside, claiming that the fight was merely a quarrel between the urban and rural bourgeoisie and not an opportunity for revolution, as Moscow insisted.

The 1923 coup brought an outbreak of vengeful barbarism and horrible mutilations. Stambolisky was beheaded and dismembered. A bourgeois coalition under Professor Alexander Tsankov took power, launching a white terror and shifting Bulgaria's international position. It moved away from links to France—because of French ties to Yugoslavia—and tilted toward Italy, where Benito Mussolini and his Fascists had just come to power. The Soviets saw the new direction as another threat of encirclement. At Moscow's demand, the Bulgarian Communists reversed themselves and launched an uprising, accepting the Soviet analysis that the time had come for a decisive confrontation between the peasant masses and the elites.

But the revolt was poorly prepared and badly executed. For ten days, Communist insurgents established themselves in the northwestern corner of the country. Then they fled abroad, some to become important leaders in the Comintern (Communist International), Moscow's organization to coordinate and command Communist parties in the rest of the world. Despite their failure, the attempt earned Bulgarian Communists a reputation for "Bolshevik discipline" and courage in Soviet eyes. By the same token, Tsankov appeared to the Western powers as a staunch bulwark against communism. But he pursued the terror against internal opponents so ferociously that revulsion against his regime's brutality came to outweigh political sympathy.

Having lost much of its grain production with the transfer of southern Dobrudja to Romania, Bulgaria became dependent on tobacco exports. The sudden fall of tobacco prices plunged Bulgaria into depression even before the rest of the world was hit. By 1934, the country's national income was 61.4 percent of what it had been in 1929. Strikes, terrorism, corruption, police excesses and general government incompetence brought a second military coup in 1934, this time scarcely resisted by an exhausted and disheartened population. Tsar Boris pushed the successful plotters aside with his own coup in January 1935, suspending the constitution. He was in fact a dictator, but he cleverly eschewed the trappings that went with the role in the 1930s. His sympathies were with Nazi Germany and Fascist Italy, but he resisted Hitler's demands for full collaboration. When German armies invaded Yugoslavia and Greece, he allowed them to use Bulgarian territory and participated in the subsequent occupation but not in the war. The lure of territorial gains proved irresistible to his nationalist ambitions. With cold cynicism, he acquiesced to Nazi demands for the deportation of Jews from the occupied areas, which meant their death. Bulgarian Jews were persecuted but not deported, which meant their survival.

German insistence and the appearance of coming German victory persuaded Tsar Boris to declare war on the Western Allies in December 1941, at the same time the United States entered the war. But it was a token adhesion to the Axis cause. He never declared war on the Soviet Union. Shortly after a stormy meeting with Hitler, Boris suddenly died, at the age of forty-nine, on August 28, 1943. He was succeeded by a regency council. Gradually, the country's leaders realized that once again Bulgaria had chosen the wrong side in war and that the territorial gains which had tempted it were endangered. As Soviet troops advanced, there was a coup d'état in Romania attempting to change to the Allied side. That was in August 1944, two months after D-Day reopened the western front. That spring and summer, Bulgarian authorities had secretly sought an armistice with London and Washington, hoping to avert the imminent Soviet occupation. By that time, an active resistance movement had been organized within the country, the Fatherland Front. It encompassed four clandestine groups, including the Communists, who ensured liaison with the Red Army.

Daily from Moscow, the veteran Communist Georgi Dimitrov broadcast exhortations to fight "the fascists and their lackeys." On September 5, 1944, the Soviet Union declared war on Bulgaria, and on September 8, Soviet troops crossed the border. A new government, formed by a coup in Sofia a few days earlier, desperately sought an armistice with the Allied powers and declared war on Germany. It was much too late. Marshal Fedor Tolbukhin, at the head of the Red Army, was pushing south from the Danube. Units of the Fatherland Front emerged from the underground to greet the Russians and open the way to the capital. They proclaimed a new regency council headed by a Communist, Todor Pavlov, and established their own government on September 9, ostensibly a coalition but in fact dominated by the Communists.

Though he remained in Moscow until April 1945, Dimitrov was the key figure. A stubby, determined man with fiery eyes and a big moustache, he was one of the first members of the Bulgarian Communist Party, founded in 1909, when he was twenty-seven years old. The son of a Macedonian peasant, he had moved to the city to become a factory worker and been exposed to intense political discussion most of his life. Too poor to plan on a university education, Dimitrov went to work for a printer when he was fourteen and soon plunged into revolutionary politics. In 1913, he was the first worker ever elected to a parliament in southeastern Europe. But during half the time that he held the mandate, until 1923, he spent underground or in prison for opposing the war policy. After participating in the 1923 uprising, Dimitrov escaped to Yugoslavia. He returned but was forced to flee again in 1925 after an attempted putsch in which a bomb was placed in the Sveta Nedelia Cathedral, killing 140 people. Condemned to death in absentia, Dimi-

trov then devoted himself to working for the Comintern in various parts
of Europe. Arrested in Berlin, he was made the main defendant in the
1933 Leipzig trial, charged with setting fire to the Reichstag to provoke
revolutionary upheaval.

The trial was to have been a staged spectacle, in which Hitler sought
to prove that Germany's shield against a Communist menace had to be
support for his Nazi Party. Later evidence indicated that the fire had
been a Nazi plot to frighten the German middle class. Dimitrov, asserting his innocence, conducted his own defense. He was a bold, flamboyant figure in the dock, turning the tables on his accusers and attacking
the Nazi leaders. "Who does not want to be the anvil must be the
hammer," he declared, proclaiming himself the defender of working
people everywhere they were oppressed. Committees were organized in
his support, and telegrams demanding his release poured in from all
over the world. He was acquitted. When the Soviets gave him citizenship in 1934, he left immediately for Moscow. "He is the purest of the
Marxist pure," one Western admirer wrote of the new antifascist hero.
In 1935, he became general secretary of the Comintern, a man of great
weight in the world Communist movement. At times, he had disputes
with Stalin but composed them "for the sake of October," the Bolshevik
revolution.

However, it was neither Dimitrov's stature nor the strength of the
Bulgarian Communists but the Red Army's occupation of the country
which assured the communization of Bulgaria. After the Potsdam Conference, in the summer of 1945, the Western Allies succeeded in persuading the Soviets to broaden the provisional government and hold
elections. The Fatherland Front won an overwhelming victory, though
the circumstances were dubious, at the least. "People's Tribunals" were
established as window dressing for a vast, bloody purge in which 18,197
people were sentenced, 2,138 of them executed. An estimated 30,000 to
50,000 were killed without the formality of trial. After a forcefully
organized referendum in September 1947, the monarchy was abolished and the People's Republic of Bulgaria was proclaimed. Non-
Communist leaders were swept aside, even those who had cooperated
with the Soviets. By the end of the year the new regime was so well
implanted that the occupation was brought to an end.

There was no more Bulgarian politics. After that, as in the Soviet
Union, what political debate was allowed to exist took place in the
secret conclaves of the Communist hierarchy. A new constitution was

proclaimed before the Red Army withdrew, modeled on Stalin's Soviet constitution of 1936 and providing "eternal friendship with the Soviet Union." Most farmland was organized into Soviet-style collectives; industry, banks and mines were nationalized. Thousands of Soviet "advisers" and "specialists" stayed on to help form the new Communist state. The intimate interconnections of the Soviet and Bulgarian secret police were established, never since broken.

There had been 8,000 members of the Bulgarian Communist Party when it left the underground in September 1944. Four years later there were 500,000. Possession of a party card had become the entry fee for jobs, university admission and social benefits. But it was not enough. Bulgaria was one of the first to conduct the internal party purges ordered by Stalin throughout Eastern Europe after the break with Yugoslavia's Tito. The most prominent victim was Traicho Kostov, a close friend of Dimitrov's and an old Communist who was nonetheless judged likely to be more nationalist. He was charged with the usual litany of show-trial crimes, including "enemy of the Soviet Union," "agent of imperialism" and "Titoist." There was an almost eerie repetition of Dimitrov's Leipzig trial, for on the first day Kostov refused to confess and proclaimed himself innocent in open court. But the similarity of the two spectacles ended there. Kostov was executed in December 1949, six months after an emotionally broken, exhausted Dimitrov had died, still head of a Communist Party that was consuming itself. The purge was expanded, affecting 30 percent of the party members.

Dimitrov was succeeded by his brother-in-law, Vulko Chervenkov, an old Communist. Another period of terror and widespread persecution ensued, this time initiated by the Bulgarian Communists against their own comrades, as in Stalin's Moscow purges of the 1930s. Chervenkov had spent twenty years in the Soviet Union. As an unadulterated Stalinist, he was remorseless in his pursuit of revisionists. But his position was weakened after Stalin's death in 1953, and he was compelled to accept some loosening of his absolute controls. Party and state leadership jobs were separated. Chervenkov remained as Prime Minister, but Todor Zhivkov took over as First Secretary of the party in 1954.

Then only forty-three, Zhivkov was not considered a real successor but a seat warmer while the new power establishment was being formed. He maneuvered astutely. By definition, the Communist system with its unbreakable principle of "the leading role of the party"—in effect, the Communist Party's monopoly of power—tips the scale in favor of the First Secretary whenever there is an attempt to disperse responsibility within the leadership. Zhivkov made a decisive bargain with Moscow which assured his supremacy. In exchange for pledges that Bulgarian policy and the consolidation of Bulgarian communism would faithfully follow the Kremlin's lead, local Communists who had not spent years under direct Soviet tutelage were allowed to rise again in the hierarchy. And Moscow promised to support Bulgaria's economic development. That was the relation which led outsiders to call Bulgaria "the sixteenth Soviet Socialist Republic."

Zhivkov was not a "Muscovite," as those who had spent the underground years and the war in the Soviet Union were called. He never left Bulgaria until after the war. He was born in 1911 to a poor peasant family in a village near Sofia. His mother was devoutly religious. But he came in contact with Communists when he went to study at a technical school in the capital and then went to work as a printer. At first, political activity was a sideline. "For twelve years I was a printer," he said later. "Then in 1938, I took up revolution as a profession." He said he was imprisoned and tortured at one period, without giving dates. During the war he was a Partisan leader, using the *noms de guerre* Ianko and Marko. When the Soviet Union declared war on Bulgaria in 1944, he took part in the Sofia uprising. Then a colonel, he was put in command of the People's Militia, the new regime's security force which conducted the bloody campaign against those tagged as fascists or anti-Communists. Rising through the Communist Party as a protégé of Chervenkov and making himself known as a loyal Stalinist, he seemed to be only a figurehead for two years after becoming First Secretary.

But by 1956 he had become a protégé of the new Soviet leader, Nikita Khrushchev. After Moscow's Twentieth Party Congress that year, at which Khrushchev made his secret de-Stalinization speech, Zhivkov attacked Chervenkov for his "cult of personality" and other failings. Like Khrushchev before him, Zhivkov then proceeded to isolate an "antiparty group" in the leadership and got rid of Chervenkov and others in 1961. His success baffled unofficial biographers, who called him lackluster, plodding, stodgy. One said his "greatest asset was precisely his mediocrity," for it pleased Moscow to have a reliable, steady follower with no sign of imagination or vanity.

When Khrushchev was ousted in 1964, Zhivkov managed to adapt once more to the power center. Bulgaria loyally joined in the Soviet invasion of Czechoslovakia in 1968 and ran a campaign at home against

"revisionism" and Western influence. Then, in the 1970s, came détente, and Bulgaria followed that line too. Relations were improved
with Greece and Turkey. Calls were issued for a "Balkan nuclear-free
zone." Zhivkov began to travel widely, especially in the third world and
Asia, but a scheduled trip to West Germany in 1984 was cancelled at
the last minute, after a sudden visit from the Kremlin's Mikhail Gorbachev, who became Soviet General Secretary the following year.

There were advantages and disadvantages for the Bulgarians in their
dependency. Over the years, their repeatedly frustrated but persistent
sense of national identity began to reassert itself. Forty years after the
new regime, one Bulgarian grumbled that "before the war, when we
said something was very good it was in German, *sehr gut*. Now, it's in
Russian, *chorosho*. When is it ever going to be *mnogo dobre* in plain
Bulgarian?" Nowhere else in Eastern Europe were complaints phrased
so mildly, so submissively, nowhere was the problem about how to say
"very good." But it was a reflection of a will to greater autonomy nonetheless. That included a different kind of conformity, a reach toward
what was considered the European mainstream from which the country
had been so long excluded. Blue jeans and discothèques, bowling alleys
and pop songs as well as industrial technology, new methods of irrigation and nuclear energy were all part of it. Of course, there was no
whisper of change in politics. Given Bulgaria's experience with political
turmoil, however, iron stability did not seem such an intolerable burden.

By the perverse good fortune of its backwardness, Bulgaria was allowed to escape the initial pattern of development, focused on huge,
heavy-industry complexes, which Stalin imposed on the rest of Eastern
Europe. In the interwar period under German influence, the economy
had moved toward commercializing agriculture and the industries associated with it. That was permitted to continue, making Bulgaria the
truck garden of the bloc and gradually giving its people a variety of diet
which was the envy of its neighbors. The improvement was particularly
marked after the emergence of Solidarity in Poland in 1980, in response
to workers' complaints about food shortages. But once the decision was
made on high to assure a good table, it was sustained. Growth was
steady, without dazzling advances and also without the disastrous set-
backs which afflicted more ambitious Communist regimes. Transport
and shipbuilding were developed into major industries. Soviet willingness to accept a balance-of-trade deficit with Bulgaria over many years,

in effect a subsidy which built up into billions of dollars of cheap debt, enabled Sofia to avoid the harsh impact of the world market economy's debt crisis in the 1980s. It had the lowest Western debt of Eastern Europe because, unlike the other countries, it had never made an attempt to leap forward on the basis of massive Western credits.

But that also meant its economic dependence on the Soviets was much greater. Almost three-quarters of Bulgaria's trade in the mid-1980s was with the Comecon countries of the Eastern bloc, over half with the Soviet Union, thus producing low earnings of hard currency. Modest economic reforms, going beyond anything allowed in the Soviet Union but far short of those decreed in some other Communist countries, sought joint ventures with Western companies and investment-for-product deals in order to increase trade opportunities with non-Communist states. A specialty of selling key-in-hand factories in the third world, using Bulgaria's relative sophistication over still quite backward economies, provided another outlet into the world market. Bulgaria's success in avoiding the economic shoals of other Eastern European states, one Western diplomat said tartly, was achieved by capitalizing one commodity—absolute fealty to Moscow's policies in both foreign and domestic affairs.

There was something in it, as the rough winter of 1984–85 showed. The Soviets cut back on oil and gas deliveries, and Bulgarians went without electricity and fuel. Homes went unheated and plants shut down. It was a warning of the fragility underlying the apparently healthy economic surface. After Mikhail Gorbachev came to power in Moscow, the Soviets also grew more demanding for better-quality goods which might otherwise have been reserved for hard-currency trade. A new phrase came into use, making the distinction not only between "hard" and "soft" (that is, nonconvertible) currency, but also between "hard" and "soft" goods, those acceptable only in noncompetitive markets. The Soviets were also less indulgent of Bulgaria's debt to Moscow, which Sofia had almost come to take for granted as its due, as a teenager given an allowance relies upon it as a right. But on balance, any reforms enhancing economic efficiency and providing incentives in the Soviet Union were likely to benefit Bulgaria as well. Its economy was essentially complementary to the Soviets' and so far integrated that improvements would both spill over and give more political leeway for domestic economic initiative.

Thus in his long rule Zhivkov did preside over substantial progress in a country at the end of Europe's train to modernity. He managed in later years to achieve a certain aura of benignity, eschewing the extravagant personal glorification that had been the mark of Communist leaders when he reached power.

But the old aura of mystery and violence still marked Bulgaria. There was the peculiar incident of the killer umbrella in London in 1978. Georgi Markov, a Bulgarian who worked for the BBC, was jostled on the street by a stranger who jabbed him with an umbrella, apparently accidentally. He fell terribly ill and died four days later. Doctors discovered he had been injected with a fatal poison. In 1983, a defector gave a revealing account of arms and drug trafficking through Bulgaria arranged by the secret police in collusion with shady Turkish criminals and thugs, and other large-scale clandestine but officially supported arms deals. The charges of a "Bulgarian connection" in the 1981 assassination attempt against Pope John Paul II led to investigations which developed highly credible evidence of the state-sponsored illicit trade. Mehmet Ali Agça, the Turkish terrorist who tried to kill the Pope, was rambling and contradictory in his account of that conspiracy. But it all added up to a dark picture of a country which organized crime and kept impenetrable secrets.

Bulgaria's life at home was little known and little noticed in the rest of the world. Abroad, the country was seen as above all a Soviet proxy, accepting intelligence and dirty-tricks assignments, training third world students expected to become missionaries of Marxism, helping build up Communist parties and police establishments in areas where Moscow saw good prospects. In terms of foreign policy, Bulgaria's only real national concern was relations within the Balkans, no longer a world hot spot as before World War II, but one where many embers were still banked and glowing. The country had survived and prospered, relative to the past. Its future depended more on the world outside than on its own inclinations and decisions.

YUGOSLAVIA
The Undone Puzzle

IT HAS BEEN SAID that Yugoslavia is more a state of mind than a state. Yugoslavs wince in irritation when they hear that from a foreigner, but among themselves they find it painfully near the truth. In a census taken a few years ago, only 5.4 percent of the people gave Yugoslav as their nationality. All the others answered Serb or Croat or Slovene or one of the many minorities.

When Yugoslavs talk of a "national" institution or problem, they are referring to one of the Federation's constituent republics. Agreements among the republics are called "international." They have not been able to agree on a national anthem, so they sing an old one, "O Slavs, our ancestors' words still live." There is a state flag, horizontal stripes of blue, white and red with a big gold star in the middle, and a capital and a currency and all the usual accouterments of a nation-state. But the wry countdown of the country goes: Yugoslavia is composed of six republics, five nations, four languages, three religions, two alphabets and one party. The party is the Communist League of Yugoslavia, the only one allowed, and ostensibly it is the force that holds the country together. But like most things, it has tended toward fragmentation lately. The Balkan Peninsula, of which Yugoslavia comprises about one-third, gave its name to mean the process of breaking something into bits, and Yugoslavia is certainly the most balkanized of the region's states.

The name means "country of the South Slavs," but their history has almost always emphasized the diversity and rivalries among them rather than molding cohesion. And there are important non-Slavic ethnic groups. The largest is the glum Albanian minority, suspected by the others of both wanting to break away and attach their autonomous province of Kosovo to neighboring Albania, and of threatening eventually to dominate the Slavs by outbreeding them. The ethnic Albanian birthrate is three times that of other Yugoslavs, who are not reproducing in sufficient numbers to maintain the current total population of 23 million in future generations. Although they belong to the same ethnic family as the Russians, Poles, Czechoslovaks and Bulgarians, and their dominant language, Serbo-Croatian, has similar roots and structure, for essentially political reasons the Yugoslavs insist that they are not a part of Eastern Europe. They do not quite fit in any category, tensely divided among themselves, a Communist-ruled state unlike any other, perched on the line between East and West.

Most of the country is mountainous, with snowy peaks and verdant valleys in the north, rugged, harsh and breathtakingly beautiful farther south. Yugoslavs are scrappy, tough, fiercely independent-minded, steeped in local traditions and difficult to unite. For a mere three years, from 1945 to 1948, Yugoslavia was part of the Soviet Union's war-born European empire. But except for a brief detour to Belgrade by Soviet tanks toward the end of the war, Yugoslavs made their own revolution. The Red Army did not stay. The proud, stubborn leader, Marshal Tito, soon fell out with Stalin, who expelled Yugoslavia from the Soviet bloc in hopes of overturning the regime and replacing it with one that was more docile. He failed. So Yugoslavia became the first Communist country to have fallen under Soviet tutelage and then escape to devise its own formula of Marxism-Leninism, a system with a good deal more freedom and flexibility than the others but by no means a Western-style democracy.

Because of its capacity to tinker with orthodoxy and experiment with reforms in defiance of Soviet views, Yugoslavia was an ideological curiosity and a magnet for many disappointed Marxists of the postwar generation. Later, after the death of Mao Tse-tung, China took on more importance as the workshop of Marxist revision and redefinition. But Yugoslavia remained a special, and especially interesting, case of the way Communist doctrine and practice can evolve with the responsibility and privileges of power.

The nationality issue, the Yugoslavs' central problem, shaped the

approach to the question of living under communism. It is so overwhelming that economics, politics, culture, everything is entangled
in this strain between ethnic separatism and the attempt to maintain
a nation-state. It is deeply rooted in the history of the South Slavs
and their incessant struggle against a variety of foreign dominations
until, in accordance with President Woodrow Wilson's vision of self-
determination after World War I, their state was created. World War I
began with the assassination of Austrian Archduke Ferdinand in the
Bosnian city of Sarajevo by a nationalist opposed to imperial rule from
Vienna. He relit the fuse of the proverbial "Balkan powder keg." When
it ended, the Austro-Hungarian Empire was destroyed. Now, ironically,
some Yugoslavs look back with nostalgia on a time when unity of rule,
a free flow of trade and travel, a vast organized polity between the forces
of Germany and Russia were assured by the alien Habsburgs, overriding
nationalism. But which particular part of history matters most is an
element of the current national tensions. Each group's memory reflects
its own point of view. And each republic runs its own educational
system with its special versions of history and literature.

The oldest identified inhabitants of the region were the Illyrians,
tribes who settled along the magnificent eastern Adriatic coast. Present-
day Albanian is believed to be a descendant of their language, but it has
disappeared elsewhere. The northern area, present Croatia-Slavonia,
was the Roman province of Pannonia. The Slavs apparently arrived
sometime in the seventh century, from the area of the Dniester River
in Russia. They were encouraged to settle by Byzantium, but they were
soon caught in the long struggle for dominance between Rome and
Constantinople. They organized in clans and engaged in constant
struggles for succession and power, so there was a recurring cycle of
attempts at union followed by decentralization and rivalries. From the
eighth to the twelfth centuries, most Serbs lived under Bulgarian or
Greek dominion, most Croats under Venice or Hungary. It turned
them in opposite directions, a division which persists to this day and is
reflected in religion and script, though not in language, which is the
same but pronounced with regional variations. The Croats, and the
Slovenes in the fertile mountain valleys to the east, are Roman Catholics and use the Latin alphabet. The Serbs are Orthodox Catholics and
use the Cyrillic alphabet, adapted by Bulgarian monks to fit Greek
letters to Slavic phonetics.

The first Croatian national kingdom was consolidated by Duke Tomislav in 924, two centuries before the first Serbian kingdom. Demetrius Zvonimir, who died in 1089, was crowned King of Croatia by an envoy of Pope Gregory VII only after dedicating himself and his lands to the Roman church. The last national king of Croatia was Petrus, who died on the battlefield in 1097. From that time, the land was parceled among neighbors or absorbed under the Hungarian and later Austrian crown. Except for a brief period during World War II as a Nazi puppet state, Croatia was never again independent, although the people maintained a strong sense of identity. During the French Revolutionary Wars, there was a revival of Croatian nationalism. Napoleon proclaimed the state of Illyria. But the Austrians drove the French out in 1813, even before Napoleon's downfall, and absorbed Dalmatia, the coastal province, and the city-state of Dubrovnik, both of which had been heavily influenced by Venice in the glory days of the doges. A Hungarian campaign to force the Croatian populace to be assimilated as Hungarians turned local sympathies away from the rulers in Budapest toward Vienna as a source of protection. And Austria, less despotic, brought models of administration, education and economic development to Croatia and the small neighboring province of Slovenia. It was to prove a lasting advantage.

The first Serbian kingdom was founded in 1159 by Stephen Nemanja, though he never took the title of king, contenting himself with Great Zhupan, chief of all the chiefs of the clans. Medieval Serbia endured as a kingdom, but almost always at war, its borders and alliances shifting constantly, its people intensely conscious of their nationality and ambitious for its triumph in the peninsula. In 1346, Stephen Dushan was crowned Emperor of the Greeks and Serbs at Skoplje, a union organized to resist the advancing Turks. It disintegrated when he died. Attempts to create a Christian front of resistance brought more Turkish attacks. After overrunning Bulgaria, the Turks defeated the Serbs at the Battle of Kosovo Field in 1389. Much of the Serbian aristocracy and both the Serbian and Turkish leaders perished on the field. The story of the battle is the subject of heroic folk ballads still sung with great emotion.

For the next four centuries, the Turkish sultans were the masters. Serbian art and culture, which had flourished in the Byzantine period, survived only in monasteries, since the Turks gave local power to religious leaders. Many Serbs fled north to the areas ruled by Hungary. A local saying goes, "Where the Turk has trod, no grass grows." It is a bitter summation of the impoverishment, the backwardness, the help-lessness endured under the sultans, whose delegated rule brought a system that was cruel, arbitrary and corrupt. Only the Church and the language kept national feeling alive, a memory that goes well beyond piety in binding the Serbs to their Orthodox religion, as Poles are bound to the Roman church for national reasons. But in Bosnia, many Ser-bian nobles converted to Islam to save their lands and peasants. Wild, mountainous, uncontrollable Montenegro in the south escaped the Turks' heavy hand, but at the price of constant battle, which toughened the people and kept them poor. There was little chance for the values and material benefits of peaceful life to develop, at a time when the Renaissance was spreading knowledge and skills and taming brute spir-its in other parts of Europe.

The failure of Austrian attempts to push back Turkish forces in the eighteenth century led the Serbs to pin their hopes on the expanding Russia of Catherine the Great. But, meanwhile, the decay of central Turkish authority left bands of insubordinate and rapacious soldiers to vie for power in the Sultan's provinces, adding to the despair of the populace. A turning point came in 1805, when the Serbian warrior Karageorge defeated the pasha of Bosnia and later reached Belgrade, the Serbian capital. The fortunes of war ebbed and flowed for a decade. Another Serbian leader, Miloš Obrenović, finally made peace, accept-ing Turkish suzerainty but with the right to local rule. It is said that he won concessions from the Sublime Porte, the European diplomatic name for the court of the Ottoman Empire, by arranging the secret assassination of Karageorge, who was demanding full independence from Turkey. True or not, the dynastic feud that resulted between the two families for the right to the crown of Serbia lasted for a century, one more reason to keep up the pitch of intrigue, hatred and violence. The diplomats of the European powers, Britain, France, Austria, Rus-sia, involved themselves closely in the Balkan struggles, shifting their favors as they perceived their own advantage.

After the upheavals of the mid-nineteenth century, Alexander Kara-georgević came to the throne. He encouraged a cultural revival, with education and a reform of the written language which enabled the emergence of literature. Peace treaties and international guarantees were signed, followed by more wars and treaties and guarantees, with the powers jockeying for influence. Sometimes the Serbs looked to Austria for support, sometimes to Russia, as the status and boundaries of the lands in the area kept changing. Austria gained Bosnia in 1878, and in 1882 the revival of the independent kingdom of Serbia was proclaimed. The Obrenović dynasty prevailed, with the help of a great deal of secret diplomacy and connivance in Vienna and elsewhere. But King Milan was a moody, probably deranged man. It was a time of great turbulence and misrule, not eased under his successor, King Alexander, who shocked his subjects and the courts of Europe by marrying his elderly mistress instead of arranging a useful political alliance. Demands for liberalization and more parliamentary power were mounting. Conservative monarchs everywhere felt a rising tide of threat, as they had during the French Revolution. There were surges of repression and resistance, murder and terrorism. The assassination of Alexander in 1903 ended the Obrenović dynasty.

Peter Karageorgević came to the throne, also aided by international intrigue. But beneath their façades of pomp and splendor, the empires of Europe were crumbling, and the advance waves of their impending catastrophe came from the Balkans. The once fierce regime in Turkey was already collapsing in anarchy, to be followed by Russia and Austro-Hungary. There was a series of uprisings, massacres and secret pacts, which led to the Balkan War of 1912. On May 30, 1913, the Treaty of London was signed, consecrating the ouster of the Turks from Europe except for a strip of land at the Bosporus. But how were the spoils to be divided? Again, alliances shifted, rivalries sharpened, agreements could not be implemented.

It has become a commonplace among late twentieth-century statesmen that Europe stumbled into World War I by accident, as though the balance might have been maintained happily and peacefully if the leaders had been a bit more alert and less impulsive. But there was plenty of warning from the violence-prone Balkans, and social signals everywhere that the old conservative imperial order was losing its grip and the European power balance was askew. After the assassination of Archduke Ferdinand at Sarajevo, Austro-Hungary sent Serbia an ultimatum demanding concessions which it could not have expected Belgrade to accept. The rush to war released explosive forces which had long been building up.

Vienna declared war on Serbia on July 28, 1914, and the first shots of World War I were from Austrian artillery bombarding Belgrade on July 29. Exhausted by the wars of the preceding years, all but abandoned by their French and British allies, the Serbs fought hard but were soon overpowered.

The catastrophic war demolished three empires—Germany, Austro-

Hungary and Ottoman Turkey—and overturned a fourth, Russia, by revolution. The map of Europe had to be redrawn. President Woodrow Wilson, attempting to inject what was considered American morality into the greedy habits of old Europe's diplomacy, did what he could to prevent territorial reassignments for reward and revenge and to promote the principle of national self-determination. The war was seen as a victory for the forces of enlightenment, democracy, freedom and national independence. The Balkans and Central Europe were too much of an ethnic muddle to draw lines that could satisfy everybody, however. Inevitably, minorities were left in many cases. The solution found by the South Slavs was to create a multinational state, named Yugoslavia, in hopes that they could learn to live in harmony together. Independence was proclaimed on December 1, 1918, under the Serbian king, who took the name Peter I.

But the new state did not have a smooth passage into the world. There were border disputes with Italy and with Albania, which had been proclaimed independent at the London Conference of 1913 only to be overwhelmed during the war. Once again, in 1920, isolated, ancient Albania became a state. Its borders were only fixed in 1925, leaving as many Albanians outside the country as within, most of them in Yugoslavia. They had long considered the Slavs their hereditary foes.

Pockets of ethnic Hungarians, Romanians and Germans were included within Yugoslavia's frontiers along with the long-feuding Slavs, who clung to their divisions as Serbs, Croats, Slovenes, Montenegrins and Macedonians. In an attempt to bring unity under Serbian dominance, Peter organized his kingdom into administrative fragments, thirty-three oblasts, arranged so that the non-Serb nationalities could not coalesce and assert autonomy. The imposition of centralized authority provoked constant unrest, political intrigue and assassinations. In 1928, a Montenegrin murdered the Croatian leader Stephen Radić and others in parliament. The Croats withdrew from the coalition government. The country seemed ungovernable.

In the name of creating national unity, promoting efficiency and stopping corruption, King Alexander, who came to the throne in 1921, arranged a coup and established a dictatorship in 1929. He died, alongside French Foreign Minister Louis Barthou, from the bullets of a Macedonian assassin in Marseille on October 9, 1934. The Depression and the rise of fascism were roiling Europe, and the threat of war from Italy had been worrying Alexander. He had gone to France to seek help in mediation. His son, who became Peter II, was only eleven years old. The regime was placed under the regency of Peter's uncle, Paul, who for fear of Italy looked for support from the new Nazi regime of Adolf Hitler in Germany.

It was a time of much violence and terrorism. A Croatian terrorist group, the Ustachi, under the homicidal maniac Ante Pavelić, established itself in Mussolini's Italy to fight the dominating Serbian dictatorship. Some Serbs and Croats cooperated with each other politically, but they were the ones who favored democracy and opposed both fascist powers. The combination of ethnic and political conflict kept the country in turmoil. There were two efforts to strengthen resistance to mounting external threats by diplomacy—the Little Entente, which grouped Yugoslavia, Czechoslovakia and Romania and was supported by France, and the Balkan Entente of Turkey, Greece, Romania and Yugoslavia, which leaned to Germany. They made for a great deal of activity and friction, public and secret, but the storms of Europe were growing too menacing for small countries to find shelter in loose alliances.

The Yugoslav government proclaimed neutrality when World War II broke out with the German invasion of Poland on September 3, 1939. The Germans pressed Belgrade to sign the Axis pact, but the people were opposed to the fascist dictatorships and Paul feared a general uprising if he agreed. Policy was paralyzed. There was too much pro-Allied feeling in the country to permit cooperation with Berlin, but there was too much desire for appeasement in the government to make any serious preparations for defense against the Axis powers. Berlin stepped up the pressure and finally, in March 1941, Belgrade signed the Axis pact of alliance with Germany, Italy and Japan. An outraged Serbian populace and part of the army overthrew the government. Paul fled to Greece. Peter, then eighteen, proclaimed the regency ended and himself King Peter II.

But by then the country was surrounded. German troops had moved into Hungary, Romania and Bulgaria. On April 10, 1941, Germany invaded Yugoslavia, supported by Italian, Hungarian and Bulgarian forces, all of whom had been promised territorial spoils at Yugoslavia's expense. The army, which had not been mobilized and properly supplied during the period of appeasement, was unable to continue organized resistance after two weeks. Peter II took refuge in London as the head of a Yugoslav government-in-exile.

With German and Italian support, Ante Pavelić returned to Zagreb and proclaimed an independent Croatian republic, allied with the Nazis. His Ustachi cooperated with the Gestapo in a reign of terror and revenge. Two resistance forces arose. One, the Chetniks under General Draža Mihajlović, supported the King and the government in London. The other, the Partisans, was led by a former Comintern official named Josip Broz, who had taken the pseudonym Tito and maintained contact with Moscow and Soviet military intelligence. Tito never hid the fact that he was a Communist and that his Partisan war was not only to rid the homeland of the invaders but to make a revolution.

The effect was that a terrible civil war raged across the country throughout the occupation, massacring and devastating far more than the foreign troops did. The fratricidal fury unleashed atrocities on a vast scale, venting old hatreds and creating solid reason for new ones. Yugoslavia suffered proportionally more casualties than any other combatant country, with an estimated 1.7 million killed, half in the civil war rather than in resisting the invader. Altogether, the population loss was one in eight, a total of 2.2 million people. Families and communities were riven by the bitter hostilities, adding to the legacy of division by ethnicity, religion and politics. The youth of bourgeois families, moved by patriotism and idealism, often joined the revolutionary Partisans. Some working-class young joined the fascist Ustachi.

Gradually word got out to Allied leaders that Tito's fighters were considerably more active in attacking the Germans, while the Mihajlović forces tended to make local accommodations with the occupiers, hoarding their strength for encounters with the Partisans. Britain's Winston Churchill sent his agents to Yugoslavia, including his son Randolph, to check on the reports that Tito was the more effective anti-German force there, more deserving of Allied support in the drive to victory than the underground loyal to the exiled government. The secret British mission sent back recommendations in favor of Allied support for the Partisans, and at the Teheran meeting of Churchill, Roosevelt and Stalin in late November 1943, the shift of Allied support from Mihajlović to Tito was officially endorsed.

By the beginning of 1944, some 6,000 tons of arms and ammunition were being parachuted to the Partisans each month, and by the summer of 1944 Allied intelligence estimated that the Western powers were supplying half of the Partisans' military equipment. Nonetheless, a fierce German offensive in the spring of 1944 came near to capturing

Tito. He fled to southern Italy, by then out of the war, and the British flew him back to the Yugoslav island of Vis so he could continue to command his forces from Yugoslav soil. Later, on August 12, he flew to Italy again for a secret meeting with Churchill at Caserta. Churchill believed he had obtained pledges that Allied supplies would not be used in the civil war but only against the Germans and that Tito would not forcibly impose communism after the war.

There remains a great deal of controversy about whether the Communists would have won without this help, and whether their claim to be so much more active in the resistance than the Chetniks was justified. Mythmaking was an important part of the military and political struggle in the guerrilla war. In any event, the Partisans did win, and took power in Belgrade. A socialist republic was proclaimed. Peter II and his ministers and aides remained in permanent exile.

The establishment of communism continued the violence and exaction of vengeance in the ravaged country after the defeat of Germany in 1945. It is estimated that in the following five years the vicious Communist purges claimed 300,000 Croatian victims—of whom 1,000 were Roman Catholic priests—70,000 Germans, 17,000 Slovenes, 6,000 Montenegrins and 3,000 Serbs. On their side, the Croatian Ustachi had killed some 500,000 Orthodox Serbs, and the Serbs retaliated.

Some Croats who fled to Western Europe and the United States never abandoned terrorism, conducted abroad, in their opposition to the Communist regime. In the immediate postwar period, American agents used the "rat lines," escape routes established by a Croatian priest in Italy, to smuggle abroad Nazis who had gone to work for U.S. intelligence after the war. This was documented two generations later when the Department of Justice investigated how Klaus Barbie, whom the French called "the Butcher of Lyon" for atrocities committed during the occupation, managed to avoid prosecution for war crimes and to settle in Bolivia.

Though the Red Army never stopped in Yugoslavia, as it did in neighboring Bulgaria, Romania, Hungary and Austria, communism was imposed just as mercilessly by its indigenous adherents. Tito supported the Communist guerrillas in Greece in the civil war which continued there after liberation, and seemed a loyal ally of Stalin. Europe held its breath when the Yugoslavs forced down an American plane in 1946, an incident which signaled the coming Cold War and could have led to conflict. But behind the scenes, Tito and Stalin were moving toward confrontation. Stalin wanted full hegemony over the newly Communist countries. He forced those occupied by the Red Army to remodel themselves on the Soviet pattern and expected their leaders to kowtow to his commands. Tito refused.

The Comintern (Communist International), which Moscow had built to control and abet Communist parties around the world between the wars, had been dissolved in deference to President Roosevelt while the United States and the Soviet Union were allies. But in 1947 it was revived in a new shape with a new name, Cominform (Communist Information Bureau), with headquarters at first in Belgrade, then moved to the Romanian capital of Bucharest. Suddenly, on June 29, 1948, the Cominform announced that Yugoslavia had been expelled. That was Stalin's way of pronouncing anathema on Tito and trying to provoke his replacement by a puppet. A Soviet embargo was placed on Yugoslavia, a drastic pressure because as a member of the Soviet bloc it had turned entirely to Moscow for economic cooperation. Like other new Communist regimes, it had rejected America's Marshall Plan for vast reconstruction aid.

Within a short time, the country was brought to a halt. Simple necessities like needles and soap were unavailable. Scarcities were worse than in wartime. But Yugoslavia was not brought to its knees. Tito's determination to resist, backed by all but a few pro-Soviet compatriots, brought economic and eventually military aid from the West. Slowly, the country was rebuilt and reformed.

The state's stormy first twenty years, the World War II experience and Tito's personality and his break with Stalin shaped the modern Yugoslavia. The struggle to keep power despite Stalin's machinations led Tito to experiment with reforms before the other Communist regimes dared think of it. A system of worker self-management was devised as a way of providing some incentives and responsibility in the factories without impinging on the Marxist requirement that there must be no private ownership of the means of production. People were allowed to emigrate. There was a period of rapid growth, aided by remittances from Yugoslav workers abroad. The campaign against the churches was gradually eased. A modicum of freedom of expression was allowed.

In the search for an international political refuge that would not absorb Yugoslavia into the anti-Communist West but would buffer it against the Soviets, Tito joined with India's Nehru, Egypt's Nasser and

Indonesia's Sukarno to found the nonaligned movement. This was the original third world, not meant in terms of lack of development but as a third way between the Soviet and Western blocs. Nonalignment became the cornerstone of Yugoslav foreign policy and, more than in some member states, Yugoslavia interpreted it as a need to keep a careful balance between East and West. At the 1979 Havana summit of the nonaligned, an ailing but stern Tito led the opposition to Fidel Castro's attempt to redefine the movement as the "natural ally" of the Soviet Union.

The West responded with considerable indulgence, to a point that irritated Yugoslav dissidents, such as the writer Mihajlo Mihajlov. He complained that Tito's image as a nationalist hero was too easily accepted, citing Western film stars, invited by Tito for lavish visits, who were gulled into overlooking the fact that he ran a tough Communist regime. Western banks poured out loans, an important element in the boom which gathered momentum in the 1960s and 1970s. But it was also a factor in the intensity of the economic crisis of the early 1980s when world recession hit, export markets dried up and interest rates soared. Yugoslavia tried to reach something of an equilibrium in its trade with the East and the West. But that was hard to maintain. As Belgrade officials had to admit, "It's easy to buy West and easy to sell East," given the state contracts and low quality demands of the Communist markets. The importance of Western equipment to improve quality and revive growth sharpened the quarrels among the republics over the use of their quite unequal earnings of hard currency.

Somehow, so long as Tito was there, the disputes were resolved and the dimension of the problems hidden. He acquired such power and prestige, an almost magical aura, that when he died in 1980, at age eighty-eight after a lingering illness, there were widespread fears for the survival of the state. Many thought the Soviets might invade once his towering strength had fallen. That did not happen. He had prepared for government after-Tito, but within a few years there was so much trouble in keeping the economy and administration going that Yugoslavs began to realize they hadn't so much devised an original political-social system as they had learned to lean on one man.

In his late years, Tito was a staunch, heavy figure, square of face and body. He liked to wear dazzling uniforms, and he walked ponderously, radiating authority. He had become a world figure, of far greater importance on the international scene than his small country, a name to reckon with on every continent. He had created himself, giant-sized. He was born in 1892, the seventh child of a Croatian peasant named Franjo Broz. In World War I he served in the Austrian army but was quickly taken prisoner on the Russian front. The result was to involve him in the Bolshevik revolution, and for three years, 1917–20, he fought in the Russian civil war with the Red forces. In 1919, he joined the Yugoslav section of the Soviet Communist Party, and when he returned home it was as a Soviet agent and organizer of the illegal Yugoslav party. He was caught and imprisoned in 1928.

According to Milovan Djilas, long his closest comrade but later his prime opponent, it was not just a political arrest. He was charged with planning terrorism, and bombs were found in his possession. After six years in jail, he was able to return to the Soviet Union, where he worked in 1934–36 for the Comintern in Moscow. That was when he took Tito as a pseudonym, though some accounts say it was his nickname as a child. Then, when the Spanish Civil War broke out in 1936, he was assigned to organize the Yugoslav section of the International Brigades on the Republican side. He did not fight in Spain himself, but dispatched recruits from Paris. Much of Tito's story remains mysterious, despite the flood of books, films and articles about him. The outpouring was deliberately generated to create a cult, in the Stalin pattern. Efforts at demythification have had little material to build on.

After the war in Spain, he returned clandestinely to Zagreb to take up his post as head of the illegal Communist Party. He had been installed as chief by the Soviets, after many members of the Yugoslav Central Committee were purged in 1937. He took to the mountains when the Axis powers occupied the country, to lead the Partisan resistance. Those were days of great sacrifice, great deprivation, the kind of fight which unites victorious survivors with deep bonds of loyalty and fraternity. Just because the struggle was so terrible, it is remembered by Tito's adherents in glory and boundless pride. As Mao's leadership of the Long March in China consecrated him during his lifetime as the Great Helmsman of his country, Tito's guerrilla heroics gave him unchallengeable status once his side had won. He proclaimed himself a marshal during the war, and used the title ever after. By accident of wartime geography, the Italian troops in Yugoslavia surrendered to Tito's Partisans when Rome left the war in 1944, an enormous advantage in equipment and security for the Communist guerrillas in their continuing struggle with the Chetniks. Tito proclaimed a new republic on November 29, 1945. But, although World War II was over, the fighting did not stop.

Tito was ruthless in his determination to put his Communist regime on a solid foundation, which meant building a vast, uninhibited secret police force on the Soviet model. Djilas, in his biography *Tito: The Story from Inside*, reports that Stalin complained to the Poles about their lack of vigor in wiping out "class enemies," giving Yugoslavia as a comparison. Stalin is quoted as saying, "Good for Tito—he shot them." When the break with Moscow came in 1948, however, perception of the main internal enemy shifted. It was local Communists suspected of maintaining primary allegiance to Moscow. Some fifteen thousand were rounded up and sent to concentration camps. This is still a period hidden in shadow, and there is no figure on how many survived. The camps were closed in 1956, after Stalin's successor, Nikita Khrushchev, had traveled to Belgrade for a reconciliation.

By then, Tito was unassailable. He had developed an opulent way of life, residing in Belgrade in the former royal White Palace and taking over for his personal pleasure all the royal estates. Just how many palaces he used around the country wasn't known. He loved hunting and maintained vast game preserves. He took over the whole island of Brioni, in the Adriatic, as a private retreat, flattering foreign friends and dignitaries with coveted invitations to one of the world's most exclusive and lavish resorts. He wore diamonds and a heavy solid-gold belt buckle. He had an eye for women and indulged it. In the capitalist world, he would have been seen and no doubt admired as a great, self-made tycoon, the lack of scruples overwhelmed by the glamour and totality of his success. In the Communist world, it was not much different. He knew what he wanted, and he knew how to do it. The people were encouraged to show adulation, and they did. He was an authentic hero; he had saved the nation's independence, and he had held it together.

But the revolution fell far short of its ideals. Ordinary people grumbled, though not openly. The police were omnipresent. It came as almost as much of a shock as Tito's break with Stalin when his closest comrade, Djilas, turned against him. Djilas resigned from the party in 1954 and began to write articles critical of the regime. He was imprisoned by Tito, for the first of many times, in 1956. His book *The New Class*, published in the West in 1957, was the first systematic critique by a participant of the new "people's democratic" regimes installed in

Eastern Europe after the war. He spoke from inside, with firsthand knowledge of the dirty secrets, from a committed Communist's point of view. Given his record alongside Tito during the war and the period of consolidating power, no one could accuse him of being reactionary, bourgeois, antisocialist. But his complaints were not so different from those of ideological critics. Far from wiping out class distinctions, Djilas said, the regime had elevated a "new class" of the privileged, self-indulgent and corrupt, defending their power with force. There was no democracy, no freedom. This was not the revolution that he had had in mind. Many other people had harbored the same thoughts, but until Djilas spoke out the silence had been unbroken.

In an ideological regime, the gravest breach comes not from enemies but from fissure within the ideology. Tito put Djilas in jail as a heretic, but whether he refrained from executing the unexpected opponent because of their long comradeship-in-arms, or because it would have been impolitic in view of Tito's fight with Moscow, is not clear. Djilas received very harsh treatment, which he withstood with a stoic will as great as Tito's own, never deigning to recant a word. Still, there was always a certain ambiguity in the way Tito handled him, releasing him after five years, imprisoning him again, isolating him as a nonperson but restoring certain limited rights to continue working on his books, see foreigners discreetly and publish abroad. Djilas spent a total of nine years in jail, part in solitary confinement, but emerged strong and se-rene. After Tito died, Djilas remained Yugoslavia's most eminent non-person, a name to strike awe, feared and hated by the regime but treated with circumspection. He lived with his wife in a small Belgrade apartment, well furnished with traditional pieces, under constant police surveillance, unbowed, undaunted.

One leading Yugoslav official expressed the country's dilemma as "nationality interests versus class interests." In theory, class interests are supposed to be the same throughout the supposedly classless soci-ety. But the leaders had come to recognize more or less openly that economic and social problems were inextricably tied to the regional rivalries. In an attempt to overcome the historic tensions of centraliza-tion and fear of Serbian dominance, Tito's new constitution of 1974 established far-reaching regional autonomy under Communist power. The six republics are Slovenia, Croatia, Bosnia, Serbia, Montenegro and Macedonia, with Voivodina and Kosovo having the status of auton-omous provinces of the Serbian republic. And, in an attempt to prevent a battle for the succession or the rise of a new central figure who might revert to the Soviet pattern, Tito legated a collective presidency and a collective rule of the party, with the top person rotating among the republics' delegates each year. The care with which they watched each other to prevent one individual emerging to special prominence was shown by the requirement that a visiting head of state must be received by all members of the presidency. There could be no pictures of two great men shaking hands in front of their flunkies. When a foreign correspondent asked to interview one of the leaders, they had to agree among themselves to designate whose turn it would be. The star system was not to be introduced through the back door by the foreign press.

In each republic, the government and the party have full control. They decide on investments and run the banks, the educational system, the post office, the railroads, and so on. Some of the anomalies are ludicrous. The train from Belgrade to Zagreb must stop at the Serbo-Croatian border to change locomotives. Zwornik and Mali Zwornik, two charming towns on the banks of the Drina, are connected by a bridge which the residents cross frequently. But not the mailman. Zwornik is in Bosnia and Mali Zwornik is in Serbia. The towns do not have an agreement on sharing postal expenses, so letters between them have to be detoured through the national capitals for proper accounting. Power grids do not cross republic borders. Croatia sells electricity to Italy and Austria because distributing it to other parts of Yugoslavia, where it is needed, would provoke disputes.

Some of the anomalies are intolerable. Each republic keeps its own foreign exchange account, and borrows abroad. When economic crisis came, nobody knew the total of Yugoslavia's foreign debt. It took the International Monetary Fund to go through all the separate totals to discover the debt was $20 billion, higher per capita than even Poland's. Plants are built, at great cost, where they are not needed in order to assuage local pride and ambition. Materials and equipment cannot be imported where they are needed, because the local republic does not have access to foreign exchange earned in other parts of the country. While Tito was alive, he arbitrated or forced settlements. After him, there was paralysis and stagnation.

One trouble is that, despite the constitution, the republics are not equal. Slovenia, with its fertile valleys, educated population and advanced tradition, has 8 percent of the people but produces 17 percent of the GNP and 28 percent of the hard-currency exports. It is a green, sunny land, proud of its ancient language and its totally European tradition. The capital, Ljubljana, is a pleasant city of 360,000, with old churches and Austrian-style palaces on the hilltop. The city officials deliberately resisted mass urbanization, and the town lives in close contact with the surrounding countryside. Everybody wanders off to climb a mountain, pick mushrooms or tend a vineyard on the weekends. There is a balanced pace of hard work and a leisurely love of nature. It is the smallest, and richest, republic. Instead of exporting labor to Western Europe, it attracts workers from Bosnia and Kosovo. That creates the same kinds of problems that northern Europe has experienced. The Albanians from Kosovo work hard, even on Sunday, live poorly and send most of their earnings back home. There is little intermarriage. The nationality code blocks pressures for assimilation, but that leaves language problems. Seventy-five percent of the local bus drivers are not Slovenes and cannot speak to their passengers.

Croatia, with its long, gorgeous coastline, has flourished with tourist income. Before the collapse of Austro-Hungary, its port of Fiume (now Rijeka) served as the major access to the sea for the trade of Central Europe. Zagreb, the capital, is a bustling commercial and cultural center, modern in parts, drearily so in the mass housing suburbs, but still graced with eighteenth- and nineteenth-century avenues and buildings, some dilapidated. After the Slovenes, the Croats have the highest living standard and industrial development. Since the country's borders were opened as part of the liberalizing process, millions of foreigners flow through the area every year. And there are some 750,000 Yugoslavs, many from Croatia, working in Western Europe, free to come and go as they please. The movements of so many people enhance Croatia's westward-looking tradition and spur it to be up to date. The "English beach" on the island of Rab, so named because King Edward VIII and his future American wife, Wallis Simpson, swam there in the nude in the summer of 1936, is now one of many nature camps that dot the coast. The bright sun and glittering turquoise water are irresistible to northern Europeans, and they have brought their manners and tastes.

Bosnia-Herzegovina, much poorer and a bit smaller than Croatia, was dominated by the Turks longer than other areas and is still orientalized. Apart from some Turks who stayed, its Moslems are Serbs who were converted to Islam and took up its habits, sipping tiny cups of coffee served on embossed brass trays, wandering through the bazaar, haggling and gossiping. Sarajevo, the capital, is set against bleak, dark mountains. Its filigreed minarets and the blanched white of the Moslem cemetery contrast with the dull ring of socialist-realist apartment buildings surrounding the city. It was the site of the 1984 winter Olympics, which left some handsome modern buildings and new sports facilities in the otherwise sleepy town. Croats and Slovenes complain that the benefits of their industrious efficiency are drained off to subsidize backward areas like Bosnia with overambitious investments which cannot pay their way. But some economists say they draw advantage from cheap raw materials and a captive market.

Serbia, the largest republic, is resented by all the others, who accuse it of ambitions for hegemony. The capital is Belgrade, a dusty inland city at the confluence of the Danube and the Sava. It was destroyed so many times in the endless Balkan wars that little remains of charm or historic interest. The look is simply prosaic or dated. There are elegant villas with large gardens in the suburb of Dedinje on a hill above the city, the site of Tito's White Palace, and an amusing cobblestoned section called Skadarlija, lined with taverns and handsome iron lanterns. Gypsy bands roam through. People stay late at night to eat *cevapcici*, spicy grilled meat patties which are the local version of oriental kebab, drink the light Serbian wine and sing rousing ballads. The girls are striking, with shining dark eyes. With the limited introduction of private commerce, discothèques have sprouted in other parts of town, and a rash of pizzerias, which, one Belgrade resident said contemptuously, are hives of police agents.

As autonomous provinces within the Serbian republic, Voivodina and Kosovo are restive at what they consider unequal treatment. The large Hungarian minority lives mostly in Voivodina, an extension of the Hungarian plains with the potential for a thriving agriculture. Kosovo, on the Albanian border, has a large majority of ethnic Albanians, many with irredentist yearnings. An uprising in 1981 was brutally repressed. The capital, Priština, has been called a city of soldiers, students and police spies. Sullen, grim young people stalk up and down Marshal Tito Boulevard in the evenings, speaking Albanian and glaring at the clusters of militiamen at every corner. An official of Albanian origin told a visitor, "It is political nonsense to talk about a ubiquitous enemy manipulated by Albania. In reality, the enemy is our sons and daughters." The region is half the size of Wales. People say that Tito told Albania's Communist leader Enver Hoxha in 1946 that "Kosovo and other areas inhabited by Albanians belong to Albania. We will give them back, but not now, because Serbian opinion would not accept such a thing." Because of the much higher Albanian birthrate and the increasing emigration of Serbs, whose minority status makes them feel insecure, the Albanian majority in the province is almost 80 percent. The border to Albania itself is closed to all but a trickle of authorized traffic, but people do slip across the difficult mountains. Lake Scutari, on the border south of Titograd, mostly in Albania, is a marvel of green water half covered by water lilies. Isolation has made the area Europe's greatest nature preserve, daunting, largely undeveloped and untouched.

Montenegro, on the southern part of the coastline, is a land where rosy and ocher cliffs drop precipitously into an azure sea. It is poor but very proud, with a warrior tradition that persists. The people are tall and handsome, their faces rugged as the mountains. They speak Serbo-Croatian. The American detective story writer Rex Stout was a Montenegrin, and he often included violent local lore and spicy local recipes in his thrillers.

Macedonia is inland, on the mountainous borders with Greece and Bulgaria, and has its own classical traditions and language. The capital, Skoplje, was ravaged by an earthquake in 1979. It is an unattractive city, built too fast and too shoddily. The border and nationality dispute with Bulgaria has never been settled.

After Tito's break with Stalin and the need to improve relations with the West, Yugoslavia's long-standing frontier conflict with Italy was resolved by an agreement which can be considered permanent. But the quarrels with Bulgaria and Albania remain open and festering, held in check essentially by the shadow of the Soviet army and the taut East-West relation. Tito established a large army and a local defense system which could support a guerrilla war so as to deter any thought of attack on Yugoslavia after his death. But there has always been a haunting fear that Croatian fanatics might turn to Moscow for armed support to oust the regime. While the Croats have produced some of the most violent anti-Communists, they also tend to supply the hard-liners in the continuing struggle within the League of Yugoslav Communists on how far to go toward liberal reform. It is difficult to say how much of these tensions is generated by ideology and how much by the nationality and religious rivalries. It is an element of Yugoslav politics ripe for exploitation. And although intermarriage, development and the rise of a new generation have brought some fusion and consensus, the old hatreds are still handed down.

However, it is improbable that the degree of freedom evolved over the years of Tito's rule can be reversed short of a general conflagration. The press is censored but relatively independent compared to Eastern Europe's. Workers' self-management, while unsatisfactory in many ways, is too firmly established to be wiped out and replaced by orthodox central planning. Above all, the right to travel and to possess foreign currency is too highly prized. "That is what makes us different from the East," said a Croatian banking official. A Serbian journalist remembered vividly the day she first received a passport. "I had been applying for five years, and I didn't have any special travel plans. But I went right off to London just to prove I could. With my passport in my pocket, I felt free at last."

The creeping crisis of the system after Tito's death nonetheless forced consideration of how to manage better. Decentralization in a country with so much inequality between the regions brought economic blockage. The choice of ways to overcome it was either to revert to fierce authoritarian control at the center, in effect a return to Stalinism with all the implications of terror, or to abandon Marxist controls and let a free market guide the flow of investment, trade and enterprise.

In the mid-1980s, Yugoslavia was edging toward liberal reform. There was a ferment of ideas, and fears that they would race away and explode the regime, or even the state. But it had become clear both that the revolution had not solved the country's major problems, and that it was only the exhaustion from invasion and civil war which had made it possible to impose the regime. Intellectuals in all parts of the country, modern-minded men and women, were looking for ways to dilute the burden of ideology. Occasionally, they were repressed. There was a trial in 1984–85 of a group who merely met from time to time and discussed the country's troubles. Officials complained when the case received international attention, denouncing what they called "the foreign press campaign against us." One asked, "Why are you suddenly talking about Yugoslavia?"

There wasn't any campaign. The answer was that the trial was news because the world no longer expected people to be jailed in Yugoslavia for expressing moderate criticism. That was how far the country had come. Sooner or later, it seemed clear, it would move farther. There were no outstanding leaders, no charismatic personalities to break the impasse. But there were a great many people thinking hard, arguing, hoping that eventually the country could produce the democracy it was promised in 1919 but had never known.

CONCLUDING
COMMENTS

THE NEW ERA began with the end of the Second World War. Not everything changed. Surveying the monarchical Europe of the eighteenth century, the Duc de Montesquieu said, "Europe is a state composed of many provinces, but it is not amenable to the creation of a unified empire." Two centuries later that was still the case, but the great historic difference was that Europeans no longer considered war a tolerable means for achieving unity. War had always been a scourge, but once it had been seen as rewarding, ennobling, the highest measure of valor and the highest form of patriotism. In some other parts of the world the old romantic vision persisted, but not in Europe, whose entire history had been one of conquest, combat, and upheaval. Pacifists remained a minority, and, as NATO's Secretary General Lord Carrington said, the continent had become "the arena for the largest concentration of military might the world has ever witnessed." But if there were any who wanted the guns to be used, they dared not say so.

This lesson, and the accompanying Western European lesson of the value of cooperation, were the message now from a mature Europe which once forced the world to accept its dominion. The world would not again be at Europe's feet, but Europe was not on its knees. There was still some nostalgia for the glory days of supremacy, and glum foreboding that the decline would continue in the age of a new industrial revolution based on high technology. But a sturdy base remained, economically, politically, culturally, scientifically. It had only to be organized and galvanized. The means and the brains were available.

Still, the shining postwar vision of a vigorous new power, a United States of Europe, receded beyond the horizon. There was too much nationalism, too much of what Montesquieu considered provincial spirit braking the drive for integration, which, nonetheless, Europeans knew to be the best motor for a new dynamism.

Yet the push toward the vision of unity was there, in the form of consent, association, mutual support. It was reflected in the change in politics, originally the outgrowth of wars and revolutions. Militant, violent ideologies lost their attraction. The argument about the viability and value of democracy, a central issue in the years before the war, had disappeared. Defeat and the revelation of Nazi Germany's abomination fully discredited fascism. Communism maintained an appeal for some a generation or so longer, preaching its ideals of equality and fraternity and the belief that a political system could perfect man and society. That faded too as everyday evidence on the contrast between life in the East and the West became too obvious to deny. The spread of instant and abundant information made it difficult to ignore reality. Western Europe settled comfortably and assuredly on democratic premises, even in Greece and Spain and Portugal, where into the 1970s dictatorships had been proclaimed the only system capable of maintaining order. The Soviet Union lost all moral and philosophical magnetism, one result of détente and a waning sense of inevitable confrontation which had seemed to force a polarized choice. Consensus developed among Western Europeans on the fundamentals of society. They have become moderates, pushing extremists to the margins.

Europe felt unaccustomedly small. For the Eastern Europeans, the Soviet hegemony became an insuperable obstacle to this kind of evolution. For the West, keenly aware of the Soviet shadow but spared a Soviet presence, the important change on the international scene was that America had become a superpower. Necessarily this affected attitudes. America had been seen as the land of refuge and opportunity, generous liberator and warrantor of a truly new and different world. As reliance on U.S. help dwindled, there was a feeling of constraint and excessive dependency. Europeans had considered themselves the pacesetters of the world, the arbiters of culture and style. At first they were irritated to find themselves caught up in what they called "Coca-colonization." Supermarkets, fast food, bottled soft drinks, obtrusive advertising, comic strips, a greatly accelerated pace of life and a reversal of the direction of respect from age to youth, had all come from America.

The innovations jostled customs and sensitivities. But the changes were soon assimilated and accepted for what they were—modernity, just as potatoes and tobacco and sweet corn had been brought from the New World and become familiar and domestic to the Old.

Ambivalent feelings toward the United States were bound to persist. There was a strong sense of common fate. But America's size and power cast shadows, on some occasions a welcome umbrella but much of the time a limit on others' place in the sun. Europeans felt as free to criticize U.S. government policies as Americans did. That was not anti-Americanism at all, but rather a reflection of the implicit sense of partnership in an ill-defined community called the Western world. There was fear, lest the American giant tire of the quarreling company and shrug Europe off, or lest the giant swagger or stumble into catastrophe and drag it in.

And there was satisfaction that Europe had come to resemble America in material success, a great achievement of the modern world. Never before had so many people been enabled to live so well. But the very ease and comfort defined an aching void. André Malraux once said, "The twenty-first century will be spiritual or it won't be." It was a reference to the failure to add a new dimension to human thought and feeling to match the new power of the nuclear arsenal. The incompleteness of life so centered on materialism has stirred many countermovements, some inchoate, some destructive. The youth upheaval of 1968 was a signal of yearning. But the rebels who thought up the witty cry "Imagination in power" weren't able to imagine a satisfactory balance embracing both material and spiritual needs.

The search for inspiring illusion is inherently human. It will not be abandoned. Fundamentalists look for it in a mythologized past, in old verities, in rejection of new ideas and knowledge and conduct which have come to trouble their self-assurance. Europeans who once produced so much intolerance and righteousness and paid an awesome cost for it have not developed that kind of movement. It is possible that out of the long familiarity with civilization, scarred with the terrible wounds of attempting to defy it, Europe can bring forth a new tempered spirit to comfort the twenty-first century. There are no clear signs as yet. There are sparks here and there, as there are in America and elsewhere. But there is fertile ground, seeded with great culture and mulched with the lessons of great pain. It is just possible.

EUROPEAN INSTITUTIONS

SHORTLY AFTER THE SECOND WORLD WAR, Britain's bluff Foreign Minister Ernest Bevin announced his hopes for Europe. The goal would be fulfilled, he said, "when I can go down to Victoria Station, buy a ticket for any place on the continent, and then just go." Things did not quite work out to that vision of reviving an old European order before the nineteenth- and twentieth-century barriers of nationalism were built up into blockades. But neither did they revert to the prewar system. The fundamental changes in the organization of Europe were the East-West partition and the proliferation of institutions, some continent-wide but the important ones established in East or West, essentially as rivals. The Western institutions were built on the new principle of cooperation. Those in the East were arranged to underpin the new principle of Soviet hegemony. Neither set fully achieved its initial goals, but even partially completed they transformed the political, economic, and military dynamics of the continent. They are the foundation stones of modern Europe's international relations, the basic difference from what had been before.

A brief outline of the major institutions:

WEST

EUROPEAN ECONOMIC COMMUNITY
(Common Market)

FOUNDED: 1957, with signing of the Treaty of Rome by France, West Germany, Italy, Belgium, Netherlands, and Luxembourg.

CURRENT MEMBERSHIP: in addition to founders, Britain, Ireland, Denmark, Greece, Spain, and Portugal.

POPULATION: 320 million.

ORGANIZATION: A commission, established in Brussels, with a staff of 9,000 international civil servants (Eurocrats). It has administrative responsibility for the Community and its own budget. Contributions are assessed on member states and expenditures determined by policies set in common.

Council of Ministers: Representatives of member governments, usually foreign ministers or others as appropriate. The presidency rotates among member states every six months, in alphabetical order. Heads of government meet three times a year, once in the capital of each successive president and once in Brussels.

Parliament: Elected directly by voters in each country, according to national rules. Meets in Strasbourg for debates and resolutions, but has no effective power.

FUNCTION: To create, step by step, a single market with a single external tariff and with goods and people moving freely within. Great advances have been made toward integrating economies, and five members (West Germany, France, Belgium, Holland, and Luxembourg) have a monetary agreement tying their exchange rates to each other. There are still many barriers to a fully integrated market, scheduled to be established by 1992. There are provisions for coordination of national economic, monetary, and foreign policy, but the Community has not been able to advance toward institutionalized joint policies in these areas. On matters of vital importance, each country has a veto. The ultimate aim, still far distant, is political unity, a United States of Europe.

ASSOCIATED INSTITUTIONS: European Coal and Steel Community (forerunner of the EEC), Euratom for nuclear affairs, Court of Justice, Court of Auditors, European Investment Bank, and many consultative committees and special funds.

ORGANIZATION FOR ECONOMIC COOPERATION AND DEVELOPMENT (OECD)

FOUNDED: 1961, as successor to Marshall Plan's Organization for European Economic Cooperation (1948).

CURRENT MEMBERSHIP: twenty-five states—twenty in Europe plus U.S., Canada, Japan, Australia, and New Zealand.

ORGANIZATION: Secretariat, in Paris, which studies worldwide economic trends and makes predictions. Governed by the board of member states.

FUNCTION: Operates primarily as a monitoring, reporting, and forecasting body. Many subgroups deal with crises or special issues, such as energy policy and aid to developing countries.

NORTH ATLANTIC TREATY ORGANIZATION (NATO)

FOUNDED: 1949, with seat in Paris; moved to Brussels after General de Gaulle removed France from integrated military command in 1966. Twelve original members—U.S., Canada, Britain, France, Italy, Belgium, Holland, Luxembourg, Denmark, Norway, Iceland, and Portugal.

CURRENT MEMBERSHIP: founders plus West Germany, Greece, Turkey, and Spain.

ORGANIZATION: A secretariat and permanent diplomatic representatives of member states in Brussels, directed by semiannual meetings of Defense and Foreign Ministers. Supreme Command headquarters in Mons, Belgium, which integrates forces contributed by members, directs regional commands, and organizes planning, deployment, training, maneuvers, etc.

FUNCTION: To provide a permanent alliance among interested European states and the U.S. and Canada so as to assure any aggressor that an attack on one will bring a response by all. The proclaimed purpose is exclusively defensive—the integration of forces in peacetime to guarantee wartime coordination. The area covered is the territory of member states and the North Atlantic sea-lanes. Members consult on security problems outside the NATO area but are not committed to joint action.

WESTERN EUROPEAN UNION (WEU)

FOUNDED: 1954, on the basis of the unproductive Brussels treaty of 1948 pledging France, Britain, Belgium, Holland, and Luxembourg to cooperate for collective defense and economic, social, and cultural programs.

CURRENT MEMBERS: founders plus West Germany.

ORGANIZATION: Small secretariat in Paris, governed by ministerial meetings.

FUNCTION: Originally to set constraints on the rearmament of Germany and ease its entry into NATO. Now used desultorily to launch ideas for independent European defense cooperation.

COUNCIL OF EUROPE

FOUNDED: 1949, with ten members; gradually expanded to twenty-one when Lichtenstein joined in 1978.

ORGANIZATION: Small secretariat in Strasbourg, regular large meetings of delegates.

FUNCTION: Intended to foster democratic values and human rights in Europe. Essentially a debating society, including neutrals, but its European Court of Human Rights has played a significant role in establishing standards.

EAST

COMMUNIST INFORMATION BUREAU
(Cominform)

FOUNDED: 1947, as successor to prewar Communist International (Comintern), with headquarters in Belgrade; moved to Bucharest when Tito's Yugoslavia was expelled by Stalin in 1948. Members were Soviet Union and newly Communist-ruled states of Eastern Europe. Disbanded in 1956.

COUNCIL FOR MUTUAL ECONOMIC ASSISTANCE
(CMEA or Comecon)

FOUNDED: 1949 by Soviet Union, Bulgaria, Romania, Hungary, Czechoslovakia, German Democratic Republic, and Poland.

CURRENT MEMBERSHIP: founders plus Mongolian People's Republic, Cuba, and Vietnam. Nicaragua attends as observer.

ORGANIZATION: Secretariat in Moscow, with regular members' meetings.

FUNCTION: Originally to help mold economies of new Communist states to Soviet model, later to promote division of labor within Soviet bloc and trade among members. State-controlled trade and lack of convertible currencies prevent development of free-trade-area kind of organization. Most exchanges remain bilateral.

WARSAW PACT

FOUNDED: 1955, in Warsaw, consolidating mutual defense treaties which the Soviet Union had signed with Czechoslovakia, Poland, Bulgaria, East Germany, Hungary, Romania, and Albania. Albania withdrew in 1968.

ORGANIZATION: Occasional top-level political meetings, Combined General Staff and planning staff in Moscow. Military headquarters at Legnica, in western Poland.

FUNCTION: Organize Soviet military command and planning with allies, legitimize Soviet military presence after end of war. Romania succeeded in getting Soviet troops to withdraw in 1957 but remains a Pact member.

ALL-EUROPEAN

ECONOMIC COMMISSION FOR EUROPE (ECE)

FOUNDED: 1947, in Geneva, as regional arm of United Nations Economic and Social Council. All European members of U.N. plus U.S. and Canada are members.

FUNCTION: Because of East-West antagonism, reduced to essentially non-controversial studies and recommendations on pollution, transport policy, energy plans, etc.

CONFERENCE ON SECURITY AND COOPERATION IN EUROPE
(Helsinki Accords)

FOUNDED: 1975, in Helsinki; accords signed as Final Act of conference. Members are all European states (thirty-three) except Albania, plus U.S. and Canada.

ORGANIZATION: Essentially no formal structure, but subsequent "review" conferences in Belgrade, Madrid, and Vienna have established a pattern which has taken root. A subsidiary conference on disarmament in Stockholm produced agreements on military measures.

FUNCTION: The Helsinki accords endorsed postwar European borders and recommended measures to build confidence and reduce the risk of war, to spur economic cooperation, and to foster respect for human rights. The accords are not formal treaties and have no enforcement provisions, but the "Helsinki process" has developed political importance in East-West relations.

BRIEF FACTS

AUSTRIA

AREA: 32,375 square miles.

POPULATION: 7.55 million. 56% urban. 233 persons per square mile.

RELIGION: Mostly Roman Catholic.

CAPITAL: Vienna (1.5 million).

OTHER CITIES: Graz, Linz, Salzburg, Innsbruck.

LANGUAGE: German.

FLAG: Three horizontal stripes of red, white and red.

GOVERNMENT: Parliamentary democracy. Republic established in 1919. Absorbed by Nazi Germany in 1938. Occupied after WWII by Americans, Soviets, British and French. Independence recovered in 1955 under State Treaty signed by Austria, US, UK, USSR and France. Permanently neutral.

GEOGRAPHY: Mountainous. Eastern Alps, Alpine and Carpathian foothills, and Danube Basin. The Danube flows through Austria for 220 miles. Highest mountain: Grossglockner (12,465 feet). Forests cover 44.22% of total land area.

ECONOMY: Main agricultural products are wheat, barley, oats, maize and potatoes. Vineyards are famous. Major industrial products: steel, petroleum, nonferrous metals, chemicals, construction materials, machinery, vehicles, textiles.

BELGIUM

AREA: 11,781 square miles.

POPULATION: 9.8 million. 95% urban. 839 persons per square mile, one of the most densely populated countries in the world.

RELIGION: Mostly Roman Catholic.
CAPITAL: Brussels (1 million, including suburbs).
OTHER CITIES: Antwerp, Ghent, Charleroi, Liège, Malines, Ostend.
LANGUAGES: French and Flemish. Brussels is bilingual.
FLAG: Three vertical stripes of black, yellow and red.
GOVERNMENT: Constitutional monarchy, parliamentary democracy. Member of NATO.
GEOGRAPHY: Mostly flat (average altitude: 526 feet). Two distinct regions separated by the Meuse and Sambre rivers; fertile and level west, hilly, wooded and less fertile southeast (Ardennes).
ECONOMY: Intensive agriculture, horses and dairy cows. Highly industrialized manufacture. No natural resources except coal. Major products: coal, steel, electricity, heavy engineering, chemicals and pharmaceuticals, textiles. Member of EEC.

BRITAIN (United Kingdom of Great Britain and Northern Ireland)

AREA: 94,247 square miles.
POPULATION: 55.9 million. 593 persons per square mile. England and Wales 77.7% urban, Scotland 70%, Northern Ireland 54.7%.
RELIGION: Mainly Church of England (Protestant Episcopalian) in England and Wales. Roman Catholic, Moslem and Jewish minorities. Scotland is mainly Presbyterian. Northern Ireland is two-thirds Protestant, one-third Catholic.
CAPITAL: London (7 million).
OTHER CITIES: Birmingham, Glasgow, Leeds, Sheffield, Liverpool, Manchester. Regional capitals: Cardiff, Wales; Edinburgh, Scotland; Belfast, Northern Ireland.
LANGUAGE: English, with some Welsh and Gaelic.
FLAG: The "Union Jack": red, white and blue diagonally converging stripes.
GOVERNMENT: Constitutional monarchy, parliamentary democracy. Member of NATO.
GEOGRAPHY: Mostly rolling land in England; Scotland occupies northern third of the main British island with southern uplands, northern highlands and islands (Hebrides, Orkney, Shetland, etc.) and heavily indented coast; Wales, in the west, hilly and verdant.
ECONOMY: Oldest industrial nation. Manufacturing and trading; metals and metal-using industries (machinery, autos, trucks, iron and steel), chemicals, textiles, arms, whisky. Large oil and gas fields in the North Sea, related industries. Engineering, shipbuilding in Scotland (Glasgow) and Northern Ireland (Belfast). Fishing and farming. Member of EEC.

BULGARIA
AREA: 42,823 square miles.
POPULATION: 9 million. 69% urban. 212 persons per square mile.
RELIGION: Mainly Orthodox, 10% Moslem.
CAPITAL: Sofia (1.08 million).
OTHER CITIES: Plovdiv, Varna, Ruse, Burgas.
LANGUAGE: Bulgarian.
FLAG: Three horizontal stripes of white, green and red; coat of arms in upper left-hand corner with red star symbolizing communism.
GOVERNMENT: Communist people's republic since 1946. Member of Warsaw Pact.
GEOGRAPHY: Mostly mountainous (Balkan, Rila, and Rhodope ranges). Fertile valleys and plains.
ECONOMY: Nationalized, centrally planned. Largely rural country: cereal growing and vineyards in southern valley, world's main producer of attar of roses. Exports food products and tobacco. Engineering industry accounts for two-thirds of exports: electric trucks and motors, pumps, ships, machine tools, weapons; also chemicals and textiles.

CZECHOSLOVAKIA
AREA: 49,370 square miles.
POPULATION: 15.6 million. 66% urban. 310 persons per square mile.
RELIGION: Mainly Roman Catholic; also Lutherans, Orthodox.
CAPITAL: Prague (1.1 million).
OTHER CITIES: Bratislava (capital of Slovakia), Brno, Plzeň, Ostrava, Kosiče.
LANGUAGES: Czech and Slovak.
FLAG: White and red horizontal stripes with a blue triangle on the left.
GOVERNMENT: Communist federal socialist republic composed of Czech and Slovak Socialist Republics. Independent state since 1918. Communist coup in February 1948. Member of Warsaw Pact.
GEOGRAPHY: Rugged mountains, rolling hills and fertile plains. Bohemia in the west is a plateau surrounded by mountains. Moravia is hilly. Slovakia in the east is the most mountainous area (Tatras range). Large Danube plain in southwest Slovakia.
ECONOMY: Nationalized, centrally planned. Main crops: sugar beets, potatoes, cereals. Industry: steel, machinery and transportation equipment. Glass industry in northern Bohemia. Breweries at Plzeň.

DENMARK
AREA: 16,633 square miles.
POPULATION: 5.1 million. 86% urban. 311 persons per square mile.
RELIGION: Lutheran.

CAPITAL: Copenhagen (483,000; 1.3 million including suburbs).
OTHER CITIES: Arhus, Odense, Alborg.
LANGUAGE: Danish.
FLAG: Red, with white cross.
GOVERNMENT: Constitutional monarchy, parliamentary democracy. Member of NATO.
GEOGRAPHY: Jutland Peninsula and 482 islands. Extension of the great northern European plain, flat or gently rolling country, averages only 98 feet above sea level. Many small lakes and white coastal beaches. Farmland covers three-quarters of the country.
ECONOMY: Highly efficient agriculture based on cooperatives. Trade centered on farm and dairy products: butter, cheese, bacon, ham. Fishing. Major industries: machinery, textiles, furniture, electronics. Member of EEC.

EAST GERMANY (German Democratic Republic)

AREA: 41,825 square miles.
POPULATION: 16.8 million. 78% urban. 401 persons per square mile.
RELIGION: 80% Protestant, 11% Roman Catholic, though government discourages religious practice.
CAPITAL: East Berlin.
OTHER CITIES: Leipzig, Dresden, Karl Marx-Stadt, Magdeburg, Halle.
LANGUAGE: German.
FLAG: Three horizontal bands of black, red and gold, with a hammer, compass and sheaf of corn at the center.
GOVERNMENT: Communist republic. In 1945 the area became the Soviet occupation zone of defeated Germany. In 1949 GDR was established as a state. Member of Warsaw Pact.
GEOGRAPHY: Mostly on the North German plain. Lakes in the north; Harz Mountains, Elbe Valley and sandy soil of Brandenburg in the center; highlands in the south.
ECONOMY: Nationalized, centrally planned, highly industrialized. Mining: copper, iron ore, lignite, potash. Manufacturing: chemicals and petrochemicals, machine tools, shipbuilding and transportation equipment, electronic and engineering equipment, precision tools, optical goods.

FINLAND

AREA: 130,552 square miles.
POPULATION: 4.8 million. 67% urban. 36 persons per square mile.
RELIGION: Lutheran.
CAPITAL: Helsinki (482,800).

OTHER CITIES: Tampere, Turku.
LANGUAGES: Finnish, some Swedish.
FLAG: White with a blue cross.
GOVERNMENT: Republic, parliamentary democracy. Neutral.
GEOGRAPHY: Densely forested (70%), thousands of lakes (9%), long, deeply indented coastline. Only 10% of the land is cultivated. Finnish Lapland stretches from south of the Arctic Circle almost to the edge of the Arctic Ocean. In the extreme north, midnight sun for two months, no sun for two months.
ECONOMY: Forestry remains the backbone of the economy, accounts for 40% of exports (paper and other forest products). Other industries: metalworking, shipbuilding, engineering, electronics, textiles, glass, ceramics, furniture, chemicals, pharmaceuticals.

FRANCE

AREA: Metropolitan France (mainland and Corsica): 211,208 square miles.
POPULATION: 54.6 million. 80% urban. 259 persons per square mile.
RELIGION: Mainly Roman Catholic.
CAPITAL: Paris (2.1 million; 8.7 million including suburbs).
OTHER CITIES: Marseille, Lyon, Toulouse, Lille, Bordeaux, Nice.
LANGUAGE: French.
FLAG: The "Tricolor": three vertical bands of blue, white and red.
GOVERNMENT: Republic, combination of presidential and parliamentary democracy. Member of NATO.
GEOGRAPHY: Extremely varied. Flat or rolling plains in the northern and western regions; hills and mountains in the eastern, central and southern parts. Mountains: Massif Central, Vosges, Jura, Alps, Pyrenees. Forests cover 20% of country. 2,300 miles of coastline.
ECONOMY: Extensive agriculture in the north and northeast, grasslands and orchards in the west. Major products: wheat, sugar beets, wine, fruits and vegetables. World-famous vineyards. Manufacturing: iron and steel, aluminum, chemicals, tires, cars, aeronautics, textiles, processed foods, high technology. Perfume and fashion industries. Member of EEC.

GREECE

AREA: 51,182 square miles. Mainland is 41,382 square miles; rest is islands.
POPULATION: 9.9 million. 66% urban. 194 persons per square mile.
RELIGION: Predominantly Greek Orthodox.
CAPITAL: Athens (1.3 million).
OTHER CITIES: Piraeus, Salonika.

LANGUAGE: Greek.

FLAG: Blue and white stripes with a white cross on a blue field in left-hand corner.

GOVERNMENT: Republic, parliamentary democracy. 1974 referendum abolished the monarchy. Military dictatorship 1967–73. Member of NATO.

GEOGRAPHY: Mountainous (80% of the country). Rocky, with little fertile soil. Islands are 20% of land area. 9,333 miles of coastline.

ECONOMY: Largely agricultural country despite poor soil (one-third of the work force). Main products: tobacco, wheat, cotton, olives, citrus fruits, raisins. Livestock raising (cattle, goats, sheep). Manufacturing remains weak, concentrated in the Athens area. Main industries: tobacco, processed foods, clothing, aluminum, chemicals, cement, glass, shipbuilding. Member of EEC.

HUNGARY

AREA: 35,919 square miles.

POPULATION: 10.8 million. 59% urban. 300 persons per square mile.

RELIGION: Mainly Roman Catholic.

CAPITAL: Budapest (over 2 million).

OTHER CITIES: Miskolc, Debrecen.

LANGUAGE: Hungarian (Magyar).

FLAG: Horizontal stripes of red, white and green.

GOVERNMENT: Communist people's republic. Member of Warsaw Pact.

GEOGRAPHY: Mostly flat. Fertile plain in the east, hilly and mountainous in the west and north (Mount Kekes: 3,300 feet). Danube River flows through the center of the country, north to south. Tisza River, 360 miles long.

ECONOMY: Nationalized, centrally planned, but since 1968 some liberalization of market. Collectivized agriculture unusually successful. Manufacturing, especially in Budapest area: chemicals, bauxite processing, food and beverages, machinery, steel, textiles, transportation equipment.

IRELAND (Eire)

AREA: 27,136 square miles.

POPULATION: 3.6 million. 61% urban. 132 persons per square mile.

RELIGION: Roman Catholic.

CAPITAL: Dublin (525,882).

OTHER CITIES: Cork, Limerick, Dun Laoghaire, Waterford.

LANGUAGES: English and Gaelic (Irish).

FLAG: Three vertical stripes of green, white and orange.

GOVERNMENT: Republic, parliamentary democracy. Ireland does not recognize Britain's incorporation of the six northern counties (Ulster) in
the UK. Neutral.

GEOGRAPHY: Mostly lowlands, pastures and peat bogs. Mountains near the
coast (Donegal in the northwest, Mayo and Connemara in the west,
Kerry in the southwest, Wicklow in the east). Lakes in the west. River
Shannon, longest river in the British Isles.

ECONOMY: Fertile soil in plains, humid climate good for stock raising: cattle,
sheep, pigs, horses. Pastures are main natural resource. Manufactures
mainly in the Dublin and Cork areas: alcoholic beverages, chemicals,
clothing, tobacco, machinery, auto assembly, metal and paper processing. Member of EEC.

ITALY

AREA: 116,314 square miles.

POPULATION: 57 million. 72% urban. 490 persons per square mile.

RELIGION: Roman Catholic.

CAPITAL: Rome (2.82 million).

OTHER CITIES: Milan, Naples, Turin, Genoa, Bologna, Florence, Palermo
(Sicily), Cagliari (Sardinia).

LANGUAGE: Italian.

FLAG: Three vertical stripes of green, white and red.

GOVERNMENT: Republic, parliamentary democracy. Member of NATO.

GEOGRAPHY: Rugged and mountainous, with two large plains of Emilia-
Romagna in the north, Apulia in the south. A long, boot-shaped peninsula stretching from the Alps to the Mediterranean, with the islands
of Sicily and Sardinia. The Appenine Mountains run through the center.

ECONOMY: Great regional differences between the north—one of the most
advanced industrial areas in Western Europe—and the much less developed south. Agriculture mainly in the fertile Po Valley; pastureland,
citrus fruits and olives in the south. Manufacturing: machinery, chemicals, textiles (fashion industry), steel. Leading tourist industry in Western Europe. Member of EEC.

LUXEMBOURG

AREA: 998 square miles.

POPULATION: 368,000. 82% urban. 378 persons per square mile.

RELIGION: 97% Catholic, 1% Protestant.

CAPITAL: Luxembourg 78,400.

OTHER CITIES: Esch-sur-Alzette, Dudelange, Differdange.

LANGUAGES: French and German are the official languages. Luxembour-
geois, or Letzeburgesch, is the everyday language.
FLAG: A tricolor of red, white and blue horizontal stripes.
GOVERNMENT: Constitutional monarchy.
GEOGRAPHY: Rugged uplands of the Ardennes plateau in the north. Undulating terrain with broad valleys in the south. Chief rivers: Moselle and
Sûre.
ECONOMY: The production of iron and steel remains the cornerstone of the
economy. Other industries: chemicals, rubber, fertilizer, food processing. Agricultural exports include dairy products, roses, and white
wines.

NETHERLANDS

AREA: 15,892 square miles.
POPULATION: 14.5 million. 88% urban. 912.4 persons per square mile.
RELIGION: 40% Catholic, 33% Protestant, 4% other, 23% no religion pro-
fessed.
CAPITAL: Amsterdam (687,397).
OTHER CITIES: Rotterdam, The Hague (seat of government), Utrecht, Eind-
hoven.
LANGUAGE: Dutch.
FLAG: Three horizontal bands of red, white and blue.
GOVERNMENT: Constitutional monarchy, parliamentary democracy. Member of NATO.
GEOGRAPHY: Flat and low, averaging 37 feet above sea level. Much land
below sea level reclaimed and protected by 1,500 miles of dikes. Criss-
crossed by canals and connecting rivers. Southwestern part made up
of islands and peninsula in the North Sea.
ECONOMY: Efficient, modern agriculture based on cooperatives. Dairy farming. Heavily industrialized: food processing, engineering, electronics,
petrochemicals, plastics, textiles, iron and steel based on imported
ores. Natural gas in the northeast (Groningen). Trade, banking and
shipping are traditionally important activities. Member of EEC.

NORTHERN IRELAND (Ulster) Part of United Kingdom

AREA: 5,463 square miles.
POPULATION: 1.5 million. 54.7% urban. 275 persons per square mile.
RELIGION: 67% Protestant, 33% Roman Catholic.
CAPITAL: Belfast (322,900).
OTHER CITIES: Londonderry, Bangor.
LANGUAGE: English.

FLAG: United Kingdom's Union Jack.
GOVERNMENT: Regional government suspended, under direct rule from London.
GEOGRAPHY: Flat or rolling farmland, mountains in south.
ECONOMY: Livestock and dairy goods. Shipbuilding industry centered in Belfast. Linen manufacture, rope and twine, engineering, electronics.

NORWAY

AREA: 125,057 square miles.
POPULATION: 4.1 million. 57% urban. 34 persons per square mile. Half the population lives in villages of under 200 persons.
RELIGION: Lutheran.
CAPITAL: Oslo (500,000).
OTHER CITIES: Bergen, Trondheim, Stavanger, Kristiansand.
LANGUAGES: Norwegian, Lapp.
FLAG: Red, with white-bordered blue cross.
GOVERNMENT: Constitutional monarchy, parliamentary democracy. Member of NATO.
GEOGRAPHY: Mountains and plateaus cover most of the country. 25% forested, only 2.3% cultivated. Average altitude more than 1,500 feet. Jagged coastline, tens of thousands of islands, long narrow inlets of the sea called fjords. 1,650 miles of coastline, about 13,265 miles including all the fjords and peninsulas. Northern third of the country is above the Arctic Circle.
ECONOMY: Dairy farming and livestock production, fishing. Industry based mainly on abundant hydroelectric power: chemicals, metals, processed foods, wood pulp and paper. Leading producer of aluminum. Oil and gas fields offshore in the North Sea, related products and services. Main exports: crude oil and gas, fish, paper.

POLAND

AREA: 120,725 square miles.
POPULATION: 37.1 million. 59% urban. 300 persons per square mile.
RELIGION: Roman Catholic.
CAPITAL: Warsaw (1.5 million).
OTHER CITIES: Lódź, Cracow, Wrocław, Poznań, Gdańsk.
LANGUAGE: Polish.
FLAG: Two horizontal stripes of white and red.
GOVERNMENT: Communist people's republic. Member of Warsaw Pact.
GEOGRAPHY: Flat plains and gently rolling hills. Rugged mountains in the south. Many lakes in the north.

ECONOMY: Nationalized, centrally planned. After failure of collectivization of agriculture, about 85% of farmland in private hands. Industry geared to producing capital rather than consumer goods: chemicals, iron and steel, machinery, shipbuilding, textiles. One of the leading coal-mining countries in the world.

PORTUGAL

AREA: 35,510 square miles, including the Azores and Madeira Islands.
POPULATION: 10 million. 66% rural. 282 persons per square mile.
RELIGION: Roman Catholic.
CAPITAL: Lisbon (818,000; metropolitan area 2 million).
OTHER CITIES: Oporto, Coimbra, Leiria.
LANGUAGE: Portuguese.
FLAG: Two vertical bands of green and red, bearing coat of arms.
GOVERNMENT: Republic. Dictatorship 1926–74, overthrown by military officers, parliamentary democracy since then. Member of NATO.
GEOGRAPHY: Mostly flat and low, with mountain ranges in the northeastern, central and southwestern regions. Douro and Tagus rivers cross country from east to west. Vast cork forests.
ECONOMY: Mostly agricultural, fishing. Exports: cork, fish, wood pulp, wine. Moderately industrialized: textiles, shoes, machinery, foodstuffs, but also a few heavy industries (metals, steel, shipbuilding, petrochemicals). Member of EEC.

ROMANIA

AREA: 91,700 square miles.
POPULATION: 23 million. 52% urban. 254 persons per square mile.
RELIGION: Mainly Orthodox, some Roman Catholics (Hungarians).
CAPITAL: Bucharest (2 million).
OTHER CITIES: Braşov, Timişoara, Constantsa, Cluj.
LANGUAGE: Romanian.
FLAG: Three vertical stripes of blue, yellow and red, coat of arms with a red star in the center.
GOVERNMENT: Communist people's republic. Member of Warsaw Pact.
GEOGRAPHY: Fertile flatlands, mountainous in north and central regions. Sunny east coast along the Black Sea. The Danube flows for about 900 miles through country.
ECONOMY: Nationalized, centrally planned. Based on agriculture before the 1960s, and oil deposits, forests and timber. Then rapid industrialization, overinvestment in energy-intensive heavy industry (petrochemicals) to the neglect of agriculture. Industrial machinery and mining.

SOVIET UNION (Union of Soviet Socialist Republics)

AREA: 8.65 million square miles, the largest country in the world.

POPULATION: 278 million. More than 100 nationalities, 65% urban. 32 persons per square mile.

RELIGION: Officially atheist, but Orthodox, Moslem and Jewish religions practiced.

CAPITAL: Moscow (8.39 million).

OTHER CITIES: Leningrad, Kiev, Tashkent, Baku, Kharkov, Gorky, Novosibirsk, Minsk, Vladivostok.

LANGUAGES: Russian is the dominant language, but other Slavic and many non-Slavic languages are spoken.

FLAG: Red, with a yellow hammer and sickle and a yellow outlined star in the upper left corner.

GOVERNMENT: Communist since the 1917 revolution. Nominally a federation consisting of 15 republics, the largest being the Russian Soviet Federated Socialist Republic. Leader of the Warsaw Pact.

GEOGRAPHY: Ural Mountains mark the traditional divide between European and Asian Russia. Broad, low plain in the European part, crossed by many rivers (Dnieper, Volga), with the Urals to the east and the Caucasus Mountains to the south. In the Asian part, deserts in Central Asia, vast lowlands and barren highlands in Siberia. Tundra covers the extreme north.

ECONOMY: Nationalized, centrally planned. Poor agricultural performance, permanent shortages of key crops (grain). Heavy industry: iron and steel, metals, chemicals. Exports oil, gold, weapons.

SPAIN

AREA: 196,700 square miles, including the Balearic and Canary islands.

POPULATION: 38.8 million. 77% urban. 199 persons per square mile.

RELIGION: Roman Catholic.

CAPITAL: Madrid (3.1 million).

OTHER CITIES: Barcelona, Bilbao, Valencia, Seville, Zaragoza.

LANGUAGES: Castilian Spanish official language, also Catalan and Basque.

FLAG: Three horizontal stripes of red, yellow and red.

GOVERNMENT: Constitutional monarchy and parliamentary democracy, after Franco's death in 1975 (dictatorship 1939–75). Seventeen autonomous regions have their own parliaments and governments. Separatist movements, especially in the Basque country. Member of NATO.

GEOGRAPHY: Mostly a rugged, high plateau (the Meseta). Plains broken by hills and low mountains. Mountain barrier of the Pyrenees to the north. Regional variations in topography and climate, from austere Castile to fertile Valencia.

ECONOMY: Main agricultural products: olives, oranges, wheat and wine, but imports large quantities of food. Rapid industrialization in the '50s and '60s (construction, mining, manufacturing), heavy foreign investment. Industries: automobiles, ships, cement, chemicals, shoes, clothing, steel, mainly in the northern provinces. Member of EEC.

SWEDEN

AREA: 173,436 square miles.
POPULATION: 8.3 million. 89% urban. 49 persons per square mile.
RELIGION: Lutheran.
CAPITAL: Stockholm (650,000; 1.4 million including suburbs).
OTHER CITIES: Göteborg, Malmö, Uppsala.
LANGUAGE: Swedish.
FLAG: Yellow cross on blue background.
GOVERNMENT: Constitutional monarchy, parliamentary democracy. Neutral.
GEOGRAPHY: Mountains along the northwest border. Flat or rolling terrain in the center and south, with large lakes. Forests cover half the country.
ECONOMY: Abundant natural resources: forests, mineral deposits, water power. Dairy farming. Manufacturing: iron and steel, engineering, chemical industry based on imports. Exports specialized machinery, explosives, fertilizers, plastics, safety matches.

SWITZERLAND

AREA: 15,950 square miles.
POPULATION: 6.39 million. 60% urban. 401 persons per square mile.
RELIGION: Over 50% Protestant, 45% Roman Catholic.
CAPITAL: Bern (145,700).
OTHER CITIES: Zurich, Basel, Geneva, Lausanne.
LANGUAGES: German, French and Italian are official languages. Romansch is a fourth, national language.
FLAG: Red, with white cross.
GOVERNMENT: Federal republic. Decentralized democracy. 23 cantons, 3 subdivided, making 26 in all. Neutral.
GEOGRAPHY: The most mountainous country in Europe. Alps cover 61%, Jura 12%. Major lakes: Maggiore, Zurich, Neuchâtel, Geneva. Forests cover about 25% of country.
ECONOMY: Few crops, dairy farming. Food importer. Tourism, banking and insurance. Highly industrialized, high-quality export products. Watchmaking (95% exported), chemicals, paper, processed foods, textiles.

WEST GERMANY (Federal Republic of Germany)

AREA: 96,011 square miles.

POPULATION: 61 million, including West Berlin. 86% urban. 637 persons per square mile.

RELIGION: 50% Lutheran, nearly 50% Roman Catholic.

CAPITAL: Bonn (292,900).

OTHER CITIES: West Berlin, Hamburg, Düsseldorf, Munich, Cologne, Essen, Frankfurt.

LANGUAGE: German.

FLAG: Three horizontal stripes of black, red and gold.

GOVERNMENT: Federal republic, parliamentary democracy. Ten states (*Länder*) plus West Berlin. The FRG grew out of the fusion of the three Western occupation zones after the division of Germany in the postwar era, gained sovereignty in May 1955. Member of NATO.

GEOGRAPHY: Alps in the south; Bavarian plain, sloping gently to Danube Valley; plateaus, rugged gorges and deep forests (Black Forest) between Rhine Valley and Bohemian Forest; northern plain, low, flat, drained by broad rivers.

ECONOMY: A leading industrial nation. Cut off from its main food-producing areas because of the division of Germany, imports one-third of its food. Main industries: coal mining, iron and steel, machine tools, cars, trucks, electrical equipment, optical equipment, chemicals, textiles, high technology. Member of EEC.

YUGOSLAVIA

AREA: 98,725 square miles.

POPULATION: About 23 million. 42% urban. 234 people per square mile.

RELIGION: Orthodox, Roman Catholic and Moslem.

CAPITAL: Belgrade (1.5 million).

OTHER CITIES: Zagreb, Skoplje, Sarajevo, Ljubljana.

LANGUAGES: Serbo-Croatian; also Slovenian, Macedonian, and Albanian.

FLAG: Three horizontal bands of blue, white and red, with a gold-trimmed red star in the center.

GOVERNMENT: Communist federation of six socialist republics and two autonomous regions. Nonaligned.

GEOGRAPHY: Varied, largely mountainous. Thickly wooded alpine regions in the northwest (Slovenia); narrow, rocky coastal region; bare hills, gorges and forests in Bosnia-Herzegovina.

ECONOMY: Agriculture employs 40% of all workers. 85% of the land is privately owned. Exports forest products, livestock, machinery, plastics, textiles. Tourism is important.

BIBLIOGRAPHY

The following list is intended more as a guide for further, specialized reading than as a list of sources. In addition, much of the material comes from personal experience and interviews, daily and weekly publications in several countries, government publications and standard reference works.

Albrecht-Carrié, René. *A Diplomatic History of Europe Since the Congress of Vienna*. New York: Harper & Row, 1973.
———. *The Unity of Europe: An Historical Survey*. New York: Doubleday, 1965.
Andersson, Ingvar. *A History of Sweden*. New York: Praeger, 1970.
Andrews, William G., and Hoffmann, Stanley, eds. *The Fifth Republic at Twenty*. Albany: State University of New York Press, 1981.
Ardagh, John. *France in the 1980s*. New York: Penguin Books, 1983.
Arendt, Hannah. *The Origins of Totalitarianism*. New York: Harcourt, Brace and Company, 1951.
Aron, Raymond. *Mémoires*. Paris: Julliard, 1983.
Ash, Timothy Garton. *The Polish Revolution: Solidarity*. New York: Scribner's, 1984.
Bailby, Edouard. *L'Espagne vers la démocratie*. Paris: Gallimard, 1976.
Barzini, Luigi. *The Europeans*. New York: Penguin, 1984.
———. *The Italians*. New York: Atheneum, 1977.
Beevor, Antony. *The Spanish Civil War*. London: Orbis, 1982.
Beloff, Nora. *Tito's Flawed Legacy: Yugoslavia and the West, 1939 to 1984*. London: Victor Gollancz Ltd., 1985.

Bender, Peter. *Das Ende des Ideologischen Zeitalters: die Europ-Aiserung Europas.* Severin & Siedler, 1981.

Bernard, Henri. *Terre commune. Histoire des pays de Bénélux, microcosme de l'Europe.* Brussels: Brepols, 1962.

Bethell, Nicholas. *Gomulka: His Communism.* New York: Holt, Rinehart & Winston, 1969.

Biagi, Enzo. *Italia.* Milan: Rizzoli Editore, 1975.

Bjol, Erling. *Nordic Security.* London: IISS, 1983 (Adelphi Paper).

Bocca, Giorgio. *In che cosa credono gli italiani?.* Milan: Longanesi, 1982.

———. *Storia della repubblica italiana, dalla caduta del fascismo a oggi.* Milan: Rizzoli Editore, 1982.

Bracher, Karl Dietrich. *The German Dictatorship. The Origins, Structure, and Effects of National Socialism.* New York: F. A. Praeger, 1970.

———. *The German Dilemma: The Throes of Political Emancipation.* New York: Praeger, 1975.

Brandys, Kazimierz. *A Warsaw Diary: 1978–81.* New York: Random House, 1983.

Brown, James F. *Bulgaria Under Communist Rule.* New York: Praeger, 1970.

———. *The New Eastern Europe: The Khrushchev Era and After.* New York: Praeger, 1966.

Brown, Terence. *Ireland. A Social and Cultural History 1922–1979.* London: Fontana Paperbacks, 1981.

Brus, Wladzimierz. *Processus de "Normalization" en Europe Centrale Soviétisée: Hongrie, Tchécoslovaguie, Pologne.* Cologne: Ed. Index, 1983.

Burdick, Charles; Jacobsen, Hans-Adolf; and Kudszus, Winfried, eds. *Contemporary Germany: Politics and Culture.* Boulder, Colorado: Westview Press, 1984.

Calleo, David Patrick. *The German Problem Reconsidered: Germany and the World Order 1870 to the Present.* New York: Cambridge University Press, 1978.

Cambridge Economic History of Europe. General Editors: M. Postan, D. C. Coleman and Peter Mathias. New York: Cambridge University Press, 1941.
Volume 4: *The Economy of Expanding Europe in the 16th & 17th Centuries.* Rich, E. E., and Wilson, C. H., 1967.
Volume 5: *The Economy Organization of Early Modern Europe,* Rich, E. E., and Wilson, C. H., 1977.
Volume 6: *The Industrial Revolutions and After: Incomes, Population and Technological Change.* Habakkuk, H. J., and Postan, M. M. (eds.), 1965.
Volume 7: *The Industrial Economies: Capital, Labour and Enterprise. Britain, France, Germany and Scandinavia.* Mathias, Peter, and Postan, M. M. (eds.), 1978.

Carr, Raymond. *Modern Spain: 1875–1980.* New York: Oxford University Press, 1980.

———. *The Republic and the Civil War in Spain.* New York: St. Martin's Press, 1971.

Carrère d'Encausse, Hélène. *Decline of an Empire*. New York: Newsweek Books, 1979.

———. *A History of the Soviet Union 1917–1953*. New York: Longman, 1982.

Castles, Francis Jeoffrey. *The Social Democratic Image of Society: A Study of the Achievements and Origins of Scandinavian Social Democracy in Comparative Perspective*. Boston: Routledge and Kegan Paul, 1978.

Caute, David. *Communism and the French Intellectuals 1914–1960*. New York: Macmillan, 1964.

———. *The Fellow-Travelers: A Postscript to the Enlightenment*. New York: Macmillan, 1973.

Childs, David. *The GDR: Moscow's German Ally*. Boston: George Allen & Unwin, 1983.

———, and Johnson, Jeffrey. *West Germany: Politics and Society*. London: Croom Helm, 1981.

Childs, Marquis William. *Sweden: The Middle Way*. New Haven: Yale University Press, 1936.

———. *Sweden: The Middle Way on Trial*. New Haven: Yale University Press, 1980.

Clapham, Sir John Harold. *The Economic Development of France and Germany: 1815–1914*. Cambridge: Cambridge University Press, 1923.

———. *An Economic History of Modern Britain*. 3 vols. Cambridge: Cambridge University Press, 1926, 1932, 1938.

Clark, Kenneth. *Civilisation*. New York: Harper & Row, 1970.

Clark, Martin. *Modern Italy: 1871–1982*. New York: Longmans, 1984.

Colign, Helen. *Of Dutch Ways*. Minnesota: Dillon Press, Inc., 1980.

Connery, Donald. *The Scandinavians*. London: Eyre and Spottiswoode, 1961.

Cook, Don. *Charles de Gaulle: A Biography*. New York: Putnam, 1984.

Crozier, Brian. *Franco: A Biographical History*. London: Eyre and Spottiswoode, 1967.

Custine, Astolphe (Marquis de). *Journey for Our Time: The Russian Journals of the Marquis de Custine*. New York: Pellegrini and Cudahy, 1951.

Dahl, Robert A. *Dilemmas of Pluralist Democracy: Autonomy Versus Control*. New Haven: Yale University Press, 1982.

———, ed. *Political Oppositions in Western Democracies*. New Haven: Yale University Press, 1966.

Dahrendorf, Ralf. *Society and Democracy in Germany*. New York: W. W. Norton, 1979.

Dangerfield, George. *The Strange Death of Liberal England*. New York: G. P. Putnam, 1980.

Davies, Norman. *God's Playground: A History of Poland*. New York: Oxford University Press, 1982.

———. *Heart of Europe: A Short History of Poland*. New York: Oxford University Press, 1984.

Dawidowics, Lucy S. *The War Against the Jews: 1933–1945*. New York: Holt, Rinehart and Winston, 1975.

Deaglio, Mario, and DeRita, Giuseppe. *Il punto sull'Italia*. Milan: Mondadori, 1983.

DeFelice, Renzo. *Interpretations of Fascism*. Cambridge, Massachusetts: Harvard University Press, 1977.

——. *Mussolini*. 3 vols. Torino: G. Einaudi, 1965.

——. *Fascism: An Informal Introduction to Its Theory and Practice. An Interview with Michael Ledeen*. New Brunswick: Transaction Books, 1976.

DePorte, A. W. *Europe Between the Superpowers: The Enduring Balance*. New Haven: Yale University Press, 1979.

Derry, Thomas Kingston. *A History of Modern Norway: 1814–1972*. Oxford: Clarendon Press, 1973.

——. *A History of Scandinavia: Norway, Sweden, Denmark, Finland and Iceland*. Boston: George Allen and Unwin, 1979.

Djilas, Milovan. *Conversations with Stalin*. New York: Harcourt Brace Jovanovich, 1962.

——. *Memoirs of a Revolutionary*. New York: Harcourt Brace Jovanovich, 1973.

——. *The New Class*. New York: Harcourt Brace Jovanovich, 1957.

——. *Tito: The Story from Inside*. New York: Harcourt Brace Jovanovich, 1980.

Doder, Dusko. *The Yugoslavs*. New York: Random House, 1978.

Donhoff, Marion Gräfin. *Foe into Friend: The Makers of the New Germany from Konrad Adenauer to Helmut Schmidt*. New York: St. Martin's Press, 1982.

Dumont, Georges-Henri. *Histoire de la Belgique*. Paris: Hachette, 1977.

Edinger, Lewis Joachim. *Politics in West Germany*. Boston: Little, Brown, 1977.

Elder, Neil Colbert McAuley. *The Consensual Democracies? The Government and Politics of the Scandinavian States*. Oxford: M. Robertson, 1982.

Engellan, Patrick, and Henning, Ulf, eds. *Nordic Views and Values*. 2nd ed. Stockholm: Nordic Council, 1984.

Eyck, F. Gunther. *The Benelux Countries: An Historical Survey*. New York: D. Van Nostrand, 1959.

Fejtö, François. *Behind the Rape of Hungary*. New York: D. MacKay Co., 1957.

——. *Budapest 1956*. Paris: Julliard, 1956.

——. *A History of the Peoples' Democracies: Eastern Europe Since Stalin*. New York: Praeger, 1971.

——, and Fisera, Vladimir-Claude, *Le Coup de Prague, 1948*. Paris: Le Seuil, 1976.

Fischer-Galati, Stephen, ed. *Eastern Europe in the Sixties*. New York: F. A. Praeger, 1963.

——. *The Socialist Republic of Rumania*. Baltimore: Johns Hopkins University Press, 1969.

————. *Twentieth Century Rumania*. New York: Columbia University Press, 1970.

Fitzmaurice, John. *Politics in Denmark*. London: G. Hurst, 1981.

————. *The Politics of Belgium: Crisis and Compromise in a Plural Society*. London: G. Hurst, 1983.

Floyd, David. *Rumania: Russia's Dissident Ally*. New York: F. A. Praeger, 1965.

Fontaine, André. *History of the Cold War*. 2 vols. New York: Pantheon, 1968–69.

Gage, Nicholas. *Hellas: A Portrait of Greece*. Villard Books/Random House, 1987.

Gallagher, Tom. *Portugal: A Twentieth Century Interpretation*. Dover, N.H.: Manchester University Press, 1983.

Gaus, Günter. *Wo Deutschland liegt: eine Ortsbestimmung*. Hamburg: Hoffmann und Campe, 1983.

Georgescu, Vlad, ed. *Romania: 40 Years, 1944–1984*. New York: Praeger, 1985.

Germany and Eastern Europe Since 1945: From the Potsdam Agreement to Chancellor Brandt's "Ostpolitik." New York: C. Scribner, 1973.

Gillard, Charles. *A History of Switzerland*. London: George Allen and Unwin, 1955.

Gilmour, David. *The Transformation of Spain: From Franco to the Constitutional Monarchy*. New York: Quartet Books, 1985.

Girardet, Raoul. *L'Idée coloniale en France, 1871–1962*. Paris: Table Ronde, 1972.

Graham, Lawrence Sherman. *Portugal: The Decline and Collapse of an Authoritarian Order*. Beverly Hills: Sage Publications, 1975.

————. *Romania: A Developing Socialist State*. Boulder, Colorado: Westview Press, 1982.

————, and Makler, Harry M. *Contemporary Portugal: The Revolution and its Antecedents*. Austin: University of Texas Press, 1979.

Graham, Robert. *Spain: Change of a Nation*. London: Joseph, 1984.

Gramont, Sanche de. *The French: Portrait of a People*. New York: G. P. Putnam, 1969.

Griffith, William E., ed. *Communism in Europe*. Cambridge, Massachusetts: M.I.T. Press, 1964.

Griffiths, Richard T., ed. *The Economy and Politics of the Netherlands Since 1945*. The Hague: M. Nijhoff, 1980.

Grosser, Alfred. *Germany in Our Time*. New York: Praeger, 1971.

————. *L'Allemagne en Occident: La Republique Fédérale 40 Ans Après*. Paris: Fayard, 1985.

————. *The Western Alliance: European-American Relations Since 1945*. New York: Continuum, 1980.

Harvey, Robert. *Portugal: Birth of a Democracy*. London: Macmillan, 1978.

Hayek, Friedrich August Von. *The Road to Serfdom*. Chicago: University of Chicago Press, 1976.

Hermet, Guy. *L'Espagne au XVième Siècle*. Paris: PUF, 1986.

Hillenbrand, Martin Joseph. *Germany in an Era of Transition*. Paris: Atlantic Institute for International Affairs, 1983.

Hillgruber, Andreas. *Deutsche Geschicht: 1945–1982. Die "Deutsche Frage" in der Weltpolitik*. Stuttgart: Kohlhammer, 1983.

Hobsbawm, E. J. *Industry and Empire*. Baltimore: Penguin, 1969.

Hoffmann, Stanley. *Decline or Renewal? France Since the 1930s*. New York: Viking Press, 1974.

———, and Hoffmann, Inge. "The Will to Grandeur: DeGaulle as Political Artist," in *Daedalus*, Summer 1968.

———, and Maier, Charles. *The Marshall Plan: A Retrospective*. Published in cooperation with the Center for European Studies, Harvard University. Boulder, Colorado: Westview Press, 1984.

———, et al. *In Search of France*. Cambridge, Massachusetts: Harvard University Press, 1963.

Holborn, Hajo. *Republic to Reich: The Making of the Nazi Revolution*. New York: Pantheon Books, 1972.

Jancar, Barbara Wolfe. *Czechoslovakia and the Absolute Monopoly of Political Power: A Study of Political Power in a Communist System*. New York: F. A. Praeger, 1971.

Jelavich, Barbara. *History of the Balkans*. 2 vols. New York: Cambridge University Press, 1983.

Jelen, Christian. *Les Normalisés*. Paris: Albin Michel, 1975.

John, Brian Stephen. *Scandinavia: A New Geography*. London: Longmans, 1984.

Johnson, Owen V. *Slovakia 1918–1938: Education and the Making of a Nation*. East Europe Monographs, Boulder, distributed by Colventra University Press, New York, 1985.

Johnson, Paul. *Modern Times: The World from the 20s to the 80s*. New York: Harper & Row, 1983.

Joll, James. *Europe Since 1870: An International History*. New York: Harper & Row, 1973.

Jutikkala, Eino, and Pirinen, Kauko. *A History of Finland*. New York: F. A. Praeger, 1962.

Kardelj, Edvard. *Democracy and Socialism*. London: The Summerfield Press, 1978.

———. *Reminiscences: Struggle for Recognition and Independence*. London: Blond and Briggs, 1982.

Keizer, Bernard. *Le Modèle Economique Allemand: Mythes et Réalités*. Paris: La Documentation Française, 1979.

Kennedy, Paul. *The Realities Behind Diplomacy: Background and Influences on British External Policy, 1865–1980*. Boston: G. Allen and Unwin, 1981.

Kohler, Beate. *Political Forces in Spain, Greece and Portugal*. Boston: Butterworth, 1982.

Kolodziej, Edward. *French International Policy Under de Gaulle and Pompidou*. Ithaca: Cornell University Press, 1974.

Kuisel, Richard F. *Capitalism and the State in Modern France: Renovation and Economic Management in the Twentieth Century*. Cambridge: Cambridge University Press, 1981.

Kundera, Milan. *The Book of Laughter and Forgetting*. New York: Alfred
    A. Knopf, 1981.
────. *The Joke*. New York: Harper & Row, 1982.
────. *The Unbearable Lightness of Being*. New York: Harper & Row,
    1985.
Kusin, Vladimir Victor. *From Dubček to Charter 77: A Study of Normali-
    zation in Czechoslovakia, 1968–1978*. Edinburgh: Q Press, 1978.
Lacouture, Jean. *DeGaulle*. 3 vols. Paris: Le Seuil, 1984, 1985, 1986.
────. *Mendes France*. New York: Holmes and Meier, 1984.
Lafontaine, Oskar. *Der andere Fortschritt. Verantwortung statt Verweige-
    rung*. Hamburg: Hoffmann und Campe, 1985.
Lange, Peter. *Studies on Italy: 1943–1975. Select Bibliography of American
    and British Materials in Political Science, Economics, Sociology and
    Anthropology*. Torino: Fondazione Giovanni Agnelli, 1977.
Laqueur, Walter Zéev. *Germany Today: A Personal Report*. London: Wei-
    denfeld and Nicholson, 1985.
Lavau, Georges. *A quoi sert le parti communiste français?* Paris: Fayard,
    1981.
Lazitch, Branko. *Tito et la révolution yougoslave, 1937–1949*. Paris: Fas-
    quello, 1957.
Ledeen, Michael Arthur. *Italy in Crisis*. Beverly Hills: Sage Publications,
    1977.
Leonhard, Wolfgang. *Child of the Revolution*. Chicago: H. Regnery, 1958.
Levi, Arrigo. *Ipotesti sull'Italia: undici diagnosi per una crisi*. Bologna: il
    Mulino, 1983.
Lewis, Flora. *A Case History of Hope (Poland)*. New York: Doubleday,
    1958.
────. *One of Our H'-Bombs Is Missing*. New York: McGraw-Hill, 1967.
────. *Red Pawn*. New York: Doubleday, 1965.
Lichtheim, George. *Europe in the Twentieth Century*. New York: Praeger,
    1972.
────. *Imperialism*. New York: F. A. Praeger, 1971.
Liehm, Antonin. *The Politics of Culture*. New York: Grove Press, 1971.
Lijphart, Arend. *The Politics of Accommodation: Pluralism and Democracy
    in the Netherlands*. 2nd ed. Berkeley: University of California Press,
    1975.
Loebl, Eugène, and Pokorny, Dusan. *Stalinism in Prague: The Loebl Story*.
    New York: Grove Press, 1969.
Lottman, Herbert R. *The Left Bank: Writers, Artists and Politics from the
    Popular Front to the Cold War*. Boston: Houghton Mifflin, 1982.
Lowenthal, Richard. *World Communism: The Disintegration of a Secular
    Faith*. New York: Oxford University Press, 1966.
Mack Smith, Denis. *Italy: A Modern History*. Ann Arbor: University of
    Michigan Press, 1959.
────. *Mussolini*. London: Weidenfeld and Nicholson, 1981.
Mann, Golo. *The History of Germany Since 1789*. New York: F. A. Praeger,
    1968.
Maravall, José Maria. *The Transition to Democracy in Spain*. New York:
    St. Martin's Press, 1982.

Markovits, Andrei S., ed. *The Political Economy of West Germany: "Modell Deutschland."* New York: Praeger, 1982.

Marques, Antonio Henrique de Oliveira. *History of Portugal.* New York: Columbia University Press, 1972.

Masaryk, Thomas Garrigue. *The Meaning of Czech History.* Edited and with an introduction by René Wellek. Chapel Hill: University of North Carolina Press, 1974.

Mayer, Arno J. *The Persistence of the Old Regime: Europe to the Great War.* New York: Pantheon Books, 1981.

————. *Politics and Diplomacy of Peacemaking: Containment and Counter Revolution at Versailles, 1918–1919.* New York: Alfred A. Knopf, 1967.

McCauley, Martin. *The German Democratic Republic Since 1945.* London: Thames and Hudson, 1972.

Mead, William Richard, and Hall, Wendy. *Scandinavia.* New York: Walker Publications, 1972.

Meier, Charles S.; Hoffmann, Stanley; and Gould, Andrew, eds. *The Rise of the Nazi Regime: Historical Reassessments.* Boulder, Colorado: Westview Press, 1986.

Méray, Tibor. *That Day in Budapest, October 23, 1956.* New York: Funk and Wagnalls, 1969.

Merritt, Anna, and Merritt, Richard. *Politics, Economics and Society in the Two Germanies: 1945–1975; a Bibliography of English-Language Works.* Champaign-Urbana: University of Illinois Press, 1978.

Milza, Pierre. *Le fascisme italien: 1919–1945.* Paris: Editions du Seuil, 1980.

Mlynar, Zdenek. *Nightfrost in Prague: The End of Humane Socialism.* New York: Karz, 1980.

Molnar, Miklos. *Budapest 1956. A History of the Hungarian Revolution.* London: George Allen and Unwin, 1971.

Monnet, Jean. *Mémoires.* Garden City, New York: Doubleday, 1978.

Monthias, John M. *Background and Origins of the Rumanian Dispute with Comecon: Soviet Studies, XVI, 1964.*

Newton, Gérald. *The Netherlands: An Historical and Cultural Survey: 1795–1977.* Boulder, Colorado: Westview Press, 1978.

Nissen, Henrik S. *Scandinavia During the Second World War.* Minneapolis: University of Minnesota Press, 1983.

Noelle-Neumann, Elizabeth. *Eine demoskopische Deutschstunde.* Zurich: Interfrom; Osnabruck: Fromm, 1983.

Northedge, F. S. *Descent from Power: British Foreign Policy, 1945–1973.* London: George Allen and Unwin, 1974.

Padovani, Marcelle. *Vivre avec le terrorisme: le modèle italien.* Paris: Calmann-Levy, 1982.

Pakula, Hannah. *The Last Romantic.* New York: Simon and Schuster, 1985.

Pattison de Menil, Lois. *Who Speaks for Europe? The Vision of Charles de Gaulle.* London: Weidenfeld & Nicholson, 1977.

Paul, David W. *Czechoslovakia: Profile of a Socialist Republic at the Crossroads of Europe.* Boulder, Colorado: Westview Press, 1981.

Paxton, Robert Owen. *Vichy France: Old Guard and New Order: 1940–1944.* New York: Columbia University Press, 1982.

Payne, Stanley George. *Franco's Spain.* New York: Crowell, 1967.

———. *A History of Spain and Portugal.* Madison: University of Wisconsin Press, 1973.

Petrow, Richard. *The Bitter Years: The Invasion and Occupation of Denmark and Norway, April 1940–May 1945.* New York: Morrow Quill Paperbacks, 1979.

Pierre, Andrew J. *The Global Politics of Arms Sales.* Princeton: Princeton University Press, 1982.

Polanyi, Karl. *The Great Transformation.* New York: Rinehart and Company, 1944.

Rémond, René. *The Right Wing in France from 1815 to de Gaulle.* Philadelphia: University of Pennsylvania Press, 1969.

Robinson, Richard, and Hodgson, Alan. *Contemporary Portugal: A History.* Boston: George Allen and Unwin, 1979.

Robinson, Ronald; Gallagher, John; and Denny, Alice. *Africa and the Victorians: The Official Mind of Imperialism.* New York: St. Martin's Press, 1961.

Robinson, William F. *The Pattern of Reform in Hungary: A Political, Economic and Cultural Analysis.* New York: Praeger, 1973.

Romano, Sergio. *Histoire de l'Italie du Risorgimento à Nos Jours.* Paris: Editions du Seuil, 1977.

———. *Italie.* Paris: Editions du Seuil, 1979.

Ronchey, Alberto. *Libro bianco sull'ultima generazione: tra candore e terrore.* 2nd ed. Milan: A Garzanti, 1978.

Ruehl, Lothar. *La politique militaire de la Cinquième République.* Paris: Presses de la Fondation Nationale des Sciences Politiques, 1976.

Rupnik, Jacques. *Histoire du parti communiste tchécoslovague: des origines à la prise du pouvoir.* Paris: Presses de la FNSP, 1981.

Rusconi, Gian Enrico, and Scamuzzi, Sergio. *Italy Today: An Eccentric Society.* London: Sage Publications, 1981.

Sandoz, Gérard, ed. *Les allemands sans miracle.* Paris: A Colin, OFAJ, 1983.

Schaufele, William E., Jr. *Polish Paradox: Communism and National Renewal.* New York: Foreign Policy Association, 1981.

Schneider, Eberhard. *The GDR: The History, Politics, Economy and Society of East Germany.* New York: St. Martin's Press, 1978.

Scobbie, Irene. *Sweden.* London: E. Benn, 1972.

Seton-Waston, Hugh. *The East European Revolution.* 3rd ed., rev. London: Methuen and Company, 1956.

Shawcross, William. *Dubček.* New York: Simon and Schuster, 1970.

Sherwen, Nicholas, ed. *NATO's Anxious Birth: The Prophetic Vision of the 1940s.* New York: St. Martin's Press, 1985.

Singleton, Frederick Bernard. *Twentieth Century Yugoslavia.* London: Macmillan, 1976.

———. *Yugoslavia: The Country and Its People.* London: Queen Ann Press, 1970.

Smith, Gordon R. *Democracy in West Germany: Parties and Politics in the Federal Republic.* New York: Holmes and Meier, 1979.

Stankovic, Slobodan. *The End of the Tito Era: Yugoslavia's Dilemmas.* Stanford: Hoover Institute Press, 1981.

Steele, Jonathan. *Inside East Germany: The State That Came In From the Cold.* New York: Urizen Books, 1977.

Sugar, Peter F., and Lederer, Ivo J. *Nationalism in Eastern Europe.* Seattle: University of Washington Press, 1969.

Szulc, Tad. *Czechoslovakia Since World War II.* New York: Viking Press, 1971.

Taylor, A. J. P. *English History.* New York: Oxford University Press, 1965.

———. *The Hapsburg Monarchy 1809–1918: A History of the Austrian Empire and Austria-Hungary.* Harmondworth: Penguin Books, 1964.

———. *The Origins of the Second World War.* Greenwich: Fawcett Books, 1963.

———. *The Struggle for Mastery in Europe: 1848–1918.* Oxford: The Clarendon Press, 1954.

Tigrid, Pavel. *Le printemps de Prague.* Paris: Le Seuil, 1968.

———. *Why Dubček Fell.* London: Macdonald and Co., 1971.

Tuchman, Barbara. *A Distant Mirror.*

———. *The March of Folly: From Troy to Vietnam.* New York: Alfred A. Knopf, 1984.

Volgyes, Ivan. *Hungary: A Nation of Contradictions.* Boulder, Colorado: Westview Press, 1982.

Von Beyme, Klaus, and Schmidt, Manfred G., eds. *Policy and Politics in the Federal Republic of Germany.* Aldershot: Gower, 1985.

Voslensky, Michael. *Nomenklatura.* Vienna: Verlag Fritz Molden, 1980.

Wiener, Martin J. *English Culture and the Decline of the Industrial Spirit, 1850–1980.* New York: Cambridge University Press, 1981.

Williams, Philip M. *Crisis and Compromise Politics in the Fourth Republic.* New York: Longman Group, Ltd., 1972.

Zeldin, Theodore. *France: 1848–1945.* New York: Oxford University Press, 1979–81. 2 vols.

———. *The French.* New York: Pantheon, 1982.

Ziegler, Jean. *Switzerland: The Awful Truth.* New York: Harper & Row, 1979.

INDEX

ABOUT THE AUTHOR

Flora Lewis's "Foreign Affairs" column appears twice weekly on the Op Ed page of *The New York Times*. She has written for the AP on the United States and other parts of the world. She has written about Europe for, among others, *Time, The Economist* of London, *France-Soir* of Paris, *The Atlantic, The New Yorker, Life, The Washington Post* and *The New York Times*. She was chief of the *Times*'s Paris bureau from 1972 to 1980. Ms. Lewis's awards include the National Press Club's 13th Annual Fourth Estate Award, three from the Overseas Press Club and the Columbia Journalism School's 50th Anniversary Award. Flora Lewis is author of *Case History of Hope, Red Pawn* and *One of Our H-Bombs Is Missing*. She lives in Paris.